FRANCISCAN INTERNATIONAL STUDY CENTRE

JESUS AND THE WOMEN OF THE GOSPELS

Séamus Mulholland OFM

Published by:
Franciscan International Study Centre
Giles Lane, Canterbury CT2 7NA
www.franciscans.ac.uk

Printed in Sittingbourne, England by:
Orbital Print Ltd.
www.orbitalprint.co.uk

978-0-9566568-6-5

For
The Vocations Sisters

CONTENTS

ACKNOWLEDGEMENTS

I would like to thank a few people who, in one way or another, helped me in the formulation of this work. Margaret, as always for her interest, Pauline for her usual helpful suggestions with the text, Melissa and Christian for their listening and support. I would also like to thank the Vocations Sisters who showed a great deal of interest and encouragement. Dave for all his work; the Franciscan International Study Centre for permission to incorporate materials from my book, *Meeting Jesus in the Gospel of Mark*, Vol. 1&2. Fr. Felix Just SJ, for granting gracious permission to utilise materials on his website, catholic-resources.org. I would also like to thank the CSA Sisters in Font Du Lac, USA for gracious permission to use the painting of the Visitation from their web site, csasisters.org. Finally, the friars of my own community who are always unstinting in their interest, support and encouragement.

JESUS AND THE WOMEN OF THE GOSPELS

INTRODUCTION

At the outset, it needs to be stated what this book is not: it is a not an examination or an exploration of the role/s (or lack thereof) of women in the contemporary Church. It will not examine the question of ordained ministry for women in the Church or even ask the question. Having said what it is not, I had better, perhaps, say what it is! It is a simple, straightforward presentation of the encounters that Jesus has with the various women who make their appearance in all four gospels and the meaning of those encounters both then and now. Undoubtedly some of the encounters Jesus has with women in the gospels are very brief, cameos almost, then they exit 'stage left', e.g., Simon's mother-in-law (Mk. 1.29-31 Others are more profound, more intense, e.g., the Samaritan Woman (Jn. 4.4-26); Martha at the raising of Lazarus (Jn. 11.20-27). In most cases the names of the women are not recorded, e.g., we do not know the name of Simon's mother-in-law (Mk. 1.29-31), the Samaritan Woman (Jn. 4.4-26) the woman with the issue of blood (Mk. 5.21-34), the woman caught in adultery (Jn. 7.53-8.11), the widow of Nain (Lk. 7.11-18), or those who met Jesus on the road to Calvary (Lk. 23.28-31). Others, of course, are named and their names are synonymous with care, concern, ministration, service and discipleship, faith and love: Mary, mother of Jesus, Mary Magdalene, Susanna, Joanna, Mary the sister of Martha (Marys abound in the gospels). But each of these women, named or otherwise, are of crucial importance in the Jesus story regardless of how intense or fleeting his encounters with them are. In essence then, this small work is a reflection on the gospel texts and some of the extraordinary characters who populate them. The book will obviously have to say something about how women and their role in society during the time of Jesus was understood and what some of the social conventions in relation to interaction between males and females was, as well as some words about the Jewish purity laws, so we can better contextualise these encounters. However, regardless of how presumptuous it may sound, the book is written so that we may be challenged and taught by these women and what they can inspire in us and teach us concerning matters of openness, receptivity, willingness, care, concern, gentleness, strength, tenacity, faith, and a deep and ever abiding love of Jesus. Thus, it is not a book on scriptural exegesis, though this does figure, it is not a work that debates what to some is the contentious issue of women's ministry in the Church, it is not a book that seeks to demonstrate how radical and revolutionary Jesus was in his dealings with women, i.e., it is not a presentation of Jesus the 'feminist'. It is rather a presentation of the Jesus who allowed himself to be cared for, ministered to, believed in, followed and loved by these extraordinary, warm, affectionate, caring women who followed him, ministered to his needs and loved him with a deep abiding passion and who in all cases at times were his closest, and just as faithful, disciples as the men he had called to be *with him*, i.e., the Twelve. This, surely, is what we all seek after as we too struggle to follow Jesus in faith and love today as his obedient and humble little servants.

CHAPTER ONE

JESUS AND THE WOMEN IN MATTHEW

Female Characters in Matthew's Gospel

Episode	Matthew
Mt. 8.14-15	Healing of Simon's Mother-in-Law
Mt. 12.46-50	Concern of Jesus' Family: Mother and Brothers
Mt. 9.18-19, 23-26	The Daughter of Jairus
Mt. 9.20-22	A Woman with a flow of blood
Mt. 13.55-56	Jesus is called "Son of Mary"; ref. to his sisters
Mt. 14.3-12	John the Baptist's Death: Herodias and her daughter
Mt. 15.21-28	The Syro-Phoenician Woman's Daughter
Mt. 19.3-12	On Divorce
Mt. 19.19	Jesus quotes the Decalogue: 'Honour Your Father and Mother'
Mt. 19.29	'No one who has left house or brothers or sisters or mother or father or children or fields for my sake...'
Mt. 22.23-33	The Case of a woman who had seven husbands
	The Widow's Mite
Mt. 10.21	Apocalyptic Discourse: Children rise against their parents
Mt. 24.19	'Alas for those with child or nursing'
Mt. 26.6-13	Anointing at Bethany: Anonymous Woman
Mt. 26.69-75	Peter's Denial: The Serving Girl

Mt. 27.55-56	Women at the Cross: Mary Magdalene, Mary mother of James & Joses, and Salome
Mt. 27.61	Women See Jesus Buried
Mt. 28.1-8	Women Go to Jesus' Tomb
Mt. 28.9-10	(Jesus Appears to Mary Magdalene / Women)

Additional References to Women in Matthew:
(References found only in Matthew)

Passage	Brief Description
Mt. 1.3, 5, 6	Genealogy of Jesus: '...and Judah the father of Perez and Zerah by Tamar... and Salmon the father of Boaz by Rahab, and Boaz the father of Obed by Ruth... and David was the father of Solomon by the wife of Uriah.'
Mt. 1.16	Genealogy of Jesus: '...Joseph the husband of Mary, of whom Jesus was born.'
Mt. 1.18-25	Birth of Jesus: 'When his mother Mary had been engaged to Joseph, but before they lived together, she was found to be with child from the Holy Spirit... 'Behold, the virgin shall conceive and bear a son.' ' (cf. Is. 7:14)
Mt. 2.11	Magi's Visit: 'On entering the house, they saw the child with Mary his mother; and they knelt down and paid him homage.'
Mt. 5.27-28	Sermon on the Mount, on Adultery: 'You have heard that it was said, 'You shall not commit adultery.' But I say to you that everyone who looks at a woman with lust has already committed adultery with her in his heart.'
Mt. 5.31-32	Sermon on the Mount, on Divorce: 'It was also said, 'Whoever divorces his wife, let him give her a certificate of divorce.' But I say to you that anyone who divorces his wife, except on the ground of unchastity, causes her to commit adultery; and whoever marries a divorced woman commits adultery.' (cf. Mark 10:2-12 and par.)
Mt. 14.21	Feeding of the 5000: 'Those who ate were about five thousand

	men, besides women and children.'
Mt. 15.38	Feeding of the 4000: 'Those who had eaten were four thousand men, besides women and children.'
Mt. 18.25	Parable of the Unforgiving Servant: '...his lord ordered him to be sold, together with his wife and children and all his possessions, and payment to be made.'
Mt. 21.5	Jesus' Entrance into Jerusalem: 'Tell the daughter of Zion, Look, your king is coming to you, humble, and mounted on a donkey, and on a colt, the foal of a donkey. (cf. Is. 62:11; Zech. 9:9; John 12:15)
Mt. 25.1-13	Parable of the Ten Bridesmaids and Their Lamps (actually Torches)
Mt. 27.19	Pilate's Wife: 'While he was sitting on the judgement seat, his wife sent word to him, 'Have nothing to do with that innocent man, for today I have suffered a great deal because of a dream about him.''

References found in Matthew and Luke
(From the "Q" Source):

Reference	Brief Description	Cross Reference
Mt. 10.35	Divisions within Households: 'For I have come to set a man against his father, and a daughter against her mother, and a daughter-in-law against her mother-in-law;'	cf. Lk. 12.53
Mt. 10.37	Conditions of Discipleship: 'Whoever loves father or mother more than me is not worthy of me; and whoever loves son or daughter more than me is not worthy of me;'	cf. Lk. 14.26
Mt. 11.11	Jesus Speaks about John the Baptist: 'Truly I tell you, among those born of women no one has arisen greater than John the Baptist; yet the least in the kingdom of heaven is greater than he.'	cf. Luke 7.28

Mt. 12.42	Seeking Signs: 'The Queen of the South will rise up at the judgement with this generation and condemn it, because she came from the ends of the earth to listen to the wisdom of Solomon, and see, something greater than Solomon is here!'	cf. Luke 11.31
Mt. 13.33	New Parable: 'The kingdom of heaven is like yeast that a woman took and mixed in with three measures of flour until all of it was leavened.'	cf. Luke 13.20-21
Mt. 23.37b	Lament over Jerusalem: 'How often have I desired to gather your children together as a hen gathers her brood under her wings, and you were not willing!'	cf. Luke 13.34
Mt. 24.38	Apocalyptic Discourse: 'For as in those days before the flood they were eating and drinking, marrying and giving in marriage, until the day Noah entered the ark.'	cf. Luke 17.26-27
Mt. 24.41	Apocalyptic Discourse: 'Two women will be grinding meal together; one will be taken and one will be left.'	cf. Luke 17.35

The Women In The Infancy Narrative of Matthew
The Matthean Infancy Narrative: Mt. 1-2

Common Elements in Both Infancy Narratives:

- Main characters: *Mary, Joseph, Jesus*
- Supporting characters: *Angels, Holy Spirit*
- Titles attributed to Jesus: *Christ, son of David*
- Heritage: *children of Abraham/Israel, house of David*
- Place names: *Nazareth in Galilee, Bethlehem in Judea*
- Historical period: *during the reign of King Herod* .

Different Contents of the Two Accounts:

Matthew 1–2 (only 48 verses, including genealogy)	Luke 1–2 (total of 132 verses, plus 16 more in genealogy)
1.1: Title of the Gospel	1.1-4: Literary introduction to the Gospel
1.2-17: The Genealogy of Jesus (from Abraham to King David to Exile to Joseph)	(*Genealogy included later, in Luke 3.23-38*)
	1.5-25: Angel Gabriel announces John the Baptist's birth
1.18-24:An unnamed angel announces Jesus' birth *to Joseph in a dream*	1.26-38: Angel Gabriel announces Jesus' birth *to Mary while awake*
	1.39-56: Mary visits Elizabeth (*including* Mary's *'Magnificat'*)
	1.57-58: Elizabeth gives birth to her son (John the Baptist)
	1.59-80: John the Baptist is circumcised & named (*incl. Zechariah's 'Benedictus'*)
	2.1-5: Joseph & Mary journey to Bethlehem for the census
1.25 & 2.1a: Mary's son is born in Bethlehem of Judea, and named Jesus	2.6-7: Mary gives birth to her son in Bethlehem of Judea
	2.8-14: Angels appear to some shepherds (*incl. the 'Gloria' of the angels*)
	2.15-20: Shepherds visit Mary & Joseph & the infant lying in a manger
	2.21: The infant is circumcised & named Jesus
	2.22-38: Jesus is presented to God in the Temple (*incl. Simeon's 'Nunc Dimittis'*)
2.1b-12: Magi from the East come; they first visit Herod, then Jesus	
2.13-21: Joseph & Mary flee to Egypt with the child Jesus; the Innocents are	

murdered; the Holy Family returns to Israel	
2.22-23: They journey to Nazareth	2.39-40: The family returns to Nazareth
	2.41-52: At age twelve, Jesus & his parents visit the Jerusalem Temple

Different Theological Emphases of Each Narrative:

	Matthew 1–2	Luke 1–2
Driving Force:	*Hebrew Scriptures* are fulfilled (1.22-23; 2.5-6, 15, 17-18, 23)	*Holy Spirit* is at work (1.1, 35, 41, 67; 2.25-27)
Jesus' Heritage:	Son of *David*, son of *Abraham* (1.1-17) Legal son of Joseph, but child of the Holy Spirit (1.18-25)	Son of *God*, son of *Mary* by the Holy Spirit (1.26-38) Heir to David's throne, over the house of Judah (1.32-33; 2.4)
Names & Titles	Messiah(1.1,16-18;2.4) Jesus: 'For he will save his people from their sins' (1.21, 25) *Emmanuel*. 'God with us' (1.23) *King of the Jews* (2.2) 'A ruler who is to shepherd my people Israel' (2.6) Nazorean (2.23)	Jesus (1.31; 2.21) Son of the Most High; Son of God (1.32, 35) He will be great, holy, full of wisdom and grace (1.32,35; 2.40) 'Of his kingdom there will be no end'(1.33) A *Saviour* is born... who is Messiah and *Lord* (2.11, 26) A light for revelation to Gentiles and for glory to Israel (2.32)
Characters Emphasised	*Men.* King David, Joseph of Nazareth, Magi from the East, King Herod, chief priests & scribes, Ethnarch Archelaus	*Women.* Virgin Mary of Nazareth, Elizabeth, Anna *Poor & Aged.* Shepherds, Zechariah, Simeon
Themes:	obstacles, conflict, fear, murder, politics	glory, praise, joy; poverty, humility, faith
OT Parallels	Dreamer Joseph (Genesis 37–	Birth of Samson (Judges 13)

	41)Baby Moses (Exodus 1–2)	Birth of Samuel (1 S 1–2)
Number Symbolism	(King) David = 14 (DVD = 4+6+4); three groups of 14 generations in genealogy; focus on royalty	70 weeks from Gabriel's first Annunciation to Presentation in Temple? related to: 70-week prophecy by angel Gabriel in Dan 9.24-27

Old Testament Quotations and Allusions in Matthew's Infancy Narrative

Matthew's Gospel	Old Testament Texts
Mt. 1.3b–6a: (direct quotation of ten generations from Perez to David)	Ruth 4.18-22: (ten generations from Perez to David)
Mt. 1.22-23: All this took place to <u>fulfil</u> what had been spoken by the Lord through the prophet. 'Look, the virgin shall conceive and bear a son, and they shall name him Emmanuel,' which means, 'God is with us.'	Is. 7.14: 'Therefore the Lord himself will give you a sign. Look, the young woman is with child and shall bear a son, and shall name him 'Immanuel'
	Is. 8.8b, 10: 'It (the Assyrian army) will sweep on into Judah as a flood, and, pouring over, it will reach up to the neck; and its outspread wings will fill the breadth of your land, O Immanuel... Take counsel together, but it shall be brought to naught; speak a word, but it will not stand, for God is with us.'
Mt. 2.2: (Magi ask Herod). 'Where is the child who has been born king of the Jews? For we observed his star at its rising, and have come to pay him homage.' (cf. 2.8)	Num. 24.17-19: 'I see him, but not now; I behold him, but not near-- a star shall come out of Jacob, and a *sceptre shall rise out of Israel;* it shall crush the borderlands of Moab, and the territory of all the Shethites. Edom will become a possession, Seir a

	possession of its enemies, while Israel does valiantly. *One out of Jacob shall rule*, and destroy the survivors of Ir.'
Mt. 2.5-6: (scribes tell King Herod where the Messiah will be born). 'In Bethlehem of Judea; for so it has been written by the prophet. 'And you, Bethlehem, in the land of Judah, are by no means least among the rulers of Judah; for from you shall come a ruler who is to shepherd my people Israel."	Mic. 5.2: 'But you, O Bethlehem of Ephrathah, who are one of the little clans of Judah, from you shall come forth for me one who is to rule in Israel, whose origin is from of old, from ancient days.'
Mt. 2.11b: Then, opening their treasure chests, they offered him gifts of gold, frankincense, and myrrh.	Is. 60.3, 6: 'Nations shall come to your light, and kings to the brightness of your dawn... A multitude of camels shall cover you, the young camels of Midian and Ephah; all those from Sheba shall come. They shall bring gold and frankincense, and shall proclaim the praise of the LORD.'
Mt. 2.14-15: Then Joseph got up, took the child and his mother by night, and went to Egypt, and remained there until the death of Herod. This was to <u>fulfil</u> what had been spoken by the Lord through the prophet, '*Out of Egypt I have called my son*.'	Hos.11.1: 'When Israel was a child, I loved him, and *out of Egypt I called my son*.'
Mt. 2.17-18: Then was <u>fulfilled</u> what had been spoken through the prophet Jeremiah. '*A voice was heard in Ramah, wailing and loud lamentation, Rachel weeping for her children; she refused to be consoled, because they are no more*.'	Jer. 31.15: 'Thus says the LORD. *A voice is heard in Ramah, lamentation and bitter weeping. Rachel is weeping for her children; she refuses to be comforted* for her children, *because they are no more*.'

Mt. 2.23:	Is. 11.1:
There (in Galilee) he (Joseph) made his home in a town called Nazareth, so that what had been spoken through the prophets might be <u>fulfilled</u>, 'He will be called a Nazorean.'	'A shoot shall come out from the stump of Jesse, and a branch (*nezer*) shall grow out of his roots.'

The Women of the Matthean Infancy Narrative

a. The Gospel Tradition

We begin at the beginning which is the proper place to begin and, of course, is the only place to begin for where else do we, should we, or could we begin but at the beginning. The first book of the Scripture makes that very point for, *In the beginning God created the heavens and the earth* (Gen. 1.1); the written gospel tradition begins the beginning of the literary genre of the gospel with the words *the beginning of the good news of Jesus Christ* (Mk. 1.1), and the final work of the (canonical) gospel literary tradition begins with, *in the beginning was the Logos* (Jn. 1.1). Beginning at the beginning, therefore, is the place to begin. And we begin our exploration of the women in the gospels with the woman who was there when it all began: Mary, the Mother of Jesus, whom we shall refer to as Mary of Bethlehem and then Nazareth (according to Matthew) or Mary of Nazareth (according to Luke). Mary of Nazareth is a good place to begin because she is at the beginning: the beginning of the unfolding of the Jesus event in the annunciation (Matthew/Luke), the beginning of Jesus' revelation of his glory (the Wedding Feast of Cana, Jn. 2.1.1-12[1]), the beginning of the new

---

[1] On the third day there was a wedding in Cana of Galilee, and the mother of Jesus was there. Jesus and his disciples had also been invited to the wedding. When the wine gave out, the mother of Jesus said to him, 'They have no wine.' And Jesus said to her, 'Woman, what concern is that to you and to me? My hour has not yet come.' His mother said to the servants, 'Do whatever he tells you.' Now standing there were six stone water-jars for the Jewish rites of purification, each holding twenty or thirty gallons. Jesus said to them, 'Fill the jars with water.' And they filled them up to the brim. He said to them, 'Now draw some out, and take it to the chief steward.' So they took it. When the steward tasted the water that had become wine, and did not know where it came from (though the servants who had drawn the water knew), the steward called the bridegroom and said to him, 'Everyone serves the good wine first, and then the inferior wine

community at the foot of the cross when she becomes the mother of the 'Beloved Disciple' and he her son (Jn. 19.26-27[1]) and the beginning of the Church (Pentecost, Acts 2.1-4[2]). Over the pages of this work we shall look at these 'beginnings' and the role Mary of Nazareth plays in the Jesus story. But, let us begin at the very beginning, i.e., with what Christians traditionally refer to as the 'Annunciation'. The 'Annunciation' is that part of the gospels of Matthew and Luke that we commonly call the 'Infancy Narratives' (Mt. 1-2; Lk. 1-3). However, Matthew has no 'annunciation' as such (though it is quite legitimate to take his 'genealogy' of Jesus as an 'annunciation'). Matthew simply says (Mt. 1.18-21),

> Now the birth of Jesus the Messiah took place in this way. When his mother Mary had been engaged to Joseph, but before they lived together, she was found to be with child from the Holy Spirit. Her husband Joseph, being a righteous man and unwilling to expose her to public disgrace, planned to dismiss her quietly. But just when he had resolved to do this, an angel of the Lord appeared to him in a dream and said, 'Joseph, son of David, do not be afraid to take Mary as your wife, for the child conceived in her is from the Holy Spirit. She will bear a son, and you are to name him Jesus, for he will save his people from their sins

So Matthew gives us no angel Gabriel, as Luke does, (we shall come to this presently) and no angels singing Glory to God!, no shepherds, no 'guest room', (the only appearance of angels in Matthew's 'annunciation' is to Joseph). It is not so much that Matthew 'ignores' Mary of Nazareth, (in other

---

after the guests have become drunk. But you have kept the good wine until now.' Jesus did this, the first of his signs, in Cana of Galilee, and revealed his glory; and his disciples believed in him.

[1] When Jesus saw his mother and the disciple whom he loved standing beside her, he said to his mother, 'Woman, here is your son.' Then he said to the disciple, 'Here is your mother.' And from that hour the disciple took her into his own home.

[2] When the day of Pentecost had come, they were all together in one place. And suddenly from heaven there came a sound like the rush of a violent wind, and it filled the entire house where they were sitting. Divided tongues, as of fire, appeared among them, and a tongue rested on each of them. All of them were filled with the Holy Spirit and began to speak in other languages, as the Spirit gave them ability.

words, that he reduces her to the traditional biological understanding of women, i.e., that they produced children for the husband to ensure his posterity), it is rather that Matthew's focus is on Joseph who we are told is a 'righteous' man (I shall come to importance of this in a moment). But this does not mean to say that Matthew has no interest in Mary or that she is simply the 'wife' of Joseph, far from it, for Matthew makes an almost throw away remark which is of profound significance and importance in relation to Mary. But I shall come back to this. Above I said that Matthew's focus is on Joseph but of course Matthew's focus is always on Jesus, what I meant by Matthew focusing on Joseph can be readily explained if we know a little about who Matthew was writing his gospel for.

The message of Jesus and the stories in relation to him were in circulation about thirty five to forty years before the gospels were written. Our first piece of 'canonical' New Testament is Paul's First Letter to the Thessalonians which is dated to 50-51 (Brown 1997:457) AD, if we accept that Jesus dies c.29-30 AD, then the stories and recollections of Jesus and his message and the understanding of who he was (the Messiah, I shall explain this term later) had been circulating for over twenty years. And during this twenty year or so period groups of people had come together to reflect on, pray to, acclaim Jesus as Messiah (and perhaps even at this early stage 'Son of God' though this term should not be understood in the sense that the Council of Nicea defined it in 325 AD but more as a Messianic title) and to do as he commanded and break bread and drink wine in memory of him (the Eucharist). The majority of New Testament scholars now accept that the first gospel to be written was the gospel we commonly call 'Mark' and a great deal of ink has been used in trying to determine who this Mark was. The ancient tradition was that somehow Mark was connected to Paul and may have accompanied him on some of his early missionary journeys and that eventually Mark ended up in Rome where he became associated with Peter who was in Rome and wrote down Peter's memoirs (i.e., the gospel). Tradition says that Peter was martyred during the persecutions of Nero when Nero used the early Christians as a scapegoat for the Great Fire of Rome in 64 AD. These are ancient traditions which we who are Catholic know well and while we may not doubt that Peter was certainly in Rome in the latter half of the first century, we can certainly raise questions as to whether he was the 'first Pope', i.e., Bishop of Rome. But this present work is not concerned with the details of the historicitical accuracy of ancient traditions (interesting and challenging as they are).

The tradition then arose that Mark wrote his gospel (the memoirs of Peter) for the Roman Christians who were suffering fierce persecution under Nero and who were the proto-martyrs of the Church either through being burned alive (Nero for example lit the grounds of his palace for a party with the bodies of crucified Christians which he had set alight) or being put to death by other means, e.g., being used as sport in the Colosseum. Marks' gospel, therefore, was understood to be an encouragement in the face of suffering since Mark presents Jesus as the Son of Man, the Messiah who suffers and as the Master suffered and was victorious (the Resurrection), so too shall the followers of Jesus be victorious in and through their suffering. Of course, we now know through nearly two thousand years of study and scholarship that the issue is a lot more complex than that. And it seems more likely that Mark was written sometime between 60-75 AD (Brown 1997:126) somewhere in the Roman Empire either during or just after the First Jewish War (66-73 AD) for a group of Christians who were either currently undergoing or had just undergine a period of great suffering. Though it is the first gospel to be written, Mark does not have an 'infancy narrative' or an 'annunciation' as we would understand it (though I would argue the opposite since we can take John the Baptist's preaching about the 'one who comes after me' as a 'prologue', or 'annunciation' of the coming of Jesus). However, Mark does mention Mary of Nazareth on a number of occasions and not in an especially good light but we shall come to that in a while. So Mark's gospel was the first gospel to be written and seems to have been written for a group of Gentile (non-Jewish Christians) somewhere in the Roman Empire (some scholars think Antioch) between 64-74 AD.

The second gospel to be written was Matthew. When we open a New

Testament we will always find the four gospels listed as: Matthew, Mark, Luke and John which has a nice rhythmic quality about and that rhythm was probably the reason why so many of us were able to learn one of our first prayers: 'Matthew, Mark, Luke and John, bless the bed that I lie on, if I should die before I wake I pray the Lord my soul to take' (and I was able to type that while sitting writing this without recourse to Wikipedia!). The reason for this is that for a long time the magnificent, stately gospel of Matthew was considered to have been written first and that Mark was an abbreviation of Matthew. Also, 'Matthew' is the name of one of the Apostle's (Levi-Mk.) and so it was taken that the Apostle Matthew was the author. We now know that this is not the case but rather that Matthew used Mark and had access to another source (written or oral) which is simply known by the initial 'Q' ('Q' derives from the first letter of the German word 'quelle' which means 'source') and that he used material specific to him, i.e., material only found in Matthew and which may have originated with the author), i.e., it is not found in Mark or Luke and this is usually referred to as 'M'. It sounds terribly complicated but it can be easily shown:

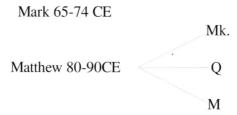

Mark 65-74 CE

Mk.

Matthew 80-90CE ← Q

M

b. The Genealogy of Jesus in Matthew

It seems that Matthew was writing for a community that was made up primarily of Jewish-Christians and it is considered to be the most 'Jewish' of the gospels. For example, he emphasises that the Law is not destroyed by Jesus but fulfilled by him; he has a high regard for the Jewish prophetic tradition (especially in the 'Infancy Narrative' and at the baptism of Jesus for when John is hesitant to baptise Jesus, Matthew has Jesus say, *Do this so that all righteousness might be fulfilled*'). As we shall see later where Luke's 'genealogy' (history of Jesus' origins) goes back to Adam, Matthew traces it back to Abraham, the 'father' of the Jews. He has a high regard for Moses (the Lawmaker) and seems to present Jesus as the 'new' Moses, the 'new' Lawgiver (indeed his 'Infancy Narrative' can be read as the story of Moses rewritten in Jesus where Jesus is type of Moses/Israel). And his gospel is generally considered to have five major sections or blocks of material which may be a deliberate construct by the writer to mirror the Pentatuech (the Five Books of Moses, or the Five Books of the Law, the Torah). Further, Matthew's community seems to have been strict in keeping their Jewish inheritance to the extent that they perhaps felt they had to 'outdo' the Pharisees and scribes in their 'righteousness' on these two groups placed great emphasis. It was definitely written after 70 AD (the destruction of the Temple) and maybe (and a *big maybe*!) as late as 90 AD. So, once we realise that Matthew is writing for Jewish-Christians and places great stress on the Jewishness of Jesus and *righteousness*, then we are in a better position to understand why he places his emphasis (as a Law abiding Jew Christian) on the centrality of Joseph in his 'Infancy Narrative' rather than Mary, since from Joseph Matthew can claim Jesus' descent from Abraham (so he is a Jew) and David (so of the messianic house) but Matthew faces a problem because he has not said that Joseph 'begot Jesus who is the Messiah'. We shall come to this seeming problem in a moment.

As I said above this does not mean that Matthew ignores Mary, far from it, her role and place is central in the story Matthew tells. However, it might be noted here that Mary is not the only woman who figures in Matthew's 'infancy/annunciation' narrative. Since we are beginning at the beginning, then let us go to the beginning of Matthew's gospel to see how and where Mary figures in Matthew's story of the advent of Jesus and look at the other women he mentions, where he mentions them and why. At first it may seem strange to be talking about Jesus and the women of the gospels when he has not even been born yet but this is to take too literally the idea of 'encounter' for Jesus is encountered quite radically even before his birth! Sometimes in contemporary social convention when we are introduced to someone they shake our hands and say something along the lines of, 'Nice to meet you' or other words to that effect. It is a polite, pleasant, social convention. If conversation continues to develop they will want to know a bit more about us, who we are and where we are from and what we do. So they might just ask that: 'Where are you from? What do you do for a living'. It allows them get get a 'sense' of us, to place us in the world so to speak, to place us in society and above all, to place us in the immediate environment of the company we are in. One of the most popular television programmes at the moment is 'Who Do You Think You Are?' where 'celebrities' or well known figures trace their ancestry and in some cases often with very surprising results.

Genealogies were especially important to the Jewish people. Israel's king had to be a Jew, and not a foreigner (Deut. 17.15). Later on it was revealed that he must be a descendant of David (2 S 7.14). When the Jews returned from the Babylonian captivity, it was important for these returned exiles to show that their roots were Jewish and could be traced through the genealogies. No one could serve as priest whose name could not be found in the genealogical records (Ez. 2.62). Bruner writes that the famous rabbi Hillel was proud that he could trace his genealogy all the way back to King David. He further indicates that Josephus began his autobiography with his own pedigree. Then there was Herod the Great, who was half-Jew and half-Edomite. Obviously his name was not in the official genealogies, and thus he ordered that the records be destroyed. If he could not be found there, he did not want to be upstaged by anyone else (Green 1989:37)

Matthew does exactly the same in his genealogy of Jesus (which he probably derives from earlier sources, cf. (Davies and Allison 1988:190-95); he asks the question about Jesus: 'who do you think you are? And then answers it for us by placing Jesus in the world and in society; he tells us 'where' he is from and 'how' he is from it, and thus shows where he belongs and why (Johnson 1988:209-10). He opens his gospel with the words (Mt. 1.1):

> the book of the origins/beginning (genesis) of Jesus the Messiah,
> Son of David, Son of Abraham.

Now in a real sense, Matthew has already told everything we need to know about Jesus: he is the Messiah, of the royal house of David (Son of David) and a Jew (a descendant of Abraham). His 'genealogy', the account of his origins/ancestry, then follows (Davies and Allison 1988:186). Traditionally, descent took place through the father, hence Matthew repeats 'so and so was the *father* of so and so and so begot so and so..who was the *father* of so and so who begot so and so..'

c. Tamar, Rahab, Ruth, Bathsheba

The ancestry of Jesus has all sorts of characters in it including kings but rather strangely and remarkably for a Jewish genealogy, Matthew's genealogy has five women in it:

> Tamar
> Rahab
> Ruth
> Bathsheba
> Mary, the mother of Jesus.

The question is, of course, what are women doing in a Jewish genealogy? There is another question beyond this: why these women? There are other great women in the Biblical tradition, Sarah, Rebecca, Leah, wives of the patriarchs, Abraham, Isaac, Jacob respectively, all of whom were great women and morally acceptable whereas Tamar, Rahab, and Bathsheba ('the wife of Uriah') each in their own way may not have been so morally acceptable by Jewish standards (but as I shall discuss later, their moral character or the fact that they may have been perceived as sinners, other than Ruth, may have nothing to do with their inclusion in the genealogy (cf.

Nolland 2005:65–87): Tamar for her 'deceit of Judah' (Gen. 38[1]); Rahab (Josh. 2.1-21;[2] 6.22-25), a Canaanite (and so a Gentile), who was a 'harlot' or 'prostitute' in Jericho and helped the Israelites capture the city through hiding their spies (Josh. 2.1-7[3]) (there is some dispute over the spelling of the name of this woman which has led some to think that the Rahab of the genealogy is not the same Rahab/Rachab of the Joshua story (cf. Bauckham: 1995:313–329). For helping the Israelites capture the city, Rahab and her family were spared and incorporated into the Jewish people. Ruth's importance in the story is that through the Levirite marriage of Boaz she is the mother of Obed who is the father of Jesse, so making him the grandfather of David which places Ruth (a Moabite and thus a Gentile) in

---

[1]   In course of time the wife of Judah, Shua's daughter, died; when Judah's time of mourning was over, he went up to Timnah to his sheep-shearers, he and his friend Hirah the Adullamite. When Tamar was told, 'Your father-in-law is going up to Timnah to shear his sheep', she put off her widow's garments, put on a veil, wrapped herself up, and sat down at the entrance to Enaim, which is on the road to Timnah. She saw that Shelah was grown up, yet she had not been given to him in marriage. When Judah saw her, he thought her to be a prostitute, for she had covered her face. He went over to her at the roadside, and said, 'Come, let me come in to you', for he did not know that she was his daughter-in-law. She said, 'What will you give me, that you may come in to me?' He answered, 'I will send you a kid from the flock.' And she said, 'Only if you give me a pledge, until you send it.' He said, 'What pledge shall I give you?' She replied, 'Your signet and your cord, and the staff that is in your hand.' So he gave them to her, and went in to her, and she conceived by him. Then she got up and went away, and taking off her veil she put on the garments of her widowhood.

[2]   Joshua said to the two men who had spied out the land, 'Go into the prostitute's house, and bring the woman out of it and all who belong to her, as you swore to her.' So the young men who had been spies went in and brought Rahab out, along with her father, her mother, her brothers, and all who belonged to her, they brought all her kindred out, and set them outside the camp of Israel. They burned down the city, and everything in it; only the silver and gold, and the vessels of bronze and iron, they put into the treasury of the house of the Lord. But Rahab the prostitute, with her family and all who belonged to her, Joshua spared. Her family has lived in Israel ever since. For she hid the messengers whom Joshua sent to spy out Jericho.

[3]   Then Joshua son of Nun sent two men secretly from Shittim as spies, saying, 'Go, view the land, especially Jericho.' So they went, and entered the house of a prostitute whose name was Rahab, and spent the night there. The king of Jericho was told, 'Some Israelites have come here tonight to search out the land.' Then the king of Jericho sent orders to Rahab, 'Bring out the men who have come to you, who entered your house, for they have come only to search out the whole land.' But the woman took the two men and hid them. Then she said, 'True, the men came to me, but I did not know where they came from. And when it was time to close the gate at dark, the men went out. Where the men went I do not know. Pursue them quickly, for you can overtake them.' She had, however, brought them up to the roof and hidden them with the stalks of flax that she had laid out on the roof. So the men pursued them on the way to the Jordan as far as the fords. As soon as the pursuers had gone out, the gate was shut.

the Davidic line.

Bathsheba (2 S 11-12) was the mother of Solomon through her adulterous liaison with David who, motivated by lust, got Bathesheba pregnant, tried to convince Uriah her husband to sleep with her and thus think the child was his, and when this failed David had him killed by putting him in 'harm's way' during a battle. God did not like this one bit, so he sent Nathan the prophet to David who told the story of the rich man who stole the little lamb of his poor neighbour (2 S 12.1-23[1]). When David heard the story he was incandescent with fury at the rich man and Nathan applied the parable to David who immediately admitted his sin and began to do penance. However, the child from the union died shortly after birth which David took to be a sign from God and the prophet also said that David's house would find no peace. This came to pass with the revolt that David's son, Absolom, led against him. We can pass over how Absolom tried to make it clear that he was the rightful king. Later when David was older, Bathsheba ensured that Solomon, her son, rather than Adonijah, David's oldest surviving son, succeeded to the throne. Other than Ruth, these women would not be considered to be the best of characters. But finally Matthew arrives at Joseph who he says was *the husband of Mary, of whom*

---

[1]   And the Lord sent Nathan to David. He came to him, and said to him, 'There were two men in a certain city, one rich and the other poor. The rich man had very many flocks and herds; but the poor man had nothing but one little ewe lamb, which he had bought. He brought it up, and it grew up with him and with his children; it used to eat of his meagre fare, and drink from his cup, and lie in his bosom, and it was like a daughter to him. Now there came a traveller to the rich man, and he was loath to take one of his own flock or herd to prepare for the wayfarer who had come to him, but he took the poor man's lamb, and prepared that for the guest who had come to him.' Then David's anger was greatly kindled against the man. He said to Nathan, 'As the Lord lives, the man who has done this deserves to die; he shall restore the lamb fourfold, because he did this thing, and because he had no pity.' Nathan said to David, 'You are the man! Thus says the Lord, the God of Israel: I anointed you king over Israel, and I rescued you from the hand of Saul; I gave you your master's house, and your master's wives into your bosom, and gave you the house of Israel and of Judah; and if that had been too little, I would have added as much more. Why have you despised the word of the Lord, to do what is evil in his sight? You have struck down Uriah the Hittite with the sword, and have taken his wife to be your wife, and have killed him with the sword of the Ammonites. Now therefore the sword shall never depart from your house, for you have despised me, and have taken the wife of Uriah the Hittite to be your wife. Thus says the Lord: I will raise up trouble against you from within your own house; and I will take your wives before your eyes, and give them to your neighbour, and he shall lie with your wives in the sight of this very sun. For you did it secretly; but I will do this thing before all Israel, and before the sun

Jesus' was born, who is called the Messiah. So Matthew has made his point since these women, even given their questionable moral status and being non-Jews, have played their part in the formation of the Messianic line (Hutchinson 2001:158)

d. Mary in Matthew

Matthew begins his gospel with the words, the *book of the origins/beginnings of Jesus the Messiah, son of David, son of Abraham* (Mt. 1.1) and ends with Jesus, the Messiah, who is the son of Mary, who is the wife of Joseph. So through the genealogy, Matthew has demonstrated the 'Jewishness' of Jesus and the Davidic descent (Bathsheba) (Kingsbury 1975:12; Longenecker 1975:141-43). But it is interesting that when he comes to Joseph he says, *Jacob was the father of Joseph, who was the husband of Mary* etc., he does not then say (according to the genealogical method) *Joseph was the father of Jesus who is the Messiah*. The answer to the question as to why he does not do that is found in the almost throw away remark Matthew makes about Mary at Mt. 1.18 which is then clarified at Mt. 1.23. Matthew says,

> Now the birth of Jesus the Messiah took place in this way. When his mother Mary had been engaged to Joseph, but before they lived together, she was found to be with child from the Holy Spirit. Her husband Joseph, being a righteous man and unwilling to expose her to public disgrace, planned to dismiss her quietly.

When we read this we do something of a double take: Mary and Joseph are betrothed but they are not living together, then Mary is discovered to be pregnant but Matthew has already given Jesus' line of descent as a *son of David* and *son of Abraham*. But on the last page I said that Matthew faces a problem: if Joseph is not the biological father of Jesus (since Mary is found to be pregnant while engaged but before the came to live together) then how can Matthew say that Jesus is of the Davidic house? Mary is of the Davidic house surely, but patrimony does not descend through the mother only through the father but Joseph, who is a son of David and therefore of the line of David, is not the biological father. So this is a bit of a conundrum. Matthew however, has a ready solution to this difficulty but once again I will leave it there and tantalise the reader until we come to Matthew's rather brilliant and perfectly acceptable solution to the problem. For the moment let us stay with Mary and Joseph being 'engaged' and Mary found to be pregnant, Joseph's response to this and its consequences for him and Mary not forgetting, of course, the consequences for the child at the centre of it all.

To all intents and purposes, Matthew proclaims in an 'announcement' to the whole world how Jesus the Messiah's birth took place and it is through the activity of God. Mary, engaged/betrothed to Joseph is found to be *with child through the Holy Spirit*. Ancient peoples thought that sometimes the gods, under various forms, mated with earthly women (we think of Zeus and Leah) but here there is no suggestion of any kind of sexual activity even 'spiritual' sexual activity. There is no suggestion that Mary does anything positive towards the child's conception, nor is there any suggestion of sexual activity, it is just something that happens to her. Mary is simply *found to be with child*. That lack of sexual activity is confirmed by Matthew in the phrase *through the Holy Spirit* and so the Spirit is seen by Matthew to be co-operating with Mary in the conception and the birth but not impregnating her. It is from this point onwards that Joseph begins to dominate Matthew's story of Jesus' beginnings, but this does not mean that Mary is simply set aside (Matthew will make a remarkable statement about her) it is simply that this is where Matthew places his emphasis given that he is writing predominantly for Jewish-Christians.

Mary is said to be *betrothed to Joseph* who is of the royal line and therefore he is heir to the throne of David and so Matthew immediately presents Joseph as honourable and of noble blood. This is a good 'catch' for Mary who may have been as young as thirteen when she was betrothed

(Jeremias 1969:365). So they are 'betrothed' and this was a state from which one could only be released through divorce because it was during the betrothal that the 'dotted line' was signed on, the covenant agreement was made, and all settlements were made (Gundry 1988:21). The actual wedding itself would have been the end of the process, the confirmation of all the arrangements and agreements that had been made beforehand. In this respect then, it would have been frowned upon by both families if any sexual activity had taken place between the couple. Since their marriage had already been arranged Joseph and Mary would have had little to do with one another and she would still be living at her father's house (Safrai 1974-1976:756-57; Finkelstein 1962:1.45. The way Matthew writes it, it seems that Mary did not notify Joseph that she was pregnant but rather that it emerged, or came out, or was discovered, which Matthew may be hinting at in *she was found to be with child*. Joseph would then have been informed and seeing the condition of Mary and being a *righteous man* (in other words, one who would act according to the Law), he sought to divorce her.

Joseph had no choice, he was of noble blood, an honourable family, and Matthew has designated him as a man of righteousness, so he would have to act to save the family honour and in accord with the Law and decency (cf. Keener 1991a:31, 156). If Joseph did not divorce her then he (and thus his family) would be little thought of, no matter how liberally minded he or they might be because that would be to act contrary to the Law which no 'righteous' man would do because the Law said that Mary now belonged to the man who had had sexual relations with her. Mary had been made 'one' with Joseph (Gen. 2.24-25;[1] 1 Cor. 6.15-16[2]) and this was also made clear in the Mishnah (a collection of Jewish legal material compiled in Palestine between 160 AD and 200 AD). Joseph may well have loved Mary but in a real sense it had nothing to do with the 'business' of

---

[1] Therefore a man leaves his father and his mother and clings to his wife, and they become one flesh. And the man and his wife were both naked, and were not ashamed.

[2] Do you not know that your bodies are members of Christ? Should I therefore take the members of Christ and make them members of a prostitute? Never! Do you not know that whoever is united to a prostitute becomes one body with her? For it is said, 'The two shall be one flesh.

betrothal and thus would not have entered the equation and it would have been even more so if Mary had been raped.

But Joseph is being set before the Matthean community as an example of true righteousness that must be deeper than that of the scribes and Pharisees (Mt. 5.20) so:

> being a righteous man and unwilling to expose her to public disgrace, planned to dismiss her quietly.

He did not want to subject her to a public investigation (Num. 5.11-31) and so bring shame and humiliation on her so he decided it would all be done on the quiet. He would issue her with a writ of divorce before two witnesses (as Law required) and Mary would then continue to live at her father's home until someone suitable could be found to marry her, which may be difficult since she would be considered 'soiled goods' (see Delaney 1987:42). In doing this Joseph would probably not be able to get get any of the marriage settlements back which the parents had agreed on or take her marriage dowry. Joseph knew the child was not his (and through this Matthew again emphasises that no sexual activity had taken place between he and Mary) unless he actually pushed for a trial, it was not necessary. So, if it were all done quietly, Mary's family could then accept any offer that might be made to them and the best she could hope for would be an older person looking for a young nubile second wife who would know her place. Mary's situation, therefore, is not looking all that good. And so Mary can, at the surface level, be ranked along with the other women of the genealogy (other than Ruth) whose moral character appears to be less than savoury. However, the reader of the gospel knows more than Joseph because the reader knows that this young woman is *with child through the Holy Spirit*. Joseph, as a 'righteous' man is not only acting according to the Law but also, in his desire to spare Mary public humiliation, is being presented as a caring, considerate, and compassionate man. In contemporary parlance, Mary has lost a 'good 'un'.

For the moment, let us follow Matthew's concentration on Joseph so that we can see how he resolves the genealogical problem I mentioned earlier and also to spend some time on the crucial importance of his almost 'throwaway' remark about Mary referred to earlier. It is obvious that Joseph had been reflecting on these things for Matthew goes on to write (Mt. 1.20):

> But just when he had resolved to do this, an angel of the Lord appeared to him in a dream and said, 'Joseph, son of David, do not be afraid to take Mary as your wife, for the child conceived in her is from the Holy Spirit.

The appearance of angels in dreams is not common in the New Testament; they do not, for example, appear in Luke, indeed, Matthew is the only place where angels in dreams appears. In the dream Joseph is addressed by the *angel of the Lord* and it is an unusual phrasing in the New Testament and in Matthew there are four other such occurrences of the angel appearing in a dream (Mt. 1.20, 24[1]; 2.13, 19). In the Old Testament, the *angel of the Lord* is synonymous with God (but not always) and such confrontations are always on a face-to-face basis, so Matthew's description here is unique (MacDonald 1989:324-35). Matthew is the only evangelist who describes it as an *angel of the Lord* which is further evidence of his Jewishness. Of course, it did not always follow that those who received messages from the *angel of the Lord* in a dream were happy about what they heard but it was the way in which God communicated important information (Gen. 28.12;[2] 31.24; 1 K 3.5[3]) and the ancient Israelite would fully have expected such information to come in dreams (Num. 12.6; Deut. 13.1; 1 S 28.6[4]) even

---

[1] But just when he had resolved to do this, an angel of the Lord appeared to him in a dream and said, 'Joseph, son of David, do not be afraid to take Mary as your wife, for the child conceived in her is from the Holy Spirit; When Joseph awoke from sleep, he did as the angel of the Lord commanded him; he took her as his wife.

[2] And he dreamed that there was a ladder set up on the earth, the top of it reaching to heaven; and the angels of God were ascending and descending on it.

[3] At Gibeon the Lord appeared to Solomon in a dream by night; and God said, 'Ask what I should give you.'

[4] And he said, 'Hear my words: When there are prophets among you, I the Lord make myself known to them in visions; I speak to them in dreams; If prophets or those who divine by dreams appear among you

though it was understood as another way rather than the primary way in which God communicated (Num. 12.6-8). There were cautions given about placing too much store in dreams and being a 'dream dreamer' (Deut. 13.1-5) so in the New Testament dreams are rare (Acts 2.18). In the New Testament visions rather than dreams are the vehicles for such revelations (Acts 9.10;[1] 10.3; 16.9; 18.9) and a 'vision in the night' may not necessarily be a 'dream'. As Matthew presents it, it cannot be a coincidence that Joseph, therefore, receives so much information in dreams from the *angel of the Lord* over a period of time. One may suggest that perhaps Joseph had the gift that Acts 2.18[2] refers to. Certainly the Magi and Pilate's wife in Matthew's gospel receive information in dreams (Mt. 2.12; 27.19[3]) but in the strict understanding of the term, they were not 'believers' (though the Magi appear to be on the path to being so); unbelievers never received visions directly and when they did it was with a view to them being made believers. Warnings to unbelievers, therefore, normally came through dreams as they had to people like Laban (Gen. 31.29[4]).

The command given to Joseph is that he be not afraid to take Mary *as his wife* and in normal circumstances to take a woman who was pregnant with another's child would have been degrading and it would be the equivalent of adultery. Joseph was not considering such a thing but reassurance is given to Joseph that what has happened to Mary is through the power of God. The Holy Spirit occasionally is connected with matters related to birth in the Old Testament (Job 33.4; Ps. 104.30[5]) but it is a

---

and promise you omens or portents; When Saul inquired of the Lord, the Lord did not answer him, not by dreams, nor by Urim, nor by prophets.

[1] Now there was a disciple in Damascus named Ananias. The Lord said to him in a vision, 'Ananias.' He answered, 'Here I am, Lord.'

[2] Even upon my slaves, both men and women, in those days I will pour out my Spirit; and they shall prophesy.

[3] And having been warned in a dream not to return to Herod, they left for their own country by another road.; While he was sitting on the judgement seat, his wife sent word to him, 'Have nothing to do with that innocent man, for today I have suffered a great deal because of a dream about him.'

[4] It is in my power to do you harm; but the God of your father spoke to me last night, saying, "Take heed that you speak to Jacob neither good nor bad."

[5] The spirit of God has made me, and the breath of the Almighty gives me life; When you send forth your spirit, they are created; and you renew the face of the ground.

totally different concept here for the Spirit takes over completely in its creative power and Mary is simply the passive instrument.

However, I mentioned earlier that Matthew's focus is on Joseph and that Mary's role is in the background but this does not mean to say that Mary is not important to Matthew for he says two very crucial things about her. The first is that (Mt. 1.21)

> she will bear a son, and you are to name him Jesus, for he will save his people from their sins.'

Even though it is Joseph who is to 'name' the child (which I shall come to presently), it is Mary who will bear the child and that child will be the saviour and his name is to be called Ye-sous, ('God is salvation', cf. Brown-Driver-Briggs:1996), *for he will save his people from their sins.* We can compare here Ps. 130.8, where it is said, *and he* (God) *shall redeem Israel from all her iniquities.* So Jesus is to act on behalf of God as a Saviour. As in Luke, the emphasis is on a Saviour acting on behalf of God <u>the</u> Saviour (cf. Lk. 1.47; 2.11[1]). Here at the very beginning of the gospel then we have the declared purpose of his coming. It is for the salvation of people from their sins (from their comings short, their missing the mark), and from the consequences of their sins. Its deliberate connection with his name means that the idea is thus to be seen as emphasised throughout the whole Gospel wherever the name of Jesus is mentioned. Therefore, we can always replace the name 'Jesus' with 'God the Saviour' (e.g., Mt. 20.28[2] cf. Mt. 10.22; 24.13, 22[3]). Mary, therefore, while she may be in the background of Matthew's infancy narrative, is nevertheless of crucial and central significance for she is to be the mother of the one who will save his people *from their sins* (this is the only place in the New Testament where 'saves his

---

[1] And my spirit rejoices in God my Saviour; to you is born this day in the city of David a Saviour, who is the Messiah, the Lord.

[2] Just as the Son of Man came not to be served but to serve, and to give his life a ransom for many.'

[3] And you will be hated by all because of my name. But the one who endures to the end will be saved; But anyone who endures to the end will be saved; And if those days had not been cut short, no one would be saved; but for the sake of the elect those days will be cut short.

people' appears with 'sins'.(cf. Gowan 2003:453). In the popular imagination of the people, *saving from sins* was understood to be a function of the Messiah but it was not the main one and certainly not as central as it is made to be here by Matthew.

It was, without doubt, part of the hope that Israel had for the future (Is. 1.18; 43.25; 44.22[1]) but it was not a major element of the Messiah's work, which was essentially understood to establish justice and judgement (Is. 11.1-4;[2] Pss. Sol. 17.28-29, 41[3]). Justice and judgement may well involve some understanding or experience of forgiveness but forgiveness was not a prominent idea and that is why Jesus emphasises that as he is the Son of Man on earth, then he has the right to forgive sins (Mt. 9.6). This is to be a different Messiah than the one expected, one who would equate with Isaiah's Servant and who would suffer on behalf of the people (Mt. 9.2; 26.28[4]; cf. Is. 53; Jer. 31.31-34;[5] Ezek. 36.24-31[6]) and forgiveness of sins is

---

[1]   Come now, let us argue it out, says the Lord: though your sins are like scarlet, they shall be like snow; though they are red like crimson, they shall become like wool; I, I am He who blots out your transgressions for my own sake, and I will not remember your sins. I have swept away your transgressions like a cloud, and your sins like mist; return to me, for I have redeemed you;

[2]   A shoot shall come out from the stock of Jesse, and a branch shall grow out of his roots. The spirit of   the Lord shall rest on him, the spirit of wisdom and understanding, the spirit of counsel and might, the spirit of knowledge and the fear of the Lord. His delight shall be in the fear of the Lord.

[3]   He will distribute them in their tribes upon the land; the sojourner and the foreigner will no longer dwell beside them. He will judge peoples and nations in the wisdom of his righteousness.

[4]   And just then some people were carrying a paralysed man lying on a bed. When Jesus saw their faith, he said to the paralytic, 'Take heart, son; your sins are forgiven.'

[5]   The days are surely coming, says the Lord, when I will make a new covenant with the house of Israel and the house of Judah. It will not be like the covenant that I made with their ancestors when I took them by the hand to bring them out of the land of Egypt, a covenant that they broke, though I was their husband, says the Lord. But this is the covenant that I will make with the house of Israel after those days, says the Lord: I will put my law within them, and I will write it on their hearts; and I will be their God, and they shall be my people. No longer shall they teach one another, or say to each other, 'Know the Lord', for they shall all know me, from the least of them to the greatest, says the Lord; for I will forgive their iniquity, and remember their sin no more.

[6]   I will take you from the nations, and gather you from all the countries, and bring you into your own land. I will sprinkle clean water upon you, and you shall be clean from all your uncleannesses, and from all your idols I will cleanse you. A new heart I will give you, and a new spirit I will put within you; and I will remove from your body the heart of stone and give you a heart of flesh. I will put my spirit within you, and make you follow my statutes and be careful to observe my ordinances. Then you shall live in the land that I gave to your ancestors; and you shall be my people, and I will be your God. I will save you from all your uncleannesses, and I will summon the grain and make it abundant and lay no famine upon you. I will make

central to the ministry of Jesus later (cf. Mt. 6.12, 14-15). Mary, therefore, is not only the mother of the Messiah but of a Messiah who will be utterly different from peoples' expectations. The second important thing Matthew says about Mary is to be found in the first of his 'fulfilment formula citations' for he writes that all the things he has thus far described take place (Mt. 1.22-23):

> to fulfil what had been spoken by the Lord through the prophet:
> 'Look, the virgin shall conceive and bear a son, and they shall
> name him Emmanuel', which means, 'God is with us.'

e. The Prophecy of Isaiah 7.14

Though Matthew has in mind the prophecy of Is. 7.14,[1] he does not mention Isaiah by name. When he does mention Isaiah's name it is in a very specific context based on the fulfilment of the prophecy used here: the coming of the Messiah (Mt. 4.14-16[2]) and Servant (Mt. 8.17;[3]) which is preparing for the revelation and reinterpretation of his Messiahship in Mt. 16.16, 21,[4] his revelation in glory in Mt. 17.1-8,[5] and the confirmation of his

---

the fruit of the tree and the produce of the field abundant, so that you may never again suffer the disgrace of famine among the nations. Then you shall remember your evil ways, and your dealings that were not good; and you shall loathe yourselves for your iniquities and your abominable deeds.

[1] Therefore the Lord himself will give you a sign. Look, the young woman is with child and shall bear a son, and shall name him Immanuel.

[2] So that what had been spoken through the prophet Isaiah might be fulfilled: 'Land of Zebulun, land of Naphtali, on the road by the sea, across the Jordan, Galilee of the Gentiles, the people who sat in darkness have seen a great light, and for those who sat in the region and shadow of death light has dawned.'

[3] This was to fulfil what had been spoken through the prophet Isaiah, 'He took our infirmities and bore our diseases.'

[4] Simon Peter answered, 'You are the Messiah, the Son of the living God.'; From that time on, Jesus began to show his disciples that he must go to Jerusalem and undergo great suffering at the hands of the elders and chief priests and scribes, and be killed, and on the third day be raised.

[5] Six days later, Jesus took with him Peter and James and his brother John and led them up a high mountain, by themselves. And he was transfigured before them, and his face shone like the sun, and his clothes became dazzling white. Suddenly there appeared to them Moses and Elijah, talking with him. Then Peter said to Jesus, 'Lord, it is good for us to be here; if you wish, I will make three dwellings here, one for you, one for Moses, and one for Elijah.' While he was still speaking, suddenly a bright cloud overshadowed them, and from the cloud a voice said, 'This is my Son, the Beloved; with him I am well pleased; listen to him!' When the disciples heard this, they fell to the ground and were overcome by fear. But Jesus came

redemptive servanthood in Mt. 20.28.[1] Matthew, therefore, regarded Isaiah's word as of profound significance and importance. The reason that Matthew emphasises the words, *the Lord,* here and at Mt. 2.15[2], is because what he is describing is God's *direct* action through the son Mary is to bear. The point that Matthew is making is that God himself is bringing his son into the world and Mary is his mother. This son will bring his people 'out of Egypt', i.e., as God saved the people in Egypt, so too Jesus will save the people by bringing them out of darkness and into the kingdom. The word *fulfilled* here has the meaning of 'filled to completion, to be brought to a destined end.' In Matthew this is more than simply a fulfilling of a prophecy but rather the completion of a great purpose (Blomberg 1992:60; Keener 1993:48).

The almost 'throwaway' remark that I have mentioned earlier is to be found here, Matthew refers to Mary as a *virgin* (Craig 1986:114 cf. Borg 1987:33-34; Meier 1994:11,519-21; Brown 1994:143-44). It is the first and only mention of this word in the Matthean text. He has not mentioned Mary as a 'virgin' up to this point: he has simply stated: *this is how the birth of the Jesus the Messiah took place, his mother Mary....*and this *formula citation* (Matthew is always very careful in his use of them) is significant because it is one of two moments when Matthew uses the phrase *spoken by the Lord* (the other is Mt. 2.15). Therefore, this citation must be understood as of crucial importance. Matthew does say where he gets this idea from; it does not appear in Mark or 'Q' and may be part of a tradition unknown to Mark and John or 'Q', i.e., the M tradition, the Matthean community (?) We simply do not know where or how this tradition arose and the nature of its historicity, if any. Greco-Roman biographies, or 'lives,' frequently included birth narratives (Aune 1987:65), including miraculous signs such as dreams when appropriate (Schuler 1982:94). Thus it is not surprising that Matthew would focus on such events, although his birth narratives do not perfectly fit

---

and touched them, saying, 'Get up and do not be afraid.' 8And when they looked up, they saw no one except Jesus himself alone.

[1] Just as the Son of Man came not to be served but to serve, and to give his life a ransom for many.'

[2] And remained there until the death of Herod. This was to fulfil what had been spoken by the Lord through the prophet, 'Out of Egypt I have called my son.'

this genre, since they lack the typical structure of miracle stories (see Theissen 1991:123). The basic account of the 'virgin birth' (a traditional way of referring to it, though it is a virginal *conception* in the first instance) is earlier than either of the Gospels that describe Jesus' infancy; neither Gospel is clearly dependent on the other (see, Brown 1977:162;Drury 1976:123-25). Reliable sources also stand behind the account; Jesus' birth is likely one of the stories whose reliability Luke investigated (Lk. 1.3). Members of Jesus' family remained in positions of prominence in early Christianity (1 Cor 15.7; Gal 1.19; 2.9) when this pre-Matthew tradition (shared with Luke) was circulating. But Matthew is less concerned to prove the virgin birth to his audience, which both accepted Jesus as Messiah and acknowledged the miraculous. Matthew is more interested in teaching, and an important lesson this narrative teaches is that Jesus fulfils scripture (Mt.1.22-23). The text is taken from Is. 7.14 and while I shall come to this in a moment in more detail, a few general observations might be made first.

In the Isaiah text the birth of the heir to the throne of David (Is. 9.6-7[1]) would happen through the conception by an '*almah*' which in the Septuagint (LXX) is translated as *virgin*, though as I shall discuss in a moment, it means an 'unmarried woman of marriageable age who was assumed to be a virgin'. This was because the *house of David* in the person of Ahaz had been rejected by God because of the refusal to ask for a miraculous sign that God had offered simply because Ahaz did not want to do what God asked of him. Ahaz placed his trust in Assyria without fully realising or understanding what that would mean. So, a miraculous sign was forced on him, one which would spell the end of his house: that he must recognise that the future hope of the house of David would no longer be in his line because the one who would come would be born of a virgin: God would bypass the current house of David. So, *God himself will give you a*

---

[1] For a child has been born for us, a son given to us; authority rests upon his shoulders; and he is named Wonderful Counsellor, Mighty God, Everlasting Father, Prince of Peace. His authority shall grow continually, and there shall be endless peace for the throne of David and his kingdom. He will establish and uphold it with justice and with righteousness from this time onwards and for evermore. The zeal of the Lord of hosts will do this.

sign really meant: God will give you a sign which will be expressed in the words that are now spoken to you by him. There will be a future wonder which will be clearly indicative of your rejection. This wonder will be greater than what you could ask from heaven or earth; it will happen through God's power, and because the one who comes will not be born of human seed, it will signal the end of your house.

The 'almah' would bear a son without a father and so the line of Ahaz would be no more and this child would be called *God with us* (Emmanuel). God would be among his people through this child but he would no longer be with Ahaz and what Ahaz had lost through his lack of belief, the child would bring about. Thus, the sign of the 'almah' conceiving and bearing a son, is not something that Ahaz can draw hope from, rather, the child would be a sign of his rejection. When it was to happen God, through Isaiah, does not say but it will happen because God has spoken his word. Matthew is saying that in the virginal conception of Jesus that prophecy is fulfilled. Thus, Jesus truly is Emmanuel: God with us as saviour.

The 'almah'-Emmanuel prophecy is crucial to understanding Matthew's Christology but it is also crucial for understanding the central role he presents Mary as playing, even given his emphasis on Joseph and his placing of Mary in the background. It need not be gainsaid that this text in Matthew has been the subject of great debate. This is not the place to go into a detailed account of issues surrounding the virginal conception but an examination of the Isaiah prophecy and some of the interpretations of it might serve to be useful, especially given the fact that for some Christian traditions the virginal conception is the basis for many other statements, doctrines, and proclamations about Mary of Nazareth.

The first thing to note is that the verse in Matthew refers to a *virgin* (Gk. 'parthenos') who will give birth to a son *conceived by the Holy Spirit'* and Matthew makes it clear that Mary did not have sexual intercourse with her husband (Joseph) until after she had given birth to this child (Mt. 1.24-25[1]). Matthew, therefore, is making it clear that in his mind this is a virginal

---

[1] When Joseph awoke from sleep, he did as the angel of the Lord commanded him; he took her as his wife,

conception and birth and even more so that there is a supernatural element which has involved only one party (Holy Spirit). It is important to grasp this: it highlights the fact that for Matthew, writing within the world view that predominated his time, there is no comparison or parallel with the other 'virgin births' found in the extant literature and which are often cited as indicating that the virginal conception of Jesus is not unique, i.e., the gods often mated with human women, such comparisons are inadequate (see, Davies and Allison 1988:214-15) and so are totally absent here. Matthew's writing, therefore, has to be considered as coming from a completely different, if not new, context: that this child is the result of the miraculous working of the 'Holy Spirit' without any suggestion of 'divine sexual' activity and thus it is not based on any ancient or contemporaneous pagan virgin-birth myth.

Matthew may have in mind Old Testament figures such as Sarah and Hannah (Gen. 21.1-2;[1] 1 S 1.20[2]) but even this is unlikely since in both these cases though there was divine aid, the conception of the children took place through sexual intercourse and are more readily taken as parallels with the conception of John the Baptist (which we shall deal with in when exploring Mary in Luke). How then is the birth of Jesus to be seen as 'fulfilling' or filling full to completion' the words of the Lord? In the Isaian prophecy the promise was that an 'almah' (Hebrew) a young woman of marriageable age presumed to be a 'parthenos' (virgin=Greek LXX) would bear a child which would show that God was with Israel and that the house of Ahaz had been rejected. 'Almah' is never used of a non-virgin or a married woman but mainly seems to indicate a young woman, unmarried and with burgeoning sexual desires and who is thus assumed to be a virgin. The word 'almah' is used in Song of Songs 6.8-9 where it is contrasted with queens and concubines and very clearly refers to those who are in the same

---

but had no marital relations with her until she had borne a son; and he named him Jesus.

[1]   The Lord dealt with Sarah as he had said, and the Lord did for Sarah as he had promised. Sarah conceived and bore Abraham a son in his old age, at the time of which God had spoken to him.

[2]   In due time Hannah conceived and bore a son. She named him Samuel, for she said, 'I have asked him of the Lord.'

situation as the loved one, unmarried and virginal and v.9 associates it with the 'daughters' of their mothers as they have not left their own households so that the many is compared with the one. 'Almah', therefore, is a word which contains the notion of sexual purity and without the taint that had come to be associated with the word 'bethula', quite often translated as virgin. This term was very specifically linked with the deities of dubious morality at Ugarit (where the famous Ras Shamra texts were found) and was used to describe the fertility goddesses, who were certainly not virgins. It did not strictly mean a 'pure virgin' at the time of the Isaian prophecy whatever it came to mean later, for example in Joel 1.8[1] a 'bethulah' is mourning the husband of her youth and there are no grounds at all for considering that they had only been betrothed.

Some have sought to use Prov. 30. (18)-19[2] as an example of 'almah' being used to refer to a non-virgin when it speaks of the *way of a man with a maid* but this does not mean that it is referring to sexual activity, indeed the opposite is more clearly indicated. There the writer is dealing with the movements of different creatures. Using sexual movements as an example of someone's movements, as being watched by others, would, with an innocent couple in view, have been severely frowned upon. And we only have to look at what it is being compared with to recognise that it is being paralleled with flight and directional movement which is watched by others. The thought is thus more of a couple on the move in their flirtatious activity, or even of a man's behaviour of which the young woman is not much aware, the onlookers being amused as he trails her trying to be noticed by her. In this case, it supports the use of 'almah' for an unmarried maiden than the opposite. It can therefore be understood why the LXX used 'parthenos' (virgin) to translate 'almah', just as it is in Gen. 24.43[3] because they recognised the emphasis that Isaiah was placing on this woman as being

---

[1] Lament like a virgin dressed in sackcloth for the husband of her youth.

[2] Three things are too wonderful for me; four I do not understand: the way of an eagle in the sky, the way of a snake on a rock, the way of a ship on the high seas, and the way of a man with a girl.

[3] I am standing here by the spring of water; let the young woman who comes out to draw, to whom I shall say, 'Please give me a little water from your jar to drink,'

unmarried and pure (cf. Sweeney:1996, 161-162). At the same time it has to be admitted that 'parthenos' does not always refer to 'virgin' as we would understand it today, i.e., an intact virgin who has not had relations with a man, but nevertheless behind it always lies the idea of purity (cf. Brown, Achtemeier 1978: 92). The term could, for example, be rightly applied to the sacred prostitutes in the temples who were certainly not virgins. However, those who wrote of them understood them to have their own special kind of 'purity' since they were the daughters of the gods and not prostitutes in the commonly accepted understanding of the term and all that it implied, they were considered to be 'holy'. But on the other hand they were certainly not 'virgins' and furthermore, after Dinah was raped (Gen. 34.1-2[1]) in the LXX she is still referred to as 'parthenos' in Gen. 34.3. She was considered 'pure' even though she had been violated and was technically not intact. In Is. 47.1 the *virgin daughter of Babylon* could lose her children and be brought in to widowhood (Is. 47.8-9[2]). In none of these instances are the 'parthenoi' (pl. parthenos) virgins in the understood sense of the term but the idea of purity may lie behind all of them.

The next thing to be noted is that this almah/parthenos of the Isiaian prophecy is to bring forth a child who will be a sign of the rejection of the house of Ahaz (indicated by the assault of Assyria in Is. 7.17[3]) and also that God do what he says and empty the land of both his enemies (which will be a warning to him) for what can be done to his enemies can also be done to him. The question now is: who then is this *son* who will be this sign? Among the many suggestions made three are of particular note:

---

[1] Now Dinah the daughter of Leah, whom she had borne to Jacob, went out to visit the women of the region. When Shechem son of Hamor the Hivite, prince of the region, saw her, he seized her and lay with her by force.

[2] Now therefore hear this, you lover of pleasures, who sit securely, who say in your heart,'I am, and there is no one besides me; I shall not sit as a widow or know the loss of children' both these things shall come upon you in a moment, in one day: the loss of children and widowhood shall come upon you in full measure, in spite of your many sorceries and the great power of your enchantments.

[3] The Lord will bring on you and on your people and on your ancestral house such days as have not come since the day that Ephraim departed from Judah, the king of Assyria.'

- It was a child born of the royal house, or Isaiah's wife, whose very birth would act as a sign.
- It was any child born at the time and the emphasis is on the fact that before it was weaned what God had said would happen.
- It was a child described in Is. 9.7[1], the coming one who would be greater than David, a Wonderful Counsellor, Mighty God, Everlasting Father, Prince of Peace and who would rule over the whole world.

So, which one is meant? To determine this we have to look at the context. God had offered help to Ahaz to put him under his protection and to give him assurance in the face of what confronted him. God had offered him a sign of truly miraculous proportions (in Is. 38.5-8[2], for example, the sun goes back ten degrees under Hezekiah). God says (Is. 7.11):

> ask a sign of the Lord whether it be as high as the heaven or as deep as Sheol

Ahaz rejects the offer whereas had he accepted it in faith, this sign would have shown that Ahaz had been established. So the sign is not only related to the promise of deliverance from the current threat, but it is also a guarantee of the future establishment of the house of David through the line of Ahaz, so protecting him from all who would threaten him. It is on the basis of his refusal of God's offer that God says he will still give him a sign but the sign that he will give will not be one to his liking, for it will be a sign of Assyria

---

[1] His authority shall grow continually, and there shall be endless peace for the throne of David and his kingdom. He will establish and uphold it with justice and with righteousness from this time onwards and for evermore. The zeal of the Lord of hosts will do this.

[2] Go and say to Hezekiah, Thus says the Lord, the God of your ancestor David: I have heard your prayer, have seen your tears; I will add fifteen years to your life. I will deliver you and this city out of the hand of the king of Assyria, and defend this city. 'This is the sign to you from the Lord, that the Lord will do this thing that he has promised: See, I will make the shadow cast by the declining sun on the dial of Ahaz turn back ten steps.' So the sun turned back on the dial the ten steps by which it had declined.

falling on him and so he will not be 'established' and the sign will be that a child will be born of an 'almah'. The first thing that must be noticed here is that these words seem to indicate that God does intend to give a sign that will be higher than the heavens and deeper than Sheol even though the sign will be of no benefit to Ahaz. Only such a sign could demonstrate the certainty that the house of Ahaz had no future and if that were to be so then only a virgin birth would meet the requirements (Childs 2001:65). It was the virgin birth of the child which would guarantee that he would not be of Ahaz's line, and that, instead of being so, God himself would have intervened in the production of the royal child.

In turning to the first of the suggestions above as to the identity of the child, a few observations might be made. The first is that the birth of a royal prince in the normal course of events (and bear in mind Hezekiah has already been born) or to the prophetess could hardly have been such as sign as God described above. No one would have believed a child could be born of a virgin and indeed, it was not possible for the prophetess to produce a child in this way since she was no longer a 'virgin'. Certainly the prophetess bears two sons both of whom by their names will be signs to Judah/Israel (as would their father, Is. 8.18[1]) but while the prophetess is mentioned earlier in respect of one of the sons (Is. 8.3[2]) she is not mentioned in v.18 where there is reference to 'signs and portents' referring to both sons and their father. There is, therefore, no emphasis on it being the prophetess who bears both sons who were 'signs and portents' in Israel (along with their father) even though she in fact done so. The emphasis here falls on the father. However, the argument is often that this is the point. The emphasis is in fact on her bearing one of the sons, Maher-shalal-hash-baz (Is. 8.3), who will be a sign of the devastation of the two kingdoms, something which in Is. 7.16[3] was to be gathered from the sign of the 'almah with child. But here

---

[1]   See, I and the children whom the Lord has given me are signs and portents in Israel from the Lord of hosts, who dwells on Mount Zion.

[2]   And I went to the prophetess, and she conceived and bore a son. Then the Lord said to me, Name him Maher-shalal-hash-baz.

[3]   For before the child knows how to refuse the evil and choose the good, the land before whose two kings you are in dread will be deserted

we should note that in Is. 8.3 this is not in fact specifically described as a sign. It is rather seen as a prophetic acting out of what was to be, which is not quite the same thing. Of course, we may accept that it was an indication of what was to be, and in that sense a sign.

However, it was equally certainly not the kind of sign that the Lord had originally spoken of, a sign of startling proportions. Nor is it said to relate to the now greater matters that were involved: that Ahaz's house would no longer be established, and that the king of Assyria was about to descend on him and his land because he had forfeited the Lord's protection. We may therefore justifiably see the birth of Maher-shalal-hash-baz as a partial sign, but not as the great sign. The child's birth, through the name given to him, was indeed a sign that the kingdom would be destroyed from their lands within a short while, and that was all that he is described as being. But he was not born of an 'almah, and he is not said to be a sign of the larger matter in hand: the rejection of the house of Ahaz as manifested by the coming of Assyria and devastation of Judah. Nor is he said to be the sign of the coming of a king who would achieve what Ahaz has failed to achieve (Is. 9.7[1]), that is, of the fulfilment of the promises to the house of David. (A fact that will later be made even clearer by the rejection of his son Hezekiah and his seed cf. Is. 39.5-7[2]). The same problems as these lie with any attempt to relate the birth of the child to the birth of any child in the house of Ahaz. The birth of such a child would hardly rank as an unusual sign, and would be even less significant than that born to the prophetess. For we must remember that the heir, Hezekiah, had already been born before this happened.

In turning to the suggestion that it refers to any child born at the time, the emphasis being on the fact that before it was weaned what God had said

---

[1]   His authority shall grow continually, and there shall be endless peace for the throne of David and his kingdom. He will establish and uphold it with justice and with righteousness from this time onwards and for evermore. The zeal of the Lord of hosts will do this.

[2]   Then Isaiah said to Hezekiah, 'Hear the word of the Lord of hosts: Days are coming when all that is in your house, and that which your ancestors have stored up until this day, shall be carried to Babylon; nothing shall be left, says the Lord. Some of your own sons who are born to you shall be taken away; they shall be eunuchs in the palace of the king of Babylon.'

would happen, again this idea can be challenged. This suffers from even more disadvantages than the first, for it does not even have the partial support in context that the first interpretation has when related to the prophetess. It is fine as evidence of how short a time it will be before both of Ahaz's opponents are devastated, but it has nothing to say about the non-establishment of the house of Ahaz or of the coming of the king of Assyria, nor could it possibly be seen as in any way parallel with the kind of sign that the Lord had spoken about. For the truth is that if the Lord made his great declaration about 'a sign almost as beyond the conception of man as it could possibly be', and then gave one which was merely a birth in the usual run of things, it would appear to all that what he had offered was something mediocre. And this is especially so because in the past he had specialised in 'special' births in that a number of past 'greats' had been born miraculously (even though not from an 'almah), and almost with the same words. Thus:

- Isaac was born 'miraculously' (Gen. 18.10-11, 14; 21.2: *conceived and bore a son*)
- Samson was born 'miraculously'(Judg.13.3: *will conceive and bear a son*)
- Samuel was born 'miraculously'(1 S 1 5,20: *conceived and bore a son*)

And all these births would be engraved on Israelite hearts. But there is no suggestion that they were born of 'almahs', nor was the child of the prophetess in fact born 'miraculously', even though she 'conceived and bore a son'. Indeed she had already previously had another son. It will be noted that the only exact parallel to '*will* conceive and bear a son' in the whole of the Old Testament is Judg. 13.3, 5, 7,[1] and that of a birth that was certainly

---

[1]   And the angel of the Lord appeared to the woman and said to her, 'Although you are barren, having borne no children, you shall conceive and bear a son; for you shall conceive and bear a son. No razor is to come on his head, for the boy shall be a nazirite to God from birth. It is he who shall begin to deliver Israel from the hand of the Philistines.'; but he said to me, "You shall conceive and bear a son. So then drink no wine or strong drink, and eat nothing unclean, for the boy shall be a nazirite to God from birth to the day of his

unusual and unexpected. Finally, the third suggestion that it refers to the child described in Is. 9.6-7,[1] the coming One who would be greater than David, who would be called:

> Wonderful, Counsellor, Mighty God, Everlasting Father, Prince of Peace,

and would rule over the whole world, thus indicating that he would be miraculously born of an 'almah ('parthenos', virgin). There can be no question that this suggestion of the virgin birth of the coming hope of the house of David has the most going for it from an Israelite's point of view and from the point of view of the context. It would tie in with the past history of conceiving and bearing a 'miraculous child' as being signs to Israel. It would tie in with the Lord's promise that he would give a remarkable miraculous sign. It would tie in with the following description of the 'birth of a child' in Is. 9.6. It would give full weight to the use of 'almah. It would explain why it demonstrated that 'God is with us'. It would confirm that the hope of the house of David was indeed coming, in spite of present appearances, even though Ahaz's house would be excluded. And in the context of Matthew it would explain why he would be able to save his people from their sins. And as no one knew when the child would be born (it could be at any time) the indication that both kings would be devastated before the child could possibly grow to boyhood was a sufficient indicator of time, especially when associated with the actual example of the birth of the son to the prophetess. Indeed the only question that it might raise is, how could such a birth in the future possibly be a sign to Ahaz?

The answer to this question lies in the nature of the sign. It should be noted that it was no longer intended to be a sign to Ahaz that he was to be

---

death." '

[1] For a child has been born for us, a son given to us; authority rests upon his shoulders; and he is named Wonderful Counsellor, Mighty God, Everlasting Father, Prince of Peace. His authority shall grow continually, and there shall be endless peace for the throne of David and his kingdom. He will establish and uphold it with justice and with righteousness from this time onwards and for evermore. The zeal of the Lord of hosts will do this

established (Is. 7.9[1]). But what it certainly was a sign of the fact that he would not be established, and while that did not really require a great present miracle at the time then current, God was determined that the one who had refused a miraculous sign would be given one which would demonstrate the fact in an inescapable way. Ahaz lived at a time when all hopes were on the coming of the future triumphant son of David, who would be of the line of David, and who would rule the world (Ps. 2.6-7[2]) and Ahaz would pride himself in the fact that it would be of his seed. Thus to inform Ahaz that he was now receiving God's words as a sign that this coming David would actually in fact be born of a virgin, and not be of his seed, was indeed a sign that he would not be established and was an unwelcome sign indeed. It was an indication vouchsafed by the word of God that the future throne would go to one not born of Ahaz's seed. The sign was thus now not a matter of when the child would be born, but of what his birth would signify as regards the hopes for the future. Furthermore, we have a good example in the past of precisely such an idea that was given as a sign to its recipient, with the actual working out of the sign being a future event (Ex. 3.12[3]). There the sign that Moses had been sent would be the fact that the people to whom he went would one day *serve God on this mountain*. The sign was a promise of a better future that had to be believed in, and that they could hold on to, and in which they had to continue to believe. It was a sign that had to be accepted on the basis of God's promise. It was a sign of a future which would actually be the result of their response of faith, just as this sign in Is. 7.14[4] was a similar promise of a better future in which the people were called on to believe, in contrast to Ahaz (Is. 7.9).

Strictly speaking, in fact, Ahaz did not want or merit a sign. He had

---

[1] The head of Ephraim is Samaria, and the head of Samaria is the son of Remaliah. If you do not stand firm in faith, you shall not stand at all.

[2] 'I have set my king on Zion, my holy hill.' I will tell of the decree of the Lord: He said to me, 'You are my son; today I have begotten you.

[3] He said, 'I will be with you; and this shall be the sign for you that it is I who sent you: when you have brought the people out of Egypt, you shall worship God on this mountain.'

[4] Therefore the Lord himself will give you a sign. Look, the young woman is with child and shall bear a son, and shall name him Immanuel.

refused it. He had already made up his mind to look to Assyria. Thus the point here is that he was now to receive a verbal sign that he did not want, which demonstrated the very opposite of what the original promised sign would have indicated. And that sign was God's own word that the Coming One would now be born of a virgin, and not of the seed of Ahaz. It demonstrated his rejection by God. Meanwhile, Israel could indeed be confident that one day it would receive its promised king whose coming would prove that God was with them, but they would now know that he would not be born of the seed of Ahaz, but would rather be born of a virgin. We should also note that while this might cause problems to our scientific age, it would have caused no problems to Israelites, or indeed to Matthew. They would not be looking for some interpretation that avoided the 'miraculous'. They would have seen no difficulty in the idea of the Creator bringing about a virgin birth. This being so, it is quite reasonable to see that to Matthew, Isaiah was seen as promising that the great Son of David would be born of a virgin and therefore it directly related to what had happened in the case of Jesus, who, as that Son of David, had indeed been born of a virgin. Matthew thus saw his birth from a virgin as 'filling in full' the prophecy which had only partly been fulfilled by Maher-shalal-hash-baz. Mary's importance to Matthew (despite his lack of emphasis on her in the narrative) is therefore crucial. We need not delve into the rest of Matthew's infancy narrative since Matthew continues to focus on Joseph and his dreams and Mary has only a 'cameo' role. However, following Matthew's formula citation of Is. 7.14, he writes (Mt. 1.24-25):

> When Joseph awoke from sleep, he did as the angel of the Lord commanded him; he took her as his wife, but had no marital relations with her until she had borne a son; and he named him Jesus.

And so when the events of the Magi, the plans to destroy Jesus by Herod, the flight into Egypt, the return from Egypt and the settling in Nazareth occur, Matthew no longer has Mary betrothed to Joseph: now she is his wife and the mother of his son whom he has named *Jesus* as he has been told

CHAPTER TWO

The Women of Matthew

The Syro-Phoenician Woman (Mt. 15.22-28)

The Narrative Context

Matthew places this story immediately after the teaching of Jesus to the disciples on issues related to purity (Mt. 15.10-20[1]) as does Mark (Mk. 7.24-30[2]). Jesus' encounter with this Gentile woman brings out the implications the Evangelists find in his view of purity: Gentiles will no longer be separated from Israel (cf. Acts 10.15, 28;[3] 11.9-18[4]). Like the

---

[1] Then he called the crowd to him and said to them, 'Listen and understand: it is not what goes into the mouth that defiles a person, but it is what comes out of the mouth that defiles.' Then the disciples approached and said to him, 'Do you know that the Pharisees took offence when they heard what you said?' He answered, 'Every plant that my heavenly Father has not planted will be uprooted. Let them alone; they are blind guides of the blind. And if one blind person guides another, both will fall into a pit.' But Peter said to him, 'Explain this parable to us.' Then he said, 'Are you also still without understanding? Do you not see that whatever goes into the mouth enters the stomach, and goes out into the sewer? But what comes out of the mouth proceeds from the heart, and this is what defiles. For out of the heart come evil intentions, murder, adultery, fornication, theft, false witness, slander. These are what defile a person, but to eat with unwashed hands does not defile.'

[2] From there he set out and went away to the region of Tyre. He entered a house and did not want anyone to know he was there. Yet he could not escape notice, but a woman whose little daughter had an unclean spirit immediately heard about him, and she came and bowed down at his feet. Now the woman was a Gentile, of Syrophoenician origin. She begged him to cast the demon out of her daughter. He said to her, 'Let the children be fed first, for it is not fair to take the children's food and throw it to the dogs.' But she answered him, 'Sir, even the dogs under the table eat the children's crumbs.' Then he said to her, 'For saying that, you may go, the demon has left your daughter.' So she went home, found the child lying on the bed, and the demon gone.

[3] The voice said to him again, a second time, 'What God has made clean, you must not call profane.' ;and he said to them, 'You yourselves know that it is unlawful for a Jew to associate with or to visit a Gentile; but God has shown me that I should not call anyone profane or unclean.

[4] But a second time the voice answered from heaven, "What God has made clean, you must not call profane." This happened three times; then everything was pulled up again to heaven. At that very moment three men, sent to me from Caesarea, arrived at the house where we were. The Spirit told me to go with them and not to make a distinction between them and us. These six brothers also accompanied me, and we entered the man's house. He told us how he had seen the angel standing in his house and saying, "Send to Joppa and bring Simon, who is called Peter; he will give you a message by which you and your entire household will be saved." And as I began to speak, the Holy Spirit fell upon them just as it had upon us at the beginning. And I remembered the word of the Lord, how he had said, "John baptised with water, but you will be baptised with the Holy Spirit." If then God gave them the same gift that he gave us when we

Centurion in Matthew's Gospel (Mt. 8.10[1]), this woman becomes an illustration of faith (Rhoads 1994:348-52). Also like the Centurion, this outsider's faith compares favourably with that of some religious insiders among Jesus' contemporaries (Mt. 15.1-20[2]). Matthew reinforces this point by specifying exactly what Mark's Hellenistic *Syro-Phoenician* woman (Mk. 7.26[3]) means (see, Theissen 1991:66-80). She is a descendant of the ancient Canaanites, the bitter biblical enemies of Israel whose paganism had often led Israel into idolatry (cf. *Jub.* 22.20-22[4]). If *Tyre and Sidon* (Mt. 15.21[5]) lead some readers to recall Jezebel, others must recall instead the

---

believed in the Lord Jesus Christ, who was I that I could hinder God?' When they heard this, they were silenced. And they praised God, saying, 'Then God has given even to the Gentiles the repentance that leads to life.'

[1] When Jesus heard him, he was amazed and said to those who followed him, 'Truly I tell you, in no one in Israel have I found such faith

[2] Then Pharisees and scribes came to Jesus from Jerusalem and said, 'Why do your disciples break the tradition of the elders? For they do not wash their hands before they eat.' He answered them, 'And why do you break the commandment of God for the sake of your tradition? For God said, "Honour your father and your mother," and, "Whoever speaks evil of father or mother must surely die." But you say that whoever tells father or mother, "Whatever support you might have had from me is given to God", then that person need not honour the father. So, for the sake of your tradition, you make void the word of God. You hypocrites! Isaiah prophesied rightly about you when he said: "This people honours me with their lips, but their hearts are far from me; in vain do they worship me, teaching human precepts as doctrines." ' Then he called the crowd to him and said to them, 'Listen and understand: it is not what goes into the mouth that defiles a person, but it is what comes out of the mouth that defiles.' Then the disciples approached and said to him, 'Do you know that the Pharisees took offence when they heard what you said?' He answered, 'Every plant that my heavenly Father has not planted will be uprooted. Let them alone; they are blind guides of the blind. And if one blind person guides another, both will fall into a pit.' But Peter said to him, 'Explain this parable to us.' Then he said, 'Are you also still without understanding? Do you not see that whatever goes into the mouth enters the stomach, and goes out into the sewer? But what comes out of the mouth proceeds from the heart, and this is what defiles. For out of the heart come evil intentions, murder, adultery, fornication, theft, false witness, slander. These are what defile a person, but to eat with unwashed hands does not defile.'

[3] Now the woman was a Gentile, of Syrophoenician origin. She begged him to cast the demon out of her daughter.

[4] Beware my son Jacob, of taking a wife from any seed of the daughters of Canaan; For all his seed is to be rooted out of the earth. For, owing to the transgression of Ham, Canaan erred, And all his seed shall be destroyed from off the earth and all the residue thereof, And none springing from him shall be saved on the day of judgement. And as for all the worshippers of idols and the profane. There shall be no hope for them in the land of the living; And there shall be no remembrance of them on the earth; for they shall descend into Sheol, And into the place of condemnation shall they go, as the children of Sodom were taken away from the earth So will all those who worship idols be taken away.

[5] Jesus left that place and went away to the district of Tyre and Sidon.

widow who supported Elijah (1 K 17.8-24;[1] Lk. 4.25-26[2]; see, Derrett 1973:16). The narrative thus constitutes another of Matthew's invitations to the Gentile mission (e.g., Mt. 2.1-11;[3] 8.5-13[4]) reinforcing the message of Mt. 11.21-24[5] (where Tyre and Sidon were more open to repentance than Galilean towns were, cf. Gnilka, 1978:1.291) (Mt. 15.22-28):

> Jesus left that place and went away to the district of Tyre and Sidon. Just then a Canaanite woman from that region came out and

---

[1]   Then the word of the Lord came to him, saying, 'Go now to Zarephath, which belongs to Sidon, and   live there; for I have commanded a widow there to feed you.' So he set out and went to Zarephath. When he came to the gate of the town, a widow was there gathering sticks; he called to her and said, 'Bring me a little water in a vessel, so that I may drink.' As she was going to bring it, he called to her and said, 'Bring me a morsel of bread in your hand.' But she said, 'As the Lord your God lives, I have nothing baked, only a handful of meal in a jar, and a little oil in a jug; I am now gathering a couple of sticks, so that I may go home and prepare it for myself and my son, that we may eat it, and die.' Elijah said to her, 'Do not be afraid; go and do as you have said; but first make me a little cake of it and bring it to me, and afterwards make something for yourself and your son. For thus says the Lord the God of Israel: The jar of meal will not be emptied and the jug of oil will not fail until the day that the Lord sends rain on the earth.' She went and did as Elijah said, so that she as well as he and her household ate for many days. The jar of meal was not emptied, neither did the jug of oil fail, according to the word of the Lord that he spoke by Elijah After this the son of the woman, the mistress of the house, became ill; his illness was so severe that there was no breath left in him. She then said to Elijah, 'What have you against me, O man of God? You have come to me to bring my sin to remembrance, and to cause the death of my son!' But he said to her, 'Give me your son.' He took him from her bosom, carried him up into the upper chamber where he was lodging, and laid him on his own bed. He cried out to the Lord, O Lord my God, have you brought calamity even upon the widow with whom I am staying, by killing her son?' Then he stretched himself upon the child three times, and cried out to the Lord, 'O Lord my God, let this child's life come into him again.' The Lord listened to the voice of Elijah; the life of the child came into him again, and he revived. Elijah took the child, brought him down from the upper chamber into the house, and gave him to his mother; then Elijah said, 'See, your son is alive.' So the woman said to Elijah, 'Now I know that you are a man of God, and that the word of the Lord in your mouth is truth.'

[2]   But the truth is, there were many widows in Israel in the time of Elijah, when the heaven was shut up for three years and six months, and there was a severe famine over all the land; yet Elijah was sent to none of them except to a widow at Zarephath in Sidon.

[3]   In the time of King Herod, after Jesus was born in Bethlehem of Judea, wise men from the East came to Jerusalem, asking, 'Where is the child who has been born king of the Jews? For we observed his star at its rising, and have come to pay him homage.' When King Herod heard this, he was frightened, and all Jerusalem with him; and calling together all the chief priests and scribes of the people, he inquired of them where the Messiah was to be born. They told him, 'In Bethlehem of Judea; for so it has been written by the prophet: "And you, Bethlehem, in the land of Judah, are by no means least among the rulers of Judah; for from you shall come a ruler who is to shepherd my people Israel." ' Then Herod secretly called for the wise men and learned from them the exact time when the star had appeared. Then he sent them to Bethlehem, saying, 'Go and search diligently for the child; and when you have found him, bring me word

started shouting, 'Have mercy on me, Lord, Son of David; my daughter is tormented by a demon.' But he did not answer her at all. And his disciples came and urged him, saying, 'Send her away, for she keeps shouting after us.' He answered, 'I was sent only to the lost sheep of the house of Israel.' But she came and knelt before him, saying, 'Lord, help me.' He answered, 'It is not fair to take the children's food and throw it to the dogs.' She said, 'Yes, Lord, yet even the dogs eat the crumbs that fall from their masters' table.' Then Jesus answered her, 'Woman, great is your faith! Let it be done for you as you wish.' And her daughter was healed instantly.

a. The Syro-Phoenician Woman's Character

It would appear that Jesus has moved into the region of Tyre and Sidon for his own safety or to get some peace and quiet (though there were many in that area who had shown an interest in hearing him, cf. Mk. 3.8;[1] Lk. 6.17[2], it must not be automatically assumed that this is the beginning of

---

so that I may also go and pay him homage.' When they had heard the king, they set out; and there, ahead of them, went the star that they had seen at its rising, until it stopped over the place where the child was. When they saw that the star had stopped, they were overwhelmed with joy. On entering the house, they saw the child with Mary his mother; and they knelt down and paid him homage. Then, opening their treasure-chests, they offered him gifts of gold, frankincense, and myrrh

[4] When he entered Capernaum, a centurion came to him, appealing to him 6and saying, 'Lord, my servant is lying at home paralysed, in terrible distress.'And he said to him, 'I will come and cure him.' The centurion answered, 'Lord, I am not worthy to have you come under my roof; but only speak the word, and my servant will be healed. For I also am a man under authority, with soldiers under me; and I say to one, "Go", and he goes, and to another, "Come", and he comes, and to my slave, "Do this", and the slave does it.' When Jesus heard him, he was amazed and said to those who followed him, 'Truly I tell you, in no one in Israel have I found such faith. I tell you, many will come from east and west and will eat with Abraham and Isaac and Jacob in the kingdom of heaven, while the heirs of the kingdom will be thrown into the outer darkness, where there will be weeping and gnashing of teeth.' And to the centurion Jesus said, 'Go; let it be done for you according to your faith.' And the servant was healed in that hour.

[5] 'Woe to you, Chorazin! Woe to you, Bethsaida! For if the deeds of power done in you had been done in Tyre and Sidon, they would have repented long ago in sackcloth and ashes. But I tell you, on the day of judgement it will be more tolerable for Tyre and Sidon than for you. And you, Capernaum, will you be exalted to heaven? No, you will be brought down to Hades. For if the deeds of power done in you had been done in Sodom, it would have remained until this day. But I tell you that on the day of judgement it will be more tolerable for the land of Sodom than for you.'

[1] Hearing all that he was doing, they came to him in great numbers from Judea, Jerusalem, Idumea, beyond the Jordan, and the region around Tyre and Sidon.

[2] He came down with them and stood on a level place, with a great crowd of his disciples and a great

a mission to the Gentiles). But if we take his own words at face value *I was sent only to the lost sheep of the house of Israel* (Mt. 15.24) then it would also appear that Jesus had a life changing experience during his encounter with this remarkable woman, for Jesus comes to the realisation that his ministry must now include the Gentiles (cf. Mt. 12.18, 21[1]; Is. 42.1-4, 6[2]; 49.6[3]). This is a strong willed woman because at the beginning of the narrative, Jesus is decidedly unwilling to help her but she persists with her request. In this context the Syro-Phoenician woman becomes a model of the faith of the Gentiles. The woman has approached Jesus of her own volition (like the woman with the haemorrhage in Mk. 5.25-34[4]) and takes the risk of being condemned because she utterly ignores the religious and social barriers in seeking help from a Jew (like the woman with the haemorrhage in relation to the purity laws). So Matthew expands Mark's description of her simply as a 'Syro-Phoenician' by telling us she was a 'Canaanite'. This is the only use of this term in the New Testament, (Mt. 10.4[5]; Mk. 3.18[6]). In

---

multitude of people from all Judea, Jerusalem, and the coast of Tyre and Sidon.

[1] 'Here is my servant, whom I have chosen, my beloved, with whom my soul is well pleased. I will put my Spirit upon him, and he will proclaim justice to the Gentiles; And in his name the Gentiles will hope.'

[2] Here is my servant, whom I uphold, my chosen, in whom my soul delights; I have put my spirit upon him; he will bring forth justice to the nations. He will not cry or lift up his voice, or make it heard in the street; a bruised reed he will not break, and a dimly burning wick he will not quench; he will faithfully bring forth justice. He will not grow faint or be crushed until he has established justice in the earth; and the coastlands wait for his teaching; I am the Lord, I have called you in righteousness, I have taken you by the hand and kept you; I have given you as a covenant to the people, a light to the nations

[3] It is too light a thing that you should be my servant to raise up the tribes of Jacob and to restore the survivors of Israel; I will give you as a light to the nations, that my salvation may reach to the end of the earth.'

[4] And a large crowd followed him and pressed in on him. Now there was a woman who had been suffering from haemorrhages for twelve years. She had endured much under many physicians, and had spent all that she had; and she was no better, but rather grew worse. She had heard about Jesus, and came up behind him in the crowd and touched his cloak, for she said, 'If I but touch his clothes, I will be made well.' Immediately her haemorrhage stopped; and she felt in her body that she was healed of her disease. Immediately aware that power had gone forth from him, Jesus turned about in the crowd and said, 'Who touched my clothes?' And his disciples said to him, 'You see the crowd pressing in on you; how can you say, "Who touched me?"' He looked all round to see who had done it. But the woman, knowing what had happened to her, came in fear and trembling, fell down before him, and told him the whole truth. He said to her, 'Daughter, your faith has made you well; go in peace, and be healed of your disease.'

[5] Simon the Cananaean, and Judas Iscariot, the one who betrayed him.

[6] And Andrew, and Philip, and Bartholomew, and Matthew, and Thomas, and James son of Alphaeus, and

Mk. 7.26 she was called a *Syro-Phoenician woman*, who in the modern world would be a woman from southern Lebanon. She is thus obviously non-Jewish. To Jewish readers of this gospel, the fact that the woman is described as a 'Canaanite' would have spoken volumes.

The Canaanites were the hereditary enemies of Israel, and were forbidden any part in the faithful of Israel. They were either to be driven out or cut off. Thus this woman had less right even than the Gentiles to expect help from a Jewish prophet. Mark gives a further description of her when he says that she was 'Hellénis', i.e., a female Greek, a Gentile (Mk. 7.26). The region of Tyre originally had been an island but it was made into a peninsula when Alexander conquered it in 322 AD. It had stayed relatively free from interference in its economic activities under the Romans. It was wealthy, cosmopolitan and its fame in the ancient world was legendary both for its maritime expertise and its trading in exports and imports, and one of its imports was foodstuffs from Galilee which it bordered. There was a Jewish diaspora there but the relations between the Jews and Tyre and its surrounds were very sour (Josephus tells us that during the Jewish War against Rome in 66 AD Tyre imprisoned and killed many Jews, cf. *Ag. Ap.* 1.70; *Jewish Wars* 2.478). So the Jews in this region lived under the threat of constant harassment, if not persecution.

She is a woman of considerable means since Mark tells us that when she went home she found her daughter *lying on the bed and the demon had gone* (Mk. 7.30). The word for 'bed' used by Mark is 'kline' rather than the mats ('krabbatos') of Mk. 2.4,[1] (cf. 2.9, 12; 6.55[2]) that the poor used and while Matthew makes no reference to the 'bed' it can be assumed that this was what she was lying on. The Syro-Phoenician woman in Matthew, therefore, is wealthy, of high social standing, a sophisticated Hellenic

---

Thaddaeus, and Simon the Cananaean

[1] And when they could not bring him to Jesus because of the crowd, they removed the roof above him; and after having dug through it, they let down the mat on which the paralytic lay.

[2] Which is easier, to say to the paralytic, "Your sins are forgiven", or to say, "Stand up and take your mat and walk"?; And he stood up, and immediately took the mat and went out before all of them; so that they were all amazed and glorified God, saying, 'We have never seen anything like this!'; and rushed about that whole region and began to bring the sick on mats to wherever they heard he was.

Gentile and of some influence. Jesus is an itinerant Jewish preacher and so he and the Syro-Phoenician woman are worlds apart in many different ways (see, Theissen 1991:72-75). The woman is defined not just by race, social standing and culture but also by her daughter's condition. This is similar to Simon's mother-in-law, Jairus' daughter and the woman with the haemorrhage, they are all unnamed and all defined by their human condition. Further, as Jairus has moved 'outside' the world of the synagogue to seek help from Jesus, so too the Syro-Phoenician woman has moved 'outside' her world, her comfort zone, to seek help from Jesus. Thus, the world in which they live cannot help them and so forces them to seek help from outside it and to do things which under ordinary circumstances they would not do. The Syro-Phoenician woman is forced to seek help from an itinerant Jewish preacher and in doing so ignores the social conventions and, in a real sense, her own safety (on the freedom of 'respectable' women to move about the Graeco-Roman world, see, Clark 1989:17-21).

Aside from the social proprieties (respectable women were not expected to talk to strangers, most especially male strangers, nor indeed, were they expected to be unaccompanied or unchaperoned if and when they did so), there was also personal safety issues: a woman of substance and position like the Syro-Phoenician woman would have been an easy target for robbers, kidnappers or worse. She shows her defiance and dismissal of these social and safety concerns for the sake of the health of her child. In this way she can be placed along side the woman with the haemorrhage who disregards the purity laws to encounter Jesus (Mk. 5.24-34) and the woman who causes such horror among the males when she bursts into the room where they are gathered to anoint Jesus (Mk. 14.3-9[1]).

---

[1]   While he was at Bethany in the house of Simon the leper, as he sat at the table, a woman came with an alabaster jar of very costly ointment of nard, and she broke open the jar and poured the ointment on his head. But some were there who said to one another in anger, 'Why was the ointment wasted in this way? For this ointment could have been sold for more than three hundred denarii, and the money given to the poor.' And they scolded her. But Jesus said, 'Let her alone; why do you trouble her? She has performed a good service for me. For you always have the poor with you, and you can show kindness to them whenever you wish; but you will not always have me. She has done what she could; she has anointed my body beforehand for its burial. Truly I tell you, wherever the good news is proclaimed in the whole world, what

b. The Woman Makes Her Request (Mt. 15.21-23)

Mark (7.24-30[1]) and Matthew are the only evangelists who have this narrative, Luke does not include it. If Luke *had* known about the incident which had taken place, it seems strange that he chose to omit it along with the second feeding of the crowds which also took place on Gentile soil for what we know about the reason for the Gospel's compilation (Lk. 1.1-4[2]), would prompt us to consider Jesus' ministry into these areas as being indications that Jesus was willing to reach out to the non-Jew even on a limited basis before the establishing of the Church and of its commission to reach 'all nations'. There can be no doubt that Gentile readers would be vitally interested in the account but, for a reason which appears to now be indeterminable, Luke misses this passage out in his Gospel.

The two parallel passages are so different in what they describe and record that it is necessary at this point to make some attempt at a harmonisation before we go on to consider the actual text. Mark begins his account by stating that Jesus was attempting to stay in the region unnoticed and that he entered *a house* (Mk. 7.24[3]). This, however, seems to be the final throw of the dice for the woman who comes in to Jesus and falls down at his feet to beg him for the deliverance that her daughter needed. Prior to this, it appears that the woman had been following both Jesus and the

---

she has done will be told in remembrance of her.'

[1] From there he set out and went away to the region of Tyre. He entered a house and did not want anyone to know he was there. Yet he could not escape notice, but a woman whose little daughter had an unclean spirit immediately heard about him, and she came and bowed down at his feet. Now the woman was a Gentile, of Syrophoenician origin. She begged him to cast the demon out of her daughter. He said to her, 'Let the children be fed first, for it is not fair to take the children's food and throw it to the dogs.' But she answered him, 'Sir, even the dogs under the table eat the children's crumbs.' Then he said to her, 'For saying that, you may go, the demon has left your daughter.' So she went home, found the child lying on the bed, and the demon gone.

[2] Since many have undertaken to set down an orderly account of the events that have been fulfilled among us, just as they were handed on to us by those who from the beginning were eyewitnesses and servants of the word, I too decided, after investigating everything carefully from the very first, to write an orderly account for you, most excellent Theophilus, so that you may know the truth concerning the things about which you have been instructed.

[3] From there he set out and went away to the region of Tyre. He entered a house and did not want anyone to know he was there. Yet he could not escape notice.

disciples around the area and crying after Jesus to have mercy on her daughter (Mt. 15.22), to which Jesus had chosen to remain absolutely silent (Mt. 15.23). Then the disciples begin to get aggravated with her persistent wailing after them and beg Jesus to send her away (Mt. 15.23-24[1]) (possibly they would have her receive her healing and begone but they also appear to be concerned to get some peace). There may be an element of feeling which is not too concerned whether this is given to her and Jesus answers their request with an enigmatic reply which seems to presume that the disciples were requesting that she be sent away with the appeal for the healing granted to her (Mt. 15.24). The woman then follows Jesus into the house (which is where Mark begins his account, Mk. 7.24) and falls down before him, imploring him to cast the demon out from her daughter (Mk. 7.26; Mt. 15.25[2]). It must have seemed quite intolerable to the disciples that she had not been excluded from the house and that she is now in their midst with her wailing reverberating off the hard walls where they are trying to get some rest! The disciples do not figure in this scene any more and the two characters that are now focused on are Jesus and the woman. Jesus gives the woman an explanation of why he cannot heal her daughter (Mt. 15.26; Mk. 7.27[3]) before she responds with a remarkable statement that ignores the reproach which is in Jesus' words (Mt. 15.27; Mk. 7.28[4]). Jesus then grants the woman's request (Mt. 15.28; Mk. 7.29) and the story closes with the fulfilment of Jesus' words (Mt. 15.28, Mk. 7.30[5]).

While Jesus was in the region of Tyre and Sidon a woman came from

---

[1] And his disciples came and urged him, saying, 'Send her away, for she keeps shouting after us.'

[2] From there he set out and went away to the region of Tyre. He entered a house and did not want anyone to know he was there. Yet he could not escape notice, but a woman whose little daughter had an unclean spirit immediately heard about him, and she came and bowed down at his feet: But she came and knelt before him, saying, 'Lord, help me.'

[3] He answered, 'It is not fair to take the children's food and throw it to the dogs.'; He said to her, 'Let the children be fed first, for it is not fair to take the children's food and throw it to the dogs.'

[4] She said, 'Yes, Lord, yet even the dogs eat the crumbs that fall from their masters' table.';But she answered him, 'Sir, even the dogs under the table eat the children's crumbs.'

[5] Then Jesus answered her, 'Woman, great is your faith! Let it be done for you as you wish.' And her daughter was healed instantly; Then he said to her, 'For saying that, you may go, the demon has left your daughter.' So she went home, found the child lying on the bed, and the demon gone.

her home and approached the area where he was. The fact that she *cried out* and that later the disciples said that she *cries after us* (v.23) suggests that she did not come too close. Perhaps as a Canaanite and a woman she was afraid to approach a Jewish prophet. But nevertheless she was not to be denied, and she cried (Mt. 15.22):

> Have mercy on me, O Lord, you son of David. My daughter is grievously vexed with a demon

Her cry to him as the *Son of David* in connection with a case of demon possession suggests that she connected him with Solomon, who had had close ties with Tyre and Sidon, and a reputation for remedies which aided those possessed by evil spirits. He too was regularly called a 'son of David'. This is in fact more likely than that she was specifically using a Messianic title, although to many Jews it may well have been a Messianic title, for it is found as such in the Psalms of Solomon. Thus, this may be seen as one of a number of examples in Scripture of 'unconscious prophecy' (for the title with 'Lord' added cf. Mt. 20.30, 31,[1] and contrast Mt. 9.27). On her lips 'Lord' used in this way must be given a high significance. It was the Gentile way of addressing supreme rulers and deities. She is thus paying Jesus due honour, and acknowledging his high status and connections, *But he did not answer her at all* (Mt. 15.23a).

It should be noted in this regard that she was not addressing him face to face but calling from a distance, so that there was nothing impolite about it. No doubt, in fact, Jesus often heard people calling things out from a distance, and could not respond to all who did so. But there was another time when Jesus 'did not answer', and that was in the case of the woman taken in adultery (Jn. 8.6[2]). It may suggest therefore deep thought in the face

---

[1] There were two blind men sitting by the roadside. When they heard that Jesus was passing by, they shouted, 'Lord, have mercy on us, Son of David!' The crowd sternly ordered them to be quiet; but they shouted even more loudly, 'Have mercy on us, Lord, Son of David!'

[2] They said this to test him, so that they might have some charge to bring against him. Jesus bent down and wrote with his finger on the ground.

of a dilemma: he was not quite sure what to do, for the reason shortly to be given. Meanwhile she continued to call after them (Mt. 15.23b-c) and:

> his disciples came and begged him, saying, "Send her away, for
> she continually calls after us.

The disciples seemingly saw no reason why he should not do as she requested and send her away. Indeed they were clearly getting very embarrassed. They were in foreign parts and she was drawing too much attention to them.

c. Jesus' Response (Mt. 15.24)

Jesus had left Jewish territory because the masses crowded him and he needed a short break to rest with and teach his disciples (Mt. 15.21; cf. Mt. 16.13[1]); but this stage of his mission was for Israel alone (compare Mt. 28.19[2]). So, when his disciples ask him to send the woman away (Mt. 15.23), he notes the limitation of his mission (Mt. 15.24;[3] cf. Mt. 10.6; Rom. 15.8[4]). Yet he did not send her away as his disciples requested, which may have encouraged her to persevere (cf. Mt. 19.13; 20.31[5]). To her own insistent entreaty (Mt. 15.25[6]) Jesus responds with almost equal firmness (Mt. 15.26[7]). Some Jewish teachers would have tried to have converted the woman (cf. Josephus. *Antiquities* 20.34-36; *Apion* 2.210; *m. 'Abot* 1.12;

---

[1] Just then a Canaanite woman from that region came out and started shouting, 'Have mercy on me, Lord, Son of David; my daughter is tormented by a demon.' ; Now when Jesus came into the district of Caesarea Philippi, he asked his disciples, 'Who do people say that the Son of Man is?'

[2] Go therefore and make disciples of all nations, baptising them in the name of the Father and of the Son and of the Holy Spirit.

[3] He answered, 'I was sent only to the lost sheep of the house of Israel.'

[4] But go rather to the lost sheep of the house of Israel; For I tell you that Christ has become a servant of the circumcised on behalf of the truth of God in order that he might confirm the promises given to the patriarchs.

[5] Then little children were being brought to him in order that he might lay his hands on them and pray. The disciples spoke sternly to those who brought them; The crowd sternly ordered them to be quiet; but they shouted even more loudly, 'Have mercy on us, Lord, Son of David!'

[6] But she came and knelt before him, saying, 'Lord, help me.'

[7] He answered, 'It is not fair to take the children's food and throw it to the dogs.'

Goppelt 1964:54); Jesus simply snubs her. He then turned in answer to his disciples' requests and gave the reason for his lack of response. he declared, *I was sent only to the lost sheep of the house of Israel* (Mt. 15.24). At this point we must remember who *the lost sheep of the house of Israel* were. They were not the whole of Israel without exception. Jesus was quite clear on the fact that many Jews would deliberately refuse to listen to them and would turn them away. In such cases the disciples were to shake the dust off their feet and go elsewhere. They were not to go to them; they were not to cast their pearls before swine (Mt. 7.6[1]). But others would welcome them with open hearts because of their sense of need, and their desire to know God. It was to them that they must go, they were *the lost sheep of the house of Israel.*

Indeed who the lost sheep of the house of Israel were has already been explained in Mt. 9.36.[2] They were the large crowds who were tending to follow him because their hearts were unsatisfied and the Jewish leadership had failed them. There were many like them waiting in the towns and cities longing for a way of salvation. In Mt. 9.36, Jesus had seen them as *distressed and scattered, as sheep not having a shepherd.*' The great crowds that gathered around Jesus had touched his heart. He was 'moved with compassion' towards them. The word for compassion used there was a word solely used of Jesus in the Gospels apart from when he uses it in his own parables. It is at the heart of the kingdom of God, for he saw these people as distressed and scattered, like sheep without a shepherd. This description of sheep without a shepherd is firmly based on the Old Testament (e.g., 1 K 22.17;[3] Ezek. 34.6, 12,[4]). And the description of Israel as sheep is even

---

[1] 'Do not give what is holy to dogs; and do not throw your pearls before swine, or they will trample them under foot and turn and maul you.

[2] When he saw the crowds, he had compassion for them, because they were harassed and helpless, like sheep without a shepherd.

[3] Then Micaiah said, 'I saw all Israel scattered on the mountains, like sheep that have no shepherd; and the Lord said, "These have no master; let each one go home in peace."

[4] My sheep were scattered, they wandered over all the mountains and on every high hill; my sheep were scattered over all the face of the earth, with no one to search or seek for them; As shepherds seek out their flocks when they are among their scattered sheep, so I will seek out my sheep. I will rescue them from all the places to which they have been scattered on a day of clouds and thick darkness.

more common (2 S 24.17;[1] Pss. 23; 74.1; 78.52;[2] Is. 53.6;[3] Jer. 23.1;[4] Mic. 2.12[5]). Without a shepherd sheep are in a hopeless condition. The scattering of sheep was a picture of the exile (Ps. 44.11; Jer. 50.17; Ezek. 34.6, 12) and of persecution (Zech. 13.7[6]).

Thus, Jesus looked on these people as in their own kind of exile, an exile from which he had himself come in order to deliver them (Mt. 2.15[7]). A group of scattered sheep without a shepherd would soon have found themselves in great distress in Palestine, especially in the dry summers. Unlike goats they were not good at looking after themselves. And what with thorn bushes, and predators, and scavenging dogs, and a disinclination to forage, and shortage of water, their situation, if left to themselves, would be desperate. In a similar way that was how Jesus saw these people: as scattered and distressed sheep, because their shepherds had failed them. It was because of their spiritual hunger and thirst that they had flocked to John and were now flocking to him. They were the ordinary people left bewildered by the arguments of the Pharisees and the Sadducees. They were seen as 'distressed and scattered.' Various alternative translations have been suggested for the Greek words used here, 'worried and helpless', 'harassed and helpless', 'distressed and downcast', 'harassed and dejected', 'bullied and unable to escape', 'mishandled and lying helpless', partly depending on whether we are thinking primarily of the sheep, or of the people that they

---

[1] When David saw the angel who was destroying the people, he said to the Lord, 'I alone have sinned, and I alone have done wickedly; but these sheep, what have they done? Let your hand, I pray, be against me and against my father's house.'

[2] The Lord is my shepherd, I shall not want. He makes me lie down in green pastures; he leads me beside still waters; he restores my soul. He leads me in right paths for his name's sake; O God, why do you cast us off for ever? Why does your anger smoke against the sheep of your pasture?; Then he led out his people like sheep, and guided them in the wilderness like a flock.

[3] All we like sheep have gone astray; we have all turned to our own way, and the Lord has laid on him the iniquity of us all.

[4] Woe to the shepherds who destroy and scatter the sheep of my pasture! says the Lord.

[5] I will surely gather all of you, O Jacob, I will gather the survivors of Israel; I will set them together like sheep in a fold, like a flock in its pasture; it will resound with people.

[6] 'Awake, O sword, against my shepherd, against the man who is my associate,' says the Lord of hosts. Strike the shepherd, that the sheep may be scattered; I will turn my hand against the little ones.

[7] And remained there until the death of Herod. This was to fulfil what had been spoken by the Lord through the prophet, 'Out of Egypt I have called my son.'

represent. But in the end they were all saying the same thing. They were a 'lost' people.

But there were also many Israelites in some of those towns and cities who were not *lost sheep of the house of Israel* (Mt. 10.14-15). It is true that theologically they were lost, and that they were Israelites, (although now to be rejected Israelites), but their hearts were closed towards him. They were quite happy with their shepherds, and did not know that they were lost. They did not think of themselves as lost. And when his messengers arrived they refused to give them a hearing. Thus in Mt. 10 the disciples had been told not to go to them but rather to shake their dust off their feet, a sign that in God's eyes they were not true members of Israel. These Israelites were not the *lost sheep of the house of Israel*. In contrast the lost sheep of the house of Israel were those whose hearts were open to receiving the disciples and hearing their message. Jesus could have said with Paul, *They are not all Israel who are Israel* (Rom. 9.6). But what did Jesus mean by his words here and why did he say it at this moment? It in fact points to his dilemma.

- If he does what this woman asks he will be opening the way to many Gentiles who will then feel that they too can bring their sick ones to be healed by the Jewish prophet. Thus he will begin to be seen as a healer, and not as a Jewish Prophet. And credit for the healings will then be given to their own gods, a complete contradiction to his mission.
- The consequences could then be that the ministry to those who were aware of their 'lostness' in Israel, the healing of whom was the purpose for which he was sent, would be hindered. In their eyes his ministry would be tarnished.

Jesus feels that what this woman is asking is outside his mission, and it was something that required deep thought. It had been one thing to heal Gentiles who were in deep sympathy with Judaism while he was among the Jews in Galilee, where the full credit would go to the God of Israel, it would be quite another to do it in a Gentile environment when the credit could go anywhere, and false ideas and beliefs could be fostered. And to him truth was central. At present his ministry was to those of the house of Israel who were like sheep without a shepherd, and he knew that that ministry was not yet complete and must not be hindered. He was not here as a Wisdom teacher. He was here as a prophet, yes, and more than a prophet. This is a salutary reminder to us that Jesus did not have precognition of everything and instantly know what to do in his earthly life (e.g., the Temptations). As he lived out his life he was rather dependent on what was revealed to him and on the Scriptures. Furthermore, he was conscious that he had come to this place for peace and quiet and not in order to arouse the neighbourhood. He did not want the floodgates to open. It was not yet time. There may also be the thought here that he cannot grant her request when by doing so he may be allowing her to go back to give thanks to her pagan gods. What part has she in the son of David and in the God of Israel?

The woman, however, shows both her determination and her strength of character when *she came and knelt before him, saying, 'Lord, help me'* (Mt. 15.25). In our culture we might consider this woman rude, but ancient Mediterranean judges were sometimes so corrupt that among the poor only a persistent, desperate, otherwise powerless woman could obtain justice from them (Lk. 18.2-5[1]). Both men and women in the Old Testament

---

[1]   He said, 'In a certain city there was a judge who neither feared God nor had respect for people. In that city there was a widow who kept coming to him and saying, "Grant me justice against my opponent." For a while he refused; but later he said to himself, "Though I have no fear of God and no respect for anyone, yet because this widow keeps bothering me, I will grant her justice, so that she may not wear me out by continually coming." '

(Gen.18.22-32; 32.26-30;[1] Ex. 33.12-23[2]; 1 K 18.36-37; 2 K 2.2; 4.14-28[3]) and in the Gospel tradition (Mk. 5.28-29;[4] Jn. 2.3-5[5]) courageously refuse to take 'No!' for an answer to a desperate need. Jairus had pleaded with Jesus in the same way and later in Mark the father of the epileptic boy will also plead with him (Mk. 9.14-27[6]). In both these cases they plead as loving, concerned parents for their children and Jesus responds, yet here there seems to be at best a reluctance on his part and at worst a downright refusal. The daughter of Jairus is *at the point of death* (Mk. 5.23), the 'demon'

---

[1] So the men turned from there, and went towards Sodom, while Abraham remained standing before the Lord. Then Abraham came near and said, 'Will you indeed sweep away the righteous with the wicked? Suppose there are fifty righteous within the city; will you then sweep away the place and not forgive it for the fifty righteous who are in it? Far be it from you to do such a thing, to slay the righteous with the wicked, so that the righteous fare as the wicked! Far be that from you! Shall not the Judge of all the earth do what is just?' And the Lord said, 'If I find at Sodom fifty righteous in the city, I will forgive the whole place for their sake.' Abraham answered, 'Let me take it upon myself to speak to the Lord, I who am but dust and ashes. Suppose five of the fifty righteous are lacking? Will you destroy the whole city for lack of five?' And he said, 'I will not destroy it if I find forty-five there.' Again he spoke to him, 'Suppose forty are found there.' He answered, 'For the sake of forty I will not do it.' Then he said, 'Oh do not let the Lord be angry if I speak. Suppose thirty are found there.' He answered, 'I will not do it, if I find thirty there.' He said, 'Let me take it upon myself to speak to the Lord. Suppose twenty are found there.' He answered, 'For the sake of twenty I will not destroy it.'Then he said, 'Oh do not let the Lord be angry if I speak just once more. Suppose ten are found there.' He answered, 'For the sake of ten I will not destroy it.' And the Lord went his way, when he had finished speaking to Abraham; and Abraham returned to his place;

[2] Moses said to the Lord, 'See, you have said to me, "Bring up this people"; but you have not let me know whom you will send with me. Yet you have said, "I know you by name, and you have also found favour in my sight." Now if I have found favour in your sight, show me your ways, so that I may know you and find favour in your sight. Consider too that this nation is your people.' He said, 'My presence will go with you, and I will give you rest.' And he said to him, 'If your presence will not go, do not carry us up from here. For how shall it be known that I have found favour in your sight, I and your people, unless you go with us? In this way, we shall be distinct, I and your people, from every people on the face of the earth.' The Lord said to Moses, 'I will do the very thing that you have asked; for you have found favour in my sight, and I know you by name.' Moses said, 'Show me your glory, I pray.' And he said, 'I will make all my goodness pass before you, and will proclaim before you the name, "The Lord"; and I will be gracious to whom I will be gracious, and will show mercy on whom I will show mercy. But', he said, 'you cannot see my face; for no one shall see me and live.' And the Lord continued, 'See, there is a place by me where you shall stand on the rock; and while my glory passes by I will put you in a cleft of the rock, and I will cover you with my hand until I have passed by; then I will take away my hand, and you shall see my back; but my face shall not be seen.'

[3] At the time of the offering of the oblation, the prophet Elijah came near and said, 'O Lord, God of Abraham, Isaac, and Israel, let it be known this day that you are God in Israel, that I am your servant, and that I have done all these things at your bidding. Answer me, O Lord, answer me, so that this people may know that you, O Lord, are God, and that you have turned their hearts back.' ; Elijah said to Elisha, 'Stay here; for the Lord has sent me as far as Bethel.' But Elisha said, 'As the Lord lives, and as you yourself live,

possessed epileptic boy is *often cast him into the fire and into the water,* as the 'demon' seeks *to destroy him* (Mk. 9.22) and the daughter of the Syro-Phoenician woman is 'tormented' by a demon (Mt. 15.22). This is the only description we get of the child's condition but Matthew's audience would have understood what being 'tormented' by a demon meant.

The daughter of the Syro-Phoenician woman is in a state of uncleanness since any demon possession renders a person unclean (in

---

I will not leave you.' So they went down to Bethel; He said, 'What then may be done for her?' Gehazi answered, 'Well, she has no son, and her husband is old.' He said, 'Call her.' When he had called her, she stood at the door. He said, 'At this season, in due time, you shall embrace a son.' She replied, 'No, my lord, O man of God; do not deceive your servant.' The woman conceived and bore a son at that season, in due time, as Elisha had declared to her. When the child was older, he went out one day to his father among the reapers. He complained to his father, 'Oh, my head, my head!' The father said to his servant, 'Carry him to his mother.' He carried him and brought him to his mother; the child sat on her lap until noon, and he died. She went up and laid him on the bed of the man of God, closed the door on him, and left. Then she called to her husband, and said, 'Send me one of the servants and one of the donkeys, so that I may quickly go to the man of God and come back again.' He said, 'Why go to him today? It is neither new moon nor Sabbath.' She said, 'It will be all right.' Then she saddled the donkey and said to her servant, 'Urge the animal on; do not hold back for me unless I tell you.' So she set out, and came to the man of God at Mount Carmel. When the man of God saw her coming, he said to Gehazi his servant, 'Look, there is the Shunammite woman; run at once to meet her, and say to her, Are you all right? Is your husband all right? Is the child all right?' She answered, 'It is all right.' When she came to the man of God at the mountain, she caught hold of his feet. Gehazi approached to push her away. But the man of God said, 'Let her alone, for she is in bitter distress; the Lord has hidden it from me and has not told me.' Then she said, 'Did I ask my lord for a son? Did I not say, Do not mislead me?'

4   For she said, 'If I but touch his clothes, I will be made well.' Immediately her haemorrhage stopped; and she felt in her body that she was healed of her disease.

5   When the wine gave out, the mother of Jesus said to him, 'They have no wine.' And Jesus said to her, 'Woman, what concern is that to you and to me? My hour has not yet come.' His mother said to the servants, 'Do whatever he tells you.'

6   When they came to the disciples, they saw a great crowd around them, and some scribes arguing with them. When the whole crowd saw him, they were immediately overcome with awe, and they ran forward to greet him. He asked them, 'What are you arguing about with them?' Someone from the crowd answered him, 'Teacher, I brought you my son; he has a spirit that makes him unable to speak; and whenever it seizes him, it dashes him down; and he foams and grinds his teeth and becomes rigid; and I asked your disciples to cast it out, but they could not do so.' He answered them, 'You faithless generation, how much longer must I be among you? How much longer must I put up with you? Bring him to me.' And they brought the boy to him. When the spirit saw him, immediately it threw the boy into convulsions, and he fell on the ground and rolled about, foaming at the mouth. Jesus asked the father, 'How long has this been happening to him?' And he said, 'From childhood. It has often cast him into the fire and into the water, to destroy him; but if you are able to do anything, have pity on us and help us.' Jesus said to him, 'If you are able!— All things can be done for the one who believes.' Immediately the father of the child cried out, 'I believe;

Mark's version of the story the demon is specified as 'unclean' Mk. 7.25[1]). Destructive, outside 'forces' have possessed this child and it should be noted that her mother, the Syro-Phoenician woman, has left her side to find Jesus. Further, no matter how unpalatable we may find it, girls were less 'valuable' than boys (Miller 2001:128); they were a costly commodity to have since dowries needed to be provided for them but this does not deter the Syro-Phoenician woman in her pursuit of the well being of her daughter. She is prepared to leave her side, get on her knees and humiliate herself even as a noble woman of high social standing and importance in order to beg an itinerant foreign preacher of a race which despised her to help her daughter. The pathos of the Syro-Phoenician woman's daughter is further heightened by the fact that while these two adults 'haggle' over her well being, she is alone being *tormented* by a demon. Jairus' daughter, the epileptic boy, the daughter of the Syro-Phoenician woman all indicate the vulnerability of children to disease and suffering which are realities of the eschatological age yet at the same time it is children who are the first beneficiaries of the new age instituted by Jesus (cf. Mk. 9.1; 13.13[2]). His reluctance or refusal to help in this instance then is curious.

d. Feeding Crumbs To The Dogs (Mt. 15.26-28)

Before coming to the actual healing of the Syro-Phoenician woman's daughter and its meaning, some time needs to be spent on examining the nature of the reply that Jesus gives to her insistent pleading. The response of Jesus to her maternal pleading for the life of her child seems both baffling

---

help my unbelief!' When Jesus saw that a crowd came running together, he rebuked the unclean spirit, saying to it, 'You spirit that keep this boy from speaking and hearing, I command you, come out of him, and never enter him again!' After crying out and convulsing him terribly, it came out, and the boy was like a corpse, so that most of them said, 'He is dead.' But Jesus took him by the hand and lifted him up, and he was able to stand.

[1] but a woman whose little daughter had an unclean spirit immediately heard about him, and she came and bowed down at his feet.

[2] And he said to them, 'Truly I tell you, there are some standing here who will not taste death until they see that the kingdom of God has come with power.'; and you will be hated by all because of my name. But the one who endures to the end will be saved.

and shocking (Donahue and Harrington:2002, 2.233), (Mt. 15.26):

> It is not fair to take the children's food and throw it to the dogs

'Dog' was a term of offensive insult used by some Jews when speaking about the Gentiles. Dogs were regarded as unclean and to touch them was to be made unclean through them. The dog image is used elsewhere by Jesus (Lk. 16.19-21[1] and elsewhere in the Old Testament, cf. 1 S 24.14; 2 K 8.12-13[2]). The term 'dog', therefore, is deliberately used by Jesus and it is shocking. Attempts are made to soften it by saying the actual Greek noun used by Matthew, 'kunarion', ('little dogs', 'house dogs', 'pups') is the diminutive of *kuon* (dog) and is thus being used by Jesus in a playful, affectionate way (Pokorny 1995:337). However, it seems hardly less insulting to be called a *little dog* or *pup* than a 'dog' (O Hanlon 2004:79; Burkill 1967:173) but Matthew is not using it in a playful, affectionately diminutive way and most people who read this section of Matthew's gospel are at a loss to understand why Jesus would use such a derogatory, insulting and even racist term (Miguel 2009:9). One can, therefore, understand why hearers/readers would want to soften it: after all, Jesus will have interaction with other Gentiles who make requests for help for him and most especially the Roman Centurion who comes to him, and though a member of the detested oppressors of the Jews, is not insulted, rebuffed or dismissed by him (Lk. 7.2-10[3]). The insulting term is all the more baffling given what Jesus has

---

[1] 'There was a rich man who was dressed in purple and fine linen and who feasted sumptuously every day. And at his gate lay a poor man named Lazarus, covered with sores, who longed to satisfy his hunger with what fell from the rich man's table; even the dogs would come and lick his sores.

[2] Against whom has the king of Israel come out? Whom do you pursue? A dead dog? A single flea?; Hazael asked, 'Why does my lord weep?' He answered, 'Because I know the evil that you will do to the people of Israel; you will set their fortresses on fire, you will kill their young men with the sword, dash in pieces their little ones, and rip up their pregnant women.' Hazael said, 'What is your servant, who is a mere dog, that he should do this great thing?' Elisha answered, 'The Lord has shown me that you are to be king over Aram.'

[3] A centurion there had a slave whom he valued highly, and who was ill and close to death. When he heard about Jesus, he sent some Jewish elders to him, asking him to come and heal his slave. When they came to Jesus, they appealed to him earnestly, saying, 'He is worthy of having you do this for him, for he loves our people, and it is he who built our synagogue for us.' And Jesus went with them, but when he was not far from the house, the centurion sent friends to say to him, 'Lord, do not trouble yourself, for I am not worthy

already said about 'clean' and 'unclean' food (Mt. 15.10-20;[1] Mk. 7.1-23[2]) and the fact that he has crossed over into Gentile territory and may even be in a Gentile house. If all these 'boundaries' have been crossed by Jesus the use of this offensive, prejudiced term by him is all the more strange. And herein may be the point: the term, coming off the lips of Jesus when it does, has a shock value which forces the reader to seek to understand it. Images of bread (the Feeding of the Five Thousand, Mt. 14.13-21[3]) and food (the clean/unclean debate) have led to discussions about what constitutes clean and unclean and how people are made unclean and who is unclean. The

---

to have you come under my roof; therefore I did not presume to come to you. But only speak the word, and let my servant be healed. For I also am a man set under authority, with soldiers under me; and I say to one, "Go", and he goes, and to another, "Come", and he comes, and to my slave, "Do this", and the slave does it.' When Jesus heard this he was amazed at him, and turning to the crowd that followed him, he said, 'I tell you, not even in Israel have I found such faith.' When those who had been sent returned to the house, they found the slave in good health.

[1] Then he called the crowd to him and said to them, 'Listen and understand: it is not what goes into the mouth that defiles a person, but it is what comes out of the mouth that defiles.' Then the disciples approached and said to him, 'Do you know that the Pharisees took offence when they heard what you said?' He answered, 'Every plant that my heavenly Father has not planted will be uprooted. Let them alone; they are blind guides of the blind. And if one blind person guides another, both will fall into a pit.' But Peter said to him, 'Explain this parable to us.' Then he said, 'Are you also still without understanding? Do you not see that whatever goes into the mouth enters the stomach, and goes out into the sewer? But what comes out of the mouth proceeds from the heart, and this is what defiles. For out of the heart come evil intentions, murder, adultery, fornication, theft, false witness, slander. These are what defile a person, but to eat with unwashed hands does not defile.'

[2] When he had left the crowd and entered the house, his disciples asked him about the parable. He said to them, 'Then do you also fail to understand? Do you not see that whatever goes into a person from outside cannot defile, since it enters, not the heart but the stomach, and goes out into the sewer?' (Thus he declared all foods clean.) And he said, 'It is what comes out of a person that defiles. For it is from within, from the human heart, that evil intentions come: fornication, theft, murder, adultery, avarice, wickedness, deceit, licentiousness, envy, slander, pride, folly. All these evil things come from within, and they defile a person.'

[3] Now when Jesus heard this, he withdrew from there in a boat to a deserted place by himself. But when the crowds heard it, they followed him on foot from the towns. When he went ashore, he saw a great crowd; and he had compassion for them and cured their sick. When it was evening, the disciples came to him and said, 'This is a deserted place, and the hour is now late; send the crowds away so that they may go into the villages and buy food for themselves.' Jesus said to them, 'They need not go away; you give them something to eat.' They replied, 'We have nothing here but five loaves and two fish.' And he said, 'Bring them here to me.' Then he ordered the crowds to sit down on the grass. Taking the five loaves and the two fish, he looked up to heaven, and blessed and broke the loaves, and gave them to the disciples, and the disciples gave them to the crowds. And all ate and were filled; and they took up what was left over of the broken pieces, twelve baskets full. And those who ate were about five thousand men, besides women and children.

imagery of *bread, dogs, children, table* etc. set this story within a household during meal time and given the previous debate about clean and unclean food and how this reflects issues within the early Christian community in relation to Gentiles played out in the context of table fellowship, the use of the term *dogs* reflects a prejudice against Gentiles as unclean which may still have been present in early communities (Collins 2007:366-7). Nevertheless, Matthew places the term on the lips of Jesus and closer examination of the conversation in this encounter may reveal that he is doing so to directly challenge such prejudices and move the discussion on to a wider plane about prejudice, faith, and religious expression. A similarly styled discussion takes place in John when Jesus encounters another woman who is the subject of prejudice and regarded as unclean. In the Samaritan Woman narrative (Jn. 4.7-42), Jesus, in his conversation with this attractive and remarkable woman, shifts the discussion of the right place for worship onto a completely different level by making it clear that physical *place* is being replaced by his physical *presence* since it is he who is now the place where true worshippers will worship in spirit and truth. As in that discussion when Jesus makes it clear that *salvation is of the Jews*, so too his use of the words *throw it to the dogs* in his initial response to the Syro-Phoenician woman indicates that there is a process of salvation through him which is open to everyone. It is this idea which the Gentile noblewoman picks up on in her response to Jesus' reply to her request (Mt. 15.27):

> Yes, Lord, yet even the dogs eat the crumbs that fall from their masters' table

which makes it clear that his understanding of *children* refers to the Jews (Jeremias 1958:30; Rhoads and Michie 1982:131). Israel, as God's 'child', is a dominant biblical image which is never used of Gentiles nor is the designation 'child/children' ever accorded to them Deut. 14.1; Hos. 11.1[1]).

---

[1] You are children of the Lord your God. You must not lacerate yourselves or shave your forelocks for the dead; When Israel was a child, I loved him, and out of Egypt I called my son.

The *children* (Jews) have already been fed with bread (the Feeding of the Five Thousand) in the desert and all of them were filled and it is not fair that their 'bread' be taken from them and thrown to those who are not in the purview of Jesus' mission and ministry, i.e., the Gentiles (bearing in mind that Jesus has not crossed into Gentile territory with the express intention of ministry there). In other words Jesus' ministry, as he has already told her, is primarily to Israel (Mt. 15.21-24[1]). 'Bread' is a biblical image used for the word of God and closely connected to the image of 'child/children'. The 'Bread of the Presence', the twelve loaves placed in the Tabernacle, eaten by the priests, represent the Twelve Tribes of Israel (the child of God). It showed that all belonged to God and to take this bread and give it to the Gentiles would have been an unthinkable sacrilege (Mulholland 2011:1.203). But bread was also the very stuff of life and it was an image of the Torah and images of God feeding the children of Israel with bread are prevalent in the Prophets.

When the disciples ask Jesus to teach them to pray (among other things) he tells them to ask God *to give us today the bread for tomorrow* and he refers to himself as the *bread of life* (Jn. 6.35) until finally at the Last Supper *bread* is the very self of Jesus (Mk. 14.22; Mt. 26.26[2]). Bread, therefore, represents the word of life and truth which Jesus both proclaims and is, and first and foremost this 'bread' is for his own people. However, the use of *throw it to the dogs* leaves open the possibility that when the children of Israel have been fed others may also be fed, though it must be said that even this hardly transforms Jesus' image into an encouraging compliment (Lane 1974:262; Anderson 1976:191). At the feeding of the 'children' (the Five Thousand) *twelve baskets* of crumbs were collected that

---

[1]   Jesus left that place and went away to the district of Tyre and Sidon. Just then a Canaanite woman from that region came out and started shouting, 'Have mercy on me, Lord, Son of David; my daughter is tormented by a demon.' But he did not answer her at all. And his disciples came and urged him, saying, 'Send her away, for she keeps shouting after us.' He answered, 'I was sent only to the lost sheep of the house of Israel.'

[2]   While they were eating, he took a loaf of bread, and after blessing it he broke it, gave it to them, and said, 'Take; this is my body.' ; While they were eating, Jesus took a loaf of bread, and after blessing it he broke it, gave it to the disciples, and said, 'Take, eat; this is my body.'

nothing should be lost so that it should be available to those who believe in Jesus in the future (Mulholland 2011:1.79.). It might be noted here that the Syro-Phoenician woman has asked Jesus to heal her *child* and Jesus has replied with a food metaphor; the woman picks the metaphor up and develops it through pointing out to Jesus that she is more skilled and knowledgeable about household matters than he is (!) and makes it clear that the *children* are indeed fed first, and thus she would not contemplate that children be denied their food but that what she is asking for is not the *food* but the *crumbs* that fall from the table. The woman is pointing out to Jesus that while he can talk about feeding the *children* first (the Jews), her daughter is also a *child* (Miller 2002:138).

e. Jesus' Response To The Woman's Faith (Mt. 15.28)

Impressed by her faith, and aware that she has now acknowledged where any benefit will come from, Jesus replies with a commendation (Mt. 15.28):

> Woman, great is your faith! Let it be done for you as you wish.'
> And her daughter was healed instantly.'

This is the second time that Jesus has been impressed by the faith of a Gentile (Mt. 8.9[1]). And her daughter was healed from that hour (Mt. 8.13b). There are parallel echoes here to Mt. 8.5-13 where the Gentile centurion also demonstrated great faith, and his servant was healed at a distance *in that hour*. They are thus both seen to be on a parallel. Does this then mean that her faith, and that of the centurion, were greater than that of the disciples who were of 'little faith'? The comparison is not fair. The disciples are seen as *of little faith* in the face of great obstacles (Mt. 14.31;[2]). His point there was that their faith was small compared with what it should have

---

[1]   For I also am a man under authority, with soldiers under me; and I say to one, "Go", and he goes, and to another, "Come", and he comes, and to my slave, "Do this", and the slave does it.'

[2]   But he said vehemently, 'Even though I must die with you, I will not deny you.' And all of them said the same.

been, but it was nevertheless a faith that kept them following him faithfully, and was great enough to have enabled them to perform wonders in his name. Thus their faith and hers must be seen as measured on a different basis. But there seems little doubt from what follows that this incident has opened Jesus' eyes to the further outreach God has now shown he must engage in. And he is thus not described as returning to Jewish territory until Mt.15.39[1].

It would seem, therefore, that the ministry that follows is intended by Matthew to be seen as on Gentile territory, fulfilling the words of Mt. 12.18, 21.[2] That the crowds which will be mentioned included many Jews we need not doubt, for all the areas around Galilee were well inhabited with Jews. But nor can we doubt that they would have included many Gentiles, who would be in the majority in these areas. It would not be true to human nature not to recognise that a wonder-worker of such magnitude would not be an object of interest to all. In attempting to teach this attractive woman a lesson about the nature of salvation, Jesus himself has been instructed and received an insight. The 'table' from which the food (the word) is given may be in the house of the Jews but others (the Gentiles) can be fed from it and receive the life of salvation. The images of bread, feeding, clean and unclean food, crumbs etc. have dominated this section of Mark's gospel and will continue to do so since this encounter with the woman from Syro-Phoenician opens the way for more healings and the feeding of the multitude in the Gentile territories. Jesus may have crossed the boundaries of what is clean and unclean and even abolished them but this encounter demonstrates that the Gentiles are not outside the saving reach of God through him and so a Jesus who in this instance may have adopted a more 'conservative' approach to the Law is taught a salutary lesson about the wider reach of salvation (Loader 1996:45-61). The Syro-Phoenician woman has become a template of the faith in Jesus that the Gentiles will come to and the house where her sick child now lies restored becomes the locus for

---

[1]   After sending away the crowds, he got into the boat and went to the region of Magadan.
[2]   'Here is my servant, whom I have chosen, my beloved, with whom my soul is well pleased. I will put my Spirit upon him, and he will proclaim justice to the Gentiles; And in his name the Gentiles will hope.'

salvation among the Gentiles. And Matthew may have the Old Testament stories of Elijah (1 K 17.8-16[1]) and Elisha (2 K 4.20, 31-37[2]) in mind here. The word of the woman, though not explicitly stated as such, is the word of faith and it is through that word of faith that her daughter is healed at a distance. The woman, like the Roman Centurion, accepts the words of Jesus and finds her daughter just as he said she would be. In a sense there are two faith experiences here: there is the faith of the woman in the word of Jesus and the faith of Jesus in his response to the woman's word and what this opens up for salvation among the Gentiles.

The Anointing of Jesus

The anointing of Jesus appears in all four gospels. Matthew, Mark and John locate it at Bethany, Luke places it in Galilee. Matthew and Mark say that it was at the house of Simon the Leper and Luke makes Simon a Pharisee, John at the home of Lazarus, and in John's account it is Mary who anoints Jesus. In Matthew and Mark the woman is anonymous, in Luke the woman is described as a repentant sinner. Matthew and Mark intercalate the

---

[1]   Then the word of the Lord came to him, saying, 'Go now to Zarephath, which belongs to Sidon, and live there; for I have commanded a widow there to feed you.' So he set out and went to Zarephath. When he came to the gate of the town, a widow was there gathering sticks; he called to her and said, 'Bring me a little water in a vessel, so that I may drink.' As she was going to bring it, he called to her and said, 'Bring me a morsel of bread in your hand.' But she said, 'As the Lord your God lives, I have nothing baked, only a handful of meal in a jar, and a little oil in a jug; I am now gathering a couple of sticks, so that I may go home and prepare it for myself and my son, that we may eat it, and die.' Elijah said to her, 'Do not be afraid; go and do as you have said; but first make me a little cake of it and bring it to me, and afterwards make something for yourself and your son. For thus says the Lord the God of Israel: The jar of meal will not be emptied and the jug of oil will not fail until the day that the Lord sends rain on the earth.' She went and did as Elijah said, so that she as well as he and her household ate for many days. The jar of meal was not emptied, neither did the jug of oil fail, according to the word of the Lord that he spoke by Elijah.

[2]   Gehazi went on ahead and laid the staff on the face of the child, but there was no sound or sign of life. He came back to meet him and told him, 'The child has not awakened.' When Elisha came into the house, he saw the child lying dead on his bed. So he went in and closed the door on the two of them, and prayed to the Lord. Then he got up on the bed and lay upon the child, putting his mouth upon his mouth, his eyes upon his eyes, and his hands upon his hands; and while he lay bent over him, the flesh of the child became warm. He got down, walked once to and fro in the room, then got up again and bent over him; the child sneezed seven times, and the child opened his eyes. Elisha summoned Gehazi and said, 'Call the Shunammite woman.' So he called her. When she came to him, he said, 'Take your son.' She came and fell at his feet, bowing to the ground; then she took her son and left.

incident between the plot to kill Jesus and Judas' betrayal. Luke places the incident much earlier in his gospel. In Matthew and Mark it is the disciples who object to her actions, in Luke it is Simon himself who judges her in his heart; in John it is Judas who objects on the basis on the amount of money involved. There are, of course, similarities between the accounts, e.g., a woman and Jesus, an anointing, ointment, a house setting, affirmation of the woman's actions by Jesus, disquiet from various sources. But there are also differences: the woman is anonymous (Matthew and Mark), she is Mary of Bethany (John), it happens at Bethany (Mark and John), the ointment is described in similar ways (Mark and John) it happens at a meal with Simon the Leper and is associated with the Passover and Passion (Matthew and Mark (Miller 200:175). In Luke the story bears no time relationship to the Passover. Jesus' feet are anointed (Luke and John), hair is used to dry his feet (Luke and John). The woman is stated as being a woman of the city, a sinner; Jesus' feet rather than head is anointed; Simon is a Pharisee, not a leper; Simon the Pharisee brings the objection rather than the disciples; Luke omits any mention of the poor. Many different theories about these similarities and differences are proposed, e.g., the anointing of Jesus' head is the original version (Elliott 1974:105-7), the anointing of his feet is the original version (Holst 1976:435-46) it is a symbolic action for his burial (Munro 1979:128), it is an act of affection, it is two separate accounts fused together. Whatever one is to make to the actual sources and presentation of the story it does seem to be more the case that this was a story which stood on its own and which was preserved within the tradition. Each of the accounts of the anointing will be dealt with in this work and each of the Evangelists intention explored. It suffices here to highlight the similarities and difference in the story in itself and to focus on the role of the woman, the action and its meaning.

f. The Anointing of Jesus In Matthew: (Mt. 26.6-13)

Now while Jesus was at Bethany in the house of Simon the
leper, a woman came to him with an alabaster jar of very costly
ointment, and she poured it on his head as he sat at the table.
But when the disciples saw it, they were angry and said, 'Why
this waste? For this ointment could have been sold for a large
sum, and the money given to the poor.' But Jesus, aware of this,
said to them, 'Why do you trouble the woman? She has
performed a good service for me. For you always have the poor
with you, but you will not always have me. By pouring this
ointment on my body she has prepared me for burial. Truly I
tell you, wherever this good news is proclaimed in the whole
world, what she has done will be told in remembrance of her.'

Matthew says this incident took place in the *house of Simon the Leper*, (Mt.
26.6) though it would be more accurate to say Simon the 'ex leper'. The
name probably indicates the momentous event that had occurred in his life
(his healing of leprosy) and thus his restoration to the community of Israel.
Though the text is silent, it would not be unreasonable to assume that Jesus
himself had healed him, hence, Simon inviting Jesus and his disciples to
dine with him. Matthew does not name the woman, simply referring to her
as *a woman* (Mt. 26.7). She comes with an *alabaster jar of very costly
ointment* (Mt. 26.7) Mark says its was *nard* (Mk. 14.3) which she pours
over the head of Jesus. The ointment was imported from the east and was
costly because of the expense of importing it from India (Lane 1974:492)
and to ship it it was placed in alabaster jars which were only broken when it
was to be used (Argyle 1963:195). This ointment was not just for any
purpose but was generally used for important guests or visitors on whom a
host wished to bestow a great honour. Such an anointing would have been
an unusual, rare gesture and a great deal of pleasure would have been
experienced by the guest anointed with such expensive ointment. The value
of the ointment would probably be the equivalent of what a working man

could earn in a year (Jn. 12.5;[1]Lane1974:491). The action which the woman performs here is special to the point of being extremely rare and the cost of such a substance declares the respect in which Jesus was held by the woman (see, Gnilka 1979:2.224 for a different perspective).

The response of the disciples is anger and indignation (Mt. 26.8-9;[2] John tells us Judas was the vocal one, Jn. 12.4-5[3]). On the one hand the indignation of the disciples is justified (it might be noted here that their indignation and anger is not directed towards the woman herself but to the expensive extravagance of her gesture), after all, Jesus himself had commanded them to deny themselves everything and to think of others (Mt. 16.24; 20.26-27[4]) and selling everything to give it to the poor and following after Jesus was the fulfilment of the command given to the rich young man (which he had been unable to do, cf. Mt. 19.21[5]). But what the disciples have failed to see is that the woman has just performed a prophetic act concerning his death (Tasker 1962:112). The disciples have been told about this time and again by Jesus yet they have failed to understand it (Mt. 26.1-2[6]) but the woman seems to have an intuitive grasp of the significance of Jesus' death. It may be stretching it to say that the woman has a 'revelation' about it but it is equally possible that Jesus himself understood it as a prophetic declaration that the disciples would pay special attention to which would reinforce his previous words to them. Her aim in anointing his head

---

[1] 'Why was this perfume not sold for three hundred denarii and the money given to the poor?'

[2] But when the disciples saw it, they were angry and said, 'Why this waste? For this ointment could have been sold for a large sum, and the money given to the poor.'

[3] There they gave a dinner for him. Martha served, and Lazarus was one of those at the table with him. Mary took a pound of costly perfume made of pure nard, anointed Jesus' feet, and wiped them with her hair. The house was filled with the fragrance of the perfume. But Judas Iscariot, one of his disciples (the one who was about to betray him), said, 'Why was this perfume not sold for three hundred denarii and the money given to the poor?'

[4] Then Jesus told his disciples, 'If any want to become my followers, let them deny themselves and take up their cross and follow me; It will not be so among you; but whoever wishes to be great among you must be your servant, and whoever wishes to be first among you must be your slave.

[5] Jesus said to him, 'If you wish to be perfect, go, sell your possessions, and give the money to the poor, and you will have treasure in heaven; then come, follow me.'

[6] When Jesus had finished saying all these things, he said to his disciples, 'You know that after two days the Passover is coming, and the Son of Man will be handed over to be crucified.'

was possibly in order to reveal that she saw him as the Messiah (the *Lord's Anointed,* cf. 2 K 9.3[1]), but she may not have been fully conscious of that, and the stress therefore on the anointing of the head may rather be Matthew's and Mark's, who may also have had in mind his High Priesthood (Ex. 29.7; Lev.8.12; 21.10[2]). They may well have seen this as God's way of pointing ahead to his coronation (Mt. 28.18[3]). The fact that she also anointed his body (v.12) and his feet (Jn. 12.3) suggests that for her it was an act of overwhelming love, made with a desire to pay him due honour.

But the emphasis here is in fact not on her love but on what she has done for Jesus. She has encouraged him and prepared him for a proper burial. Not only does the anointing proclaim his death but it also, according to most commentators, declares that such an honour in death would be unable to be fully given him because of the need to seal the stone of the tomb before the Sabbath dawned (Mk. 16.1[4]). But Joseph of Arimathea and Nicodemus certainly appear to have performed what was necessary to fulfil the Jewish burial customs (Jn. 19.38-40[5]). It is wrong to state that Jesus' body would not be buried with proper ceremony (though the women who ministered to him also seemed to have wanted to give Jesus the *honour* which had been lacking in their approach of the tomb on the Sunday morning). It is incorrect, therefore, to say that *nothing* would be done for the body of Jesus at the time of his burial (or, better, at the time of his entombment) (see, Carson 1996:2, 118)) and it may be that the anointing

---

[1]   Then take the flask of oil, pour it on his head, and say, "Thus says the Lord: I anoint you king over Israel." Then open the door and flee; do not linger.'

[2]   You shall take the anointing-oil, and pour it on his head and anoint him; He poured some of the anointing-oil on Aaron's head and anointed him, to consecrate him; The priest who is exalted above his fellows, on whose head the anointing-oil has been poured and who has been consecrated to wear the vestments, shall not dishevel his hair, nor tear his vestments.

[3]   And Jesus came and said to them, 'All authority in heaven and on earth has been given to me.

[4]   When the Sabbath was over, Mary Magdalene, and Mary the mother of James, and Salome bought spices, so that they might go and anoint him

[5]   After these things, Joseph of Arimathea, who was a disciple of Jesus, though a secret one because of his fear of the Jews, asked Pilate to let him take away the body of Jesus. Pilate gave him permission; so he came and removed his body. Nicodemus, who had at first come to Jesus by night, also came, bringing a mixture of myrrh and aloes, weighing about a hundred pounds. They took the body of Jesus and wrapped it with the spices in linen cloths, according to the burial custom of the Jews.

specified in Mark's Gospel (Mk. 16.1) was done as a mark of great honour which was superfluous to Jewish requirements. Ointments and fragrances may have been repeatedly brought into the tomb (perhaps to restrict the stench of the rotting corpse and to stifle the smell of putrefaction) but it does not appear to have been the norm to anoint the body once it had been dead almost two full days (or, three parts of days) or, at least, there does not appear to be any directions concerning such a practice. But it seems strange that the two men who saw to his entombment and who seem to have had a high regard for him, should not adhere to Jewish custom when they were of the opinion that he was no ordinary person. I would venture to suggest that, if the Scriptures indicate their assessment of Jesus correctly, the only reason for failing to *anoint* the body (which would probably be the saturation of the skin before wrapping it in the linen strips for burial, cf. Jn. 19.38-40[1]) would be the time involved and this does not appear to have been a problem.

This entire discussion has centred around the assertion that the anointing with the spikenard which took place at this meal was solely for the preparation of *the body* because of the circumstances surrounding Jesus' death. This certainly appears to be the meaning which is inherent in the verb used in the Greek but it may equally be possible that Jesus was speaking of his own *personal* preparation for death and that the action of the woman focused his mind on the final outcome of his own life. This is no more than supposition, I admit, but that Jesus was given a burial in accordance with Jewish custom is apparent from John's Gospel previously cited and the haste with which he was buried does not appear to be what is being spoken about here at the meal. That the woman anointed Jesus to 'prepare him for burial' should not be construed as inferring that she believed that he was soon to die. What the point seems to be is that the honour that was being given to

---

[1] After these things, Joseph of Arimathea, who was a disciple of Jesus, though a secret one because of his fear of the Jews, asked Pilate to let him take away the body of Jesus. Pilate gave him permission; so he came and removed his body. Nicodemus, who had at first come to Jesus by night, also came, bringing a mixture of myrrh and aloes, weighing about a hundred pounds. They took the body of Jesus and wrapped it with the spices in linen cloths, according to the burial custom of the Jews.

him at this meal was taken by him to bring the cross and his death into sharp focus. As such, it became a prophetic announcement of his imminent death and something which should have also woken the disciples up to the statement he had very recently made concerning the event (Mt. 26.2[1]).

g. Jesus' Response To The Anointing (Mt. 26.10-13)

Jesus immediately intervenes to quash this attitude among the disciples and says to them (Mt. 26.10):

> Why do you trouble the woman? She has performed a good
> service for me.

Jesus knew what was in the heart of the woman in the same way he knew what was in the heart of others. This woman has done a *good service* literally 'worked a good work' (The noun 'deed/service' and the verb are from the same root. It intensifies the statement or was an idiom (cf. Jn. 3.21; 6.28; 9.4;[2] Acts 13.41;[3] I Cor. 16.10[4]) and it connects with Mt. 5.16:

> That they may see your good works and glorify your Father who is
> in heaven.

This woman has 'worked a good work' to the glory of God. Jesus then turns to their criticism that such an expensive perfume could be sold and given to the poor. His response is *you always have the poor with you, but you will not always have me* (Mt. 26.11). Almsgiving was associated with the Passover

---

[1] 'You know that after two days the Passover is coming, and the Son of Man will be handed over to be crucified.'

[2] But those who do what is true come to the light, so that it may be clearly seen that their deeds have been done in God.' ; Then they said to him, 'What must we do to perform the works of God?'; We must work the works of him who sent me while it is day; night is coming when no one can work;

[3] "Look, you scoffers! Be amazed and perish, for in your days I am doing a work, a work that you will never believe, even if someone tells you." '

[4] If Timothy comes, see that he has nothing to fear among you, for he is doing the work of the Lord just as I am.

and the disciples in their criticism seem to be looking to Jesus for some support of their position and also seem to be implying a criticism of Jesus for allowing such expensive ointment to be used on him (Lane 1974:493). But Jesus turns the criticism back on the disciples to highlight the responsibility they have to the poor: the disciples criticise the woman yet they do little to help the poor themselves. This response of Jesus should not be taken to mean that Jesus has no concern for the poor (Gnilka 1979:2.225) indeed, the opposite is the case since he is the one who has come to serve and not be served and has ministered to the poor and the outcast. The poor have always been there and ever will be but Jesus will not be, so the contrast is not between Jesus and the poor but rather in always having the poor but not always having Jesus. The woman has recognised this and has demonstrated her love and therefore she was not to be criticised.

Soon Jesus would be gone and they would not be able to demonstrate their love for him, indeed, that love will be in short supply as they will abandon him, flee from him and leave him to face his fate alone without any support. Indeed, in his arrest, Passion and Death, Jesus is one of the poor: alone, abandoned, outcast (Danker 1966:468). In the mind of Jesus, at least, this is a preparation for *burial* (Mt. 26.12[1]) for as a condemned criminal his body would not be anointed when the time came and that she anointed his *body* (Mt. 26.11) comes out here (John says she also anointed his feet, cf. Jn. 12.3). Jesus points out, therefore, that the woman, perhaps unknowingly, has prepared him for burial (cf. Taylor 1957:533). Jesus then prophecies that whenever (Mt. 26.13):

> this good news is proclaimed in the whole world, what she has
> done will be told in remembrance of her

Jesus thus reminds the disciples that the gospel is to be proclaimed through the whole world and that her action will be remembered as an act of love (Miller 2002:178). The good news of his death and burial as expressed in

---

[1] By pouring this ointment on my body she has prepared me for burial.

this anointing, good news because it would deal for ever with the problem of sin (Mt. 20.28; 26.28[1]), will then lead on to his resurrection. Indeed it was because of the supreme importance of his death that this that she had done was so important, and that was why she would ever be remembered for it. It was a prophetic acting out of what was to come. The irony here, of course, is that the woman's action has been remembered but not her name (see, Schüssler Fiorenza xliii-xliv). But in a real sense her name is not important, it is her action which is important and it is her action which is to be remembered and lauded and in this sense she stands as representative of all those unnamed who follow Jesus and also those who have 'cameo' roles that are indicative of support of Jesus (e.g., Simon of Cyrene, Joseph of Arimathea, cf. Mk. 15.21; 15.43[2]). This remarkable account, followed as it is by an increasing emphasis on women, is a deliberate indication of the new worth being put on women by the Gospel (Mt. 15.21-28; 27.19, 55-56, 61; 28.1-11[3]). Just as Matthew had emphasised the move from *the lost sheep of*

---

[1] For this is my blood of the covenant, which is poured out for many for the forgiveness of sins.

[2] They compelled a passer-by, who was coming in from the country, to carry his cross; it was Simon of Cyrene, the father of Alexander and Rufus; Joseph of Arimathea, a respected member of the council, who was also himself waiting expectantly for the kingdom of God, went boldly to Pilate and asked for the body of Jesus.

[3] Jesus left that place and went away to the district of Tyre and Sidon. Just then a Canaanite woman from that region came out and started shouting, 'Have mercy on me, Lord, Son of David; my daughter is tormented by a demon.' But he did not answer her at all. And his disciples came and urged him, saying, 'Send her away, for she keeps shouting after us.' He answered, 'I was sent only to the lost sheep of the house of Israel.' But she came and knelt before him, saying, 'Lord, help me.' He answered, 'It is not fair to take the children's food and throw it to the dogs.' She said, 'Yes, Lord, yet even the dogs eat the crumbs that fall from their masters' table.' Then Jesus answered her, 'Woman, great is your faith! Let it be done for you as you wish.' And her daughter was healed instantly; While he was sitting on the judgement seat, his wife sent word to him, 'Have nothing to do with that innocent man, for today I have suffered a great deal because of a dream about him.'; Mary Magdalene and the other Mary were there, sitting opposite the tomb; Many women were also there, looking on from a distance; they had followed Jesus from Galilee and had provided for him. Among them were Mary Magdalene, and Mary the mother of James and Joseph, and the mother of the sons of Zebedee; After the Sabbath, as the first day of the week was dawning, Mary Magdalene and the other Mary went to see the tomb. And suddenly there was a great earthquake; for an angel of the Lord, descending from heaven, came and rolled back the stone and sat on it. His appearance was like lightning, and his clothing white as snow. For fear of him the guards shook and became like dead men. But the angel said to the women, 'Do not be afraid; I know that you are looking for Jesus who was crucified. He is not here; for he has been raised, as he said. Come, see the place where he lay. Then go quickly and tell his disciples, "He has been raised from the dead, and indeed he is going ahead of you to

the house of Israel to an interest in the Gentiles, so now he brings out the growing importance of women (something also very important to Luke).

h. The Woman As An Example of Discipleship

What follows in this section is equally applicable to Mark and Luke so it will not be repeated when Mark and Luke's version of this story is dealt with. Matthew says (Mt. 26.7):

> the woman came to him (Jesus) with an alabaster jar of very costly ointment, and she poured it on his head as he sat at the table

Matthew makes no mention of her 'breaking' the jar as Mark does (Mk. 14.3[1]) but since the jar would have been sealed it could only be opened through breaking thus allowing the ointment to pour out. Mark's use of the Greek verb 'suntripsasa' ('having broken into pieces', 'having crushed') indicates that the jar is shattered into pieces and so cannot be used again. It does not appear, therefore, that there was any left over that might have been sold which reinforces the severity of the disciples' criticism (Lane:1974, 492). So the woman has 'poured out' everything she has in her possession which is what Jesus has asked the disciples to do. Jesus praises her because what 'she had she has done' (Mk. 14.8 'eschen epoiēsen', cf. Mt. 26.10) and this recalls Jesus' words that whoever does the will of God is his brother and sister (Mk. 3.35[2]) i.e., his disciple. The woman came to Jesus with an alabaster jar of *costly ointment* (Mt. 26.7) which Mark and John tell us (Mk. 14.4; Jn. 12.4) was worth three hundred denarii (a year's salary for a labourer) and even what was left would have fetched a tidy sum, but she

---

Galilee; there you will see him." This is my message for you.' So they left the tomb quickly with fear and great joy, and ran to tell his disciples. Suddenly Jesus met them and said, 'Greetings!' And they came to him, took hold of his feet, and worshipped him. Then Jesus said to them, 'Do not be afraid; go and tell my brothers to go to Galilee; there they will see me.'

[1]   Whoever does the will of God is my brother and sister and mother.'

[2]   Truly I tell you, wherever the good news is proclaimed in the whole world, what she has done will be told in remembrance of her.';

pours all of it over Jesus so that she has given everything she had, all her 'riches'. So before the encounter with Jesus she had everything (the expensive perfume) after the encounter she has nothing (a broken empty jar); she has given everything in an act of love to him. This is a total loss on her part but it precisely this for which she will be remembered (Mk. 14.9; Mt. 26.13[1]).

There is a real sense in which the woman's action is a microcosm of the Passion and Death of Jesus: she 'pours out' everything she has, just as Jesus pours out everything he has at his death; her actions are criticised by those who oppose her, just as Jesus' action are criticised by those who oppose him (Barton 1993:232-33). She remains silent in the face of the criticism levelled against her, just as Jesus remains silent in the face of the criticisms and accusations levelled against him (Mk. 14.61; 15.5; Mt. 27.14[2]). Jesus vindicates the woman and her actions just as he will be vindicated by the action of God at the resurrection (Mk. 16.1-9; Mt. 28.1-10; Lk. 24.1-12; Jn. 20.1-10). The woman's action in the anointing can also be seen as an acknowledgement of his Messiahship on a par with Peter's so called 'confession of faith' (Mk. 8.27-28;[3] Mt. 16.13-20; Lk. 9.18-20) but whereas Peter fails to grasp the reality of the suffering of Jesus, the woman, with this anointing *for burial,* has perceived it. The praise that Jesus lavishes on her and her action (Mt. 26.13):

> Truly I tell you, wherever this good news is proclaimed in the
> whole world, what she has done will be told in remembrance of
> her

is more than anything Jesus has said to the disciples. In the section that

---

[1]

[2] But he was silent and did not answer. Again the high priest asked him, 'Are you the Messiah, the Son of the Blessed One?'; But Jesus made no further reply, so that Pilate was amazed; But he gave him no answer, not even to a single charge, so that the governor was greatly amazed.

[3] Once when Jesus was praying alone, with only the disciples near him, he asked them, 'Who do the crowds say that I am?' They answered, 'John the Baptist; but others, Elijah; and still others, that one of the ancient prophets has arisen.' He said to them, 'But who do you say that I am?' Peter answered, 'The Messiah of God.'

follows the anointing the name of the betrayer of Jesus is recorded (Mt. 26.14; Mk. 14.10[1]) but the woman remains anonymous for she is to be remembered *not by her name* but *by her action* and her gift of 'anointing'. It is this which will be proclaimed throughout the world as the gospel is proclaimed throughout the world. She grasps something of the nature of Jesus' future, whereas the disciples have no perception, no understanding, and no intuition to see the reality of the situation Jesus moves towards. Her name, therefore, is not important but her action of recognition, anointing, love and solidarity with the suffering Jesus is important (as the women at the cross stand in solidarity with the suffering Jesus, Mt. 27.55-56; Mk. 15.40-41; Lk. 23.49[2]) for this is what the true disciple of Jesus is called to.

---

[1] Then one of the twelve, who was called Judas Iscariot, went to the chief priests.

[2] Many women were also there, looking on from a distance; they had followed Jesus from Galilee and had provided for him. Among them were Mary Magdalene, and Mary the mother of James and Joseph, and the mother of the sons of Zebedee; There were also women looking on from a distance; among them were Mary Magdalene, and Mary the mother of James the younger and of Joses, and Salome. These used to follow him and provided for him when he was in Galilee; and there were many other women who had come up with him to Jerusalem; But all his acquaintances, including the women who had followed him from Galilee, stood at a distance, watching these things.

CHAPTER THREE

JESUS AND THE WOMEN OF MARK

Female Characters in Mark's Gospel

MARK	CHARACTER / EPISODE
1.29-31	Healing of Simon's Mother-in-Law
3.19b-21, 31-35	Concern of Jesus' Family: Mother and Brothers
5.21-24, 35-43	The Daughter of Jairus
5.25-34	A Woman with a Flow of Blood
6.3	Jesus is called "Son of Mary"; ref. to his sisters
6.17-29	John the Baptist's Death: Herodias and her daughter
7.24-30	The Syro-Phoenician Woman's Daughter
10.2-12	On Divorce
10.19	Jesus quotes the Decalogue: "Honour Your Father and Mother"
10.29-30	"No one who has left house or brothers or sisters or mother or father or children or fields for my sake..."
12.18-27	The Case of a Woman Who Had Seven Husbands
12.41-44	The Widow's Mite
13.12	Apocalyptic Discourse: Children Rise against their Parents
13.17	'Alas for those with child or nursing'
14.3-9	Anointing at Bethany: Anonymous Woman
14.66-72	Peter's Denial: The Serving Girl
15.40-41	Women at the Cross: Mary Magdalene, Mary mother of James & Joses, and Salome
15.47	Women See Jesus Buried
16.1-8	Women Go to Jesus' Tomb

The Women of Mark

It is generally agreed that the gospel known as Mark was the first of the canonical gospels to be written sometime c.64-77AD with possible locations being Rome or Antioch (Brown 1999:127; cf. also Marcus 1992: 446-48). Since this is the first gospel to be written, Mark's presentation of women and Jesus' interaction with them is important. His presentation is important in that it allows us to gain some insight into how Mark (and the Markan community) viewed women both in themselves and in their response to Jesus. While the gospel of Luke is sometimes known as the *gospel of the women*, Mark's gospel also has some striking encounters between Jesus and women and the gospel is 'well populated' with female characters, some of whom have a 'cameo' role and some who have central roles. The women in the gospel of Mark are presented in three distinct but complementary ways: faith, service and discipleship (cf. Schmitt 1981: 231;Beavis 1988:8). It is interesting to note that the first 'physical' healing of Jesus in Mark takes place in the 'house' of Simon in an act that is briefly told but deeply significant, the cure of Simon's mother-in-law from a 'fever' after which she 'serves' Jesus (Mk. 1.29-31) and the gospel closes with the women at the tomb (Mk. 16.8). One could suggest therefore that the whole of Mark's gospel is played out between these two encounters.

Some of the women in Mark are strong and determined characters: the woman with the haemorrhage (Mk. 5.21-43), the Syro-Phoenician woman (Mk. 7.24-30), the servant girl who challenges Peter (Mk. 14.53-54; 66-72); some are children, the daughter of Jairus (Mk. 5.21-43), the daughter of the Syro-Phoenician woman (Mk. 7.24-30). Some are cold and scheming, Herodias and her daughter (Mk. 6.14-29). Some are warm, tender and compassionate, the woman who anoints Jesus at Bethany (Mk. 14.3-9). Some misunderstand his ministry and try to prevent it, his mother and sisters and brothers (Mk. 3.20-35) and some provide Jesus with opportunities to teach and instruct, the poor widow (Mk. 12.41-44); and some love and grieve for him, the women at the crucifixion and burial (Mk. 15.40-41,47). Women in Mark, therefore, in the main, appear at central and significant moments and highlight and illustrate aspects both of Jesus' teaching and his instruction and serve as open and receptive respondents to Jesus' demands for service and discipleship (see, Kopas 1985:920). Contrast can be made, of course, between the way in which the 'Twelve' males respond to Jesus and the way in which the women respond to Jesus for Mark consistently portrays the Twelve as failing to understand or grasp the true significance and meaning of Jesus both in himself and of his teaching and as ultimately abandoning Jesus in his most desperate hour of need (cf. Schüssler Fiorenza 1985:320-22).

The women in Mark (setting Herodias and her daughter and the family of Jesus aside for the moment) are *with* Jesus more constantly and, it appears, with greater fidelity and it is they who are with him at the end and beyond the end. Is Mark saying, therefore, that the women are 'better' disciples than the men? That they are more faithful and constant through their attentiveness to him and in their following of him? One might note, for example, that as the disciples run away in fear from Jesus and abandon him in Gethsemane and are silent during his Passion and death (Mk. 14.50[1]), so too the women run away in fear from the empty tomb and are silent about the resurrection (Mk. 16.8[2]) in which case both the males and the females are presented as failures as disciples. Whether these comparisons of 'negative males' and 'positive females' in pictures of service and discipleship are useful is a matter of some debate and it does not follow that this is Mark's primary intention. The distinctive and important contribution and role of women in the Markan-Jesus narrative may be lost if they serve only as comparisons to the male disciples in the gospel (Dewey 1994:508). Mark interweaves women throughout the whole of his narrative and does so within the context of his world view wherein Jesus comes to tear down dehumanising structures whether it is the 'kingdom' of Satan (characterised by disease, possession, sickness) or the 'kingdom' of stultifying legalism (characterised by his often contentious encounters with representatives of

---

[1]   All of them deserted him and fled.

[2]   So they went out and fled from the tomb, for terror and amazement had seized them; and they said nothing to anyone, for they were afraid.

Jerusalem and the Temple), liberate from sin and all its associations, and renew the hearts of men and women in preparation for the eschatololgical realisation of the reign of God and the encounters with women in the gospel are to be seen in this light.

Simon's Mother-in-Law (Mk. 1.29-31)

The Narrative Context

a. Establishing Identity (Mk. 1.9-11)

The healing of Simon's mother-in-law in the gospel of Mark takes up only two verses but it is of profound significance and importance. Before coming to the story itself, it is necessary to set it in context by providing the 'lead up' to it. Mark has begun his story of Jesus with the ministry of John the Baptist (Mk. 1.1-8[1]), which is immediately followed by the baptism of Jesus (Mk. 1.9-11[2]). Everything that follows from this point onwards is contextualised by the baptism of Jesus (which is followed by the Temptation and the call of the disciples Mk. 1.12-13; 16-20[3]). It is while John is baptising at the Jordan (and whom Mark quite clearly presents as Elijah, the

---

[1] The beginning of the good news of Jesus Christ, the Son of God. As it is written in the prophet Isaiah, 'See, I am sending my messenger ahead of you, who will prepare your way; the voice of one crying out in the wilderness:"Prepare the way of the Lord, make his paths straight" John the baptiser appeared in the wilderness, proclaiming a baptism of repentance for the forgiveness of sins. And people from the whole Judean countryside and all the people of Jerusalem were going out to him, and were baptised by him in the river Jordan, confessing their sins. Now John was clothed with camel's hair, with a leather belt around his waist, and he ate locusts and wild honey. He proclaimed, 'The one who is more powerful than I is coming after me; I am not worthy to stoop down and untie the thong of his sandals. I have baptised you with water; but he will baptise you with the Holy Spirit.'

[2] In those days Jesus came from Nazareth of Galilee and was baptised by John in the Jordan. And just as he was coming up out of the water, he saw the heavens torn apart and the Spirit descending like a dove on him. And a voice came from heaven, 'You are my Son, the Beloved; with you I am well pleased.'

[3] And the Spirit immediately drove him out into the wilderness. He was in the wilderness for forty days, tempted by Satan; and he was with the wild beasts; and the angels waited on him; As Jesus passed along the Sea of Galilee, he saw Simon and his brother Andrew casting a net into the lake—for they were fishermen. And Jesus said to them, 'Follow me and I will make you fish for people.' And immediately they left their nets and followed him. As he went a little farther, he saw James son of Zebedee and his brother John, who were in their boat mending the nets. Immediately he called them; and they left their father Zebedee in the boat with the hired men, and followed him.

one who would herald the coming of the new age with the advent of the Messiah, Mk. 1.2-8; cf. 9.13; Mt. 11.10-14;[1] 17.12; Lk. 1.17), that Jesus comes to him to be baptised (Mk. 1.9). Jesus comes to John (as had the people) and when he is baptised the Spirit comes upon the one who will inaugurate the time of the Spirit. As Jesus comes out of the water a voice from heaven proclaims (Ps. 2.7; Is. 42.1[2]):

> You are my beloved Son, in you I am well pleased

While the baptism of Jesus is undoubtedly historical (see, Harrington 2202:32-34) it is the theological-Christological meaning that is more important. In Mark's brief account of Jesus' baptism by John, Jesus is being presented as Son of God and Servant of God. Ps. 2 in the first instance refers to the heirs of David as the 'adopted' sons of God but it is essentially about the king who comes, God's anointed *one* (Messiah, Ps. 2.2) who will bring the rule of God over the nations (Ps. 2.8-9). Is. 42.1-4[3] (cf. Is. 49.1-6; 50.4-8; 52.13-53.12) images the great Servant of the Lord who will achieve the purposes of God through suffering.

Up to this point John has mainly attracted the interest of the Judaeans and Jerusalemites, so the coming of a Galilean indicates the identification by Jesus of himself with John's ministry: Jesus comes to show that John's present ministry and his own future ministry are part of God's purpose. In coming to John, Jesus identifies with all the people who are freely

---

[1] This is the one about whom it is written,"See, I am sending my messenger ahead of you, who will prepare your way before you." Truly I tell you, among those born of women no one has arisen greater than John the Baptist; yet the least in the kingdom of heaven is greater than he. From the days of John the Baptist until now the kingdom of heaven has suffered violence, and the violent take it by force. For all the prophets and the law prophesied until John came; and if you are willing to accept it, he is Elijah who is to come.

[2] I will tell of the decree of the Lord: He said to me, 'You are my son; today I have begotten you. Ask of me, and I will make the nations your heritage, and the ends of the earth your possession. You shall break them with a rod of iron, and dash them in pieces like a potter's vessel.'

[3] Here is my servant, whom I uphold, my chosen, in whom my soul delights; I have put my spirit upon him; he will bring forth justice to the nations. He will not cry or lift up his voice, or make it heard in the street; a bruised reed he will not break, and a dimly burning wick he will not quench; he will faithfully bring forth justice. He will not grow faint or be crushed until he has established justice in the earth; and the coastlands wait for his teaching.

responding to John's ministry (see, McBride 1996:30-31). And this is deliberate on Mark's part; he does not mention or even point to the seeming incongruity of Jesus undergoing a baptism that is the outward sign of repentance when Jesus needs no repentance for he is without sin (cf. Mt. 3.14). Jesus is identifying himself with sinners for it is they he has come to save. John, however, sees the incongruity in two ways: first, his own sense of unworthiness to baptise the one who was greater than he, and secondly, John understood that he himself needed the baptism of Jesus who baptised with the Spirit. How then could John baptise the baptiser in the Spirit, how could the less baptise the greater? Jesus does not suffer from the same angst as John; certainly there is no need of repentance, admission of and forgiveness for sin in his case but those were the preparatory acts for baptism, without them there could be no baptism. They preceded the baptism, they did not symbolise it. Once these other acts had taken place, baptism took place as a seal of what the people had professed in their repentance etc. and were now ready to receive the drenching of the Spirit that Jesus would bring.

Jesus, therefore, does not need to repent but he does stand with the people to affirm and confirm the God given authority of John's ministry. He presents himself to John as one ready and willing to receive the outpouring of the spirit on their behalf and so, *it is fitting that we should fulfil all righteousness* (Mt. 3.15). As the representative human, Jesus has to do what a righteous person must do, i.e., participate in that which points to the coming work of the Spirit. So by this act Jesus is very clearly identifying himself with those for whom he has come, affirming John as one sent by God and affirming and confirming the authenticity of his baptism and that the outpouring of the Spirit was coming (Byrne 2008:30). When Jesus comes up out of the waters of the Jordan he sees (Mk. 1.10-11):

> the heavens torn apart and the Spirit descending like a dove on him. And a voice from heaven said, 'You are my Son, the Beloved; with you I am well pleased.'

Here we get an insight into Jesus' personal religious (mystical) experience, only he hears the voice and sees the Spirit descending *like a dove* on him. As he come sup from the waters, he experiences activity in the heavens. He image of the heavens *opening* of *being rent asunder* (a metaphor for the ripping open of the canopy above the earth) was frequently used but not in the same dramatic way in which Mark presents it here. Mark may be seeking to link this *rending/tearing* open of the heavens at the baptism where Jesus is proclaimed *Beloved Son* with the *rending/tearing* of the Temple veil in Mk. 15.38,[1] (Mullins 2005:66) a dramatic moment of divine revelation, at the death of Jesus where he is proclaimed *Son of God* by the Centurion. Is. 64.1,[2] may also be in view here given that Is. 63-64 has interesting connections with Mark's narrative here. Is. 63.11 speaks of the leaders of Israel *coming up from the water* when God put the Spirit in the midst of them and then Israel was brought through the wilderness (Is. 63.13-14[3]) only to fail in their response to God's call (Is. 63.19[4]). God is now *rending the heavens* (as Isaiah had implored) in the expectation of a much better result.

Jesus was aware of some presence (Luke specifies it as the *bodily form of a dove* (Lk. 3.22)(Maloney 2002:36-37) which had descended on him in the same way that Isaiah speaks of the Spirit descending on the king, (Is. 11.1-4[5]) the Servant (Is. 42.1-4) and the anointed prophet (Is. 61.1-3[6]).

---

[1] And the curtain of the temple was torn in two, from top to bottom.

[2] O that You would rend the heavens and come down.

[3] Who led them through the depths? Like a horse in the desert, they did not stumble. Like cattle that go down into the valley, the spirit of the Lord gave them rest. Thus you led your people, to make for yourself a glorious name.

[4] We have long been like those whom you do not rule, like those not called by your name.

[5] A shoot shall come out from the stock of Jesse, and a branch shall grow out of his roots. The spirit of the Lord shall rest on him, the spirit of wisdom and understanding, the spirit of counsel and might, the spirit of knowledge and the fear of the Lord. His delight shall be in the fear of the Lord. He shall not judge by what his eyes see, or decide by what his ears hear; but with righteousness he shall judge the poor, and decide with equity for the meek of the earth; he shall strike the earth with the rod of his mouth, and with the breath of his lips he shall kill the wicked.

[6] The spirit of the Lord God is upon me, because the Lord has anointed me; he has sent me to bring good news to the oppressed, to bind up the broken-hearted, to proclaim liberty to the captives, and release to the

According to the gospel of John, the Baptist also has an awareness of this presence (Jn. 1.32). The crowds (at least in Matthew) may have heard *This is my beloved Son* and given that that it would have been spoken in Aramaic both translations would be acceptable in Greek: to Jesus, *You are my beloved Son*, to John, *This is my beloved Son* (in Aramaic it may simply have been rendered as, *My beloved Son* with the pronoun understood) (see, Martin 2007:13;Mulholland 2012:1.34). Jesus, therefore, identifies himself with the repentant, expectant people who await the eschatological coming of the kingdom and in this he is 'showered in the Spirit' and empowered by God whose *beloved Son* he is (Lk. 4.1 says he is *full of the Holy Spirit*) and whose approval he has and John receives the confirmation that this is the one who will soak humanity in the Spirit (Jn. 1.33[1]) like soothing, quenching rain (Is. 32.15; 55.10[2]). The impression that Jesus has is that the presence is *as a dove*, not literally but impressionistically and perhaps the intention here is to connect it with Gen. 1.2 where the Spirit *broods* over the impending creation. Thus is would be a symbol of the impending creative work of God *in the beginning* (Gen. 1.1) as his gospel is the *beginning* of the Good News (Mk. 1.1) so that Jesus is the inaugurator of a new (apocalyptic age) creation. One might also call to mind the dove which brings back the branch (sign of new life) following the flood so that it would emphasise the mercy of God to allow humanity to begin again in a new creation (Gen. 8.11-12[3]). It was a symbol, therefore, of new life and new hope and new beginnings. The *voice* which speaks from the heavens has

---

prisoners; to proclaim the year of the Lord's favour, and the day of vengeance of our God; to comfort all who mourn; to provide for those who mourn in Zion—to give them a garland instead of ashes, the oil of gladness instead of mourning, the mantle of praise instead of a faint spirit. They will be called oaks of righteousness, the planting of the Lord, to display his glory.

[1] I myself did not know him, but the one who sent me to baptise with water said to me, "He on whom you see the Spirit descend and remain is the one who baptises with the Holy Spirit."

[2] Until a spirit from on high is poured out on us, and the wilderness becomes a fruitful field, and the fruitful field is deemed a forest; For as the rain and the snow come down from heaven, and do not return there until they have watered the earth, making it bring forth and sprout, giving seed to the sower and bread to the eater.

[3] And the dove came back to him in the evening, and there in its beak was a freshly plucked olive leaf; so Noah knew that the waters had subsided from the earth. Then he waited another seven days, and sent out the dove; and it did not return to him any more.

sometimes be likened to the *bat kol'* (daughter of the voice), a far off voice that came from God who spoke it in the heaven of heavens but which had not been heard in Israel for four hundred years when the last prophetic voice, Micah, has sounded. But this was not the *bat kol'* this, rather, was God in direct communication with his own voice resolutely and definitively affirming who Jesus was and what his mission was: the heavens had been *rent asunder* and Jesus was well aware of it.

The voice proclaims to Jesus, *you are my beloved Son, in you I am well pleased*. As noted above, this echoes Ps. 2.7, which in its original setting spoke of the adoption of the Davidic king by God, and Is. 42.1[1] which is spoken to the coming Servant to the nations (Dowd and Malbon 2006:273-274). In this proclamation, God confirms that Jesus is *the* true son of David, the Messiah promised and expected, and God's faithful Servant. But the words have a much deeper meaning and significance here because they show that Jesus is <u>the</u> beloved son in a way which far transcends any conception of the sonship of the Davidic King. Ps. 2 was probably used at the coronation ceremony of the king of Judah and perhaps at an annual renewal ceremony and it gives voice to the hope that the Davidic king, God's chosen, would one day reign over the world as his chosen king (see Mullins 2005:69). Ps. 2.7 reads:

you are my son, today I have begotten you

However, the change to *beloved* in Mark indicates that Jesus was not 'adopted' but unique. It reflects the idea of *only begotten* (in the LXX it is used of Abraham's *only son* and Jephthah's *only daughter*) but it distinguishes Jesus from the earlier Davidic king as the one whom God uniquely and essentially loved: his only beloved son (cf. Mk. 9.7; 12.6[2]). Is. 42.1 connects Jesus with the Servant of Isaiah's prophecies and Mt. 3.17 is

---

[1]   Here is my servant, whom I uphold, my chosen, in whom my soul delights;I have put my spirit upon him; he will bring forth justice to the nations.

[2]   Then a cloud overshadowed them, and from the cloud there came a voice, 'This is my Son, the Beloved; listen to him!'

of special interest here since it also contains a reference to Jesus as *beloved son* (see Mulholland 2012:1.37;Martin 2007:13;Mc Bride 1996:33-34). Initially, this referred to Israel and then to *faithful* Israel (Is. 49.3[1]) who would restore *Jacob* and *Israel* and bring the nations to God, the Servant became a prophetic figure who would suffer at the hands of his enemies who would not hear him (Is. 53.8[2]), and who would eventually suffer for the sins of the people (Is. 52.13-53.12). Though not connected to the Davidic King, he nevertheless had royal bearing (Is. 52.13[3]) and later Jesus would connect himself with this suffering Servant (Lk. 22.37[4]) as well as making a messianic claim (cf. Jn. 4.25-26[5] where the title is not misleading to the hearers), the son of David and the suffering Son of Man. So Jesus became aware at his baptism that this was the moment when he had to reveal himself as the Son, Servant and Messiah of God: his mission of service, suffering and royal authority was now to begin (see Byrne 2008:33;Meier 1994:2.1-7-108 for fuller theological explanation).

b. The War With Satan Begins (Mk. 1.12-13)

This account of the temptation of Jesus is brief compared to Mt. 4.1-11 and Lk. 4.1-13. In these accounts the purpose of the temptation is clear: how would Jesus use his Messianic powers to accomplish his redemptive task But what could Mark's brief account mean? (see, Best 1980:15) It is possible that this event may be seen as a symbol of Jesus' defeat of evil (i.e., by the empowering of the Spirit), a foreshadowing of the Passion Week (Matera 1988:3-4). But this is only speculation. The text itself gives no clue except the event's timing, just after Jesus' (1) enduing by the Spirit and (2) affirmation by the Father, but before his public ministry. This is one of the

---

[1] And he said to me, 'You are my servant, Israel, in whom I will be glorified.'

[2] By a perversion of justice he was taken away. Who could have imagined his future? For he was cut off from the land of the living, stricken for the transgression of my people.

[3] See, my servant shall prosper; he shall be exalted and lifted up, and shall be very high.

[4] For I tell you, this scripture must be fulfilled in me, "And he was counted among the lawless"; and indeed what is written about me is being fulfilled.'

[5] The woman said to him, 'I know that Messiah is coming' (who is called Christ). 'When he comes, he will proclaim all things to us.' Jesus said to her, 'I am he, the one who is speaking to you.'

three events mentioned before Jesus' public ministry

1.   John's ministry
2.   John's baptism
3.   Satan's temptation

This is an essential part of the introduction. It is a reminder that the way ahead will not be smooth. Jesus has not come simply to reveal the power of God. His coming involves him in being fully involved in temptation, for the battle is in the end a moral one. And it is a reminder that as a human being, and as God's Anointed One, he must face the consequences of being involved in a sinful world, and must overcome, whether it be over Satan and his testings, or over the wild beasts of unredeemed mankind (Dan. 7.3; Rev. 13.1, 11[1]; cf. Gibson 1994:21-32). Mark's version of the Temptation is simply (Mk. 1.12-13):

> And the Spirit immediately drove him out into the wilderness.
> He was in the wilderness for forty days, tempted by Satan; and
> he was with the wild beasts; and the angels waited on him.

He opens his brief account up with the statement that it was the *Spirit* that *drove* Jesus into the wilderness/desert *immediately* after the Baptism. The word *immediately/straight away* here is a Markan literary device which serves to move the action quickly forward and to connect different narratives rather than as an indication of chronology (cf. Mauser 1963:80). It is frequently present in Mk. 1.9-2.12 where it quickly moves the reader through Jesus' initial activity in one smooth moment. The implication behind this verse is clear: the Spirit who has come on Jesus is now directing his life. His past life is over, and his new life has begun; he is now being *driven* by

---

[1]   And four great beasts came up out of the sea, different from one another; And I saw a beast rising out of the sea, having ten horns and seven heads; and on its horns were ten diadems, and on its heads were blasphemous names; Then I saw another beast that rose out of the earth; it had two horns like a lamb and it spoke like a dragon.

the Holy Spirit (cf. Luke 4.1). The word *driven/impelled/throw out* is a strong word (often used of exorcisms, cf., e.g., Mk. 1.34; 3.15; 6.13; 7.26; 9.18[1]) and implies that there is a divine compulsion: Jesus is driven by one whom he cannot resist (Byrne 2008:34). In the Old Testament the wilderness was a time of testing for Israel, but also a time of intimate fellowship. The rabbis called the wilderness wandering period the *honeymoon between God and Israel*. Elijah and John the Baptist grew up in the wilderness. It was a place of seclusion for training, meditation, and preparation for active ministry (Mullins 2005:70). This period was crucial for Jesus' preparation (cf. Heb. 5.8[2]). He was driven into the wilderness because he too must be a prophetic figure like John was, and in the wilderness he would meet God. John had prepared the way in the wilderness. Now he for whom John was preparing the way must go into that wilderness as he approached his future. It was to be a time of preparation and challenge. The temptations that followed suggest that one of the main reasons for the move was to consider how he should approach his ministry. This time of pondering the future inevitably provided opportunity for Satan to introduce his false suggestions. Others see the driving into the wilderness as being because there he could face up to all the powers of evil that some thought to be in the desert. But there is little evidence of the Jews thinking like that (Mulholland 2012:1.37). The thought then would be that he went there precisely to meet them face to face. But if that were so we might have expected further reference to it somewhere. The impression given is that it was Satan alone, and his temptations, that he had to face, and that he had to face them, as it were, man to man (but see, Gundry 1993:54-62).

Jesus is in *the wilderness/desert* for *forty days* and is *tempted by Satan* though succinct, these are strong images that have significant meaning. The

---

[1] And he cured many who were sick with various diseases, and cast out many demons; and he would not permit the demons to speak, because they knew him; and to have authority to cast out demons; They cast out many demons, and anointed with oil many who were sick and cured them; Now the woman was a Gentile, of Syrophoenician origin. She begged him to cast the demon out of her daughter; and whenever it seizes him, it dashes him down; and he foams and grinds his teeth and becomes rigid; and I asked your disciples to cast it out, but they could not do so.'

[2] Although he was a Son, he learned obedience through what he suffered;

wilderness/desert was the place where God and prophet met; both Moses and Elijah spent *forty days* with God in the desert (and here was one greater than both); Jesus is *tempted by Satan*, i.e., tested as to his future plans (the easy way or God's way); and he is *with the wild beasts* away from human contact, society and civilisation, his only company being the wild beasts; and the *angles ministered to him*, he is under the protection of God. Jesus is *in the wilderness/desert for forty days* (this is used both literally and figuratively in the Bible. It denotes a long indeterminate period of time i.e., longer than a lunar cycle, but shorter than a seasonal change) as Moses was on the mountain in the wilderness/desert for forty days and forty nights to be given the covenant and to have the plans of God revealed to him (Ex. 24.18; 34.28[1]); Elijah was in the wilderness/desert for forty days and forty nights when he was running for his life and while there God renewed his prophetic commission (1 K 19.8[2]; cf. Guelich 1989: 38.). Both these were forty days and forty nights and Matthew (Mt. 4.2[3]) makes this connection while Mark simply abbreviates it. Jesus, therefore, is in the tradition of Moses and Elijah (the most honoured of the prophets, cf. Mk. 9.2). It is important to note that Moses and Elijah are both figures who were expected to come in the future, or rather the like of them: the *prophet like Moses* would know God face-to-face and God's words would be in his mouth (Deut. 18.15, 18[4] cf. 34.10) and the Elijah who would *prepare the way of the Lord* for both represented the prophetic Law (Torah=*instruction*) and the prophetic speech (cf. Drury 1985:25-36). Now here was one who was greater than both. Mark gives us no information about the actual temptations themselves but he clearly sees the temptation of Jesus as connected with his mission, and, as is known from the other gospels, the temptations concerned themselves with precisely

---

[1]   Moses entered the cloud, and went up on the mountain. Moses was on the mountain for forty days and forty nights; He was there with the Lord for forty days and forty nights; he neither ate bread nor drank water. And he wrote on the tablets the words of the covenant, the ten commandments.

[2]   He got up, and ate and drank; then he went in the strength of that food for forty days and forty nights to Horeb the mount of God.

[3]   He fasted for forty days and forty nights, and afterwards he was famished.

[4]   The Lord your God will raise up for you a prophet like me from among your own people; you shall heed such a prophet.

how Jesus would fulfil his mission: misuse his powers? Use extraordinary means to win people to his cause? Avoid suffering through compromise? (Mt. 4.1-11; Lk. 4.1-13). Ultimately, the temptations are about choosing 'my way' or God's way to follow or not to follow the path of God. We should note however that Mark gives the impression of continual temptation. Jesus is tempted throughout the forty days. In Matthew the final temptations come at the end. But this must surely be because those final temptations were the earlier temptations finally crystallised into a solid and specific form. The continual temptations are seen as having finally brought Jesus to the point of dealing with the three major ones then crystallised in his mind by the subtleties of Satan. And, after a short break (Lk. 4.13[1]), the temptations will continue throughout his life (e.g. Mt. 16.23[2]).

The noun *Satan* means 'the adversary' and also called 'the Devil' ('diabolos' - 'the accuser', 'the slanderer', used in LXX to translate 'Satan'). He appears in the Old Testament as a heavenly being who leads humanity astray and who attacks God's servants in the presence of God, opposing God's purposes (1 Chron. 21.1;[3] Job 1.6-2.7; Zech. 3.1[4]). When he is cast down from that position it is a cause of great rejoicing (Rev. 12.9-10[5]). While in the wilderness being tempted by the Adversary, Jesus is *with the wild beasts*. In Ps. 91.11-13[6] domination of wild beasts goes hand in hand with the ministration of angels. Thus the thought here may well include the idea that he need not be afraid of them; he was with them, but because of

---

[1] When the devil had finished every test, he departed from him until an opportune time.

[2] But he turned and said to Peter, 'Get behind me, Satan! You are a stumbling-block to me; for you are setting your mind not on divine things but on human things.'

[3] Satan stood up against Israel, and incited David to count the people of Israel;

[4] Then he showed me the high priest Joshua standing before the angel of the Lord, and Satan standing at his right hand to accuse him.

[5] The great dragon was thrown down, that ancient serpent, who is called the Devil and Satan, the deceiver of the whole world, he was thrown down to the earth, and his angels were thrown down with him. Then I heard a loud voice in heaven, proclaiming,'Now have come the salvation and the power and the kingdom of our God and the authority of his Messiah, for the accuser of our comrades has been thrown down, who accuses them day and night before our God.

[6] For he will command his angels concerning you to guard you in all your ways. On their hands they will bear you up, so that you will not dash your foot against a stone. You will tread on the lion and the adder, the young lion and the serpent you will trample under foot.

his relationship of love with God they are subject to his control. They cannot touch him (see, Heil 2006:63-78). We can compare Daniel's words, *My God sent his angel and shut the lions' mouths* (Dan. 6.22).

But the idea is also surely that he was away from human contact with no one but the wild beasts for company (and the angels, see below). The wild beasts are met with in desolate places (Is. 34.14[1]). In other Jewish literature (*The Testament of the Twelve Patriarchs*) there appears to be a connection between wild beasts in desert places and demonic forces. Some have therefore suggested that there may thus be in this a further hint at his battle with Satanic forces, so, these wild beasts may also be compared with the later antagonism of Jesus' adversaries (Mk. 3.22[2]; see, Kingsbury 1989:64-65;Malbron 1989:419-41)) just as the wild beasts which represented the godless nations were contrasted with the 'son of man' and the true people of God who truly served him in Daniel 7. From the beginning then, Jesus is being made aware that he has come among the *wild beasts;* the world will not welcome him and the way ahead will be rough. While Jesus is *in the wilderness/desert*, the *angels ministered to him* (cf. Heb. 1.14[3]). Whether this means being fed as Elijah was (1 K 19.5-7[4]), or protected as Elisha was (2 K 6.15-17[5]) and as the Psalmist described (Ps. 91.11-12), we do not know. But it is a reminder that in the 'heavenly places', the spiritual realm where the Christian lives and wrestles with evil

---

[1] Wildcats shall meet with hyenas, goat-demons shall call to each other; there too Lilith shall repose, and find a place to rest.

[2] And the scribes who came down from Jerusalem said, 'He has Beelzebul, and by the ruler of the demons he casts out demons.'

[3] Are not all angels spirits in the divine service, sent to serve for the sake of those who are to inherit salvation?

[4] Then he lay down under the broom tree and fell asleep. Suddenly an angel touched him and said to him, 'Get up and eat.' He looked, and there at his head was a cake baked on hot stones, and a jar of water. He ate and drank, and lay down again. The angel of the Lord came a second time, touched him, and said, 'Get up and eat, otherwise the journey will be too much for you.'

[5] When an attendant of the man of God rose early in the morning and went out, an army with horses and chariots was all around the city. His servant said, 'Alas, master! What shall we do?' He replied, 'Do not be afraid, for there are more with us than there are with them.' Then Elisha prayed: 'O Lord, please open his eyes that he may see.' So the Lord opened the eyes of the servant, and he saw; the mountain was full of horses and chariots of fire all around Elisha.

(Eph. 6.12[1]), there are those who quietly and unobtrusively, unseen and unheralded, provide sustenance and help and this will explored when considering the response of Simon's mother-in-law to being cured by Jesus.

c. The Synagogue At Capernaum (Mk. 1.21-28)

After Jesus has called the Twelve (Mk. 1.16-20[2]) he makes his way to Capernaum which seems to have been his 'headquarters' during the Galilean ministry. When the Sabbath came (Mk. 1.21-22)

> he entered into the synagogue and taught, and they were astonished
> at his teaching, for he taught them as having authority and not as
> the scribes.'

Invited to teach (Jesus never seems to have been refused this privilege in any synagogue), the teaching makes a deep impression on those who are listening for he taught them *with authority and not as the scribes*. Jesus did not quote oral tradition (i.e., Talmud). The Jews were concerned that they might break God's commands, so every verse of the Torah (the writings of Moses, Genesis – Deuteronomy) was interpreted by rabbinical discussions. Later these developed into schools, one liberal (i.e., Hillel) and one conservative (i.e., Shammai). The leading rabbis of these two ancient schools were often quoted as authorities. The scribes were the professional teachers of Judaism who interpreted the oral tradition to local situations and needs. Most scribes in Jesus' day were Pharisees. Mark's purpose here is to draw out the authority of Jesus: he defeated Satan in the desert, he appointed his own disciples, he teaches with an authority that has never been

---

[1] For our struggle is not against enemies of blood and flesh, but against the rulers, against the authorities, against the cosmic powers of this present darkness, against the spiritual forces of evil in the heavenly places.

[2] As Jesus passed along the Sea of Galilee, he saw Simon and his brother Andrew casting a net into the lake, for they were fishermen. And Jesus said to them, 'Follow me and I will make you fish for people.' And immediately they left their nets and followed him. As he went a little farther, he saw James son of Zebedee and his brother John, who were in their boat mending the nets. Immediately he called them; and they left their father Zebedee in the boat with the hired men, and followed him.

seen before (cf. Mt. 10.17; 12.19) (cf. Mullins 2005:82; Byrne:43;Mulholland 2012:1.53). Jesus is the one anointed with the Spirit who is unique as the *beloved Son*, a prophet and more than a prophet.

This authority of Jesus is revealed once again when he is confronted by a man in the synagogue who is possessed by an unclean spirit which was so disturbed by his presence that it cried out and challenged him and declared him to be the *Holy One of God*. Jesus then rebuked the spirit and it left the man with some violence. The result was amazement on the part of those who saw it, and they linked it with, and included it in, his authoritative teaching. It should be noted here that the word *authority* ('exousia) was often used in Hellenistic Greek to express the idea of a combination of supernatural power with a supernatural knowledge of divine things. Both of these things have been revealed by the Spirit-filled Jesus. The confrontation between Jesus and the spirit is quite forceful and violent (Mk. 1.23-26):

> Just then there was in their synagogue a man with an unclean spirit

The scribes and Pharisees used the term *unclean spirit* to refer to evil spirits and thereby make the contrast with the cleanness and purity of God. These spirits are excluded from the presence of God because of their uncleanness and absence of moral fitness, they are not wholesome. It might be noticed he was still in worship, keeping up appearances. The New Testament makes a distinction between physical illness and demon possession, although they often had the same symptoms. Mt. 4.24 makes a clear distinction is made between those who are diseased, those who are lunatic and those who are possessed with devils. It is wrong to think that in those days men necessarily saw all disease and madness as resulting from evil spirits. In these cases the demon controls the person. The person has lost his own will, thus the man who entered the synagogue may not even have been aware that he was possessed until 'he' was forced to cry out (I say 'he' because the spirit uses the person's lips). The Jewish world view assumed the presence of spiritual beings, good (cf. Mk. 1.13;[1] Mt. 18.10;[2] Acts 12.15;[3]) and evil (cf. Mk. 1.23[4], 26, 27; 3.11,[5] 20; 5.2,[6] 8, 13; 6.7;[7]), who affected people's lives. The man then cried out (Mk. 1.24):

> 'What have you to do with us, Jesus of Nazareth? Have you come to destroy us? I know who you are, the Holy One of God.'

The presence of the one anointed with the 'Holy' Spirit was unbearable to the unholy (unwholesome) spirit who cries out in fear (the Greek used for *cried out* indicates very strong, disturbed emotion). In that cry the unclean/unwholesome spirit recognises and proclaims Jesus' holiness as *the Holy One of God*. The presence of such holiness and wholeness in Jesus makes it terrified of idea of its own destruction (and others of its kind for notice the plural *destroy us*), for Jesus is the one with absolute authority and power who has successfully defeated Satan in the desert. So the unclean spirit confronts Jesus directly, *what have you to do with us, Jesus of Nazareth?* This is literally 'what to us and to you.' In classical Greek the phrase would mean *what have we in common?* Here, however, it corresponds to the Hebrew *Why do you meddle with us?*. This idiom is illustrated in Judg.11.12;[8] 2 S 16.10;[9] 19.22; 1 K 17:18;[10] *The Holy One of*

---

[1] He was in the wilderness for forty days, tempted by Satan; and he was with the wild beasts; and the angels waited on him.

[2] 'Take care that you do not despise one of these little ones; for, I tell you, in heaven their angels continually see the face of my Father in heaven.

[3] They said to her, 'You are out of your mind!' But she insisted that it was so. They said, 'It is his angel.'

[4] Just then there was in their synagogue a man with an unclean spirit.

[5] Whenever the unclean spirits saw him, they fell down before him and shouted, 'You are the Son of God!'

[6] And when he had stepped out of the boat, immediately a man out of the tombs with an unclean spirit met him.

[7] He called the twelve and began to send them out two by two, and gave them authority over the unclean spirits.

[8] Then Jephthah sent messengers to the king of the Ammonites and said, 'What is there between you and me, that you have come to me to fight against my land?'

[9] But the king said, 'What have I to do with you, you sons of Zeruiah? If he is cursing because the Lord has said to him, "Curse David", who then shall say, "Why have you done so?" '

[10] She then said to Elijah, 'What have you against me, O man of God? You have come to me to bring my sin to remembrance, and to cause the death of my son!'

God is the title by which Simon Peter would later address Jesus in Jn. 6.69.[1] It was not a known Messianic title (Mullins 2005:85;. But we are not dealing with Messiahship here. Whatever men thought, the evil spirits were aware of Jesus' special powers and authority, and of his unique holiness. They knew that they were dealing with one who had a supernatural background, totally separated to and infilled by God, even if they were not aware of his full deity (*Holy ones* for the Watchers in Dan. 4.13, 17, 23, and of angels in Ps. 89.7;[2] Hos. 11.12;[3] Zech. 14.5[4]).

But Jesus was greater than those 'holy ones'; he was the supreme Holy One, God's Holy One. The title *Holy One of Israel* was a title regularly used of God in the Old Testament (2 K 19.22;[5] Ps. 71.22;[6] 78.41;[7] 89.18[8] (where he was also seen as 'our King') and in Isaiah 24 times, and once as the *Holy One of Jacob*, and God as incomparable is called *the Holy One* in Is. 40.25;[9] 43.15;[10] 49.7;[11] Hos. 11.9;[12] Hab. 1.12;[13] 3.3 and in Is. 57.15 *his name is Holy* (see, O Hanlon 1994:36)So such a title has close connections with God and makes the one so uniquely designated to be of divine rank, the title being almost the equivalent of 'Son of God'. 'Your Holy One', which is the

---

[1] We have come to believe and know that you are the Holy One of God.'

[2] A God feared in the council of the holy ones, great and awesome above all that are around him?

[3] Ephraim has surrounded me with lies, and the house of Israel with deceit; but Judah still walks with God, and is faithful to the Holy One.

[4] And you shall flee by the valley of the Lord's mountain, for the valley between the mountains shall reach to Azal; and you shall flee as you fled from the earthquake in the days of King Uzziah of Judah. Then the Lord my God will come, and all the holy ones with him.

[5] 'Whom have you mocked and reviled? Against whom have you raised your voice and haughtily lifted your eyes? Against the Holy One of Israel!

[6] I will also praise you with the harp for your faithfulness, O my God; I will sing praises to you with the lyre, O Holy One of Israel.

[7] They tested God again and again, and provoked the Holy One of Israel.

[8] For our shield belongs to the Lord, our king to the Holy One of Israel.

[9] To whom then will you compare me, or who is my equal? says the Holy One.

[10] I am the Lord, your Holy One, the Creator of Israel, your King.

[11] Thus says the Lord, the Redeemer of Israel and his Holy One, to one deeply despised, abhorred by the nations, the slave of rulers,'Kings shall see and stand up, princes, and they shall prostrate themselves, because of the Lord, who is faithful, the Holy One of Israel, who has chosen you.'

[12] will not execute my fierce anger; I will not again destroy Ephraim; for I am God and no mortal, the Holy One in your midst, and I will not come in wrath.

[13] Are you not from of old, O Lord my God, my Holy One? You shall not die. O Lord, you have marked them for judgement; and you, O Rock, have established them for punishment.

equivalent of *the Holy One of God*, is found in Psalm 16.10 where it refers firstly to David as the anointed of God. It could therefore even better be applied to the coming greater David, the Messiah as evidenced by Acts 2.25-28,[1] but this latter application may have arisen from this very title used of Jesus here and in Jn. 6.69. Israel is also called *His Holy One* (Is. 10.17), possibly as a purified Israel who would burn up Assyria (cf. Obad. 1.18), but it may be that we are to see there 'the Light of Israel' as God Himself. And *holy ones* (saints) is a title sometimes applied to the people of God when thought of as living in obedience, especially in the Psalms. In all cases it denotes special, unique relationship. But Jesus is not just one of the holy ones: he is _the_ Holy One.

Jesus may well be the *Holy One of God* but he does not want nor does he require any confirmation or affirmation of this fact from an unclean spirit. The command to *be quiet* is better rendered as *be silenced/be muzzled carrying*, as it does, a much more authoritative command than a simple *be quiet*. Jesus never accepts the testimony of evil spirits and wanted no testimony from evil spirits which might give people the wrong ideas about him (cf. Mulholland 2012:1.55). He did not want to be seen as associated with them in any way. The command of Jesus that the spirit *come out of him* was clear. It must relinquish its hold on the man (Mk. 1.26):

> and the unclean spirit, tearing him and crying with a loud voice,
> came out of him.

To the awe of the watchers there was a terrible cry and the man was clearly visibly distressed and convulsed, and then the spirit was gone. The man was in his right mind. This is a regular description of release from 'spirit' possession. The response of those witching is amazement, They thought that it must be some new teaching, not in a wrong sense but in the sense of being

---

[1] For David says concerning him,"I saw the Lord always before me, for he is at my right hand so that I will not be shaken; therefore my heart was glad, and my tongue rejoiced; moreover, my flesh will live in hope. For you will not abandon my soul to Hades, or let your Holy One experience corruption. You have made known to me the ways of life; you will make me full of gladness with your presence."

more powerfully true, *what is this? A new teaching*. We might bring in *with authority* here as part of the phrase and translate, *What is this? A new authoritative teaching* (a new teaching with authority)? *He commands even the unclean spirits and they obey him?*' This would agree with what seems to be the correct text. But either way the significance is the same: *he commands the unclean spirits and they obey him.*' Jesus will himself later point out what this proved: that Satan in his strength was being defeated, and that this could only be by the Spirit of God (Mt. 12.28[1]), thus demonstrating that he himself was a man of the Spirit and a 'man of God' (see, Dillon 1995:92-113). But his claim to be 'the Stronger than he' would go even further than that. It is noteworthy that although he did this on the Sabbath it was not at this stage questioned, (but perhaps that was only because it required simply a word of command cf. McBride 1996:45).

d. Simon's Mother-in-Law (Mk. 1.29-31)

> As soon as they left the synagogue, they entered the house of Simon and Andrew, with James and John. Now Simon's mother-in-law was in bed with a fever, and they told him about her at once. He came and took her by the hand and lifted her up. Then the fever left her, and she began to serve them.

It may seem that the detailed exposition of Jesus' baptism, his testing in the desert and the confrontation with the demon in the synagogue at Capernaum have little or nothing to do with the healing of Simon's mother-in-law from her 'fever'. This would be a legitimate assumption were it not for the fact that, in a real sense, it has everything to do with it (see, Marcus 1-8:199; Mullins 2005:87). This is the first recorded healing by Jesus in the gospels. It involves a woman, it involves 'touch', it involves a 'rising', and it involves 'service'; in that context, therefore, the lead up to it (the baptism, testing, synagogue) is of central importance, since the events before the healing of

---

[1] But if it is by the Spirit of God that I cast out demons, then the kingdom of God has come to you.

Simon's mother-in-law give the reader the identity of Jesus (the Beloved Son and Anointed Servant), the first defeat of Satan's power (the Temptation), the authority of Jesus (he did not teach as the scribes did) and the routing of Satan's 'forces' with the authoritative word (the demon in the synagogue). Further, the touching, the rising, the service are all motifs which are developed and their implications and meaning teased out throughout the rest of the gospel. Mark has presented Jesus as the bringer of an apocalyptic conflict between himself and Satan and thus far Jesus is winning that conflict.

Anointed at the baptism as the *beloved Son,* he 'wins' the first battle in the 'war' between the kingdom of God and the kingdom of Satan, between freedom and tyranny, between wholeness and uncleanness, between the holy and the profane (Mulholland 2012:1.55). Satan tries to tempt Jesus into using his power as the Anointed Son and Servant in a materialistic, earthly, crass way, Jesus rejects him out of hand (the importance of the wild beasts/angels referred to in the previous pages in relation to the symbolism of the healing in Simon's house will be drawn out in a moment). Mark has shown Jesus to have the authoritative word of command to call his own disciples and to silence and banish the unholy, unclean minions of Satan's kingdom and to teach in a new and exciting way. Given the drama that has gone before it, the healing of Simon's mother-in-law does not seem to be on the same plane of significance. Nothing, however, could be further from the truth for it is a moment pregnant with multi-layered meanings.

The healing of Simon's mother-in-law is set within the context of Jesus' first day of 'public' ministry and it has been a busy and powerful one (Mk. 1.21-28[1]). But even in the quiet of the day (the Sabbath) Jesus is still

---

[1] They went to Capernaum; and when the Sabbath came, he entered the synagogue and taught. They were astounded at his teaching, for he taught them as one having authority, and not as the scribes. Just then there was in their synagogue a man with an unclean spirit, and he cried out, 'What have you to do with us, Jesus of Nazareth? Have you come to destroy us? I know who you are, the Holy One of God.' But Jesus rebuked him, saying, 'Be silent, and come out of him!' And the unclean spirit, throwing him into convulsions and crying with a loud voice, came out of him. They were all amazed, and they kept on asking one another, 'What is this? A new teaching—with authority! He commands even the unclean spirits, and they obey him.' At once his fame began to spread throughout the surrounding region of Galilee.

kept busy for he is told that Simon's mother-in-law has a *fever*; he goes into where she is, takes her by the hand, the fever *immediately* leaves her, she get us and 'ministers/serves' him (Mk. 1.29-31). At the surface level it seems a simple enough story with a warm, homely compassionate tone and feel to it. A deeper examination reveals something quite different. This is the first time in Mark's gospel that Jesus heals someone and it is a woman; that the woman gets up and 'waits on/serves/ministers' to Jesus clearly shows that the first one to 'minister' to Jesus, to meet his needs, is a woman (on the significance of this see, Maloney 2002:55). Key elements in this story are that Jesus *took her by the hand,* that she *got up,* that it was a *fever* she had and that *she served/waited/minimised* to him (cf. Mullins 2002:87). The simple story may be preserved in the early Christian tradition because of an association with Peter (Gnilka 1978-79, 1.84-85) but Peter only appears in this story in relation to the woman, or perhaps the other way around is better. The woman is anonymous and contextualised by her relationship with Peter (*mother-in-law,* Mk. 1.29;cf. Miller 2002:). The same will be true of other women in the gospel:

- the woman with the haemorrhage is unnamed (Mk. 5.25-34)
- the name of Jairus is given but not his daughter (Mk. 5.21-43)
- neither the daughter of the Syro-Phoenician woman nor she herself is named (Mk. 7.24-30)

While this may reflect the cultural and social mores whereby the names of males were recorded more frequently than that of women, it does not indicate that Mark deliberately excluded the name of Simon's mother-in-law, it may simply be that he did not know it. Further, women were frequently contextualised by their relations with males, e.g., Mary and Martha the *sisters* of Lazarus (Jn. 11.1-44), Mary the *wife* of Clopas (Jn. 19.25), Mary the *mother of Jesus* (it is also interesting to note that in Mk. 6.3, Mark gives the names of Jesus' brothers but not his sisters). The woman is characterised by her relationship to Simon (*mother-in-law*) and not by that of relation to her husband which may suggest or indicate she was a widow (Miller 2201:23). That she is in Simon's house would seem to suggest that she was living with Simon and her daughter (who is never mentioned but cf. 1 Cor. 9.5) as part of the wider family unit whereby Simon is looking after one who is of a vulnerable group viz. widows (Ex. 22.22;[1] Deut. 24.17;[2] Is. 10.2[3]). This would seem to indicate that Simon's family unit was 'functional' as opposed to the dysfunction of Jesus' own family (Mk. 3.31-35[4]). Simon appears frequently throughout this beginning stage of Jesus' ministry centred around Capernaum (Mk. 1.16.29,[5] 30) which is further emphasised by the fact that Jesus has not chosen the Twelve nor given Simon his 'nickname' of 'Peter' (the rock) and it is Simon who begins the search for Jesus the next morning (Mk. 1.35-39[6]). Other than Simon's mother-in-law no other women are mentioned but his does not mean to say that other women were not present. As noted above, Simon's wife is not mentioned but she may have been in the house perhaps as part of the group at Mk. 1.30 who tell Jesus of the woman's fever (see Byrne 2008:45;Mullins 2002:86;Miller 2002:33). Mark frequently refers to 'the crowd' who follow Jesus which also included women and as we shall see, the woman with the haemorrhage comes out of

---

[1] You shall not abuse any widow or orphan.

[2] You shall not deprive a resident alien or an orphan of justice; you shall not take a widow's garment in pledge.

[3] To turn aside the needy from justice and to rob the poor of my people of their right, that widows may be your spoil, and that you may make the orphans your prey!

[4] Then his mother and his brothers came; and standing outside, they sent to him and called him. A crowd was sitting around him; and they said to him, 'Your mother and your brothers and sisters are outside, asking for you.' And he replied, 'Who are my mother and my brothers?' And looking at those who sat around him, he said, 'Here are my mother and my brothers! Whoever does the will of God is my brother and sister and mother.'

[5] As Jesus passed along the Sea of Galilee, he saw Simon and his brother Andrew casting a net into the lake, for they were fishermen;

[6] In the morning, while it was still very dark, he got up and went out to a deserted place, and there he prayed. And Simon and his companions hunted for him. When they found him, they said to him, 'Everyone is searching for you.' He answered, 'Let us go on to the neighbouring towns, so that I may proclaim the message there also; for that is what I came out to do.' And he went throughout Galilee, proclaiming the message in their synagogues and casting out demons.

the crowd to touch Jesus' hem at Mk. 5.24-34 and Jesus includes women when he speaks of those are his 'sisters and mother' at Mk. 3.25. However, the fact that the Simon, Andrew, James and John are named allows them to act as witnesses to the healing of the woman by Jesus, while the unnamed woman acts as a symbol of all those who seek healing from Jesus and as we shall see, the healings of Jesus are on the one hand personal and for the individual, but they are also symbolic of the healing and restoration he has come to bring to all.

Jesus is told of the illness having *entered the house* (Mk. 1.29) and this is similar to his entering *the synagogue* (Mk. 1.21) because in both cases Jesus is made aware of the presence of something unwholesome and destructive: in other words, the presence of evil in any form cannot abide to be hidden in the presence of Jesus. It is important to note here that the woman is not described as simply *being sick* but that she was *lying in bed with a fever* (Mk. 1.30a). The Greek tense of the verb is the imperfect which indicates continual action, in other words, she had been ill with a *fever* for some time. Fever and its associations, burning (in the form of high temperature), and incapacity, was not considered a symptom of an illness but a serious, life threatening illness in itself. (the rabbis on occasion linked fever with demons cf. Davies and Allison 1991:35). But there may be a deeper meaning lying behind Mark's clear assertion that this was *fever* (and its fiery associations) and not just 'illness'. In the writings of the Prophets (Is. 66.24; Zech. 13.9[1]) fire is associated with the punishments of the eschaton and Jesus himself at Mk. 9.48-49 makes a connection between fire, judgement and cleansing (Mulholland 2012:1.58). The woman has been ill for some time, which clearly shows that is is not getting better; she is in the grip of something debilitating, paralysing, and life-threatening and it is easy to make a connection between this and the debilitating, paralysing, life-

---

[1] And they shall go out and look at the dead bodies of the people who have rebelled against me; for their worm shall not die, their fire shall not be quenched, and they shall be an abhorrence to all flesh; And I will put this third into the fire, refine them as one refines silver, and test them as gold is tested. They will call on my name, and I will answer them. I will say, 'They are my people'; and they will say, 'The Lord is our God.

threatening grip that Satan has over people in demon possession, sickness, or illness before Jesus arrives on the scene. That Jesus himself is aware of this is shown not only in how he wages war on these expressions of Satan's power in the Markan world view but also by the fact that in the Markan 'Little Apocalypse) (Mk. 13) he makes it clear that (Mk. 13.19-20):

> in those days there will be suffering, such as has not been from the beginning of the creation that God created until now, no, and never will be. And if the Lord had not cut short those days, no one would be saved

The healing of Simon's mother-in-law, therefore, is not simply a healing story by Mark, it is another battle in the war Jesus has engaged in with Satan and Satan's power. Simon's mother-in-law's illness is a death dealing *fever*, the healing by Jesus who *enters* the place where the power of evil is (the bedroom where she is in the fever), who shows no fear in the presence of such evil (he *takes her by the hand*), and who *raises* her up to wholeness, is nothing other than Jesus drawing the woman back from the grasp of death: where the grasp of the fever would bring her to death, the grasp of Jesus brings her back to life (Mulholland 2012:1.56).

While not wishing to engage in a detailed examination of the Greek of Mark and its grammar and syntax, this idea of Jesus 'grasping' the woman from death (symbolised by the fever) can be further demonstrated by looking at the participles and verb Mark uses. Mark uses the participle 'proselthōn', which means 'to draw near', 'approach' (Mk. 1.31). Now it is certainly true that this could simply mean that Jesus drew near the bed on which she lay but Mark seems to suggest that he literally drew her *towards him* having 'kratēsas' ('strongly taken', 'grasped', 'taken hold of') *her by the hand* and 'ēgeiren', he *raised her up* (Mullins 2005:86;Byrne 2008:46;O Hanlon 1994:46). The verb *he raised her up* is set between the two participles, *he approached, drew towards* and *he took hold of strongly*. This verb as Mark uses it here does not simply mean he raised her up from the bed: the verb will appear in other forms in Mark's narratives about Jesus' healing (Mk. 2.9,11, *stand up!*) the cure of the paralytic; Mk. 3.3, *and calling/raising him into the midst of them*, the man with the withered hand; Mk. 5.41, *talitha cum*, translated, *little girl, I tell you, get up*, Jairus' daughter). But more importantly, it is used in the resurrection prophecy at Mk. 14.28 and more especially it is used by the 'young man' at the empty tomb, *he is not here but 'ēgerthē'*, i.e., *he has been raised*. The healing of Simon's mother-in-law, therefore, is a prefigurement of the resurrection (as it is in the narrative of Jairus' daughter).

That Mark presents this healing as a 'battle' in the war between the Anointed Son and Servant, the Holy One of God who speaks the word of God with authority and the unholy ruler of a world of sin, disease and death can also be seen in the use of the verb 'kratēsas' as *taking hold of strongly*, or *with force* and in this context it can also mean 'arrest', 'seize'. John the Baptist is *arrested* (Mk. 6.17) or *taken hold of* and it is used in the same way of Jesus in Mark's Passion Narrative (Mk. 14.1, 44, 46, 49[1]). As Mark uses the verb, therefore, it suggests a forceful, strong taking and not just the *touching* of the woman's hand as in Matthew's account of this story (Mt. 8.14-15):

> when Jesus entered Peter's house, he saw his mother-in-law lying in bed with a fever; he touched her hand, and the fever left her, and she got up and began to serve him

Luke does not mention the touching but concentrates on the word of Jesus and clearly sees this as an exorcism since Jesus (Lk. 4.49):

> then he stood over her and rebuked the fever, and it left her.

[1] It was two days before the Passover and the festival of Unleavened Bread. The chief priests and the scribes were looking for a way to arrest Jesus by stealth and kill him; Now the betrayer had given them a sign, saying, 'The one I will kiss is the man; arrest him and lead him away under guard.'; Then they laid hands on him and arrested him; Day after day I was with you in the temple teaching, and you did not arrest me. But let the scriptures be fulfilled.'

Immediately she got up and began to serve them

and the word 'rebuke' is found frequently in Mark in Jesus' confrontations with demons. In Mark's story the power of Jesus' *taking her strongly, taking her forcefully* by the hand is so authoritative that the fever *departed from her* (cf. Mullins 2005:86;Byrne 2008:47) The verb, 'departed', 'send away' (aphiémi) is stronger than simply *left her* since in Mark's other stories about Jesus' conflicts with demons, they *depart* after he has commanded them to do so (Mk. 1.26; 5.13; 9.26[1]). In this sense the fever the woman suffers from is presented by Mark almost anthropomorphically as a personal force and thus its 'departure' is the same as that of the demon departing from the man in the synagogue. One of the other meanings of the Greek verb 'aphiémi' is 'to release', 'to permit to go away', and so Jesus not only heals or cures the illness he also 'releases' the woman from the destructive force that has her in its power (see, Kee 1967: 232-46).

Mark's story of the healing of Simon's mother-in-law, therefore, through the use of the participles and verbal forms, *he took took hold of her hand strongly/forcefully* and *the fever departed* suggests conflict and the struggle against the destructive forces of Satan in the form of disease which lays human beings so low as to be in a life threatening situation (just as the demon in the synagogue tormented the possessed man and as Legion torments the Gerasene Demoniac, cf. Mk. 5.1-20). Simon's mother-in-law is presented as suffering from a fever that 'torments' her and she is 'released' from that and restored to health *immediately*. Mark does not present it as an exorcism as such, since exorcisms shatter the power of evil (and in Mark these are shown first, then healings, but together they show the power of Jesus to break the chains that bind humanity and restore them to full 'health'

---

[1] And the unclean spirit, throwing him into convulsions and crying with a loud voice, came out of him; So he gave them permission. And the unclean spirits came out and entered the swine; and the herd, numbering about two thousand, rushed down the steep bank into the lake, and were drowned in the lake; After crying out and convulsing him terribly, it came out, and the boy was like a corpse, so that most of them said, 'He is dead.'

cf., e.g., Mk. 5.1-20;[1]) but he does present it almost as if Jesus has physically reached into the woman and *strongly taken hold* of the fever and pulled it from her thus *raising* her up to fully restored health.

The fact that *she got up* and *began to serve them* shows that she was fully restored (Mulholland 2012:57). She did not need a period of rest or recuperation, not it appears, and she did not need food to aid her to full health. Her recovery is absolute and total. The point is that the outcome of this encounter with Jesus is immediate, as was the response of the disciples who had *immediately* left everything to follow him (Mullins 2205:87; Mulholland 2012:1.58;Martin 2005.:25). Jesus had demonstrated his power and authority over the kingdom of Satan in preternatural creatures with a word, now he demonstrates his power over sickness with a touch.

e. The Woman As A Disciple

The response of the woman to Jesus' healing is an act of service. In this sense the woman is not unlike others who respond with some type of activity when they have been cured by Jesus: the paralysed man *carries his*

---

[1] They came to the other side of the lake, to the country of the Gerasenes. And when he had stepped out of the boat, immediately a man out of the tombs with an unclean spirit met him. He lived among the tombs; and no one could restrain him any more, even with a chain; for he had often been restrained with shackles and chains, but the chains he wrenched apart, and the shackles he broke in pieces; and no one had the strength to subdue him. Night and day among the tombs and on the mountains he was always howling and bruising himself with stones. When he saw Jesus from a distance, he ran and bowed down before him; and he shouted at the top of his voice, 'What have you to do with me, Jesus, Son of the Most High God? I adjure you by God, do not torment me.' For he had said to him, 'Come out of the man, you unclean spirit!' Then Jesus asked him, 'What is your name?' He replied, 'My name is Legion; for we are many.' He begged him earnestly not to send them out of the country. Now there on the hillside a great herd of swine was feeding; and the unclean spirits begged him, 'Send us into the swine; let us enter them.' So he gave them permission. And the unclean spirits came out and entered the swine; and the herd, numbering about two thousand, rushed down the steep bank into the lake, and were drowned in the lake. The swineherds ran off and told it in the city and in the country. Then people came to see what it was that had happened. They came to Jesus and saw the demoniac sitting there, clothed and in his right mind, the very man who had had the legion; and they were afraid. Those who had seen what had happened to the demoniac and to the swine reported it. Then they began to beg Jesus to leave their neighbourhood. As he was getting into the boat, the man who had been possessed by demons begged him that he might be with him. But Jesus refused, and said to him, 'Go home to your friends, and tell them how much the Lord has done for you, and what mercy he has shown you.' And he went away and began to proclaim in the Decapolis how much Jesus had done for him; and everyone was amazed.

bed (Mk. 2.12); the daughter of Jairus *walks* (Mk. 5.49); however, it might also be noted that these responses are part of the command of Jesus: the paralysed man is told to *get up, take up your bed and walk* (Mk. 2.9); Jairus' daughter gets up in response to Jesus' command that she *get up* (Mk. 5.49). Here, however, the woman *serves* Jesus of her own volition as a response to what Jesus has done for her. While it is true that there are some similarities between these stories of healing, for example, Jesus commends the faith of the friends of the paralysed man (Mk. 2.5[1]), responds to Jairus' faith in him, responds immediately to the leper (Mk. 1.41[2]) and eventually meets the request of the Syro-Phoenician woman (Mk. 7.29[3]) and the father of the epileptic boy both of who demonstrate faith in Jesus.

However, the healing of Simon's mother-in-law differs in one key respect: the story is not about faith and nowhere is faith mentioned in the story and we are not given any of the traditional responses to such 'miracles' or Jesus, i.e., there is no wonder, amazement, or questioning who Jesus Is. Those present *in the house* tell Jesus about her but she herself has not heard or seen Jesus so there is not, strictly speaking, even a 'coming to faith' by the woman. However, there is a definite response and it is one which is paradigmatic for issues of discipleship and service which follow in the gospel. At the beginning of Mark's story Simon's mother-in-law is utterly powerless since she had the fever for a long time. However, after her healing she *immediately* gets up as *serves* those present. This indicates that her healing was total and complete and that she needed not time to rest or recover any further. The act of the woman serving Jesus, though not specified, would seem to indicate the preparation and serving of a meal at table (cf. Krause 2001:1.29-31). The verb Mark uses, 'diakoneó' means 'to serve', 'wait at table' (Beyer, TDNT2: 85), though it can also mean 'to give care to' and was regarded as 'woman's work' or the work of a slave and was never carried out by 'free' men. However, it is worth noting that in the Old

---

[1] When Jesus saw their faith, he said to the paralytic, 'Son, your sins are forgiven.'
[2] Moved with pity, Jesus stretched out his hand and touched him, and said to him, 'I do choose. Be made clean!'
[3] Then he said to her, 'For saying that, you may go, the demon has left your daughter.'

Testament this type of service is viewed very positively as in, for example, Abraham and Sarah serving the visitors at Gen. 18.1-8[1] and Elijah and Elisha (1 K 17.6-18; 2 K 4.8[2] interestingly these women who serve the prophets are 'rewarded' by acts of healing).

In the New Testament the verb is also used with the meaning 'to serve at table'. the cognate noun 'diakonos' is used of the servants in the parable of the wedding feast (Mt. 22.13[3]) and in the account of the wedding at Cana (Jn. 2.5, 9[4]). In John's gospel, Martha is depicted as *serving at the table*, while her brother Lazarus joins Jesus at the dinner (Jn. 12.2[5]). Jesus uses the verb to describe himself as *one who serves* and his 'service' is the giving of his life (Mk. 10.45). The 'giving' of Jesus' own life gives life to others so images of *giving, receiving, serving* (Davies and Allison 1991:2.32) indicate the mutuality of Mark's understanding of redemption. As the woman has been 'redeemed' from Satan (in the form of the life-threatening fever) and 'raised up' to life by Jesus, so now she takes the role of 'servant' and her role of service is a symbol of how the disciples should act (Mullins 2005:87;Miller 2002:33-35). However, whether this 'service' is to be seen as an act of discipleship qua discipleship can be discussed and debated though to suggest that this is the case may be reading too much into the text given

---

[1] The Lord appeared to Abraham by the oaks of Mamre, as he sat at the entrance of his tent in the heat of the day. He looked up and saw three men standing near him. When he saw them, he ran from the tent entrance to meet them, and bowed down to the ground. He said, 'My lord, if I find favour with you, do not pass by your servant. Let a little water be brought, and wash your feet, and rest yourselves under the tree. Let me bring a little bread, that you may refresh yourselves, and after that you may pass on—since you have come to your servant.' So they said, 'Do as you have said.' And Abraham hastened into the tent to Sarah, and said, 'Make ready quickly three measures of choice flour, knead it, and make cakes.' Abraham ran to the herd, and took a calf, tender and good, and gave it to the servant, who hastened to prepare it. Then he took curds and milk and the calf that he had prepared, and set it before them; and he stood by them under the tree while they ate.

[2] At the end of the seven years, when the woman returned from the land of the Philistines, she set out to appeal to the king for her house and her land.

[3] Then the king said to the attendants, "Bind him hand and foot, and throw him into the outer darkness, where there will be weeping and gnashing of teeth."

[4] His mother said to the servants, 'Do whatever he tells you.' ; When the steward tasted the water that had become wine, and did not know where it came from (though the servants who had drawn the water knew), the steward called the bridegroom.

[5] There they gave a dinner for him. Martha served, and Lazarus was one of those at the table with him.

that Simon's mother-in-law does not accompany Jesus on any of his travels around Galilee (though we would not be being unreasonable that she continued to *serve* Jesus when he returned to Capernaum after those journeys but see below).

Mark makes reference to 'service' of Jesus at other points in the gospel: he has already mentioned the angels ministering to Jesus after the desert temptation (Mk. 1.13[1]) and at the end of the gospel the women minister to Jesus (Mk. 15.41[2]). All this suggests that one of the primary roles of the women in Mark is to be the sustainers of Jesus from the beginning to the end of his mission. The mission of Jesus in Mark, therefore, is the mid section of a triptych with acts of service by women on either side of it (see, Wainwright 2006:111 cf.106-110,112)). Thus in this sense, it is possible to see the verb that Mark uses for 'service', 'diakoneó' ('I serve at table') as a term of discipleship. More interestingly, this verb is used only of women in the gospel, e.g., it is used of the women who were with Jesus to Jerusalem and were present at the crucifixion (Mk. 15.40-41).

Mark says that *she began to serve them* (Mk. 1.31) whereas Matthew says that she *began to serve him* (Mt. 8.15) (in Matthew Jesus is always the subject-object of the verb 'diakoneó'). Mark began the short narrative of the healing of Simon's mother-in-law by saying that *they told him about her* (Mk. 1.30) and closes the narrative with *she began to serve them* which suggests that it was not Jesus alone who was served (as in Matthew) and while it may mean Jesus and the newly called disciples, it is more likely that the act of service includes the group who told Jesus of her condition. Thus, the woman's act of service may be seen as a response to the 'good news': as the woman has been personally healed, so now she serves the 'community' gathered around Jesus (Gnilka 1978:183). In this context the woman's service after her healing and restoration by Jesus, who comes to serve and not to be served (Mk. 10.45) and who restores to life by word, touch and

---

[1]   He was in the wilderness for forty days, tempted by Satan; and he was with the wild beasts; and the angels waited on him.

[2]   These used to follow him and provided for him when he was in Galilee; and there were many other women who had come up with him to Jerusalem.

presence, is paradigmatic of the restoration of the whole 'community' by Jesus in his 'service' as the announcer of the good news.

CHAPTER FOUR

THE WOMEN IN MARK

The Woman with the Haemorrhage and Jairus' Daughter

(Mk. 5.21-43)

a. The Narrative Context

In the narrative of the woman healed of her bleeding and the raising of Jairus' daughter from the dead, Mark has composed a complex structured narrative where the two central characters are juxtaposed in a number of ways. While in essence the two stories concern themselves with faith, there are other features to these stories which give insight into how the women are presented by Mark. The context of the story is quite important, so we will consider this first and then move into exploring the narrative and the role of the women within them.

The two narratives that have preceded Mk.5.21-43 are the traditionally named, 'Calming of the Storm' (Mk. 4.35-41[1]) and the 'Gerasene Demoniac' (Mk. 5.1-20[2]). In the first narrative Jesus demonstrates his power over

---

[1]   On that day, when evening had come, he said to them, 'Let us go across to the other side.' And leaving the crowd behind, they took him with them in the boat, just as he was. Other boats were with him. A great gale arose, and the waves beat into the boat, so that the boat was already being swamped. But he was in the stern, asleep on the cushion; and they woke him up and said to him, 'Teacher, do you not care that we are perishing?' He woke up and rebuked the wind, and said to the sea, 'Peace! Be still!' Then the wind ceased, and there was a dead calm. He said to them, 'Why are you afraid? Have you still no faith?' And they were filled with great awe and said to one another, 'Who then is this, that even the wind and the sea obey him?'

[2]   They came to the other side of the lake, to the country of the Gerasenes. And when he had stepped out of the boat, immediately a man out of the tombs with an unclean spirit met him. He lived among the tombs; and no one could restrain him any more, even with a chain; for he had often been restrained with shackles and chains, but the chains he wrenched apart, and the shackles he broke in pieces; and no one had the strength to subdue him. Night and day among the tombs and on the mountains he was always howling and bruising himself with stones. When he saw Jesus from a distance, he ran and bowed down before him; and he shouted at the top of his voice, 'What have you to do with me, Jesus, Son of the Most High God? I adjure you by God, do not torment me.' For he had said to him, 'Come out of the man, you unclean spirit!' Then Jesus asked him, 'What is your name?' He replied, 'My name is Legion; for we are many.' He begged him earnestly not to send them out of the country. Now there on the hillside a great herd of swine was feeding; and the unclean spirits begged him, 'Send us into the swine; let us enter them.' So he gave them permission. And the unclean spirits came out and entered the swine; and the herd, numbering about two thousand, rushed down the steep bank into the lake, and were drowned in the lake. The swineherds ran off

nature and in the second he demonstrates his power over evil characterised not by an individual evil spirit but by a 'Legion' of them. Further, both these narratives have as an underlying theme the question of Jesus' identity. In the 'Calming of the Storm', the disciples are *in the boat* with Jesus (Mk. 4.35-40) and the other boats are on the Sea of Galilee *with him* (Mullins 2005:159). Here to be *in the boat* may carry the same weight as being *inside the house* with Jesus, i.e., it may stand as a metaphor for discipleship. Similarly the other boats 'with him' may also be read as a metaphor for discipleship. In other words, the storm narrative begins with a positive description of discipleship but it ends with a description of the disciples failure (Mk. 4.40-41[1]cf. Kelber 1979:31). In the demoniac narrative, the central issue again is the identity of Jesus and the response to the people to the exorcism (Mulholland 2012:1.51). It is possible to read both the storm and demoniac narratives as 'exorcisms' in so far the ancients often thought that storms and sea swells were the 'demons' of the air or sea at work (cf. Byrne 2005:94;Marcus 2000:38;O Hanlon 1996:64)) Jesus 'rebuked' the wind and sea, i.e., he used the same language that he used of the demoniac in the synagogue (Mk. 1.25[2]), so reading the storm narrative as an exorcism is a legitimate reading, though, of course, traditionally not the primary reading.

However, given the response that Jesus makes to the fear of the disciples and his challenge to them about faith (Mk. 4.40), and the question of the disciples, *who is this that even wind and sea obey him* (Mk. 4.41) the narrative also highlights the issue of faith in Jesus as well as the continuing

---

and told it in the city and in the country. Then people came to see what it was that had happened. They came to Jesus and saw the demoniac sitting there, clothed and in his right mind, the very man who had had the legion; and they were afraid. Those who had seen what had happened to the demoniac and to the swine reported it. Then they began to beg Jesus to leave their neighbourhood. As he was getting into the boat, the man who had been possessed by demons begged him that he might be with him. But Jesus refused, and said to him, 'Go home to your friends, and tell them how much the Lord has done for you, and what mercy he has shown you.' And he went away and began to proclaim in the Decapolis how much Jesus had done for him; and everyone was amazed.

[1]   He said to them, 'Why are you afraid? Have you still no faith?' And they were filled with great awe and said to one another, 'Who then is this, that even the wind and the sea obey him?'

[2]   But Jesus rebuked him, saying, 'Be silent, and come out of him!'

questions regarding who he really is (cf. Byrne:2008:94-95;OHanlon 1996:67). In the demoniac narrative Legion announces the identity of Jesus, *Son of the Most High,* as did the demoniac in the synagogue (Mk. 1.24), which, of course, Jesus ignores as he wants no affirmation or proclamation of his identity from the likes of an evil spirit. While essentially concerned with the exorcism of a particularly destructive demonic force, the narrative has at its heart the restoration to life of a person alienated at every level: from himself, from his community, from society and from God, as can be seen in the description that Mark gives of the demoniac (Mk.5.3-5[1]). In this sense, therefore, the calming of the storm and the healing of the Gerasene demoniac demonstrate the power of Jesus at every level of being, i.e., the natural and the supernatural. Both these 'miracles' take place through the power of Jesus' word; in the story of the woman with the haemorrhage, it is the power of Jesus' presence that affects the cure and in Jairus' daughter, it is again his touch and word together. Having demonstrated his power over nature and the forces of evil, Jesus will now demonstrate his power over life and death through his interaction with two women: one old (or at least more mature) and the other a child on the verge of adulthood (Mulholland 2012:1.133).

Before coming to the narratives in themselves one or two contextual questions might be asked here, the first being how does Mark understand the two women here? It is difficult to make any accurate assessment of Jairus' daughter in the sense that she does not appear until the end of the narrative, does not speak and is not named. She is presented at the beginning of the narrative as 'at the point' of death (Mk.5.23) and then midway through the narrative Jairus is told, *your daughter is dead* (Mk. 5.35), however, by examining the embedded narrative of the woman with the haemorrhage, the narrative of Jairus' daughter and her role in it becomes much more clearly focused. How then, does Mark present the woman? In

---

[1]   He lived among the tombs; and no one could restrain him any more, even with a chain; for he had often been restrained with shackles and chains, but the chains he wrenched apart, and the shackles he broke in pieces; and no one had the strength to subdue him. Night and day among the tombs and on the mountains he was always howling and bruising himself with stones.

the main Mark presents the woman in a very positive light: she fights her way through the crowds to touch the 'hem' of Jesus' garment, she has enough faith to believe that even if she does only this some good will be come from it, she openly confesses to Jesus that it was she who touched him, and she is commended for her faith. There is some suggestion that the cure of the woman is not complete until she places herself at Jesus' feet and admits that it was her (Selvidge 1989:623) but this is tenuous given that the moment she touches Jesus' hem her *bleeding dried up immediately* (Mk. 5.29). Further, Jesus does not condemn her for touching him even though through her action he would have been considered ritually unclean, but rather commends her for her faith (Mk. 5.34) (see, Swartley, 1989:19). In view of the fact that most scholars regard this as menstrual bleeding, it is possible to view the narrative within the context of the Jewish purity laws and so suggest that Jesus is setting such purity laws aside, or that the narrative reflects the abandonment of those laws by Mark's community (Tolbert 1992:262-263). The purity laws of Lev. 15.19-30 were quite specific and stringent:

> When a woman has a discharge of blood that is her regular discharge from her body, she shall be in her impurity for seven days, and whoever touches her shall be unclean until the evening. Everything upon which she lies during her impurity shall be unclean; everything also upon which she sits shall be unclean. Whoever touches her bed shall wash his clothes, and bathe in water, and be unclean until the evening. Whoever touches anything upon which she sits shall wash his clothes, and bathe in water, and be unclean until the evening; whether it is the bed or anything upon which she sits, when he touches it he shall be unclean until the evening. If any man lies with her, and her impurity falls on him, he shall be unclean for seven days; and every bed on which he lies shall be unclean. If a woman has a discharge of blood for many days, not at the time of her impurity, or if she has a discharge beyond the time of her impurity, for all the days of the discharge she shall continue in uncleanness; as in the days of her impurity, she shall be unclean.

> Every bed on which she lies during all the days of her discharge shall be treated as the bed of her impurity; and everything on which she sits shall be unclean, as in the uncleanness of her impurity. Whoever touches these things shall be unclean, and shall wash his clothes, and bathe in water, and be unclean until the evening. If she is cleansed of her discharge, she shall count seven days, and after that she shall be clean. On the eighth day she shall take two turtle-doves or two pigeons and bring them to the priest at the entrance of the tent of meeting. The priest shall offer one for a sin-offering and the other for a burnt-offering; and the priest shall make atonement on her behalf before the Lord for her unclean discharge.

As already noted, Jesus does not condemn the woman for touching him. However, this also presumes that during Jesus' ministry women on their menstrual cycle were 'quarantined' (for want of a better word) but the evidence for this is thin. This practice is mentioned in Jewish writings only as late as the sixth century (Cohen 1991:278-8). However, Josephus says that menstruating women were not allowed to enter the Temple or celebrate Passover (*Jewish Wars,* 5.227; 6.426-27) but how rigorously this was enforced is difficult to say. It may have been that there were different understandings of the Levitical code and so for example the wives/women of Pharisees may have been more rigorous in this practice than say, for example, the wives/women of the Sadducees (Miller 2002:70). It may be suggested that the narrative is nothing to do with the purity laws since they were applicable only in Jerusalem and the Temple but elements of the narrative, e.g., the fact that it was bleeding, her hesitancy, her fear, all indicate that the woman is ritually unclean and a vocabulary comparison between Mark's narrative and Lev.15 bears this out.

The narrative also focuses on the touch of Jesus: 'If only I can *touch* the hem of his garment', she *touched* him', 'who *touched* me' (Mk. 5.28, 30, 31) and the Leviticus text makes it clear that anyone who touched a woman regarded as ritually unclean was unclean themselves. Given that Jesus says nothing about her touching him but rather praises it (even though she would consciously know that she was making Jesus unclean and seemed more than willing to do it) and it can be suggested that this sets the precedent for any abandonment of the purity laws by Mark's community (if such a theme is indeed underlying the narrative).

b. The Woman's Encounter With Jesus (Mk. 5.21-34)

As the discussion above on the context of the narrative shows, Jesus has demonstrated his power over nature and evil in the 'Calming of the Storm' (Mk. 4.35-41), and 'The Gerasene Demoniac' (Mk. 5.1-20) encounters. Now he will demonstrate the power of his touch and his power over death itself through the raising of Jairus' daughter. It cannot be doubted that Jairus' daughter was dead because Jairus is told this by those who were present (see below). Then girls is twelve years old and the woman with the blessing has had the condition for twelve years so this must be seen as significant: since twelve is the number of the tribes of Israel both the woman and the girl stands as metaphors for the plight of Israel, desperately in need (Mulholland 2012:1.135).

The fact that Jesus says she is only 'sleeping' is of no significance since he says the same about Lazarus (Jn. 11.11-14[1]) before making it clear that what he meant by 'sleeping' was that Lazarus was dead. By the time Jesus left Jairus' daughter she was no longer dead but very much alive. However, the narrative of Jairus' daughter is intercalated with the story of the woman with the bleeding. In a real sense, she too was 'dying' for she had had her condition for twelve years, as the twelve year of daughter of Jairus was 'at the point of death'. The girl had survived twelve years and now was at the *point of death*, the woman had her blood loss for *twelve years* and was 'dying' in the sense that she was cut off from the Temple and society by her uncleanness. So, both were representative of the people: dying in sin and

---

[1] After saying this, he told them, 'Our friend Lazarus has fallen asleep, but I am going there to awaken him.' The disciples said to him, 'Lord, if he has fallen asleep, he will be all right.' Jesus, however, had been speaking about his death, but they thought that he was referring merely to sleep. Then Jesus told them plainly, 'Lazarus is dead.

unclean before God.

c. Jairus Approaches Jesus (Mk. 5.21-14)

It is after Jesus has *crossed* to the other side of the lake that he is approached by Jairus who Mark says was a *one of the leaders of the synagogue* (Mk. 5.22). That Mark names Jairus is of significance since names rarely appear in Mark and may be indicative of his societal status as the 'leader' of the synagogue. The name 'Jairus' (it is omitted in a few manuscripts but perhaps accidentally) has a great deal of support. It may be derived from 'Jair' which appears in the Old Testament (Num. 32.41; Judg. 10.3) and Est. 2.5 (LXX), 'Jair' is translated as 'Jairus'. The name itself may have some symbolic significance since it means 'he enlightens', or 'he awakens'. However, even given the fact that by the end of the narrative Jairus' faith has been 'enlightened' or 'awakened' after his anguish at hearing the news of his daughter's death (Mk. 5.35) when Jesus tells him, *Do not be afraid, only have faith*, the meaning of his name should not be overstressed (Guelich 1989:295).

In the strict sense of the term, 'leaders' of the synagogue is unusual since normally they were run by one leader (Lk. 8.49;[1] 13.14;[2] Acts 13.15;[3] 18.8,[4] 17; cf. Mt. 9.18, 23; Lk. 8.41; 18.18.). This 'leader' would be responsible for the administration, organisation of synagogue liturgy. There were others involved, a council of elders also called 'leaders' who would have been men of some social and religious importance in the local community. Jairus may well have been one of these (Mulholland 2012:1.136). Whatever the case may be, this socially and religious

---

[1] While he was still speaking, someone came from the leader's house to say, 'Your daughter is dead; do not trouble the teacher any longer.'

[2] But the leader of the synagogue, indignant because Jesus had cured on the Sabbath, kept saying to the crowd, 'There are six days on which work ought to be done; come on those days and be cured, and not on the Sabbath day.

[3] After the reading of the law and the prophets, the officials of the synagogue sent them a message, saying, 'Brothers, if you have any word of exhortation for the people, give it.'

[4] Crispus, the official of the synagogue, became a believer in the Lord, together with all his household; and many of the Corinthians who heard Paul became believers and were baptised.

important man comes to Jesus, an itinerant rabbi, and begs him to come to his 'little' daughter who is 'at the point of death'. One may ask the question as to why Jairus was not at his daughter's beside if she was 'at the point of death'. It may be precisely because she was 'at the point of death' and having heard about Jesus decided that he would approach him. Given that Jairus is a person of some importance, his actions in coming to Jesus and *falling at his feet* (Mk. 5.22) begging him *repeatedly* (Mk. 5.23) to come to his *little daughter* are those of a desperate man (like the father of the epileptic boy in Mk. 9.14-29[1] or the Syro-Phoenician woman in Mk. 7.24-30[2]).

Jairus already has some kind of faith, even if it is in desperation, since he does approach Jesus and pleads with him, and as the end of the narrative demonstrates, had he not done so his 'little daughter' would have remained dead. The message is clear: if Israel would submit to Jesus then life would be given to it. The placing of this narrative before Jesus return to his home

---

[1] When they came to the disciples, they saw a great crowd around them, and some scribes arguing with them. When the whole crowd saw him, they were immediately overcome with awe, and they ran forward to greet him. He asked them, 'What are you arguing about with them?' Someone from the crowd answered him, 'Teacher, I brought you my son; he has a spirit that makes him unable to speak; and whenever it seizes him, it dashes him down; and he foams and grinds his teeth and becomes rigid; and I asked your disciples to cast it out, but they could not do so.' He answered them, 'You faithless generation, how much longer must I be among you? How much longer must I put up with you? Bring him to me.' And they brought the boy to him. When the spirit saw him, immediately it threw the boy into convulsions, and he fell on the ground and rolled about, foaming at the mouth. Jesus asked the father, 'How long has this been happening to him?' And he said, 'From childhood. It has often cast him into the fire and into the water, to destroy him; but if you are able to do anything, have pity on us and help us.' Jesus said to him, 'If you are able!— All things can be done for the one who believes.' Immediately the father of the child cried out, 'I believe; help my unbelief!' When Jesus saw that a crowd came running together, he rebuked the unclean spirit, saying to it, 'You spirit that keep this boy from speaking and hearing, I command you, come out of him, and never enter him again!' After crying out and convulsing him terribly, it came out, and the boy was like a corpse, so that most of them said, 'He is dead.' But Jesus took him by the hand and lifted him up, and he was able to stand. When he had entered the house, his disciples asked him privately, 'Why could we not cast it out?' He said to them, 'This kind can come out only through prayer.'

[2] From there he set out and went away to the region of Tyre. He entered a house and did not want anyone to know he was there. Yet he could not escape notice, but a woman whose little daughter had an unclean spirit immediately heard about him, and she came and bowed down at his feet. Now the woman was a Gentile, of Syrophoenician origin. She begged him to cast the demon out of her daughter. He said to her, 'Let the children be fed first, for it is not fair to take the children's food and throw it to the dogs.' But she answered him, 'Sir, even the dogs under the table eat the children's crumbs.' Then he said to her, 'For saying that, you may go, the demon has left your daughter.' So she went home, found the child lying on the bed, and the demon gone.

town where *he could work no miracle* and where he was *amazed at their lack of faith* (Mk. 6.1-6[1]) is also significant. These two stories highlight the need for faith in Jesus both in his own person (the touch of the woman) and in his word (Jairus' daughter). But few were willing to do what Jairus did, deliberately seek Jesus out and ask for that life. The pathos of this encounter between Jesus and Jairus is thrown into relief by Jairus calling here *my little daughter*. While not disputing that parents loved their sons and daughters, nevertheless, the birth of a daughter was something of disappointment, Sir. 22.3:

> It is a disgrace to be the father of an undisciplined son, and the
> birth of a daughter is a loss,

and the tannaitic tradition (the oral tradition) (*Gen. Rab.* 45: 2) writes,

> Anyone who does not have a son is as if dead

There are, however, much more positive and wholesome references to daughters in other writings. The relationship between God and Israel is often depicted as that between a father and a daughter (cf. e.g., *Song Rab.*1.9.5) and one might refer to the story told by Rabbi Hanina ben Dosa in *b.Yeb.*12.1b (cf. *b.B.Qam.* 50A). Later the reader will be told that the girl was *twelve years old*, so right on the cusp of womanhood. The rabbis often said that girls should marry shortly after puberty (*b.Sanh* 76a) and the age for this was twelve and a half (*m.Nid.* 5:6-8). Trying to determine what the illness of Jairus' daughter is not entirely useful since it would add nothing to the central focus of the story which concerns itself itself with faith in Jesus.

---

[1] He left that place and came to his home town, and his disciples followed him. On the sabbath he began to teach in the synagogue, and many who heard him were astounded. They said, 'Where did this man get all this? What is this wisdom that has been given to him? What deeds of power are being done by his hands! Is not this the carpenter, the son of Mary and brother of James and Joses and Judas and Simon, and are not his sisters here with us?' And they took offence at him. Then Jesus said to them, 'Prophets are not without honour, except in their home town, and among their own kin, and in their own house.' And he could do no deed of power there, except that he laid his hands on a few sick people and cured them. And he was amazed at their unbelief.

This, as noted above, corresponds to the *twelve years* the woman had with her bleeding which suggests that it is ongoing and that therefore she was zabah (that she transmits uncleanness to anything she touches or sits on) and that any man who had sexual relations with her was deemed unclean (Lev 15.24ff.;[1] Pss. Sol. 8.12[2]). This allows us to understand that like Jairus, the woman was desperate and though she had consulted *many doctors* (Mk. 5.25) her condition had got worse, thus all the help she had sought had been a failure, indeed, as all help is gone for Jairus' daughter. Jairus *falls* at Jesus' feet and begs him to come and *lay your hands on her*. The *I beg you* is read into the text since the Greek would assume such an idea. It is read as 'in order that having come you would lay hands on her', signifying 'please, having come, lay your hands on her' (the imperative use of 'hina'). Jairus had clearly seen Jesus in action or heard about him and so was aware of how he healed (Mk. 6.5;[3] 7.32;[4] 8.23,[5] 25). Jairus begs Jesus to come so that *she may be made whole,* i.e., 'be saved' (regularly used of healing) *and she shall live.* The life of the *little daughter* was in the balance, everything now depended on Jesus restoring her before it was too late, and Jairus had faith enough to believe that Jesus could this.

d. The Woman Touches Jesus' Garment (Mk. 5.25-34)

Jesus instantly responds for he *went with him* (Mk. 5.24) and a *great crowd* was *pressing* in around him. That Mark mentions the *great crowd* as he begins the woman with the haemorrhage narrative, allows him to recall it when Jesus asked the question, *Who touched me?* (Mk. 5.31c) which then

---

[1] If any man lies with her, and her impurity falls on him, he shall be unclean for seven days; and every bed on which he lies shall be unclean.

[2] They trode the altar of the Lord, (coming straight) from all manner of uncleanness; And with menstrual blood they defiled the sacrifices, as (though these were) common flesh.

[3] And he could do no deed of power there, except that he laid his hands on a few sick people and cured them.

[4] They brought to him a deaf man who had an impediment in his speech; and they begged him to lay his hand on him.

[5] He took the blind man by the hand and led him out of the village; and when he had put saliva on his eyes and laid his hands on him, he asked him, 'Can you see anything?'

sets the context for the woman to admit to him that it was her. Mark then introduces the woman at Mk. 5.25 as having had the haemorrhage for *twelve years* and that she had *endured much* and *spent all she had* on doctors only to be left in a worse condition (Mk. 5.26). It may be noted here that only the rich could afford doctors, so it may have been that at one time the woman was quite wealthy but now, as a result of doctors' fees, she was left in poverty, having *spent all she had* on them. Mark does not name her so she is anonymous and surreptitious in her approach to Jesus, whereas Jairus is rich (his daughter, for example, has a separate room whereas the poor only had a one room house), and is a leading member of the community, while the woman is ritually excluded from the community, and he approaches Jesus in full view of everyone. The woman touches the 'hem' of Jesus' clothes, Jairus asks that he come to the house, Jesus calls the woman forward in full view of the *great crowd* but will expel everyone from Jairus' house. These two stories, therefore, are carefully interwoven by Mark and also in Matthew and Luke and this may indicate that they were interwoven in the very early tradition.

Although the woman touches his clothes in secret she does seem to be part of the *great crowd* that followed him because she had *heard about Jesus* (Mk. 5.27) but as someone ritually unclean she knew that she could not approach him directly, so the crowd provided her with anonymity for she said, *If I but touch his clothes, I will be made well'* (Mk. 5.28). One or two observations might be made about this: the woman has faith, but it is an odd faith, perhaps even superstitious, but it is enough: she is ritually unclean and would know that in touching him she would render him unclean also, so there is a certain selfishness here but desperation requires desperate measures sometimes (see below). She fights her way through the crowd and touches the tassels on the end of his robe (Mt. 9.20;[1] Lk. 8.44[2]). It was a *great crowd* but only she *touched* him. The tassel which she touched was required by Law. Probably what she touched was his prayer shawl, used by

---

[1]   Then suddenly a woman who had been suffering from haemorrhages for twelve years came up behind him and touched the fringe of his cloak,

[2]   She came up behind him and touched the fringe of his clothes, and immediately her haemorrhage stopped.

men for covering their heads during worship. It was called the Tallith (Num.15.38-40;[1] Deut. 22.12[2]) to remind the people of the commandments by which they were bound. Now two desperate people were depending on him at the same time. Mark then writes (Mk. 5.29):

> Immediately her haemorrhage stopped; and she felt in her body
> that she was healed of her disease

The healing is total and complete for *immediately* the bleeding stopped and the woman knew it instantly. She did not simply 'recover', or 'begin to feel better', like Simon's mother-in-law the healing effect was instantaneous and she was made whole, complete and well. No one who ever called on Jesus in faith was ignored. Mark then writes (Mk. 5.30):

> Immediately aware that power had gone forth from him, Jesus
> turned about in the crowd and said, 'Who touched my clothes?

This repetition of *immediately* reinforces the nature of the healing, the moment the woman touched his tassel and was healed Jesus knew something had happened, exactly what he did not know but he knew *power had gone from him* (Mulholland 2012:1.136). This is something of a unique situation for normally Jesus knows who he is healing since they have approached him and so the healing is in full view of the crowds who follow him or directly concerned with the person, as in the healing of the leper (Mk. 1.40-45) or the healing of the paralytic (Mk. 2.1-12[3]). Here, no public

---

[1] Speak to the Israelites, and tell them to make fringes on the corners of their garments throughout their generations and to put a blue cord on the fringe at each corner. You have the fringe so that, when you see it, you will remember all the commandments of the Lord and do them, and not follow the lust of your own heart and your own eyes. So you shall remember and do all my commandments, and you shall be holy to your God.

[2] You shall make tassels on the four corners of the cloak with which you cover yourself.

[3] When he returned to Capernaum after some days, it was reported that he was at home. So many gathered around that there was no longer room for them, not even in front of the door; and he was speaking the word to them. Then some people came, bringing to him a paralysed man, carried by four of them. And when they could not bring him to Jesus because of the crowd, they removed the roof above him; and after having dug through it, they let down the mat on which the paralytic lay. When Jesus saw their faith, he said

approach is made so in a sense Jesus heals without his consent or intention to do so. But even though the woman has been healed, Jesus cannot leave it at that and so his question, *Who touched me?* because he is *aware* that *power* has gone out of him. Arguments that the woman has a belief in magic (since she believes that by touching his clothes she will be healed) are not convincing. At Mk. 6.56, Mark gives other indications of those who touched Jesus' clothes and were healed. Acts 19.12 says:

> God did extraordinary miracles through Paul, so that when the handkerchiefs or aprons that had touched his skin were brought to the sick, their diseases left them, and the evil spirits came out of them

And in Acts 5.14-15 we read:

> Yet more than ever believers were added to the Lord, great numbers of both men and women, so that they even carried out the sick into the streets, and laid them on cots and mats, in order that Peter's shadow might fall on some of them as he came by

The clothes of Jesus, therefore, are not just what he wears, they are part of his person. So it does not follow that what motivates the woman is a belief in magic.

At his baptism, Jesus is anointed with the Spirit (Mk. 1.9-11[1]) and is

---

to the paralytic, 'Son, your sins are forgiven.' Now some of the scribes were sitting there, questioning in their hearts, 'Why does this fellow speak in this way? It is blasphemy! Who can forgive sins but God alone?' At once Jesus perceived in his spirit that they were discussing these questions among themselves; and he said to them, 'Why do you raise such questions in your hearts? Which is easier, to say to the paralytic, "Your sins are forgiven", or to say, "Stand up and take your mat and walk"? But so that you may know that the Son of Man has authority on earth to forgive sins'—he said to the paralytic— 'I say to you, stand up, take your mat and go to your home.' And he stood up, and immediately took the mat and went out before all of them; so that they were all amazed and glorified God, saying, 'We have never seen anything like this!'

[1] In those days Jesus came from Nazareth of Galilee and was baptised by John in the Jordan. And just as he was coming up out of the water, he saw the heavens torn apart and the Spirit descending like a dove on him. And a voice came from heaven, 'You are my Son, the Beloved; with you I am well pleased.'

full of the Spirit (Mk. 1.24[1]) so that he is the *Holy One of God* (Mk. 1.24) what is unclean cannot stand to be in the presence of the pure and holy (Mk. 1.23-26;[2] 5.1-13[3]),as the woman is unclean' she risks annihilation by touching the incomparably pure and holy. But, as it is with the case of the leper that Jesus 'touches' (Mk. 1.40-45) nothing unclean can defile Jesus. But he is aware that the 'power' has gone out of him; the Spirit moves from the person of Jesus and heals the woman, her realisation that something has happened is physical and existential (Mk. 5.25), Jesus' realisation is internal and spiritual (Mk. 5.30). Mark's use of the word *power* ('dunameis') is of significance. This is the word that is associated with Jesus' miracles (Mk. 6.2), it is the power of God that is recognised even by Herod (Mk. 6.14[4]) and in Mk. 9.1; 13.26[5] it is used with an eschatological meaning. This 'power' therefore, has as one of its primary characteristics, a moving out: Jesus is inaugurating a new age; a time when there will be no sickness and disease; a time when the power of Satan (manifested in sickness, disease,

---

[1] and he cried out, 'What have you to do with us, Jesus of Nazareth? Have you come to destroy us? I know who you are, the Holy One of God.'

[2] Just then there was in their synagogue a man with an unclean spirit, and he cried out, 'What have you to do with us, Jesus of Nazareth? Have you come to destroy us? I know who you are, the Holy One of God.' But Jesus rebuked him, saying, 'Be silent, and come out of him!' And the unclean spirit, throwing him into convulsions and crying with a loud voice, came out of him.

[3] They came to the other side of the lake, to the country of the Gerasenes. And when he had stepped out of the boat, immediately a man out of the tombs with an unclean spirit met him. He lived among the tombs; and no one could restrain him any more, even with a chain; for he had often been restrained with shackles and chains, but the chains he wrenched apart, and the shackles he broke in pieces; and no one had the strength to subdue him. Night and day among the tombs and on the mountains he was always howling and bruising himself with stones. When he saw Jesus from a distance, he ran and bowed down before him; and he shouted at the top of his voice, 'What have you to do with me, Jesus, Son of the Most High God? I adjure you by God, do not torment me.' For he had said to him, 'Come out of the man, you unclean spirit!' Then Jesus asked him, 'What is your name?' He replied, 'My name is Legion; for we are many.' He begged him earnestly not to send them out of the country. Now there on the hillside a great herd of swine was feeding; and the unclean spirits begged him, 'Send us into the swine; let us enter them.' So he gave them permission. And the unclean spirits came out and entered the swine; and the herd, numbering about two thousand, rushed down the steep bank into the lake, and were drowned in the lake.

[4] King Herod heard of it, for Jesus' name had become known. Some were saying, 'John the baptiser has been raised from the dead; and for this reason these powers are at work in him.'

[5] And he said to them, 'Truly I tell you, there are some standing here who will not taste death until they see that the kingdom of God has come with power.' ; Then they will see "the Son of Man coming in clouds" with great power and glory.

possession, death) will be destroyed. His *power*, therefore, points to the kingdom of God being realised in his present work and in the future. In this sense, then, the presence of Jesus is the power of God's healing of the world present in his person as well as in his words and actions.

This self-awareness of Jesus is further highlighted by the very reasonable observation of the disciples that (Mk. 5.31):

> You see the crowd pressing in on you; how can you say, "Who touched me?

Jesus, however, ignores their facile comment and scans the crowd intently, *to see who had done it* (Mk. 5.32). The woman then throws herself at the feet of Jesus and admits that it was she who touched him (Mk. 5.33). Mark says that woman came before Jesus in *fear and trembling* (Mk. 5.33). Fear and trembling is often the response to Jesus' miracles, e.g., the disciples are filled with *great fear* when Jesus calms the storm (Mk. 4.41), the women at the tomb are *filled with fear* at the empty tomb (Mk. 16.8).

While this may reflect the proper attitude of awe towards Jesus' miracles, Mark, however, presents this fear as a lack of trust and faith and therefore as a failure and while it may seem that the woman's *fear and trembling* may seem to indicate the proper response to what has been done to her, it has, in fact, nothing to do with this attitude. The woman's fear is grounded solidly in the fact that she has been found out and therefore she is guilty of contaminating a Jewish male with her own ritual impurity contrary to the Law. However, it is also clear that the woman is somehow 'emboldened' by what has happened to her (Mk. 5.33) she could have crept away back into the anonymity of the crowd from which she emerged but she does not do so, she comes forward in front of the whole crowd. If the woman was expecting condemnation from Jesus, it does not come. Instead he addresses her as *daughter* and this recalls Jairus' plea to Jesus to come because his *little daughter* is at the point of death. Jesus is fond of using these terms of affection but in essence they are terms of relationship. In the story of the paralytic, he addressed the paralytic as *son* (Mk. 2.5) and when Jesus is teaching the disciples about how they are to be in his community he uses these terms that speak of relationship (Mk. 3.31-35):

> And he replied, 'Who are my mother and my brothers?' And looking at those who sat around him, he said, 'Here are my mother and my brothers! Whoever does the will of God is my brother and sister and mother.'

The term, therefore, indicates not simply that the woman has been restored to her 'local' community from which she had previously been excluded but she is also welcomed into the new community of faith. And it is this for which she is commended (Mk. 5.34):

> your faith has made you whole, go in peace and be whole from your illness

The woman had already exhibited faith (regardless of how superstitious it may have been) in believing that even if she touched the tassels on his robe she would be cured, it is this faith that Jesus highlights and he affirms it in the use of *daughter* and the reassurance he gives her (the giving of peace was a recognised way of giving reassurance, cf. Ex. 4.18;[1] 1 S 1.17;[2] 29.7;[3] 2 S 15.9;[4] Lk. 7.50;[5] Acts 16.36[6]). This dismissal may also mean *go into* peace and can further indicate that the woman (and others dismissed by

---

[1] Moses went back to his father-in-law Jethro and said to him, 'Please let me go back to my kindred in Egypt and see whether they are still living.' And Jethro said to Moses, 'Go in peace.'

[2] Then Eli answered, 'Go in peace; the God of Israel grant the petition you have made to him.'

[3] So go back now; and go peaceably; do nothing to displease the lords of the Philistines.'

[4] The king said to him, 'Go in peace.' So he got up, and went to Hebron.

[5] And he said to the woman, 'Your faith has saved you; go in peace.'

[6] And the jailer reported the message to Paul, saying, 'The magistrates sent word to let you go; therefore come out now and go in peace.'

Jesus in this way, cf. Mk. 1.44;[1] 5.19;[2] 10.52[3]) is now entering a new state of life, one of restoration and wholeness. This can be seen in the use of the verb 'soze' which means 'to heal', 'to make whole' and thus to make new. Mark shows Jesus destroying the old age and inaugurating the new age. The miracles of Jesus, therefore, are the signs that the kingdom of God is pressing in on people. Jesus makes no mention of the purity laws, indeed, as in other cases (the healing of the leper, Mk. 1.40-45), he simply ignores them and when he comes to Jairus' daughter he will ignore the purity laws about touching the dead.

e. The Little Daughter of Jairus is Raised (Mk. 5.35-45)

It is while Jesus is dealing with the woman with the haemorrhage, that the news is brought to Jairus that his *little daughter* is dead. This is what Jairus feared and this is what he was dreading. The messengers adopt a very pragmatic approach to this when they tell him not to *trouble the master any longer* (Mk. 5.35). Jairus has come to beg Jesus for help, the delay with the woman has proved devastatingly costly. But Jesus was concerned which is why he agreed to go in the first place and (Mk. 5.36):

> overhearing what they said, Jesus said to the leader of the synagogue, 'Do not fear, only believe

The Greek word given for *overhearing* (cf. Hooker 1991:149) here means to 'hear beside' or 'to hear and disregard' Jesus plainly does not 'disregard' Jairus but turns to the despairing father encouraging him not to have any fear (the way the Greek is constructed here it would read as 'stop this present act of fear which you have at the moment') and to believe. Jairus

---

[1] Saying to him, 'See that you say nothing to anyone; but go, show yourself to the priest, and offer for your cleansing what Moses commanded, as a testimony to them.'

[2] But Jesus refused, and said to him, 'Go home to your friends, and tell them how much the Lord has done for you, and what mercy he has shown you.

[3] Jesus said to him, 'Go; your faith has made you well.' Immediately he regained his sight and followed him on the way.

had faith when he originally approached Jesus for it was that belief in Jesus' power which led him to fall at Jesus' feet and plead that he come, Jesus encourages this faith in him in this present moment. Here we can take the other meaning of 'parakousas' ('I refuse to hear', 'I pretend not to hear') as 'hear but not regard', 'not pay any heed to' and say that Jesus has not only disregarded the actual hearing of the message but also its content, that is, he takes no notice of the fact that the child is dead (Mulholland 2012:1.138). This is not to suggest that the child is not dead but rather that Jesus is confident in his power: the power to save, make whole and restore. Jesus dismisses the crowd and takes with him Peter, James and John, his 'inner circle' (Byrne 2008:102; Mullins 2005:163)

When he arrives at the house, Jesus is confronted with mourning and weeping and *people wailing loudly* (Mk. 5.38). It is unlikely that these are 'professional' mourners (Gnilka 1978-79:1.217) but rather members of the household since there would have been no time to organise professional mourners (Taylor 1957:295) (though Matthew calls them *professional mourners* Mt. 9.23). That the grieving had already begun indicates that the death of the child was expected, which emphasises Jairus' desperation in seeking out Jesus. The group may have included 'professional mourners' who wailed and groaned publicly so giving the family the opportunity to grieve in private. When Jesus enters he acknowledges the grief but then asks why they weep so much, *the child is not dead but sleeping.' And they laughed at him.*

'Sleep' is a metaphor used for death in the Old Testament and it is also found in the teaching of the Pharisees who believed in the resurrection of the dead: *You will sleep, but you will not die (Gen. Rab.* on Genesis 47.30). The word used for 'sleeping' is 'katheudo' which often means 'sleep' but means *death* in Ps. 87.5-6 LXX[1] (88.5 in MT); 1 Thess. 5.10.[2] Thus here, 'not dead but in a temporary sleep of death' (see, Boring 2006:162). There is a play on the two meanings of the word and Jesus describes Lazarus as

---

[1] Free among the dead, as the slain ones cast out, who sleep in the tomb; whom you remember no more; and they are rejected from thy hand. They laid me in the lowest pit, in dark places, and in the shadow of death.

[2] Who died for us, so that whether we are awake or asleep we may live with him.

'sleeping' in John (Jn. 11.11[1]) and as Jesus went to the grave of Lazarus to confront death so too now he goes to the house of Jairus to do the same (see, Byrne, 1991:41,49,84-89). Jesus' response to this laughter is to throw everyone out of them room. The verb 'ekballō' is the same verb that Mark uses when he is describing Jesus 'casting out' or 'driving out' evils spirits. So this is more than simply asking people to leave; Jesus 'drives' them out very forcefully (Mulholland 2012:1.138;Byrne 2005:102). Jesus has told Jairus to have faith and this group have no faith and where there is no faith Jesus cannot act (. Mark, therefore, is making a distinction between those on the 'outside' of the 'house' who have no faith in Jesus and those on the 'inside' so he violently removes those who oppose him in their lack of faith (Marshall 1989:98).

Jesus takes with him Peter, James and John, his 'inner circle'.(Mk. 5.37[2]). He wanted 'witnesses' to the action he was about to perform (as these three were witnesses to the Transfiguration later cf. Mk.9.2[3]). However, the injunction to silence at the end of the story would seem to discount this. This may be another example of the so-called Markan *'Messianic Secret'* (cf. Wrede 1971 (1901):50-51): Jesus did not want to be known simply as a healer, even a healer who could raise the dead, but as something much more profound (Mk.5.41):

> He took her by the hand and said to her, 'Talitha cum', which
> means, 'Little girl, get up!

Mark has already shown that nothing that is unclean (touching the leper, touching a dead body) can make Jesus unclean, once again he demonstrates this in having Jesus take the child by the hand and telling her to get up. There are many Aramaic phrases used in the gospel (*Sabbata*, 3.4; *Boanerges*, 3.17; *Satan*, 3.23; *Ephphatha*, 7.35; *Gehanna*, 9.43, 45, 47;

---

[1] After saying this, he told them, 'Our friend Lazarus has fallen asleep, but I am going there to awaken him.'

[2] He allowed no one to follow him except Peter, James, and John, the brother of James.

[3] Six days later, Jesus took with him Peter and James and John, and led them up a high mountain apart, by themselves. And he was transfigured before them.

pascha, 14.14; *Abba*, 14.36; *Eloi, Eloi, lamasabachthani*, 15.34) and the fact that Mark has to translate them indicates that he is writing for a Gentile audience (cf. O Hanlon 2004:85). Any suggestion that the preservation of the words of Jesus in the original language indicates that the early community were interested in magical formulae is to be resoundingly rejected. Mark then uses his favourite word to show the impact of Jesus' command (Mk. 5.40):

> And <u>immediately</u> the girl got up and began to walk about (she was twelve years of age)

There are similarities here with the healing of Simon's mother-in-law: the going into where the child was, Peter James and John, the taking by the hand, and the immediate impact of Jesus healing. But whereas Simon's mother-in-law was sick, this child is dead but the response of both to Jesus' command was immediate: Simon's mother-in-law got up and began to minister to them and the child got up and began to walk, indicating that the restoration is total, complete and absolute. In healing Simon's mother-in-law, Jesus 'reached in' and almost physically wrenched the life-threatening fever from her, but here he wrenches the little girl from death itself. The language that Mark uses here has close similarities with that which he will use for the resurrection: Jesus commands the little girl to *rise, get up* (Mk. 5.41), the same verb will be used at Mk. 16.6, *he is risen*. The little girl, *got up* and began to walk (Mk. 5.42), the same verb will be used to speak of the resurrection (Mk. 8.31;[1] 9.31;[2] 10.34[3]). The command that she be given something *to eat* (Mk. 5.43) echoes the meal that Simon's mother-in-law prepared for Jesus and those present after her healing and suggests the eschatological banquet (Miller 2002:83). This there are deeper similarities with Simon's mother-in-law than may first appear: both are touched by

---

[1] Then he began to teach them that the Son of Man must undergo great suffering, and be rejected by the elders, the chief priests, and the scribes, and be killed, and after three days rise again.

[2] For he was teaching his disciples, saying to them, 'The Son of Man is to be betrayed into human hands, and they will kill him, and three days after being killed, he will rise again.'

[3] They will mock him, and spit upon him, and flog him, and kill him; and after three days he will rise again.'

Jesus, both are physically raised by him, both respond immediately, both get up and walk about, both are associated with a meal (indeed, it may be possible to suggest that is a celebratory meal since Jesus has vanquished the power that Satan had over both of them). Mark, therefore, clearly foreshadows the resurrection of Jesus in this narrative but links it also with the Cross: suffering (woman with haemorrhage) and death (the child) (Marshall, 1989:99).

Furthermore, we should recognise that this was not an isolated incident: he also raised the widow's son at Nain (Lk. 7.11-17[1]) and both Mt. 11.4-6[2] and Lk. 7.22-23[3] mention him as raising the dead generally, to say nothing of the raising of Lazarus (Jn. 11.1-44, cf. Mullins 2005:164). But the taking apart of the favoured three emphasises that in the case of Jairus' daughter a lesson was meant to be learned, perhaps as a preparation for them to believe in his own resurrection (cf. Byrne 2008:102). And it is this which makes sense of Jesus' seemingly outrageous command when he, *strictly ordered them that no one should know this* (Mk. 5.43). Given that the response of all those present *were overcome with amazement,* it is difficult to see how Jesus could reasonably make such a request, even if it is another example of the so-called 'Messianic Secret' (and most especially since his commands to silence were generally ignored)? Mark's intention here must be seen in the light of the resurrection faith of the Markan community: Jairus comes to Jesus in a humble moment of faith (regardless of the fact

---

[1]   Soon afterwards he went to a town called Nain, and his disciples and a large crowd went with him. As he approached the gate of the town, a man who had died was being carried out. He was his mother's only son, and she was a widow; and with her was a large crowd from the town. When the Lord saw her, he had compassion for her and said to her, 'Do not weep.' Then he came forward and touched the bier, and the bearers stood still. And he said, 'Young man, I say to you, rise!' The dead man sat up and began to speak, and Jesus gave him to his mother. Fear seized all of them; and they glorified God, saying, 'A great prophet has risen among us!' and 'God has looked favourably on his people!' This word about him spread throughout Judea and all the surrounding country.

[2]   Jesus answered them, 'Go and tell John what you hear and see: the blind receive their sight, the lame walk, the lepers are cleansed, the deaf hear, the dead are raised, and the poor have good news brought to them. And blessed is anyone who takes no offence at me.'

[3]   And he answered them, 'Go and tell John what you have seen and heard: the blind receive their sight, the lame walk, the lepers are cleansed, the deaf hear, the dead are raised, the poor have good news brought to them. And blessed is anyone who takes no offence at me.'

that it is human desperation which brings him, he nevertheless believes Jesus can do 'something' (cf. Hooker 1991:111;Moloney 2002:111). He comes as a synagogue official, someone of importance, someone with high social and community standing in Judaism. But for all this, Judaism (synagogue) has not been able to help him but in leaving that 'place' and coming to Jesus he experiences a saving action which is greater than anything he could possibly hope for (Mulholland 2012:1.139;Trainor 2201:118-120)). The same is true for the older woman who had tried everything and no one was able to help her and Judaism had said she was 'unclean', i.e., outside society and community, outside 'life'. In Jesus both have found new life and as Jesus tells the older woman that her *faith* has saved her, so it is the *faith* of Jairus which has saved his daughter and in ordering that the child be given *something to eat*, Mark reinforces the totality of the healing not in the sense that the miracle of the raising of the child be sustained by anything 'earthly' (food) but rather in this act of sensitive gentleness Jesus acknowledges the child's needs and meets them both at a human level having already met them at a much more profound level.

Another answer to the command to silence may lie in what Jesus says after the Transfiguration (Mk. 9.9):

> As they were coming down the mountain, he ordered them to
> tell no one about what they had seen, *until after the Son of Man*
> *had risen from the dead*

This suggests that there is a 'time limit' on the command to silence. It is also interesting to note that at the Transfiguration Jesus has with him, Peter, James and John (Mk. 9.2) as he will have at the garden of Gethsemane (Mk. 14.32-42[1]). At the Transfiguration there is the three disciples, as there is at

---

[1] They went to a place called Gethsemane; and he said to his disciples, 'Sit here while I pray.' He took with him Peter and James and John, and began to be distressed and agitated. And he said to them, 'I am deeply grieved, even to death; remain here, and keep awake.' And going a little farther, he threw himself on the ground and prayed that, if it were possible, the hour might pass from him. He said, 'Abba, Father, for you all things are possible; remove this cup from me; yet, not what I want, but what you want.' He came and found them sleeping; and he said to Peter, 'Simon, are you asleep? Could you not keep awake one hour?

the raising of Jairus' daughter; there is the command to secrecy, as there is at the raising of Jairus' daughter (Wrede 1971(1901):50-51). At the Transfiguration Jesus is transformed (Mk. 9.2-3) in the presence of the three disciples, as Jairus' daughter is transformed from death to life with the same disciples present (see, Marshall 1989:99). This transformation is emphasised in the description of the clothing *and his clothes became dazzling white, such as no one on earth could bleach them* (Mk. 9.3) which recalls Rev.7.9,

> After this I looked, and there was a great multitude that no one could count, from every nation, from all tribes and peoples and languages, standing before the throne and before the Lamb, robed in white, with palm branches in their hands

and Rev.7.13-14,

> Then one of the elders addressed me, saying, 'Who are these, robed in white, and where have they come from?' I said to him, 'Sir, you are the one that knows.' Then he said to me, 'These are they who have come out of the great ordeal; they have washed their robes and made them white in the blood of the Lamb.

At the resurrection the young man at the tomb is also described in terms of his garments (Mk. 16.5):

> As they entered the tomb, they saw a young man, dressed in a white robe, sitting on the right side; and they were alarmed.

These descriptions indicate the heavenly and transcendent nature of the events within which they are described. The Transfiguration clearly indicates the resurrection. Further, at the Transfiguration Jesus appears with

---

Keep awake and pray that you may not come into the time of trial; the spirit indeed is willing, but the flesh is weak.' And again he went away and prayed, saying the same words. And once more he came and found them sleeping, for their eyes were very heavy; and they did not know what to say to him. He came a third time and said to them, 'Are you still sleeping and taking your rest? Enough! The hour has come; the Son of Man is betrayed into the hands of sinners. Get up, let us be going. See, my betrayer is at hand.'

Moses and Elijah at his side (Mk. 9.4[1]) with the disciples looking on; at the crucifixion Jesus will be 'lifted up' on the cross with two others at his side (Mk. 15.27[2]), with the women (and the 'Beloved Disciple' in John's account, Jn. 19.25b-27[3]) looking on (Mk. 15.40-41[4]). At his mocking, Jesus is dressed in the garments of a ruler, emperor, king, and hailed as such (Mk. 15.16-18):

> Then the soldiers led him into the courtyard of the palace (that is, the governor's headquarters); and they called together the whole cohort. And they clothed him in a purple cloak; and after twisting some thorns into a crown, they put it on him. And they began saluting him, 'Hail, King of the Jews!'

and the inscription above him is *'The King of the Jews.'* (Mk. 15.26b). The connection between these images and the raising of Jairus' daughter is the fact that kings would often travel with and be flanked by their counsellors or servants or retainers. As Moses and Elijah fill this function at the Transfiguration (Thrall 1970:311) and the two bandits at the crucifixion, the regal garnet and the proclamation above his head all indicate the kingship of Jesus and at the raising of Jarius' daughter he is flanked by two retainers, i.e., the mother and father of the little girl (Mk. 5.40):

> Then he put them all outside, and took the child's father and mother and those who were with him, and went in where the child was

The raising of Jairus' daughter clearly foreshadows Jesus' own death and

---

[1]   And there appeared to them Elijah with Moses, who were talking with Jesus.

[2]   And with him they crucified two bandits, one on his right and one on his left.

[3]   Meanwhile, standing near the cross of Jesus were his mother, and his mother's sister, Mary the wife of Clopas, and Mary Magdalene. When Jesus saw his mother and the disciple whom he loved standing beside her, he said to his mother, 'Woman, here is your son.' Then he said to the disciple, 'Here is your mother.' And from that hour the disciple took her into his own home.

[4]   There were also women looking on from a distance; among them were Mary Magdalene, and Mary the mother of James the younger and of Joses, and Salome. These used to follow him and provided for him when he was in Galilee; and there were many other women who had come up with him to Jerusalem.

resurrection and her raising to life can only be understood in that light and by those who are on the 'inside' with Jesus in terms of faith and not those on the 'outside' in terms of unbelief.

f. Faith and Discipleship

As with the case of the healing of Simon's mother-in-law, it is possible to explore the healing of the woman with the haemorrhage in terms of faith and discipleship and to see the woman as an example of both. At first sight, however, it may appear as if too much is being read into the text but a closer examination of the framework of the narrative reveals that seeing the woman as an example of faith and discipleship is a legitimate reading. The first thing to be noticed is that the woman comes up 'behind' Jesus (Mk. 5.27[1]). The only other time 'behind' will be used is when Jesus rebukes Peter for his presumption (Mk. 8.33[2]), Jesus is telling Peter in no uncertain terms that his place as a disciple is 'behind' Jesus since it is Jesus who leads while others follow (Mulholland 2012:2.59-60). The disciples, therefore, 'follow behind' Jesus and most especially as he makes his way to the suffering of the cross (Mk. 8.34[3]). In this context of Jesus' sufferings, it is possible to draw some comparisons with the woman (Selvidge 1989:99). The sufferings of the woman can be compared with the sufferings of Jesus; the woman is alienated and isolated in her society because of the purity laws, as Jesus is isolated and alienated in his trials and suffering because of a perceived violation of the Law (blasphemy). The particular suffering of the woman (menstrual bleeding) is a stigma within her society, just as crucifixion was also considered a stigma, as Lev. 21.22-23 points out,

> When someone is convicted of a crime punishable by death and
> is executed, and you hang him on a tree, his corpse must not

---

[1] She had heard about Jesus, and came up behind him in the crowd and touched his cloak.

[2] But turning and looking at his disciples, he rebuked Peter and said, 'Get behind me, Satan! For you are setting your mind not on divine things but on human things.'

[3] He called the crowd with his disciples, and said to them, 'If any want to become my followers, let them deny themselves and take up their cross and follow me.

remain all night upon the tree; you shall bury him that same day, for anyone hung on a tree is under God's curse. You must not defile the land that the Lord your God is giving you for possession.

The word 'suffering' is used of the woman, as it is used of Jesus, indeed, other than Jesus, the word is used of no one else in the gospels except the woman. The woman, therefore, follows Jesus in her suffering, is isolated and alienated from her community, just as Jesus is from the 'community' of the disciples (Miller 2002:88). The woman has given all she had to those who could not help her and is willing to risk judgement and condemnation to touch Jesus' tassels, just as Jesus is judged and condemned by a perversion of the Law. The woman suffers at the hands of Satan and evil, as characterised by her illness, just as Jesus will suffer at the hands of Satan through human instruments of evil. The woman was 'dead' but through Jesus she is brought to life, just as Jairus' daughter was dead and through Jesus was brought to life. The woman steps forward to be honest with Jesus when he asks who touched him and so, though fearful, is empowered by her already present faith (regardless of how superstitious it may seem). The woman is saved by Jesus, as is Jairus' daughter, but Jesus cannot save himself. The woman and Jairus' daughter are the first recipients of the 'ransom' which Jesus says is his own life *for many* (Mk. 10.45).

The woman with the haemorrhage, therefore, is an example of faith and following of Jesus in suffering and restoration. Further, if the gospel of Mark was written for a community that was currently suffering persecution (Rome 64 AD?) or had just come through a period of persecution and suffering (somewhere in the Roman Empire during the First Jewish War 66-73 AD), then the woman and Jairus himself become examples of endurance in suffering and faith that in Jesus such suffering and even death can be overcome. The woman comes up 'behind' Jesus (see above) because she believes that even his tassel can restore her to wholeness of life (Mk. 5.28, and Jairus is urged by Jesus not to give up and *only have faith* (Mk. 5.36). Jairus may well be representative of those who had lost family members during persecution. The story of the woman with the haemorrhage and Jairus' daughter, then, can be seen as a story which juxtaposes faith and fear. Fear is characteristic of the disciples: in the 'Calming of the Storm' the disciples, struggling in the boat against the storm are filled with fear (Mk. 4.38-40):

> But he was in the stern, asleep on the cushion; and they woke him up and said to him, 'Teacher, do you not care that we are perishing?' He woke up and rebuked the wind, and said to the sea, 'Peace! Be still!' Then the wind ceased, and there was a dead calm. He said to them, 'Why are you afraid? Have you still no faith?'

And here fear is seen to be a lack of faith in Jesus who is 'in the boat with them'. After the 'Feeding of the Five Thousand' (Mk. 6.45-52) the disciples are terrified when they see Jesus walking on the water and are immediately reassured by him when he says, *Do not be afraid, it is I* (Mk. 6.50). And even at the end the women leave the empty tomb and tell *no one because they were* afraid (Mk. 16.8). At Mk. 13.9 Jesus says,

> As for yourselves, beware; they will hand you over to councils;
> you will be beaten in synagogues; you will stand before
> governors and kings because of me, as a testimony to them.

This may already have been happening in the Markan community which confessed Jesus as the Messiah and that confession split families asunder (Mk. 13.13),

> Brother will betray brother to death, and a father his child, and
> children will rise against parents and have them put to death;
> and you will be hated by all because of my name. But the one
> who endures to the end will be saved.

But even through all this suffering the good news still had to be proclaimed, *And the good news must first be proclaimed to all nations* (Mk. 13.10). In the face of such suffering Jesus reassures them that their fear will be overcome because (Mk. 13.11):

> When they bring you to trial and hand you over, do not worry
> beforehand about what you are to say; but say whatever is given
> you at that time, for it is not you who speak, but the Holy Spirit

and the final reassurance is that *who endures to the end will be saved* (Mk. 13.13). Prior to the advent of Jesus fear, suffering, and distress dominated; the forces of Satan and evil held sway but with the coming of Jesus the new age has dawned and suffering, evil, and death itself are confronted head on a decisively defeated (the demon in the synagogue, the leper, the paralysed man, the Gerasene demoniac, the woman with the haemorrhage, Jairus' daughter). In these confrontations what Satan brings is waste and death, i.e., destruction, what Jesus brings is wholeness, restoration and life, i.e., salvation. The healing of the woman with the haemorrhage and the raising of Jairus' daughter, therefore, are both identified with Jesus in his sufferings and death and also stand as examples of what faith in Jesus can do even in the most desperate of circumstances. They further represent the power of the Spirit that goes 'out' of Jesus as he inaugurates the eschatological kingdom of God.

CHAPTER FIVE

JESUS AND THE WOMEN IN MARK

The Widow at the Treasury (Mk. 12.41-44)

and

The Anointing At Bethany (Mk. 14.3-9)

The Widow At The Treasury (Mk. 12.41-44)

Narrative Context

The story of the 'Widow's Mite', or 'Widow's Gift' at the Temple Treasury throws interesting light on the attitude of Jesus to such giving to the Temple. In the main, this story is often interpreted as an example of generous, selfless giving from one who is in dire circumstances who thus becomes paradigmatic of what generosity and selflessness is all about. The woman is seen to be an example of Christian discipleship and absolute self giving; she is pious and devoted and is commended by Jesus for her noble generosity, indeed, after observing the widow he goes on to make a significant statement about alms giving. These interpretations may well be accurate, but the story has a deeper and much more subversive connotation than the overly spiritualised way it is often presented. The reflection that Jesus offers on the widow's gift is his last in the Temple. The significance of this should not be lost for his teaching in the Temple following his entry into Jerusalem has been met with intensified opposition, attempts to trap him into saying something foolish and rash, and contentious and adversarial encounters with the Temple elite. It is this attitude of the Temple to Jesus' teachings that forms the context for his reflection on the widow's gift and his reflection is far from an affirmation of the widow's generosity but is rather a searing indictment and condemnation of the Temple itself. The story of the 'Widow's Mite/Gift', therefore, cannot be viewed in isolation from what precedes it, indeed, its significance can only be fully understood by examining those incidents that lead up to it, usually referred to as the 'Temple Controversies'. In this way, Jesus' observations and comments on the widow's generosity become much less an extolling of her virtues (of which, undoubtedly, she has many) than a scathing indictment of the superficiality and lifelessness of its intended destination.

The Temple Controversies

Following what is traditionally called the 'Triumphal Entry Into Jerusalem' (Mk. 11.1-11a) Jesus makes his way to the Temple. On entering the Temple he 'looks around at everything' (Mk. 11.11b). This suggests that he is almost like a tourist but the verb used for 'looked around' is much stronger, 'periblépō' means 'to survey', 'to closely observe with a sweeping look', or to put it in more concrete terms the translation would be better rendered as, 'Jesus went to the Temple and when he had glowered around at everything...'(This explains why 'periblépō' is always in the Greek *middle* voice which accents the *personal concern* – like the movement of the eyes expressed with the looking (Mulholland 2012:2.171-173). Jesus goes to the Temple and does not like what he sees then leaves with his intention clear (see Byrne 2005:177). It is when he leaves the Temple that we are told of the curious incident of the 'Cursing of the Fig Tree' (Mk. 11.12-14).

a. The Cursing of the Fig Tree (Mk. 11.12-14)

Given that it was not the season for figs, Jesus' action in cursing the fig tree for not providing fruit out of season seems on the surface somewhat petulant. A closer look at the small narrative reveals something much more profound cf. Cotter 1986:62-66). Having surveyed the Temple so closely and finding it lacking any 'fruit' with which to feed the people, he surveys the fig tree in the same way and finding it too lacking in fruit, he curses it never to bear fruit again (Mk. 11.14). His surveying of the fig tree is closely associated with his surveying of Temple: finding no fruit in either case, he sees nothingness but barrenness; 'pruning' will not work and so the only thing left is that the fig tree/Temple have to be destroyed (see, Hooker . Judgement would fall on Jerusalem because it was withered and dead. So as the fig tree was cursed to barrenness *now and forever*, so too Temple worship would never flower again (Mulholland 2012:2.173; cf. Meier 2001:2.885-889 for the place of this episode in the gospel).

b. The Cleansing of the Temple (Mk. 11.15-20)

Having surveyed the Temple, cursed the fig tree and made his decision, Jesus re-enters the Temple and gives vent to the fury that has been building in him since the previous day and begins to

> drive out those who were selling and those who were buying in the temple, and he overturned the tables of the money-changers and the seats of those who sold doves.

The Greek verb Mark uses is 'ekballō' and means, 'I drive out', 'I cast out', 'I banish' and it is the term he uses when Jesus is casting out demons (Mk. 1.32-34). It is possible, therefore, to view Jesus' action as having the air of an exorcism about it: the driving out of something that is not of God, not wholesome, that does not lead to or give life (Byrne 2005:178). Jesus targets first *those who were buying and those who were selling*. People who came to the Temple needed various things for their sacrifices, e.g., animals, wine, oil, salt, incense. These had to pass the test of suitability and they could be purchased from merchants licensed by the chief priests and approved with a certificate of guarantee of their suitability. Often, animals brought by the pilgrims themselves for sacrifice would be inspected, found wanting and deemed not suitable for sacrifice and so the pilgrims were left with no choice but to buy from the Temple traders (Mulholland 2012:2.179). Further, the poor could buy doves or birds which were also used in the purification rites for women after childbirth (Lk. 2.22-24[1]). All these could

---

[1] When the time came for their purification according to the law of Moses, they brought him up to Jerusalem

be bought in an area known as the 'Court of the Gentiles.' This was an area of the Temple which was separated from the Temple proper by a high wall and, as the name indicates, it was a space where Gentiles (especially those who were converting to Judaism) were permitted to be. They were not allowed to enter the Temple itself (even Jesus, as a Jew, would have disapproved of this) but in this space they could have some access to the God of Jews.

All this activity necessary for worship at the Temple required a great deal of money being exchanged but the money had to be of a religiously approved coinage so given that many foreigners (Gentiles) would come to the Temple, money changers were necessary (Mullins 2005:303). The Book of Exodus (Ex.30.13-16[1]) stipulated that adults had to pay half a shekel as an atonement and for the upkeep of the 'tent of meeting' (this was replaced eventually after the settlement with the Temple). The Temple levy/tax had to be paid in Tyrian coinage since this had no images on it (either of humans or animals) it was the closest coin to the old Hebrew shekel and was the equivalent of just over a day's wage (see, Donahue and Harrington 2002:327-328). The money changers sat at tables and exchanged other coinage for it. This involved a large fee and if change were to be given then another fee was imposed. The intention was to extract from the pilgrims coming to Jerusalem as much money as possible and since many who came were poor this led to a great deal of resentment. The sight of Jesus overturning these tables would, no doubt, have caused great delight with the crowds. In effect, this activity of the money changers in the Court of the Gentiles meant that instead of being overcome with awe at the sight of the

---

to present him to the Lord (as it is written in the law of the Lord, 'Every firstborn male shall be designated as holy to the Lord'), and they offered a sacrifice according to what is stated in the law of the Lord, 'a pair of turtle-doves or two young pigeons.'

[1] This is what each one who is registered shall give: half a shekel according to the shekel of the sanctuary (the shekel is twenty gerahs), half a shekel as an offering to the Lord. Each one who is registered, from twenty years old and upwards, shall give the Lord's offering. The rich shall not give more, and the poor shall not give less, than the half-shekel, when you bring this offering to the Lord to make atonement for your lives. You shall take the atonement money from the Israelites and shall designate it for the service of the tent of meeting; before the Lord it will be a reminder to the Israelites of the ransom given for your lives.

Temple, Gentiles were subjected to what for all intents and purposes was a market place. And there may have been the attitude that since these worshippers were *only* Gentiles, then it did not really matter but that was not the attitude of Jesus.

Jesus' concern was for the sanctity and purity of the Temple, hence Mark says, *he would not allow anyone to carry anything through the Temple.* This phrase is unique to Mark and indicates that the Temple forecourts were being used as short-cut passages for those moving about that area of the city. The Mishnah tractate, *m. Berakot 9.5* reads,

> one may not enter the holy mount with his staff, or with his sandal, or with his belt-pouch, or with dust on his feet, and do not make a short cut, And spitting is forbidden, as deduced from lesser to greater

and the carrying of money bag was also not allowed. With so much money changing hands, these bags of coins would have to be ferried to safe places and so taken through the Temple forecourt. Jesus' concern, therefore, is that the Temple is seen and experienced as a place of awe and worship and not a place where commerce and commercial activity is undertaken. This is further emphasised by his combination of utterances by the prophets Isaiah and Jeremiah when he says (Mk. 11.17):

> He was teaching and saying, 'Is it not written,"My house shall be called a house of prayer for all the nations"? But you have made it a den of robbers.'

The first part of the quote is from Is. 56.7 and the second part from the speech of Jeremiah against this kind of commercial activity in the Temple (Jer.7.1-11[1]). This is especially relevant since it took place precisely in the

---

[1] The word that came to Jeremiah from the Lord: Stand in the gate of the Lord's house, and proclaim there this word, and say, Hear the word of the Lord, all you people of Judah, you that enter these gates to worship the Lord. Thus says the Lord of hosts, the God of Israel: Amend your ways and your doings, and let me dwell with you in this place. Do not trust in these deceptive words: 'This is the temple of the Lord,

Court of the Gentiles which was where those non-Jewish searchers after God could come and believe and pray and worship. Jesus is emphasising that this was the divine intention for *My house of prayer* is a house of prayer *for all the nations*, but this was not what was being experienced so what opportunity did the Gentiles have if instead of quiet reverential awe they were met with the din of what was in essence now a bustling market place? John has Jesus clear the Temple and tell those present to stop turning it into an 'emporion': 'a market-place', 'a place of commerce', 'a shop' but Jesus' term is much stronger, he calls it 'a cave of brigands' (Byrne 2008:179;Mullins 2005:307-308).

Implicit in this on the part of Jesus may well be a condemnation of the oppression of the poor and the vulnerable by the priests and other Temple authorities (chief priests?) who all got their share of the transactions. This is important when considering the 'Widow's Mite'. Couple this with the fussy or rigorous demands about the purity of the animals being sacrificed, that the proper money be used for the Temple tax and it would appear that Jesus is making a statement about exploiting the poor for financial gain under the auspices of proper cultic worship, so that what should have been a place of worship of and awe in the presence of God is now no more than a place where brigands, robbers and thieves assemble and hide. But there may be more to it than this: the fact that this activity takes place in the 'Court of the Gentiles' seems to be implying that this does not matter because after all, as noted above, this is the place where the *Gentiles* come, the uncircumcised,

---

the temple of the Lord, the temple of the Lord.' For if you truly amend your ways and your doings, if you truly act justly one with another, if you do not oppress the alien, the orphan, and the widow, or shed innocent blood in this place, and if you do not go after other gods to your own hurt, then I will dwell with you in this place, in the land that I gave of old to your ancestors for ever and ever. Here you are, trusting in deceptive words to no avail. Will you steal, murder, commit adultery, swear falsely, make offerings to Baal, and go after other gods that you have not known, and then come and stand before me in this house, which is called by my name, and say, 'We are safe!'—only to go on doing all these abominations? Has this house, which is called by my name, become a den of robbers in your sight? You know, I too am watching, says the Lord.

those not of Israel and thus not of the 'holy people' and so are the 'unholy.' (cf. Evans 1993:93-110) In this context then, the Temple was 'divided' with a 'them' and 'us' mentality, between the 'holy' and the 'unholy' and since the phrase Mark uses is 'drives out', 'casts out', a term used for expelling demons (the unholy) there may be a suggestion here that there is an 'exorcistic' dimension to Jesus 'cleansing' of the Temple thereby implying that the action of Jesus is an attack on the 'demonic' (the perversion of the purpose of the Temple) (cf. Byrne 2008:180).

It is small wonder then, given all this, that the chief priests and other Temple authorities would be angry at Jesus' actions (Mk. 11.18-19[1]). They controlled the Temple, its liturgies, its ministries and its financial activities and received a great deal of money from them. Jesus had not only hit 'at their pockets' but he had also (intentionally or otherwise) undermined their authority before the people and implicitly condemned them by calling them *brigands*. Their response to Jesus is to look for *a way to kill him* which calls the mind of the reader back to Mk. 3.6 where the same intentional plot against Jesus was begun. The response of the authorities should not surprise the reader, the Temple occupied the central place in Jewish worship and its economic life and thus it was the power base of those who controlled it, this action of Jesus, therefore, is not just a symbolic prophetic action, it is an 'attack' on the religious and social basis of the power of the Jewish leaders and authorities.

c. The Greed of the Scribes is Condemned (Mk. 12.38-40)

Though the scribes were not a religious grouping as such, their influence with and over the people was significant. As experts in biblical and legal matters, especially those of a moral and spiritual nature, would have placed them in sympathy with the Pharisee movement. Having bested the best of them Jesus now feels compelled to caution the people against

---

[1] And when the chief priests and the scribes heard it, they kept looking for a way to kill him; for they were afraid of him, because the whole crowd was spellbound by his teaching. And when evening came, Jesus and his disciples went out of the city.

them. Matthew's account of this warning (Mt. 23.1-5) seems to be an expansion of Mark who gives what is, to all intents and purposes, a summary statement. In the three sections of Mark that follows three contrasts are made:

> 1. The scribes are those who devour the *widows' houses* and depicted as eager for such gifts. (Mk. 12.38-40)
> 2. Following from this, the widow is described as having given her all to God contrasting with the greed of the scribes. (Mk. 12.41-44)
> 3. The disciples of Jesus admire the Temple, when they should have been admiring the widow. (Mk. 13.1-2)

There is another, often overlooked, contrast to be made here between the requirement that Jesus makes of the 'good' scribe to love the Lord your God with all your heart, soul, mind and strength in all aspects of one's life, and the picture Jesus draws of these men who love *themselves* with all their soul, mind, heart and strength. Throughout the ministry of Jesus the scribes (and Pharisees) have dogged at his heels; they have challenged his teaching, his disciples, his authority to forgive sins, his teaching on the Sabbath, questioned the source of his authority, plotted against him, sought to entrap him before the crowd and in all this Jesus has patiently endured their endless questions, carping and criticisms. Now he goes on the attack by warning the people against their greed, self seeking and over stated sense of self-importance (cf. Taylor 1957:493;Byrne 2008:193;Mullins 205:335). The temporal connection between Mk. 12:25-27 and vv. 38-40 is uncertain. Obviously he is addressing the same category of leaders (i.e., scribes) but it is uncertain if the scribes of vv. 35-37 are being addressed or other scribes who like to flaunt their religion. Surely Jesus' words also relate to the Sadducees and the Pharisees who put on a religious show in order to be recognised by the people? Undoubtedly there were scribes who were holy and righteous, as his encounter with the 'good' scribe demonstrates, but many of them had become spiritually vain and self-seeking. The *long robes* Jesus mentions refers to the ornate festal gowns of the day: the distinctive white linen *tallith* with large blue tassels worn by the scribes.

The Talmud taught that one is required to stand in the presence of a rabbi, so these men would expect to be greeted with the title 'Rabbi' ('great teacher', e.g., Mt. 23.6-7) and they would seek after the *best seats in the synagogues*. The *best seats* ('the chief seat', 'the most honourable seat') probably refers to the row of elevated seats immediately in front of the ark which contained the sacred scrolls and facing the rest of the congregation. The same idea is present in the image of the *places of honour at banquets*, they would sit at the highest level so that even their peers would think they were important. But sometimes this was not always the case for it could happen that there was someone recognised as being more important than them and they had to face the humiliation of being 'demoted' to a lower place (Lk. 14.7-9[1]). All this is about the search for recognition and adulation of the people and it is a stark contrast to the attitude of Jesus himself: the scribes do not teach the people with authority, Jesus does. The scribes seek the admiration of the people, Jesus seeks to be with them and shepherd them with compassion; the scribes seek the respect of people, Jesus is one who serves and has taught his disciples to be the same as he and to have attitudes and values antithetical to those of the scribes (Mk. 10.42-45;[2] Mt. 20.26-28;[3]). The self-seeking and approval for their piety and righteousness that the scribes engage in is self-important pomposity which can be laughingly dismissed but Jesus turns his attention to a much more destructive tendency in them and severely censures them for it.

---

[1] When he noticed how the guests chose the places of honour, he told them a parable. 'When you are invited by someone to a wedding banquet, do not sit down at the place of honour, in case someone more distinguished than you has been invited by your host; and the host who invited both of you may come and say to you, "Give this person your place", and then in disgrace you would start to take the lowest place.

[2] And whoever gives even a cup of cold water to one of these little ones in the name of a disciple—truly I tell you, none of these will lose their reward.'

[3] It will not be so among you; but whoever wishes to be great among you must be your servant, and whoever wishes to be first among you must be your slave; just as the Son of Man came not to be served but to serve, and to give his life a ransom for many.'

The biblical tradition in the shape of the Law (Deut. 24.17-18[1]) and the Prophets (Is. 1.17;[2] Jer. 7.5-7;[3] Zech. 7.8-11;[4] Mal. 3.5[5]) has always spoken with reverence and respect for widows, the orphan and the stranger because they are the ones who most need justice and protection and God was seen to be their defender par excellence (Deut. 22.21-24[6]). The scribes were not allowed to receive money for their expertise since what they did was seen to be a service to God and for his greater glory and generosity and hospitality to them was seen as an act of kindness and piety. But there were ways around this and it resulted in some very unsavoury and unscrupulous practices. Jesus severely condemns the scribes for (Mk. 12.40)

> they devour widows' houses and for the sake of appearance say
> long prayers.

This was probably done through a manipulation of Jewish inheritance laws where the one entrusted to administer the estate of the widow, orphan, in

[1] You shall not deprive a resident alien or an orphan of justice; you shall not take a widow's garment in pledge. Remember that you were a slave in Egypt and the Lord your God redeemed you from there; therefore I command you to do this.

[2] Learn to do good; seek justice, rescue the oppressed, defend the orphan, plead for the widow.

[3] For if you truly amend your ways and your doings, if you truly act justly one with another, if you do not oppress the alien, the orphan, and the widow, or shed innocent blood in this place, and if you do not go after other gods to your own hurt, then I will dwell with you in this place, in the land that I gave of old to your ancestors for ever and ever

[4] The word of the Lord came to Zechariah, saying: Thus says the Lord of hosts: Render true judgements, show kindness and mercy to one another; do not oppress the widow, the orphan, the alien, or the poor; and do not devise evil in your hearts against one another. But they refused to listen, and turned a stubborn shoulder, and stopped their ears in order not to hear.

[5] Then I will draw near to you for judgement; I will be swift to bear witness against the sorcerers, against the adulterers, against those who swear falsely, against those who oppress the hired workers in their wages, the widow, and the orphan, against those who thrust aside the alien, and do not fear me, says the Lord of hosts.

[6] Then they shall bring the young woman out to the entrance of her father's house and the men of her town shall stone her to death, because she committed a disgraceful act in Israel by prostituting herself in her father's house. So you shall purge the evil from your midst. If a man is caught lying with the wife of another man, both of them shall die, the man who lay with the woman as well as the woman. So you shall purge the evil from Israel. If there is a young woman, a virgin already engaged to be married, and a man meets her in the town and lies with her, you shall bring both of them to the gate of that town and stone them to death, the young woman because she did not cry for help in the town and the man because he violated his neighbour's wife. So you shall purge the evil from your midst.

fact uses it for this own advantage (cf. Derret 1972:118-27). Or Mark may be referring here to the way in which the vulnerable were persuaded to give up their inheritance (and thus their livelihood) to the Temple. Without any means of support, the widows and orphans were left destitute. This may be why Mark links this practice of deceiving widows with the *appearance* of *long prayers*. Scribes frequented the market places and in their reputation for piety and being *greeted obsequiously* they built up a clientèle and so won the confidence of those who needed their legal expertise. The *long prayers* (false piety) can be seen as part of the 'long con' of confidence tricksters (Mullins 2005:336). They are used to lure someone in (in this case the vulnerable widow) by giving them the impression of piety, devotion, holiness and trust only for the widow (or vulnerable) to find themselves without anything. Jesus' response to this is to say that these scribes will *receive greater condemnation* because they claimed to be teachers (rabbis) yet they use their learning as a cloak for hypocrisy hence their crime is all the greater and so will be their punishment at the judgement (Mt. 10.14;[1] 11.20-24;[2] 18.7;[3] Lk. 12.47-48[4]). Jesus may be using a form of oriental hyperbole which he was fond of doing to both make and illustrate his point but the outcome remains the same: God, the special defender of the widow, will not idly stand by and not act against such hypocritical exploitation.

One interesting question may be raised here: are the scribes the only

---

[1] If anyone will not welcome you or listen to your words, shake off the dust from your feet as you leave that house or town.

[2] Then he began to reproach the cities in which most of his deeds of power had been done, because they did not repent. 'Woe to you, Chorazin! Woe to you, Bethsaida! For if the deeds of power done in you had been done in Tyre and Sidon, they would have repented long ago in sackcloth and ashes. But I tell you, on the day of judgement it will be more tolerable for Tyre and Sidon than for you. And you, Capernaum, will you be exalted to heaven? No, you will be brought down to Hades. For if the deeds of power done in you had been done in Sodom, it would have remained until this day. But I tell you that on the day of judgement it will be more tolerable for the land of Sodom than for you.'

[3] Woe to the world because of stumbling-blocks! Occasions for stumbling are bound to come, but woe to the one by whom the stumbling-block comes!

[4] That slave who knew what his master wanted, but did not prepare himself or do what was wanted, will receive a severe beating. But one who did not know and did what deserved a beating will receive a light beating. From everyone to whom much has been given, much will be required; and from one to whom much has been entrusted, even more will be demanded.

ones in Jesus' sights or does he have in mind a wider group? Jesus has been in conflict situations with the religious and Temple authorities since he arrived in Jerusalem. They have challenged, questioned and sought to discredit him. And one of the first things Jesus did on arriving at the Temple was to clear it of money changers. In condemning this activity Jesus was also condemning those who got their 'cut' (does Jesus have this group in mind also when he is condemning the greed of the scribes)? Given that these contentious issues have been examined and explored in the area of the Temple, it is not unreasonable to make the suggestion that while specifically criticising the scribes, Jesus is casting his eye wider. This idea of a deeper meaning in Jesus' condemnation of the scribes may be strengthened by the narrative which immediately followed.

d. The Widow At The Treasury (Mk. 12.41-44)

The previous sections were necessary so as to highlight the antagonism that has grown among the religious leaders and Jesus situated, as they are, in the Temple. In understanding the narrative context which relates to the end of Temple worship and the refusal of the religious leadership to accept the authority of Jesus, coupled with their outright hostility to him masked by sycophantic appeals to his righteousness and Godliness, the small narrative of the 'Widow's Mite' can be seen in a much more profound light than simply Jesus praising the widow for her 'gift' (cf. Wright 1982:261-263). There is no doubt that Jesus praises the widow for generosity but in doing so he is also condemning its destination and making it clear that the Temple treasury is not the best recipient of such generosity but is in fact, corrupt, greedy and coming to an end. Jesus (Mk. 10.41):

> sat down opposite the treasury, and watched the crowd putting
> money into the treasury. Many rich people put in large sums

The *Treasury* probably indicates the thirteen large, trumpet shaped receptacles against the wall of the 'Court of the Women' which the Mishnah speaks of (Byrne 2008:194) (*m.Sheqalim* 6.5, though there has never been found any physical evidence of these nor any other literary confirmation beside the Mishnah of their existence.). Each of these had a specific purpose, e.g., one for the upkeep of the Temple, one for sacrifices, etc. the money was dropped in to one of these trumpet shaped receptacles and undoubtedly the amount put in would have determined how much clanging the money would have made: the more the money, the longer the clanging; the more the clanging, the more the approval and admiration for the one throwing it in see Mullins 2005:337-338). Finally (Mk. 10.42):

> A poor widow came and put in two small copper coins, which are worth a penny.

In the case of the widow, there was no display and no ostentation, just a simple putting in of *two small copper coins*. Mark tells us they were kodrantés. The quadrans was the smallest Roman copper coin, a quarter of an as, the sixteenth part of a sesterius, i.e., the same as a *farthing*, equal to two *lepta* (mites). In other words, not a very great amount at all. The sound this would make as it was deposited into the treasury would be difficult to hear and since it appears that her offering was for the upkeep of the Temple, then it was insignificant indeed (Mullins 2005:227;Maloney 2002:247). Mark mentions there were *two coins*, she could have kept one of them for her own needs but she did not. No one noticed her donation except Jesus. On seeing this, Jesus (Mk. 12.43-44):

> called his disciples to him and said to them, 'Truly I tell you, this poor widow has put in more than all those who are contributing to the treasury. For all of them have contributed out of their abundance; but she out of her poverty has put in everything she had, all she had to live on.'

The calling of the disciples *to him* meant that what he was about so say was for their ears. He was again teaching and instructing them in the ways of discipleship with seriousness for he prefaces his remarks with *Amen* (truly) which always indicates solemnity and perhaps he had in mind their earlier discussions *on the road* about what constituted greatness and true humility (Mt. 9.33-37) rather than self-seeking and serving or the lust for position and prestige. Jesus makes a quite deliberate contrast between the greed of the scribes whom he has just castigated and the widow who has given *all* she had to God and he also contrasts the ostentatious giving with the almost embarrassing unobtrusiveness of the widow. But is Jesus simply using the widow and her action as an exemplar for the disciples or is there more to it than this? Is Jesus also lamenting or grieving the widow's donation?

The question, of course, is why would Jesus grieve or lament? (Mullins 2005:338) The simple answer is because he knows her to be exploited by the Temple and possibly by the Temple authorities whose rapaciousness Jesus has already challenged and whose end he will 'prophesy' in Mk. 13. On the one hand Jesus is definitely commending the widow and on the other he deplores what she has done because she is a victim of the way in which the Temple administration preys upon the vulnerable to gain from them not just what they can afford but also what they cannot. The Temple 'flourishes' because it has taken *all she had to live* on while the widow (and others like her) go without because in pious devotion they had given *all* (they) *had to live on*. Mark certainly emphasises the exemplary nature of the widow's actions here but the underlying theme of Jesus lamenting the state of Temple religion is a legitimate reading cf. Sugirtarajah 1991:42-43). If for nothing else it paves the way for the prophesy of the Temple's fall in a moment. The complete trust and faith in God which the widow has shown is contrasted with the superficiality and hypocritical flamboyance of the scribes who *devour the property of widows* and the rich donors. Her donation also serves to highlight the exploitation that she is the victim of.

So on the one hand, there are the morally and spiritually bankrupt Temple authorities and money grabbing scribes and the ostentatiously generous who contribute for show and on the other the poor widow (and those like her) who gives her all: both very different and opposing understandings and expressions of religion and faith. But there is a further contrast: as the disciples leave the Temple they point out its many splendours; they had missed the meaning of the widow's total giving and, it seems, not even heard what Jesus had said. In this respect they failed to see that it was because of such giving by the likes of the widow that the Temple could be so splendid. But Jesus is not concerned with the Temple but with the widow's gift and when he does turn his attention to splendour of the Temple it is to prophesy its doom.

In his meetings with the religious leadership in the Temple, Jesus has been the subject of scrutiny, challenge, subtle and not so subtle plots to trap him into saying the wrong thing and he has referred to the Temple as a 'den of thieves'. The greedy grasping of the scribes has been condemned outright and the image that Jesus leaves us with is not that of the 'Good Scribe' (Mk. 12.28-34[1]) but of those who (Mk. 12.40):

> devour widows' houses and for the sake of appearance say long
> prayers

The widow, however, gives everything she has, puts her faith and trust in God and so stands in contrast to the greedy scribes. As with Simon's mother-in-law, the woman with the haemorrhage, the widow is alone and emerges from the crowd who are throwing their money into the treasury receptacles (Miller 2002:152). Mark, however, highlights the fact that she is a 'widow.' The Old Testament makes frequent reference to the especial care

---

[1] One of the scribes came near and heard them disputing with one another, and seeing that he answered them well, he asked him, 'Which commandment is the first of all?' Jesus answered, 'The first is, "Hear, O Israel: the Lord our God, the Lord is one; you shall love the Lord your God with all your heart, and with all your soul, and with all your mind, and with all your strength." The second is this, "You shall love your neighbour as yourself." There is no other commandment greater than these.' Then the scribe said to him, 'You are right, Teacher; you have truly said that "he is one, and besides him there is no other"; and "to love him with all the heart, and with all the understanding, and with all the strength", and "to love one's neighbour as oneself",this is much more important than all whole burnt-offerings and sacrifices.' When Jesus saw that he answered wisely, he said to him, 'You are not far from the kingdom of God.' After that no one dared to ask him any question.

God has for widows, Ps. 68.5, says that God is, *the father of orphans and the judge of widows*; Deut. 10.18 notes that God, *executes justice for the orphan and the widow*; Ps. 146.9 says that God *upholds* them. The widow (and the orphan) stand as metaphors for the poorest and most underprivileged in society, not just in Israel, but in the ancient near east. kings who wished to be considered wise and kind rulers highlighted the fact that they especially looked after widows and even among the rich and elite humaneness was characterised by how they treated widows (Job 31.16-17[1]). Widows, therefore, were seen in a positive light because of their perceived destitution, poverty elicits sympathy, kindness, compassion. These are Godly traits and so the widow came to be understood as someone completely dependant on God. Many widows did not have a life of comfort; they could be forced to contract debts they were unable to redeem and so could lose everything (2 K 4.1;[2] Deut. 24.17;[3] Job 24.3[4]) and the fact that such actions had to be prohibited by law indicates that it was widespread and some widows ever resorted to begging (Job 31.16).

A great number of widows, then, appear to have been lacking any means of subsistence. It is possible that in Israel, the Temple offered help to widows, a version of 'social security' since the Temple organised the redistribution of tithes from which the widows benefited (Deut. 14.28-29;[5] Deut. 26). While most widows stayed in their own villages or towns some may have stayed within the precincts of the Temple (Lk. 2.36-38[6]).

---

[1] 'If I have withheld anything that the poor desired, or have caused the eyes of the widow to fail, or have eaten my morsel alone, and the orphan has not eaten from it

[2] Now the wife of a member of the company of prophets cried to Elisha, 'Your servant my husband is dead; and you know that your servant feared the Lord, but a creditor has come to take my two children as slaves.'

[3] You shall not deprive a resident alien or an orphan of justice; you shall not take a widow's garment in pledge.

[4] They drive away the donkey of the orphan; they take the widow's ox for a pledge.

[5] Every third year you shall bring out the full tithe of your produce for that year, and store it within your towns; the Levites, because they have no allotment or inheritance with you, as well as the resident aliens, the orphans, and the widows in your towns, may come and eat their fill so that the Lord your God may bless you in all the work that you undertake.

[6] There was also a prophet, Anna the daughter of Phanuel, of the tribe of Asher. She was of a great age, having lived with her husband for seven years after her marriage, then as a widow to the age of eighty-four. She never left the temple but worshipped there with fasting and prayer night and day. At that moment she

However, not all widows in Israel were poor. Judith was left gold, silver, male and female slaves, cattle and land (Jud. 8.7[1]); Abigail, who was married to David after the death of her husband, was in charge of a large estate (1 S 25.18[2]); the mother of Micah owned something like eleven hundred pieces of silver and that she could spend it without reference to her husband suggests she was a widow (Judg. 17.1-4[3]) and the widow of Zarapthath was a the mistress of a household (1 K 17.17[4]). Poverty, therefore, does not necessarily belong to the definition of a widow but it was so closely associated with her that she is often described as a 'poor widow' (which is how she is described by Mk. 12.42, 43). The widow of the Markan narrative is not only a widow but she does appear to be a *poor widow* since she has only two small coins to her name (Mk. 12.42) and Mark highlights this further when he makes the contrast between the *poor widow* and the *many rich people* who put in *large sums* (Mk. 12.41). Passover was traditionally a time for alms giving which would account for the large number of rich people putting in money. Like the woman with the haemorrhage, who is defined by her illness and Jairus; daughter who is defined by her closeness to death, the widow is defined by her poverty since she puts in *everything she had to live on.* (Mk. 12.44). While the rich are designated as 'many' the widow is alone, solitary and therefore unnoticed in the crowd except by Jesus. There is no meeting between her and Jesus,

---

came, and began to praise God and to speak about the child to all who were looking for the redemption of Jerusalem.

[1] She was beautiful in appearance, and was very lovely to behold. Her husband Manasseh had left her gold and silver, men and women slaves, livestock, and fields; and she maintained this estate.

[2] Then Abigail hurried and took two hundred loaves, two skins of wine, five sheep ready dressed, five measures of parched grain, one hundred clusters of raisins, and two hundred cakes of figs. She loaded them on donkeys

[3] There was a man in the hill country of Ephraim whose name was Micah. He said to his mother, 'The eleven hundred pieces of silver that were taken from you, about which you uttered a curse, and even spoke it in my hearing, that silver is in my possession; I took it; but now I will return it to you.' And his mother said, 'May my son be blessed by the Lord!' Then he returned the eleven hundred pieces of silver to his mother; and his mother said, 'I consecrate the silver to the Lord from my hand for my son, to make an idol of cast metal.' So when he returned the money to his mother, his mother took two hundred pieces of silver, and gave it to the silversmith, who made it into an idol of cast metal; and it was in the house of Micah.

[4] After this the son of the woman, the mistress of the house, became ill; his illness was so severe that there was no breath left in him.

unlike Simon's mother-in-law, the woman with the haemorrhage, or Jairus' daughter. In Mk. 7.25, the Syro-Phoenician woman comes to Jesus because she has heard of him, as Jairus comes to Jesus because he has undoubtedly heard of him, as has the woman with the haemorrhage (Mk. 5.27). Thus there are no reassuring or comforting words from Jesus, she remains unaware of Jesus' presence and she leaves the scene poorer than she arrived, for she had to *small coins* at the beginning (Mk. 12.42) but by the end she has *given everything she had to live on* (Mk. 12.44).

e. The Widow as Example of Discipleship.

As noted above, people seek Jesus out, they 'come' to him whether deliberately or from the anonymity of the crowd and there is some kind of interaction between them and Jesus. Here the only interaction is Jesus' observation of the 'poor widow' who, in a sense has stood out or emerged from the 'crowd' of the rich to make her offering of 'everything she had' which has caught Jesus' close attention. But in a real sense, interaction is not needed for it is Jesus who is not only the great and astute observer of human behaviour and intentions but also their great interpretor, for Mark writes that on seeing this Jesus (Mk. 12.43-44):

> called his disciples to him and said to them, 'Truly I tell you, this poor widow has put in more than all those who are contributing to the treasury. For all of them have contributed out of their abundance; but she out of her poverty has put in everything she had, all she had to live on.'

In other words, he has noticed, been attentive, and offered his observations on the meaning of the widow's actions. He was 'sitting' watching what was happening and 'sitting' is the traditional posture of a teacher (Mk. 4.1; 13.3). The 'calling' of the disciples *to him* meant that what he was about so say was for their ears (Jesus 'calling' the disciples to him is a favourite Markan expression cf. Mk. 3.13,[1] 23; 6.7;[2] 8.1,[3] 34; 10.42[4]). He then begins to teach and instruct them in the ways of discipleship with seriousness for he prefaces his remarks with *Amen* (truly) which always indicates solemnity and perhaps he had in mind their earlier discussions *on the road* about what constituted greatness and true humility (Mk. 9.33-37[5]) rather than self-seeking and serving or the lust for position and prestige. Jesus makes a quite deliberate contrast between the greed of the scribes whom he has just castigated and the widow who has given *all* she had to God and he also contrasts the ostentatious giving with the almost embarrassing unobtrusiveness of the widow (Byrne 2008:194-195;Mullins 2002:228-339).

But is Jesus simply using the widow and her action as an exemplar for the disciples or is there more to it than this? Is Jesus also lamenting or grieving the widow's donation? The question, of course, is why would Jesus grieve or lament? The simple answer is because he knows her to be exploited by the Temple and possibly by the Temple authorities whose rapaciousness Jesus has already challenged and whose end he will 'prophesy' in Mk. 13.1-8.[6] On the one hand, Jesus is definitely commending the widow

---

[1] He went up the mountain and called to him those whom he wanted, and they came to him.

[2] He called the twelve and began to send them out two by two, and gave them authority over the unclean spirits.

[3] In those days when there was again a great crowd without anything to eat, he called his disciples and said to them.

[4] So Jesus called them and said to them, 'You know that among the Gentiles those whom they recognise as their rulers lord it over them, and their great ones are tyrants over them.

[5] Then they came to Capernaum; and when he was in the house he asked them, 'What were you arguing about on the way?' But they were silent, for on the way they had argued with one another about who was the greatest. He sat down, called the twelve, and said to them, 'Whoever wants to be first must be last of all and servant of all.' Then he took a little child and put it among them; and taking it in his arms, he said to them, 'Whoever welcomes one such child in my name welcomes me, and whoever welcomes me welcomes not me but the one who sent me.'

[6] As he came out of the temple, one of his disciples said to him, 'Look, Teacher, what large stones and what large buildings!' Then Jesus asked him, 'Do you see these great buildings? Not one stone will be left here upon another; all will be thrown down.' When he was sitting on the Mount of Olives opposite the temple, Peter, James, John, and Andrew asked him privately, 'Tell us, when will this be, and what will be the sign that all these things are about to be accomplished?' Then Jesus began to say to them, 'Beware that no one leads you astray. Many will come in my name and say, "I am he!" and they will lead many astray. When you hear of wars and rumours of wars, do not be alarmed; this must take place, but the end is still to come.

and on the other hand he deplores what she has done because she is a victim of the way in which the Temple administration preys upon the vulnerable to gain from them not just what they can afford but also what they cannot. The Temple 'flourishes' because it has taken *all she had to live* on while the widow (and others like her) go without because in pious devotion they had given *all* (they) *had to live on*. Mark certainly emphasises the exemplary nature of the widow's actions here but the underlying theme of Jesus lamenting the state of Temple religion is a legitimate reading (Miller 2002:156-157). If for nothing else it paves the way for the prophesy of the Temple's fall. The complete trust and faith in God which the widow has shown is contrasted with the superficiality and hypocritical flamboyance of the scribes who *devour the property of widows* and the rich donors. Her donation also serves to highlight the exploitation that she is the victim of.

So on the one hand, there are the morally and spiritually bankrupt Temple authorities and money grabbing scribes and the ostentatiously generous who contribute for show and on the other the poor widow (and those like her) who gives her all: both very different and opposing understandings and expressions of religion and faith. But there is a further contrast: as the disciples leave the Temple they point out its many splendours. They had missed the meaning of the widow's total giving and, it seems, not even heard what Jesus had said. In this respect they failed to see that it was because of such giving by the likes of the widow that the Temple could be so splendid. But Jesus is not concerned with the Temple but with the widow's gift and when he does turn his attention to splendour of the Temple it is to prophesy its doom.

The small narrative of the 'Widow's Mite/Gift', is therefore crucially placed in the Temple sequence following the entry into Jerusalem. The widow serves as an example of discipleship and sacrifice to the disciples and thus the Markan community most of which may have been made up of the poor. The widow can be contrasted with the rich man who comes to Jesus in

---

For nation will rise against nation, and kingdom against kingdom; there will be earthquakes in various places; there will be famines. This is but the beginning of the birth pangs.

Mk. 10.17-22:[1] he 'lacks' one thing in his life of richness and undoubtedly holiness and striving for goodness and righteousness (Mk. 10.20), the widow 'lacks' everything in her poverty. The rich man cannot sacrifice everything and follow Jesus (Mk. 10.21), the widow sacrifices *all she had to live on*, i.e., her life (the Greek noun Mark uses at 12.44, 'bios', can mean 'life' or 'livelihood') in an act of selfless generous giving. In this way the widow is commended by Jesus for she acts out of the nothingness of her life, whereas the rich (including the rich man of Mk. 10.17-22) act out of their surplus and the rich man seems to be trying to out God under an obligation to give him eternal life, *What must I do to inherit eternal life?* When Jesus gives him the answer, he readily admits that he has done 'all these things' since his youth but when challenged to give the entirety of himself to God through following Jesus in poor discipleship, he goes away 'sad' (Mk. 10.22). The riches of the man have become his stumbling block to the eternal life he seeks in his original question to Jesus, the widow, however, gives all she has freely and without hesitation and therefore, by implication, she is 'rich' in 'eternal life' (i.e., the kingdom of God). The widow has given 'everything' freely to God, just as the disciples have given freely given everything to follow Jesus (Mk. 10.28) and the rewards of that are infinitely greater than material wealth (Mk. 10.29-31).

This giving of *'everything, all she had to live* (bios) *on'* can also be understood as a metaphor for the free giving of Jesus in his Passion and Death. In the Markan Passion Narrative, Jesus faces death alone, he is 'destitute' of friends and followers, as the woman is destitute materially; Jesus gives his 'bios' to God as a ransom for man (Mk. 10.45) as the woman gives her 'bios' to God (Miller 2002:156. As the disciple must give

---

[1] As he was setting out on a journey, a man ran up and knelt before him, and asked him, 'Good Teacher, what must I do to inherit eternal life?' Jesus said to him, 'Why do you call me good? No one is good but God alone. You know the commandments: "You shall not murder; You shall not commit adultery; You shall not steal; You shall not bear false witness; You shall not defraud; Honour your father and mother." ' He said to him, 'Teacher, I have kept all these since my youth.' Jesus, looking at him, loved him and said, 'You lack one thing; go, sell what you own, and give the money to the poor, and you will have treasure in heaven; then come, follow me.' When he heard this, he was shocked and went away grieving, for he had many possessions.

everything they have to follow Jesus, even their life ('bios') (Mk. 8.35), so too the widow gives her everything in an act of generosity to God (Miller 2002:158-159;Byrne 2008:195). In the destitution of death, Jesus is uncared for since he receives none of the customary treatment of the dead that was so important among the Jews, instead he receives a wrapping in a makeshift burial shroud and a tomb belonging to someone else (Mk. 15.42-46). The prophets had called for widows to be cared for but this woman has been ignored. Her poverty and self-giving is juxtaposed with the greed of the scribes and the rich who give of their surplus. He commends the widow for her generosity but condemns its destination which he has already made clear is a *den of brigands* (Mk. 11.17). At the same time, the widow stands as a metaphor for the total self-giving expected of a disciple of Jesus, even to the point of their lives as Jesus himself gives his life in total self-giving which is his stated purpose in the world (Mk. 10.45[1]) (see, Painter 1996:169). There is a risk in following Jesus as a disciple but in the example of the widow, Jesus shows the rewards of that risk: the woman with the haemorrhage risked everything to touch Jesus' tassel (having already placed herself in a situation of destitution since she had spent *all she had* on doctors, Mk. 5.26), the Syro-Phoenician woman (Mk. 7.24-30[2]) risked reputation and status is coming to Jesus who was of a different race and religion. It seems somehow that the women of Mark are willing to risk everything. The generosity of the widow, who gives *all she had to live on* as an act of selflessness to God, is contrasted with the rich who give out *of their abundance* (Mk. 12.44) and the rich man who could not 'give all' he had to live on (i.e., his 'life'); further the widow's *giving* is a metaphor for the

---

[1] For the Son of Man came not to be served but to serve, and to give his life a ransom for many.

[2] From there he set out and went away to the region of Tyre. He entered a house and did not want anyone to know he was there. Yet he could not escape notice, but a woman whose little daughter had an unclean spirit immediately heard about him, and she came and bowed down at his feet. Now the woman was a Gentile, of Syrophoenician origin. She begged him to cast the demon out of her daughter. He said to her, 'Let the children be fed first, for it is not fair to take the children's food and throw it to the dogs.' But she answered him, 'Sir, even the dogs under the table eat the children's crumbs.' Then he said to her, 'For saying that, you may go, the demon has left your daughter.' So she went home, found the child lying on the bed, and the demon gone.

totality of the giving demanded of disciples which is exemplified by Jesus himself in his Passion and Death (Miller 2002:154;Byrne 2008:195). It night further be noted that while the widow is commended, she arrived at the Temple treasury in a better condition than when she left it: she had 'everything' when she arrived (the two 'lepton' *all she had to live on*) and when she left she had nothing, in other words, she was absolutely poor since she has given it all away. Finally, Jesus does nothing to resolve her poverty and it can be presumed, therefore, that she did indeed live as a *poor widow* in Israel but a poor widow who had fully and completely entered the kingdom. In this sense then, the example of the widow who gives her 'life' is a fitting end to Jesus' public ministry and teaching.

f. The Anointing At Bethany (Mk. 14.3-9)

> While he was at Bethany in the house of Simon the leper, as he sat at the table, a woman came with an alabaster jar of very costly ointment of nard, and she broke open the jar and poured the ointment on his head. But some were there who said to one another in anger, 'Why was the ointment wasted in this way? For this ointment could have been sold for more than three hundred denarii, and the money given to the poor.' And they scolded her. But Jesus said, 'Let her alone; why do you trouble her? She has performed a good service for me. For you always have the poor with you, and you can show kindness to them whenever you wish; but you will not always have me. She has done what she could; she has anointed my body beforehand for its burial. Truly I tell you, wherever the good news is proclaimed in the whole world, what she has done will be told in remembrance of her.'

Mark deliberately places this incident between the plotting of the chief priests and scribes (Mk. 14.1-2[1]) and the betrayal of Judas (Mk. 14.10-11[2]) to emphasise that Jesus is being anointed as Messiah for his burial (Byrne 2008:216; Mullins 2005:375; Miller 2002:172). Having highlighted the scheming of the chief priests and then later showing the devastation of the betrayal of Jesus by a close friend, this singular action on the part of the woman is presented by Mark as both an act of discipleship and an act of love. John places it when Jesus first arrives in Jerusalem and before his entry to the city and Luke provides greater detail (Lk. 7.36-50[3]). Mark sets the action within the context of a meal at the house of Simon the Leper, who apparently had been cured, possibly by Jesus himself (Byrne 2008:217). It is during this meal that (Mk. 14.3b):

> a woman came with an alabaster jar of very costly ointment of nard, and she broke open the jar and poured the ointment on his head.

---

[1] It was two days before the Passover and the festival of Unleavened Bread. The chief priests and the scribes were looking for a way to arrest Jesus by stealth and kill him; for they said, 'Not during the festival, or there may be a riot among the people.

[2] Then Judas Iscariot, who was one of the twelve, went to the chief priests in order to betray him to them. When they heard it, they were greatly pleased, and promised to give him money. So he began to look for an opportunity to betray him.

[3] One of the Pharisees asked Jesus to eat with him, and he went into the Pharisee's house and took his place at the table. And a woman in the city, who was a sinner, having learned that he was eating in the Pharisee's house, brought an alabaster jar of ointment. She stood behind him at his feet, weeping, and began to bathe his feet with her tears and to dry them with her hair. Then she continued kissing his feet and anointing them with the ointment. Now when the Pharisee who had invited him saw it, he said to himself, 'If this man were a prophet, he would have known who and what kind of woman this is who is touching him—that she is a sinner.' Jesus spoke up and said to him, 'Simon, I have something to say to you.' 'Teacher,' he replied, 'speak.' 'A certain creditor had two debtors; one owed five hundred denarii, and the other fifty. When they could not pay, he cancelled the debts for both of them. Now which of them will love him more?' Simon answered, 'I suppose the one for whom he cancelled the greater debt.' And Jesus said to him, 'You have judged rightly.' Then turning towards the woman, he said to Simon, 'Do you see this woman? I entered your house; you gave me no water for my feet, but she has bathed my feet with her tears and dried them with her hair. You gave me no kiss, but from the time I came in she has not stopped kissing my feet. You did not anoint my head with oil, but she has anointed my feet with ointment. Therefore, I tell you, her sins, which were many, have been forgiven; hence she has shown great love. But the one to whom little is forgiven, loves little.' Then he said to her, 'Your sins are forgiven.' But those who were at the table with him began to say among themselves, 'Who is this who even forgives sins?' And he said to the woman, 'Your faith has saved you; go in peace.'

Mark refers to her simply as *a woman* perhaps to emphasise the fact that she stands as an archetype for all the women who followed Jesus (and she is often confused with Mary Magdalene, cf. Lk. 8.2-3[1]) (cf. Munro 1982:240). So Mark is drawing attention not to her identity but to her action and its symbolic significance. Mark gives a detailed description of the action, it is an *alabaster jar*, it is *costly ointment*, it is *pure nard*, the woman *broke open the jar*. The Greek word, 'pistikos' ('genuine','trustworthy') which Mark uses here may refer to the oil of the pistachio nut which was used as the base for perfumes but it may also refer to 'pino' so indicating that it was in liquid form (Mulholland 2013:2.284). The woman *broke open the jar*, probably at the neck, and so gave everything to Jesus since this was an *alabaster jar* and therefore expensive. This was not just an act of love but like the widow who put in the two copper coins *(everything she* had), it was the sacrificing of everything the woman possessed in an act of unspeakable love. *Nard* was a very expensive perfume made from a rare plant in India and women sometimes wore a little phial of it around their necks with which to freshen up after working (cf. Mullins 2005:378). Mark says she *poured the ointment on his head*. This is a symbolically powerful action on the part of the woman for this was how kings, priests and prophets were anointed (e.g., 1 S 10.1;[2] 2 K 9.3;[3]). It was also an action performed on important and distinguished guests (Lk. 7.46;[4] Ps. 141.5[5]). Mark emphasises that the woman anointed Jesus' head because he wants to draw attention to Jesus as Messiah thus

---

[1]   As well as some women who had been cured of evil spirits and infirmities: Mary, called Magdalene, from whom seven demons had gone out, and Joanna, the wife of Herod's steward Chuza, and Susanna, and many others, who provided for them out of their resources.

[2]   Samuel took a phial of oil and poured it on his head, and kissed him; he said, 'The Lord has anointed you ruler over his people Israel. You shall reign over the people of the Lord and you will save them from the hand of their enemies all around. Now this shall be the sign to you that the Lord has anointed you ruler over his heritage:

[3]   Then take the flask of oil, pour it on his head, and say, "Thus says the Lord: I anoint you king over Israel." Then open the door and flee; do not linger.'

[4]   You did not anoint my head with oil, but she has anointed my feet with ointment.

[5]   Let the righteous strike me; let the faithful correct me. Never let the oil of the wicked anoint my head, for my prayer is continually against their wicked deeds.

setting him apart as God's 'Anointed One' (Ps. 2.2;[1] Dan. 9.25[2]) Jesus has already been confessed as the 'Anointed One' at his baptism and by Peter at Ceasarea Philippi (Mk. 8.29[3]) and blind Bartimaeus had proclaimed his messianic kingship with *Son of David* which the crowds had echoed in his entry to Jerusalem (Mk. 11.1-10[4]) (on the idea that this is an anointing for kingship cf. Hooker 1991:238; Moloney 2002:281). Now the full meaning of that messiah-kingship is proclaimed by the actions of the woman: Jesus is being anointed for burial which means he will die and his prophesies/predictions of his own passion and death at the hands of the *chief priests and scribes and elders* are recalled. John says that the woman also anointed his feet thus confirming that Jesus is being anointed for burial since the whole of the dead body would have been anointed.

This incident occurred earlier than it is placed at Mk. 14.1 than may be first realised (Matera 1982:74; Mulholland 2013:2.187). Mark says that it happened *while he was staying at Bethany* which means it could have happened at any time after his arrival there and by placing it here he highlights its meaning in relation to the secret plots being formed against Jesus. John says it happened before the entry into Jerusalem (Jn. 12.1-8[5])

---

[1] The kings of the earth set themselves, and the rulers take counsel together, against the Lord and his anointed

[2] Know therefore and understand: from the time that the word went out to restore and rebuild Jerusalem until the time of an anointed prince, there shall be seven weeks; and for sixty-two weeks it shall be built again with streets and moat, but in a troubled time.

[3] He asked them, 'But who do you say that I am?' Peter answered him, 'You are the Messiah.'

[4] When they were approaching Jerusalem, at Bethphage and Bethany, near the Mount of Olives, he sent two of his disciples and said to them, 'Go into the village ahead of you, and immediately as you enter it, you will find tied there a colt that has never been ridden; untie it and bring it. If anyone says to you, "Why are you doing this?" just say this, "The Lord needs it and will send it back here immediately." ' They went away and found a colt tied near a door, outside in the street. As they were untying it, some of the bystanders said to them, 'What are you doing, untying the colt?' They told them what Jesus had said; and they allowed them to take it. Then they brought the colt to Jesus and threw their cloaks on it; and he sat on it. Many people spread their cloaks on the road, and others spread leafy branches that they had cut in the fields. Then those who went ahead and those who followed were shouting,'Hosanna! Blessed is the one who comes in the name of the Lord! Blessed is the coming kingdom of our ancestor David! Hosanna in the highest heaven!'

[5] Six days before the Passover Jesus came to Bethany, the home of Lazarus, whom he had raised from the dead. There they gave a dinner for him. Martha served, and Lazarus was one of those at the table with him. Mary took a pound of costly perfume made of pure nard, anointed Jesus' feet, and wiped them with her

which followed his coming to Bethany. Mark places it here for theological purposes and it may well be that in Mark's original sources vv.10-11 immediately followed vv.1-2. However, not everyone was as impressed with the action of the woman as Jesus was because (Mk. 14.4-5):

> some were there who said to one another in anger, 'Why was the ointment wasted in this way? For this ointment could have been sold for more than three hundred denarii, and the money given to the poor.' And they scolded her.

At one level the complaint is justified since it reflected the concern for the plight of the poor which was an important feature of Jewish spirituality and the reply of Jesus (perhaps with Deut. 15.11[1] in mind) does not dispute the reality of poverty and the suffering it brings. But Mark presents those at table, *some,* (John says the questioner was Judas) and with Jesus, perhaps even the disciples (Matthew states clearly it was the disciples) as almost engaging in the same secret conversations that he has described the chief priests and scribes undertaking in their plotting for *they said to one another.* They mention the amount that it could have been sold for *three hundred denarii* and given that a denarius was a day's wages, this was a very great deal of money (Byrne 2008:217; Mullins 2005:378). Jesus' reply, however, is a rebuke to them: he is well aware of the condition of the poor and well aware of the consequences of such poverty, he has not long ago highlighted as an example to them the self sacrifice of the widow at the Temple treasury. His reply seems to be saying to them, 'Well, I know the plight of the poor and so do you but instead of complaining about this woman's actions, ask yourselves what you have done for the poor lately?'

---

hair. The house was filled with the fragrance of the perfume. But Judas Iscariot, one of his disciples (the one who was about to betray him), said, 'Why was this perfume not sold for three hundred denarii and the money given to the poor?' (He said this not because he cared about the poor, but because he was a thief; he kept the common purse and used to steal what was put into it.) Jesus said, 'Leave her alone. She bought it so that she might keep it for the day of my burial. You always have the poor with you, but you do not always have me.'

[1] Since there will never cease to be some in need on the earth, I therefore command you, 'Open your hand to the poor and needy neighbour in your land.'

If the disciples (or those at table) have not understood the meaning and significance of the woman's action then Jesus points it out to them by telling them to (Mk. 14.6-8)

> 'Let her alone; why do you trouble her? She has performed a good service for me. For you always have the poor with you, and you can show kindness to them whenever you wish; but you will not always have me. She has done what she could; she has anointed my body beforehand for its burial.

Jesus defends the woman's actions which he sees as prophetic fulfilment of his forthcoming death and in his mind this was a *good work* or a *beautiful* work ('kalon', 'beautiful') for *she did what she could*. Jesus will not receive the traditional washing and anointing of the dead body which was so important to the Jews but this woman now provides it for him in anticipation of his death. This is more than the disciples will do for Jesus: when John the Baptist was killed by Herod the disciples of John asked for his body and buried it with all reverence. When Jesus dies, it is not the close disciples who will go to Pilate but Joseph of Arimathea. As they fail Jesus in his death, so now they fail him in the recognition of the anticipation of that death. So what this woman has done is *good work,* again in keeping with Jewish spirituality. Good works were alms giving and charity and the care of the dead for burial was seen as a charitable work. Jesus reminds them that while they may the poor, *you will not always have me* which calls to mind Jesus' words at Mk. 2.19[1] about the Bridegroom being taken away. Jesus then tells them with a solemn pronunciation (Mk. 14.9):

> Truly....wherever the good news is proclaimed in the whole world, what she has done will be told in remembrance of her.'

---

[1] Jesus said to them, 'The wedding-guests cannot fast while the bridegroom is with them, can they? As long as they have the bridegroom with them, they cannot fast.

This highlights the uniqueness of Jesus because he makes it clear that the good news which he himself proclaimed (Mk. 1.14-15[1]) will be preached to the *whole world* and what she has done will be forever remembered as a *good work* and as the kind, generous, loving action of a committed, faithful disciple or one of those who seem to have only 'cameo' roles in the gospel but whose interaction with Jesus is important (like the Samaritan woman in John, the Syro-Phoenican woman, the father of the epileptic boy, the Centurion with the sick servant, blind Bartimaeus). Further, the fact that Mark records the incident in his gospel (still preached today throughout the world) is indicative of the fulfilment of Jesus' words and one might suggest that John's remembrance of the 'aroma' of the perfume also demonstrates this.

---

[1] Now after John was arrested, Jesus came to Galilee, proclaiming the good news of God, and saying, 'The time is fulfilled, and the kingdom of God has come near; repent, and believe in the good news.'

CHAPTER SIX

JESUS AND THE WOMEN OF LUKE

Women are mentioned frequently in all four of the New Testament Gospels, but they are especially prominent in Luke:

Sources: L = only in Luke;
Q = also in Matthew, but not Mark;
Mk = also in Mark (and usually also Matthew)
Note: When Luke mentions 'disciples' or 'they,' do *not* assume the reference is *only* to men; it may *also* include women!

Passage (Source)	Brief Description
Lk. 1.5-7 (L)	Zechariah's wife Elizabeth is named; both are righteous and old
Lk. 1.13, 18 (L)	Gabriel and Zechariah each mention Elizabeth briefly
Lk. 1.24-25 (L)	Elizabeth conceives & praises God for taking away her 'disgrace' (of being barren)
Lk. 1.26-38 (L)	Annunciation: Gabriel visits Mary to proclaim Jesus' birth; Mary agrees to cooperate
Lk. 1.39-56 (L)	Mary visits Elizabeth; Elizabeth praises Mary; Mary praises God in the 'Magnificat'
Lk. 1.57-61 (L)	Elizabeth gives birth to John & she names him
Lk. 2.5-7 (L)	Mary goes with Joseph to Bethlehem; there she gives birth to her first-born child
Lk. 2.15-20 (L)	Shepherds visit Mary & Joseph; Mary treasures all things in her heart (v. 19)
Lk. 2.22 & 27 (L)	'They' go to Jerusalem for 'their' purification; Simeon

	speaks to both 'parents'
Lk. 2.33-35 (L)	Simeon speaks directly to Mary: a sword shall pass through her heart
Lk. 2.36-38 (L)	Prophet-widow Anna praises God and speaks to the people about Jesus
Lk. 2.41-51 (L)	Both 'parents' take Jesus to Jerusalem; his Mother speaks (v. 48) and 'treasures' all (v. 51)
Lk. 3.19 (Mk)	Wicked Herodias mentioned only very briefly (contrast Mark 6:17-29)
Lk. 4.25-26 (L)	Jesus uses as examples the OT stories of the widows of Israel & the widow of Zarephath
Lk. 4.38-39 (Mk)	Jesus heals Simon's mother-in-law; she then immediately serves them all
Lk. 7.11-17 (L)	Jesus has compassion for a widow in Nain, and so restores her only son to life
Lk. 7.28 (Q)	'Among those born of women, no one is greater than John (the Baptist)
Lk. 7.35 (L)	'Wisdom is vindicated by all her children'
Lk. 7.36-50 (Mk)	A sinful woman anoints Jesus and is forgiven; she is contrasted to Simon the Pharisee
Lk. 8.1-3 (L)	Several women are named who accompany Jesus and provided for the disciples
Lk. 8.19-21 (Mk)	Jesus' mother & brothers come; those who hear & do God's word are his mother/brothers
Lk. 8.40-42, 49-56 (Mk)	Jesus restores Jairus' daughter to life; child's parents both mentioned (vv. 51, 56)
Lk. 8.43-48 (Mk)	Jesus heals a haemorrhaging woman; she takes the initiative and is praised for her faith
Lk. 10.38-42 (L)	Martha serves & complains while Mary sits at Jesus' feet (like a disciple!) and is praised
Lk. 11.27-28 (L)	A woman says, 'Blessed is the womb that bore you and the breasts that nursed you!'

Lk. 11.31 (Q)	The Queen of the South used as a positive example; she came to hear Solomon's wisdom
Lk. 12.45 (L)	In a parable, both men & women slaves are beaten by a wicked manager
Lk. 12.53 (Q)	Families will be divided: father/son, mother/daughter, mother-in-law/daughter-in-law
Lk. 13.10-17 (L)	On a Sabbath, Jesus cures a woman crippled for 18 years
Lk. 13.20-21 (Q)	Parable of the Kingdom of God being like a woman mixing yeast & flour
Lk. 13.34 (Q)	Jesus wants to gather Jerusalem's children like a mother hen protects her brood
Lk. 14.26 (Q)	Disciples must 'hate' father, mother, wife, children, brothers, sisters
Lk. 15.8-10 (L)	Parable of a woman who lost and found a coin, then rejoices with her friends
Lk. 16.18 (Mk)	Brief saying against men divorcing their wives or marrying divorced women
Lk. 17.26-27 (Q)	In the days of Noah, people were marrying and giving in marriage
Lk. 17.32 (L)	'Remember Lot's wife.'
Lk. 17.35 (Q)	Two women will be grinding grain: one will be taken, one left
Lk. 18.1-8 (L)	Parable of a widow fighting for her rights against an unjust judge
Lk. 18.20 (Mk)	'Honour your father and mother' (cited from Ex. 20:12)
Lk. 18.28-30 (Mk)	Disciples who have left wives, brothers, parents, children, etc. will be rewarded
Lk. 20.27-36 (Mk)	Sadducees question the resurrection with story of a woman who had seven husbands
Lk. 21.1-4 (Mk)	Poor widow's small offering is worth more than the offerings of rich people
Lk. 21.23-24	Alas for pregnant and nursing women in the days of

(Mk)	Jerusalem's destruction
Lk. 22.56-57 (Mk)	Peter's first denial comes after a servant girl challenges him
Lk. 23.26-31 (L)	Jesus speaks to wailing women in the crowd on the way to his crucifixion
Lk. 23.49 (Mk)	The women from Galilee watch Jesus' crucifixion from a distance
Lk. 23.55-56 (Mk)	The women see where Jesus is buried and prepare spices & ointments
Lk. 24.1-11 (Mk & L)	The women find Jesus' tomb empty; two messengers speak with them; they remember Jesus' words and go tell the other disciples, who don't believe them
Lk. 24.22-24 (L)	Two disciples on the road to Emmaus (two men? a married couple? 'Cleopas' named in 24:18) tell Jesus how some women of their group went to the tomb that morning and saw vision of angel

In a time when women were either ignored or treated differently from men socially and religiously, Luke conscious strives to show them on equal par with men as far as the Gospel is concerned (a tendency which may well go back to Jesus himself). This can be illustrated by taking the above table and expanding it and showing how Luke places his texts concerning women in relation to men. Some of these examples, as the above table shows are common to Mark (which demonstrates that Mark does the same). It might also be noted that in a number of cases the women come first, where the order could equally have been reversed (this applies also to the examples cited from Jesus):

| Lk. 1-2 | Luke gives women, both Elizabeth and Mary, an equal say with Zacharias |
| Lk. 2.25-40 | Jesus' visit to Jerusalem is witnessed to by both Simeon and Anna the Prophetess, and it is Mary and not Joseph |

	who is prominent in the description of Jesus' visit to the Temple in His youth.
Lk. 4.23-27	Jesus gives two examples of God's blessing on Gentiles in the Old Testament, one concerning a woman, the widow of Zarephath, and one concerning a man, Naaman the Syrian.
Lk. 7	He alternates stories of the Roman centurion, the widow of Nain, John the Baptiser, and the sinful woman.
Lk. 8.1-2	He introduces first the twelve, and then the women who accompanied Jesus, some by name.
Lk. 8	The man Jairus with his daughter, intermingled with which is the woman with the issue of blood.
Lk. 10-11	The Lord's prayer is surrounded by two examples of a prayerful attitude, on one side is Mary (with Martha), and on the other the visit of the male friend at midnight.
Lk. 11.29-32	He cites two examples of Gentiles who listened to the word of God in the Old Testament, the queen of the south and the men of Nineveh
Lk. 11.24-28	The man with the unclean spirits is followed by the woman who blesses Jesus.
Lk. 12.22-32	In the sermon on the plain, his examples of those that God provides for are the masculine ravens and the feminine flowers.
Lk. 13.6-17	The man who planted a fig tree is followed by the woman who could not straighten herself
Lk. 13.18-21	The man who sowed the mustard seed who is paralleled with the woman who inserted the leaven into the flour, both illustrations of the successful advance of the Kingly Rule of God.
Lk. 15	The parable of the shepherd and the lost sheep is followed by that of the woman and the lost coin.
Lk. 17.34-35	The examples of the men in bed are followed by the

	women grinding.
Lk. 18	The example of the woman who prayed is followed by the example of the men who prayed.
Lk. 20.45-21.4	The example of the men who devoured widows' houses is followed by the example of the widow who gave her all.

It will be apparent from a consideration of these examples that some are the result of Jesus' own emphasis on the equality of women in God's sight, and some are more deliberately the work of Luke. If this table is broken down in to sub divisions then it is possible to identify five groups or classes of women which dominate Luke's narrative:

1. **The women of the Birth/Infancy narratives:**
   - Mary (Lk. 1.27-2.52)
   - Elizabeth (Lk. 1.5-2.66)

2. **Widows:**
   - Anna (Lk. 2.36-38) and
   - The widow at Zarephath (Lk. 4.25-30).
   - The widow of Nain (Lk. 7.11-17),
   - Widow in Lk. 18.1-8
   - Widow at the treasury (Lk. 21.1-4)

3. **Sinners/Sick**
   - The woman who came to Jesus at the Pharisee's house (Lk. 7.36-50),
   - Jairus' daughter (Lk. 8.40-55)
   - The woman with the haemorrhage (Lk. 8.40-55).
   - The woman who was a cripple (Lk. 13.10-17).
   - Parables about the kingdom include the woman and

leaven.
- the woman and the lost coin (Lk. 15.8-10).

4. Women who ministered or responded:
- Simon's mother-in-law(Lk. 4.38-39),
- The women who travelled with Jesus (Lk. 8.2-3),
- Jesus' mother (and brothers) (Lk. 8.19-21),
- Mary and Martha who were visited by Jesus (Lk. 10.38-42),
- The women along the road who declared Mary's womb and breasts blessed (Lk. 11.27-28).

5. Women in the Passion Narrative:
- Women on the way to Calvary (Lk. 23.27-31),
- women at the crucifixion (Lk. 23.49),
- women at the burial (Lk. 23.55-56a),
- women at the tomb (Lk. 24.1-12)
- women who witness that Jesus forgives sins (Lk. 24.13-56).
-

The Women in Infancy Narrative of Luke:
Lk. 1-2: Elizabeth, Mary and the Old Testament Women

Overview of the Contents of Luke 1—2

Lk. 1.1-4	Prologue: Literary Introduction to the Gospel
Lk. 1.5-25	Angel Gabriel appears to Zechariah to announce the birth of John (the Baptist)
Lk. 1.26-38	Angel Gabriel appears to Mary to announce the birth of Jesus (the *'Annunciation'*)
Lk. 1.39-56	Mary visits her cousin Elizabeth (the *'Visitation'*; including Mary's

	'Magnificat')
Lk. 1.57-80	The Birth of John the Baptist (incl. Zechariah's *'Benedictus'*)
Lk. 2.1-5	Joseph and Mary journey to Bethlehem
Lk. 2.6-7	The Birth of Jesus in Bethlehem of Judea (the *'Nativity'*)
Lk. 2.8-14	Angels appear to some shepherds (incl. the angels' *'Gloria'*)
Lk. 2.15-20	Shepherds visit the baby Jesus
Lk. 2.21	Jesus is circumcised & given his name
Lk. 2.22-38	Jesus is presented to God in the Jerusalem Temple (the *'Presentation'*)
Lk. 2.39-40	Jesus' family returns to Nazareth
Lk. 2.41-52	The boy Jesus is found in the Temple (incl. Simeon's *'Nunc Dimittis*

Parallels in Biblical Birth Narratives

	Birth of Ishmael (Gen 16.7-13)	Birth of Samson (Judg 13.2-25)	Birth of Samuel (1 S1.1—2.11)	Birth of John (1.5-25, 57-80)	Birth of Jesus (1.26-38; 2.1-40)
Mother's Situation	Sarai. old, barren (16.7-8)	Anonymous Wife. barren	Hannah. barren	Elizabeth. barren, old	Mary. virgin, not yet married
Father's Role	Abram.	Manoah. dialogues with wife	Elkanah. comforts Hannah	Zechariah. priest in temple	Joseph. no major role
Child Requested		*(not explicit)*	by Hannah's prayer	by Zechariah's prayer *(implicit)*	*(not requested)*
Announcement		by an angel to			

			by Eli's assurance to Hannah	by angel Gabriel to Zechariah	by angel Gabriel to Mary
of Birth		the woman	by Eli's assurance to Hannah	by angel Gabriel to Zechariah	by angel Gabriel to Mary
Initial Reaction		Woman tells her husband	Eli thinks Hannah is drunk	Zechariah questions / doubts	Mary questions / believes
Result of Announcement		Angel appears again to both	Hannah conceives from husband	Elizabeth conceives from husband	Mary conceives from Holy Spirit
Birth of Child		brief mention (13.24a)	very brief mention (1.20)	brief narration (1.57-58)	extensive narration (2.1-20)
Circumcision		(*not mentioned*)	(*not mentioned*)	extensive narration (1.59-79)	brief mention (2.21)
Boy's Name		Samson (13.24a)	Samuel (1.20)	John (1.13, 59-63)	Jesus (1.31, 35; 2.21)
Reaction Praising God		(*sacrifice offered before birth*)	by Hannah (2.1-10)	by Zechariah (1.67-79)	by Mary (1.46-55); by angels (2.8-14); by shepherds (2.20) by Simeon (2.28-32)
Child Grows		mentioned	(1.24-28; 2.11)	mentioned	incident at

		briefly (13.24b-25)		only briefly (1.80)	age twelve (2.40-52)

The main emphasis of this section will focus on Mary in Luke's 'Infancy Narrative', which is not to say that Luke does not mention her in other places. Indeed, Luke's gospel is often called the 'gospel of the women' because of the tenderness with which he speaks of and presents women both on their own and in their interactions with Jesus. As Matthew was writing for a predominantly Jewish-Christian group, Luke was writing for a predominantly Gentile group. Most scholars accept that Luke was written 85 AD and that the author may have been a physician/doctor and a companion of Paul. Luke appears to be a well educated speaker of Greek and had a thorough knowledge of the LXX (Septuagint=the Jewish Scriptures in Greek) but he was not an eye-witness to the events he describes in his gospel. He does not appear to have been a Palestinian or to have been brought up as a Jew, which has led some scholars to believe that he may have been a convert to Judaism before becoming a Christian. His gospel seems to have been destined for churches either founded directly by Paul or indirectly through others associated with Paul's missionary activity. As Matthew drew on Mark and the 'Q' source, so too Luke drew on Mark and Q and seems to have had other sources available to him either written or oral. So Luke's sources can be outlined like this:

Luke's presentation of Jesus markedly differs from that of Matthew and Mark while essentially keeping the same 'format' as Matthew and Mark (hence they are referred to as the 'Synoptics' ('same eye', 'same view', 'same perspective'). Jesus is the universal Saviour, gracious, generous and filled with warmth and tenderness for those who suffer, who is open and responsive to the needs of all who come to him. And women figure more highly in Luke's gospel than any other of the Synoptics and we shall come to these when we examine Jesus and women in Luke. Our attention at this stage of Luke's presentation of women will be focused on Mary (and by extension Elizabeth) in his 'Infancy Narrative' (Lk. 1.5-2.52). The Infancy Narrative of Luke can be tabled thus:

The Infancy of the Son of Man (Lk.1.5–2:52)

- Annunciation of birth of John and Jesus (Lk.1.5; 1.56)
- The Gospel Canticles (Lk.1.46-55)
- Birth, Circumcisions, Naming of John and Jesus (Lk.1.57-2.40)
- The Finding in the Temple (Lk.2.41-52)

a. Elizabeth and John (Lk. 1.5-25)

Following his introductory remarks about why he is writings his gospel and to whom, Luke opens his Infancy Narrative with the story of Elizabeth and Zechariah and the conception of John the Baptism. For four hundred years no prophetic voice had been heard among the people And the last words had been (Mal.4.5-6):

> Behold I will send you Elijah the prophet before the great and terrible day of the Lord come. And he will turn the heart of the fathers to the children, and the heart of the children to their fathers, lest I come and smite the land with a curse"

Now those dark days are ending, God was about to make good his words through the prophet for someone has come in the 'spirit and power of Elijah' to fulfil the words of Malachi. It is interesting to observe that these words are spoken by Malachi, a name which means 'my messenger' and the prophecy of Malachi, the *messenger* is to be fulfilled in another who is designated as *my messenger* (Lk. 7.27;[1] Mt. 11.10; Mk. 1.2[2]). Where one 'messenger' spoke the word that was followed by silence, now the new 'messenger' speaks the new word that will be followed by the proclamation about the coming one and the proclamation of the arrival of the kingdom by the one who comes. Luke immediately situates his story in history but situating it *in the days of Herod* (see below) and by naming Zechariah, a priest, and Elizabeth, his wife, also of priestly descent. Further, both of these Israelites were 'righteous' before God, who both observed the Law and were 'blameless'. Herod (the Great), king of Judea (and Judaea here must be understood in its broadest sense to encompass Samaria, Galilee and Peraea (Acts 2.9;[3] 10.37[4]; cf. Brown 1977:257). Josephus says that Herod was king from 37-5/1 BC. But the dating of this depends on whether the coins issued by his sons were dated correctly and which lunar eclipse Josephus is speaking of. If the census he speaks of in Lk. 2.1 was that of the time of the twenty-fifth anniversary of the Emperor Augustus which happened in 3 BC then 1 BC would be the accurate time of Herod's death which would place it two years after the events described in Mt. 2.16. This was a very difficult time for the Jews; they were under the occupation of the Romans and they had a Idumaen king and despite the fact that he had begun the Temple building programme, he was only a half Jew and had erected pagan buildings in the land. He was considered a tyrant and as dangerous to his children as he was to others. But he was obedient and submissive to Rome, otherwise he would not have held on to his kingdom for long. Luke, therefore, is making it clear that it is *in the days of Herod*,(see Fitzmyer 1978:402-405 for more details on precise dating) bloodthirsty, dangerous, traitorous and worldly days, that God revealed his plan to bring the true 'Son of David' to the throne and the contrast between the two could not have

---

[1] This is the one about whom it is written,"See, I am sending my messenger ahead of you, who will prepare your way before you."

[2] As it is written in the prophet Isaiah,
'See, I am sending my messenger ahead of you, who will prepare your way;

[3] Parthians, Medes, Elamites, and residents of Mesopotamia, Judea and Cappadocia, Pontus and Asia,

[4] That message spread throughout Judea, beginning in Galilee after the baptism that John announced.

been greater.

Like Matthew, Luke, for the moment, focuses on Zechariah who as a priest in the line of Abijah. The priesthood in Israel had been split into twenty four 'lines' or 'moments' since the time of David and though the progress of history had done serious damage to these lines, they, nevertheless, had been re-established (Fitzmyer 1978:322. Marshall 1978:53. Jeremais 1969: 198-207). Each line took its 'moment' to preside at Temple liturgies, usually about a week twice a year and because priests were ten a penny, presiding at Temple liturgies (for which lots were drawn) would be seen as a 'lottery win!' (see, Coleridge 1993:33;Green 1997:68). Therefore, as Luke presents it, Zechariah is in a once-in-a-lifetime moment (cf. Mc Bride 1982:24). At this point, Luke introduces Elisabeth, his wife who as descended from the line of Aaron, so both of these pious Jews are of priestly families. The Jews considered it a great blessing for a woman to marry into a priestly family and for a priest to marry a woman who was herself descended from a priestly family was a highly respected and honourable thing to do and reflected the priest's dedication to God. So Zechariah and Elizabeth are presented by Luke as true and righteous Israelites and of equal importance (see, Reid 1996:57). Luke is not saying that they were perfect even though (Lk. 1.6):

> Both of them were righteous before God, living blamelessly
> according to all the commandments and regulations of the Lord

but like Noah (Gen. 9.6[1]), they sought to please God and to obey his word (the Law). There was one area in which they would not be considered perfect, i.e., they had no children because *Elizabeth was barren* and to many people this would have looked as if Zechariah and Elizabeth were not everything they seemed to be or that their response to God was not quite as fulsome as it appeared. To be barren was seen to be under the disapproval

---

[1] Whoever sheds the blood of a human, by a human shall that person's blood be shed; for in his own image God made humankind.

of God and to Elizabeth this would have been particularly saddening as she had not been able to give her husband a son. It is nigh on impossible for us to understand what a stigma this was for a 'righteous' couple; people would see them and silently shake their heads. The rabbis would silently condemn them because in their minds a childless couple was a couple who were under God's severe reproach (see the interesting approach by Dornisch 1996:16. Yet this very experience of what her society understood as divine disapproval would be her vindication for she was to bear the 'messenger' who would proclaim the coming of the Messiah and prepare his way.

Luke tells us that Zechariah had been on duty in the Temple all week as he had been selected by lot to offer the incense at the hour of prayer (Lk. 1.9). This was made twice a day by the priests. Given that this would happen only once in a lifetime, since having been already chosen he would be excluded from further 'lots', Zechariah was both fortunate and privileged to find himself in this position. It should be noted here that Luke is highlighting the importance of both place and time here: the declaration of the conception and birth of John would take place at the most solemn time in Temple worship (the evening offering of incense, cf. Nolland 1993:29) so that everyone would know that the child was a direct gift from God (see argument of Coleridge 1993:33). Luke, therefore, is making it clear to Israel John's importance and how his coming is the response to the prayers of Israel which were offered at the time of incense (cf. Ps. 141.2[1]). Thus, everything about this announcement was sacred and to be remembered. It is during this time when the (Lk. 1.11-12):

> angel of the Lord appeared to him standing at the right side of
> the altar And Zachariah was troubled when he saw him, and
> fear fell on him.

But the angel replies in the standard reassurance formula, *Do not be afraid, Zachariah* (Lk. 1.11-12): and then imparts the news to him that his

---

[1]   Let my prayer be counted as incense before you, and the lifting up of my hands as an evening sacrifice.

supplication is heard, and his wife (Lk. 1.13):

Elizabeth will bear you a son, and you will call his name John

Deliverance was to come to Israel and both Zechariah and his wife would be central to its coming for a child would be given to them and his named would be called 'John' (Yo-annen='God is gracious') because through the child God would act *graciously*. The coming of the child will bring great joy not just to Zechariah and his wife but to the whole people and he will be filled with the Holy Spirit even before his birth (Lk. 1.14-15). And the work and ministry of this child will be such that many will be brought to repentance because it is for this reason that he is being sent: he is coming to bring people back to God and to prepare them for the day of deliverance (cf. Is. 49.6; cf. Benoit 1956-57:169-194). The turning back of the people to God is a constant theme in the Old Testament and was a sine qua non for the advent of the Messiah (e.g. Is. 30.15;[1] 31.6; 44.22; Is. 59.20; Jer. 3.14;[2] 24.7; Ezek. 33.11;[3] Dan. 12.3; Hos. 3.5;[4] 6.1; 12.6; 14.1-2; Joel 2.12-13,[5] 28-32; Zech. 1.3;[6] Mal. 3.7;[7] 4.6;). And Zechariah's and Elizabeth's child (Lk. 1.17):

---

[1] For thus said the Lord God, the Holy One of Israel: In returning and rest you shall be saved; in quietness and in trust shall be your strength. But you refused

[2] Return, O faithless children, says the Lord, for I am your master; I will take you, one from a city and two from a family, and I will bring you to Zion.

[3] Say to them, As I live, says the Lord God, I have no pleasure in the death of the wicked, but that the wicked turn from their ways and live; turn back, turn back from your evil ways; for why will you die, O house of Israel?

[4] Afterwards the Israelites shall return and seek the Lord their God, and David their king; they shall come in awe to the Lord and to his goodness in the latter days.

[5] Yet even now, says the Lord, return to me with all your heart, with fasting, with weeping, and with mourning; rend your hearts and not your clothing. Return to the Lord, your God, for he is gracious and merciful, slow to anger, and abounding in steadfast love, and relents from punishing.

[6] Therefore say to them, Thus says the Lord of hosts: Return to me, says the Lord of hosts, and I will return to you, says the Lord of hosts.

[7] Ever since the days of your ancestors you have turned aside from my statutes and have not kept them. Return to me, and I will return to you, says the Lord of hosts. But you say, 'How shall we return?'

> will go before his face in the spirit and power of Elijah, to turn
> the hearts of the fathers to the children, and the disobedient to
> walk in the wisdom of the just, to make ready for the Lord a
> people prepared for him

Elijah was a prophet who was closely connected the Spirit and the spirit of Elijah was passed on to Elisha (2 K 2.9,[1] 15) and now it was to be passed on to the son of Zechariah and Elizabeth and the end in view of all this would be the preparing of a people whose hearts were ready to receive the Lord.

There is no definite reference to the Messiah here because the description is probably based on Mal. 4.5 where there is no reference to the Messiah. The stress here falls on the fact that the child John will be the expected Elijah and since Elijah was to come before the *great and terrible Day of the Lord* the connection with the Messiah is hardly doubted and the connection with the Messiah in Lk. 1.67-79 is made very clear. And Elizabeth did conceive (Lk. 1.24-25):

> and she hid herself five months, saying, "Thus has the Lord
> done to me in the days on which he looked on me, to take away
> my reproach among men

She kept to her private room for five months with joy in her heart at the thought that her 'reproach' had been removed, and no doubt let it be known to some that God had heard their cry and given them a son (Reid 1996:61). He had graciously looked on her and taken away her 'reproach'. The five months of retirement, like Zachariah's enforced silence, (Lk. 1.20) would indicate that something especially remarkable was happening about which she wished to retain silence. Indeed the sign of Zachariah's dumbness might have made them feel that God did not want them to spread about what was happening. But with such a remarkable birth foretold she would also want

---

[1] When they had crossed, Elijah said to Elisha, 'Tell me what I may do for you, before I am taken from you.' Elisha said, 'Please let me inherit a double share of your spirit.'

time to meditate and prepare herself. We must not underestimate the sense of awe that must have filled her at the thought of what God had promised concerning her baby. She would clearly feel that such a privilege required special preparation, especially in view of the restriction on John. Perhaps she felt that he must not be tainted by the world while in her womb, for his necessary separation from the world had been revealed by the injunction laid on him to avoid wine and strong drink (1 S 1.15;[1] Judg. 13.4[2]). It was the same sense that would drive John into the wilderness.

It may be significant that 'five' is the number of the Covenant (see, Mulholland 2012:1.152-154). She was to be seen as revealing her covenant faithfulness. But there may have been another explanation. Elizabeth was known to be past the child bearing age and for some time she would not be able to say whether what the angel had said was true and perhaps she hid herself from the prying questions that would inevitable be asked. Her period of isolation came to an end *in the sixth month* (Lk. 1.26) because that was when Mary visited her and Elizabeth received her. But even in this there was significance because the first to come in contact with Elizabeth's newly conceived child in her womb (Lk. 1.41) was the one who was to be the mother of the Messiah, of whom Elizabeth's child was immediately aware and to whom one day her child would give witness. The promise had been given of the coming of the one who would prepare the way of the Lord, the birth had now taken place and so the next event could be the promise and the coming of the Messiah himself.

b. Mary and Jesus (Lk. 1.26-38)

Luke now momentarily interrupts the narrative of Elizabeth and John and begins his narrative of the annunciation and birth of Jesus. Luke's focus here is quite clearly on Mary and her role in the annunciation and birth of the Messiah and, of course, this is contrasted with Matthew's focus on

---

[1] But Hannah answered, 'No, my lord, I am a woman deeply troubled; I have drunk neither wine nor strong drink, but I have been pouring out my soul before the Lord.

[2] Now be careful not to drink wine or strong drink, or to eat anything unclean.

Joseph. Luke will later bring the story of Elizabeth and Mary and their children together when he narrates the moment traditionally referred to as 'The Visitation', (Lk. 1.39-56) then go on to complete the Elizabeth and John narrative with the birth of John (Lk. 1.57-65) and then complete the Mary and Jesus narrative with the birth and childhood of Jesus (Lk. 2.1-52). The two birth narratives, therefore, share certain characteristics with both Elizabeth and Mary playing important central roles (Brown 1977:295-297; Fitzmyer 1983:334; Marshall 1978:62). Lk. 1.26-38 can be understood as a unit within themselves and connected with the phrase *in the sixth month*. It might be noted here that the emphasis in this section is not on the virginal conception as such but on how this will actually come about since the woman who is to conceive is a virgin.

While Mary has an important role in this and while Luke does make her the focus of the angel's message and annunciation, she is, nevertheless, in the background since the section is firmly centred on the one who is to be born and who he is: the only *Son of God, Son of the Most High* who is not conceived as the result of a human father. Having said that, however, Mary's role cannot simply be sidelined as a 'walk on part' or a cameo: her response to the angel's message is crucial. The birth of the 'Son of the Most *High'* *from* a virgin is without doubt in this passage and her purity and virginity is seen as necessary for what has been promised and what will actually happen. In this sense, therefore, God's activity will take place through a pure and untouched 'source' and in titling the child as *Son of the Most High* and *Son of God*, Luke is also emphasising the 'otherness' of Jesus. The name *Mary* (Miriam, Maria) probably means 'exalted/favoured one' which is how the angel Gabriel addresses her.

In 1.26-27 Luke describes the sending of the angel Gabriel and does so through the use of key words: the *angel Gabriel, Galilee, Nazareth, Virgin, house of David*, and in doing so not only sets the scene for what follows but also shows how unbelievable it was. Gabriel is sent to *Nazareth* in *Galilee* immediately any self-respecting Jew would be raising their eyebrows for nothing *good can come from Galilee* (Jn. 1.46) and certainly no prophet ever came from Galilee (Jn. 7.52[1]). This was *Galilee of the nations*, which while it may be Jewish, it was only just so (cf. 1 Macc.5.15;Is.9.1). It was a place to be despised; they were an agricultural people, unsophisticated and barely comprehensible with their thick easily recognisable accents (Mk. 14.70). The rabbis considered them as lacking in the appropriate behaviour and Nazareth itself was a nothing town, insignificant and meaningless. On top of this, Galilee was a place that would launch into a rebellion at the drop of a hat. It was 'different' from the rest of Judea because although it was controlled by the Romans, it was ruled by the even more despised Herod who himself was not even a true Jew. So the idea of Gabriel, who stood in the presence of God, making an appearance at Nazareth in Galilee was an idea too ridiculous to even contemplate. But it was so, because it was from Nazareth that God would choose to bring forth the one who was greater than any of the prophets.

Gabriel had come to a *virgin* and the fact that Luke states this twice (*to a virgin...and the virgin's name..*) indicates that he wants to emphasise this important point and leave the reader in no doubt that Gabriel is sent to a virgin, i.e., one who has not had sexual relations (Green 1992:464;Ilan 1995:68). Mary is a *betrothed* virgin, i.e., though not yet married she was, nevertheless, legally bonded to her future husband (Loewe :22-23). The normal period of betrothal was about a year and while sexual relations between a betrothed couple was not forbidden, it was, however, frowned upon. But Luke makes it clear that there was no such behaviour in this case (Fitzmyer 1978:56).

Mary is betrothed to Joseph who, Luke tells us, is *of the House of David* which means that Joseph, as a son of David, was heir to the royal throne. This was why at Lk. 2.4 he had to return to Bethlehem his home town, the site of his lands and place of his family. But it is important that Luke states that Joseph is of David's house and so as the legal father of Jesus that would mean that his 'adopted' son was also a son of David and therefore

---

[1] They replied, 'Surely you are not also from Galilee, are you? Search and you will see that no prophet is to arise from Galilee.'

heir to the promise. Other than Mary was a 'virgin' and that she came from Nazareth, nothing else is known of her but it maybe that the genealogy in Lk. 3.23-38 is of Mary which would then mean that she too was of the house of David and given that Luke says her son will be of the line of David there may be some substance in this.

The angel greets Mary with, *Hail, highly favoured one, the Lord is with you* Lk. 1.28). *Hail* is probably Luke's rendering of the Hebrew 'shalom' thus he is making it clear that Gabriel has come to make an announcement for Greeks too but since this was also the manner in which the Emperor was addressed perhaps Mary is being addressed like an Emperor in recognition of the annunciation of the nature of the child she is to bear (*Son of the Most High, Son of God*). Every woman in Israel wanted to be the mother of the Messiah and with the appearance of Gabriel in this backwater town the mother of the Messiah had been chosen and so Mary is *highly favoured* (see, Coleridge 1993:55 for full discussion on what this means). This was not because Mary was perfect for later on she would rebuke Jesus after finding him in the Temple (Lk. 2.48-49) and later on, motivated by anxiety and worry for her son's mental health, she would try to interfere with his ministry and have to be put straight on that issue (Mk. 3.21, 31-35; Jn. 2.4), but God saw deeper than that and knew her to be a fitting mother for his son. The term could also be used of physical beauty (Eccl. 9.8) or moral excellence (Eccl. 18.17) but it does not mean it is something hat can be passed on or signify 'full of grace' in that sense. The *Lord is with* Mary and this is an Old Testament idea (Ruth 2.4;[1] 2 Chron. 15.2;[2] Zech. 8.23[3]) and can therefore be contrasted with the *Hail* thus allowing Luke to emphasise the universality of the angel's message. Mary would be the mother of a child without a father; she was betrothed, there would be shame, humiliation,

---

[1] Just then Boaz came from Bethlehem. He said to the reapers, 'The Lord be with you.' They answered, 'The Lord bless you.'

[2] He went out to meet Asa and said to him, 'Hear me, Asa, and all Judah and Benjamin: The Lord is with you, while you are with him. If you seek him, he will be found by you, but if you abandon him, he will abandon you.

[3] Thus says the Lord of hosts: In those days ten men from nations of every language shall take hold of a Jew, grasping his garment and saying, 'Let us go with you, for we have heard that God is with you.'

suspicion, mistrust, hurt and disappointment and perhaps even public divorce proceedings against her. But the Lord was *with her* in a way in which he was with no other woman for from her would come the human child Jesus who would be the divine Son of God.

We need to tread carefully here and not see this as an over exaltation of Mary, the emphasis here is on the child she will conceive and give birth to, Mary is favoured because of the extraordinary part she will play in all this, she is *highly* favoured, more so than Elizabeth, more so than any other woman before or after her but the favour is from God and she is its recipient. Mary's response to this encounter is to be *greatly troubled* and to wonder *what this greeting could mean* (Lk. 1.29). The words *greatly troubled* have been used as Lk. 1.12 but here they have a stronger meaning (on the theories about the source of this alarm see, Coleridge 1993:58;. Something great is about to be asked of Mary and so something great will be expected of her and perhaps her mind recalled other women who had angelic visitors with both the joy and sorrow that came from such visits: Sara, the wife of Abraham the prospective mother of Isaac who had had to be rebuked because she had not believed (Gen. 18.10-15[1]), and the wife of Manoah (Judg. 13.3-5,[2] 9). Mary would have known of these great women of Israel's past and what they had been through and Mary did not feel she could measure up to them for she was only a teenage girl from a nowhere and so desperately she searched her mind and heart for what all this meant (see, Nolland 1993:87 for a more cautious approach).

Gabriel, however, immediately reassures her: she was favoured by God

---

[1]   Then one said, 'I will surely return to you in due season, and your wife Sarah shall have a son.' And Sarah was listening at the tent entrance behind him. Now Abraham and Sarah were old, advanced in age; it had ceased to be with Sarah after the manner of women. So Sarah laughed to herself, saying, 'After I have grown old, and my husband is old, shall I have pleasure?' The Lord said to Abraham, 'Why did Sarah laugh, and say, "Shall I indeed bear a child, now that I am old?" Is anything too wonderful for the Lord? At the set time I will return to you, in due season, and Sarah shall have a son.' But Sarah denied, saying, 'I did not laugh'; for she was afraid. He said, 'Oh yes, you did laugh.'

[2]   And the angel of the Lord appeared to the woman and said to her, 'Although you are barren, having borne no children, you shall conceive and bear a son. Now be careful not to drink wine or strong drink, or to eat anything unclean, for you shall conceive and bear a son. No razor is to come on his head, for the boy shall be a nazirite to God from birth. It is he who shall begin to deliver Israel from the hand of the Philistines.'

and God wanted to bless her and now he reveals to her what God expects of her. She is to *conceive,* to bring forth *a son* and call his name *Jesus* (Lk. 1.30) and the very way in which this is said implied a birth from a virgin for she was not married, young and had had no sexual relations with a man: she was to conceive in her own womb and bring forth her own son. The word reflects Is. 7.14 in the LXX (Septuagint):

> Behold the virgin shall conceive in her womb and bear a son,
> and will call his name Emmanuel

(when this is read in the Greek the wording is very similar to that here of Luke and may even had had a translation for Is. 7.14 which was even closer). Mary has already been declared a *virgin* in Lk. 1.27 and it may be this similarity that raises in her mind the questions she asks at Lk. 1.34. The name of the child is to be *Jesus* (Ye-sous) which means 'God is salvation' and the naming of Jesus recalls and parallels the naming of John indicating that both these children are under the protection of God and just as the child in Is. 7.14 is named by God so too is John and so too is Jesus and the names they are given reflect the nature of what they will be when they are born. Mary's child will

- be great
- be called the son of the Most High.
- receive from the Lord God the throne of his father David.
- reign for ever over the house of Jacob.
- have a kingdom of which there will be no end.

The child of Mary will be *great*, as John was said to be *great in the sight of the Lord* at Lk. 1.5 but the child of Mary will be great because of who he is: *Son of the Most High*. The attribute *great* is used in the Acts (8.9-

10^1) by the Jews to describe God; it is used in Pss. 48.1;[2] 76.1;[3] 86.10;[4] 96.4;[5] 99.2;[6] 135.5;[7] 145.3;[8] 147.5.[9] The description therefore has divine overtones, especially in parallel with *the Son of the Most High*. In the annunciation of John's birth it was said that the son of Elizabeth would be the *prophet of the Most High* (Lk. 1.76) (a startling statement since there had been no prophets in Israel after Malachi some four hundred years before this announcement) but here the son of Mary is the *Son of the Most High* and thus far outranks John in glory.

This is highlighted again by Luke in his version of the 'Parable of the Tenants' (Lk. 20.9-18[10]) where *after the prophets came the son* so the distinction between Jesus and John is drawn at the very beginning. There are no references to the Messiah ever being 'the Son of God' so what is being stated here goes far beyond simply being the Messiah. The title *Most High* is first used of God in Gen. 14.18,[11] 19, 20, 22 in connection with

---

[1] Now a certain man named Simon had previously practised magic in the city and amazed the people of Samaria, saying that he was someone great. All of them, from the least to the greatest, listened to him eagerly, saying, 'This man is the power of God that is called Great.'

[2] Great is the Lord and greatly to be praised in the city of our God. His holy mountain,

[3] In Judah God is known, his name is great in Israel.

[4] For you are great and do wondrous things; you alone are God.

[5] For great is the Lord, and greatly to be praised; he is to be revered above all gods.

[6] The Lord is great in Zion; he is exalted over all the peoples.

[7] For I know that the Lord is great; our Lord is above all gods.

[8] Great is the Lord, and greatly to be praised; his greatness is unsearchable.

[9] Great is our Lord, and abundant in power; his understanding is beyond measure.

[10] He began to tell the people this parable: 'A man planted a vineyard, and leased it to tenants, and went to another country for a long time. When the season came, he sent a slave to the tenants in order that they might give him his share of the produce of the vineyard; but the tenants beat him and sent him away empty-handed. Next he sent another slave; that one also they beat and insulted and sent away empty-handed. And he sent yet a third; this one also they wounded and threw out. Then the owner of the vineyard said, "What shall I do? I will send my beloved son; perhaps they will respect him." But when the tenants saw him, they discussed it among themselves and said, "This is the heir; let us kill him so that the inheritance may be ours." So they threw him out of the vineyard and killed him. What then will the owner of the vineyard do to them? He will come and destroy those tenants and give the vineyard to others.' When they heard this, they said, 'Heaven forbid!' But he looked at them and said, 'What then does this text mean:"The stone that the builders rejected has become the cornerstone"? Everyone who falls on that stone will be broken to pieces; and it will crush anyone on whom it falls.'

[11] And King Melchizedek of Salem brought out bread and wine; he was priest of God Most High.

Melchizedek (Heb.7.1[1]) and again at Num. 24.16[2] in connection with Balaam. Moses used it of God in Deut. 32.8.[3] In Ps. 82.6[4] the judges in Israel were called *elohim* (gods) and *sons of the Most High* because they acted in the place of God. But the son of Mary will be the unique son. Outside the Psalms (e.g., Pss. 18.13;[5] 78.35;[6] 89.27[7]) it is used mainly by foreigners and the most emphatic use of it is to be found in Dan. 7 where *saints of the Most High* will receive the everlasting kingdom from God through a 'son of man' who will come with the clouds of heaven to the throne of God and receive it. That this approaching 'son of man' must be the representative of Israel is clear in the passage, and would undoubtedly bring to mind Israel's king, the son of David. Thus *Son of the Most High* may well also have in mind this earthly/heavenly figure who acts on behalf of 'the saints of the Most High', thus already connecting Jesus with the Son of Man, and with the saints of the Most High. The same connection seems to be being made here by Luke: the son of Mary is *the Son of the Most High* which clearly reveals his highly exalted status but in Lk. 6.35[8] the people of God are urged to reveal themselves as son of the *Most High* by their unselfish generosity and loving their enemies, in the same way God is kind to the ungrateful and the selfish (Evans 1990:25) The *sons* of the Most High are those who look to <u>the</u> Son of the Most High and seek to be like him in the same way the *saints* of the Most High looked to the 'son of man'.

The son of Mary will receive the *throne of his father David* and to Mary this would have simply meant that he would be restored to the throne

---

[1] This 'King Melchizedek of Salem, priest of the Most High God, met Abraham as he was returning from defeating the kings and blessed him'

[2] The oracle of one who hears the words of God, and knows the knowledge of the Most High, who sees the vision of the Almighty, who falls down, but with his eyes uncovered

[3] When the Most High apportioned the nations, when he divided humankind, he fixed the boundaries of the peoples according to the number of the gods

[4] I say, 'You are gods, children of the Most High, all of you.

[5] The Lord also thundered in the heavens, and the Most High uttered his voice.

[6] They remembered that God was their rock, the Most High God their redeemer.

[7] I will make him the firstborn, the highest of the kings of the earth.

[8] But love your enemies, do good, and lend, expecting nothing in return. Your reward will be great, and you will be children of the Most High; for he is kind to the ungrateful and the wicked.

that was his by right of birth. But his reign would be *for ever* and this is certainly not a reference to a millennium reign (cf. Rev. 20.1-6.[1] It might be noted here that Jesus never alludes to a 'limited' messianic reign). What is envisaged here is an eternal kingdom (Ps. 45.7;[2] 93.2;[3] Is. 9.6,7;[4] Dan. 7:14,[5] 18) and this would indicate to Mary at least some element of the supernatural. Her child would be more than an 'earthly' Messiah and in Ezek. 37.25[6] and 2 S 7.13, 16[7] the king who was to come would rule forever which may, of course, mean that it was the *house* that would rule forever. But here it is made clear to Mary that her child is to reign everlastingly (Is. 9.7) since he is born through supernatural birth with a supernatural future clearly in view. It is not being suggested here that Mary fully understood all this nor indeed would she fully understand her child in the future but it was being made clear to her that this is more than an earthly kingship. Her son would be the expected Messiah, an everlasting Messiah and more: in her child, heaven would break through into everlastingness.

Mary's response to this is both tenderly innocent and practical: how is

---

[1] Then I saw an angel coming down from heaven, holding in his hand the key to the bottomless pit and a great chain. He seized the dragon, that ancient serpent, who is the Devil and Satan, and bound him for a thousand years, and threw him into the pit, and locked and sealed it over him, so that he would deceive the nations no more, until the thousand years were ended. After that he must be let out for a little while. Then I saw thrones, and those seated on them were given authority to judge. I also saw the souls of those who had been beheaded for their testimony to Jesus and for the word of God. They had not worshipped the beast or its image and had not received its mark on their foreheads or their hands. They came to life and reigned with Christ for a thousand years. (The rest of the dead did not come to life until the thousand years were ended.) This is the first resurrection. Blessed and holy are those who share in the first resurrection. Over these the second death has no power, but they will be priests of God and of Christ, and they will reign with him for a thousand years.

[2] You love righteousness and hate wickedness. Therefore God, your God, has anointed you with the oil of gladness beyond your companions

[3] Your throne is established from of old; you are from everlasting.

[4] For a child has been born for us, a son given to us; authority rests upon his shoulders; and he is named Wonderful Counsellor, Mighty God, Everlasting Father, Prince of Peace.

[5] O him was given dominion and glory and kingship, that all peoples, nations, and languages should serve him. His dominion is an everlasting dominion that shall not pass away, and his kingship is one that shall never be destroyed.

[6] They shall live in the land that I gave to my servant Jacob, in which your ancestors lived; they and their children and their children's children shall live there for ever; and my servant David shall be their prince for ever.

[7] He shall build a house for my name, and I will establish the throne of his kingdom for ever;

all this to happen since *I know not a man* (i.e., a virgin). The word *know* in Hebrew implies an intimate, personal relationship (cf. Jer. 1.5[1]), even a sexual union (cf. Gen. 4.1;[2] 1 S 1.19[3]). This same idiom is used in the same sense in the Septuagint (cf. Judg. 11.39;[4] 21.12[5]). Mary stands there as a teenage girl listening high-powered, complex theological ideas and responds with the only practical difficulty that she can see to it: since she was betrothed, not married and had no husband and thus had not had sexual intercourse, how was this going to happen? (on the nature of this question see, Coleridge 1993:64; Brown 1977:280). The fact that Mary asks the question would seem to indicate that there is an immediacy about this event.

These words are central to the passage which is constructed around them. So, when the normal interpretation is applied to this it can only mean one thing: a remarkable conception and birth which would produce a unique human being who would be like the God called *holy* in Is. 57.15. as God's Son, the child would be of the same nature of God. Mary may well have been utterly bewildered and confused by this and unable to understand what was being proposed to her at the time but there was only one place in scripture that this could be applied: the prophecy of Is. 7.14 where the failure of the sons of David meant that they would be replaced by one not born of the heirs of David but born miraculously from a woman, pure and unmarried of marriageable age, i.e., a virgin. Her son would be called *Everlasting God* and would rule over God's everlasting kingdom (Is. 9.6-7). No one can fully appreciate the significance of this, so how a teenage girl could is beyond any comprehension for it is way beyond the limited mind of humanity.

---

[1] 'Before I formed you in the womb I knew you, and before you were born I consecrated you; I appointed you a prophet to the nations.'

[2] Now the man knew his wife Eve, and she conceived and bore Cain, saying, 'I have produced a man with the help of the Lord.'

[3] They rose early in the morning and worshipped before the Lord; then they went back to their house at Ramah. Elkanah knew his wife Hannah, and the Lord remembered her.

[4] Jephthah said to the elders of Gilead, 'If you bring me home again to fight with the Ammonites, and the Lord gives them over to me, I will be your head.'

[5] And they found among the inhabitants of Jabesh-gilead four hundred young virgins who had never slept with a man and brought them to the camp at Shiloh, which is in the land of Canaan.

It would be by the power of the *Most High* who would come upon her and cast his shadow over her, not a man but the *Holy Spirit*. This is why the one born from her would be *Son of the Most High,* because the one in whose power the child would be conceived was holy and thus her child would be a holy thing who would be a man and yet be called *the Son of God* because though born of Mary he would be begotten of the Holy Spirit and so begotten of God (Jn. 1.14, 18;[1] 1 Jn. 5.1[2] Le Verdiere 1984:19)). The reply from Gabriel was because the Holy Spirit would *overshadow* her and so the child who she would give birth to would be called *holy*, the *Son of God.* *Overshadow* seems to be related to the Old Testament 'shekinah' cloud of the wilderness wanderings which symbolised God's presence (cf. LXX Exod. 40.35[3]). The same term in Greek is used of God's presence overshadowing the inner circle of Apostles at the Transfiguration (cf. Mt. 17.5;[4] Mk. 7.9; Lk. 9.34), it showed his personal presence and power.

As already noted, this was not a sexual experience for God or Mary; the Spirit does not have a physical, human body. There is a parallel relationship between: *The Holy Spirit will come upon you* and *the power of the Most High will overshadow you.* In this context it is not the person of the Spirit that is emphasised but that Old Testament concept of the Spirit as the power of God that goes forth to do God's bidding (cf. Gen. 1.2[5]). As the power of God *came upon* Mary to accomplish its purposes, so too did it come upon the early church (cf. Acts 1:8). Mary's child, therefore,

---

[1] And the Word became flesh and lived among us, and we have seen his glory, the glory as of a father's only son, full of grace and truth; No one has ever seen God. It is God the only Son, who is close to the Father's heart, who has made him known.

[2] Everyone who believes that Jesus is the Christ has been born of God, and everyone who loves the parent loves the child.

[3] And Moses was not able to enter into the tabernacle of testimony, because the cloud overshadowed it, and the tabernacle was filled with the glory of the Lord.

[4] While he was still speaking, suddenly a bright cloud overshadowed them, and from the cloud a voice said, 'This is my Son, the Beloved; with him I am well pleased; listen to him!'

[5] the earth was a formless void and darkness covered the face of the deep, while the Spirit of God swept over the face of the waters.

> in Mark's words would be *Son of God*,
> in John's words, *Word made flesh*,
> in Luke's words, *Son of the Most High*,
> in Matthew's words, *Son of Abraham, Son of David*

It should be noted here that we are told of what will happen, Luke does not describe Mary's actual physical experience because it it not susceptible to a human description. This was the result of the power of God probably without Mary even being aware of it in that she would not even know the moment when conception took place. The Holy Spirit was to fill John from his mother's womb, but the one described here comes because the Holy Spirit comes on Mary and works within her in divine power, before he is in the womb, producing one who is in his manhood 'of the Spirit' even in his conception.

The son of Elizabeth and the son of Mary are then seen as being contrasted in a number of ways as the following table outlines:

The Son of Elizabeth	The Son of Mary
The messenger is called Yo-annen (God is gracious, Lk. 1.13)	The Son is called Ye-sous (God is salvation, Lk. 1.31).
The messenger is called 'the prophet of the Most High' (Lk. 1.76)	The Son is called 'the Son of the Most High' (Lk. 1. 32).
The messenger is filled with the Holy Spirit after he is conceived (Lk. 1.15),	The Son is conceived by the Holy Spirit (Lk. 1. 35).
The messenger comes to proclaim the One Who is coming,	The Son comes in order to be the Coming One, the everlasting King.
The messenger would be 'great in the sight of the Lord' (Lk. 1.15),	The Son would essentially *be* great (Lk. 1.32), great in every way.

As if to emphasise the power of the divine in this conception, Gabriel informs Mary that (Lk. 1.36-37):

> your relative Elizabeth in her old age has also conceived a son;
> and this is the sixth month for her who was said to be barren.
> For nothing will be impossible with God.

This statement refers to Lk. 1.36, but also to Gabriel's message to Mary (Lk. 1.26-35). Elizabeth's pregnancy was a way of confirming God's supernatural actions in human conception (cf. LXX of Gen. 18.14[1]). This phrase *nothing will be impossible with God* is an Old Testament idiom of God's power accomplishing his purposes (cf. Job 42.2;[2] Jer. 32.17;[3] Zech. 8.6[4]). It may be an allusion to Gen. 18.14, which deals specifically with the birth of Isaac (another supernatural, but not virgin, birth). It also occurs in a similar affirmation in Mk. 10.27[5] and Lk. 18.27.[6] Mary may have already known about Elizabeth but Gabriel is not simply providing Mary with information, he was pointing out the significance of the two conceptions and births for he points out that Elizabeth conception in her old age was just as God had promised through the word spoken by Gabriel himself.

That word had been effective and demonstrated that no word of God was ever without power and Mary, therefore, could be sure that the word spoken to her by God through Gabriel would be just as effective. But there is also compassion in Gabriel's words for Mary's world was about to be turned upside down, as had Elizabeth's, and if Mary needed to speak to someone then who better than a female relative whose own world had been turned upside down by the same power of God. After hearing all this Mary's response is open, generous and willing (Lk. 1.38):

---

[1] Shall anything be impossible with the Lord? At this time I will return to thee seasonably, and Sarrha shall have a son.

[2] 'I know that you can do all things, and that no purpose of yours can be thwarted.

[3] Ah Lord God! It is you who made the heavens and the earth by your great power and by your outstretched arm! Nothing is too hard for you.

[4] Thus says the Lord of hosts: Even though it seems impossible to the remnant of this people in these days, should it also seem impossible to me, says the Lord of hosts?

[5] Jesus looked at them and said, 'For mortals it is impossible, but not for God; for God all things are possible.'

[6] He replied, 'What is impossible for mortals is possible for God.'

> Here am I, the servant of the Lord; let it be with me according
> to your word.

Here Mary is presented as an example of faith showing complete trust in the word that has just been announced to her and she accepts the word and responds generously (Coleridge 1993:69; McBride 1982:27). The way would not be easy, of course, and she would make mistakes, not understand sometimes and even attempt to block her son's ministry but the Lord was with her and her faith was solidly grounded.

Mary and Elizabeth (Lk. 1.39-55)

a. Elizabeth's Response To Mary (Lk. 1.39-45)

In terms of the narrative, this meeting expands Luke's characterisation and is the pivot of the chapter (see Green 1992:468). Although it is the two women who meet, the narrative is really about the meeting of the two children. Elizabeth's time of retreat is partly interrupted by Mary in its sixth month (which explains why it is only five months) but it is not a source of irritation for Elizabeth because the arrival of Mary brings with it a sign from God of the relationship that will exist between Jesus and John (on the unusualness of Mary's journey cf. Reid 1996:70; Green 1997: 94-95). It is being made clear that the revelations continue through the outpouring of the Spirit and it demonstrates that the times of the Spirit being poured out is nearly upon the world, for these are the first fruits of prophecy that will be poured out on the world. No reason is given why Mary left and went to Elizabeth in *haste* but it may have been because the teenage Mary was in an anxious state and wanted the advice of the older and wiser Elizabeth (see Brown 1977:341). Elizabeth does seem to be aware of something about Mary's condition for as soon as Mary greets her the *child in* her (*my*) *womb* leaps *for joy* (Lk. 1.41a). Luke has already told us that John was *filled with the Holy Spirit in his mother's womb* (Lk. 1.15) and even at six months old was aware of the one who would bring the *Son of the Most High* into the world.

The rabbis had asserted that children in the womb could respond to spiritual things and a lot in this passage parallels Gen. 25.22-26, though there are some major differences. In Genesis there is internal tension as Jacob and Esau struggle for supremacy in the womb. Here there is a total absence of tension: John *leaped for joy* (Lk. 14.1, 44) at the presence of Jesus' mother, who bears Jesus in her womb (see for discussions around this issue, Brown 1977:365; Green 1997:95; Nolland 1993:66; Fitzmyer 363). John's ministry starts in the womb; he is a forerunner even as he responds in Elizabeth's womb to the presence of the newly conceived Jesus (Lk. 1.14-15). The next note of fulfilment of the angelic promises comes at Lk. 1.42b-45 when Elizabeth *filled with the Holy Spirit* becomes a spontaneous prophetess lifts up her voice and she expresses the mind of God when she exclaims with a loud cry (cf. McBride 1982:29) (which indicates her emotive state) (Lk. 1.42-45):

> Blessed are you among women, and blessed is the fruit of your womb. And why has this happened to me, that the mother of my Lord comes to me? For as soon as I heard the sound of your greeting, the child in my womb leapt for joy. And blessed is she who believed that there would be a fulfilment of what was spoken to her by the Lord.

Elizabeth is exemplary in her response, (cf. Reid 1996:72) she is the *amazed saint*. Her attitude is summarised in the question, *Why am I so favoured?* (Lk. 1.43) Here is humble amazement at being able to participate directly in God's plan and see him at work (2 S 6.9; [1]24.21[2]). Elizabeth's emphasis here is on *the Lord* just as Mary's response will also be in a moment for Elizabeth and Mary are not exalting each other but *the Lord* as they are both humbled by what has happened to them (McBride 1984:29-30). *Blessed..blessed* are

---

[1] David was afraid of the Lord that day; he said, 'How can the ark of the Lord come into my care?'

[2] Araunah said, 'Why has my lord the king come to his servant?' David said, 'To buy the threshing-floor from you in order to build an altar to the Lord, so that the plague may be averted from the people.'

both exclamatory forms (Hebrew and Aramaic), like Ps. 1.1 (no verbs). These are also both perfect passive participles. Mary is blessed for a divine purpose. The world is blessed because of her child (cf. Gen. 3.15[1]). Mary is truly *blessed among all women* because she is the one chosen to be the mother of the Messiah. At this time and in this culture women saw one of their primary functions to be that of wife and mother; it was what they saw themselves as living for, their primary purpose in life and so Mary is *blessed* by being given this great privilege. Mary is blessed because of *there will be a fulfilment of the things spoken to her* (Lk. 1.45); these things spoken to her will come to their end. Mary is not blessed because of what she is in herself, she is not being exalted here. Later in Luke (Lk. 11.27-28[2]) when a woman in crowd cries out that Mary is blessed because she is his mother, Jesus will reject the idea and rather blessed those who heard the word of God and kept it. Elizabeth immediately turns to what she knows is more important than the mother: the child she bears. And here is the idea of the fuller, undefined blessing, here is the one to be exalted and Elizabeth's humility shines out here (Lk. 1.43):

> why has this happened to me, that the mother of my Lord comes to me?

Elizabeth is using the theologically significant term *Lord* (cf. Ex. 3.14;[3] Ps. 110.1[4]) to refer to the unborn Messiah (cf. Lk. 2.14). The filling of the Spirit has clearly opened her eyes as he did for Simeon in Lk. 2.26;[5] for Anna in

---

[1] I will put enmity between you and the woman, and between your offspring and hers; he will strike your head, and you will strike his heel.'

[2] While he was saying this, a woman in the crowd raised her voice and said to him, 'Blessed is the womb that bore you and the breasts that nursed you!' But he said, 'Blessed rather are those who hear the word of God and obey it!'

[3] God said to Moses, 'I am who I am.' He said further, 'Thus you shall say to the Israelites, "I am has sent me to you." '

[4] The Lord says to my lord,'Sit at my right hand until I make your enemies your footstool.'

[5] It had been revealed to him by the Holy Spirit that he would not see death before he had seen the Lord's Messiah.

Lk. 2.36-38;[6] for Nathanael in Jn. 1.49;[7] and for Peter in Mt. 16.16.[8] Elizabeth uses the same Greek term, *Lord*, of God in vv.45 and vv. 46-47 (by means of his messenger angel). In later Jewish worship the Jews were nervous of pronouncing the covenant name for God, YHWH, so they substituted the Hebrew term *Adon* (husband, owner, master, lord) for it in their reading of Scripture. This in turn affected later translations like the English ones, which use Lord for YHWH and Lord for *Adon* (cf. Ps. 110.1[9]). So here in Elizabeth is the open recognition that the child forming in the womb of Mary is already her *Lord*. Elizabeth blesses Mary again when she says (Lk. 1.45):

> And blessed is she who believed that there would be a fulfilment
> of what was spoken to her by the Lord.

This is a different Greek word for *blessed* ('makaria') than in v.42 (twice), which is 'eulogeō'. The term in v.42 is used only of God (once of Mary in 1.42), while the term in v.45 is used of humans (cf. Lk. 6.20-23;[8] Mt. 5.3-11[9]). Here is the essence of the response to God, to trust his word to be true

---

[6]   There was also a prophet, Anna the daughter of Phanuel, of the tribe of Asher. She was of a great age, having lived with her husband for seven years after her marriage, then as a widow to the age of eighty-four. She never left the temple but worshipped there with fasting and prayer night and day. At that moment she came, and began to praise God and to speak about the child to all who were looking for the redemption of Jerusalem.

[7]   Nathanael replied, 'Rabbi, you are the Son of God! You are the King of Israel!'

[8]   Simon Peter answered, 'You are the Messiah, the Son of the living God.'

[9]   The Lord says to my lord,'Sit at my right hand until I make your enemies your footstool.'

[8]   Then he looked up at his disciples and said:'Blessed are you who are poor, for yours is the kingdom of God. 'Blessed are you who are hungry now, for you will be filled.'Blessed are you who weep now, for you will laugh.'Blessed are you when people hate you, and when they exclude you, revile you, and defame you on account of the Son of Man. Rejoice on that day and leap for joy, for surely your reward is great in heaven; for that is what their ancestors did to the prophets.

[9]   'Blessed are the poor in spirit, for theirs is the kingdom of heaven. 'Blessed are those who mourn, for they will be comforted. 'Blessed are the meek, for they will inherit the earth. 'Blessed are those who hunger and thirst for righteousness, for they will be filled. 'Blessed are the merciful, for they will receive mercy. 'Blessed are the pure in heart, for they will see God. 'Blessed are the peacemakers, for they will be called children of God. 'Blessed are those who are persecuted for righteousness' sake, for theirs is the kingdom of heaven. 'Blessed are you when people revile you and persecute you and utter all kinds of evil against you falsely on my account.

and live in the light of that belief. To be *blessed* is to be happy because God has touched one's life. Such divine benefit rains down on those who trust him and his promises. Blessing emerges from God's ability to bring his promises to completion, but to share the benefits, we must be confident that God does what he says. The first sign of such faith in Mary was her willingness to let God use her (Lk.1.38). The second was her immediate visit to Elizabeth (*with haste*), who herself served as a sign that God keeps his word and can give life (Lk.1.36, 39). Elizabeth's joy is shared by Mary, who will utter a hymn of praise to God for his gracious work on her behalf. Mary's psalm also comes from the heart of a grateful believer.

b. Mary's Response: Magnificat (Lk. 1.46-55)

The response that Mary gives to Elizabeth's welcome and greeting of her her is full of spontaneous joy and echoes Old Testament language with a perspective that sees the present in light of God's consistent activity throughout time (see McBride 1984:30). The 'Magnificat' clearly echoes the ideas in the song of Hannah (1 S 2.1-11[1]) and reflects Old Testament thought continuously (e.g., 98.3;[2] 111.9;[3] 103.17;[4] 107.9;[5] and see

---

[1]   Hannah prayed and said,'My heart exults in the Lordmy strength is exalted in my God.My mouth derides my enemies, because I rejoice in my victory. 'There is no Holy One like the Lord, no one besides you; there is no Rock like our God. Talk no more so very proudly, let not arrogance come from your mouth; for the Lord is a God of knowledge, and by him actions are weighed. The bows of the mighty are broken, but the feeble gird on strength. Those who were full have hired themselves out for bread, but those who were hungry are fat with spoil. The barren has borne seven, but she who has many children is forlorn. The Lord kills and brings to life; he brings down to Sheol and raises up. The Lord makes poor and makes rich; he brings low, he also exalts. He raises up the poor from the dust; he lifts the needy from the ash heap, to make them sit with princes and inherit a seat of honour. For the pillars of the earth are the Lord's, and on them he has set the world. 'He will guard the feet of his faithful ones, but the wicked shall be cut off in darkness; for not by might does one prevail. The Lord! His adversaries shall be shattered; the Most High will thunder in heaven. The Lord will judge the ends of the earth; he will give strength to his king, and exalt the power of his anointed.'

[2]   He has remembered his steadfast love and faithfulness to the house of Israel. All the ends of the earth have seen the victory of our God.

[3]   He sent redemption to his people; he has commanded his covenant for ever. Holy and awesome is his name.

[4]   He made known his ways to Moses, his acts to the people of Israel.

[5]   For he satisfies the thirsty, and the hungry he fills with good things.

comparative chart at beginning of this work). We need not go into the area of sources and composition of the 'Magnificat' or the other canticles in Lk.2 (cf. Johnson 1991:43-44; Tannehill 1974:263-275; Brown 1997:233;), but allow the 'Magnificat' to stand simply as a text within Luke's narrative 'spoken' by Mary (lest we find ourselves side-tracked into source and text critical issues and this work is not concerned with that). So, taking the text as it stands, it is immediately noticeable that there is no self-exaltation from Mary in this exclamation. She does not even refer to the great favour (to be the mother of the Messiah) that has been shown her (unless *he has looked with favour on the lowliness of his servant* is to be considered as such but is unlikely in the context) all Mary's thoughts are focused on God. What is key in this hymn/song/poem is that the promises of God to save his people are already in the process of being realised (Lk. 1.46b-50):

> My soul magnifies the Lord,
> and my spirit rejoices in God my Saviour,
> for he has looked with favour on the lowliness of his servant.
> Surely, from now on all generations will call me blessed;
> for the Mighty One has done great things for me,
> and holy is his name.
> His mercy is for those who fear him
> from generation to generation.

The dominant tones of this poem/hymn are joy and praise, Mary's whole being is open to God as she praises him continually, her whole being (*soul* and *spirit*) magnifies *the Lord;* her words acknowledge God's greatness and they bring the focus of all on him and that same wholeness of being rejoices in *God* her *saviour* (Pss. 24.5;[1] 25.5;[2] Mic. 7.7;[3] Hab. 3.18[4]) and she, in her song and life, makes his name great (Lk. 1.46b-47). Through her God is fulfilling his promises of salvation and like all women and men Mary

---

[1]   They will receive blessing from the Lord, and vindication from the God of their salvation.
[2]   Lead me in your truth, and teach me, for you are the God of my salvation; for you I wait all day long.
[3]   But as for me, I will look to the Lord, I will wait for the God of my salvation; my God will hear me.
[4]   yet I will rejoice in the Lord; I will exult in the God of my salvation.

needed to be saved and she rejoices because God is, indeed, her *saviour*. She acknowledges her *lowly* state because she is his servant and so she acknowledges God as her sovereign (cf. v.38; 2 K 14.26;[1] Ps. 9.11-14;[2] 25.16-18[3]). She acknowledges God as the *almighty* or *mighty one* (Deut. 10.21;[4] 34.11;[5] Pss. 44.4-8;[6] 89.8-10;[7] 111.2,[8] 9; Zeph. 3.17[9]), but she does not fear precisely because God is her *saviour* (Ps. 25.5-6;[10] Is. 12.2;[11] Mic. 7.7[12]). Yet though God has looked on her *lowly* state and *poverty;* he has also lifted her high to where *all generations will* declare how *blessed* she is (e.g., Pss. 21.6;[13] 34.8;[14] 128.1;[15] Lk. 1.48[16]) because they will see that the promises made to her have already been fulfilled. Elizabeth has already

---

[1] For the Lord saw that the distress of Israel was very bitter; there was no one left, bond or free, and no one to help Israel.

[2] Sing praises to the Lord, who dwells in Zion.Declare his deeds among the peoples. For he who avenges blood is mindful of them; he does not forget the cry of the afflicted. Be gracious to me, O Lord.See what I suffer from those who hate me; you are the one who lifts me up from the gates of death, so that I may recount all your praises, and, in the gates of daughter Zion, rejoice in your deliverance.

[3] Turn to me and be gracious to me, for I am lonely and afflicted. Relieve the troubles of my heart, and bring me out of my distress. Consider my affliction and my trouble, and forgive all my sins.

[4] He is your praise; he is your God, who has done for you these great and awesome things that your own eyes have seen.

[5] He was unequalled for all the signs and wonders that the Lord sent him to perform in the land of Egypt, against Pharaoh and all his servants and his entire land

[6] You are my King and my God; you command victories for Jacob. Through you we push down our foes; through your name we tread down our assailants. For not in my bow do I trust, nor can my sword save me. But you have saved us from our foes, and have put to confusion those who hate us. In God we have boasted continually, and we will give thanks to your name for ever.

[7] O Lord God of hosts, who is as mighty as you, O Lord? Your faithfulness surrounds you. You rule the raging of the sea; when its waves rise, you still them. You crushed Rahab like a carcass; you scattered your enemies with your mighty arm.

[8] Great are the works of the Lord, studied by all who delight in them.

[9] The Lord, your God, is in your midst, a warrior who gives victory; he will rejoice over you with gladness, he will renew you in his love; he will exult over you with loud singing

[10] Lead me in your truth, and teach me, for you are the God of my salvation; for you I wait all day long. Be mindful of your mercy, O Lord, and of your steadfast love, for they have been from of old.

[11] Surely God is my salvation; I will trust, and will not be afraid, for the Lord God is my strength and my might; he has become my salvation.

[12] But as for me, I will look to the Lord, I will wait for the God of my salvation; my God will hear me.

[13] You bestow on him blessings for ever; you make him glad with the joy of your presence.

[14] O taste and see that the Lord is good; happy are those who take refuge in him.

[15] Happy is everyone who fears the Lord, who walks in his ways.

[16] For he has looked with favour on the lowliness of his servant. Surely, from now on all generations will call me blessed.

blessed her twice and this will be repeated through all time because of the significance of the child she bears. Mary will be seen as *blessed* because of the *great things* God has done in and through her in the birth of her son, the Messiah, in the same way as that same mercy is applied to all who fear him of all generations in the way now about to be described, and especially so through the son that will be born from her. Mary's blessedness will thus be shared by all.

But it is God who is unique, for his name is *holy* (among the ancient peoples the name of a thing or person indicated something about them substantially or essentially), for her, his name is wonderful because his character is true. In this declaration of Mary, there is no sense of over exaltation of her personally; she is righteous and has been highly *favoured* by God in what is about to happen but not as one who in any sense has become superior to others in humanity. She is the model of belief and in contrast to Zechariah she believes the word of God when it is spoken to her (Lk. 1.37-38); she is the favoured one of God (Lk. 1.30); she is thoughtful (Lk. 1.39); she is obedient (Lk. 1.38); she is believing and worship full (Lk. 1.46-46). Mary then universalises her praise for she recognises and acknowledges that the love and mercy which has been shown to her, revealed from *generation to generation*, will continue to be revealed to *those who love him* (Lk. 1.50) and they shall experience his graciousness.

In this is shown God's *hesed*. Such love is faithful as well as gracious (Ps. 103. 2-6,[1] 8-11, 13, 17). Loyal love is the hymn's basic theme, and God's treatment of Mary is but one example. We gain from her words something of Mary's theology. God is her Lord, her Saviour, he is the *Mighty One*, His *Name* (that is, as he essentially is) is *holy*, and he is compassionate and merciful. But what she understands of his saving work is very practical. And this is what is proclaimed in the second part of Mary's hymn (Lk. 1.51-55):

---

[1] Bless the Lord, O my soul, and do not forget all his benefits who forgives all your iniquity, who heals all your diseases, who redeems your life from the Pit, who crowns you with steadfast love and mercy, who satisfies you with good as long as you live so that your youth is renewed like the eagle's.

He has shown strength with his arm;
he has scattered the proud in the thoughts of their hearts.
He has brought down the powerful from their thrones,
and lifted up the lowly;
he has filled the hungry with good things,
and sent the rich away empty.
He has helped his servant Israel,
in remembrance of his mercy,
according to the promise he made to our ancestors,
to Abraham and to his descendants for ever.

The poetic description of how God has shown his loyal love to *generation to generation* is strong: he has *shown strength with his arm* (Deut. 4.34;[1] Ps. 44.3;[2] 89:13;[3] 118.15[4]).The promise of God's judgement here recalls the Exodus, when God exercised his power in total judgement (Ex. 6.1,[5] 6; Deut. 3.24;[6] 7.19[7]). Before the divine authority, all earthly power with its arrogant pride has been *scattered* (Is. 29.20-21[8]); rulers and princes have been brought down *from their thrones* (1 S 15.28;[9] Ps. 68.1;[10] 89.10[11]) and

---

[1] Or has any god ever attempted to go and take a nation for himself from the midst of another nation, by trials, by signs and wonders, by war, by a mighty hand and an outstretched arm, and by terrifying displays of power, as the Lord your God did for you in Egypt before your very eyes?

[2] For not by their own sword did they win the land, nor did their own arm give them victory; but your right hand, and your arm, and the light of your countenance, for you delighted in them.

[3] You have a mighty arm; strong is your hand, high your right hand.

[4] There are glad songs of victory in the tents of the righteous: 'The right hand of the Lord does valiantly.

[5] Then the Lord said to Moses, 'Now you shall see what I will do to Pharaoh: Indeed, by a mighty hand he will let them go; by a mighty hand he will drive them out of his land.'

[6] 'O Lord God, you have only begun to show your servant your greatness and your might; what god in heaven or on earth can perform deeds and mighty acts like yours!

[7] The great trials that your eyes saw, the signs and wonders, the mighty hand and the outstretched arm by which the Lord your God brought you out. The Lord your God will do the same to all the peoples of whom you are afraid.

[8] For the tyrant shall be no more, and the scoffer shall cease to be; all those alert to do evil shall be cut off, those who cause a person to lose a lawsuit, who set a trap for the arbiter in the gate, and without grounds deny justice to the one in the right.

[9] And Samuel said to him, 'The Lord has torn the kingdom of Israel from you this very day, and has given it to a neighbour of yours, who is better than you.

[10] Let God rise up, let his enemies be scattered; let those who hate him flee before him.

[11] You crushed Rahab like a carcass; you scattered your enemies with your mighty arm.

in opposite and contrast to this he has *lifted up the lowly* (1 S 2.7;[1] Ps. 147.6[2]). Those who hunger are filled with all good things (1 S 2.5;[3] Ps. 107.9;[4]) but the rich have been sent away empty handed (Job 15.29;[5] Jer.17.11[6]). Ordinarily on earth it is the rich who are filled with good things, and it is the hungry who are turned away. But God turns such things on their heads. For the rich also tend to be the unbelieving and disobedient (Pss. 39.6;[7] 49.6;[8] 52.7;[9] 73.12[10] etc.), and the poor those who respond to God and do His will. This is certainly the emphasis of the Psalms where the poor are regularly seen as synonymous with the Godly (Pss. 9.18;[11] 14.6;[12] 34.6;[13] 69.29;[14] 72.13;[15] 74.19,[16] 21; 86.1;[17] 107.41;[18] 109.31;[19] 140.12[20]).

In the Greek of Luke all these verbs are in the aorist tense, in other words, God has not only *acted* in this way but he *is acting now* and Mary is evidence of this. God continues his saving action on behalf of the poor and downtrodden, those who wait on him in hope for deliverance, the 'remnant',

---

[1] The Lord makes poor and makes rich; he brings low, he also exalts.

[2] Who executes justice for the oppressed; who gives food to the hungry.

[3] Those who were full have hired themselves out for bread, but those who were hungry are fat with spoil. The barren has borne seven, but she who has many children is forlorn.

[4] For he satisfies the thirsty, and the hungry he fills with good things.

[5] they will not be rich, and their wealth will not endure, nor will they strike root in the earth

[6] Like the partridge hatching what it did not lay, so are all who amass wealth unjustly; in mid-life it will leave them, and at their end they will prove to be fools.

[7] Surely everyone goes about like a shadow. Surely for nothing they are in turmoil; they heap up, and do not know who will gather

[8] Those who trust in their wealth and boast of the abundance of their riches?

[9] 'See the one who would not take refuge in God, but trusted in abundant riches, and sought refuge in wealth!'

[10] Such are the wicked; always at ease, they increase in riches.

[11] For the needy shall not always be forgotten, nor the hope of the poor perish for ever.

[12] You would confound the plans of the poor, but the Lord is their refuge.

[13] Your righteousness is like the mighty mountains, your judgements are like the great deep; you save humans and animals alike, O Lord.

[14] But I am lowly and in pain; let your salvation, O God, protect me.

[15] He has pity on the weak and the needy, and saves the lives of the needy.

[16] Do not deliver the soul of your dove to the wild animals; do not forget the life of your poor for ever.

[17] Incline your ear, O Lord, and answer me, for I am poor and needy.

[18] But he raises up the needy out of distress, and makes their families like flocks.

[19] For he stands at the right hand of the needy, to save them from those who would condemn them to death.

[20] I know that the Lord maintains the cause of the needy, and executes justice for the poor.

those whom the Old Testament call the 'anawim' (Pss. 9.11-12,[1] 17-20; 10.1-4;[2]). It should be noted here that it is those who look and turn to God who are the objects of his blessing. Though the blessings of Lk. 1.50-53 come to those in need, they are not a carte blanche offer to all the poor and hungry, but only to those who look to God for care. His divine loyalty requires his action on behalf of the beloved and those who stand in opposition to him will face his might and power and authority to bring them down.

We should note also in this Mary's recognition of what type of Messiah is coming and it is not one who will exalt the powerful but one who will go to the meek and lowly; not one who will invite the rich to his table, but one who will go to the poor and the maimed and the blind (Is. 29.18-19;[3] 35.5-6;[4] 61.1-2[5]). He will be the Messiah of the people, the one who does not *break the bruised reed or extinguish the dimly burning wick* (Is. 42.3). What is being expressed here is the hope of Israel that those oppressed by foreign rulers would one day be liberated. In the past God's actions reflected his mercy and they do so again now for he helped his *servant Israel* (this reference recalls a major motif from Isaiah e.g., 45.4;[6] 49.3.[7] Later Luke will describe Jesus in terms that picture the Servant (cf.

---

[1] Sing praises to the Lord, who dwells in Zion. Declare his deeds among the peoples. For he who avenges blood is mindful of them; he does not forget the cry of the afflicted.

[2] Why, O Lord, do you stand far off? Why do you hide yourself in times of trouble? In arrogance the wicked persecute the poor, let them be caught in the schemes they have devised. For the wicked boast of the desires of their heart, those greedy for gain curse and renounce the Lord. In the pride of their countenance the wicked say, 'God will not seek it out';all their thoughts are, 'There is no God.'

[3] On that day the deaf shall hear the words of a scroll, and out of their gloom and darkness the eyes of the blind shall see. The meek shall obtain fresh joy in the Lord, and the neediest people shall exult in the Holy One of Israel.

[4] Then the eyes of the blind shall be opened, and the ears of the deaf unstopped; then the lame shall leap like a deer, and the tongue of the speechless sing for joy.

[5] The spirit of the Lord God is upon me, because the Lord has anointed me; he has sent me to bring good news to the oppressed, to bind up the broken-hearted, to proclaim liberty to the captives, and release to the prisoners; to proclaim the year of the Lord's favour, and the day of vengeance of our God; to comfort all who mourn

[6] In your majesty ride on victoriously for the cause of truth and to defend the right; let your right hand teach you dread deeds.

[7] My mouth shall speak wisdom; the meditation of my heart shall be understanding.

Lk. 22.37;[1] Acts 8.32-33[2]) and Mary seeks that God will remember *his mercy*, promised to *our fathers*. God had committed himself to such loyalty and compassion in the promised blessing to Abraham for his seed (Gen. 12.1-3[3]) now God was fulfilling that promised blessing in Mary's son, the one who would be the help of Israel.

The Birth and Naming of John (Lk. 1.57-66)

Luke now returns to the older woman, Elizabeth and her husband Zechariah to show how, with the birth of John, God is continuing to fulfil the promises of Lk. 1.5-25. As in Lk. 1.39-56, where there was a meeting (1.39-45) and then a hymn (1.46-56), John's birth is followed by a hymn. In each case the hymn details the significance of the previous event. The difference is that Mary's hymn focused on how God deals with his people, while Zechariah's hymn will highlight the main players who bring such blessing on humanity (see McBride 1984:32-35). When the time comes for Elizabeth to give birth there family and friends gather round to help and support her because (Lk. 1.58):

> the Lord had shown his great mercy to her, and they rejoiced with her.

Great history changing events may well be taking place but there is also the impact of the divine on personal lives. In the case of Elizabeth, God has

---

[1] And saying, 'If you are the King of the Jews, save yourself!'

[2] Now the passage of the scripture that he was reading was this:'Like a sheep he was led to the slaughter, and like a lamb silent before its shearer, so he does not open his mouth. In his humiliation justice was denied him. Who can describe his generation? For his life is taken away from the earth.'

[3] Now the Lord said to Abram, 'Go from your country and your kindred and your father's house to the land that I will show you. I will make of you a great nation, and I will bless you, and make your name great, so that you will be a blessing. I will bless those who bless you, and the one who curses you I will curse; and in you all the families of the earth shall be blessed.'

shown her mercy and magnified her (cf. Gen 19.19;[1] 24.12;[2] 40.14;[3] 47.29;[4] Ruth 1.8;[5] 4.13[6]) and those who once shared her sorrow at being childless now share her joy. God's love is not an abstract notion or theological idea: it is action in the real circumstances of lives. But there is also a surprise: Elizabeth insisted on a name which no one in her family had and Zechariah would emphasise the name by making the same insistence and (Lk. 1.64)

> immediately his mouth was opened and his tongue freed, and
> he began to speak, praising God.

With the birth and circumcision of John the long prophetic silence was over, Israel was no longer 'dumb', God now had a 'tongue' through which he could speak. After John is born (Lk. 1.59):

> on the eighth day they came to circumcise the child, and they
> were going to name him Zechariah after his father

Every son in Israel was circumcised on the eighth day otherwise he would have been considered to be cut off from the people. Circumcision could be carried out by a woman if necessity dictated and it could be done on the Sabbath. The circumcision was also a time when the child was named (though children were often named at birth cf. Gen. 29.32-35[7]) Luke

---

[1]   Your servant has found favour with you, and you have shown me great kindness in saving my life; but I cannot flee to the hills, for fear the disaster will overtake me and I die.

[2]   And he said, 'O Lord, God of my master Abraham, please grant me success today and show steadfast love to my master Abraham.

[3]   But remember me when it is well with you; please do me the kindness to make mention of me to Pharaoh, and so get me out of this place.

[4]   When the time of Israel's death drew near, he called his son Joseph and said to him, 'If I have found favour with you, put your hand under my thigh and promise to deal loyally and truly with me. Do not bury me in Egypt.

[5]   But Naomi said to her two daughters-in-law, 'Go back each of you to your mother's house. May the Lord deal kindly with you, as you have dealt with the dead and with me.

[6]   So Boaz took Ruth and she became his wife. When they came together, the Lord made her conceive, and she bore a son.

[7]   She conceived again and bore a son, and said, 'This time I will praise the Lord'; therefore she named him Judah; then she ceased bearing.

indicates that both Elizabeth and Zechariah were present and thus shows them to be devout and pious Jews (Gen. 21.4;[1] Lev.12.3[2]). John's name had already been given him but not it was known because of Zechariah's dumbness and Elizabeth's retirement, so the crowd of family and friends would expect that custom to be followed and that the boy be named after his father, Zechariah (Fitzmyer 1981:380) (sometimes boys were named after their grandfathers cf. 1 Macc. 1:1-2;[3] Josephus, *Life* 15; *Antiquities* 14.1.3 10; 20.9.1 197; *Jub.* 11.15[4]). Elizabeth, however, ignores the expectations of the crowd and simply states, *'No; he is to be called John.'* (Lk. 1.60b). How Elizabeth knew that he was to be called John Luke does not say, Zechariah may have indicated as such in writing (as he will do in a moment) but it is not an important issue. What is important is that God himself has named the child and when God names a child (e.g., Jesus) then that child is of importance and significance in God's plans.

Elizabeth's insistence on the name John indicates her obedience to God. This surprises the crowd, *None of your relatives has this name* (Lk. 1.61). At such family gatherings there are always those who want to be 'helpful', there are those who are 'organisers', there are 'busybodies' and those who 'know best', the same seems to be true of the celebration of John's circumcision. Not satisfied with Elizabeth's response (Lk. 1.62):

> they began motioning to his father to find out what name he
> wanted to give him

As the father, Zechariah would have the final say and he was the one with authority, the mother of the child was being awkward and stubborn. The

---

[1]   And Abraham circumcised his son Isaac when he was eight days old, as God had commanded him.

[2]   On the eighth day the flesh of his foreskin shall be circumcised.

[3]   After Alexander son of Philip, the Macedonian, who came from the land of Kittim, had defeated King Darius of the Persians and the Medes, he succeeded him as king. (He had previously become king of Greece.) He fought many battles, conquered strongholds, and put to death the kings of the earth.

[4]   And the child began to understand the errors of the earth that all went astray after graven images and after uncleanness, and his father taught him writing, and he was two weeks of years old, and he separated himself from his father, that he might not worship idols with him.

fact that they *motion* to Zechariah may indicate that he was also deaf, so Zechariah asks for a tablet and with the same insistence writes, *'His name is John.'* (Lk. 1.63b). The fact that Zechariah writes his name *is* John indicates that the child is already bearing the name given him by God through the angel's words, Zechariah follows God's word and command not the word and desire of custom of tradition understood by the onlookers. This amazes them for no one in the family has that name (the word for 'amazed' is the Greek term 'thaumazō', which is used often by Luke (e.g., 8.25;[1] 9:43;[2] Acts 2.7;[3] 3.12;[4] 4.13;[5]). Luke's vocabulary is influenced by the Septuagint and this word is also found in several Old Testament contexts (Gen. 19.21;[6] Lev.19.25;[7] 26.32;[8] Deut. 10.17;[9] Job 41.4;[10] Dan. 8.27[11]). The noun form is used of God's miracles (cf. Ex. 3.20;[12] Deut. 34.12;[13] Judgs. 6.13;[14] and I Chron.16.9[15]). No sooner does Zechariah write what the child's name is than (Lk. 1.64):

[1] Then Jesus asked, 'Who touched me?' When all denied it, Peter said, 'Master, the crowds surround you and press in on you.'

[2] And all were astounded at the greatness of God.

[3] Amazed and astonished, they asked, 'Are not all these who are speaking Galileans?

[4] When Peter saw it, he addressed the people, 'You Israelites, why do you wonder at this, or why do you stare at us, as though by our own power or piety we had made him walk?

[5] Now when they saw the boldness of Peter and John and realized that they were uneducated and ordinary men, they were amazed and recognised them as companions of Jesus.

[6] He said to him, 'Very well, I grant you this favour too, and will not overthrow the city of which you have spoken.

[7] But in the fifth year you may eat of their fruit, that their yield may be increased for you: I am the Lord your God.

[8] I will devastate the land, so that your enemies who come to settle in it shall be appalled at it.

[9] For the Lord your God is God of gods and Lord of lords, the great God, mighty and awesome, who is not partial and takes no bribe.

[10] Will it make a covenant with you to be taken as your servant for ever?

[11] So I, Daniel, was overcome and lay sick for some days; then I arose and went about the king's business. But I was dismayed by the vision and did not understand it.

[12] So I will stretch out my hand and strike Egypt with all my wonders that I will perform in it; after that he will let you go.

[13] And for all the mighty deeds and all the terrifying displays of power that Moses performed in the sight of all Israel.

[14] Gideon answered him, 'But sir, if the Lord is with us, why then has all this happened to us? And where are all his wonderful deeds that our ancestors recounted to us, saying, "Did not the Lord bring us up from Egypt?" But now the Lord has cast us off, and given us into the hand of Midian.'

[15] Sing to him, sing praises to him, tell of all his wonderful works.

> immediately his mouth was opened and his tongue freed, and he
> began to speak, praising God

Zechariah's first action on getting back the power of speech is to praise God and the judgement visited by God on Zechariah ends. The silence of Zechariah, a metaphor for the prophetic silence in Israel since Micah some four hundred years before, is now ended with the fulfilment of God's word and the meaning is plain: believe (as Elizabeth and Mary did) and understand that God fulfils the promises in his word. Three important things have happened here:

> 1.   An old man and woman well past child producing/bearing age have had a son.
> 2.   The child has a strange name not found anywhere else in the Old Testament.
> 3.   Zechariah's loss of speech (and hearing?) have been taken away and his first words are praises of God.

These are strange, unusual events and they cause the crowd to fear, wonder, and reflect (Lk. 1.65-66):

> Fear came over all their neighbours, and all these things were talked about throughout the entire hill country of Judea. All who heard them pondered them and said, 'What then will this child become?' For, indeed, the hand of the Lord was with him.

The people are afraid for Judea was a land steeped in religion and everything was seen and interpreted in the light of that religion. This fear (a better word would be *awe*) is the common human response to the presence of the supernatural. These neighbours, family, and friends recognised God's special presence and divine purpose (Lk. 1.66) in this conception and birth, so the question, *'What then will this child become?'* would be asked from a religious point of view and Luke certainly wants his reader/s (Theophilus and us) to ask the same question, *For, indeed, the hand of the Lord was with him* (see, Marshall 1978:90; Stein 1992:98). When God's hand is referred to in the Old Testament it usually indicates that an opportunity for deliverance is around the corner (e.g., Ps. 28.5;[1] 80.17;[2] 1 K 18.46;[3] 1 Chron. 28.19;[4] Ezek.1.3;[5] 3.14, 22[6]) and Zechariah, in his silence, has learned to believe God and be obedient to his word rather than to the customs and practices of the people.

a. Zehariah's Hymn: The 'Benedictus' (Lk. 1.67-80)

I am aware that this reflection is meant to be concerned with Jesus and the *women* of the gospels and that at first sight inserting Zechariah's great hymn may not be 'on task'. However, John is the child not just of Elizabeth, the old woman past child bearing age but favoured of God, he is also the child of Zechariah, the old man past child producing age, and Zechariah is an important part of the Lukan Elizabeth-John narrative (Oliver, 1963/64: 205-15). Aside from that, the Benedictus is stunningly beautiful and needs no excuse to be inserted into a work on gospel literature! Further, Zechariah's hymn describes the *universal* and *cosmic* dimension of God's saving work which is to be continued in role of his and Elizabeth's child as the prophetic forerunner of Mary's child (see Dillon 2006:457-80). The hymn views the drama of God's salvation through the lens of the forerunner (John) and the anointed David heir (Jesus) and God is blessed for the works that he does through these two and rejoices that the *horn* of David has been lifted up to carry out his work of salvation which is both spiritual and

---

[1] Because they do not regard the works of the Lord, or the work of his hands, he will break them down and build them up no more.

[2] But let your hand be upon the one at your right hand, the one whom you made strong for yourself.

[3] But the hand of the Lord was on Elijah; he girded up his loins and ran in front of Ahab to the entrance of Jezreel.

[4] All this, in writing at the Lord's direction, he made clear to me, the plan of all the works.'

[5] The word of the Lord came to the priest Ezekiel son of Buzi, in the land of the Chaldeans by the river Chebar; and the hand of the Lord was on him there.

[6] The spirit lifted me up and bore me away; I went in bitterness in the heat of my spirit, the hand of the Lord being strong upon me.

earthly (Lk. 1.71-75;[1] 78-79[2]). *Zechariah was filled with the Holy Spirit* when he proclaimed this hymn of blessing and elsewhere in Luke, the presence of the Holy Spirit is behind other prophetic proclamations (Acts 2.17-18;[3]11.27-28;[4]). This particular prophetic hymn is a sustained reflection on God's saving history which is particularised now in John, who is the prophet of the *Most High* the forerunner of the *Son of the Most High*; so, just as John points to Jesus, so too does Zechariah's hymn (Brown 1977:377-92).

Zechariah's hymn opens with a *blessing* (Lk. 1.68) as is the custom among the Jews (cf. e.g., Pss. 41.13;[5] 72.18;[6] 106.48[7]). The birth of John means that God is once again actively working to bring his promise to fulfilment (Lk. 1.72-73). God has *come* to his people or another way of putting it, *has looked favourably* on his people as he has with Elizabeth and Mary. This 'coming' of God is a visitation (Lk. 1.78;[8] 7:16;[9] 19.44;[10] Acts 15.14[11]) and Zechariah's hymn is a hymn of praise in both thanks and

---

[1] That we would be saved from our enemies and from the hand of all who hate us. Thus he has shown the mercy promised to our ancestors, and has remembered his holy covenant, the oath that he swore to our ancestor Abraham, to grant us that we, being rescued from the hands of our enemies, might serve him without fear, in holiness and righteousness before him all our days.

[2] By the tender mercy of our God, the dawn from on high will break upon us, to give light to those who sit in darkness and in the shadow of death, to guide our feet into the way of peace.'

[3] "In the last days it will be, God declares, that I will pour out my Spirit upon all flesh, and your sons and your daughters shall prophesy, and your young men shall see visions, and your old men shall dream dreams. Even upon my slaves, both men and women, in those days I will pour out my Spirit; and they shall prophesy.

[4] At that time prophets came down from Jerusalem to Antioch. One of them named Agabus stood up and predicted by the Spirit that there would be a severe famine over all the world; and this took place during the reign of Claudius.

[5] Blessed be the Lord, the God of Israel, from everlasting to everlasting. Amen and Amen.

[6] Blessed be the Lord, the God of Israel, who alone does wondrous things.

[7] Blessed be the Lord, the God of Israel, from everlasting to everlasting. And let all the people say, 'Amen.' Praise the Lord!

[8] By the tender mercy of our God, the dawn from on high will break upon us,

[9] Fear seized all of them; and they glorified God, saying, 'A great prophet has risen among us!' and 'God has looked favourably on his people!'

[10] They will crush you to the ground, you and your children within you, and they will not leave within you one stone upon another; because you did not recognize the time of your visitation from God.'

[11] Simeon has related how God first looked favourably on the Gentiles, to take from among them a people for his name.

celebration for this *visiting* by God in the person of the Messiah (Lk. 2.26-32). God is *working redemption* on behalf of the people and coming to them as a deliverer and saviour both earthly, politically since he has come to deliver the people from those who persecute and spiritual as the hearts of the people will be turned back towards him. God would save to the greatest degree for he was sending this salvation to his own people (Ps. 111.9[1]). In the promised Messiah God has raised up a *mighty saviour*. This is the way in which it is usually translated but the literal translation is better: God has:

> raised up a horn of salvation for us in the house of David his servant

The key term is *house* and the key context is 2 Samuel 7, from this Messianic promise comes Ps. 132.17[2] and Is. 11.1.[3] The Messiah will be from the tribe of Judah (cf. Gen. 49) and the family of Jesse (cf. Mt. 1.1;[4] Lk. 1.32;[5] Jn. 7.42;[6] Acts 13.23;[7] Rom. 1.3;[8] Rev. 22.16[9]). *Servant* was an Old Testament title of honour and is used of Moses and Joshua. In the past God has *raised up* prophets (Deut. 1.15[10]), judges (Judg. 3.9, 15[11]), priests

---

[1] He sent redemption to his people; he has commanded his covenant for ever. Holy and awesome is his name.
[2] There I will cause a horn to sprout up for David; I have prepared a lamp for my anointed one.
[3] A shoot shall come out from the stock of Jesse, and a branch shall grow out of his roots.
[4] An account of the genealogy of Jesus the Messiah, the son of David, the son of Abraham.
[5] He will be great, and will be called the Son of the Most High, and the Lord God will give to him the throne of his ancestor David.
[6] Has not the scripture said that the Messiah is descended from David and comes from Bethlehem, the village where David lived?'
[7] Of this man's posterity God has brought to Israel a Saviour, Jesus, as he promised.
[8] The gospel concerning his Son, who was descended from David according to the flesh.
[9] 'It is I, Jesus, who sent my angel to you with this testimony for the churches. I am the root and the descendant of David, the bright morning star.'
[10] So I took the leaders of your tribes, wise and reputable individuals, and installed them as leaders over you, commanders of thousands, commanders of hundreds, commanders of fifties, commanders of tens, and officials, throughout your tribes.
[11] But when the Israelites cried out to the Lord, the Lord raised up a deliverer for the Israelites, who delivered them, Othniel son of Kenaz, Caleb's younger brother.

(1 S 3.10[1]) and kings (2 S 3.10[2]). Luke is quite taken by this idea since its demonstrates how the unfolding of God's plan is directed entirely by him (Acts 3.22, 26;[3] 13.22[4]). And this salvation is a mighty weapon (*horn*), the anointed of the *house of David*, God's servant. In Ps. 18.2 the *horn of my salvation* is God himself delivering him from all his afflictions. A *horn* was a sign of power and strength and it was through that horns that earthly animals showed their power and strength and used them to defeat their enemies, e.g., the ox (Deut. 33.17[5]); the image is also used for a warrior (2 S 22.3;[6] Pss. 75.4-5,[7] 10; 148.14[8]) and the Davidic king was also seen as a *horn* of God's salvation (cf. Num. 24.8;[9] 1 S 2.10;[10] Ps. 132.17[11]), Luke is very clearly thinking of Jesus in kingly terms. But this is not predominantly, or even simply about a political deliverer because the coming of the son of David will not only bring deliverance, it will also open up the floodgates for forgiveness from sin and uncleanness (Zech.13.1[12]). All this was in accord with what God *spoke by the mouth of his holy prophets of old* (Lk. 1.70) for prophecy was now in the immediacy of being fulfilled and as the Jewish scriptures were known and venerated by man people (including non-Jews)

[1] Now the Lord came and stood there, calling as before, 'Samuel! Samuel!' And Samuel said, 'Speak, for your servant is listening.'

[2] To transfer the kingdom from the house of Saul, and set up the throne of David over Israel and over Judah, from Dan to Beer-sheba.'

[3] Moses said, "The Lord your God will raise up for you from your own people a prophet like me. You must listen to whatever he tells you.

[4] When he had removed him, he made David their king. In his testimony about him he said, "I have found David, son of Jesse, to be a man after my heart, who will carry out all my wishes."

[5] A firstborn bull, majesty is his! His horns are the horns of a wild ox; with them he gores the peoples, driving them to the ends of the earth; such are the myriads of Ephraim, such the thousands of Manasseh.

[6] My God, my rock, in whom I take refuge, my shield and the horn of my salvation, my stronghold and my refuge, my saviour; you save me from violence.

[7] All the horns of the wicked I will cut off, but the horns of the righteous shall be exalted.

[8] He has raised up a horn for his people, praise for all his faithful, for the people of Israel who are close to him.

[9] God, who brings him out of Egypt, is like the horns of a wild ox for him; he shall devour the nations that are his foes and break their bones. He shall strike with his arrows.

[10] The Lord! His adversaries shall be shattered; the Most High will thunder in heaven. The Lord will judge the ends of the earth; he will give strength to his king, and exalt the power of his anointed.'

[11] There I will cause a horn to sprout up for David; I have prepared a lamp for my anointed one.

[12] On that day a fountain shall be opened for the house of David and the inhabitants of Jerusalem, to cleanse them from sin and impurity.

any prophetic fulfilment of them would have been seen as of central importance and significance. The theological thrust is that the Messiahship of Jesus was not a recent invention, but ancient, inspired prophecy. He would bring physical (Old Testament) and spiritual (New Testament) salvation to Israel and beyond (cf. Mt. 28.18-20;[1] Lk. 24.47;[2] Acts 1.8[3]). And this is *salvation from our enemies, and from the hand of all who hate us* (Lk. 1.71). These words can be read in the light of Ps. 106.10:

> so he saved them from the hand of the foe, and delivered them
> from the hand of the enemy.

The popular understanding was that this involved some kind of socio-political liberation or deliverance when the Messiah came so that the Jews would be able to serve God fully and faithfully without hindrance. The Messiah would, of course, bring liberation and deliverance but it would be different from what Zechariah and Elizabeth and Mary and Joseph, i.e., the *expectant people*, understood and Luke in his gospel will go on to show what type of deliverance the Messiah does bring: liberation from Satan, evil and sin for his kingdom is not of this world. The whole of Israel understood the promises of God within the context of Abraham (Lk. 1.72-75). God's *covenant* with Abraham was *holy* because God had initiated it and had promised that Abraham's descendants would be *blessed*. And this meant that they would be brought into a situation of peace, *when they had been delivered out of the hand of* (our) *enemies* and they being righteous could serve God fully, without fear and in holiness all the days of their lives (Lk. 1.77 shows how this is possible). This was the ultimate fulfilment:

---

[1] And Jesus came and said to them, 'All authority in heaven and on earth has been given to me. Go therefore and make disciples of all nations, baptising them in the name of the Father and of the Son and of the Holy Spirit, and teaching them to obey everything that I have commanded you. And remember, I am with you always, to the end of the age.'

[2] And that repentance and forgiveness of sins is to be proclaimed in his name to all nations, beginning from Jerusalem.

[3] But you will receive power when the Holy Spirit has come upon you; and you will be my witnesses in Jerusalem, in all Judea and Samaria, and to the ends of the earth.'

deliverance outside and fulfilment inside. But there was no thought that this deliverance could be achieved without a change of heart (and the angel had described this is what Elizabeth and Zechariah's child would do, i.e., call them to repentance of sins, Lk. 1.15-17).

God would fulfil these promises made to Abraham though Mary's child but his teaching would emphasise the heavenly, not the earthly, kingdom and this would be a period of tribulation leading up to the final deliverance (Jn. 16.33;[1] Acts 14.22[2]). Luke, therefore, in this hymn combines two sets of divine promises: those about David's son and those made to Abraham. What God will do for his people he does through the Messiah. The fresh fulfilment of both covenants begins with Jesus' arrival. So Zechariah prays that God will remember his *holy covenant* and bring them to a position where they can live in peace and safety, and live righteously before him (Ps.106.45;[3]Lev.26.42,45[4]; Jer.14.21[5]; Ezek.16.60[6]). Zechariah's hymn now turns its attention to the agents of this work of God: John, who *will be called the prophet of the Most High* (Lk. 1.76a) and Jesus, the *sun/dawn from on high.* He will be great indeed, in his part in the purposes of God. Yet his greatness pales before that of *the Son of the Most High* (v.32).

As already noted, prophecy was silent in Israel since the time of Micah and among the Jews the next prophet expected was the return of Elijah who would be in the harbinger of the last days (Mic. 4.5[7]). So this hymn-

---

[1] I have said this to you, so that in me you may have peace. In the world you face persecution. But take courage; I have conquered the world!'

[2] There they strengthened the souls of the disciples and encouraged them to continue in the faith, saying, 'It is through many persecutions that we must enter the kingdom of God.'

[3] For their sake he remembered his covenant, and showed compassion according to the abundance of his steadfast love.

[4] Then will I remember my covenant with Jacob; I will remember also my covenant with Isaac and also my covenant with Abraham, and I will remember the land.

[5] Do not spurn us, for your name's sake; do not dishonour your glorious throne; remember and do not break your covenant with us.

[6] Yet I will remember my covenant with you in the days of your youth, and I will establish with you an everlasting covenant.

[7] For all the peoples walk, each in the name of its god, but we will walk in the name of the Lord our God for ever and ever.

prophecy from Zechariah is an announcement that the last days have arrived and Jesus would make clear, John was the Elijah who was to come (Mt. 11.14[1]) since he came in the spirit and power of Elijah. So the child is the one who goes *ahead* of the Lord (lit. *Before the face of the lord*) and this can mean something that is happening right before God's eyes (Gen. 19.13;[2] 1 S 26.20[3]); or it can mean that God is ready to act and that he is turning his face before something (Ps. 34.16[4]); or people place themselves before *the face of the Lord* in repentance (Lam. 2.19[5]). Any of these are possible with the first two being the more likely but in essence the emphasis is on the preparation. God is *preparing* because John is not the final answer, there is one who comes after John whose way John prepares (Acts. 19.1-6[6]). John is to bring (Lk. 1.77):

> to give knowledge of salvation to his people by the forgiveness
> of their sins

Forgiveness is a major theme of Luke's gospel (Lk. 24.47;[7] Acts 2.38;[8]

---

[1] And if you are willing to accept it, he is Elijah who is to come.

[2] For we are about to destroy this place, because the outcry against its people has become great before the Lord, and the Lord has sent us to destroy it.'

[3] Now, therefore, do not let my blood fall to the ground, away from the presence of the Lord; for the king of Israel has come out to seek a single flea, like one who hunts a partridge in the mountains.'

[4] The face of the Lord is against evildoers, to cut off the remembrance of them from the earth.

[5] Arise, cry out in the night, at the beginning of the watches! Pour out your heart like water before the presence of the Lord! Lift your hands to him for the lives of your children, who faint for hunger at the head of every street.

[6] While Apollos was in Corinth, Paul passed through the inland regions and came to Ephesus, where he found some disciples. He said to them, 'Did you receive the Holy Spirit when you became believers?' They replied, 'No, we have not even heard that there is a Holy Spirit.' Then he said, 'Into what then were you baptised?' They answered, 'Into John's baptism.' Paul said, 'John baptised with the baptism of repentance, telling the people to believe in the one who was to come after him, that is, in Jesus.' On hearing this, they were baptised in the name of the Lord Jesus. When Paul had laid his hands on them, the Holy Spirit came upon them, and they spoke in tongues and prophesied.

[7] And that repentance and forgiveness of sins is to be proclaimed in his name to all nations, beginning from Jerusalem.

[8] Peter said to them, 'Repent, and be baptised every one of you in the name of Jesus Christ so that your sins may be forgiven; and you will receive the gift of the Holy Spirit.

5.31;[1] 10.43;[2] 13.38;[3] 26.18[4]). In the revelation of salvation, the people will become aware of their sins and find forgiveness in them. This is why John's baptism will called *a baptism of repentance for the forgiveness of sins* (Lk. 3.3). He is to be the 'preparer' of *the way of the Lord* that people might become aware of their sins and find forgiveness from them. That is why his baptism will be called *a baptism of repentance* (change of mind and heart) *for the forgiveness of sins* (Lk. 3.3). He is to make ready the way of the Lord by turning the peoples' hearts to God in repentance and faith (compare vv. 16-17) so that they will come within God's offered sphere of salvation. The *giving of the knowledge of salvation* is also an Old Testament motif (cf. Ps. 98.2[5]) and the giving of knowledge of salvation in the forgiveness of sins reflects Ex. 34.7;[6] Num. 14.18;[7] Is. 43.25;[8] It was the prayer for Israel of the scion of the Davidic house (1 K 8.36, 50[9]). All this will happen (Lk. 1.79):

> because of the tender mercy of our God, whereby the day-spring
> from on high will visit us, to shine on those who sit in darkness
> and the shadow of death, to guide our feet into the way of peace

[1] God exalted him at his right hand as Leader and Saviour, so that he might give repentance to Israel and forgiveness of sins.

[2] All the prophets testify about him that everyone who believes in him receives forgiveness of sins through his name.'

[3] Let it be known to you therefore, my brothers, that through this man forgiveness of sins is proclaimed to you.

[4] To open their eyes so that they may turn from darkness to light and from the power of Satan to God, so that they may receive forgiveness of sins and a place among those who are sanctified by faith in me."

[5] The Lord has made known his victory; he has revealed his vindication in the sight of the nations.

[6] Keeping steadfast love for the thousandth generation, forgiving iniquity and transgression and sin, yet by no means clearing the guilty, but visiting the iniquity of the parents upon the children and the children's children, to the third and the fourth generation.'

[7] "The Lord is slow to anger, and abounding in steadfast love, forgiving iniquity and transgression, but by no means clearing the guilty, visiting the iniquity of the parents upon the children to the third and the fourth generation."

[8] I, I am He who blots out your transgressions for my own sake, and I will not remember your sins.

[9] Then hear in heaven, and forgive the sin of your servants, your people Israel, when you teach them the good way in which they should walk; and grant rain on your land, which you have given to your people as an inheritance. and forgive your people who have sinned against you, and all their transgressions that they have committed against you; and grant them compassion in the sight of their captors, so that they may have compassion on them

The one who is coming will be like the dawn of a new day, the Sun of Righteousness (Mal. 4.2[1]) who is coming on visitation of the world in redemption and who will shine on those who *sit in darkness*. The Davidic horn (v.69) is an image of light (Num.24.17;[2] Is. 11.10[3]). The image of light will be important in Acts (13.47; 26.17-20) as well as in Luke (Lk. 2.32). The picture is of a world cloaked in darkness and death, desperate for someone to lead it into light and life. For Zechariah, this rescue is Messiah's mission for is is he who is the *day-spring*. In Greek this is 'anatole' which literally means, 'rising' or 'that which rises' and in the Old Testament it translates the *branch* in Jer. 23.5;[4] Zech. 3.8;[5] 6.12[6] and so it is a messianic motif. As it also used to describe the rising of the sun or moon, it is an abbreviation for the equivalent of the rising of the sun or moon. This ties in with Malachi's *Sun of Righteousness,* so the image is of one who comes like the rising sun of righteousness who shines in the darkness in which his people sit (cf. Jn. 3.19-21[7]).We can also compare here the idea in Is. 60.1[8] where Israel is compared to a light which is to 'arise and shine', and this as a result of the glory of the Lord which rises ('anatello') on them. This would make 'the rising' here the rising of the glory of the Lord which shines on His people who sit in darkness calling on them also to arise and shine.

---

[1] But for you who revere my name the sun of righteousness shall rise, with healing in its wings. You shall go out leaping like calves from the stall.

[2] I see him, but not now; I behold him, but not near, a star shall come out of Jacob, and a sceptre shall rise out of Israel; it shall crush the borderlands of Moab, and the territory of all the Shethites.

[3] On that day the root of Jesse shall stand as a light to the peoples; the nations shall inquire of him, and his dwelling shall be glorious.

[4] The days are surely coming, says the Lord, when I will raise up for David a righteous Branch, and he shall reign as king and deal wisely, and shall execute justice and righteousness in the land.

[5] And this is the judgement, that the light has come into the world, and people loved darkness rather than light because their deeds were evil. For all who do evil hate the light and do not come to the light, so that their deeds may not be exposed. But those who do what is true come to the light, so that it may be clearly seen that their deeds have been done in God.'

[6] Say to him: Thus says the Lord of hosts: Here is a man whose name is Branch: for he shall branch out in his place, and he shall build the temple of the Lord.

[7] And this is the judgement, that the light has come into the world, and people loved darkness rather than light because their deeds were evil. For all who do evil hate the light and do not come to the light, so that their deeds may not be exposed. But those who do what is true come to the light, so that it may be clearly seen that their deeds have been done in God.'

[8] Arise, shine; for your light has come, and the glory of the Lord has risen upon you.

Alternately we may consider Is. 60.19 in LXX reads:

> And you will no more have the sun for a light by day, Nor will
> the rising (anatole) of the moon lighten your night, But the Lord
> will be your everlasting light, And God your glory.'

This may be seen by inverted parallelism as signifying that the Lord Who is their everlasting light parallels the 'rising' of the moon to lighten the night and was therefore 'the rising from on high' (with the sun paralleling 'God your glory'). In all these examples the 'rising' is the rising of the Lord on His people in order to bring them light in the darkness. For he is to be like a light shining on those who sit in darkness and the shadow of death (Is. 9.2):

> The people who walked in darkness have seen a great light, those
> who dwell in the land of the shadow of death, on them has the light
> shined

which was also spoken in the context of the coming everlasting King (49.6;[1] for sitting in darkness, cf. Ps. 107.10[2]). Jesus elsewhere also likens himself to a light shining on those in darkness (Jn. 3.19-21; 8.12[3]). The Christ then is the bearer of forgiveness as his day dawns. Once his day dawns, the light of the 'Sun' never sets. He is the one who guides *our feet into the path of peace*. Even the righteous Zechariah recognises the need to be totally dependent on the one God will send. Those who are righteous know that the only true journey in life is the one taken in the hands of God. In Luke 1, Zechariah has grown from a figure of doubt to an example of dependence. And he comes to *guide our feet into the way of peace*. The 'way of peace' there is the way of righteousness, of godliness, of avoidance of violence, of

---

[1] 'It is too light a thing that you should be my servant to raise up the tribes of Jacob and to restore the survivors of Israel; I will give you as a light to the nations, that my salvation may reach to the end of the earth.'

[2] Some sat in darkness and in gloom, prisoners in misery and in irons,

[3] Again Jesus spoke to them, saying, 'I am the light of the world. Whoever follows me will never walk in darkness but will have the light of life.'

the kind of behaviour that finally leads to peace for all men (Lk. 2.14). This peace was to be the result of the coming of the everlasting King, the prince of peace, in order to guide our feet (Is. 9.6-7) and is the fruit of the Spirit (Gal. 5.22[1]). And Elizabeth and Zechariah's child (Lk. 1.80):

> grew and became strong in spirit, and he was in the wilderness
> until the day he appeared publicly to Israel

So John began to develop and grow, and became strong in the Spirit (he was full of the Holy Spirit from his mother's womb (v 15). And he went into the wildernesses (the plural is typical of LXX) there to prepare for the day when he would be revealed to Israel as the prophet and preparer of the way. Even if we translate 'spirit' with a small 's', signifying that his own spirit was made strong, verse 15 makes quite clear the source of his strength, as indeed it was intended to do (cf. Lk. 2.52;[2] Judg.13.24[3] and 1 S 2.26.[4]

Some have suggested that John was connected with the Qumran community, but it must be recognised that if so his emphasis was totally different from theirs. They certainly would not have agreed with his view of himself as the herald preparing the way for the Coming One, nor with his preaching of righteousness instead of asceticism, nor with his going among the people (they kept themselves separate in order to avoid defilement), nor with his baptism as a symbol of the pouring out of the Holy Spirit. It is probable therefore that he lived as a solitary, although that is not to deny that he may have had contact with them. They would appreciate his asceticism and separation from society. But his teaching was not like theirs. Then Luke turns the story's spotlight from John and his birth and shines it on the star of his narrative, Jesus, the son of Mary, the Davidic horn and king who delivers his people into the light.

---

[1] By contrast, the fruit of the Spirit is love, joy, peace, patience, kindness, generosity, faithfulness.
[2] And Jesus increased in wisdom and in years, and in divine and human favour.
[3] The woman bore a son, and named him Samson. The boy grew, and the Lord blessed him.
[4] Now the boy Samuel continued to grow both in stature and in favour with the Lord and with the people.

The Birth and Early Childhood of Jesus (Lk. 2.1-52)

a. The Birth of Mary's Son (Lk. 2.1-7)

If ever there was an opportunity for God to enact his plan with a majestic flourish, it was at Jesus' birth. But God did not presume upon humanity when he stepped in to redeem it. There was no pretence in this arrival. Rather, God chose to identify in the humblest way with those made in his image. The story of Jesus' birth in Luke mixes praise with simplicity. Its contrast to the birth of John the Baptist is remarkable. John's birth was announced in the capital, at the temple, in the centre of the Jewish nation. But Jesus arrives in rural anonymity. John is the child of a priest and his righteous wife; Jesus belongs to Jews of average social status. Yet it is Jesus' birth that draws an angelic host. Once again, appearances are deceiving. As humble as the setting is, his birth is accompanied by the attention of the heavenly host. The shepherds who are privileged to share in the moment become bearers of a story full of wonder. Jesus' birth is more than a cosmic event; it is the arrival of divine activity that should provoke joy, reflection and attentiveness. That is why Mary ponders these events and the shepherds return glorifying God.

In Lk. 2, the birth of Jesus is over in the blink of an eye, it occupies only two verses and Luke does not sentimentalise about it, perhaps because magical stories were already being invented by some (as in the apocryphal gospels). Mary's son is the *Son of the Most High*, the *Son of God* but he was also coming as a man among men and women and this is how he is to be see. Luke does not mention the Magi (Mt. 2.1-11) for Luke's narrative of the birth of Mary's son is about humility and deprivation, which is why Luke populates his narrative with the humble and the meek, so it is not wise men or women who come to visit the child but shepherds, it is those who live in the hills and fields not those who live in palaces and splendour. However, while the birth of Mary's son is presented as humble beginnings in poverty and deprivation, those who gather to witness to it are the angels and the Holy Spirit. While the earth is rapt in silence, heaven bears witness to his birth and what it means and Luke ends his narrative with the child Jesus in his *Father's house* which signals that which is to come. So the birth of Mary's son is itself a quiet event yet Luke highlights everything he needs to highlight about it in the events that surround it and by drawing attention to the fact that Jesus is born in Bethlehem as a scion of the house *of David* which is further emphasised by the background history so that it cannot be missed. There is no doubt that Luke had in his mind the prophecy of Micah 5.2 which said that the one who was to be the *governor of my people Israel* would be born in Bethlehem and would be Jesse's root (Jesse was the father of David, cf. Is. 12.1).

But unlike Matthew, Luke does not make any formula citations of this prophecy, rather he infers and allows the reader/hearer to make their own conclusions. Luke is very adept at getting his message across in silence. Lk. 1 has concentrated on Elizabeth and Zechariah and John the baptist wherein the divine intention is carefully revealed to human beings and the emphasis is on the preparation for the event of the coming of the one promised. Beginning at Lk. 2.8 the same concentration is to be found, except that it is a retrospective on the event. Yet, the extraordinary event (the birth of Jesus) is so ordinary that we might almost miss it. The son of Mary, who is all at one *Son of the Most High* and *Son of God* is coming into the world to inaugurate the kingdom of God, and Luke depicts this momentous moment in a child lying in a feeding trough wrapped in rags.

The contrast between the annunciation and birth of John and the annunciation and birth of Jesus makes us wonder who is, indeed, the One who comes? The annunciation of John's birth takes place in Jerusalem to a well respected priestly family during a profound moment of Temple liturgy; the annunciation of the birth of Jesus takes place to a betrothed peasant girl in a remote village in the dubiously though of Galilee. The parents of John have some social status, the parents of Jesus are of a decidedly more average status. But as we shall see, appearances can not only be, but most definitely are deceiving. Elizabeth's son draws a crowd of curious, bewildered people, Jesus' birth draws angelic hosts proclaiming *Glory to God in the highest*;

John's onlookers are priests and people of Jerusalem, the onlookers who gather around Mary's son are the shepherds from the hills who wondering and wondered wander to see what they have been told by the angels and then themselves become the bearers of wonder. Elizabeth's son is born in the heart of Judaism, Mary's son is born in in an animal feeding station. Elizabeth and Zechariah did not have to move far from their own place, Mary and Joseph had to go to Bethlehem under the edict of the earthly power, Rome, to be registered at the census. The father of Jesus is is shown as obedient to the earthly authority as he is to the divine authority. Yet, Luke makes it clear that whatever the events surround Mary's son, it is a moment of unspeakable joy and the irruption of the divine into a waiting world and the source of wonder and awe for all who witness it.

Luke begins the narrative of Jesus' birth with a statement of historical contextuality (Lk. 2.1):

> Now it came about that in those days, there went out a decree
> from Caesar Augustus, that all the world should be enrolled

These Roman enrolments ran in fourteen-year cycles which began under Caesar Augustus (30 BC to 14 AD, cf. Lk. 3.1; Mt. 22.17). We learn of these cycles from Egyptian papyri. They took years to finish. A second census is mentioned in Acts 5.37. An edict went out c. 3 BC on the silver jubilee of the reign of the Emperor Augustus that men of some importance were to go to their places of authority and show their loyalty or fealty to Augustus. This may well have been the *decree* that Luke is speaking of here and Joseph, an heir to the throne of David (in Jewish eyes, at least) would be required to go to his family of the Davidic house and swear that loyalty to Caesar. However, It is, possible that this was a similar enrolment organised some years prior to that event, of which as yet we have no archaeological evidence. Josephus tells us that during the last days of Herod (he died in 6 AD) 'the whole Jewish people' swore allegiance to Caesar, confirming that such an enrolment did take place, at least in Palestine, at that time. Or it may be that such an enrolment was taking place for a different reason, e.g., for the purposes of taxation (on the historical problems of this census cf. Nolland 1989:1.99-102; Marshall 1978:99-104).

Thus Luke's reference to a 'census; may simply be stating that Caesar had issued a general requirement for all to be taxed which resulted in the fact that each province carried it out as seemed best when it was suitable. It is known that from 6 AD regular taxation censuses were conducted in Judaea and elsewhere every fourteen years, and actual documents for such censuses held in Egypt have been found among papyri and exist from 20 – 270 AD. According to Josephus (*Antiquities,* 18.1-2, 26) at the tax census which was organised by the Romans and was held in Judaea in 6 AD, there was a great deal of trouble and an insurrection (cf. Acts 5.37[1]). This would be because it was carried out without regard to Jewish sensitivities (cf. Green 1997:126). The one here may have been a similar tax census fourteen years prior to that, but conducted by Herod along Jewish lines in such a way as to prevent such trouble, at which family tribal possessions were required to be registered by the tribal leaders and owners, the emphasis being on the enrolment of the tribes, and the measuring of their possessions.

At these censuses names and details were recorded together with a record of what was owned. Whichever census is being mentioned by Luke meant that Joseph had to return to his own place but this requirement would have been unusual for Rome who normally carried out such a census in the place of domicile but if it was carried out by Herod then he may have required men to return to their family lands in order to make it seem like a very Jewish enrolment and therefore a patriotic action. There is in one on the Egyptian papyri an edict by a governor of Egypt in 104 AD which demands that people return to their family homes for a census. Luke then tells us that this was the *first census made when Quirinius was in charge of Syria* (Lk. 2.2), this further emphasises the power and presence of Rome (on the census see Brown 1993:547-56).

---

[1] After him Judas the Galilean rose up at the time of the census and got people to follow him; he also perished, and all who followed him were scattered.

There is a problem with this statement and secular history. Quirinius was the civil governor of Syria in 6 AD. He was the military leader in Syria, of which Judea was a part, from 10-7 BC, however, he did not become the political leader until 6 AD. He came to Judea in 6/7 AD for the explicit purpose of registration for taxation. He was a special legate of Augustus to deal with a rebellious tribe and, therefore, was the military governor of Syria while Varas was the civil governor (Metzger and Murphy 1991:79-80) . He acted as a special representative of the Emperor from 12 BC to 16 BC, which included an administrative charge related to the census. It also asserts that he was twice governor of Syria, from 3-2 BC and again in 6-16 BC. A 'census' in 3 BC would accord with the fact that Quirinius, civil servant of Syria at the time of the census in 6 AD, is evidenced as having some kind of civil authority there c. 3 BC and it is known that he had military responsibilities there between 10-7 BC, given this, any date is possible. However, Luke says that this is his *first* census with the census in 6 AD being his second and this further emphasises Rome's power (see McBride's comment 1982:37). Luke connects the *first born* son of Mary and Joseph with the *first* census of Quirinius: the latter's census is convened on behalf of the earthly authority thus showing the subjection of Palestine under Rome, the former is an 'edict' of the divine power which demonstrates the deliverance of God's people. Rome strengthened its grip on the land of the people of God and thus the people and God moves to counteract it (cf. Moehring 1972:144-160). Luke then says (Lk. 2.3-5):

> And all went to enrol themselves, every one to his own town. And Joseph also went up from Galilee, out of the town of Nazareth, to Judaea, to the city of David, which is called Bethlehem, because he was of the house and family of David, to enrol himself with Mary, who was betrothed to him, being great with child.'

and in this gives us very detailed information about Mary and Joseph: they live in Galilee, Joseph is of the house of David, Mary is betrothed to him and heavily pregnant, and they are headed to Bethlehem, the city of David in answer to an edict from Rome. Luke's opening, therefore, emphasises that the child Jesus is born into a world ruled by Rome and his own land is ruled by Rome (no matter how indirectly) and that his life will be very much affected by the decisions made by Rome. Rome controls everything and even Herod, the 'king' is no more than a vassal puppet. Bethlehem was a small Judaean village about six miles south west of Jerusalem and, therefore, about seventy miles south of Nazareth. It was known in the Old Testament as Ephrath (cf. Gen. 35.19[1]), which became Bethlehem Ephrathah of Mic.5.2.[2] This was a way to distinguish it from a Bethlehem in the north of Israel. This city is known as the city where Boaz and Ruth, who were ancestors of King David, lived (cf. Ruth 4.11[3]). David's father, Jesse, lived here also (cf. 1 S 17.12[4]). Because it was the ancestral home of David, it was the prophesied but unexpected site of Jesus' birth (cf. Mic. 5.2; Mt. 2.5, 6;[5] Jn. 7.42[6]). Luke probably still uses the term *betrothed* in order to indicate that they had not yet consummated their marriage (although some witnesses have 'wife' or 'betrothed wife'). He is technically aware. As far as he is concerned they were not yet fully married. Matthew tells us that a marriage ceremony had taken place although Joseph did not consummate the marriage until after Jesus was born (Mt. 1.24-25[7]).

It is, however, unlikely that she would have accompanied Joseph if the

---

[1] So Rachel died, and she was buried on the way to Ephrath (that is, Bethlehem)

[2] But you, O Bethlehem of Ephrathah, who are one of the little clans of Judah, from you shall come forth for me one who is to rule in Israel, whose origin is from of old, from ancient days.

[3] Then all the people who were at the gate, along with the elders, said, 'We are witnesses. May the Lord make the woman who is coming into your house like Rachel and Leah, who together built up the house of Israel. May you produce children in Ephrathah and bestow a name in Bethlehem;

[4] Now David was the son of an Ephrathite of Bethlehem in Judah, named Jesse, who had eight sons. In the days of Saul the man was already old and advanced in years.

[5] They told him, 'In Bethlehem of Judea; for so it has been written by the prophet: "And you, Bethlehem, in the land of Judah, are by no means least among the rulers of Judah; for from you shall come a ruler who is to shepherd my people Israel." '

[6] Has not the scripture said that the Messiah is descended from David and comes from Bethlehem, the village where David lived?'

[7] When Joseph awoke from sleep, he did as the angel of the Lord commanded him; he took her as his wife, but had no marital relations with her until she had borne a son; and he named him Jesus.

wedding had not taken place. The distinctions are only technical. The chiasmus brings out that the stress is finally on the fact that Jesus was of the house and family of David, and that he therefore had to be born in Bethlehem because of his Messiahship. There is as yet no evidence that the Jews were actually previously expecting the Messiah to be born in Bethlehem. It may well be that the discovery by the 'wise men' of Jerusalem in Mt. 2.5 was the first recognition of the fact. But Luke's readers would certainly know it, and would recognise that the Scriptures had said it. It is while they are at Bethlehem that (Lk. 1.7):

> the time came for her to deliver her child. And she gave birth to
> her first born son and wrapped him in bands of cloth, and laid
> him in a manger, because there was no place for them in the
> guest room

Many of the details supplied in the Christmas telling of this story do not come from Luke. There is no indication of a long search for a place to stay or of an insensitive innkeeper who made Mary and Joseph stay outdoors. Note that he is described as *her* first born son. This emphasises the fulfilment of the promise to her, or it may be hinting at the fact that Joseph had had no part in his conception. Mary wraps her new born son in *swaddling*, long strips of cloth that would keep him warm. The 'guest room' (see below) was full so Mary and Joseph and the new born slept on the ground floor and there would have been others sleeping there also, along with the domestic animals as was the practice on Jewish homes. Animals were seen as valuable and family 'friends', they provided, for example, the daily milk supply. It was into one of these 'feeding boxes' that Mary's son was laid (see Bailey 1994:xv). This contrasts with the comfort of Caesar's palace from where he had issued the edict that had brought Mary and Joseph to be lying on a floor among the animals. There was no room for Mary and

Joseph in the 'kataluma', the 'guestroom' (Lk. 22.11;[1] Mk. 14.14[2]).

This is the same word to describe the place that Jesus and his disciples would later eat the Passover (Lk. 22.11[3]) and it could also mean a *resting place* (which could include and inn) but it is unlikely that in returning to family Mary and Joseph would sleep at an inn (cf. C. S. Keener, 1994:194; Witherington 1989:69-70). Inns were for people who had nowhere else to go and who could find no hospitality but at a time such as Luke is describing hospitality would be at its strongest and most generous. Sleeping on the ground floor was common and it was not an insult, especially when the house was full, the greater insult to Jewish customs of hospitality would have been to have had the heavily pregnant Mary and her husband stay in a stable or in the open air. The contrast between the birth's commonness and the child's greatness that Luke draws could not be greater. The promised one of God enters creation among the creation; the profane decree of a census has put the child in the promised city of messianic origin. God is quietly at work, and a stable is the Messiah's throne room.

b. The Response to the Birth of the Son of Mary (Lk. 2.8-14)

As with the birth of John we cannot ignore the rest of Luke's narrative about the birth of Mary's son simply because the present work's main preoccupation is to present the interactions that Jesus has with women in the gospels and the meaning and significance of these. The narrative that Luke now tells of the appearance of the angels to the shepherds in the fields and their response is an integral part of his Infancy Narrative about the son of Mary and therefore deserves consideration as to its meaning. One thing immediately strikes the reader here and that is that those who come to see the new born child of Mary and Joseph are not those that one would

---

[1] And say to the owner of the house, "The teacher asks you, 'Where is the guest room, where I may eat the Passover with my disciples?'"

[2] And wherever he enters, say to the owner of the house, "The Teacher asks, Where is my guest room where I may eat the Passover with my disciples?"

[3] And say to the owner of the house, "The teacher asks you, 'Where is the guest room, where I may eat the Passover with my disciples?'"

immediately expect: Matthew has the exotic Gentile magi from the mysterious east and Luke has the Jewish shepherds.

That Luke mentions the shepherds fits in with his overall depiction of Jesus as one who comes especially for the poor, for the shepherds were poor and while not exactly despised, they were nevertheless looked down upon. As shepherds they were in ongoing poverty, on top of which their work did not allow for them to observe the cleanness laws (Talmud) and to observe the Sabbath and in the main people saw them as irreligious and dishonest to the extent that their testimony was acceptable in the courts. It may well that these shepherds were those employed by the Temple to look after the sheep that had been brought for Temple offerings but even so they would still be very poor and find religious observance very difficult. These shepherds are the last of a trilogy in Luke's narrative in which angels make their appearance before the coming of the *Son of the Most* High which we might table thus:

Zechariah – Mary- Shepherds

and the first of a triology of those who welcome Jesus:

Shepherds Simeon-Anna

On the one side of the them are Zechariah and Mary and on the other side are Simeon and Anna:

Zechariah/Mary-Shepherds-Simeon/Anna

Zechariah would then represent the *priesthood*
Mary would represent *womanhood*
Simeon and Anna all *faithful men and women in Jerusalem*
Shepherds represent *all the people*

Luke moves out from the confines of the ground floor where the new born child is asleep in the manger present with his mother and father and the domestic animals, to the open countryside where the shepherds are *keeping watch over their flock by night* (Lk. 2.8b Luke may have thought night a better time for a divine revelation cf. Marshall 1978:110; Drury 1973:37; Delling 1970:1123-1126). This was where David had watched over sheep (1 S 17.15, 34-37[1]) and it was apt, therefore, that shepherds be somehow involved in the birth of the heir to David's throne (Giblin 1967:87-101; Green 1997:131). There is no reason not to doubt that even though shepherds would have found the keeping of Talmudic laws and the Sabbath difficult and have been regarded as unclean, that they did not share the hope of the Messiah who would come and so be regarded as pious men (cf. Brown 1976:528-538). It is while they are watching and talking and being on the alert for anything which might threaten the sheep that (Lk. 2.9):

> an angel of the Lord stood before them, and the glory of the
> Lord shone around them, and they were terrified

With the appearance of the angels the *glory of the Lord shone around them* and even the irreligious, despised and poor shepherds knew what the *glory of the Lord* meant: this was God revealing himself in the *shekinah*, the revealing of his *kabod* (glory) so long expected and patiently waited for by Israel, as a sign of what was yet to come. It would be revealed again at the Transfiguration (Lk. 9.29[2]) and at the Resurrection (Mt. 28.3-4[3]) and it would contrast with the darkness of the crucifixion of the son of Mary who

---

[1] but David went back and forth from Saul to feed his father's sheep at Bethlehem. But David said to Saul, 'Your servant used to keep sheep for his father; and whenever a lion or a bear came, and took a lamb from the flock, I went after it and struck it down, rescuing the lamb from its mouth; and if it turned against me, I would catch it by the jaw, strike it down, and kill it. Your servant has killed both lions and bears; and this uncircumcised Philistine shall be like one of them, since he has defied the armies of the living God.' David said, 'The Lord, who saved me from the paw of the lion and from the paw of the bear, will save me from the hand of this Philistine.' So Saul said to David, 'Go, and may the Lord be with you!'

[2] And while he was praying, the appearance of his face changed, and his clothes became dazzling white.

[3] His appearance was like lightning, and his clothing white as snow. For fear of him the guards shook and became like dead men.

would be proclaimed *Son of God* (Mk. 15.39[1]) by those who watched him die. This was the last thing that shepherds in the fields would be expecting and their response is terror.

But once again, as with Zechariah and Mary, the angel moves quickly to calm their fear and reassure them (Lk. 2.10a). The shepherds are told to not *be afraid* because the angel brings *good news* (euangelizō, cf. Lk. 1:19,[2] is a combination of the words *good* and *message*. It is used often in the Septuagint for preaching a message of gladness or joy (cf. 2 S 4.10;[3] 18.19-20,31;[4] 1 K 1.42;[5] Ps. 39.10[6]) and came to be used in a technical sense for preaching the gospel of Jesus Christ (cf., e.g., Lk. 3.18;[7] 4.18,43;[8] Acts 5.42;[9] 10.36;[10] 13.32;[11]). And this *good news* is news of *great joy* (cf. Lk. 1.14, 47, 58) for it was to be for *all the people*. This was the promise of Gen. 3.15;[12] 12.3;[13] Ex. 19.5-6;[14] and of the eighth century prophets; it is

---

[1] Now when the centurion, who stood facing him, saw that in this way he breathed his last, he said, 'Truly this man was God's Son!'

[2] The angel replied, 'I am Gabriel. I stand in the presence of God, and I have been sent to speak to you and to bring you this good news.

[3] when the one who told me, "See, Saul is dead", thought he was bringing good news, I seized him and killed him at Ziklag, this was the reward I gave him for his news.

[4] Then Ahimaaz son of Zadok said, 'Let me run, and carry tidings to the king that the Lord has delivered him from the power of his enemies.' Joab said to him, 'You are not to carry tidings today; you may carry tidings another day, but today you shall not do so, because the king's son is dead.'

[5] While he was still speaking, Jonathan son of the priest Abiathar arrived. Adonijah said, 'Come in, for you are a worthy man and surely you bring good news.'

[6] But at the time when Saul's daughter Merab should have been given to David, she was given to Adriel the Meholathite as a wife. Now Saul's daughter Michal loved David. Saul was told, and the thing pleased him

[7] So, with many other exhortations, he proclaimed the good news to the people.

[8] 'The Spirit of the Lord is upon me, because he has anointed meto bring good news to the poor.He has sent me to proclaim release to the captives and recovery of sight to the blind, to let the oppressed go free; But he said to them, 'I must proclaim the good news of the kingdom of God to the other cities also; for I was sent for this purpose.'

[9] And every day in the temple and at home they did not cease to teach and proclaim Jesus as the Messiah.

[10] You know the message he sent to the people of Israel, preaching peace by Jesus Christ, he is Lord of all.

[11] And we bring you the good news that what God promised to our ancestors.

[12] I will put enmity between you and the woman, and between your offspring and hers; he will strike your head, and you will strike his heel.'

[13] I will bless those who bless you, and the one who curses you I will curse; and in you all the families of the earth shall be blessed.'

[14] Now therefore, if you obey my voice and keep my covenant, you shall be my treasured possession out of all the peoples. Indeed, the whole earth is mine, but you shall be for me a priestly kingdom and a holy nation.

the mystery hidden in ages past, but now fully revealed in Christ (cf. Eph. 2.11-3.13). This same universal emphasis is repeated and defined in Lk. 1.32: this good news for was all classes of people not just for the righteous and the favoured and even reaches to outcast shepherds (and by implication to Luke's Gentile readers). Luke intends it to be understood in its wider connections. And the *good news* is that *in the city of David* a *saviour* is *born* who is *Christ the Lord* (Lk. 2.10). *Saviour* was used of God in the Old Testament (cf. 1.47; Is. 43.3,[1] 11; 45.15,[2] 21; 49.26;[3] 60.16[4]). In the Roman Empire it was used of Caesar (see Bovon 2009:125-126). The word in Hebrew means *deliverer* and is part of the name of Jesus (i.e., Hosea) this and Lk. 1.47 are surprisingly the only use of this term in the Synoptic Gospels. The literal meaning of *Christ* is *Anointed One* from the Greek verb 'chriō'. It refers to the Coming King (Pss. 2.2;[5] 84.9;[6] 89.49-51;[7] 132.10,17[8]) who will be called and equipped to do God's will in initiating the restoration and the new age. The Hebrew term is translated in Greek as *Christ* ('christos'). The Greek term *Lord* ('kurios') can be used in a general sense or in a developed theological sense (on how Luke may have used the term cf. Schurmann 1970:1.110). It can mean *mister, sir, master, owner, husband* or *the full God-man* (cf. Jn. 9.36,[9] 38). The Old Testament (Hebrew, 'adon') usage of this term came from the Jews' reluctance to

---

These are the words that you shall speak to the Israelites.' Then Moses went up to God; the Lord called to him from the mountain, saying, 'Thus you shall say to the house of Jacob, and tell the Israelites:

[1] For I am the Lord your God, the Holy One of Israel, your Saviour. I give Egypt as your ransom, Ethiopia and Seba in exchange for you.

[2] Truly, you are a God who hides himself, O God of Israel, the Saviour.

[3] I will make your oppressors eat their own flesh, and they shall be drunk with their own blood as with wine. Then all flesh shall know that I am the Lord your Saviour, and your Redeemer, the Mighty One of Jacob.

[4] You shall suck the milk of nations, you shall suck the breasts of kings; and you shall know that I, the Lord, am your Saviour and your Redeemer, the Mighty One of Jacob.

[5] The kings of the earth set themselves, and the rulers take counsel together, against the Lord and his anointed.

[6] Behold our shield, O God; look on the face of your anointed.

[7] Lord, where is your steadfast love of old, which by your faithfulness you swore to David? Remember, O Lord, how your servant is taunted; how I bear in my bosom the insults of the peoples, with which your enemies taunt, O Lord, with which they taunted the footsteps of your anointed.

[8] For your servant David's sake do not turn away the face of your anointed one.

[9] He answered, 'And who is he, sir? Tell me, so that I may believe in him.'

pronounce the covenant name for God, YHWH, which was from the Hebrew verb 'to be' (cf. Ex. 3.14). They were afraid of breaking the Commandment which said, *Thou shall not take the name of the Lord thy God in vain* (cf. Ex. 20.7;[1] Deut. 5.11). They thought if they did not pronounce it, they could not take it in vain, so they substituted the Hebrew word *adon*, which had a similar meaning to the Greek word *kurios* (Lord) (cf. Marshall 1978:110). The New Testament authors will use this term to describe the full deity of Christ (e.g., Lk. 2.11;[2] Jn. 20.28;[3] Acts 10.36;[4] 1 Cor. 2.8;[5] Phil. 2.11;[6] James 2.1;[7] Rev. 19.16[8]). The phrase *Jesus is Lord* was the public confession of faith and a baptismal formula of the early church (cf. Rom.10:9-13;[9] I Cor.12:3;[10] Phil.2:11[11]) and in Acts 2:36 both *Christ* and *Lord* are used of Jesus. As Messiah he fulfils all the promises in the Old Testament of a great Deliverer from the house of David. As Lord he is superior to David as his Lord (Lk. 20.41-44;[12] Ps. 110.1[13]), and Paul takes it further by seeing in the title the Name above every name, the name of YHWH (Phil. 2.9-11). So the three titles reveal his saving power, his

---

[1] You shall not make wrongful use of the name of the Lord your God, for the Lord will not acquit anyone who misuses his name.

[2] To you is born this day in the city of David a Saviour, who is the Messiah, the Lord.

[3] Thomas answered him, 'My Lord and my God!'

[4] You know the message he sent to the people of Israel, preaching peace by Jesus Christ, he is Lord of all.

[5] None of the rulers of this age understood this; for if they had, they would not have crucified the Lord of glory.

[6] And every tongue should confess that Jesus Christ is Lord, to the glory of God the Father.

[7] My brothers and sisters, do you with your acts of favouritism really believe in our glorious Lord Jesus Christ?

[8] On his robe and on his thigh he has a name inscribed, 'King of kings and Lord of lords'.

[9] Because if you confess with your lips that Jesus is Lord and believe in your heart that God raised him from the dead, you will be saved. For one believes with the heart and so is justified, and one confesses with the mouth and so is saved. The scripture says, 'No one who believes in him will be put to shame.' For there is no distinction between Jew and Greek; the same Lord is Lord of all and is generous to all who call on him. For, 'Everyone who calls on the name of the Lord shall be saved.'

[10] Therefore I want you to understand that no one speaking by the Spirit of God ever says 'Let Jesus be cursed!' and no one can say 'Jesus is Lord' except by the Holy Spirit.

[11] And every tongue should confess that Jesus Christ is Lord, to the glory of God the Father.

[12] hen he said to them, 'How can they say that the Messiah is David's son? For David himself says in the book of Psalms,"The Lord said to my Lord, 'Sit at my right hand, until I make your enemies your footstool.' " David thus calls him Lord; so how can he be his son?'

[13] The Lord says to my lord, 'Sit at my right hand until I make your enemies your footstool.'

fulfilment of prophecy, and his position as supreme Lord. The chapter began with Caesar Augustus, who was regularly called Saviour and Lord. Now we are introduced to the greater and more effective Saviour and Lord as pronounced from heaven. The announcement of the angel used the same kind of announcement/proclamation language as that used by rulers when a new heir to the throne was born; it was the announcement of the birth of a king. The birth of Augustus was also said to have been announced as *good news*; it was *good news* for all and in the case Luke uses, the words happened to be true, the birth of the son of Mary really is *good news*.

In Lk. 2.1, Augustus had proclaimed his decree, now God was issuing his as he called the shepherds to 'enrol' and give their fealty and loyalty to the new born Saviour. The great Augustus, had called the strongest in his empire to pay homage to him, here (symbolically) God calls the mightiest in *his* empire, the poor and the despised; the two empires were progressing along history side by side but the empire of the poor, the lowly, the meek and the despised would eventually conquer (cf. Laurentin 1986:184). The angels appear to shepherds in the city of David who was originally a shepherd and Matthew in his use of Mic.5.2 had said that from Bethlehem would come a *leader* to *shepherd my people Israel*. It is not without strong symbolic import, therefore, that *shepherd/shepherds/sheparding* was a recurrent motif of God's servants of his word through Old and New Testaments (Num. 27.17;[1] 1 K 22.17;[2] Jer. 23.4;[3] Ezek. 34.23;[4] 37.24;[5]

---

[1] Who shall go out before them and come in before them, who shall lead them out and bring them in, so that the congregation of the Lord may not be like sheep without a shepherd.'

[2] Then Micaiah said, 'I saw all Israel scattered on the mountains, like sheep that have no shepherd; and the Lord said, "These have no master; let each one go home in peace."

[3] I will raise up shepherds over them who will shepherd them, and they shall not fear any longer, or be dismayed, nor shall any be missing, says the Lord.

[4] I will set up over them one shepherd, my servant David, and he shall feed them: he shall feed them and be their shepherd.

[5] My servant David shall be king over them; and they shall all have one shepherd. They shall follow my ordinances and be careful to observe my statutes.

Zech. 13.7;[1] Jn. 21.15-17[2]); fellow-shepherds with God (Pss. 23.1;[3] 80.1;[4] Is. 40.11;[5] Jn. 10.11-14;[6] Heb.13.20;[7] 1 Pet.2.25;[8] 5.4[9]). Caesar wanted great leaders and men of wealth and position (Lk. 22.25), God wanted the humble and poor to be his shepherds and through whom to do great things (Lk. 22.24-27;[10] 1 Cor. 1.27[11]).

At Lk. 2.12 the angel tells the shepherds about the sign they will see which bears out the truth of what he has announced to them:

> And this is the sign to you, You will find a babe wrapped in
> swaddling clothes, and lying in a manger

They were to go, find a baby wrapped in swaddling and lying in manger:

[1.] Awake, O sword, against my shepherd, against the man who is my associate,' says the Lord of hosts. Strike the shepherd, that the sheep may be scattered; I will turn my hand against the little ones.

[2] When they had finished breakfast, Jesus said to Simon Peter, 'Simon son of John, do you love me more than these?' He said to him, 'Yes, Lord; you know that I love you.' Jesus said to him, 'Feed my lambs.' A second time he said to him, 'Simon son of John, do you love me?' He said to him, 'Yes, Lord; you know that I love you.' Jesus said to him, 'Tend my sheep.' He said to him the third time, 'Simon son of John, do you love me?' Peter felt hurt because he said to him the third time, 'Do you love me?' And he said to him, 'Lord, you know everything; you know that I love you.' Jesus said to him, 'Feed my sheep.

[3] The Lord is my shepherd, I shall not want.

[4] Give ear, O Shepherd of Israel, you who lead Joseph like a flock! You who are enthroned upon the cherubim, shine forth

[5] He will feed his flock like a shepherd; he will gather the lambs in his arms, and carry them in his bosom, and gently lead the mother sheep.

[6] 'I am the good shepherd. The good shepherd lays down his life for the sheep. The hired hand, who is not the shepherd and does not own the sheep, sees the wolf coming and leaves the sheep and runs away and the wolf snatches them and scatters them. The hired hand runs away because a hired hand does not care for the sheep. I am the good shepherd. I know my own and my own know me,

[7] Now may the God of peace, who brought back from the dead our Lord Jesus, the great shepherd of the sheep, by the blood of the eternal covenant.

[8] For you were going astray like sheep, but now you have returned to the shepherd and guardian of your souls.

[9] And when the chief shepherd appears, you will win the crown of glory that never fades away.

[10] A dispute also arose among them as to which one of them was to be regarded as the greatest. But he said to them, 'The kings of the Gentiles lord it over them; and those in authority over them are called benefactors. But not so with you; rather the greatest among you must become like the youngest, and the leader like one who serves. For who is greater, the one who is at the table or the one who serves? Is it not the one at the table? But I am among you as one who serves.

[11] But God chose what is foolish in the world to shame the wise; God chose what is weak in the world to shame the strong.

this would be no accident for it was pre-arranged, the Son of the Most High, who holds all things together (Col. 1.17;[1] Heb. 1.3[2]), was himself held together in swaddling clothes. This would be a fitting sign to give to shepherds: a baby lying in a manger where animals fed revealed one associated with their kind of work, and so revealed one one who had come to the meek and the despised.

One wonders if this was an intentional allusion to Is. 7.14:[3] Zechariah and Mary had to believe without immediate confirmation, but these shepherds are given immediate confirmation. No sooner does the angel give this command than (Lk. 2.13-14):

> suddenly there was with the angel a multitude of the heavenly
> host praising God, and saying, Glory to God in the highest,
> And on earth peace among men in whom he is well pleased

When the Kings and emperors were born legions of their armies would be called on to give praise and to hail the birth of the new born son. But here, greater legions than those of earthly emperors came forth to hail to birth of the *Son of the Most High*, and Son *of God* and celebrate his birth. When God laid the foundations of the earth, *the morning stars sang together, and all the sons of the elohim* ('heavenly beings' or 'God') *shouted for joy* (Job 38.7). How much more fitting that when God laid his new foundation stone (1 Cor. 3.11[4]) and new cornerstone (Lk. 20.17;[5] Eph. 2.20;[6] 1 Pet. 2.6[7]) for his new heaven and earth, they should do so even more rapturously: for a moment, at

---

[1] He himself is before all things, and in him all things hold together.

[2] He is the reflection of God's glory and the exact imprint of God's very being, and he sustains all things by his powerful word. When he had made purification for sins, he sat down at the right hand of the Majesty on high.

[3] Therefore the Lord himself will give you a sign. Look, the young woman is with child and shall bear a son, and shall name him Immanuel.

[4] For no one can lay any foundation other than the one that has been laid; that foundation is Jesus Christ.

[5] But he looked at them and said, 'What then does this text mean:"The stone that the builders rejected has become the cornerstone"?

[6] Built upon the foundation of the apostles and prophets, with Christ Jesus himself as the cornerstone.

[7] For it stands in scripture: 'See, I am laying in Zion a stone, a cornerstone chosen and precious; and whoever believes in him will not be put to shame.'

least, the veil between heaven and earth is opened and heaven's view of things is revealed to the shepherds on earth (cf. 2 K 6.17[1]). The message of the angels, therefore, is not some mystical heavenly obscurity, it is concerned and connected with real events in the real world. The appear and give *Glory to God in the highest* and this is their eternal proclamation whether they are on earth or in heaven, for it is the angels who see the glory of God and know him as he truly is (Rev. 4.11;[2] 5.13[3]) but now the angels sing something different:

> and on earth peace among men in whom he is well pleased.

This language is typically Semitic and has been found in hymns among the Dead Sea Scrolls. The phrase is not a declaration of universal salvation but refers to those who are the special objects of God's grace. They are like the God-fearers Mary mentioned in Lk. 1.50-53[4], whom God will exalt with his blessing. They are the saved or the elect, those on whom God has bestowed the favour of his grace.

The coming of the son of Mary into the world offers humanity peace with God (Rom. 5.1[5]) and peace from God (Rom. 1.7[6] passim) and the peace of God which surpasses all comprehension (Phil. 4.7). This would be for all those on whom his favour rested. To bring and establish peace was a task of

---

[1] Then Elisha prayed: 'O Lord, please open his eyes that he may see.' So the Lord opened the eyes of the servant, and he saw; the mountain was full of horses and chariots of fire all around Elisha.

[2] 'You are worthy, our Lord and God, to receive glory and honour and power, for you created all things, and by your will they existed and were created.'

[3] Then I heard every creature in heaven and on earth and under the earth and in the sea, and all that is in them, singing, 'To the one seated on the throne and to the Lamb be blessing and honour and glory and might for ever and ever!'

[4] His mercy is for those who fear him from generation to generation. He has shown strength with his arm; he has scattered the proud in the thoughts of their hearts. He has brought down the powerful from their thrones, and lifted up the lowly; he has filled the hungry with good things, and sent the rich away empty.

[5] Therefore, since we are justified by faith, we have peace with God through our Lord Jesus Christ.

[6] To all God's beloved in Rome, who are called to be saints: Grace to you and peace from God our Father and the Lord Jesus Christ.

the Messiah (Is. 9.6-7;[1] Zech. 9.9-10[2]). This was indeed what the son of Mary had come to do as the prince of Peace: to save humanity and enable it to be reconciled to God through his provision for their need so that he might reveal his kindness towards them continually for evermore (Eph. 2.6-7[3]). This was why the angel had called the child, 'the Saviour'. This promise of peace and goodwill to all who found favour with God was all the more significant at the time of the child's birth because the world was in the 'Pax Romana' and 'peace' reigned over the known world and this was a remarkable achievement. But peace did not reign in the hearts of men and women and this is why, ultimately, the Pax Romana failed. The mighty Augustus might give peace from war and strife but he could not give peace of heart for which men and women yearn more than for outward peace. Only the son of Mary could bring this peace (Lk. 2.15-20):

> When the angels had left them and gone into heaven, the shepherds said to one another, 'Let us go now to Bethlehem and see this thing that has taken place, which the Lord has made known to us.' So they went with haste and found Mary and Joseph, and the child lying in the manger. When they saw this, they made known what had been told them about this child; and all who heard it were amazed at what the shepherds told them. But Mary treasured all these words and pondered them in her heart. The shepherds returned, glorifying and praising God for all they had heard and seen, as it had been told them.

In this account each set of characters plays a major role. The angels present

---

[1] For a child has been born for us, a son given to us; authority rests upon his shoulders; and he is named Wonderful Counsellor, Mighty God, Everlasting Father, Prince of Peace. His authority shall grow continually, and there shall be endless peace for the throne of David and his kingdom. He will establish and uphold it with justice and with righteousness from this time onwards and for evermore. The zeal of the Lord of hosts will do this.

[2] Rejoice greatly, O daughter Zion! Shout aloud, O daughter Jerusalem! Lo, your king comes to you; triumphant and victorious is he, humble and riding on a donkey, on a colt, the foal of a donkey. He will cut off the chariot from Ephraim and the warhorse from Jerusalem; and the battle-bow shall be cut off, and he shall command peace to the nations; his dominion shall be from sea to sea, and from the River to the ends of the earth.

[3] And raised us up with him and seated us with him in the heavenly places in Christ Jesus, so that in the ages to come he might show the immeasurable riches of his grace in kindness towards us in Christ Jesus.

the commentary of heaven on the events of Lk. 2.1-7. They identify the child and reflect the heavens' excitement that this child has come to do God's work. The shepherds have the type of response any of us should have as we contemplate these events. Their curiosity leads them to *go to Bethlehem and see this thing that has happened.* And once they had seen what they saw they went away and continually told everywhere what the angels had told them about this child, and there was great wonder everywhere as people considered what the shepherds said. They would make it known for years, it was a never to be forgotten event. Such amazement is another theme of Luke's writings (e.g. 20.26;[1] 24.12,[2] 41; Acts 2.7,[3] 12; 3.10;[4] 9.21;[5] 13.12[6]). For the Good News is truly amazing. These are the first two instances of what will become common in Luke's writings, especially in Acts, the 'spreading of the word'. The news was so wonderful that it could not be held back. As they see God's word honoured in the presence of the sign, they come to testify to God's work and tell the story of the child. This birth is no mere arrival of a new life, as poignant as each such event is. The story is not told so that hearers can identify with the new mother and father or enjoy a story of hope, of a touching birth in humble surroundings. This birth has value because of whose birth it is. The shepherds have found that the angel's words were true, that events have transpired *just as they had been told.* God's word is coming to pass; his plan is again strategically at work. They break out in praise to God because he

---

[1] And they were not able in the presence of the people to trap him by what he said; and being amazed by his answer, they became silent.

[2] But Peter got up and ran to the tomb; stooping and looking in, he saw the linen cloths by themselves; then he went home, amazed at what had happened. While in their joy they were disbelieving and still wondering, he said to them, 'Have you anything here to eat?'

[3] Amazed and astonished, they asked, 'Are not all these who are speaking Galileans? All were amazed and perplexed, saying to one another, 'What does this mean?'

[4] And they recognized him as the one who used to sit and ask for alms at the Beautiful Gate of the temple; and they were filled with wonder and amazement at what had happened to him.

[5] All who heard him were amazed and said, 'Is not this the man who made havoc in Jerusalem among those who invoked this name? And has he not come here for the purpose of bringing them bound before the chief priests?'

[6] When the proconsul saw what had happened, he believed, for he was astonished at the teaching about the Lord.

has sent Jesus, the Saviour, Lord and Christ. Mary, to whom the shepherds would have explained everything, depicts the wonder of experiencing the inbreaking of God in her life and kept what they had said, along with what the angel had said to her earlier, and everything else that she heard about those days, and *pondered on them* regularly in her heart (Lk. 2.19). They were not things easily forgotten. It was not until she got older and 'more sensible' that she tried to but a brake on Jesus' ministry (Mk. 3.21, 31-35[1]) for, godly woman though she was, like us she was only human. And as for the shepherds, they returned to the countryside, and to their flocks, glorifying and praising God for all that they had heard and seen. Such behaviour inevitably follows reception of the Good News (Lk. 5.26;[2] 7.16;[3] 13.13;[4] 17.15;[5] 18.43,[6] 23.47;[7] Acts 2.47;[8] 4.21;[9] 13.48[10]). The *glad tidings* were for all mankind and the listeners to the shepherds' report *were amazed*. Their response exemplifies the awe that should fill anyone who hears Jesus' story. Note the interesting contrasts: The hearers were filled with wonder, Mary kept it all in her heart and meditated on it, the shepherds glorified and praised God. They had no doubt about what had happened.

---

[1] When his family heard it, they went out to restrain him, for people were saying, 'He has gone out of his mind.'; Then his mother and his brothers came; and standing outside, they sent to him and called him. A crowd was sitting around him; and they said to him, 'Your mother and your brothers and sisters are outside, asking for you.' And he replied, 'Who are my mother and my brothers?' And looking at those who sat around him, he said, 'Here are my mother and my brothers! Whoever does the will of God is my brother and sister and mother.'

[2] Amazement seized all of them, and they glorified God and were filled with awe, saying, 'We have seen strange things today.'

[3] Fear seized all of them; and they glorified God, saying, 'A great prophet has risen among us!' and 'God has looked favourably on his people!'

[4] When he laid his hands on her, immediately she stood up straight and began praising God.

[5] Then one of them, when he saw that he was healed, turned back, praising God with a loud voice.

[6] Immediately he regained his sight and followed him, glorifying God; and all the people, when they saw it, praised God.

[7] When the centurion saw what had taken place, he praised God and said, 'Certainly this man was innocent.'

[8] praising God and having the goodwill of all the people. And day by day the Lord added to their number those who were being saved.

[9] After threatening them again, they let them go, finding no way to punish them because of the people, for all of them praised God for what had happened.

[10] When the Gentiles heard this, they were glad and praised the word of the Lord; and as many as had been destined for eternal life became believers.

c. Mary's Son Becomes A Son of Abraham (Lk. 2.21-24)

Reflecting the piety of obedient Jewish parents, Joseph and Mary undertake to circumcise the child on the eighth day and give him the name the angel said he should possess, Jesus. In every action this couple is showing faithfulness. They are examples of faith. As devout Jewish parents, they follow the Mosaic law (McBride 1984:42). Jesus has been born into a good family. The testimony to Jesus continues as both a prophet and a prophetess reveal God's plan. By showing how each gender among the people of God testifies to what God is doing through this child, Luke is saying that all should rejoice at his coming. And culturally it is no accident that both Simeon and Anna are advanced in years. Here is the testimony of two with a full resume of life experience.

Anna's and Simeon's prophecies share a note of hope and expectation, along with declarations that in this child God's promise is moving into realisation. Luke also reveals Jesus' superiority to John in this passage, for the testimony about John stops with his circumcision but the praise of Jesus extends long past the eighth day of life. Here two old and wise prophets of Jewish piety speak not only for the nation but for all humankind, as Simeon's prophecy mentions Jesus' relationship to the Gentiles (for the first time in the book). This passage also provides the first hint that all will not go well. Mary will experience the pain of seeing her son rejected by a divided Israel. The Law required that Mary and Jesus be purified from ritual uncleanness due to childbirth. This would take forty days (for a son, eighty for a daughter) and when this was completed offerings and sacrifices could then be made. The uncleanness of Mary is evidence of the reality of the birth and that the child was true man. The pronoun *their* has bothered Bible students because it involves a sin offering for both the mother and the child, but it was right that the son of Mary should be subject to this because the was *born under the Law* (Gal. 4.4). He was sent under the likeness of sinful flesh and for sin, becoming like the rest of humanity that he might dies for sin on their behalf (Heb. 2.17[1]); so he went through what he did not for his own sin since he was without sin (2 Cor. 5.21;[2] 1 Pet. 2.22[3]) but for humanity as representative man.

As I shall show in a moment, Simeon at Lk. 2.29-32 is in parallel with Elizabeth at Lk. 1.41-45: both prophecy under the inspiration of the Holy Spirit over Jesus: Elizabeth before his birth, and Simeon after his birth. Elizabeth and Simeon, therefore, represent the whole of humanity that acknowledges the coming of the son of Mary into the world. It might be observed here that all the people men and women who have been somehow involved in the 'Jesus event' are all ordinary people. They are people of God but there is no chief priest, scribe or elder among them; the son of Mary does not come to the great but rather to those who will receive and accept him. Jesus' parents are law-abiding Jews. They show up at the temple to perform sacrifices associated with the wife's purification after birth (Lev. 12.2-4, 6,[4] see below). Such a ceremony occurs forty days after the child's arrival (see, Fitmeyer 1981:421). At the same time the first born child is to be set aside to the Lord (Ex. 13.2, 12, 16;[5] 34.19;[6] Num. 18.15-16[7]). Jesus' parents bring the child along, though that is not necessary. They offer *a pair*

---

[1] Therefore he had to become like his brothers and sisters in every respect, so that he might be a merciful and faithful high priest in the service of God, to make a sacrifice of atonement for the sins of the people.

[2] For our sake he made him to be sin who knew no sin, so that in him we might become the righteousness of God.

[3] 'He committed no sin, and no deceit was found in his mouth.'

[4] If a woman conceives and bears a male child, she shall be ceremonially unclean for seven days; as at the time of her menstruation, she shall be unclean. On the eighth day the flesh of his foreskin shall be circumcised. Her time of blood purification shall be thirty-three days; she shall not touch any holy thing, or come into the sanctuary, until the days of her purification are completed; When the days of her purification are completed, whether for a son or for a daughter, she shall bring to the priest at the entrance of the tent of meeting a lamb in its first year for a burnt-offering, and a pigeon or a turtle-dove for a sin-offering.

[5] Consecrate to me all the firstborn; whatever is the first to open the womb among the Israelites, of human beings and animals, is mine. you shall set apart to the Lord all that first opens the womb. All the firstborn of your livestock that are males shall be the Lord's. It shall serve as a sign on your hand and as an emblem on your forehead that by strength of hand the Lord brought us out of Egypt.'

[6] All that first opens the womb is mine, all your male livestock, the firstborn of cow and sheep.

[7] The first issue of the womb of all creatures, human and animal, which is offered to the Lord, shall be yours; but the firstborn of human beings you shall redeem, and the firstborn of unclean animals you shall redeem. Their redemption price, reckoned from one month of age, you shall fix at five shekels of silver, according to the shekel of the sanctuary (that is, twenty gerahs).

of doves or two young pigeons. This offering recalls Lev. 12.8,[1] though the wording is closer to the Greek Old Testament version of Lev. 5.11.[2] Since this offering is the one usually made by the poor, Jesus is identified with the very people he reached out to save (Lk. 1.52;[3] 4.18-19;[4] 6.20;[5] 7.22-23[6]). But Joseph and Mary do not live in abject poverty, since Joseph is a carpenter by trade. This could be the offering of someone from a 'middle-class' background as well. Regardless of their precise social status, Luke is making it clear that Jesus' parents are not spiritual renegades, but Jews who are sensitive and faithful to the Mosaic law (a point reinforced in Lk. 2.40-52,[7] when they will make their customary annual pilgrimage to Jerusalem). All the persons surrounding Jesus at his birth have a heritage of devotion to God. The testimony to Jesus stands on the shoulders of a series of highly respectable figures. Luke writes (Lk. 2.21):

---

[1] If she cannot afford a sheep, she shall take two turtle-doves or two pigeons, one for a burnt-offering and the other for a sin-offering; and the priest shall make atonement on her behalf, and she shall be clean.

[2] But if you cannot afford two turtle-doves or two pigeons, you shall bring as your offering for the sin that you have committed one-tenth of an ephah of choice flour for a sin-offering; you shall not put oil on it or lay frankincense on it, for it is a sin-offering.

[3] He has brought down the powerful from their thrones, and lifted up the lowly.

[4] 'The Spirit of the Lord is upon me, because he has anointed me to bring good news to the poor. He has sent me to proclaim release to the captives and recovery of sight to the blind, to let the oppressed go free, to proclaim the year of the Lord's favour.'

[5] Then he looked up at his disciples and said:'Blessed are you who are poor, for yours is the kingdom of God.

[6] And he answered them, 'Go and tell John what you have seen and heard: the blind receive their sight, the lame walk, the lepers are cleansed, the deaf hear, the dead are raised, the poor have good news brought to them. And blessed is anyone who takes no offence at me.'

[7] Now every year his parents went to Jerusalem for the festival of the Passover. And when he was twelve years old, they went up as usual for the festival. When the festival was ended and they started to return, the boy Jesus stayed behind in Jerusalem, but his parents did not know it. Assuming that he was in the group of travellers, they went a day's journey. Then they started to look for him among their relatives and friends. When they did not find him, they returned to Jerusalem to search for him. After three days they found him in the temple, sitting among the teachers, listening to them and asking them questions. And all who heard him were amazed at his understanding and his answers. When his parents saw him they were astonished; and his mother said to him, 'Child, why have you treated us like this? Look, your father and I have been searching for you in great anxiety.' He said to them, 'Why were you searching for me? Did you not know that I must be in my Father's house?' But they did not understand what he said to them. Then he went down with them and came to Nazareth, and was obedient to them. His mother treasured all these things in her heart.

> After eight days had passed, it was time to circumcise the child;
> and he was called Jesus, the name given by the angel before he
> was conceived in the womb.

This ritual of circumcision had to be undergone by every male is they did not want to be cut off from Israel; the ritual of circumcision was considered so important that it could even be carried out on the Sabbath and wit was a sign that the child was being brought into the covenant God made with Abraham (Gen. 17.12[1]). The delay for seven days (see below) with the actual circumcision taking place on the eighth, was to fulfil the *removal by waiting* of the uncleanness of childbirth (due to contact with blood and afterbirth). The naming of the child might indicate that naming at the time of circumcision had become an established custom. For Luke, given that he makes a comment on it, this naming is important because Jesus is named with the name given by the angel before his conception and so it highlights his separation to God from before his birth. Luke continues (Lk. 2.22-24):

> When the time came for their purification according to the law
> of Moses, they brought him up to Jerusalem to present him to
> the Lord (as it is written in the law of the Lord, 'Every first
> born male shall be designated as holy to the Lord'), and they
> offered a sacrifice according to what is stated in the law of the
> Lord, 'a pair of turtle-doves or two young pigeons.'

The Law said that every first born male in Israel belonged to God for service in God's dwelling-place because they were viewed as having been redeemed by God at the Passover and so had become his. A sacrifice would be offered on the child's behalf but then so that they could be redeemed from obligation of service at the Tabernacle/Temple (this has been substituted by the Levites) five shekels had to be paid to a priest at least a

---

[1] Throughout your generations every male among you shall be circumcised when he is eight days old, including the slave born in your house and the one bought with your money from any foreigner who is not of your offspring.

full moon period after the actual birth (Ex. 13.2, 12;[1] Num.18.15;[2] cf. 1 S 1.24-28[3]). Luke, however, does not mention these actual details because his focus is on the presentation of Jesus, the son of Mary, as holy (see Marshall 1978:116-118 for some of the difficulties surrounding this). When a woman gave birth to a son she was seen to be ritually unclean for seven days. This mean that anyone who came in contact with her was unclean, and anyone who entered the room was unclean. In that forty day period the woman was not allowed to enter the Temple or to participate in any of the liturgical/religious celebration or acts but at the end of forty days her (purification would be complete after which she had to offer up a lamb as a *whole burnt offering* ('that which goes up'). This was an offering of atonement, dedication and worship and a pigeon for the *purification for sin sacrifice* (a sacrifice for dealing with and removing sin). However, two pigeons could be offered by the poor (where one of the pigeons substituted for the lamb. Details of the regulations are found in Lev.12). These regulations appear to have been slightly relaxed by Jesus' day so that two young pigeons were seen as sufficient for any woman whether poor or not (cf. Fitzmyer 1981:426;Marshall 1978:esp.119). Thus this offering need not indicate that they were poor (and Joseph was a skilled craftsman and thus not exactly poor. There was no obligation to actually bring the child to the Temple, but women who lived not far from the Temple would want to take the opportunity of showing off their babies when they came to offer their offerings. To have a male child was a triumph and an occasion for gratitude.

---

[1] Consecrate to me all the firstborn; whatever is the first to open the womb among the Israelites, of human beings and animals, is mine. you shall set apart to the Lord all that first opens the womb. All the firstborn of your livestock that are males shall be the Lord's.

[2] The first issue of the womb of all creatures, human and animal, which is offered to the Lord, shall be yours; but the firstborn of human beings you shall redeem, and the firstborn of unclean animals you shall redeem.

[3] When she had weaned him, she took him up with her, along with a three-year-old bull, an ephah of flour, and a skin of wine. She brought him to the house of the Lord at Shiloh; and the child was young. Then they slaughtered the bull, and they brought the child to Eli. And she said, 'Oh, my lord! As you live, my lord, I am the woman who was standing here in your presence, praying to the Lord. For this child I prayed; and the Lord has granted me the petition that I made to him. Therefore I have lent him to the Lord; as long as he lives, he is given to the Lord.' She left him there for the Lord.

The women could watch the ritual by looking from the Nicor gate, but they could not enter into the inner court of the Temple because

1.   they were considered ceremonially unclean
2.   they were women.

The point of these offerings were twofold: redemption and atonement because childbirth was a constant reminder of the woman's part in the sin of Eve in Eden. Every child born in Israel was a reminder of that day and so atonement was needed and the woman needed to be cleansed from impurity. On top of this, the constant contact the child had with its mother rendered it unclean, thus he/she would also need to be ritually purified. In saying that this is to fulfil the Law, i.e.,

> as it is written in the law of the Lord, "Every male which opens
> the womb shall be called holy to the Lord."

Luke is not actually citing a particular biblical verse but is rather combining ideas found in biblical texts, e.g., Ex. 13.2, 12, 15; Num.18.15. So, Mary and Joseph brought their child to the Temple to carry out everything the law demanded. *Their* may mean that of Mary and her child but it could also mean her husband since he too would be unclean from contact with his wife. It is important to distinguish here the *purifying from uncleanness* from the sacrifices which followed and which were for *atonement* (. In all these ritual actions, God's requirements were being fulfilled: Jesus was a *full* Jew as he had to be for *salvation was of the Jews* as the Hebrew scriptures made clear (cf. Jn. 4.22) and the Jews would not accept anyone who had not fulfilled the Law In all respects. Luke skirts over the detail of the ceremonial, he is more concerned to emphasise that Jesus was presented to God as one who was holy before the Lord. The ceremonial was secondary, so he makes no mention of the payment of the five shekels which released Jesus from the obligation of Temple service. He is rather concerned with the fact that Jesus was being offered to God for a greater service. Nevertheless he lays great stress on His parent's obedience to God's command in carrying out all that was required of them, emphasising their continual piety and obedience to the Law (vv. 22-24, 27, 39).

d. The Prophecy of Simeon (Lk. 2.25-35)

It is while the child new born Jesus is in the Temple that Luke introduces the first of two prophetic witnesses two prophetic witnesses to him and his destiny (Lk. 2.25):

> Now there was a man in Jerusalem whose name was Simeon;
> this man was righteous and devout, looking forward to the
> consolation of Israel, and the Holy Spirit rested on him

There have been attempts to identify Simeon, e.g., he might have been the son of Rabbi Hillel and the father of Gamaliel, but this is very doubtful. Others suppose that he was the president of the Sanhedrin. These suggestions are proposed so that Simeon would be a priest and this would be the rite of the buying back of the first born male child, but this is not in the text. Tradition says that he was old, but the text is silent. And so any attempt to thus identify him is futile and in reality beside the point that Luke is making. He is *righteous and devout* This term literally means *taking hold well,* it refers to one who is careful about religious matters, therefore, a pious person. It was used in the Septuagint in Lev. 15.31[1] and Mic. 7.2.[2] It is found only in Luke's writings in the New Testament (cf. 2.25;[3] Acts 2.5;[4]

---

[1] Thus you shall keep the people of Israel separate from their uncleanness, so that they do not die in their uncleanness by defiling my tabernacle that is in their midst.
[2] The faithful have disappeared from the land, and there is no one left who is upright; they all lie in wait for blood, and they hunt each other with nets.
[3] Now there was a man in Jerusalem whose name was Simeon; this man was righteous and devout, looking forward to the consolation of Israel, and the Holy Spirit rested on him.
[4] Now there were devout Jews from every nation under heaven living in Jerusalem.

8.2;[1] 22.12,[2] cf. Mt. 10.41;[3] 19.17;[4] 23.29, 35;[5] 2 Pet. 2.7-8):[6] Simeon is yet another witness to Jesus who possesses a vibrant walk with God. Such piety includes having an eye on the hope of God's redemption. Luke expresses this hope in national terms appropriate for this first-century saint: Simeon has been *waiting for the consolation of Israel.* He longs for the nation's deliverance, just as Zechariah had (Lk. 1.68-75;[7] Is. 40.1;[8] 49.13;[9] 51.3;[10] 57.18;[11] 61.2;[12] 2 Baruch 44.7[13]). In fact, later rabbis will call the Messiah *Menahem,* or *Comforter* (*y. Berakot* 2.3). It was such deliverance that Simeon expected. The Spirit of God directs this scene, because he had revealed to Simeon that death would not come until he *had seen the Lord's*

---

[1] Devout men buried Stephen and made loud lamentation over him.

[2] A certain Ananias, who was a devout man according to the law and well spoken of by all the Jews living there.

[3] Whoever welcomes a prophet in the name of a prophet will receive a prophet's reward; and whoever welcomes a righteous person in the name of a righteous person will receive the reward of the righteous.

[4] And he said to him, 'Why do you ask me about what is good? There is only one who is good. If you wish to enter into life, keep the commandments.'

[5] 'Woe to you, scribes and Pharisees, hypocrites! For you build the tombs of the prophets and decorate the graves of the righteous, so that upon you may come all the righteous blood shed on earth, from the blood of righteous Abel to the blood of Zechariah son of Barachiah, whom you murdered between the sanctuary and the altar.

[6] And if he rescued Lot, a righteous man greatly distressed by the licentiousness of the lawless (for that righteous man, living among them day after day, was tormented in his righteous soul by their lawless deeds that he saw and heard),

[7] 'Blessed be the Lord God of Israel, for he has looked favourably on his people and redeemed them. He has raised up a mighty saviour for us in the house of his servant David, as he spoke through the mouth of his holy prophets from of old, that we would be saved from our enemies and from the hand of all who hate us. Thus he has shown the mercy promised to our ancestors, and has remembered his holy covenant, the oath that he swore to our ancestor Abraham, to grant us that we, being rescued from the hands of our enemies, might serve him without fear, in holiness and righteousness before him all our days.

[8] Comfort, O comfort my people, says your God.

[9] Sing for joy, O heavens, and exult, O earth; break forth, O mountains, into singing! For the Lord has comforted his people, and will have compassion on his suffering ones.

[10] For the Lord will comfort Zion; he will comfort all her waste places, and will make her wilderness like Eden, her desert like the garden of the Lord; joy and gladness will be found in her, thanksgiving and the voice of song.

[11] I have seen their ways, but I will heal them; I will lead them and repay them with comfort, creating for their mourners the fruit of the lips.

[12] To proclaim the year of the Lord's favour, and the day of vengeance of our God; to comfort all who mourn;

[13] For if you endure and persevere in His fear, And do not forget His law, The times shall change over you for good. And you shall see the consolation of Zion.

Christ. Promise, fulfilment and God's direction stand behind the prophecy of this old saint. Lk. 2.22 tells us that Simeon, took the child in his arms and praised God, saying (Lk. 2.29-32):

> Master, now you are dismissing your servant in peace, according to your word; for my eyes have seen your salvation, which you have prepared in the presence of all peoples, a light for revelation to the Gentiles and for glory to your people Israel

Simeon's prayer is one of the deepest gratitude for in his arms was the Messiah he had longed for and for whom Israel had waited and having witnessed this his request is that he now be allowed to *depart* (die) in peace (for fuller details see, Grelot 1986:481-509). Simeon's task of praying for and preparing for the coming of the long awaited Messiah was now complete, he was no longer needed in this life. Simeon had seen and witnessed to God's *salvation* in the child he held, a salvation that would be for Jew and Gentiles (*the nations*) alike (cf. Ps. 98.2-3;[1]Is. 52.10[2]). Mary's son was to be *a light for revelation to the Gentiles* and to be the *glory of* his *people, Israel*, the light of God would come to both. God's work is for *all people (*'laon'*)*. As in Lk. 2.10, the reference to the people ultimately is broad, encompassing both Jew and Gentile, as v.32 makes clear. In fact, Jesus is *light (*'phos'*)*, an image that recalls the description of the Davidic son as the *dayspring* or bright morning star in Lk. 1.78-79. But Jesus serves as light in two distinct ways. For Gentiles he is a *revelation*. This term refers to his opening up the way of salvation to the nations in a way unknown before his coming (for a fuller exploration see, Green 1997:144-148). But for Israel, God's people, Jesus is *glory,* that is, his activity represents the realisation of promises made by God and thus shows Israel's special place in

---

[1]   The Lord has made known his victory; he has revealed his vindication in the sight of the nations. He has remembered his steadfast love and faithfulness to the house of Israel. All the ends of the earth have seen the victory of our God.

[2]   The Lord has bared his holy arm before the eyes of all the nations; and all the ends of the earth shall see the salvation of our God.

his heart (Is. 46.13[1]). The remarks in this verse recall Is. 60.1-3,[2] which in turn recall imagery surrounding the promised Servant of the Lord. Thus, in Mary's son, the *Shekinah* would come to Israel (Is. 60.19[3] cf. 46.13) and also to the far off Gentiles as Isaiah had spoken (Is. 42.6;[4] 49.6[5]). The word Luke places on Simeon's lips for *Lord* is 'despota', ('Master', cf. Acts 4.24;[6] Rev.6.10[7]) and is used of a master with his slave. As it used here it refers to God as Simeon's *Master* and he as God's slave and so it indicates God's sovereignty and his right to obedience from all his servants. Now that Simeon's task is done for his *despota,* he asks that he be given permission to *depart in peace* because his eyes have *seen the salvation,* i.e., the saviour God has sent.

Mary and Joseph *marvelled* (Lk. 2.33) at what was being said about their child and Luke intends that the reader of his gospel continues to marvel at what is being said about him. This marvelling was continual and was deepening because this is the first time in Luke's narrative that so great an emphasis had been laid upon the fact that the child was to be a *light to the Gentiles* and that the salvation he was and he had come to bring was for all men and women. The son of Mary is a gift to the whole world and not Just Israel, so this was no 'national' Messiah but a universal one. But Simeon is not finished yet, there is one more thing he has to pronounce before he can *depart in peace* and it is an ominous prophecy full of foreboding. To this

---

[1] I bring near my deliverance, it is not far off, and my salvation will not tarry; will put salvation in Zion, for Israel my glory.

[2] Arise, shine; for your light has come, and the glory of the Lord has risen upon you. For darkness shall cover the earth, and thick darkness the peoples; but the Lord will arise upon you, and his glory will appear over you. Nations shall come to your light, and kings to the brightness of your dawn

[3] The sun shall no longer be your light by day, nor for brightness shall the moon give light to you by night; but the Lord will be your everlasting light, and your God will be your glory.

[4] I am the Lord, I have called you in righteousness, I have taken you by the hand and kept you; I have given you as a covenant to the people, a light to the nations

[5] He says,'It is too light a thing that you should be my servant to raise up the tribes of Jacob and to restore the survivors of Israel; I will give you as a light to the nations, that my salvation may reach to the end of the earth.'

[6] When they heard it, they raised their voices together to God and said, 'Sovereign Lord, who made the heaven and the earth, the sea, and everything in them

[7] They cried out with a loud voice, 'Sovereign Lord, holy and true, how long will it be before you judge and avenge our blood on the inhabitants of the earth?'

moment everything has been joy, happiness, rejoicing, blessing but Luke now introduces the other side of the coin: all that the child would achieve would be done only after great suffering and tribulation. Many in Israel would *rise* and many others would *fall* (Lk. 2.34b) because they would refuse to acknowledge him. Mary's son would not be welcomed by all, he would arouse opposition as well as joyous fervour, he would be accepted by some and rejected by others, he would be a stumbling block for some, and the source of salvation and liberation to others. The source for these images of *rising* and *falling* are to be found in Is. 8.14-15:

> he will become a sanctuary and a stone of offence, many will stumble and they will fall and be broken) and 28.13-16 (that they may go and fall backward, I am laying in Zion for a foundation stone, a tested stone, a precious cornerstone of a sure foundation)

These Old Testament texts are frequently alluded to in the New Testament (e.g., 1 Pet 2.6-8;[1] Lk. 20.17-18,[2]). The point Luke is making is that the son of Mary will divide the nation between those who will respond to his call and rise and those who will reject it and fall. He will be a sign from God but many will speak against him: to be with Jesus will bring pain and suffering and Luke references this when he speaks of a *sword piercing* the heart of Mary. This refers to the large sword which was carried by the Romans. This is a metaphorical reference to Jesus' rejection and crucifixion; Mary was present at Jesus' crucifixion (cf. Jn. 19.26-27[3]). This phrase seems to be

---

[1] For it stands in scripture:'See, I am laying in Zion a stone, a cornerstone chosen and precious; and whoever believes in him will not be put to shame.' To you then who believe, he is precious; but for those who do not believe,'The stone that the builders rejected has become the very head of the corner', and' A stone that makes them stumble, and a rock that makes them fall.' They stumble because they disobey the word, as they were destined to do.

[2] But he looked at them and said, 'What then does this text mean: "The stone that the builders rejected has become the cornerstone"? Everyone who falls on that stone will be broken to pieces; and it will crush anyone on whom it falls.'

[3] When Jesus saw his mother and the disciple whom he loved standing beside her, he said to his mother, 'Woman, here is your son.' Then he said to the disciple, 'Here is your mother.' And from that hour the disciple took her into his own home.

addressed to Mary specifically: she would know a great deal of pain and suffering, doubt and fear in her own life because of her son until she would experience the greatest suffering of all, the loss of her child through death. All this would happen because *he would lay bare the heart of many*: the hearts of men and women would be an open book to him and those hearts would themselves be filled with joy because of their acceptance of him or sorrow because of their rejection of him.

e. The Widow Anna In The Temple (Lk. 2.36-38)

Having had 'mankind' prophecy about the impact Jesus would have on the world, Luke now has 'womankind' prophecy through the words of Anna:

> There was also a prophet, Anna the daughter of Phanuel, of the tribe of Asher. She was of a great age, having lived with her husband for seven years after her marriage, then as a widow to the age of eighty-four. She never left the temple but worshipped there with fasting and prayer night and day. At that moment she came, and began to praise God and to speak about the child to all who were looking for the redemption of Jerusalem.

No actual words of Anna's prophecy are recorded but she completes the cycle of male/female witnesses to the birth and future of Jesus. Anna had dedicated her life to God following the death of her husband by serving in the temple *night and day* (see, Brown 1993:467; Green 1997:151). Luke says she *never left the temple* and some have taken this to mean she lived there (cf. Creed 1930:43)! But it is hyperbole, it simply means that her life now was a life of service of God in prayer and fasting (see Marshall 1978:124). Anna was of the tribe of Asher and thus a true Israelite and as a 'prophetess' (Reid 1996:90) may have been the focus of attention for the women who came to the Temple (on the significance of this see, Fitzmyer 1978:430; Coleridge 1993:179). And coming up to where they were at that very hour (we may presume guided by the Spirit) she gave thanks to God, and then immediately she went away, her heart thrilled, in order to 'continue to proclaim' the news of his coming to all the faithful, those who were especially looking for redemption in Israel. By this we are reminded that beneath all the pageantry and formal ritual and machinations of the Temple, and all the stultifying regulations of the Pharisees, there was still a righteous and godly remnant in Israel whose worship was true and pure and spiritual, and who had not bowed the knee to Mammon or religious bigotry or formalism (on fasting as a protest, cf. Neyrey 1991:375).

Anna speaks to all who would listen and who longed for *the redemption of Jerusalem*. Here we might call to mind Is. 52.9 which, speaking of the future deliverance, declares:

> God has comforted (consoled) his people, he has redeemed Jerusalem.

Note how here it ties in with Simeon's *consolation of Israel*. Both have in mind the activity of the Messiah. Redemption in the Old Testament regularly meant deliverance by the exertion of power, but Is. 52.9 is immediately followed by the description of the Suffering Servant who will suffer for the sins of many (Is. 52.13-53.12). Thus it includes the deeper significance of deliverance by the payment of a price. So are described God's two witnesses to the son of Mary, the coming one who will bring consolation and redemption to Israel, the two witnesses necessary for the acceptance of their testimony. And from those two witnesses the word goes out to all whose hearts were especially right towards God in Jerusalem. When all these events have concluded and having obeyed the Mosaic law, Joseph and Mary return to Nazareth where, Luke tells us (Lk. 2.40):

> the child grew and became strong, filled with wisdom; and the favour of God was upon him

The activity of god continued in the growth and development of the infant son of Mary: John grew *strong in the Spirit* (Lk. 1.80) but Jesus became *strong* and *filled with wisdom*, and the *favour of God* was with him. Jesus did not come knowing everything: he is human and so he has to grow, develop, mature at every level. Before concluding these pages on Jesus and the women of Infancy Narratives with the narrative traditionally called *The Finding of the Boy Jesus in the Temple* (Lk. 2.41-51) a few observations about Luke's account of the many things said about Jesus by angels and men and women would not be out of place. The first observation is that Jesus has *two* parents and that they are devout Jews and faithful to the Law; secondly, he has been vouched for by *a priest in the Temple* and *circumcised according to the Law* and thus is a true *child of Abraham* (a Jew), he has also been witnessed to by *a pious man in the Temple* (Simeon) and a *devout and pious woman* (Anna).

So, there has been a threefold witness from the Temple. Thirdly, three angelic appearances have witnessed to him: *to Zechariah, to Mary, to the shepherds* and so by heaven itself. So, there has been a threefold witness from the angels. Fourthly, he has been witnessed to by *prophecy both before his birth* (Zechariah, Elizabeth, Mary) and *after his birth* (angels, Simeon, Anna) and finally, he is *witnessed to by the Holy Spirit* who has given threefold witness through Zechariah, Elizabeth and Simeon. Jesus' 'pedigree' therefore is beyond dispute: he is a true son of Abraham from devout and faithful Jewish parents, testified to by the Temple, the angels, the prophets and prophetesses and the Holy Spirit itself. One more constant should be drawn attention to, and that is the emphasis on 'salvation':

- Mary speaks of *God my Saviour* who has saved her (Lk. 1.47);
- Zacharias speaks of *a horn of salvation raised for us* (Lk. 1.69) and of *giving knowledge of salvation to His people* (Lk. 1.77);
- the initial angel speaks of *a Saviour who is Christ the Lord'* (Lk. 2.11);

- the host of angels speaks of *peace on those on whom his favour rests'* and thus of their salvation (Lk. 2.14);
- and Simeon says *my eyes have seen your Salvation* (Lk. 2.30).

The message of what is coming is therefore very much one of salvation and deliverance. Salvation is coming with and in this child: it is of God and it is of the Jews: And the content of this witness through annunciation and prophecy is also of importance.

Zechariah Lk. 1.14-17	Gabriel Lk. 1.32-33	Elizabeth Lk. 1.43	Mary Lk. 1.46-55	Simeon Lk. 1.67-79	Angel Lk. 2.10-12.
John is being sent to turn the hearts of people to God	The coming one is Son of the Most High, greater than David, Everlasting King, Son of God, conceived through the Holy Spirit	She declares that the coming one is 'My Lord'	The coming one is the one who throws down the mighty, lifts the lowly, and is the one who fulfils the covenant with Abraham	The Horn of Salvation, giver knowledge of salvation, and bringer light out of darkness, a light to the Gentiles and a glory to Israel, preparing for the theme in Acts of going first to the Jews and then to the Gentiles	He is the Messiah of the house of David, the LORD

f. The Boy Jesus in the Temple (Lk. 2.41-52)

Now every year his parents went to Jerusalem for the festival of the Passover. And When he was twelve years old, they went up as usual for the festival. When the festival was ended and they started to return, the boy Jesus stayed behind in Jerusalem, but his parents did not know it. Assuming that he was in the group of travellers, they went a day's journey. Then they started to look for him among their relatives and friends. When they did not find him, they returned to Jerusalem to search for him. After three days they found him in the temple, sitting among the teachers, listening to them and asking them questions. And all who heard him were amazed at his understanding and his answers. When his parents saw him they were astonished; and his mother said to him, 'Child, why have you treated us like this? Look, your father and I have been searching for you in great anxiety.' He said to them, 'Why were you searching for me? Did you not know that I must be in my Father's house?' But they did not understand what he said to them. Then he went down with them and came to Nazareth, and was obedient to them. His mother treasured all these things in her heart. And Jesus increased in wisdom and in years, and in divine and human favour.

As Luke's Infancy Narrative comes to a close, he makes a transition to John and Jesus' ministry through a single incident from Jesus' adolescence. This is the only such incident in the Gospels, though the non canonical gospels do include such accounts (*Infancy Gospel of Thomas* 19.1-5[1]). After the host of

---

[1] And when he was twelve years old his parents went according to the custom unto Jerusalem to the feast of the passover with their company: and after the passover they returned to go unto their house. And as they returned the child Jesus went back to Jerusalem; but his parents supposed that he was in their company. And when they had gone a day's journey, they sought him among their kinsfolk, and when they found him not, they were troubled, and returned again to the city seeking him. And after the third day they found him in the temple sitting in the midst of the doctors and hearing and asking them questions. And all men paid heed to him and marvelled how that being a young child he put to silence the elders and teachers of the

witnesses to Jesus in Lk. 1.5-2.40, Jesus now speaks for himself for the first time. This is the literary climax of Luke's initial section and shows the sense of mission and self-awareness Jesus possesses. Jesus has a unique relationship to God and a clear sense of his calling, one that transcends his relationship to his earthly parents. That this event, though strictly speaking not an infancy account, belongs in this initial literary division of Luke is indicated by the fact that it takes place in the temple, which is where the section started in Lk. 1.5 (Fitzmyer 1981:434). In addition, the note on Jesus' growth parallels the close of the discussion of John the Baptist in Luke 1:80 (cf. Smothers 1952:67-69; Laurentin 1989:141-46; Harrington 1991:60-62).

g. The Boy Jesus Goes Missing (Lk. 2.41-45)

The parents of Jesus *went to Jerusalem every year for the festival of the Passover* (Lk.2.41) because Jewish males over 21 years of age were required to attend all three major annual feasts (cf. Passover, Pentecost and Tabernacles; Ex. 23.14-17;[1] 34.23;[2] Deut. 16.16[3]). In the first century this was reduced to one feast because of the number of Jews living outside of Palestine (cf. Josephus on Passover, *Life* 345-54; *Antiquities* 17.9.3, 213-14;

---

people, expounding the heads of the law and the parables of the prophets. And his mother Mary came near and said unto him: Child, wherefore hast thou so done unto us? behold we have sought thee sorrowing. And Jesus said unto them: Why seek ye me? know ye not that I must be in my Father's house? But the scribes and Pharisees said: Art thou the mother of this child? and she said: I am. And they said unto her: Blessed art thou among women because God hath blessed the fruit of thy womb. For such glory and such excellence and wisdom we have neither seen nor heard at any time. And Jesus arose and followed his mother and was subject unto his parents: but his mother kept in mind all that came to pass. And Jesus increased in wisdom and stature and grace. Unto him be glory for ever and ever. Amen.

[1] Three times in the year you shall hold a festival for me. You shall observe the festival of unleavened bread; as I commanded you, you shall eat unleavened bread for seven days at the appointed time in the month of Abib, for in it you came out of Egypt. No one shall appear before me empty-handed. You shall observe the festival of harvest, of the first fruits of your labour, of what you sow in the field. You shall observe the festival of ingathering at the end of the year, when you gather in from the field the fruit of your labour. Three times in the year all your males shall appear before the Lord God.

[2] Three times in the year all your males shall appear before the Lord God, the God of Israel.

[3] Three times a year all your males shall appear before the Lord your God at the place that he will choose: at the festival of unleavened bread, at the festival of weeks, and at the festival of booths. They shall not appear before the Lord empty-handed.

Jewish Wars 2.1.3 10-12; 2.14.3 280). They were, however, still expected to make an effort to attend in Jerusalem at least once a year, and their being accompanied by their womenfolk had become the norm (Marshall 1978:126). This is another evidence of Jesus' parents' dedication to the law of Moses. Mary was not required by law to attend, but she wanted to (Fitzmyer 1981:440). When he was twelve years old, they went up *as usual for the festival*. Every Jewish boy came of age at thirteen from which point on he was looked on as a responsible adult and expected to fulfil his religious responsibilities, becoming 'a son of the Law' (see Harrington 1991:60; Marshall 1978:126-127. Thus the Rabbis recommended that boys who were approaching that age be brought to the feasts so that they could become acquainted with the atmosphere and with what went on (see, Green 1997:155). Jerusalem was eighty miles from Nazareth, so the trip would take three days. Though some have argued that women and children travelled separately from the men as a way to explain how Jesus got lost, there is no ancient text that describes this practice.

If the Mishnah is relevant to the first-century Jewish practice, which is likely in this case, then religious instruction would have become more intense for Jesus upon his reaching twelve (*m. Niddah* 5.6; *m. Megilla* 4.6; *m. ʾAbot* 5.12). The custom of bar mitzvah for a thirteen-year-old Jewish boy was not in place at this time. So when Jesus was twelve his parents took him up to the Feast of the Passover, and once the seven days of unleavened bread were over they set off to return to Nazareth with a large group of Galileans. However (Lk. 2.42-43):

> when the festival was ended and they started to return, the boy
> Jesus stayed behind in Jerusalem, but his parents did not know
> it. Assuming that he was in the group of travellers, they went a
> day's journey. Then they started to look for him among their
> relatives and friends

What happened appears to indicate that on the pilgrimage to Jerusalem, on which would also be all their relatives, it was quite normal during the festivities for boys of twelve, who were seen as almost mature, to go around together enjoying the festival (compare modern older teenagers who would not want to be tied to their parents), and when hungry or tired, to stay with one or other of their relatives whose son(s) would be one of them. Then, of course, when it was time to go back home, whoever they were with could be expected to see that they were included in the caravan (cf. Marshall 1978:127;. This is really the only explanation as to why Jesus had not been missed, and why they set off without him. They had had confidence in him that he would not get up to mischief, and in their relatives that whoever he was staying with would ensure that he was properly looked after and would set off back for Galilee with them. Probably in previous years this had worked very well. What they had not taken into account, and what Jesus considered that they ought to have taken into account, was that now that he was almost 'of age' it was necessary for him to go to his Father's house to learn of him. In such caravans the men would often walk together in a large group, while the women went ahead in front, and this may well have been why they did not ask each other where Jesus was. Joseph may have thought that Jesus had joined up with Mary, and Mary may have thought that he had joined up with Joseph. Or both may have been satisfied that he would be with relatives.

But, although they did not know it, Jesus had lingered in Jerusalem, for he had gone to the Temple and was listening to the great teachers (McBride 1981:42). It seems that he just assumed that when his parents wanted him they would come for him there because in his view 'they should know that he was there'. When they did not find him, they returned to Jerusalem to search for him and (Lk. 2.45-47):

> after three days they found him in the temple, sitting among the teachers, listening to them and asking them questions. And all who heard him were amazed at his understanding and his answers

But we may ask as to whether a boy, even though a 'mature' boy ('pais'), would really remain in the Temple day and night for three days without going back to his parents. There could only be two reasons why this was feasible: either it was normal for boys of his age to go about with boys of their own age during such festivals, sleeping where they liked and obtaining food from different relatives who would be there, or even from generous pilgrims, so that he did not see this as unusual, or because he had in fact tried to go back to his parents, only to discover that they had disappeared. This would leave him having to find something to do until they came back for him.

h. The Boy Jesus Is Found In The Temple (Lk. 2.46-51)

Apparently after *one day's journey back to Jerusalem and a day looking* for Jesus, it is on the third day that Joseph and Mary discover him at the temple, listening to and asking questions of the teachers. The exact location of the incident within the temple is unstated, but Jesus' discussion with the officials leaves those who listen *amazed at his understanding and his answers.* This assumes that Jesus is debating with those present in his circle and not as a passive pupil (see Green: 1997:157; on the idea Jesus was a pupil cf. Fitzmyer 1978:442; Evans 1990:225). At the tender age of twelve, Jesus already shows signs of possessing great wisdom. Clearly Luke wants the reader to develop a sense of respect for this amazing, blessed child. Luke tells us (Lk. 2.48):

> when his parents saw him they were astonished; and his mother
> said to him, 'Child, why have you treated us like this? Look,
> your father and I have been searching for you in great anxiety.'

Once again his parents were astonished. Firstly to see him standing in the crowd listening to the great Rabbis, secondly that he appeared to be oblivious of the fact that he had been left behind, and thirdly because they just could not understand why he had been so inconsiderate. This time their amazement was not that of pleasure. When the parents finally find him, it is Mary who steps forward to address the young Jesus in a way that both parents and children can appreciate. She expresses concern about the anxiety Jesus has caused by remaining at the temple and his mother asks him sternly why he had behaved like this. Did he not realise that they had been looking for him and had been very worried? The fact that Mary asked him confirms that he was in a unique position with regard to his mother. Normally the father would take the lead. Jesus' reply causes them even more astonishment (Lk. 2.49):

> 'Why were you searching for me? Did you not know that I must
> be in my Father's house?

But Jesus was equally astonished: he too uttered a kind of rebuke. Why had they had to search for him? Surely they must have known where he was? How could they possibly have needed to look for him? With the reply appears the first of many *dei* (*it is necessary*) statements in Luke (Lk. 4.43;[1] 9.22;[2] 13.33;[3] 17.25;[4] 19.5;[5]). The key phase in v. 49 is elliptical, making its meaning disputed (see Green 1997:156;Fitzmyer 1978:443;Harrington, 1981:59). The statement reads, *I must be in the . . . of my Father* (the NIV renders this *I had to be . . .*). Two views are popular:

1. I must be about my Father's affairs
2. I must be in the house of my Father

The second view also means that Jesus must be engaged in teaching God's

---

[1] But he said to them, 'I must proclaim the good news of the kingdom of God to the other cities also; for I was sent for this purpose.'

[2] Saying, 'The Son of Man must undergo great suffering, and be rejected by the elders, chief priests, and scribes, and be killed, and on the third day be raised.'

[3] Yet today, tomorrow, and the next day I must be on my way, because it is impossible for a prophet to be killed away from Jerusalem."

[4] But first he must endure much suffering and be rejected by this generation.

[5] When Jesus came to the place, he looked up and said to him, 'Zacchaeus, hurry and come down; for I must stay at your house today.'

ways, since for Luke the temple is a place where Jesus instructs (Lk. 20.1-21.4). Greek idiom supports this second view. Surely they must have realised that *it was necessary* for him to be in his Father's house? (It was so obvious to him that he could not believe that it was not obvious to them). There is an interesting parallel between this question *how is it that you searched for me?*' and the question of the angels in Lk. 24.5, *why do you seek the living among the dead?* There too they sought him where they should have known he would not be. Both indicate how blind were the eyes of those who loved him most, because he was so much beyond their understanding.

There is here a contrast between *your father and I sought you* and *I must be in my Father's house.* He is by this making it clear that supremely God is his Father and he must obey him, and that it is that filial obedience to his Father which must come first. And the implication is that he would expect his parents to agree with him. The word 'dei' (it is necessary) regularly indicates the divine necessity, as it does here. He was not here by chance. Jesus had felt that he had no option but to be here. He was hungry to learn about his Father. That surely was the purpose in coming to the Feast, that he might take every opportunity of learning about his Father. And he had expected them to realise it. He had yet to realise that others were not guided by the Spirit in the same way as he was. Jesus' parents (and Luke's readers) need to appreciate that Jesus understood his mission. From the very beginning he is reflecting on the will of God. He starts revealing himself right in the centre of Judaism's religious capital. But there is a second key detail. Jesus refers to God as his *Father.* This alludes to the sense of family relationship and intimacy Jesus has with his heavenly Father (Lk. 10.21-22[1]). Such closeness to God not only is something Jesus' parents need to appreciate but also is a point the disciples will struggle to grasp (Lk.

---

[1] At that same hour Jesus rejoiced in the Holy Spirit and said, 'I thank you, Father, Lord of heaven and earth, because you have hidden these things from the wise and the intelligent and have revealed them to infants; yes, Father, for such was your gracious will. All things have been handed over to me by my Father; and no one knows who the Son is except the Father, or who the Father is except the Son and anyone to whom the Son chooses to reveal him.'

9.59-62;[1] 14.26;[2] Mk. 10.29-30[3]). In fact, Luke makes this the first note in a series of revelations that will build the case for who Jesus Is. The infancy material stresses Jesus as Messiah, but this text is one of two hints early in Luke's Gospel that he is also much more. Luke reveals Jesus' identity gradually, bringing the reader along in an understanding of who Jesus Is. So this first clue comes from Jesus himself, the other major clue comes in the infancy section, where Jesus' divine origin is tied to the Spirit (Lk. 1.31-35[4]).

His astonishment releases him from blame. It was not that he had been careless or selfish for during the festivities of the Feast many young boys of his age apparently stayed away from their parents days at a time in order to enjoy the festival atmosphere. Their parents knew that they would not get into any trouble and that they were with their friends and that there were relatives all over the place to whom they could look, and generous-hearted people always ready to help youngsters who were hungry. They let them go and enjoy themselves (they were seen as the equivalent of older teenagers today, almost adults). They would come home when they were ready to. And to such boys time would seem to stand still. They would not realise how the days were passing. It had been the same for him, the only difference between him and them was where they spent their time. But he had been sure that his parents would know exactly where he must be, and

---

[1] To another he said, 'Follow me.' But he said, 'Lord, first let me go and bury my father.' But Jesus said to him, 'Let the dead bury their own dead; but as for you, go and proclaim the kingdom of God.' Another said, 'I will follow you, Lord; but let me first say farewell to those at my home.' Jesus said to him, 'No one who puts a hand to the plough and looks back is fit for the kingdom of God.'

[2] 'Whoever comes to me and does not hate father and mother, wife and children, brothers and sisters, yes, and even life itself, cannot be my disciple.

[3] Jesus said, 'Truly I tell you, there is no one who has left house or brothers or sisters or mother or father or children or fields, for my sake and for the sake of the good news, who will not receive a hundredfold now in this age houses, brothers and sisters, mothers and children, and fields, with persecutions and in the age to come eternal life.

[4] And now, you will conceive in your womb and bear a son, and you will name him Jesus. He will be great, and will be called the Son of the Most High, and the Lord God will give to him the throne of his ancestor David. He will reign over the house of Jacob for ever, and of his kingdom there will be no end.' Mary said to the angel, 'How can this be, since I am a virgin?' The angel said to her, 'The Holy Spirit will come upon you, and the power of the Most High will overshadow you; therefore the child to be born will be holy; he will be called Son of God.

what he must be doing, and that they would therefore have sent for him when they wanted him. He just could not understand how they could have been so misguided as to not to have known: he was genuinely puzzled. He did not feel that he was to blame. The response of his mother and father is simple confusion, *But they did not understand what he said to them* (Lk. 2.50). It was not surprising. No one else had a son who on coming to Jerusalem spent the week at the Temple learning and asking questions. Other people's sons saw themselves as on holiday, and as they got precious few of those they made the most of them and most boys looked mainly to their fathers for teaching about religion. So they could not understand that Jesus had a source of learning that went beyond that and that that was indeed the secret of his special 'wisdom' (v.52) (see, Kilgallen 1985:553-559). So his parents did not understand him (cf. Fitmeyer 1978:445). He had never behaved like this before, because he was too young. But they had failed to appreciate that now he considered himself 'grown up' religiously, and so as needing to be built up by the special wisdom that he could receive from his Father, something beyond what his father could teach him. Thus he had felt a new sense of needing to know his Father more intimately. But such a concept was beyond them.

And so in a quite unemphasised way we learn of the uniqueness of this young boy whom no one understood, a young boy who lived in such close touch with his Father that He could not understand why others did not do the same. He called him *my Father* and that demonstrated his sense of the unique relationship that there was between him and God. He knew that his relationship to God was unique (note the *my*, and compare its use in, e.g., Jn. 10.29-32;[1] 26.42,[2] all of which indicate a unique relationship with God). Note also how this incident links Jesus with the Temple. Indeed the whole of these first two chapters stress connection with the Temple. The point is

---

[1]   What my Father has given me is greater than all else, and no one can snatch it out of the Father's hand. The Father and I are one.' The Jews took up stones again to stone him. Jesus replied, 'I have shown you many good works from the Father. For which of these are you going to stone me?'

[2]   Again he went away for the second time and prayed, 'My Father, if this cannot pass unless I drink it, your will be done.'

being made that the message of Jesus did not start out with a bias against the Temple, but rather that he and his witnesses had the closest of relationships with the Temple. He was approved by the choice souls who frequented it, and he himself sought truth there. And when listing the temptations Luke placed the crucial last one in the Temple (Lk. 4.9-12[1]). All this stressed that he came from the very centre of Israel's worship. Salvation was very much of the Jews (Jn. 4.22[2]). It was only later in Luke that he would have to warn of the destruction of the Temple (Lk. 13.35;[3] 21.6[4]) because he had found out what it was really like (Lk. 19.45-46[5]), and even then he still preached there (Lk. 21.37,[6] 38). It was, however, finally the Temple that rejected him (Lk. 22.52[7] cf. Elliot 1971-1972:87-89). (Yet even so the Apostles end up praising God in the Temple (Lk. 24.53[8]), and the first acts of witness in Acts will be in the Temple). The same thing happens in Acts. The Apostles continue regularly to preach and pray in the Temple. And it is only when the Temple rejects first the Apostles, and then Paul, that they go elsewhere. Christianity was thus to be seen as springing from all that was good in the Temple (cf. Ezek. 47.1-12). In a sense it was like the 'chicken from the egg.' But once the chicken had come forth, the new Israel from the old, the eggshell could be thrown away. It was no longer needed. Luke brings his Infancy Narrative to an end with the simple statement that (Lk. 2.51-52):

---

[1] Then the devil took him to Jerusalem, and placed him on the pinnacle of the temple, saying to him, 'If you are the Son of God, throw yourself down from here, for it is written, "He will command his angels concerning you, to protect you", and "On their hands they will bear you up, so that you will not dash your foot against a stone." ' Jesus answered him, 'It is said, "Do not put the Lord your God to the test." '

[2] You worship what you do not know; we worship what we know, for salvation is from the Jews.

[3] See, your house is left to you. And I tell you, you will not see me until the time comes when you say, "Blessed is the one who comes in the name of the Lord." '

[4] 'As for these things that you see, the days will come when not one stone will be left upon another; all will be thrown down.'

[5] Then he entered the temple and began to drive out those who were selling things there; and he said, 'It is written,"My house shall be a house of prayer"; but you have made it a den of robbers.'

[6] Every day he was teaching in the temple, and at night he would go out and spend the night on the Mount of Olives, as it was called.

[7] Then Jesus said to the chief priests, the officers of the temple police, and the elders who had come for him, 'Have you come out with swords and clubs as if I were a bandit?

[8] And they were continually in the temple blessing God.

> he went down with them and came to Nazareth, and was obedient to them. His mother treasured all these things in her heart. And Jesus increased in wisdom and in years, and in divine and human favour

This is the last mention of Joseph. Christian tradition says that he died at an early age, but Mary and Joseph may have had several other children though there is difficulty with this idea for Christians of the Roman Catholic and Orthodox traditions (cf. Mt. 12.46;[1] 13.55;[2] Mk. 6.3;[3] Jn. 2.12; 7.3, 5, 10;[4] Acts 1.14;[5] 1 Cor. 9.5;[6] Gal.1.19[7]). Responding immediately to his parents Jesus went down with them to Nazareth (going from Jerusalem is always 'down', even for those who go up). And there he continued to be subject to them. There had been no intention of rebellion. He had merely been doing what he saw to be right. And his mother kept in her heart all the things that were said, (and when she was asked by Luke, unburdened them to him and by then she had gained a little more understanding). But Mary was still only in her twenties herself. While she pondered she did not fully understand. And later, when she felt that she must save her boy from himself, possibly at the instigation of his brothers (Mk. 3.21,25[8]), she was only doing what was natural for a mother. But it is a reminder to us that she too was human

---

[1] While he was still speaking to the crowds, his mother and his brothers were standing outside, wanting to speak to him.

[2] Is not this the carpenter's son? Is not his mother called Mary? And are not his brothers James and Joseph and Simon and Judas?

[3] Is not this the carpenter, the son of Mary and brother of James and Joses and Judas and Simon, and are not his sisters here with us?' And they took offence at him.

[4] After this he went down to Capernaum with his mother, his brothers, and his disciples; and they remained there for a few days; So his brothers said to him, 'Leave here and go to Judea so that your disciples also may see the works you are doing; (For not even his brothers believed in him.); But after his brothers had gone to the festival, then he also went, not publicly but as it were in secret.

[5] All these were constantly devoting themselves to prayer, together with certain women, including Mary the mother of Jesus, as well as his brothers.

[6] Do we not have the right to be accompanied by a believing wife, as do the other apostles and the brothers of the Lord and Cephas?

[7] But I did not see any other apostle except James the Lord's brother.

[8] When his family heard it, they went out to restrain him, for people were saying, 'He has gone out of his mind.' And if a house is divided against itself, that house will not be able to stand.

and so very much like us.

Meanwhile Jesus continued to grow in wisdom and in physical strength, and in favour with God and men. He did not at this stage need to go into the wilderness for he was guided in a way that even John did not know, and his goodness protected him. All acknowledged his godliness, and loved him for his open-heartedness and genuine kindness. The people loved him and God was with him. For John it was a harder struggle. He had to fight himself (this description is based on 1 S 2.26,[1] but that here we have the addition of 'wisdom'). Jesus grew like Samuel, but with the addition of special wisdom. Luke probably expects his readers to notice the addition and interpret accordingly. We can add further that by the time he was 'about thirty' his father had died, and he himself was a carpenter following in his father's footsteps; he had a number of brothers and sisters; and he had for some time probably been mainly responsible for providing for the family. Once, however, he had been able to train up his brothers, he would be able to leave the welfare of the family to them.

---

[1] Now the boy Samuel continued to grow both in stature and in favour with the Lord and with the people.

CHAPTER SEVEN

JESUS AND WOMEN IN LUKE

Luke and His Understanding and Use of Widows

Luke has five references to widow in his gospel:

- Anna (Lk. 2.36-38)
- The widow at Zarephath (Lk. 4.25-30).
- The widow of Nain (Lk. 7.11-17),
- The Widow in Lk. 18.1-8
- Widow at the treasury (Lk. 21.1-4)

Indeed, the majority of references to 'widows' in the New Testament texts is to be found in Luke's gospel (the others are to be found in 1 Cor. 7.8, 39-40;[1] James 1.27,[2] Rev. 18.7[3] and 1 Tim. 5.3-16[4] see Thurston

---

[1]   To the unmarried and the widows I say that it is well for them to remain unmarried as I am. A wife is bound as long as her husband lives. But if the husband dies, she is free to marry anyone she wishes, only in the Lord. But in my judgement she is more blessed if she remains as she is. And I think that I too have the Spirit of God.

[2]   Religion that is pure and undefiled before God, the Father, is this: to care for orphans and widows in their distress, and to keep oneself unstained by the world.

[3]   As she glorified herself and lived luxuriously, so give her a like measure of torment and grief. Since in her heart she says, "I rule as a queen; I am no widow, and I will never see grief",

[4]   Honour widows who are really widows. If a widow has children or grandchildren, they should first learn their religious duty to their own family and make some repayment to their parents; for this is pleasing in God's sight. The real widow, left alone, has set her hope on God and continues in supplications and prayers night and day; but the widow who lives for pleasure is dead even while she lives. Give these commands as well, so that they may be above reproach. And whoever does not provide for relatives, and especially for family members, has denied the faith and is worse than an unbeliever. Let a widow be put on the list if she is not less than sixty years old and has been married only once; she must be well attested for her good works, as one who has brought up children, shown hospitality, washed the saints' feet, helped the afflicted, and devoted herself to doing good in every way. But refuse to put younger widows on the list; for when their sensual desires alienate them from Christ, they want to marry, and so they incur condemnation for having violated their first pledge. Besides that, they learn to be idle, gadding about from house to house; and they are not merely idle, but also gossips and busybodies, saying what they should not say. So I would have younger widows marry, bear children, and manage their households, so as to give the adversary no occasion to revile us. For some have already turned away to follow Satan. If any believing woman has

1989:21). As noted in the section on the Widow at the Treasury in Mark (Mk.12), the experience of widows in Jewish culture was one of abandonment and marginalisation. The place of a woman was determined by the man with whom she had a relationship or to whom she was related, so since the widow had no husband she had neither representation or voice (cf. Ilan 1995:149; Thurston 1989:9) (it is interesting to note that the root word for 'widow'-almanah-is 'alem' which means 'not able to speak', 'unable to give voice'). When this is translated into Greek it becomes 'chera' the root of which means 'empty' or 'forsaken', and the original meaning was 'left without'. By the time the gospels were written it had come to mean a woman left without a husband. Thus it can mean someone whose husband has died (a widow properly understood), or someone who has no husband, and so it could mean someone who was destitute. This latter was the result of an understanding of 'widow' as one without financial support (cf. Siem 1994:98). In the Hebrew biblical tradition God had a special concern for widows (and orphans, cf. e.g., Ex. 22.23-24;[1] Deut. 10.18;[2] Deut. 27.19;[3] Pss. 68.5;[4] 94.6;[5]) as God had a special concern for the widow, so too were his people to ensure that they were cared for (Deut. 14.29;[6] 16.11,14;[7] 24.17-21[8]). The meaning of 'widow' changed over the course of the years in

---

    relatives who are really widows, let her assist them; let the church not be burdened, so that it can assist those who are real widows.

[1] If you do abuse them, when they cry out to me, I will surely heed their cry; my wrath will burn, and I will kill you with the sword, and your wives shall become widows and your children orphans.

[2] Who executes justice for the orphan and the widow, and who loves the strangers, providing them with food and clothing.

[3] 'Cursed be anyone who deprives the alien, the orphan, and the widow of justice.' All the people shall say, 'Amen!'

[4] Father of orphans and protector of widows is God in his holy habitation.

[5] They kill the widow and the stranger, they murder the orphan,

[6] The Levites, because they have no allotment or inheritance with you, as well as the resident aliens, the orphans, and the widows in your towns, may come and eat their fill so that the Lord your God may bless you in all the work that you undertake.

[7] Rejoice before the Lord your God, you and your sons and your daughters, your male and female slaves, the Levites resident in your towns, as well as the strangers, the orphans, and the widows who are among you, at the place that the Lord your God will choose as a dwelling for his name. Rejoice during your festival, you and your sons and your daughters, your male and female slaves, as well as the Levites, the strangers, the orphans, and the widows resident in your towns.

[8] You shall not deprive a resident alien or an orphan of justice; you shall not take a widow's garment in

the sense that it came to be seen as a 'venerable estate' within the early Christian communities but in his gospel Luke keeps the traditional understanding of widow as a woman whose husband had died.

Two Widows in Luke: Lk. 4.25; 7.11-17

a. Jesus At Nazareth (Lk. 4.16-21)

The Narrative Context

While it is true that Anna was a widow and may deserve consideration at this point, she has already been sufficiently explored within the women of the Infancy Narrative (Lk. 2.36). The next occasion a widow appears in Luke's gospel is at Lk. 4.25[1] where Jesus makes reference to the widow of Zarephath and Lk. 7.11-17, the famous and unusual story of the widow of Nain. In both these instances Luke presents the traditional view of widows: both had lost their husbands, both were voiceless, both were in need of compassion from God and humans. In having Jesus use the story of the widow of Zarephath, Luke shows that the compassion of God given to the widow of Zarephath by Elijah (1 K 17:17-24[2]) is similar to that given by

---

pledge. Remember that you were a slave in Egypt and the Lord your God redeemed you from there; therefore I command you to do this. When you reap your harvest in your field and forget a sheaf in the field, you shall not go back to get it; it shall be left for the alien, the orphan, and the widow, so that the Lord your God may bless you in all your undertakings. When you beat your olive trees, do not strip what is left; it shall be for the alien, the orphan, and the widow. When you gather the grapes of your vineyard, do not glean what is left; it shall be for the alien, the orphan, and the widow.

[1] But the truth is, there were many widows in Israel in the time of Elijah, when the heaven was shut up for three years and six months, and there was a severe famine over all the land.

[2] After this the son of the woman, the mistress of the house, became ill; his illness was so severe that there was no breath left in him. She then said to Elijah, 'What have you against me, O man of God? You have come to me to bring my sin to remembrance, and to cause the death of my son!' But he said to her, 'Give me your son.' He took him from her bosom, carried him up into the upper chamber where he was lodging, and laid him on his own bed. He cried out to the Lord, 'O Lord my God, have you brought calamity even upon the widow with whom I am staying, by killing her son?' Then he stretched himself upon the child three times, and cried out to the Lord, 'O Lord my God, let this child's life come into him again.' The Lord listened to the voice of Elijah; the life of the child came into him again, and he revived. Elijah took the child, brought him down from the upper chamber into the house, and gave him to his mother; then Elijah said, 'See, your son is alive.' So the woman said to Elijah, 'Now I know that you are a man of God, and that the word of the Lord in your mouth is truth.'

Jesus to the widow of Nain (on the connection Luke makes between Elijah and Jesus see, Nolland 1993:200-201; Fitzmyer 1978:538). But there is more to the compassion of Jesus than simply 'feeling sorry', or 'feeling pity.' Compassion does indeed include these features but a more radical understanding of compassion is that it is the articulation of protest. It is a form of criticism that all is not as it should be in society where there are those who suffer because suffering should never be seen as acceptable. Thus the compassion of Jesus is more than an expression of concern, it is a statement of criticism by him within his societal context in which he acts counter culturally and against the accepted social mores. Once again to better understand why Luke has Jesus refer to the story of the widow of Zarephtath, it is necessary to set it within its context. Luke sets the reference to the widow of Zarepthath within the narrative of Jesus' return to Nazareth (Lk. 4.16-30) and gives us some insight into the piety of Jesus himself for he writes (Lk. 4.16):

> on the Sabbath day he went into the synagogue as was his custom.

By the end of that visit Jesus will have become embroiled in the first of many controversies either on, or concerning, the Sabbath (e.g.,Lk. 6.1-11;[1] 13.10-17;[2] 14.1-5[3]). These controversies are a major motif in Luke's gospel:

---

[1] One Sabbath while Jesus was going through the cornfields, his disciples plucked some heads of grain, rubbed them in their hands, and ate them. But some of the Pharisees said, 'Why are you doing what is not lawful on the Sabbath?' Jesus answered, 'Have you not read what David did when he and his companions were hungry? He entered the house of God and took and ate the bread of the Presence, which it is not lawful for any but the priests to eat, and gave some to his companions?' Then he said to them, 'The Son of Man is lord of the Sabbath.'

[2] On another Sabbath he entered the synagogue and taught, and there was a man there whose right hand was withered. The scribes and the Pharisees watched him to see whether he would cure on the Sabbath, so that they might find an accusation against him. Even though he knew what they were thinking, he said to the man who had the withered hand, 'Come and stand here.' He got up and stood there. Then Jesus said to them, 'I ask you, is it lawful to do good or to do harm on the Sabbath, to save life or to destroy it?' After looking around at all of them, he said to him, 'Stretch out your hand.' He did so, and his hand was restored. But they were filled with fury and discussed with one another what they might do to Jesus.

[3] On one occasion when Jesus was going to the house of a leader of the Pharisees to eat a meal on the Sabbath, they were watching him closely. Just then, in front of him, there was a man who had dropsy. And

who represents God? But Jesus is immersed in Judaism and does not cede from it, rather he shows that his ministry is the fulfilment of all its hopes. And those hopes are being fulfilled here and now in the words, actions and very presence of Jesus himself. During the synagogue liturgy (see comment of Marshall 1978:181; cf. Crockett 1966:13-46) Jesus reads from the prophesy of Is. 61.1-2 which deals with the coming salvation of God (cf. Fitzmyer 1978:532). At this point a commentary would be offered and so *the eyes of all in the synagogue were fixed on him* (Lk. 4.20c). The commentary on the text that Jesus offers, however, is simply one sentence (Lk. 4.21),

> today this scripture has been fulfilled in your hearing

therefore, the scripture that Jesus claims (a monumental claim!) to have been fulfilled in their existential present needs careful exploration (Teide 1980:96). Jesus' first radical claim is that the *Spirit of the Lord has been given to* (him) *me* and the readers/hearers of Luke know that this is the case because Luke has shown Jesus as being 'anointed' with the Spirit at his baptism (Lk. 3.21-22); Jesus is thus an 'anointed' prophet and the one who brings the 'good news' (gospel) to the poor and the downtrodden (Fitzmyer 1978:532; Harrington 1990:81). But Jesus' reference to the poor here is not a carte blanche acceptance of the poor, nor is it as some have tried to make it, a reduction of the good news to a socio-economic humanism. At the same time Jesus does not totally exclude issues around socio-economics or class. The poor have already been the focus of Mary's 'Magnificat' (Lk. 1.50-53, 'humble') and will be mentioned at Lk. 6.20-23 and the hope which this expresses extends to those who are sensitive in spirit, to those who respond. It is the poor who are seen to be most open to God's proclamation, they are the ones who wait in their need and accept it with humility. They have no place of pre-eminence or exalted status or power. They are the

---

Jesus asked the lawyers and Pharisees, 'Is it lawful to cure people on the Sabbath, or not?' But they were silent. So Jesus took him and healed him, and sent him away. Then he said to them, 'If one of you has a child or an ox that has fallen into a well, will you not immediately pull it out on a Sabbath day?'

'anawim', the 'pious poor' (1 Cor.1.26-29;[1] James 2.5;[2] 2 S 22.28;[3] Pss. 14.6;[4] 22.24;[5] 25.16;[6] 34:6;[7] 40.17;[8] 69.29;[9] Is. 3.14-15;[10] Amos 8.4[11]) and Jesus is their hope. The second claim that Jesus makes is that he has been sent (Lk. 4.18):

> to proclaim release to the captives and recovery of sight to the
> blind, to let the oppressed go free

He has come to proclaim freedom to the captives. The picture is of deliverance and salvation. In the Old Testament the captives were those who had been oppressed by a foreign power as a judgement on their sins. Their release arose because God was having mercy on them and their sins were forgiven (cf. Jer. 29.14). Now they could return home because they had returned to God. So the prophet here is to proclaim salvation and forgiveness, deliverance from sin and from the tyranny of Satan, to those who found themselves bound and oppressed (cf. Marshall 1978:183-184). But we see from what follows that it includes deliverance from captivity by evil spirits. In Is. 42.7 it is the *Servant* of the Lord who will:

---

[1] Consider your own call, brothers and sisters: not many of you were wise by human standards, not many were powerful, not many were of noble birth. But God chose what is foolish in the world to shame the wise; God chose what is weak in the world to shame the strong; God chose what is low and despised in the world, things that are not, to reduce to nothing things that are, so that no one might boast in the presence of God.

[2] Listen, my beloved brothers and sisters. Has not God chosen the poor in the world to be rich in faith and to be heirs of the kingdom that he has promised to those who love him?

[3] You deliver a humble people, but your eyes are upon the haughty to bring them down.

[4] For he did not despise or abhor the affliction of the afflicted; he did not hide his face from me, but heard when I cried to him.

[5] Turn to me and be gracious to me, for I am lonely and afflicted.

[6] This poor soul cried, and was heard by the Lord, and was saved from every trouble.

[7] As for me, I am poor and needy, but the Lord takes thought for me. You are my help and my deliverer; do not delay, O my God.

[8] But I am lowly and in pain; let your salvation, O God, protect me.

[9] Hear this, you that trample on the needy, and bring to ruin the poor of the land,

[10] The Lord enters into judgement with the elders and princes of his people: It is you who have devoured the vineyard; the spoil of the poor is in your houses. What do you mean by crushing my people, by grinding the face of the poor? says the Lord God of hosts.

[11]

open the blind eyes, bring out the prisoners from the prison, and those who sit in darkness out of the prison house'

There, as here, the blind and the captives and those who are in darkness go together. Again in Is. 49.9 the Servant is told

in the time of favour (the acceptable time) you will say to the prisoners, "Go forth", to those who are in darkness, "Show yourselves (come in to the light)"'

and the result is that they will no longer be hungry or thirsty or needy. In Zech. 9.9, 12,[1] the coming of the King riding on his colt will result in the 'prisoners of hope' or 'hopeful prisoners' being restored. In each case the thought is of those who are out in the darkness being brought into God's favour and thus finding a new life of freedom. The similarity of phrases identify the Servant and the prophet as the same person. The *recovery of sight to the blind* goes along with this. The emphasis here is on the spiritually blind. They walk in darkness and do not know where they are going (Jn. 12.35[2]). In the reading a line is left out (*He has sent me to bind up the broken hearted*), and instead another line is added further on from Is. 58.6, (*to send forth those who are oppressed in deliverance (forgiveness)*'). It was in fact quite acceptable for the reader not to read the whole in the case of the prophets (but not of the Law of Moses which was sacrosanct). He could omit what he wished. More questionable from a Jewish point of view might be the way that Jesus incorporates, presumably from memory, a line from Is. 58.6. But we do not know that this was not permissible, and anyway Jesus as a prophet did not always see the need to follow convention. Perhaps he wanted to include the hint of forgiveness contained in that line. Or perhaps he had in mind the sending forth of his apostles (those sent

---

[1] Rejoice greatly, O daughter Zion! Shout aloud, O daughter Jerusalem! Lo, your king comes to you; triumphant and victorious is he, humble and riding on a donkey, on a colt, the foal of a donkey. Return to your stronghold, O prisoners of hope; today I declare that I will restore to you double.

[2] Jesus said to them, 'The light is with you for a little longer. Walk while you have the light, so that the darkness may not overtake you. If you walk in the darkness, you do not know where you are going.

forth). Whatever the reason it would be like underlining them for most would recognise the changes and it was intended to make them think.

The *captives, blind,* and *oppressed* in view here, then, are those who in some way have their humanity taken from them by unhealthy spiritual forces who 'imprison' humanity in sin, pain, suffering. Jesus is the one 'anointed' to announce their release in his words and actions (specifically his miracles). He will set free those held captive by their sins (Lk. 19.1-10[1]). Jesus will heal the blind (Lk. 18.35-43[2]) and bring light into the darkness that binds and chains (Lk. 1.78-79), because it is he who is the 'Physician' (Lk. 5.31-32[3]). And through the death and resurrection Jesus it will not just be humanity who will be released from its sin and darkness but the whole of creation (Rom. 8.18-39;[4] Rev.21-22). This process begins with the ministry

---

[1]   He entered Jericho and was passing through it. A man was there named Zacchaeus; he was a chief tax-collector and was rich. He was trying to see who Jesus was, but on account of the crowd he could not, because he was short in stature. So he ran ahead and climbed a sycamore tree to see him, because he was going to pass that way. When Jesus came to the place, he looked up and said to him, 'Zacchaeus, hurry and come down; for I must stay at your house today.' So he hurried down and was happy to welcome him. All who saw it began to grumble and said, 'He has gone to be the guest of one who is a sinner.' Zacchaeus stood there and said to the Lord, 'Look, half of my possessions, Lord, I will give to the poor; and if I have defrauded anyone of anything, I will pay back four times as much.' Then Jesus said to him, 'Today salvation has come to this house, because he too is a son of Abraham. For the Son of Man came to seek out and to save the lost.'

[2]   As he approached Jericho, a blind man was sitting by the roadside begging. When he heard a crowd going by, he asked what was happening. They told him, 'Jesus of Nazareth is passing by.' Then he shouted, 'Jesus, Son of David, have mercy on me!' Those who were in front sternly ordered him to be quiet; but he shouted even more loudly, 'Son of David, have mercy on me!' Jesus stood still and ordered the man to be brought to him; and when he came near, he asked him, 'What do you want me to do for you?' He said, 'Lord, let me see again.' Jesus said to him, 'Receive your sight; your faith has saved you.' Immediately he regained his sight and followed him, glorifying God; and all the people, when they saw it, praised God.

[3]   Jesus answered, 'Those who are well have no need of a physician, but those who are sick; I have come to call not the righteous but sinners to repentance.'

[4]   I consider that the sufferings of this present time are not worth comparing with the glory about to be revealed to us. For the creation waits with eager longing for the revealing of the children of God; for the creation was subjected to futility, not of its own will but by the will of the one who subjected it, in hope that the creation itself will be set free from its bondage to decay and will obtain the freedom of the glory of the children of God. We know that the whole creation has been groaning in labour pains until now; and not only the creation, but we ourselves, who have the first fruits of the Spirit, groan inwardly while we wait for adoption, the redemption of our bodies. For in hope we were saved. Now hope that is seen is not hope. For who hopes for what is seen? But if we hope for what we do not see, we wait for it with patience. Likewise the Spirit helps us in our weakness; for we do not know how to pray as we ought, but that very Spirit intercedes with sighs too deep for words. And God, who searches the heart, knows what is the mind of the

of Jesus that brings *release* to those captured by sin so that they are freed into new relationship with God. As the one who brings *release* to the captives, the *blind* and the *oppressed,* Jesus is the one in whom salvation is to be found. The third claim he makes is that he has come to proclaim the:

> acceptable year of the Lord' (the year of acceptance, the time of favour)

has in mind the year of Jubilee, and refers to that time when God was to step in and act again on behalf of his people bringing them relief and blessing. The year of Jubilee was the year of cancellation of debts and restoration of lands Sloan 1977:39-41; Lev.25.8-17; Deut. 15.1-11). God's promise for his people was that one day he would step in, in the Jubilee of all Jubilees, delivering them, removing sin, and restoring and blessing the, to the full. Thus to declare that that year was now here was to declared a ministry of the 'last days', i.e., the days in which God will do his final work. The 'last days' began here, continued in the Acts of the Apostles, and have continued even to this day. It will be noted that Jesus does not read about *the day of vengeance of your God.* That yet awaited the future for he was here to save and not to judge (Jn. 3.17), and the judgement would take place when God drew history to a close. Jesus, therefore, makes three claims:

Spirit, because the Spirit intercedes for the saints according to the will of God. We know that all things work together for good for those who love God, who are called according to his purpose. For those whom he foreknew he also predestined to be conformed to the image of his Son, in order that he might be the firstborn within a large family. And those whom he predestined he also called; and those whom he called he also justified; and those whom he justified he also glorified. What then are we to say about these things? If God is for us, who is against us? He who did not withhold his own Son, but gave him up for all of us, will he not with him also give us everything else? Who will bring any charge against God's elect? It is God who justifies. Who is to condemn? It is Christ Jesus, who died, yes, who was raised, who is at the right hand of God, who indeed intercedes for us. Who will separate us from the love of Christ? Will hardship, or distress, or persecution, or famine, or nakedness, or peril, or sword? As it is written,'For your sake we are being killed all day long; we are accounted as sheep to be slaughtered.' No, in all these things we are more than conquerors through him who loved us. For I am convinced that neither death, nor life, nor angels, nor rulers, nor things present, nor things to come, nor powers, nor height, nor depth, nor anything else in all creation, will be able to separate us from the love of God in Christ Jesus our Lord.

1. He is the one anointed with the Spirit.
2. He is the prophet of fulfilment who declares good news. This office is what theologians have called *the eschatological prophet* or the *prophet like Moses*, because Jesus proclaims the arrival of a new era of salvation, functioning as a prophet-leader.
3. He is the one who brings release as well as the one who proclaims it. He is Messiah, the Anointed One.

This last idea explains the blind man's insight into what he has been hearing about Jesus when in Lk. 18.35-43[1] he calls out to the *Son of David* for healing. The *Son of David* brings not only a future rule but also present release from sin and a reversal of the effects of Satan's presence in the world (Lk. 11.14-23[2]). In short, this is the beginning of the fulfilment of God's promise, and Jesus is the source of that fulfilment.

b. The Hearers' Response and Jesus' Statements (Lk. 4.22)

The claim by Jesus that *today this scripture is fulfilled* in their *hearing* is both a challenge and a demand. Either Jesus is the spirit anointed Prophet

---

[1] As he approached Jericho, a blind man was sitting by the roadside begging. When he heard a crowd going by, he asked what was happening. They told him, 'Jesus of Nazareth is passing by.' Then he shouted, 'Jesus, Son of David, have mercy on me!' Those who were in front sternly ordered him to be quiet; but he shouted even more loudly, 'Son of David, have mercy on me!' Jesus stood still and ordered the man to be brought to him; and when he came near, he asked him, 'What do you want me to do for you?' He said, 'Lord, let me see again.' Jesus said to him, 'Receive your sight; your faith has saved you.' Immediately he regained his sight and followed him, glorifying God; and all the people, when they saw it, praised God.

[2] Now he was casting out a demon that was mute; when the demon had gone out, the one who had been mute spoke, and the crowds were amazed. But some of them said, 'He casts out demons by Beelzebul, the ruler of the demons.' Others, to test him, kept demanding from him a sign from heaven. But he knew what they were thinking and said to them, 'Every kingdom divided against itself becomes a desert, and house falls on house. If Satan also is divided against himself, how will his kingdom stand? —for you say that I cast out the demons by Beelzebul. Now if I cast out the demons by Beelzebul, by whom do your exorcists cast them out? Therefore they will be your judges. But if it is by the finger of God that I cast out the demons, then the kingdom of God has come to you. When a strong man, fully armed, guards his castle, his property is safe. But when one stronger than he attacks him and overpowers him, he takes away his armour in which he trusted and divides his plunder. Whoever is not with me is against me, and whoever does not gather with me scatters.

or he is not and thus, either he is the one who comes to bring the good news to the poor etc., or he is not; either he is the fulfilment of God's promises or he is not. The initial reaction of his hearers is at first favourable (Lk. 4.22):

> all spoke well of him and were amazed at the gracious words
> that came from his mouth

but then they realised that Jesus was the son of Joseph, the village carpenter. To the best of their knowledge he had not attended any of the rabbinical schools, so where did the *son of Joseph* get all this wisdom from and how could he be the one whom the Spirit of the Lord had anointed? Favour soon turns to antagonism (see, Hill 1971:161-180; Reike 1973:47-55). But Jesus knows what is in their mind and hearts and responds (usually in the gospels when someone has a thought about what Jesus has said or done, his response carries a rebuke with it, cf. Lk. 7.39, 49-50;[1] 11.38-39[2]) with a well known saying, *no doubt you will say, physician heal yourself* (Lk. 4.23), in other words: prove what you are saying. Jesus reinforces this with his statement that expresses he knows what they are thinking, *do here also in your home town the things that we have heard you did at Capernaum* (Lk. 4.23c), i.e., we have heard of your miracles elsewhere now do one here. But Jesus moves on from this and quotes another saying:

> Truly I tell you, no prophet is accepted in the prophet's home
> town

This demonstrates that Jesus is only too well aware of the rejection the prophets suffered among their own people. This theme surface continually

---

[1] Now when the Pharisee who had invited him saw it, he said to himself, 'If this man were a prophet, he would have known who and what kind of woman this is who is touching him—that she is a sinner.' But those who were at the table with him began to say among themselves, 'Who is this who even forgives sins?' And he said to the woman, 'Your faith has saved you; go in peace.'

[2] The Pharisee was amazed to see that he did not first wash before dinner. Then the Lord said to him, 'Now you Pharisees clean the outside of the cup and of the dish, but inside you are full of greed and wickedness.

in Luke (cf. Lk. 11.49-52;[1] 13.32-35;[2] 20.10-12;[3] Acts 7.51-53[4]).

c. The Widow of Zarephath Illustration (Lk. 4.25-26)

It is against this narrative contextuality that Luke has Jesus illustrate the point he is making the story of the widow of Zarepath from 1 K 17. Jesus points out to them that in the history of Israel there was a great famine in the time of Elijah when God was judging the people. But Elijah had not been sent to his own people for God had moved his works of mercy outside the nation into Gentile regions, as only a widow in Sidon and Naaman the Syrian experienced God's healing (1 K 17-18; 2 K 5.1-14[5]). Following his

---

[1] Therefore also the Wisdom of God said, "I will send them prophets and apostles, some of whom they will kill and persecute", so that this generation may be charged with the blood of all the prophets shed since the foundation of the world, from the blood of Abel to the blood of Zechariah, who perished between the altar and the sanctuary. Yes, I tell you, it will be charged against this generation. Woe to you lawyers! For you have taken away the key of knowledge; you did not enter yourselves, and you hindered those who were entering.'

[2] He said to them, 'Go and tell that fox for me, "Listen, I am casting out demons and performing cures today and tomorrow, and on the third day I finish my work. Yet today, tomorrow, and the next day I must be on my way, because it is impossible for a prophet to be killed away from Jerusalem." Jerusalem, Jerusalem, the city that kills the prophets and stones those who are sent to it! How often have I desired to gather your children together as a hen gathers her brood under her wings, and you were not willing! See, your house is left to you. And I tell you, you will not see me until the time comes when you say, "Blessed is the one who comes in the name of the Lord." '

[3] When the season came, he sent a slave to the tenants in order that they might give him his share of the produce of the vineyard; but the tenants beat him and sent him away empty-handed. Next he sent another slave; that one also they beat and insulted and sent away empty-handed. And he sent yet a third; this one also they wounded and threw out.

[4] 'You stiff-necked people, uncircumcised in heart and ears, you are for ever opposing the Holy Spirit, just as your ancestors used to do. Which of the prophets did your ancestors not persecute? They killed those who foretold the coming of the Righteous One, and now you have become his betrayers and murderers. You are the ones that received the law as ordained by angels, and yet you have not kept it.'

[5] Naaman, commander of the army of the king of Aram, was a great man and in high favour with his master, because by him the Lord had given victory to Aram. The man, though a mighty warrior, suffered from leprosy. Now the Arameans on one of their raids had taken a young girl captive from the land of Israel, and she served Naaman's wife. She said to her mistress, 'If only my lord were with the prophet who is in Samaria! He would cure him of his leprosy.' So Naaman went in and told his lord just what the girl from the land of Israel had said. And the king of Aram said, 'Go then, and I will send along a letter to the king of Israel.' He went, taking with him ten talents of silver, six thousand shekels of gold, and ten sets of garments. He brought the letter to the king of Israel, which read, 'When this letter reaches you, know that I have sent to you my servant Naaman, that you may cure him of his leprosy.' When the king of Israel read the letter, he tore his clothes and said, 'Am I God, to give death or life, that this man sends word to me to

proverb Jesus' point here was that Elijah too had not been welcomed in his own country (cf. Marshall 1990:188; Fitzmyer 1990:538). It thus illustrated why he too had been able to heal in Capernaum but not in Nazareth. In Capernaum they had flocked to him. Here in Nazareth they had not stirred. We must remember that Capernaum was on a busy trade route, and was by the Sea of Galilee, with boats coming in and out. Nazareth was a quiet little town situated in the hills. Thus Capernaum probably looked down on Nazareth, ('that out of the way place') and Nazareth probably bristled at Capernaum ('those sophisticated upstarts'). They thus looked on each other as in a sense 'foreigners', and this was probably what was in Jesus' mind. (The parochial attitude of country folk was proverbial). But to a people already infuriated his words suggested that they were not as good as the Sidonians. They were thus not at all pleased. Luke would, however, be delighted to include this saying, for it was an early indication to his Gentile readers that Jesus did not see Gentiles as excluded from God's mercy. The 'good news' brought by Jesus confronts the religious understanding of the synagogue congregation both by its declaration of God's freedom to act with compassion towards the outsider and also by its claim that in Jesus the scripture finds fulfilment.

---

cure a man of his leprosy? Just look and see how he is trying to pick a quarrel with me.' But when Elisha the man of God heard that the king of Israel had torn his clothes, he sent a message to the king, 'Why have you torn your clothes? Let him come to me, that he may learn that there is a prophet in Israel.' So Naaman came with his horses and chariots, and halted at the entrance of Elisha's house. Elisha sent a messenger to him, saying, 'Go, wash in the Jordan seven times, and your flesh shall be restored and you shall be clean.' But Naaman became angry and went away, saying, 'I thought that for me he would surely come out, and stand and call on the name of the Lord his God, and would wave his hand over the spot, and cure the leprosy! Are not Abana and Pharpar, the rivers of Damascus, better than all the waters of Israel? Could I not wash in them, and be clean?' He turned and went away in a rage. But his servants approached and said to him, 'Father, if the prophet had commanded you to do something difficult, would you not have done it? How much more, when all he said to you was, "Wash, and be clean"?' So he went down and immersed himself seven times in the Jordan, according to the word of the man of God; his flesh was restored like the flesh of a young boy, and he was clean.

d. The Widow of Nain (Lk. 7.11-17)

The Narrative Context

The story of the widow in Lk. 7.11-17 (told only in Luke) is an unforgettable moment in the gospel and there are some interesting features in the text that are worth exploring.

> Soon afterwards he went to a town called Nain, and his disciples and a large crowd went with him. As he approached the gate of the town, a man who had died was being carried out. He was his mother's only son, and she was a widow; and with her was a large crowd from the town. When the Lord saw her, he had compassion for her and said to her, 'Do not weep.' Then he came forward and touched the bier, and the bearers stood still. And he said, 'Young man, I say to you, rise!' The dead man sat up and began to speak, and Jesus gave him to his mother. Fear seized all of them; and they glorified God, saying, 'A great prophet has risen among us!' and 'God has looked favourably on his people!'

The first thing to be noticed is the comparison Luke makes between the two central individuals (Jesus and the widow) and the two crowds (the one following Jesus and the other following the widow). The *large crowd* following Jesus (and his disciples) are joyful and expectant, they are filled with life; the crowd following the widow are bowed down with grief and walking in the darkness of death. The focus of one crowd was on the dead son who had been his mother's only hope since she was a widow, the focus of the other on Jesus, the giver of life and the hope of Israel. The two crowds and the two persons, one life itself, the other dead meet and the end result was that death was confronted and destroyed and Jesus is revealed as the ruler over death (whether this raising has resurrection connotations will be discuss below). However, there is another motif lying behind this story and shown in Jesus' words to the widow *do not weep* (Lk. 7.13c): a weeping widow was a symbol of Israel in its need (Jer. 31.15):

A voice is heard in Ramah, lamentation and bitter weeping,
Rachel is weeping for her children, she refuses to be comforted
for her children, because they are not

which can be combined with the promise (Is. 54.4-5)

the reproach of your widowhood you will remember no more

Thus here we see the promise of life made available to Israel through the
Messiah.

e. The Encounter With Jesus (Lk. 7.11-15)

This passage is set in partnership with the previous passage Lk. 7.1-
10[1] about the healing of the centurion's slave displaying Luke's characteristic
pairing of a male and female and more importantly for the overall symbolic
power of the narrative from 1 K 17.8-24.[2] (cf. Reid 1996:104-105) In both

---

[1] After Jesus had finished all his sayings in the hearing of the people, he entered Capernaum. A centurion there had a slave whom he valued highly, and who was ill and close to death. When he heard about Jesus, he sent some Jewish elders to him, asking him to come and heal his slave. When they came to Jesus, they appealed to him earnestly, saying, 'He is worthy of having you do this for him, for he loves our people, and it is he who built our synagogue for us.' And Jesus went with them, but when he was not far from the house, the centurion sent friends to say to him, 'Lord, do not trouble yourself, for I am not worthy to have you come under my roof; therefore I did not presume to come to you. But only speak the word, and let my servant be healed. For I also am a man set under authority, with soldiers under me; and I say to one, "Go", and he goes, and to another, "Come", and he comes, and to my slave, "Do this", and the slave does it.' When Jesus heard this he was amazed at him, and turning to the crowd that followed him, he said, 'I tell you, not even in Israel have I found such faith.' When those who had been sent returned to the house, they found the slave in good health.

[2] Then the word of the Lord came to him, saying, 'Go now to Zarephath, which belongs to Sidon, and live there; for I have commanded a widow there to feed you.' So he set out and went to Zarephath. When he came to the gate of the town, a widow was there gathering sticks; he called to her and said, 'Bring me a little water in a vessel, so that I may drink.' As she was going to bring it, he called to her and said, 'Bring me a morsel of bread in your hand.' But she said, 'As the Lord your God lives, I have nothing baked, only a handful of meal in a jar, and a little oil in a jug; I am now gathering a couple of sticks, so that I may go home and prepare it for myself and my son, that we may eat it, and die.' Elijah said to her, 'Do not be afraid; go and do as you have said; but first make me a little cake of it and bring it to me, and afterwards make something for yourself and your son. For thus says the Lord the God of Israel: The jar of meal will not be emptied and the jug of oil will not fail until the day that the Lord sends rain on the earth.' She went and did as Elijah said, so that she as well as he and her household ate for many days. The jar of meal was

stories the prophet meets the widow at the gate of the city (1 K 17.10; Lk. 17.12[1]), and in both cases the dead son is an only son. Both stories have identical wording when the prophet gives the raised son back to his mother (1 K 17.23; Lk. 7.15[2]). In both incidents the healer is the one who acts and speaks for God (1 K 17.24; Lk. 7.16[3]).Those healings took a little more effort: Elisha lay on the boy three times and Elisha touched the boy with the staff and then lay on top of him. When Jesus hands the boy back to his mother, the language recalls 1 K 17.23. So even as Luke tells the story, he points to prophetic models. Such historical background explains why the crowds come to see Jesus as a *great prophet* (see, Nolland 1993:324) The Old Testament precedents help explain the event. Given such precedents, the reader should not jump to conclusions about what such events prove about Jesus' divinity, especially since Peter and Paul will do similar works. The belief that Jesus is divine has other bases. The comparison between Jesus and Elijah has a counterpart in Acts 9.36-42 in the comparison between Peter and Elisha (cf. 2 K 4.22-36). The similarity between Jesus and Elijah identifies Jesus as a prophet of God in line with the prophets of old and makes known that the good news is to those who are socially marginalised (Fitzmyer 1981:656-657). The differences between the two passages emphasise Jesus as one who had authority, who spoke not to God in prayer, but to the dead son, who is brought back to life (see, Lindars 1965:63-79;

not emptied, neither did the jug of oil fail, according to the word of the Lord that he spoke by Elijah. After this the son of the woman, the mistress of the house, became ill; his illness was so severe that there was no breath left in him. She then said to Elijah, 'What have you against me, O man of God? You have come to me to bring my sin to remembrance, and to cause the death of my son!' But he said to her, 'Give me your son.' He took him from her bosom, carried him up into the upper chamber where he was lodging, and laid him on his own bed. He cried out to the Lord, 'O Lord my God, have you brought calamity even upon the widow with whom I am staying, by killing her son?' Then he stretched himself upon the child three times, and cried out to the Lord, 'O Lord my God, let this child's life come into him again.' The Lord listened to the voice of Elijah; the life of the child came into him again, and he revived. Elijah took the child, brought him down from the upper chamber into the house, and gave him to his mother; then Elijah said, 'See, your son is alive.' So the woman said to Elijah, 'Now I know that you are a man of God, and that the word of the Lord in your mouth is truth.'

[1] As he entered a village, ten lepers approached him. Keeping their distance

[2] The dead man sat up and began to speak, and Jesus gave him to his mother.

[3] Fear seized all of them; and they glorified God, saying, 'A great prophet has risen among us!' and 'God has looked favourably on his people!'

Brodie 1986:247-267). Jesus is the Lord (Lk. 7.13). He performs the role of God (cf. 1 K 17.21, 22).:

> Now when he drew near to the gate of the city, behold, there was carried out one that was dead, the only son of his mother, and she was a widow, and many people of the city was with her.

The location for the story is the village of Nain. Nain is the modern Nen in the plain of Jezreel six miles SSE of Nazareth and on the slope of Little Hermon. Its ancient gates have not yet been discovered, if it had any, but insufficient work has as yet been done on the site to be sure (cf. Nolland 1993:324; Green 1997:290). However 'gate' can indicate simply an entrance thought of metaphorically as a gate. Although Luke refers to it as a city, he presents more a village type atmosphere with the community mourning the loss of the widow's son. Probably this only son of a widow died earlier this same day, since Jewish tradition encouraged a quick burial in order to avoid ceremonial uncleanliness (*m. Sanhedrin* 6.5). According to custom, the bereaved family members would rend their clothes and mourn the death. The process did not begin until it was certain that death had occurred. The body was anointed to prevent deterioration. It was buried quickly and was not kept overnight at home. The corpse would be wrapped in a burial cloth and put on a burial plank for all to see. Burials took place outside towns, and burial sites have been discovered near Nain. Jesus no doubt saw many funeral processions for in those days life was uncertain. The thing, however that distinguished this one was a particular weeping woman, for she was a widow, and her only main mainstay was now dead. Life held little for her in the future. She was fairly well known for almost the whole of the town were taking part. Taking part in such an even was seen by Jews as a meritorious act. And there was also probably a great sense of sympathy with her. For a widow to lose her only son was a huge tragedy. Perhaps Jesus knew the woman. The widow, cast in the role of a traditional widow, is nameless, silent and weeping. Her only son, her means of support, the person who gave her a place in the community, is dead. She is vulnerable but she is at the centre of the narrative (Green 1997:289).

> When the Lord saw her, he had compassion for her and said to her, 'Do not weep.' Then he came forward and touched the bier, and the bearers stood still. And he said, 'Young man, I say to you, rise!'

As these two groups meet at the gate, Jesus and his followers and the widow and her followers, her situation stirs the compassion in him and three important things happen:

1. He tells her *do not weep*
2. He touches the funeral bier
3. He raises the son from the dead

The widow has not made any request from Jesus, the initiative comes from Jesus himself, *when the Lord saw her* (Lk. 7.13) he was filled with compassion and said, *do not weep* (Lk. 7.13c). This call to mind the earlier words of Jesus, *Blessed are you who weep now, for you will laugh* (Lk. 6.21). The use of *Lord* is not accidental. Here was the one who was in control of the situation, the Lord of life.(cf. Lk. 2.11 a Saviour who is Christ the Lord); Lk. 5.8 (the holy Lord); Lk. 5.12 (the Lord over disease); Lk. 5.17 (the Lord of power); Lk. 6.5 (the Lord of the Sabbath); Lk. 6.46 (the Lord of disciples who must be obeyed). It speaks of authority and power. The command *do not weep* creates in the narrative a sense of anticipation, an implied promise of action (cf. Nolland 1993:323; Fitzmyer 1981:659; Green 1997:292). This is not a command to forbid grief but is spoken in view of his coming action and it serves as a reminder to Luke's audience that the good news of salvation will turn weeping into laughter. On drawing next to the bier, *he touched it*. Normally this action would have rendered the person unclean (Num. 19.11, 16[1]). But here it is an act of someone who cannot be rendered unclean by anything, even death and, though all good Jews knew when they had become unclean, there is no consciousness of that at all on his part (Green 1997:292). Then Jesus said (Lk. 7.14):

> 'Young man, I say to you, rise!' The dead man sat up and began
> to speak, and Jesus gave him to his mother

This recalls 1 K 17.22 where the boy, having been raised from the dead, 'cried out and 1 K 17.23 where Elijah *gave him to his mother*. This makes it clear that Luke intends his reader/hearer to connect this incident with the miracle performed by Elijah and to understand that Jesus is greater than Elijah, greater than Moses and greater than all the prophets (cf. Lk. 9.10[2]; see, Teide 1988:152). We only have details of three occasions on which Jesus raised people from the dead, one a son (here), one a daughter (Lk. 8.54), and the third was Lazarus (Jn. 11). But Lk. 7.22 suggests a number of others. Eusebius quotes Quadratus (125 AD) as saying in his Apology to Hadrian,

> The persons who were healed, and those who were raised from
> the dead, by Jesus, were not only seen when they were healed
> and raised but were always present also afterwards, and not only
> during the time when the Saviour walked on the earth, but after
> His departure also, they were present for a considerable time, so
> that some of them even lived until our times

Once again, therefore, Jesus has healed by the authority of his word (*I say* to you) but whether there resurrection connotations here is difficult to say. It may be best not to see this raising of the son of the widow of Nain (even

---

[1] In the second month on the fourteenth day, at twilight, they shall keep it; they shall eat it with unleavened bread and bitter herbs. It was always so: the cloud covered it by day and the appearance of fire by night.

[2] On their return the apostles told Jesus all they had done. He took them with him and withdrew privately to a city called Bethsaida.

given its eschatological setting) through the Johannine lens of Jn. 11.25[1] as an anticipation of the eschatological raising of the dead. The main focus here seems to be the authority of Jesus, his status and his institutional role in the salvific purposes of God. The response of the crowd to what they have just witnessed is one of *fear* (which in Luke is always the natural reaction to the presence of God) and the crowd consider that Jesus is a *great prophet* and that in this great prophet, *God has looked favourably on his people!* (Lk. 7.16, cf. Lk. 1.68, 78[2]). There is the sense that God is once again active among his people. The stress on *great* should be noted here because Jesus had raised the dead. This meant that he was on a par with the greatest of the prophets and so the words of the angel at Lk. 1.32 were being fulfilled. With his account of this miracle Luke is steadily building his portrait of the many-faceted nature of Jesus. God is visiting his people (cf. Green 1997:292-293). God's visitation is a key theme in Luke (1.68, 78; 19.41-44;[3] Acts 15.14[4]). God is active through Jesus (see, Marshall 1978:286). Public opinion about Jesus is spreading and is taking on various forms. God is at work through him. Yet his activity suggests that no one label or title is sufficient to describe and explain who he Is.

Martha and Mary of Bethany (Lk. 10.38-42)

The Narrative Context

It may at first seem strange that the examination of Martha and Mary which follows is out of place. Surely it belongs in the chapters which

---

[1]   Jesus said to her, 'I am the resurrection and the life. Those who believe in me, even though they die, will live.

[2]   'Blessed be the Lord God of Israel, for he has looked favourably on his people and redeemed them. By the tender mercy of our God, the dawn from on high will break upon us.

[3]   As he came near and saw the city, he wept over it, saying, 'If you, even you, had only recognized on this day the things that make for peace! But now they are hidden from your eyes. Indeed, the days will come upon you, when your enemies will set up ramparts around you and surround you, and hem you in on every side. They will crush you to the ground, you and your children within you, and they will not leave within you one stone upon another; because you did not recognize the time of your visitation from God.'

[4]   Simeon has related how God first looked favourably on the Gentiles, to take from among them a people for his name.

examine women in the gospel of Luke? This is a legitimate argument but what I have sought to do is bring the narratives in which they appear together so that the four aspects of the narratives can be fully explored, i.e., service, discipleship and faith. Martha and Mary alone appear in Lk. 10.38-42,[1] there is no mention of Lazarus; Martha, Mary and Lazarus appear in Jn. 11.1-42 (though Lazarus is dead) and Mary appears alone at the anointing at Bethany in Jn. 12.1-8.[2] While each of these narratives express different content and intention they are linked by the presence of the two sisters (Luke) and Lazarus in relation to the two sisters as a sibling (John). For this reason, therefore, it seemed easier to examine the narratives all together and to use Luke's account of Martha and Mary so, in a sense, 'set the scene' for the introduction of the Lazarus narrative in Jn. 11 in which the two sisters have a key role.

a. Readings on the Meaning of the Narrative

Aside from Jesus, Martha and Mary there are no other characters involved in the Luke narrative which ostensibly is concerned with a moment of generous welcome and hospitality on the part of the two sisters. Mary and Martha also appear in John 11 and 12 but the Luke does not mention Lazarus (because he had no knowledge of him?), nor is the group that accompanied Jesus mentioned as being present. This short, homely and pleasant narrative can be interpreted in many ways and for a long time it was understood to refer to the roles of 'active', 'apostolic' v 'contemplative' with contemplation (specified as monastic and, or, religious life) being the 'better path' that one could choose. However, this is to make the narrative much too subject specific since while this may be a way of reading the text, it is only

---

[1]   Now as they went on their way, he entered a certain village, where a woman named Martha welcomed him into her home. She had a sister named Mary, who sat at the Lord's feet and listened to what he was saying. But Martha was distracted by her many tasks; so she came to him and asked, 'Lord, do you not care that my sister has left me to do all the work by myself? Tell her then to help me.' But the Lord answered her, 'Martha, Martha, you are worried and distracted by many things; there is need of only one thing. Mary has chosen the better part, which will not be taken away from her.'

[2]

one and a weak one at that. It has also been read as pointing to the role of women in ministry whereby Martha represents 'table ministry' and Mary 'the word'. Again, this may be a legitimate reading of the narrative but it is not as specific as some would suggest since Luke does not make any reference direct or allusive to ministries in the early church. The narrative can be explored from the point of view of the two women and the roles they adopt whereby one conforms to social gender specifics stereotyping (Martha) where the other does not (Mary). It is also significant that the narrative is set within the context of a meal where Martha, the eldest, acts as the patroness/host to Jesus as he travels on his way to Jerusalem. However, Martha is gently chastised by Jesus for her over busyness which causes her to be *distracted* (Lk. 10.40-41). But Martha was simply engaging in a role specific to the societal custom. Jesus, however, makes no comment about the specific roles within that society and gently chides Martha not for her lack of welcome, hospitality, or service but rather because that those very things are what distracts her from the *better part* (Lk. 10.42). This does not mean to say that Jesus demeans or devalues those important values and customs but that he rather acknowledges them and points out that while these are important and valuable, there are other things which are more valuable and important. This leads us then to consider what the narrative actually concerns itself with and in essence, it does not concern itself with women and their roles in society. The narrative is not about women but about discipleship and this is the key to its reading.

b. The Theme of Discipleship and Service: Martha

Without offering another specific narrative contextuality, it will be useful to examine the placing of the content of the narrative within the theme of discipleship in this section of Luke. In Lk. 9.57-62 Jesus responds to the three people who wish to follow him by telling them:

> As they were going along the road, someone said to him, 'I will
> follow you wherever you go.' And Jesus said to him, 'Foxes have

> holes, and birds of the air have nests; but the Son of Man has nowhere to lay his head.' To another he said, 'Follow me.' But he said, 'Lord, first let me go and bury my father.' But Jesus said to him, 'Let the dead bury their own dead; but as for you, go and proclaim the kingdom of God.' Another said, 'I will follow you, Lord; but let me first say farewell to those at my home.' Jesus said to him, 'No one who puts a hand to the plough and looks back is fit for the kingdom of God.

This group is, in a sense, challenged by Jesus to be absolute and single-minded in their following of Jesus: one is criticised by him for the seeming failure to understand the extreme demands of such discipleship (Lk. 9.58). The other two are criticised for placing family custom above the immediacy of following Jesus (Lk. 9.60, 62[1]), even given, for example in the case of the third person, that burial of the dead was a religious duty that took precedence over all others, including study of the Law. Burial of a father was a religious duty of utmost importance, to leave it undone was considered scandalous to a Jew. Seen in this context, Martha's service of Jesus can be seen as 'following' Jesus as he is *on the road* (since both of these incidents are set within Jesus' travelling 'on the road' to Jerusalem). But at the same time, Martha is chided by Jesus for her own adherence to custom (the proper hospitality to a visitor) and her distracted busyness. As the men have been criticised by Jesus for their adherence to Jewish family custom which results in their delay in following Jesus, so Martha is criticised for her following custom which results in her 'delay' in listening to the word of Jesus as Mary does.

Martha is certainly portrayed by Luke in the role of discipleship through her serving ('diakonein=diakoneó', 'I serve', 'I wait at table' (particularly of a slave who waits on guests); 'I serve' (generally). It can also literally mean, 'to kick up dust' because of constantly 'being on the move' which seems to be indicated here with Martha's busyness). But while Luke

---

[1] But Jesus said to him, 'Let the dead bury their own dead; but as for you, go and proclaim the kingdom of God.'; Jesus said to him, 'No one who puts a hand to the plough and looks back is fit for the kingdom of God.'

has used the same term in Lk. 4.39 (Simon's mother-in-law),

> Then he stood over her and rebuked the fever, and it left her. Immediately she got up and began to serve them.

And Lk. 8.1-3 (the women who accompanied Jesus):

> Soon afterwards he went on through cities and villages, proclaiming and bringing the good news of the kingdom of God. The twelve were with him, as well as some women who had been cured of evil spirits and infirmities: Mary, called Magdalene, from whom seven demons had gone out, and Joanna, the wife of Herod's steward Chuza, and Susanna, and many others, who provided (*diēkonoun*) for them out of their resources.

Its use here has a slightly different connotation. Martha is undoubtedly the one who is both organising and carrying out the serving while at the same time frustrated with Mary apparent lack of involvement in the traditional custom of meeting the needs of guests (which was a woman's household task) but the structure of the sentence indicates that the serving was not being undertaken for Jesus' benefit. Martha is the subject of the verb but Jesus is not the object, indeed, it is difficult to find an object in the sentence. In this context, therefore, Martha's busyness seems to be going nowhere, or to colloquially put it, it is busy work for busy work's sake. Thus Martha, unlike Mary, is not in relationship with Jesus (unlike Mary) through this busyness but carries it out to fulfil traditional custom (and customary roles, i.e., woman's work) and does so by 'kicking up dust'.

c. The Theme of Discipleship and Service: Mary

Martha's frantic activity is set against Mary's calmness as she sits at the feet of Jesus listening to the word (Lk.10.39[1]). Here, Mary is quite

---

[1] She had a sister named Mary, who sat at the Lord's feet and listened to what he was saying.

clearly seen to be a pupil learning from the master. It might be noted here that the role of the student in which Luke depicts Mary goes beyond the normal opportunity for women to hear the word other than in the environment of worship. In this narrative while traditional roles according to custom are referred to (Martha), priority is given to the role of listening to the word and within the Jewish religious and societal understanding this activity of listening to the word was the domain of men. Indeed, Luke says that Mary has *chosen the better part* (Lk. 9.42) and in the rabbinic traditions this are word is associated with teaching situations (*b.Ber IV 2b* uses 'part' in relation to a pupil at a place of teaching and about the obligation of rising early for the word of the Law, showing that it is the student's 'lot' that is good and praiseworthy. 'Lot' is further clarified as referring to the student's preference for study of the Law). Luke, therefore, firmly places a woman in a role which was the priority of men. Luke says Mary was *at the Lord's feet* and listening *to what he was saying* (Lk. 10.39) which indicates both her submissiveness and her status as a disciple. In this position she is listening *to his words* which for Luke means to join Jesus as a disciple and this is why Jesus praises Mary for having chosen the *better part* (Lk. 10.41-42). Luke has thus shown that the priority of the disciple is to listen to the word of Jesus.

The Lukan narrative, therefore, is it is not about the roles of women in society (though societal custom and tradition does contextualise the narrative content). It is a narrative on discipleship. The narrative of Mary and Martha sets the fundamental priority for discipleship: listening to the word of God proclaimed by Jesus is the basis of service or ministry. The point is not that women can get too easily caught up in the busy work of keeping the home for what is said to Martha about Mary would be equally true if Mary were male or even a child. The fact that two women dominate the story would have been shocking in the first-century context, where men often dismissed women as marginal, but the account is designed to make a point about all disciples. Further, the point is not that activity like Martha's is bad. The choice Jesus discusses with Martha is between something that is good and something that is better. Life is full of difficult choices, and Jesus is stressing the relative merits of good activities here. For conscientious people, such choices are often the most difficult and anxiety-filled. In this narrative Luke is not highlighting competing expressions of service, but the basis of discipleship. Women are called, in their own right, against the pressures of custom, to listen to the word of the Lord as the basis of their discipleship. Jesus commends the hearing of the word at his feet; to take time to relate to Jesus is important. The language of the passage recalls Deut. 8.3:

> He humbled you by letting you hunger, then by feeding you with manna, with which neither you nor your ancestors were acquainted, in order to make you understand that one does not live by bread alone, but by every word that comes from the mouth of the Lord.

In a sense Mary is preparing to partake in the 'right meal' that is enshrined in Deut. 6.1-8:

> Now this is the commandment, the statutes and the ordinances that the Lord your God charged me to teach you to observe in the land that you are about to cross into and occupy, so that you and your children and your children's children may fear the Lord your God all the days of your life, and keep all his decrees and his commandments that I am commanding you, so that your days may be long. Hear therefore, O Israel, and observe them diligently, so that it may go well with you, and so that you may multiply greatly in a land flowing with milk and honey, as the Lord, the God of your ancestors, has promised you. Hear, O Israel: The Lord is our God, the Lord alone. You shall love the Lord your God with all your heart, and with all your soul, and with all your might. Keep these words that I am commanding you today in your heart. Recite them to your children and talk about them when you are at home and when you are away, when you lie down and when you rise.

What she has done by sitting at Jesus' feet will remain with her. This meal will last. Jesus is not so much condemning Martha's activity as commending Mary's, he is saying that her priorities are in order. In Luke's mind, therefore, *to sit at the feet* of Jesus and consume his teaching is to be present at and to the more important meal: his word.

The Parable of the Widow and the Judge (Lk. 18.1-8)

> Then Jesus told them a parable about their need to pray always and not to lose heart. He said, 'In a certain city there was a judge who neither feared God nor had respect for people. In that city there was a widow who kept coming to him and saying, "Grant me justice against my opponent." For a while he refused; but later he said to himself, "Though I have no fear of God and no respect for anyone, yet because this widow keeps bothering me, I will grant her justice, so that she may not wear me out by continually coming." 'And the Lord said, 'Listen to what the unjust judge says. And will not God grant justice to his chosen ones who cry to him day and night? Will he delay long in helping them? I tell you, he will quickly grant justice to them. And yet, when the Son of Man comes, will he find faith on earth?'

The Narrative Context

This unusual parable refers back to Jesus' prophecy about himself s the coming Son of Man (Lk. 18.8b[1] cf.17.24[2]). The parable is call to his disciples to continue praying that God will sustain the cause of his people until the day of the coming of the Son of Man. But the question posed at Lk. 18.8b,:

---

[1] I tell you, he will quickly grant justice to them. And yet, when the Son of Man comes, will he find faith on earth?'

[2] For as the lightning flashes and lights up the sky from one side to the other, so will the Son of Man be in his day.

And yet, when the Son of Man comes, will he find faith on earth?'

indicates that the way is not going to be easy. It demonstrates that the disciples of Jesus will have to face many barriers and challenging experiences. One might ask the question as to why Jesus did not illustrate his teaching on the need for persistence in prayer with an image of a righteous judge? This, surely, would have been a more powerful affirmation of how God moves swiftly to help those in need. The answer is simply that Jesus wanted to incorporate into the parable ideas of delay and the need for persistence. Delay for the need for persistence would not occur if the judge were righteous. If the judge were under pressed with work then delay might occur in which case persistence would be needed, but Jesus hardly wants to give the impression that God is 'snowed under'! This highlights what the stress of the parable is: delay and need for persistence. The central point of the parable is that God will give his people justice and will answer when the time is right and this will be most especially the case at the final consummation. The future is guaranteed but it is to be in conjunction with persistence in prayer and fidelity of life (see, Harrington 1991:273-275; Marshall 1978:670). Interestingly, Luke's portrait of Jesus highlights prayer. He prays before receiving the Spirit (Lk. 3.21-22[1]), all-night prayer precedes the selecting the Twelve (Lk. 6.12[2]), and two parables focus on prayer (Lk. 11.5-13;[3] 18.1-8). The answer to the dilemma of prayer is that it is not

---

[1] Now when all the people were baptised, and when Jesus also had been baptised and was praying, the heaven was opened, and the Holy Spirit descended upon him in bodily form like a dove. And a voice came from heaven, 'You are my Son, the Beloved; with you I am well pleased.'

[2] Now during those days he went out to the mountain to pray; and he spent the night in prayer to God.

[3] And he said to them, 'Suppose one of you has a friend, and you go to him at midnight and say to him, "Friend, lend me three loaves of bread; for a friend of mine has arrived, and I have nothing to set before him." And he answers from within, "Do not bother me; the door has already been locked, and my children are with me in bed; I cannot get up and give you anything." I tell you, even though he will not get up and give him anything because he is his friend, at least because of his persistence he will get up and give him whatever he needs. 'So I say to you, Ask, and it will be given to you; search, and you will find; knock, and the door will be opened for you. For everyone who asks receives, and everyone who searches finds, and for everyone who knocks, the door will be opened. Is there anyone among you who, if your child asks for a fish, will give a snake instead of a fish? Or if the child asks for an egg, will give a scorpion? If you then,

intended to do something for God, but for us. It is one of the mechanisms of relationship that God gives to his children to be in touch with him. God may not need prayer, but we do. This parable highlights that point, as v. 1 makes clear:

> Then Jesus told his disciples a parable to show them that they
> should always pray and not give up.

Since Jesus was speaking to his disciples in Lk.17.22-37,[1] the same audience is assumed by the NIV to be present here, since the Greek says only that he told them a parable. Jesus shows that God responds to prayer and listens to his children. He does not wind up the universe like a watch, as the deists of old argued. He does not merely send the universe ticking on its merry way and sit back to observe as an uninterested spectator; God relates to his creation. This is especially the case when our prayers cry out for justice and the righteous treatment of his children. In such cases, when God acts, his response will be swift and certain (v.8).

One of the strengths of Jesus' parables is that they are filled with interesting characters. This is especially true of this parable. Two characters are central to the story: a nagging *widow* and an independent *judge* who

---

who are evil, know how to give good gifts to your children, how much more will the heavenly Father give the Holy Spirit to those who ask him!'

[1] Then he said to the disciples, 'The days are coming when you will long to see one of the days of the Son of Man, and you will not see it. They will say to you, "Look there!" or "Look here!" Do not go, do not set off in pursuit. For as the lightning flashes and lights up the sky from one side to the other, so will the Son of Man be in his day. But first he must endure much suffering and be rejected by this generation. Just as it was in the days of Noah, so too it will be in the days of the Son of Man. They were eating and drinking, and marrying and being given in marriage, until the day Noah entered the ark, and the flood came and destroyed all of them. Likewise, just as it was in the days of Lot: they were eating and drinking, buying and selling, planting and building, but on the day that Lot left Sodom, it rained fire and sulphur from heaven and destroyed all of them, it will be like that on the day that the Son of Man is revealed. On that day, anyone on the housetop who has belongings in the house must not come down to take them away; and likewise anyone in the field must not turn back. Remember Lot's wife. Those who try to make their life secure will lose it, but those who lose their life will keep it. I tell you, on that night there will be two in one bed; one will be taken and the other left. There will be two women grinding meal together; one will be taken and the other left.' Then they asked him, 'Where, Lord?' He said to them, 'Where the corpse is, there the vultures will gather.'

does not show preference to anyone. I am sure all of us know someone we would call a nag. Such persons are always complaining about something, and if there is an important issue or principle involved, they will not let it go until it is fixed. Such a woman is the example in this parable. We are to pray just as she nags, especially when we desire God's vindication of our commitment to him. We are to pray and keep praying for this. Now, of course, we need not whine in our prayers to God, but simply express our sincere desire to see him and those who are his vindicated. Often when we pray we do not share our true feelings with God (as if he does not know them already!). It gives me pause to realize that the most common type of psalm in the Psalter is the lament. The mature Old Testament saints were honest about their feelings before God. Yet often as we voice our concerns to God, he renews our faith and trust in him. So when we pray, we should express our deepest feelings, even our complaints, as we urge God to bring justice. Perhaps the prayer found in Acts 4.24-32[1] is an example. There God's people pray, in essence, 'Lord, give us boldness and show your presence.' Yet it is significant that the encouragement not to grow weary in such prayer (Lk. 18:1) indicates that God's response may not always come when we want it. We may have to wait for it. Jesus did teach that God's vindication of the saints might take some time. Prayer can help us stay in touch with God and stay patient in the interim.

a. The Characters of the Judge and Widow (Lk. 18.2-3)

Luke positions the parable after Jesus' remark on the end of the age in

---

[1] When they heard it, they raised their voices together to God and said, 'Sovereign Lord, who made the heaven and the earth, the sea, and everything in them, it is you who said by the Holy Spirit through our ancestor David, your servant:"Why did the Gentiles rage, and the peoples imagine vain things? The kings of the earth took their stand, and the rulers have gathered together against the Lord and against his Messiah." For in this city, in fact, both Herod and Pontius Pilate, with the Gentiles and the peoples of Israel, gathered together against your holy servant Jesus, whom you anointed, to do whatever your hand and your plan had predestined to take place. And now, Lord, look at their threats, and grant to your servants to speak your word with all boldness, while you stretch out your hand to heal, and signs and wonders are performed through the name of your holy servant Jesus.' When they had prayed, the place in which they were gathered together was shaken; and they were all filled with the Holy Spirit and spoke the word of God with boldness.

Lk. 17.22-37 and before the parable of the Pharisee and tax collector in Lk. 18.8-14.[1] The parable itself is found in Lk. 18.2-5.[2] It is surrounded by the narrator's comment, in Lk. 18.1, 6-10, about 'the need to pray and not lose heart'. The passage contains more than just a parable and the relation of the other verses to it, and of the whole to the preceding episode, is a matter of no little debate. It should be noted here that the parable is so important that an explanation of its meaning is given right at the very beginning (Lk. 18.1). It is given both as an incentive and encouragement to pray and to persist in that praying (Harrington 1991:274; cf. Freed 1987:38-60). The prayer is to be concern itself with God acting on behalf of his people, that he will have a careful watch over them and will bring them safely to the end. Jesus' final question at the end (Lk. 18.8b), *when the Son of Man comes, will he find faith on earth?* Is in reality an encouragement to faith rather than an expression his own doubt that the question will be answered in the affirmative. In context the emphasis is on praying continuously until the Son of Man comes; the disciple of Jesus must be continually at prayer that never ceases, and which all should be involved and that prayer should be centred on the fulfilment of his purposes (Lk. 11.1-4[3]) because that will play a part in his purposes actually becoming a reality.

---

[1] I tell you, he will quickly grant justice to them. And yet, when the Son of Man comes, will he find faith on earth?' He also told this parable to some who trusted in themselves that they were righteous and regarded others with contempt: 'Two men went up to the temple to pray, one a Pharisee and the other a tax-collector. The Pharisee, standing by himself, was praying thus, "God, I thank you that I am not like other people: thieves, rogues, adulterers, or even like this tax-collector. I fast twice a week; I give a tenth of all my income." But the tax-collector, standing far off, would not even look up to heaven, but was beating his breast and saying, "God, be merciful to me, a sinner!" I tell you, this man went down to his home justified rather than the other; for all who exalt themselves will be humbled, but all who humble themselves will be exalted.'

[2] He said, 'In a certain city there was a judge who neither feared God nor had respect for people. In that city there was a widow who kept coming to him and saying, "Grant me justice against my opponent." For a while he refused; but later he said to himself, "Though I have no fear of God and no respect for anyone, yet because this widow keeps bothering me, I will grant her justice, so that she may not wear me out by continually coming." '

[3] He was praying in a certain place, and after he had finished, one of his disciples said to him, 'Lord, teach us to pray, as John taught his disciples.' He said to them, 'When you pray, say: Father, hallowed be your name. Your kingdom come. Give us each day our daily bread. And forgive us our sins, for we ourselves forgive everyone indebted to us. And do not bring us to the time of trial.'

This parable is found only in Luke's gospel and relies for its force on both a contrast and juxtaposition of the characters of the two central figures: the judge and the widow. Luke describes the character of the judge first and so indicate to the reader what kind of formidable opposition the widow was up against (Lk. 18.2):

> In a certain city there was a judge who neither feared God nor
> had respect for people.

This is a person, then, who is resolute and absolute and who does not seem to know the words dialogue or negotiation, he is unaffected by anything and does exactly what he wants. God is like this in that he is over all and acts completely on his own without any hindrance or limitation. The difference between the judge and God, of course, is that God does what is right and just and that is an image of God from the very beginning (Gen. 18.25[1]). God is not limited by any law outside himself only by what he himself is. That the judge in the parable *feared neither God nor man* may suggest that he was non-Jewish (a legitimate reading given Luke's audience was primarily Gentile) and that the widow had moved outside the religious court structure to get justice from the highest source possible, i.e., the civil powers. These judges had a reputation for partiality and bribes opened their ears!

The phrase is to be found in extra-biblical courses (e.g., Josephus) and so may indicate someone who is 'their own man', independent, strong-minded and is not influenced by anything outside himself (e.g., the widow) (Fitzmyer 1981:1178; Green 1997:639; Tiede 1988:304). Luke then contrasts the judge (probably a local magistrate and thus a male person of important status) with the widow (Lk. 18.3):

> In that city there was a widow who kept coming to him and
> saying, "Grant me justice against my opponent."

---

[1] Far be it from you to do such a thing, to slay the righteous with the wicked, so that the righteous fare as the wicked! Far be that from you! Shall not the Judge of all the earth do what is just?'

The widow is the direct antithesis of the judge: female, of no status, poor, helpless and with no advocate to act for justice on her behalf. The only 'weapon' she had at her disposal was her persistence that justice be given her and so she *kept coming to him* in the public forum for that justice (cf. Reid 1996:191). It would be a mistake to assume that the woman in this story is old. In the ancient culture, women married in the early to mid teens, and the life expectancy for men who reached adulthood often did not exceed 'thirtysomething'. Yet being a widow, she was among the most vulnerable people in her society. In the Scriptures widows are always mentioned (along with orphans) as among the neediest, the weakest and the most dependent of people. They often have no one directly to look to but God. It is significant that Luke mentions widows nine time compared with Matthew's one mention and Mark's three. This confirms his greater emphasis on and concern about women. But Jesus' use of the idea of a widow possibly has in mind Lam.1.1. There, Israel in her need is likened to a lonely widow who weeps bitterly in the night, thus here it is a suitable picture of the people of God, especially when they are in periods of distress. She was to be cared for by others (Ex. 22.22-24;[1] Deut. 10.18;[2] 14.29;[3]). Her precarious position parallels the risk believers experience in an often hostile world. This woman, in her need, came to the judge pleading for justice, and using the only weapon that she had, persistence. The verb is sometimes translated 'avenge me', but it does not necessarily signify a desire for revenge. It is more concerned with obtaining justice. It is on this case a demand for her legal rights. She is probably wanting what is due to her, or to be protected from interference. We could possibly better translate as *give me justice against my*

---

[1] You shall not abuse any widow or orphan. If you do abuse them, when they cry out to me, I will surely heed their cry; my wrath will burn, and I will kill you with the sword, and your wives shall become widows and your children orphans.

[2] Who executes justice for the orphan and the widow, and who loves the strangers, providing them with food and clothing.

[3] The Levites, because they have no allotment or inheritance with you, as well as the resident aliens, the orphans, and the widows in your towns, may come and eat their fill so that the Lord your God may bless you in all the work that you undertake.

adversary (cf. Acts 7.24;[1] Rom.12.19;[2] 2 Cor.10.6[3]). But she knew that she had only one weapon, persistence. With her lack of influence that was the only way that she could hope to get a hearing. If in fact he was a Jewish judge she should have been first in his list, for the Old Testament makes quite clear that judges judge in the place of God (Deut. 16.18-20;[4] Ps. 82.2-4[5]) and that special care that should be taken of widows and orphans (see Deut. 10.18;[6] Ps. 68.5;[7] Is. 1.17[8]). But whether he was or not he does not take her widowhood into account. He is more concerned for an easy life. The widow's complaint may well have been a financial one in regard to which she is seeking some kind of vindication. It may be that the widow is complaining that material resources had nor been granted her or had been withheld from her. The startling image of this parable is that this is woman arguing her case before the judge. Legal matters and their resolution was the business of men and with the death of her husband responsibility for the widow's affairs would have fallen to the nearest male relative. The widow's complaint may well have been that this person who should have been both her protector and agent for her best interests was, in fact, neither. That the woman herself persists with the judge would indicate that she has no male relative to undertake her case and the fact that she has to be persistent with this judge suggests that she does not have the money for a bribe which

---

[1] When he saw one of them being wronged, he defended the oppressed man and avenged him by striking down the Egyptian.

[2] Beloved, never avenge yourselves, but leave room for the wrath of God; for it is written, 'Vengeance is mine, I will repay, says the Lord.'

[3] We are ready to punish every disobedience when your obedience is complete.

[4] You shall appoint judges and officials throughout your tribes, in all your towns that the Lord your God is giving you, and they shall render just decisions for the people. You must not distort justice; you must not show partiality; and you must not accept bribes, for a bribe blinds the eyes of the wise and subverts the cause of those who are in the right. Justice, and only justice, you shall pursue, so that you may live and occupy the land that the Lord your God is giving you.

[5] 'How long will you judge unjustly and show partiality to the wicked? Give justice to the weak and the orphan; maintain the right of the lowly and the destitute. Rescue the weak and the needy; deliver them from the hand of the wicked.'

[6] Who executes justice for the orphan and the widow, and who loves the strangers, providing them with food and clothing.

[7] Father of orphans and protector of widows is God in his holy habitation.

[8] Learn to do good; seek justice, rescue the oppressed, defend the orphan, plead for the widow

would result in a speedy settlement of her case.

b. The Widow's Vindication (Lk. 18.4-5)

The judge has already been described as one who *feared neither God nor man* (Lk. 18.2), not especially interested in justice for the widow (the tense of the verb, the imperfect active indicative translated as, *for a while he refused* ('ēthelen' indicates his ongoing refusal) which is contrary to the biblical imperative given in 2 Chron.19.6-7:

> To judge not for man but for the Lord; he is with you in giving
> judgement ... there is no perversion of justice with the Lord our
> God, or partiality, or taking bribes'

So for a while the judge ignored her pleas, putting off her case and hoping that she would go away. But when she kept coming to him continually he gave in. He recognised that she was not just going to go away and that the best thing to do in order to obtain a quiet life was to deal with her request. Her persistence had won through (Lk. 18.4c-5):

> he said to himself, "Though I have no fear of God and no
> respect for anyone, yet because this widow keeps bothering me,
> I will grant her justice, so that she may not wear me out by
> continually coming." '

The judge eventually grants her the justice she seeks but the motivation lying behind the judgement is not about the justice of the case: he decides to grant her case because of her unwavering and wearying persistence. The verbs use here are strong ones, *she keeps bothering lest she wear me down* ('kopos', 'to hit, strike' – properly, 'a strike (blow) that is so hard, it seriously weakens or debilitates'; (figuratively) 'deep fatigue', 'extreme weariness' (wearisome toil); 'hupópiazó','I strike under the eye', hence: 'I bruise', 'treat severely', 'discipline by hardship', 'molest', 'annoy', 'harass', 'worry', 'exhaust'). The picture of the judge fearful of the widow borders on the absurd. The woman is acting so out of social status that, he reflects, she may be capable of assaulting him with more than words. Jesus accents the astonishingly uncharacteristic initiative and persistence of an allegedly impotent woman in the face of injustice. But he is not concerned about about being assaulted by her reputation or even his reputation or being shamed by the widow. We can compare the principle described here with that in mind in the parable of the importunate neighbour where the same principles applied (Lk. 11.5-8[1]). But in a real sense, The judge had not been converted. He just wanted to be rid of a bothersome woman who he fears may 'blacken his eye'(wear him out). So in spite of the fact that neither the divine or human could influence this judge to do anything, he gives her justice.

The Meaning of the Parable

c. The Widow As Metaphor (Lk. 18.6-8)

There are various ways of interpreting the meaning of this parable based on the two characters of the judge and the widow. The parable itself (Lk. 18.2-5) does not appear to have any application but since the parable concludes with a statement about the coming Son of Man (Lk. 18.8b), it may be seen in relation to the teaching of the coming Son of Man at Lk. 17.22-27[2] which ends with a parable about prayer (where the meaning is

---

[1] And he said to them, 'Suppose one of you has a friend, and you go to him at midnight and say to him, "Friend, lend me three loaves of bread; for a friend of mine has arrived, and I have nothing to set before him." And he answers from within, "Do not bother me; the door has already been locked, and my children are with me in bed; I cannot get up and give you anything." I tell you, even though he will not get up and give him anything because he is his friend, at least because of his persistence he will get up and give him whatever he needs.

[2] Then he said to the disciples, 'The days are coming when you will long to see one of the days of the Son of Man, and you will not see it. They will say to you, "Look there!" or "Look here!" Do not go, do not set off in pursuit. For as the lightning flashes and lights up the sky from one side to the other, so will the Son of Man be in his day. But first he must endure much suffering and be rejected by this generation. Just as it was in the days of Noah, so too it will be in the days of the Son of Man. They were eating and drinking, and marrying and being given in marriage, until the day Noah entered the ark, and the flood came and

said to be an encouragement to the disciples to pray continuously and to be strong in hope until the parousia), as this parable ends with a statement about faith. So, it is Lk. 18.8b which supplies the application in this parable and the character of the judge is the central focus, where the meaning of the parable is to be found in the contrast between the judge and God (on possible variations of meaning of parable at this point see, Green 1997:636-638; Nolland 1983:866;). This would then mean that Jesus' words at Lk. 18.8b are directed to the disciples and whether their faith will be as unwavering as the persistence of the widow against the judge.

Another way of viewing the parable is to include Lk. 18.2-6[1] which interconnects the characters of the judge and the widow, in which case the parable would mean that if the unjust and unbending judge accedes to the persistence of the powerless and poor widow, then how much more will the just judge, God, hear the prayers of those who implore him (the disciples). Here, therefore, the judge is contrasted with God and the widow's persistence a metaphor for prayer of the disciples (see, Fitzmeyer 1981:1178; Thurston 1989:27). This would certainly be in line with the stated aim of the parable which Luke gives at Lk. 18.1:

> Then Jesus told them a parable about their need to pray always
> and not to lose heart

This would mean that the parable's main concentration is on prayer and perseverance. The widow's persistence towards the judge is a metaphor for persistent prayer from which the hearers/readers of the parable are to derive the lesson that persistence in prayer pays off. However, part of the problem with this view of the parable is that if the widow represents persistence in prayer, then the judge represents God but since the judge is said to be unjust

---

destroyed all of them.

[1] He said, 'In a certain city there was a judge who neither feared God nor had respect for people. In that city there was a widow who kept coming to him and saying, "Grant me justice against my opponent." For a while he refused; but later he said to himself, "Though I have no fear of God and no respect for anyone, yet because this widow keeps bothering me, I will grant her justice, so that she may not wear me out by continually coming." ' And the Lord said, 'Listen to what the unjust judge says.

which is contrary to everything revealed in the biblical data. It also seems to be suggesting that God 'capitulates' to persistence which does not seem to square with the biblical image of God as gracious, open and receptive to all who would come to him.

The view that the parable concerns itself with faithfulness is interesting. Here the contrast is made between the judge and God and his faithfulness and the widow and her own faithfulness in waiting for God to answer. However, the question that Jesus asks in Lk. 18.8b does not concern itself with faith as such but rather that faith (persistence) of the widow. This would mean that there is a connection, therefore, between Luke's introduction (and statement of the parable's meaning) at Lk. 18.1 and Jesus' words at Lk. 18.8b about *faith on earth,* in which case the description of the widow at Lk. 18.2-5 would parabolicly represent the life of the disciple of Jesus as they await the eschaton and the parousia. Thus the widow takes on an archetypal quality. However, it may be that it is the widow who represents God and not the judge and that the meaning of the parable concerns itself with the persistence in seeking justice. So that God, now imaged as a poor, powerless widow, is the one who resolutely pursues justice. This is an interesting, challenging and unusual interpretation and would certainly fit with the subversive ideas found in the parables of Jesus. God is the one who grants justice because he is just as opposed to the unjust judge who only grants justice not because he is just but to be rid of an annoyance. If this is granted then the actions of the widow can be set between Luke's opening verse at Lk. 18.1 about the need to pray and have heart, and the crying to God *night and day* at Lk. 18.7 in which case there is an element of 'protest' in the parable insofar as the widow is now a metaphor for the relentless and persistent pursuit of justice (Lk. 18.2-5) (Reid 1996:192).

These are all various ways of reading the parable but persistence in prayer is a key element in all of them. At Lk. 18.6, Jesus says, *Listen to what the unjust judge says.* We can compare here the use of *unrighteous* with regard to the estate manager in Lk. 16.8. In both cases it indicates that they were unscrupulous and did their own thing. They looked at things from a worldly viewpoint. So in order to get over a powerful point Jesus was not averse to using such people as illustrations, for it often made the point that he was seeking to get over clear cut, while at the same time the reference to *unrighteous* is a warning against applying it too literally to God. The point being made here is that the widow's constant pleas can be compared in some ways with genuine intercessory prayers to God, because they were effective in obtaining from the object of those pleas a ready and complete answer. The underlying lesson is that of persistence.

But because he was 'unrighteous' we are to recognise that his reasons for giving way were totally unlike those of God. God does not respond to our prayers because he is weary of them, nor will we get our own way by wearing him down. In fact, elsewhere he has stressed that he does not answer people's prayers just because of their *much speaking* (Mt. 6.7). What he does guarantee to hear are genuine prayers concerning matters which are his concern, which because they matter a great deal to the suppliant, are persistent. And what Jesus is urging here is that we continue constantly with such prayers. This is not speaking of prayers just for ourselves. It has in mind prayers for what is right, prayers concerning the well-being, and spiritual growth and protection of his people. To drive his parabolic point home Jesus asks two rhetorical questions (Lk. 18.7-8):

> And will not God grant justice to his chosen ones who cry to
> him day and night? Will he delay long in helping them?

Thus, says Jesus, 'if even an unrighteous judge gives way before continual pleading, how much more we can be certain that God, the supremely righteous Judge, will listen to the voice, not of one who is just an unknown woman, but of those whom he has chosen who are personally known to him, when they cry to him *day and night*. He may seem to delay, like the judge did, he may indeed wait for what seems to us a long time (another hint that the end will not come as soon as many expected). But of one thing we can be sure, justice will come. God's way, which is what should be the great desire of his people, will triumph, and his people will prosper and be blessed. It might be noted here that Jesus' description of God's people as his elect comes regularly in relation to the second coming (Mk. 13.20, 22, 27;[1]). The direction of our prayers as 'the elect' are therefore to be seen as having that in mind.

The verb that Luke uses in *delay long over them* is 'makrothumeó', which means 'I suffer long, have patience, am forbearing' (James 5.7[2]) and can be read as 'long suffering' (Mt. 18.26, 29;[3] 1 Cor. 13.4;[4] 1 Thess. 5.14;[5] 2 Pet. 3.9[6]) in which case the verse can be read as, *even though he is long suffering over them*, or *even though he wait a long time over them*. The idea of God's non delay has caused much discussion, given that the final judgement has still not come. Though many explanations have been offered, two are more likely. The first possibility is that rather than meaning God will not delay long over them, it means God will show patience to them. In other words, he will be patient about their request and honour it by vindicating them. This view fits Sir. 35.19 LXX,[7] which appears to be a conceptual parallel. Texts like 2 Pet. 3.8-9[8] show that God's patience reflects his merciful desire that more come to know him. Another possible meaning is that God will prevent excessive persecution of the community until the

---

[1] And if the Lord had not cut short those days, no one would be saved; but for the sake of the elect, whom he chose, he has cut short those days. False messiahs and false prophets will appear and produce signs and omens, to lead astray, if possible, the elect. Then he will send out the angels, and gather his elect from the four winds, from the ends of the earth to the ends of heaven.

[2] Be patient, therefore, beloved, until the coming of the Lord. The farmer waits for the precious crop from the earth, being patient with it until it receives the early and the late rains.

[3] So the slave fell on his knees before him, saying, "Have patience with me, and I will pay you everything." Then his fellow-slave fell down and pleaded with him, "Have patience with me, and I will pay you."

[4] Love is patient; love is kind; love is not envious or boastful or arrogant

[5] And we urge you, beloved, to admonish the idlers, encourage the faint-hearted, help the weak, be patient with all of them.

[6] The Lord is not slow about his promise, as some think of slowness, but is patient with you, not wanting any to perish, but all to come to repentance.

[7] As she cries out against the one who causes them to fall?

[8] But do not ignore this one fact, beloved, that with the Lord one day is like a thousand years, and a thousand years are like one day. The Lord is not slow about his promise, as some think of slowness, but is patient with you, not wanting any to perish, but all to come to repentance.

vindication comes. 'Patience' can refer to the delaying or putting off of a consequence of an action (Ex. 34.6;[1] Num. 14.18;[2] Joel 2.13;[3] Sir. 5.4[4]). Thus God will lighten his people's suffering until vindication comes. It is hard to be certain which of these ideas is meant, though the first option seems less subtle. Regardless, it is clear God will vindicate his saints. We may see in it here a combination of these senses. It includes the thought of delaying in order to give people time to repent because he is long-suffering, and delaying in order finally to complete what he has purposed, because nothing short of what he has purposed will do. He will not be satisfied until every one of his own is gathered in. The Shepherd is still busy. Other suggested translations are, 'Is he slow to help them?' (signifying, of course, that he is not), or, 'Is he not patient with them?' (signifying that he never gets tired of hearing the prayers of his people). Jesus then gives an absolute assurance (Lk. 18.8):

> I tell you, he will quickly grant justice to them. And yet, when
> the Son of Man comes, will he find faith on earth?'

This could mean that when it finally comes it will come with speed, it will occur suddenly, unexpectedly and without delay. And then all will be put right. And as he then makes clear, this refers to the Parousia. Alternatively it could mean 'soon'. But in that case it is to be seen as 'soon' from God's perspective. Delay will occur no longer than is necessary. (cf. 2 Pet 3.8-10[5]).

---

[1]   The Lord passed before him, and proclaimed, 'The Lord, the Lord, a God merciful and gracious, slow to anger, and abounding in steadfast love and faithfulness,

[2]   "The Lord is slow to anger, and abounding in steadfast love, forgiving iniquity and transgression, but by no means clearing the guilty, visiting the iniquity of the parents upon the children to the third and the fourth generation."

[3]   Rend your hearts and not your clothing. Return to the Lord, your God, for he is gracious and merciful, slow to anger, and abounding in steadfast love, and relents from punishing.

[4]   Do not say, 'I sinned, yet what has happened to me?' for the Lord is slow to anger.

[5]   But do not ignore this one fact, beloved, that with the Lord one day is like a thousand years, and a thousand years are like one day. The Lord is not slow about his promise, as some think of slowness, but is patient with you, not wanting any to perish, but all to come to repentance. But the day of the Lord will come like a thief, and then the heavens will pass away with a loud noise, and the elements will be dissolved with fire, and the earth and everything that is done on it will be disclosed.

And then comes the challenge, the open question, that in one way or another regularly comes at the end of what Jesus has to say. And that question is as to whether when the end comes, and Jesus comes in his glory, He will find persevering faith on earth. Whether he will find persistent and continuing prayer. It is a challenge to his listeners. It is not said, however, in order to instil doubt, but in order to encourage persistence in prayer in the face of whatever comes on them. Elsewhere it is made perfectly plain that in the last days there will be faith on earth (e.g., 1 Thess. 4.17-18;[1] Rev.11.1-13[2]). There will be many who, like the skin-diseased Samaritan who was healed, will persistently return to give glory and thanksgiving to God. And this will be so in spite of any tribulation that they might face. This is especially exemplified in the Book of Revelation where the most dreadful events are

---

[1] Then we who are alive, who are left, will be caught up in the clouds together with them to meet the Lord in the air; and so we will be with the Lord for ever. Therefore encourage one another with these words.

[2] Then I was given a measuring rod like a staff, and I was told, 'Come and measure the temple of God and the altar and those who worship there, but do not measure the court outside the temple; leave that out, for it is given over to the nations, and they will trample over the holy city for forty-two months. And I will grant my two witnesses authority to prophesy for one thousand two hundred and sixty days, wearing sackcloth.' These are the two olive trees and the two lampstands that stand before the Lord of the earth. And if anyone wants to harm them, fire pours from their mouth and consumes their foes; anyone who wants to harm them must be killed in this manner. They have authority to shut the sky, so that no rain may fall during the days of their prophesying, and they have authority over the waters to turn them into blood, and to strike the earth with every kind of plague, as often as they desire. When they have finished their testimony, the beast that comes up from the bottomless pit will make war on them and conquer them and kill them, and their dead bodies will lie in the street of the great city that is prophetically called Sodom and Egypt, where also their Lord was crucified. For three and a half days members of the peoples and tribes and languages and nations will gaze at their dead bodies and refuse to let them be placed in a tomb; and the inhabitants of the earth will gloat over them and celebrate and exchange presents, because these two prophets had been a torment to the inhabitants of the earth. But after the three and a half days, the breath of life from God entered them, and they stood on their feet, and those who saw them were terrified. Then they heard a loud voice from heaven saying to them, 'Come up here!' And they went up to heaven in a cloud while their enemies watched them. At that moment there was a great earthquake, and a tenth of the city fell; seven thousand people were killed in the earthquake, and the rest were terrified and gave glory to the God of heaven.

intermingled with the thought of the endurance of God's true people. Alternately 'ten pistin' ('thus' with the article) could signify 'those who are trusting', so placing more emphasis on the believing people rather than their faith, or it could signify 'the faith', indicating what had been taught and is believed. So Jesus urges prayer and perseverance. God will vindicate his saints. Trust him to do so and keep praying for his return, which is the vindication of the saints. We should pray because, unlike the judge in the parable, God is not grudging about granting our desires for justice. And we should keep asking for the vindication of the people of God; our patience and willingness to make this request should never run out. By continuing to make the request, we stay sensitive to the need for justice to come. So like the poor widow, just keep asking.

CHAPTER EIGHT

JESUS AND THE WOMEN OF LUKE

The Sinful Woman at the Meal (Lk. 7.36-50):

The Healing of the Crippled Woman (Luke 13:10-17)

The Sinful Woman at the Meal (Lk.7.36-50)

The Narrative Context

This chapter will concern itself with two stories in Luke that relate to issues of purity-uncleanness, love-forgiveness, sickness-healing: the sinful woman at the meal (Lk. 7.36-50 and the healing of the crippled woman on the Sabbath (Lk. 13.10-17). The narrative of the sinful woman at the meal in Luke, while it is an anointing and bears some similarities to the story in Matthew, Mark and John, is strikingly different from the narratives of the other gospels. Both stories, in their own ways, have as their context the social and religious understandings of purity and its demands. The Jewish purity laws in the first century were rooted in the idea that Israel was a 'holy people' and this contextualised their understanding of God, the 'Holy One' and their understanding of their relationship to the Holy One as a 'holy people'. Holiness is an attribute of God and the word 'holy' in Hebrew takes on the meaning 'to be set apart' and all Jews must conform to the foundational principle of the 'holiness' of the nation. The importance of this idea/ideal of holiness can also be found in the Mishnah which gives over one of its six divisions, 'Purities', entirely to the issue of ritual purity. The whole of Jewish society, therefore, was constructed along the lines of the 'degrees' of purity in relation to proximity to the Temple where the classifications of holiness move from 'outside the Temple' to inside the Temple itself (i.e., the Holy of Holies where God was). In this regard there were 'degrees of separation' in relation to holiness: priests were the highest degree and women (those without a penis) were the lowest. The inflexibility of the purity system and the near impossible demands of complying with it, meant that many people were either marginalised or ostracised from Jewish society. The poor, sick or sinner were often on the edges of society since health was seen as a blessing and sickness was seen either as unfortunate or punishment for sin. Sinners covered a broad range of types of people: those who did not keep the Law, criminals, swineherds, shepherds, pimps, prostitutes, tax collectors. The theologians and scribes considered these to be 'unclean' and thus contrary to the purity laws of Israel.

One of the most striking passages of the Old Testament is where Ezekiel says that Jerusalem has become like a prostitute who has sold herself to the highest bidder (Ezek. 16.15[1]). Then God says:

> I will remember my covenant with you in the days of your youth, and I will establish with you an everlasting covenant. Then you will remember your ways and be ashamed. I will establish my covenant with you and you shall know that I am the Lord, that you may remember and be confounded and *never open your mouth again* because of your shame, *when I forgive you all that you have done*, says the Lord God.'

In an account unique to Luke a woman 'who was a sinner' comes to Jesus' feet and does not speak but instead washes his feet with her tears and wipes them with her hair, her intimacy with Jesus produces an array of opinion. Her action forces Jesus to explain how he responds to others, especially sinners, the unclean and impure who are marginalised from society (and God) by the strict Jewish purity laws In the response he reveals both his philosophy of dealing with people and his authority. a striking image is set before the reader of the sinful people of God and their way back to forgiveness. Traditionally she has been called a prostitute, but the text is not so specific. Nor is she likely to be Mary Magdalene, who is introduced as a

---

[1] But you trusted in your beauty, and played the whore because of your fame, and lavished your whorings on any passer-by.

new figure in Lk. 8.1-3.[1] Whatever her sin, her reputation precedes her. The story of the anointing of Jesus by the sinful, therefore, is set within the context of the Jewish purity laws. In his use of Mark, Luke has kept some incidents of healing, he has drawn on the 'Q' document and has narrative unique to him. Further, he has a broad concentration on those designated as 'sinners': Luke contains six narratives of women who were 'sinners' or sick, four are from Luke himself and two from Mark and include:

- Jairus' daughter and the woman with the haemorrhage (Lk. 8.40-55),
- The account of the woman, a sinner, who attends the Pharisee's dinner (Lk. 7.36-50) and
- The healing of the crippled woman in the synagogue on the Sabbath (13.10-17).
- The story of the healing of Simon's mother-in-law (Lk. 4.38-39)
- The women from Galilee (Lk. 8.1-3)

While similar stories are found in Mk. 14.3-9, Mt. 26.6-13 and Jn. 12.1-8, the Lucan account is not a literary reshaping of Mark (see, Fitzmyer 1981:684-685; Harrington 1991:129). It is more likely the case that the story of an anointing of Jesus by a woman intruder into a dinner scene took on various forms in the during the oral tradition, which have been reflected in Matthew, Mark, Luke and John (see, Marshall 1978:305; cf. Nolland 1993:351). Features of the story that are distinctive to Luke include: The story is set in Galilee and bears no time relationship to the Passover; the woman is stated as being a woman of the city, a sinner; Jesus' feet rather than head is anointed; Simon is a Pharisee, not a leper; Simon the Pharisee

---

[1] Soon afterwards he went on through cities and villages, proclaiming and bringing the good news of the kingdom of God. The twelve were with him, as well as some women who had been cured of evil spirits and infirmities: Mary, called Magdalene, from whom seven demons had gone out, and Joanna, the wife of Herod's steward Chuza, and Susanna, and many others, who provided for them out of their resources.

brings the objection rather than the disciples; Luke omits any mention of the poor.

a. The Encounter With Jesus: (Lk. 7.36-50)

One of the Pharisees asked Jesus to eat with him, and he went into the Pharisee's house and took his place at the table. And a woman in the city, who was a sinner, having learned that he was eating in the Pharisee's house, brought an alabaster jar of ointment. She stood behind him at his feet, weeping, and began to bathe his feet with her tears and to dry them with her hair. Then she continued kissing his feet and anointing them with the ointment. Now when the Pharisee who had invited him saw it, he said to himself, 'If this man were a prophet, he would have known who and what kind of woman this is who is touching him—that she is a sinner.' Jesus spoke up and said to him, 'Simon, I have something to say to you.' 'Teacher,' he replied, 'speak.' 'A certain creditor had two debtors; one owed five hundred denarii, and the other fifty. When they could not pay, he cancelled the debts for both of them. Now which of them will love him more?' Simon answered, 'I suppose the one for whom he cancelled the greater debt.' And Jesus said to him, 'You have judged rightly.' Then turning towards the woman, he said to Simon, 'Do you see this woman? I entered your house; you gave me no water for my feet, but she has bathed my feet with her tears and dried them with her hair. You gave me no kiss, but from the time I came in she has not stopped kissing my feet. You did not anoint my head with oil, but she has anointed my feet with ointment. Therefore, I tell you, her sins, which were many, have been forgiven; hence she has shown great love. But the one to whom little is forgiven, loves little.' Then he said to her, 'Your sins are forgiven.'But those who were at the table with him began to say among themselves, 'Who is this who even forgives sins?' And he said to the woman, 'Your faith has saved you; go in peace'

Before looking at the text in more detail there is a point to be made about what lies behind this narrative (cf. Harrington 1981:129-30). At the centre of the story is the striking point that the woman was not forgiven because she loved Jesus, rather she loved Jesus because she had been forgiven. That is the point of the parable Jesus tells: each debtor loved because they had been forgiven, and the one who loved the most was the one who had been forgiven the most. This is made clear in the fact that it is her faith which saves her and thus, forgiveness comes through faith. And that brings out that when Jesus saw this disreputable woman come towards him to touch him he knew at once the reason why. It was because she had been listening to his preaching and had repented and had received forgiveness, and now wanted to reveal her gratitude (for discussions about when this forgiveness happens (cf. Seim 1994:88; Green 1997:313). That is why he did not rebuke her. The story begins with Jesus being invited to the house of *one of the Pharisees*. He appears to be on fairly good terms with Jesus, but it becomes quite apparent that while he would expect the necessary pouring of water over the hands to take place (without which he himself would not have eaten) he pays little attention to the courtesies which would be offered to an honoured guest. Here clearly was one who did not 'love the most'. He no doubt felt that he was doing enough in allowing Jesus to sit with his honoured guests. It is while he is at the meal that (Lk. 7.37-38):

> a woman in the city, who was a sinner, having learned that he
> was eating in the Pharisee's house, brought an alabaster jar of
> ointment. She stood behind him at his feet, weeping, and began
> to bathe his feet with her tears and to dry them with her hair.
> Then she continued kissing his feet and anointing them with the
> ointment.

The setting of this narrative is important for the issues that it throws up and for the response to the woman's actions on the part of the Pharisee who is concerned with purity matters (see below). Table fellowship was crucially important for determining and reinforcing religious and social boundaries in Jewish society. They defined its social systems and certain groups (cf. Neyrey 1991:364. It is during this meal that 'two worlds collide': the world of the exacting purity system (the Pharisee) and the world of the marginalised and excluded person (the sinful woman *of the city*) who represents faith (cf. Fitmyer 1991:686). As we shall see, when these two worlds collide, it throws into relief the question as to where God and forgiveness is to be found and experienced: in the world of the Temple and its exclusionary purity system, or in the world of love born of forgiveness?

It is while this meal is under way that there is a striking and unusual interruption by a woman who is characterised by her lack of moral and religious purity since she is, *of the city, a sinner*. It is customary to interpret sinner in Lk. 7.37 to mean that the woman not only failed to fulfil the demands of the Pharisees, but that she was well-known as a local whore. In Palestine prostitutes were despised not only for reasons of sexual immorality but also for religious and political reasons. The text wants to say that the sinner in Lk. 7.36-50 is a prostitute (see, Harrington 1991:127; cf. McBride 1982:108). Prostitution is understood from a social perspective rather than a moral perspective. Although prostitutes violate the will of God and are, therefore, sinners, God forgives them and is pleased with those who prevent their hardship. Lk. 7.36-50 tells of God's mercy bestowed on the prostitute, not repentance of the prostitute as a condition of forgiveness. Luke describes her as a woman with a bad reputation (Lk. 7.37). The combination of the term 'sinner' with her identification as a woman known in the city makes it more likely that Luke intends for his readers to identify her as a prostitute or more colloquially as a street walker or public woman (for scholars' opinions see, Seim 1994:90; Marshall 1978:308; Schotoff 1992:150). There is also possibility that as she is known for her promiscuity that she could also be a lower class working woman or freed woman who may have earned her freedom by prostituting herself. She may now support herself by one of the few avenues open to her.

It was probably Luke who characterised the woman as a 'woman of the city, a sinner', e.g., a prostitute (cf. Green 1997:309). The dramatic impact of the woman's actions appears most strikingly if 'sinner' is understood as a euphemism for 'prostitute' or 'courtesan'. While tradition has often thought of this unknown woman as Mary Magdalene or sometimes as Mary of Bethany, it seems best to preserve the anonymity of the sinful woman who came to Jesus. Whatever the narrative implies about the woman's status, and I would agree that she is probably to be considered a prostitute, this intrusion is an outrageous act.

Further, although her presentation is ambiguous, she embodies all the cultic impurities attached to prostitutes. Everything was against the woman, and she would know it. She had been dealing with Pharisees for years: she knew that her touch was unclean, she knew that her precious ointment had been bought with immoral earnings (or would be seen as so), she knew that she should not enter a Pharisee's house. But she was determined. No doubt she wanted to anoint Jesus' head with her ointment. And she did so because of her faith in the fact that he would be her Saviour (v. 50), and because of a consciousness of sins forgiven through her previous contact with him. It was because she knew that she was now clean that she felt that she could do what she did.

The woman is able to 'gate crash' the meal because it was normal for doors to be open during such meals (it was considered an act of charity). People who had not been invited could enter either for some food or to hear the teachers who may have been there. However, a woman such as this would not have been welcome for any reason because her untied hair would have indicated her profession and to the Jewish leaders, anyone who did not keep all the expected rules and rituals of the Talmud was considered a sinner (e.g., shepherds, tanners) therefore, she had no place even in the house of a Pharisee let alone a meal. Such meals as these were venues for men not women and as soon as the meal starts the social (and religious) conventions and mores are turned upside down. The woman does not belong here and given the description with which Luke has presented her (a *woman of the city*-prostitute) that is even more the case. The actions that she engages in with Jesus are consonant with the actions of a prostitute (however, it may also be suggested that the fact that she was a prostitute is not actually pertinent to the narrative as a whole). And here is where the two worlds collide: the world of the purity system of the Pharisee and the purity system of the woman and both of these, in a sense, are measured against the interaction each has with Jesus.

b. Simon And Jesus: Jesus and the Woman (Lk. 7.39-50)

Simon the Pharisee is astounded by what he witnesses; for him, ritual purity is crucial and the setting (a meal) is also important. This woman has flagrantly invaded both and the guest he has invited has said nothing indeed, he has colluded with her (cf. Seim 1994:91) and it is this which swirls around his head and heart (Lk. 7.39):

> Now when the Pharisee who had invited him saw it, he said to himself, 'If this man were a prophet, he would have known who and what kind of woman this is who is touching him, that she is a sinner.'

But the horrified Simon says nothing directly to the woman or to Jesus, indeed it is through his judgement of the woman that he makes a judgement about Jesus, *if this man were a prophet* because how could he be a prophet and knowingly let himself be touched by a woman of this sort since he did not seem to be making attempt at all to avoid her? (Thibeaux 1993:153-161) In a purity system based on law, the prophets in the line of Moses are guardians of society's boundaries and both know the law and recognise transgressors of it. The Greek reveals a nice literary touch here. The construction is a second-class, or contrary-to-fact, condition. The form of this sentence shows that he did not believe Jesus was a prophet (this is a unique Greek construction which would be understood as 'if this man were a prophet, which he is not, he would know who and what sort of person this woman is who is touching him, but he does not'). This Pharisee totally misunderstood Jesus and his motives, purposes, and actions (Marshall 1978:311). The Pharisee is thinking that Jesus is not a prophet; his actions (the fact that he does not rebuke this woman) indicate his lack of status.

There is a theological assumption in this evaluation: pious figures like prophets have nothing to do with sinners. Separationism is what is key: if spiritual people are to maintain purity and testimony, association with sinners is prohibited. Luke often mentions this view of the Pharisees in contexts that suggest rebuke (Lk. 5.29-32;[1] 15.1-2;[2] 18.9-14[3]). Simon does not appear to be overly concerned with his own lack of proper social respect towards Jesus (as Jesus himself will point out in a moment).

Jesus, however, shows Simon that, in fact, he is a prophet because he is able to read what is in Simon's mind and heart and on the basis of that he tells Simon a parable and in it he throws out a spoken challenge to Simon comparable to Simon's unspoken challenge to Jesus (Lk. 7.40-43):

> Jesus spoke up and said to him, 'Simon, I have something to say to you.' 'Teacher,' he replied, 'speak.' 'A certain creditor had two debtors; one owed five hundred denarii, and the other fifty. When they could not pay, he cancelled the debts for both of them. Now which of them will love him more?' Simon answered, 'I suppose the one for whom he cancelled the greater debt.' And Jesus said to him, 'You have judged rightly.'

This parable is a simple illustration but its application is much more complex. Simon demonstrates that he has listened carefully to the parable Jesus has told and replies (Lk. 7.43), *I suppose the one for whom he*

---

[1] Then Levi gave a great banquet for him in his house; and there was a large crowd of tax-collectors and others sitting at the table with them. The Pharisees and their scribes were complaining to his disciples, saying, 'Why do you eat and drink with tax-collectors and sinners?' Jesus answered, 'Those who are well have no need of a physician, but those who are sick; I have come to call not the righteous but sinners to repentance.'

[2] Now all the tax-collectors and sinners were coming near to listen to him. And the Pharisees and the scribes were grumbling and saying, 'This fellow welcomes sinners and eats with them.'

[3] He also told this parable to some who trusted in themselves that they were righteous and regarded others with contempt: 'Two men went up to the temple to pray, one a Pharisee and the other a tax-collector. The Pharisee, standing by himself, was praying thus, "God, I thank you that I am not like other people: thieves, rogues, adulterers, or even like this tax-collector. I fast twice a week; I give a tenth of all my income." But the tax-collector, standing far off, would not even look up to heaven, but was beating his breast and saying, "God, be merciful to me, a sinner!" I tell you, this man went down to his home justified rather than the other; for all who exalt themselves will be humbled, but all who humble themselves will be exalted.'

cancelled the greater debt. Jesus commends the reply. His point is obvious: great forgiveness provides the opportunity for great love. When God forgives a notorious sinner for much sin, the realisation of such bountiful forgiveness means the potential for great love. Jesus pursues sinners and welcomes association with them because of the possibility that they may realise God's gracious forgiveness. To keep separate from them would be to ignore a potentially rich harvest field. Jesus then indicates the woman to Simon and says to him (Lk. 7.44-48):

> 'Do you see this woman? I entered your house; you gave me no water for my feet, but she has bathed my feet with her tears and dried them with her hair. You gave me no kiss, but from the time I came in she has not stopped kissing my feet. You did not anoint my head with oil, but she has anointed my feet with ointment. Therefore, I tell you, her sins, which were many, have been forgiven; hence she has shown great love. But the one to whom little is forgiven, loves little.' Then he said to her, 'Your sins are forgiven.'

Up to this point Simon had probably been ignoring the woman and pretending that he had not noticed her. So Jesus pointedly draws attention to her. And then he draws attention to what she had done that Simon had left undone. There are several actions that Simon the Pharisee did not perform for Jesus that were expected of a host in Jewish culture:

1. He did not wash His feet when he entered (Lk. 7.44)
2. He did not give Him a kiss of greeting (Lk. 7.45)
3. He did not anoint Him with oil (Lk. 7.46)

When Jesus had entered his house no one had washed his feet. It was normally considered polite to arrange for the feet of guests to be washed once they had come in off the dusty road. The failure to arrange it for Jesus must have been deliberate. Perhaps Simon had wanted to make it clear to the other guests that Jesus was not here because he thoroughly approved of him, but more under sufferance; that he was not so much a guest as an invitee. He was indicating that he was wanting to find out what he had to say, but must not be thought to be too interested, or making too many concessions. It would not be a discourtesy, only an indication that Jesus was not a particularly welcome guest. The fact that Jesus drew attention to it demonstrates that he wanted to strike his conscience and give a gentle rebuke. Here was Simon criticising the woman in his mind for being a 'sinner', but in fact Simon was far more guilty than the woman. He had failed in offering basic hospitality to one whom he considered might well be a prophet of God (which did put him in the wrong. It was a discourtesy to God) (see, Fitzmyer 1981:691). The fact that there were sufficient tears to wipe his feet demonstrates the deep feeling the woman was experiencing. Her gratitude to Jesus was overflowing. And then when she had washed his feet she used her hair to dry them. In indicating the woman to Simon and saying what he does about her, Jesus is challenging Simon to see things anew and as Simon has seen sin present in the woman and her actions, he is now being asked to see God present in the parable and in the actions of Jesus (cf. Thibeuax 1993:152-153;).

Simon is being challenged by a different order of purity, not the order of Temple purity but the order of the purity of forgiveness and love, in others, a new purity that is not superficially concerned with outer cleanness but the purity of the heart and soul in which love resides through the forgiveness that has been granted to it (Reid 1996:110). In a remark that raises the stakes, Jesus proclaims that the woman's sins are forgiven because she has loved much. It is important that this statement and the parable be combined to allow Jesus' theological point to be clear. Jesus is not saying that the woman's works have saved her. Rather, the love and forgiveness that have made her feel accepted by God (the parable's point) have produced her acts of love.

Therefore, I tell you, her sins, which were many, have been forgiven; hence she has shown great love. But the one to whom little is forgiven, loves little.'

And what did all this prove? It proved that she had good reason to be grateful to Jesus. And Jesus knew the reason why. He knew that she had been burdened down by many sins, and that on hearing His words as He proclaimed the Good News she had at some stage found forgiveness for them all. This explained her love and gratitude. Her much love proved her much forgiveness. A lesser love would have indicated that she had received a lesser forgiveness. It should be noted that the fact that she was there at all, not saying anything but expressing genuine love, indicated that she felt that she owed a debt of gratitude. Why else would she love Jesus? The kind of 'love' she had been used to would not have been deserving of forgiveness, nor would it have been welcome to Jesus. What had happened here had to be because something that he had done or said had genuinely benefited her, and it had to have been something spectacular for her to humiliate herself like that. Furthermore she would have been in no doubt about the kind of welcome she would receive in the Pharisee's house, and yet she had come. Why? Because she had known in her heart that Jesus would not turn her away. She knew that he would welcome her because he would know that she had turned to God and had been forgiven. (She would not expect to be welcomed as a practising prostitute). Thus all points to an experience of having been cleansed for which she was grateful. And the parable confirms that Jesus was aware of it. *But the one to whom little is forgiven, loves little.* Is there a hint here of Simon's own failure (he had not demonstrated great love) not on a par with the woman's, perhaps, but still there?

If Jesus' reception of the sinner is a problem, his declaration of the forgiveness of sins is a massive problem (cf. Lk. 5.17-26[1]) Only God

---

[1] One day, while he was teaching, Pharisees and teachers of the law were sitting nearby (they had come from every village of Galilee and Judea and from Jerusalem); and the power of the Lord was with him to heal. Just then some men came, carrying a paralysed man on a bed. They were trying to bring him in and lay him before Jesus; but finding no way to bring him in because of the crowd, they went up on the roof and let him down with his bed through the tiles into the middle of the crowd in front of Jesus. When he saw

forgives sin. Again we see how Jesus' ministry combines ethics and theology. His behaviour is an example of how to relate to others but also reflects a unique authority that makes Jesus more than a mere instructor of morality. In saying the woman's sins are forgiven, he is clearly even greater than a prophet. Here is raw authority. The Pharisees again engage in private thoughts and theological assessment; they know the significance behind Jesus' statement. They know no mere man has the right to forgive sin, so they ask, *Who is this who even forgives sin?* The question is crucial. If Jesus has the authority to forgive sin, then he has the right to reveal how salvation occurs. Simon was worried about Jesus being a prophet, but Jesus' pronouncement of forgiveness means he is much more. Jesus closes with a declaration that deepens the message. He reassures the woman by commending the faith that led to her works, *Your faith has saved you; go in peace* (v. 50). With this he turns her earlier expression of love into evidence of saving faith. Faith has motivated the response of love and humility that was evidenced in the anointing (see, Seim 1994:91; Green 1997:314; Marshall 1978:314).

The woman's story shows that sinners can know God will respond when they turn to him. Jesus represents the messenger of God who ministers God's love. As a result, he is open to and conscious of the opportunity that exists when sinners are loved. He does not ignore the woman's sin, but he recognises that sin can be destroyed through forgiveness when God's love is received. The Pharisees' separatist-purity attitudes stands rebuked as an inappropriate model of holiness: God is ready to forgive debts when people turn humbly to him. Jesus also raises again the issue of his authority. He possesses the authority to forgive sin. Jesus is more than an example of one

---

their faith, he said, 'Friend, your sins are forgiven you.' Then the scribes and the Pharisees began to question, 'Who is this who is speaking blasphemies? Who can forgive sins but God alone?' When Jesus perceived their questionings, he answered them, 'Why do you raise such questions in your hearts? Which is easier, to say, "Your sins are forgiven you", or to say, "Stand up and walk"? But so that you may know that the Son of Man has authority on earth to forgive sins', he said to the one who was paralysed, 'I say to you, stand up and take your bed and go to your home.' Immediately he stood up before them, took what he had been lying on, and went to his home, glorifying God. Amazement seized all of them, and they glorified God and were filled with awe, saying, 'We have seen strange things today.'

who is open to sinners; he wields the gavel. He can discern the presence of faith, and he can pronounce forgiveness of sins. The sinful woman is an example of faith expressing itself in humble love even to the point of boldness. In the action of the woman and the reaction of Simon and Jesus, Luke shows that the presence of mercy, forgiveness and freedom is no longer to be found in the Temple purity system (which damned and kept the woman in her sin) but in the actions of Jesus (which freed her) and the faith of those who would be taught and healed by him. The redeemed sinful woman, therefore, stands for all those in the community (ecclesial and social) whose style of life, or way of being in the world is a source of scandal, moral horror which deserves their marginalisation but yet whose humble acknowledgement of their forgiveness because they have experienced themselves as much loved, stands as a silent accusation of failure to love and forgive against the very system that pharasaically supposes itself to be only source through which God's forgiveness can be experienced.

Healing of the Crippled Woman (Lk. 13.10-17)

Now he was teaching in one of the synagogues on the Sabbath. And just then there appeared a woman with a spirit that had crippled her for eighteen years. She was bent over and was quite unable to stand up straight. When Jesus saw her, he called her over and said, 'Woman, you are set free from your ailment.' When he laid his hands on her, immediately she stood up straight and began praising God. But the leader of the synagogue, indignant because Jesus had cured on the Sabbath, kept saying to the crowd, 'There are six days on which work ought to be done; come on those days and be cured, and not on the Sabbath day.' But the Lord answered him and said, 'You hypocrites! Does not each of you on the Sabbath untie his ox or his donkey from the manger, and lead it away to give it water? And ought not this woman, a daughter of Abraham whom Satan bound for eighteen long years, be set free from this bondage on the Sabbath day?' When he said this, all his opponents were put to shame; and the entire crowd was rejoicing at all the wonderful things that he was doing.

Narrative Context

The healing of the bent-over woman is not just another miracle in Luke. Luke has been silent about miracles since 11.14[1] and the Beelzebub controversy. He has not included a detailed miracle report since Lk. 9.37-43.[2] In the meantime he has called for repentance. This miracle repeats work Jesus did earlier in his ministry (Lk. 4.31-41;[3] 6.6-11[4]). It is a 'mirror'

---

[1]   Now he was casting out a demon that was mute; when the demon had gone out, the one who had been mute spoke, and the crowds were amazed.

[2]   On the next day, when they had come down from the mountain, a great crowd met him. Just then a man from the crowd shouted, 'Teacher, I beg you to look at my son; he is my only child. Suddenly a spirit seizes him, and all at once he shrieks. It throws him into convulsions until he foams at the mouth; it mauls him and will scarcely leave him. I begged your disciples to cast it out, but they could not.' Jesus answered, 'You faithless and perverse generation, how much longer must I be with you and bear with you? Bring your son here.' While he was coming, the demon dashed him to the ground in convulsions. But Jesus rebuked the unclean spirit, healed the boy, and gave him back to his father. And all were astounded at the greatness of God.

[3]   He went down to Capernaum, a city in Galilee, and was teaching them on the Sabbath. They were astounded at his teaching, because he spoke with authority. In the synagogue there was a man who had the spirit of an unclean demon, and he cried out with a loud voice, 'Let us alone! What have you to do with us, Jesus of Nazareth? Have you come to destroy us? I know who you are, the Holy One of God.' But Jesus rebuked him, saying, 'Be silent, and come out of him!' When the demon had thrown him down before them, he came out of him without having done him any harm. They were all amazed and kept saying to one another, 'What kind of utterance is this? For with authority and power he commands the unclean spirits, and out they come!' And a report about him began to reach every place in the region. After leaving the synagogue he entered Simon's house. Now Simon's mother-in-law was suffering from a high fever, and they asked him about her. Then he stood over her and rebuked the fever, and it left her. Immediately she got up and began to serve them. As the sun was setting, all those who had any who were sick with various kinds of diseases brought them to him; and he laid his hands on each of them and cured them. Demons also came out of many, shouting, 'You are the Son of God!' But he rebuked them and would not allow them to speak, because they knew that he was the Messiah.

[4]   On another Sabbath he entered the synagogue and taught, and there was a man there whose right hand was withered. The scribes and the Pharisees watched him to see whether he would cure on the Sabbath, so that they might find an accusation against him. Even though he knew what they were thinking, he said to the man who had the withered hand, 'Come and stand here.' He got up and stood there. Then Jesus said to them, 'I ask you, is it lawful to do good or to do harm on the Sabbath, to save life or to destroy it?' After looking around at all of them, he said to him, 'Stretch out your hand.' He did so, and his hand was restored. But they were filled with fury and discussed with one another what they might do to Jesus.

miracle, for it repeats earlier work in the hope that perhaps Jesus' warnings have been heeded. In addition, the discussion of conflict with Satan is continued in v. 16, as is the theme of God's compassion. In many ways this scene and another like it in Lk. 14.1-6[1] summarises the reaction to Jesus' ministry. Since the account is unique to Luke, we can assume it is particularly important. The setting of the miracle is important since it takes place in the synagogue on the Sabbath (Green 1997:532). 'Sabbath' is from the Hebrew word meaning, 'rest' or 'cease' It is connected to the seventh day of creation where God ceased his labour after finishing initial creation (cf. Gen. 2.1-3[2]). God did not rest because he was tired, but because (1) creation was complete and good (cf. Gen. 1.31) and (2) to give mankind a regular pattern for worship and rest. The usage as a day of worship starts with Gen. 2.2-3, where God uses his rest as a pattern for animals (cf. Ex. 23.12[3]) and mankind (humans need a regular schedule of work, rest, and worship). The Sabbath begins like all the days of Genesis 1, at twilight; therefore, twilight on Friday to twilight on Saturday was the official time period. All the details of its observance are given in Exodus (especially Ex. 16.20, 31, and 35[4]) and Leviticus (especially Ex. 23-26). The first specialised use of this day by Israel was in Ex. 16.25-26 in the gathering of manna. It then becomes part of the 'Ten Words' ('Ten Commandments' cf. Ex. 20.8-11; Deut. 5.12-15).

---

[1] On one occasion when Jesus was going to the house of a leader of the Pharisees to eat a meal on the Sabbath, they were watching him closely. Just then, in front of him, there was a man who had dropsy. And Jesus asked the lawyers and Pharisees, 'Is it lawful to cure people on the Sabbath, or not?' But they were silent. So Jesus took him and healed him, and sent him away. Then he said to them, 'If one of you has a child or an ox that has fallen into a well, will you not immediately pull it out on a Sabbath day?' And they could not reply to this.

[2] Thus the heavens and the earth were finished, and all their multitude. And on the seventh day God finished the work that he had done, and he rested on the seventh day from all the work that he had done. So God blessed the seventh day and hallowed it, because on it God rested from all the work that he had done in creation.

[3] For six days you shall do your work, but on the seventh day you shall rest, so that your ox and your donkey may have relief, and your home-born slave and the resident alien may be refreshed.

[4] But they did not listen to Moses; some left part of it until morning, and it bred worms and became foul. And Moses was angry with them. The house of Israel called it manna; it was like coriander seed, white, and the taste of it was like wafers made with honey. The Israelites ate manna for forty years, until they came to a habitable land; they ate manna, until they came to the border of the land of Canaan.

This is one example where the Ten Words in Ex. 20 are slightly different from the Ten Words in Deut. 5.6-21. Deuteronomy is preparing Israel for the settled, agricultural life in Canaan. Strict keeping of the Sabbath, along with circumcision and diet, marked the Jewish people. The Pharisees had taken these regulations and, by their oral discussions, interpreted them to include many rules. Jesus often performed miracles, knowingly violating their picky rules for two unrelated reasons:

> 1. Jesus fulfilled all Jewish requirements. Sabbath worship
> was surely one of these (cf. Gen. 2:2-3; Ex. 20.8-11).
> 2. He acted on the Sabbath to instigate dialogue with the
> religious leaders who cherished their rules and traditions
> over people. It was not the Sabbath that Jesus rejected or
> belittled, but their self-righteous legalism and lack of love.

This story is central to this section of Luke, as is demonstrated by the chiasmus. In it Jesus sets free a woman who is totally bent double and releases her from Satan's power. It is a picture of what he has come to do for Israel, and for all who will respond to him, and descriptive of what this section is all about, the making straight of people and their deliverance *from the power of Satan to God* (Acts 26.18). It is another moment when, as with the sinful woman at the meal, two worlds collide for it is a collision between a woman who was bent double and a blind man. For the ruler of the synagogue was as blind as a man could be. He had just seen an amazing miracle of deliverance, and he dismissed it as a piece of everyday work, as though people regularly 'popped' in to the synagogue to be healed because it was a surgery. He was blind to the working of God, a typical representative of the men who opposed Jesus. And glorious working it was for it was symbolic of what God will do for all who come to Jesus.

a. The Healing and The Woman's Response (Lk. 13.10-13)

The narrative opens with Jesus in the synagogue, (Lk. 13.10) and this will be the last time Jesus, often depicted as being in the synagogue, *as was his custom* (Lk. 4.16) (cf. Neyrey 1991:301), will be found in one in Luke and it recalls Jesus' visit to the synagogue in Nazareth in Lk. 4 where during worship, he outlined his messianic programme (Lk. 4.18-19[1]). That this is the last mention of Jesus teaching in a synagogue, is not necessarily decisive, for such visits are usually only mentioned at this stage when specifically connected with incidents, and Luke in the main drops the incidents too, although the latter undoubtedly carried on to the end. It was on the Sabbath day, and Jesus was there, having been invited to teach. It is while he is there (Lk. 13.11-13):

> that there appeared a woman with a spirit that had crippled her for eighteen years. She was bent over and was quite unable to stand up straight. When Jesus saw her, he called her over and said, 'Woman, you are set free from your ailment.' When he laid his hands on her, immediately she stood up straight and began praising God.

This may well indicate that he suddenly spotted her while he was teaching (cf. Seim 1994:43). This, of course, raises the further question as to whether women were allowed in the synagogue. Since the woman is seen by Jesus in the synagogue, it would seem that the assumption that women were not allowed in the synagogue is not correct. However, if women were allowed in the synagogue, then this woman should not have been there since the woman's sickness and possession would normally have brought cultic impurity and since she would have been unclean she should not have been there at all (see, Reid 1996:165). While the text in itself makes no mention of the woman being a sinner or indeed, unclean, the fact that it is a 'spirit'

---

[1]   'The Spirit of the Lord is upon me, because he has anointed me to bring good news to the poor. He has sent me to proclaim release to the captives and recovery of sight to the blind, to let the oppressed go free, to proclaim the year of the Lord's favour.'

that had *crippled her for eighteen years* would mean that she was ritually unclean. What he saw, however, was a woman who was bent double and could not straighten herself. In view of the connection with an evil spirit it was probably skoliasis hysterica, a partly psychological condition. Others see it as spondylitis ankylopoietica indicating a fusion of the spinal bones. The one may, of course, have resulted in the other. The woman had been affected in this way by an evil spirit for 'eighteen years'. A connection with the 'eighteen' who perished at Siloam may well be in mind, with the thought that she too was suffering because of sin in the world. She was bowed double and could not lift herself up. She was a picture of a world bent double by sin, and unable to stand tall. It is, therefore, more appropriate to see Luke's description of her state as grounded in 'satanic' bondage (see Green 1997:521). This highlights his overall perspective on the inseparability of physical illness and diabolic influence and thus on the inseparability of healing and liberation.

- Jesus *sees* the woman,
- *calls* her, and
- *lays hands* on her (Lk. 13.12);
- the woman *hears* Jesus,
- *comes* to him, and
- *stands up straight* (Lk. 13.13) and
- *praises God.*

His statement, *woman, you are free from your ailment* (Lk. 13.12b) is the equivalent of a command to the evil spirit to leave her, for with Jesus deliverance from evil spirit was always by his word. But Jesus is not finished, for he *lays* his hands on her because while released from the evil spirit, she had been so long in that condition that she could not straighten herself, and so Jesus went over to her and laid his hands on her and immediately she was made straight. And the not unsurprising result was that she glorified God. By this it was openly revealed that Jesus could make crooked people straight. It should be noted that nowhere else does Jesus cast out evil spirits by any other means than his word. Thus here also we should see that he casts out the evil spirit by his word before he touches her. The evil spirit is to be seen as unclean in an unusually in depth sense. The earthly Jesus wants no contact with unclean spirits, for they cannot be made clean. The laying on of hands is then used in order to heal the physical impediment so as to give assurance to the woman. In Lk. 4.16-21 the Evangelist had written:

> When he came to Nazareth, where he had been brought up, he went to the synagogue on the Sabbath day, as was his custom. He stood up to read, and the scroll of the prophet Isaiah was given to him. He unrolled the scroll and found the place where it was written: 'The Spirit of the Lord is upon me, because he has anointed me to bring good news to the poor. He has sent me to proclaim release to the captives and recovery of sight to the blind, to let the oppressed go free, to proclaim the year of the Lord's favour.' And he rolled up the scroll, gave it back to the attendant, and sat down. The eyes of all in the synagogue were fixed on him. Then he began to say to them, 'Today this scripture has been fulfilled in your hearing.'

Now in this synagogue once again these words have been fulfilled for Jesus is now seen to be the agent of God's liberation of those who are literally bowed down or oppressed and spiritually bowed down by the power of Satan. Those on the outside, the forgotten, the marginalised, the 'no people' have been called by Jesus, they have heard, and responded with praise and glory to God. And where the woman would have been deemed unclean and excommunicate from the community of Israel according to the purity laws, now she stands straight and through the word and action of Jesus she is restored not just to physical health but also to spiritual health, she is made clean and can now take her place in the community as a *daughter of*

Abraham (Lk. 13.16).

b. The Sabbath Controversy (Lk. 13.14-17)

> But the leader of the synagogue, indignant because Jesus had cured on the Sabbath, kept saying to the crowd, 'There are six days on which work ought to be done; come on those days and be cured, and not on the Sabbath day.' But the Lord answered him and said, 'You hypocrites! Does not each of you on the Sabbath untie his ox or his donkey from the manger, and lead it away to give it water? And ought not this woman, a daughter of Abraham whom Satan bound for eighteen long years, be set free from this bondage on the Sabbath day?' When he said this, all his opponents were put to shame; and the entire crowd was rejoicing at all the wonderful things that he was doing.

The response of the woman is one of joy and praise of God, the response of the ruler of the synagogue is one of intense annoyance because the healing has taken place on the Sabbath (see Harrington 1991:212;. Strictly *leader of the synagogue* would refer to the single 'ruler' who controlled the administration and especially the organisation of the service at the synagogue, but there were others who helped in the general administration and running of the synagogue, a council of elders, and these were also called leaders/rulers, men of standing in the community. The synagogue ruler here was probably one of these. The emphasis on it would seem to infer that he was an important man in the community (cf. Lk. 8.49;[1] Acts 18.8,17;[2] cf.

---

[1] While he was still speaking, someone came from the leader's house to say, 'Your daughter is dead; do not trouble the teacher any longer.'

[2] Crispus, the official of the synagogue, became a believer in the Lord, together with all his household; and many of the Corinthians who heard Paul became believers and were baptised. Then all of them seized Sosthenes, the official of the synagogue, and beat him in front of the tribunal. But Gallio paid no attention to any of these things.

Mt. 9.18, 23;[1] Lk. 8.41;[2] 18.18.[3]). But the ruler of the synagogue, who led the synagogue committee, was angry because what Jesus had done, i.e., healed, was not permissible on the Sabbath. He ignores the liberation of this woman from her pain. He ignores the release of power through Jesus that has allowed this to take place. He gives no indication of compassion or of joy that God has worked. Possibly he recognised that he might be called on by certain of the Pharisees to explain why he had allowed this to happen in his synagogue on the Sabbath day. But the fact of his anger suggests that we are to see his feeling as personal as well. And yet his anger is directed at the crowd. clamoured for more. So he covered himself by rebuking the people who were gathered there. He pointed out to them that there were six days in every seven in which men should work, and therefore that if they wished to be healed they should come on a day other than the Sabbath. The weakness of his position comes out in the fact that Jesus was not a doctor (had he been the ruler may have had a point). But everyone knew that only God could have done what had happened that day. Possibly that was what the ruler had recognised and had thus felt that it would probably be unwise to rebuke God by rebuking Jesus. He would feel that he was on safe ground in rebuking the crowd. In Pharisaic eyes, however, he was totally in the right. The only healing that was allowed on the Sabbath was dealing with possible life threatening conditions to the minimum required (see, Wilkinson 1977:195-205).

Jesus, however, indicates in quite strong language that there is another view that it is just as valid, indeed, more so. For the synagogue ruler it was necessary to be healed on the six days of the week, they could come then but it was necessary not to do these things on the Sabbath as the Law decreed (cf. Fitzmyer 1981:179; Harrington 1991:214). Jesus turns this argument on its head and shows that healing was not a 'work' undertaken on

---

[1] While he was saying these things to them, suddenly a leader of the synagogue came in and knelt before him, saying, 'My daughter has just died; but come and lay your hand on her, and she will live.' When Jesus came to the leader's house and saw the flute-players and the crowd making a commotion.

[2] Just then there came a man named Jairus, a leader of the synagogue. He fell at Jesus' feet and begged him to come to his house.

[3] A certain ruler asked him, 'Good Teacher, what must I do to inherit eternal life?'

the Sabbath but that it was just as necessary a part of God's plan to restore people to right relationship with him, to heal them spiritually as well as physically as was ceasing from work. The necessity was not to simply observe the Sabbath proscriptions but also to observe what God was doing in Jesus. Hence, Jesus' rebuke is severe and the language strong when the accuses them of double standards (Lk. 13.15c):

> Does not each of you on the Sabbath untie his ox or his donkey from the manger, and lead it away to give it water? And ought not this woman, a daughter of Abraham whom Satan bound for eighteen long years, be set free from this bondage on the Sabbath day?'

Sabbath activity such as Jesus describes was often allowed. The Mishnah lists rules allowing cattle to drink, along with the 'forty less one' practices that were prohibited on the Sabbath (*m. Sabbat* 7.2; 5.1-4; 15.1-2; *m. Erubin* 2.1-4). In contrast, at Qumran such aid was often denied to animals (Cairo Damascus Document 11:13-14). Jesus' point is simple: if animals can receive basic care on the Sabbath, how much more human beings, especially a woman of promise, a child of Abraham! In effect, Jesus says, what more appropriate day to release her than the Sabbath? What better day to reveal Satan's impotence? The synagogue leader's and Jesus' views could not be more opposed. The great division Jesus predicted is evidenced here. Jesus refers to the woman as a *daughter of Abraham* and this unique phrase is not to be found anywhere else in the New Testament (see, Seim 1994:47). The woman is already a child of Abraham and does not become one because she has been healed from an evil spirit and thus made clean. This *daughter of Abraham* has been bound for eighteen years, that is, three times six and so they should recognise that she had completed not just 'six days' but six years, three times over, and had not been loosed on any of them, because they were unable to loose her, and thus it was right that at last she be loosed by God on the 'seventh' day, the Sabbath, on a day when God was at work (cf. Marshall 1978:539). It should be noted that Jesus does not just defend his healing on the Sabbath, but seems to suggest that it was right that it happen on the Sabbath. This might be seen as confirming that to him the Sabbath pointed forward to the 'rest' of the people of God into which he wanted all to enter. It was thus the most suitable day for healing and revealing the compassion of God. After all Satan had still been at work in the woman on the Sabbath day. Was he then to have it as his sole preserve? Luke then juxtaposes two different experiences and responses to both the healing and Jesus' words, on the one hand the *shame* of his opponents (cf. Is. 45.16;[1] 50.7[2]), on the other, the *rejoicing* of the crowd who see God at work (Lk. 13.17;[3] cf. Ex. 34.10[4]). Thus the passage ends by noting the choice people must make about Jesus.

---

[1] All of them are put to shame and confounded, the makers of idols go in confusion together.

[2] The Lord God helps me; therefore I have not been disgraced; therefore I have set my face like flint, and I know that I shall not be put to shame;

[3] When he said this, all his opponents were put to shame; and the entire crowd was rejoicing at all the wonderful things that he was doing.

[4] He said: I hereby make a covenant. Before all your people I will perform marvels, such as have not been performed in all the earth or in any nation; and all the people among whom you live shall see the work of the Lord; for it is an awesome thing that I will do with you.

CHAPTER NINE

JESUS AND WOMEN IN JOHN

Women in Gospel of John

John	Pericope
2.1-11	The Mother of Jesus at the Wedding of Cana, and afterwards going with him to Capernaum
4.1-42	The Samaritan Woman at the Well encounters Jesus and later brings others to him
(8.1-11)	The Adulterous Woman is accused by others but forgiven by Jesus (not originally in John)
11.1-45	Martha and Mary ask Jesus to help their brother Lazarus, and express their faith in him
12.1-8	Mary of Bethany anoints the feet of Jesus during a dinner, and is defended by Jesus
19.25b-27	The Mother of Jesus and other Women are present at the Foot of the Cross
20.1-2	Mary Magdalene discovers the Empty Tomb and tells the disciples
20.11-18	Mary Magdalene is the first person to whom the Risen Jesus appear

There are also some shorter references to women and feminine imagery in the Fourth Gospel

John	Reference
3.4	Nicodemus asks about returning to *a mother's womb* and being born a second time
3.29	John (the Baptist) uses an analogy involving a *bride* and bridegroom
6.42	Some Jews claim that they know Jesus' "father and *mother*"
9.18-23	The parents of the man born blind (implicitly also the *mother*) are questioned by the Pharisees

12.15	The Evangelist mentions the *"daughter of Zion"* while quoting Zech 9.9
16.21	Jesus uses the image of *a woman in labour* as an analogy for sorrow turning into joy
18.16-17	The *woman gatekeeper* challenges Peter in the courtyard of the High Priest

Mary, The Mother of Jesus in John

The Wedding Feast at Cana (Jn. 2.1-11)

On the third day there was a wedding in Cana of Galilee, and the mother of Jesus was there. Jesus and his disciples had also been invited to the wedding. When the wine gave out, the mother of Jesus said to him, 'They have no wine.' And Jesus said to her, 'Woman, what concern is that to you and to me? My hour has not yet come.' His mother said to the servants, 'Do whatever he tells you.' Now standing there were six stone water-jars for the Jewish rites of purification, each holding twenty or thirty gallons. Jesus said to them, 'Fill the jars with water.' And they filled them up to the brim. He said to them, 'Now draw some out, and take it to the chief steward.' So they took it. When the steward tasted the water that had become wine, and did not know where it came from (though the servants who had drawn the water knew), the steward called the bridegroom and said to him, 'Everyone serves the good wine first, and then the inferior wine after the guests have become drunk. But you have kept the good wine until now.' Jesus did this, the first of his signs, in Cana of Galilee, and revealed his glory; and his disciples believed in him.

The Narrative Context

Mary is never mentioned by name in the gospel, she is simply referred to as *the mother of Jesus* and appears twice in the whole gospel and is mentioned or alluded to in only two other instances. John's gospel is essentially Christological and thus its central theme or subject matter is the person of Jesus and how men and women experience him and the claims he makes about himself. John presents Jesus as the enfleshed pre-existent Logos (Word) (Jn. 1.1-3[1]) who comes to reveal the Father, as the one who brings life to to those who believe in him. Redemption (life) is given to those who respond to him in faith. In this respect everything else that John presents in his gospel is secondary to this and this includes its portrait of *the mother of Jesus*. Though the *mother of Jesus* plays a secondary role in the gospel, the two moments when she does appear are of extraordinary import. The narrative of the 'Wedding Feast at Cana' (Jn. 2.1-11) is the first of the 'signs' by Jesus in John's gospel and the episode of the *mother of Jesus* at the foot of the cross (Jn. 19.25-27[2]) is the last event of his earthly life. On both occasions the *mother of Jesus* is present. One of the most important aspects or elements of the gospel of John is its symbolism, to the extent that it is permissible to say that the gospel not only contains symbolism but is itself symbolic. Understanding symbols and how symbols work is central to understanding John since in his gospel Jesus is the symbol of God and the gospel is the symbol of Jesus. And since the gospel is symbol and non-symbolic interpretation of it is not enough and so an understanding of the symbolism of John is central to any study of or within the gospel. In the narratives that concern women which follow, the symbolic element of the narrative and its content will be uppermost. Given this, in this section which deals with the *mother of Jesus* attention will be paid to symbol of Jesus' flesh and the symbol of motherhood since both have a direct bearing on how the *mother of Jesus* is presented in the gospel.

---

[1]   In the beginning was the Word, and the Word was with God, and the Word was God. He was in the beginning with God. All things came into being through him, and without him not one thing came into being. What has come into being

[2]   Meanwhile, standing near the cross of Jesus were his mother, and his mother's sister, Mary the wife of Clopas, and Mary Magdalene. When Jesus saw his mother and the disciple whom he loved standing beside her, he said to his mother, 'Woman, here is your son.' Then he said to the disciple, 'Here is your mother.' And from that hour the disciple took her into his own home.

a. The Wedding (Jn. 2.1-2)

> On the third day there was a wedding in Cana of Galilee, and the mother of Jesus was there. Jesus and his disciples had also been invited to the wedding. When the wine gave out, the mother of Jesus said to him, 'They have no wine.' And Jesus said to her, 'Woman, what concern is that to you and to me? My hour has not yet come.' His mother said to the servants, 'Do whatever he tells you.'

In Jn. 2.1, on the third day more than likely refers to the third day after the events recorded towards the end of Jn. 1. Some scholars think that the *third day* is symbolically significant here (Schnackenburg 1980a:297, 325). If Jn. 1 were taken to refer to the first week of Jesus' ministry, and therefore are a parallel with Gen. 1, then the wedding at Cana takes place on the seventh day (the old creation v the new creation) (cf. Mullins 2003:112). This section provides the setting of the story: temporal, local, and situational. The story happens *on the third day* at *Cana of Galilee* and there is a *wedding*. Literally, this is the third day from Jesus' conversation with Nathaniel (Jn.1.43-51[1]). Probably, the evangelist did not intend to date the Cana story historically but simply to bring out the sequence of events. Symbolically, *the third day* reminds any Christian of Jesus' resurrection and the day of the resurrection is the day of glory. In starting the story with *on the third day*, the evangelist already raises the expectations of the hearers/readers, making them anticipate that what will follow is a "moment

---

[1]   The next day Jesus decided to go to Galilee. He found Philip and said to him, 'Follow me.' Now Philip was from Bethsaida, the city of Andrew and Peter. Philip found Nathanael and said to him, 'We have found him about whom Moses in the law and also the prophets wrote, Jesus son of Joseph from Nazareth.' Nathanael said to him, 'Can anything good come out of Nazareth?' Philip said to him, 'Come and see.' When Jesus saw Nathanael coming towards him, he said of him, 'Here is truly an Israelite in whom there is no deceit!' Nathanael asked him, 'Where did you come to know me?' Jesus answered, 'I saw you under the fig tree before Philip called you.' Nathanael replied, 'Rabbi, you are the Son of God! You are the King of Israel!' Jesus answered, 'Do you believe because I told you that I saw you under the fig tree? You will see greater things than these.' And he said to him, 'Very truly, I tell you, you will see heaven opened and the angels of God ascending and descending upon the Son of Man.'

of glory. The situation is that of a wedding. Again, this is loaded with symbolism since the wedding feast is a well-known symbol of the messianic days (the mention of *a wedding on the third day* simply confirms and even heightens the readers' expectation that a moment of glory is about to come (Grassi 1988:84). The idea is interesting but it should not be pushed too far (Robinson 1985:163), the text of itself does not seem to carry that kind of weight in relation to the symbolic number. However, it is worth noting that Gen. 2.2-3 reads:

> By the seventh day God had finished the work he had been doing; so on the seventh day he rested from all his work. And God blessed the seventh day and made it holy, because on it he rested from all the work of creating that he had done

In later rabbinic thought (post-New Testament) the age of the world was divided up into six millennia. The seventh millennium was to be the Age of Messiah. Something similar may be behind Heb 4.9:

> There remains yet a Sabbath rest for the people of God.

But this is purely speculative and Jn. 1.1-18[1] on closer inspection does not

---

[1] In the beginning was the Word, and the Word was with God, and the Word was God. He was in the beginning with God. All things came into being through him, and without him not one thing came into being. What has come into being in him was life, and the life was the light of all people. The light shines in the darkness, and the darkness did not overcome it. There was a man sent from God, whose name was John. He came as a witness to testify to the light, so that all might believe through him. He himself was not the light, but he came to testify to the light. The true light, which enlightens everyone, was coming into the world. He was in the world, and the world came into being through him; yet the world did not know him. He came to what was his own, and his own people did not accept him. But to all who received him, who believed in his name, he gave power to become children of God, who were born, not of blood or of the will of the flesh or of the will of man, but of God. And the Word became flesh and lived among us, and we have seen his glory, the glory as of a father's only son, full of grace and truth. (John testified to him and cried out, 'This was he of whom I said, "He who comes after me ranks ahead of me because he was before me." ') From his fullness we have all received, grace upon grace. The law indeed was given through Moses; grace and truth came through Jesus Christ. No one has ever seen God. It is God the only Son, who is close to the Father's heart, who has made him known.

seem to recounting the 'first week' of Jesus' ministry; on top of this, if the numbers are so symbolically important to John then why has he not made all this a little clearer? This is no more than a thin *possibility* by the Evangelist and as mentioned above should not be pushed too far. Some have sought to see in *Cana in Galilee* a symbolic significance in the way in which 'Cana' is translated: 'ownership/possession'. The symbolic meaning here would be that Jesus is at the wedding in Cana with 'his own' (the disciples) and this is a way of referring to the disciples in John. Jesus comes to Cana, his own possession, with 'his own', the disciples who now are the true and real possession of God and it is there that 'his own' see the *greater things* he promised them in Jn. 1.50-51[1] and by emphasis of *in Galilee* because Galilee is the place where the new people of God is born. So that this, in reality, is a transitional moment visible in the 'old' (the Jewish water jars of Jn. 2.6) to the new (the wine of the Kingdom). Again, this is interesting but in a sense it is exegesis gone mad; the importance of Cana lies in the fact of its obscurity. Cana is in Galilee, where Nazareth is, where according to Nathaniel *nothing good can come from* (Jn. 1.46) (though it is recorded in Jn 21.2 that Nathaniel came from Cana) other than the Johannine sign, its claim to fame is that Josephus records he once had quarters there! It is a no place: yet it is precisely in such a no place, in precisely such an obscure place, that the Word made flesh chooses to reveal his glory (cf. Ridderbos 1991:104). Further, Cana has significance for the Evangelist in so far as the first main section of his gospel begins in Cana and ends in Cana (Jn. 4.46). In other words, the glory of the Word made flesh is made manifest in the obscurity of Galilee and not in the corridors of Jerusalemite power.

Finally, the setting also establishes the characters of the story. Contrary to expectation, the reader is not told who the bridegroom and the bride are. Instead one is told that *the mother of Jesus* is there, and Jesus and his disciples were also *invited*. Only Jesus, obviously the main character in the story, is named. All the other characters are unnamed. It is known from

---

[1] Jesus answered, 'Do you believe because I told you that I saw you under the fig tree? You will see greater things than these.' And he said to him, 'Very truly, I tell you, you will see heaven opened and the angels of God ascending and descending upon the Son of Man.'

the other gospels that his mother's name is Mary. With regard to the disciples, it is not known who the evangelist is referring to. If a synchronic reading of the text is done, then, one would say that at this point, *disciples* would simply refer to those whom Jesus has already called, namely, Andrew, John, Philip, Nathanael, and an unnamed disciple (the 'Beloved Disciple'?).

Nuptial imagery, festivity, vines, vintage, wine are all used by Jesus as images in parables and wedding imagery was also used in the Hebrew bible to express the covenant relationship between God and Israel (cf. Mullins 2002:113). Much has been written about the 'historical' circumstances of this wedding, e.g., the fact that the mother of Jesus was *there* but that Jesus and his disciples were *invited*. This has led to speculation that Mary was related to the wedding couple and that Jesus and the disciples were in attendance in a different capacity. The fact that she approaches Jesus to inform him that *they have no wine* might indicate that Mary was approached first by the stewards and then approached Jesus. The 'intercessory' role of Mary here has led to seeing her in a prominent role in this sign of John and linked her presence here (when the *hour* of Jesus has not yet come), with the *hour* that does come in the passion and death of Jesus in Jn. 18-19. Some have sought to see an Adam and Eve typology in Mary and Jesus where through Adam and Eve's disobedience the earth was no longer freely fruitful and the prophets proclaimed famine and desolation, now in Mary and Jesus in the first Johannine sign the abundance of the messianic banquet is made present in the 'new wine'. There may well be some indication of this insofar as John assumes that his community knew enough about the role and place of Mary in the life of Jesus to interpret the significance of the conversation she has with him (cf. Ridderbos 1991:104). This may be true, as the covenant imagery may well be in the mind of the Evangelist, but it should not be pushed too far. Be that as it may, the simple statement that the mother of Jesus makes *they have no wine* allows us to examine some of the social customs and responsibilities of a wedding couple which may have led to her approaching Jesus.

Weddings in humble villages in Palestine were major social events. Most people in the little villages like Cana lived in considerable poverty and survived without extravagance or frills. However, the wedding was the one time that the limitations of economy were ignored as much as possible. The stops were pulled out and a great celebration took place. The festivities usually lasted for an entire week with the host family providing food and drink for the guests. Instead of small portions twice a day (the norm in Palestine) the meals were lavish. The guests expected to eat well and to enjoy a brief reprieve from the harshness of life. In addition to the eating the wedding was a time of celebration and rejoicing through a variety of social activities. Part of the reason that weddings were the single time of breaking through the restraints of poverty is that Jews believed that weddings were very much an expression of the will of God. After all, God had started things off for the human race with a wedding. His first commandment was to be fruitful and multiply (Gen. 1.28[1]). A wedding was the beginning of a new family that would obey that commandment and produce love, happiness, and children to train up in the faith. The wedding gave social sanction to a couple to begin the life of obedience to God's design for human beings.

Within the Palestinian wedding wine was a very essential part of the celebration. The Jewish rabbis claimed, *Without wine there is no joy*. This does not mean that they were alcoholics! The wine was diluted with a considerable amount of water so that there was no drunkenness unless a person was totally immoderate in their drinking. The place of wine was so significant that failure to provide enough would have created a serious breach of hospitality (Derrett 1970:232-34). Mary's report to Jesus that the wine had run out was not just a comment about the level of the larder. Jesus would have immediately recognised that a young couple and their families would live in embarrassment for the rest of their lives for failing to provide adequately for the wedding celebration. Social failure is not easily lived

---

[1] God blessed them, and God said to them, 'Be fruitful and multiply, and fill the earth and subdue it; and have dominion over the fish of the sea and over the birds of the air and over every living thing that moves upon the earth.'

down in a small town (cf. Mullins 2002:116). Further, there was a strong element of reciprocity about weddings in the Ancient Near East: it was possible in certain circumstances to take legal action against the man who failed to provide an appropriate wedding gift. The bridegroom and family here might have been involved in a financial liability for failing to provide adequately for their guests.

b. The Wine, The Statement, The Response (Jn. 2.3-5)

When the wine gave out, the mother of Jesus said to him, 'They have no wine.' And Jesus said to her, 'Woman, what concern is that to you and to me? My hour has not yet come.' His mother said to the servants, 'Do whatever he tells you.'

This section contains the only words that the mother of Jesus uttered in the whole gospel of John, *They have no wine* and *Do whatever he tells you*, and these words have been interpreted in so many ways over the years. In the past, the interpretation of these words tended towards two extremes. One interpretation says that these words show Mary's power of intercession and they are meant to teach the reader to pray to Jesus through Mary. Another says that Mary's insistence after Jesus' refusal (i.e., *Do whatever he tells you*) proves that Mary did not really believe in Jesus and thus she is *a model of unbelief*. Today, most scholars would avoid these two extremes and rightly so (Brown et al. 1978:193). Does the mother of Jesus approach him in a moment of crisis to help save the embarrassment of this young couple? What does she expect Jesus to do about it? (see, Ridderbos 1991:104; Brown 1978:98) Is she relying on a knowledge she has of her son that no one else has? Is she expecting a miracle? (cf. Mullins 2002:116) The Evangelist gives us no details as to what is going on inside Mary's mind, but she does have a certain confidence in Jesus, though where this confidence comes from is not given to us. Her reaction to the answer Jesus gives to her statement *do whatever he tells you* seems to indicate that she knew Jesus could so something without specifying what that something was. In this reading then, her words and deeds offer an intriguing portrait of a woman as a leader and catalyst in the mission of Jesus' life with implications for women's empowerment. Mary sees that wine has run out and so acting in a decisive and confident manner, she named the need and took the initiative to seek a solution. So, far from silent, she speaks; far from passive, she acts; far from receptive to the orders of the male, she goes counter to his wishes, finally bringing him along with her; far from yielding to a grievous situation, she takes charge of it, organising matters to bring about benefit to those in need, including herself. Seen from this perspective, then, Mary stands in solidarity with women around the world who struggle for social justice for themselves and their children (Salezer 2006:112). In addition, this challenging plea from Mary addresses the conscience of the body of Christ today, especially the rich nations on earth. 'They have no wine, no food, no clean drinking water: You need to act!". When the wine runs out, Jesus' mother brings it to his notice; of course she does it with the aim of getting him to do something about it and Jesus understood her statement correctly. Mary's statement, *they have no wine*, is not just a statement of fact; it is an implied request. The question why it is Mary in particular (and not any other character in the story) who asks Jesus can best be answered not by wondering what particular position Mary had in the marriage feast (e.g., was she a relative of the bride or the groom? Was she in the kitchen? How come she knew that they ran out of wine already?) but by pointing out that the narrative probably comes from circles in which a certain authority was already ascribed to the mother of the Lord, as a matter of course. Using this interpretation, this scene can actually be used as an indication that Mary was really part of the post-resurrection church and the source of this story apparently knew this tradition. In addition, neither the bride nor the groom is shown making the request, either to Jesus or to Mary.

Mary is shown, out of her own freedom, as seeing the problem and directing Jesus' attention to it. But the response of Jesus to Mary's initial statement, *they have no wine* seems to be saying to her 'So? What has that got to do with me?' Jesus' addressing his mother as *woman* is linked with what appears to be a dismissive and negative response to her request: literally *what to me and to you?* (see, Barratt 2002:117)This phrase is a Semitism and in the main it has two meanings:

> 1. When a person who was being bothered by another considered it unjust to do so and so it could be paraphrased as *What have I done to you that you should treat me like this?*
> 2. When a person was being asked to get involved in a situation which they felt was none of their business they could ask, *What to me and to you?* Or paraphrased as, *that's your business, what has it to do with me?*

1. Has a more hostile meaning to it, whereas, 2. indicates something like disengagement or indifference. The second meaning better fits the context here. It need not of itself be offensive, though materially it does intend a rebuke, indeed many of the Greek fathers understood it in this way. Whether it is used as a rebuke to Mary here or not, it does nevertheless indicate that Jesus feels he is becoming embroiled in a situation which is none of his business (see, Giblin 1979-1980:197-211). The lack of wine is not his problem and even more so is this the case because his reply to Mary, *my hour has not yet come* gives the reason for his initial refusal to get involved and is the first reference to his *hour* saying, The *hour* is one of the key symbolic terms in the gospel of John and it refers to the moment of Jesus' return to the Father (Salezer 2006:114;). The reference to Jesus' *hour* connects this episode to the second book of the gospel, the book of glory when Jesus knew that his *hour* had come (Jn. 13,1). Consequently, the second scene where the mother of Jesus appears is also pointed to. The crucifixion is Jesus' *hour* and his mother was present in his *hour*. *My hour has not yet come* is better understood in its context as, *What business of*

mine is this thing you have bothered me with? It is not yet time for me to act.
The *hour* of Jesus is of crucial significance to the Evangelist and it occurs
throughout the gospel, e.g., 12.23;[1] 13.1;[2] 16.25;[3] and 17.1.[4] It is best seen
as a reference to the special period in Jesus' life when he is to leave this
world and return to the Father (Jn. 13.1); the hour when the Son of man is
glorified (Jn. 17.1). This is accomplished through his suffering, death,
resurrection and ascension (though this is not emphasised by John). Jn. 7.30
and Jn. 8.20 imply that Jesus' arrest and death are included. Jn. 12.23 and
Jn.17.1, referring to the glorification of the Son, imply that the resurrection
and ascension are included as part of the *hour*. But the *hour* of Jesus
understood like this means the fullness of his glory of which his passion and
death are only part, so that Jn. 2.4 would refer to all his 'future' glory. Jn.
2.11 does refer to Jesus letting 'his glory' be seen in the sign at Cana but this
would then be understood as a prophecy of that future glory so that John is
planting in the mind of his hearers/readers the idea that the full realisation
and significance of Jesus' glory are not to be found in his miracles but in his
glorification by the Father (see, Ridderbos 1991:106 and Brown's
discussion, 1978:99-100).

But at the risk of sounding too rhetorical, is this really what is implied
in the reply that Jesus gives to Mary's initial approach to tell him that the
wedding couple have no wine? When Jesus replies *what business is this of
mine my hour has not yet come* is he really saying *what business of this is
mine, the hour of my future glorification by the Father in suffering and death
has not yet arrived*? It is difficult to see in its present contextual use that
Jesus is referring to his departure at the very beginning of his public ministry
(which, in actual fact, has not begun yet because at this point he has still not
done anything about the appeal Mary makes to him). It does not seem from

---

[1] Jesus answered them, 'The hour has come for the Son of Man to be glorified.

[2] Now before the festival of the Passover, Jesus knew that his hour had come to depart from this world and
go to the Father. Having loved his own who were in the world, he loved them to the end.

[3] 'I have said these things to you in figures of speech. The hour is coming when I will no longer speak to you
in figures, but will tell you plainly of the Father.

[4] After Jesus had spoken these words, he looked up to heaven and said, 'Father, the hour has come; glorify
your Son so that the Son may glorify you.

the present context that Jesus is referring to the 'hour' which comes at the end of his life, but the 'hour' which comes at the beginning. *My hour has not yet come* in Jn. 2.4 refers to the hour of the beginning of Jesus revelation of his glory in the flesh and this 'hour' cannot seize this beginning before hand no matter who urges him to do so (in this case, his mother). In Jn. 2:4 Jesus' remark to his mother indicates that the time for this self-manifestation has not yet arrived; his identity as Messiah is not yet to be publicly revealed. Jesus awaits the will of the Father that his glory be revealed and he is aware that the time is not yet. This 'not yet' also means that as Jesus waits on the Father's time, so people must wait on Jesus' time and Mary must also await the 'hour'.

So Jesus' initial reaction is one of negativity and the form of the response is terse and dismissive. He is making it clear that whatever this situation is it is not his responsibility and it is none of his business. His reply takes us by surprise, *woman* (Jn. 2.4). In the vocative this is a term of respect or affection and Jesus uses it on a number of occasions in John, e.g. Jn. 4.21;[1] 8.10;[2] 19.26[3] and 20:15.[4] However, in Aramaic/Hebrew some qualifying adjective or title would normally be used but it was an unusual form of address for a son to use for his mother and thus appears distant and dismissive (cf. Ridderbos 1991:105; Brown 1978:1.99,102). So what is the significance of its use here? It is a gross exaggeration to say that Jesus disowns his mother with this form of address. It can be interpreted to mean that human ties and obligations in no way influence Jesus' action. Others have seen in this address a symbolic meaning. Jesus, is not addressing his mother simply as his mother but as a woman of faith making a request. He is not disowning his mother, but indicating rather that a different kind of

[1] Jesus said to her, 'Woman, believe me, the hour is coming when you will worship the Father neither on this mountain nor in Jerusalem.
[2] Jesus straightened up and said to her, 'Woman, where are they? Has no one condemned you?'
[3] When Jesus saw his mother and the disciple whom he loved standing beside her, he said to his mother, 'Woman, here is your son.'
[4] Jesus said to her, 'Woman, why are you weeping? For whom are you looking?' Supposing him to be the gardener, she said to him, 'Sir, if you have carried him away, tell me where you have laid him, and I will take him away.'

relationship, a relationship of faith, is being called upon. It is more than likely that it indicates a new relationship existing between Jesus and his mother at the outset of his public ministry. Jesus is no longer just the *son of Mary* but now the *Son of Man* and is also suggested by the use of the same term in Jn. 19.26 in the scene at the cross, where the 'Beloved Disciple' is 'given' to Mary as her 'new' son (see below).

However, given Jesus' reply to her initial comment, her action after she has spoken to him and heard his reply in Jn. 2.5 is strange *do whatever he tells you*. Mary has not understood the enigmatic reply of Jesus; quite literally, it has gone over her head. Jesus has made it clear that he will not be goaded into action by any human being, not even his mother; he will act when the time is right for him. In telling the servants to *do whatever he tells you* Mary is leaving the initiative entirely in the hands of Jesus; she awaits his time (hour) and thus leaves the decision with him. She does not and cannot know what the hour of Jesus is; she cannot enter into this hour but nevertheless she does seem to have some confidence in him. In this statement to the stewards, Mary plays her exemplary role: the hour belongs to Jesus, it is his time; no one can determine when and how he is to act but without the faith symbolised in Mary, Jesus cannot do miracles (see, Ridderbos 1991:106).

The mother has understood her son; all she can do now is to wait and so she directs the servants to do whatever he tells them. What attitude of Mary comes out from this command? This command, though short, expresses the mother's faith, trust and confidence in Jesus. It shows that Mary did not doubt that Jesus will, in the end, intervene. In Mary, the evangelist is able to demonstrate the disciple's openness to whatever may be revealed. As a result, the disciples themselves believed. So, instead of reading this verse to mean Mary's power of intercession or seeing her as a model of unbelief, scholars today read this story and see the mother of Jesus as falling into a general category of those who, despite their good intentions, misunderstood Jesus. Her implied request for a sign shows both naive trust and a lack of comprehension which ultimately leads to solid faith

c. The Water That Is Wine (Jn. 2.6-11)

> Now standing there were six stone water-jars for the Jewish rites of purification, each holding twenty or thirty gallons. Jesus said to them, 'Fill the jars with water.' And they filled them up to the brim. He said to them, 'Now draw some out, and take it to the chief steward.' So they took it. When the steward tasted the water that had become wine, and did not know where it came from (though the servants who had drawn the water knew), the steward called the bridegroom and said to him, 'Everyone serves the good wine first, and then the inferior wine after the guests have become drunk. But you have kept the good wine until now.' Jesus did this, the first of his signs, in Cana of Galilee, and revealed his glory; and his disciples believed in him.

The narrative now introduces the *stone water jars* in Jn. 2.6. These water pots were present to fulfil the rites of Jewish purification. Each of the pots held two or three 'metretes'. A metre-tes literally, (measure) was approximately 9 gallons (39.39 litres); thus each jar held 18-27 gallons (78.8-118.2 litres) and the total volume of liquid involved was 108-162 gallons (472.7-709 litres) (see, Ridderbos 1991:107; Brown 1978:100). The significance of the number should not be lost on us: this is a lot of water, so there is no shortage of water, but there is a shortage of wine. There is ample for the Jewish purification rites in the 'Jewish vessels of the law'; Jesus simply requisitions these to save the wedding from being a disaster. John wants us to be aware of the amount that was already present for the purification rites and for the abundance that Jesus will provide. The Evangelist gives us no reason as to why Jesus decided to act but the 'hour' has now come. We do not 'see' the miracle happen but two things are made clear:

> 1. The authority of Jesus, indicated in the commands to 'fill them', *Jesus said to them, fill the jars with water.*

2 The obedience and compliance of those who heard the command, *and they filled them to the brim*.

It is only when the stewards have done as they were commanded *filled to the brim* that Jesus gives them other commands *now draw* (*some out*) *and take it to the chief steward*. The moment that the stewards comply with Jesus' command is the moment of his 'hour'. Where once there was an abundant supply of water for the purification rites of the Jewish law, now there is new wine in abundance which all can draw on. But this is not just 'wine' or even 'new wine': though the Evangelist has given us the amount of wine there would be 108-162 gallons (!) his emphasis at this point is not so much on the abundance as on the *quality* of the wine. The drawn wine is taken to the chief steward who *did not know where it came from* (Jn. 2.9) but the servants *who had drawn the water did*. Thus, the steward acts as an independent objective witness to the miracle who, as chief steward can offer his own judgement of the wine. This is independent objectivity is further strengthens when the steward approaches the bridegroom and not Jesus, why should he? We have already been told he did not know where the wine came from. The chief steward is astonished at the quality of the wine and mentions this fact the bridegroom. The steward understands the custom at weddings: give the good wine first and then when the guests have had enough serve the lesser quality after that. But he compliments the bridegroom because, *You have kept the good wine until now*. The steward cannot speak about what he does not know (the provenance of the wine) but he can speak about he does know: the fact that it is there and its quality and this is precisely what he does. Thus, the Evangelist provides an objective, independent witness to Jesus' first sign.

d. The Meaning of the Sign

While this story provides a powerful picture of true discipleship, the main point is that it reveals Jesus' glory (Jn. 2.11[1]). It does this in part by

[1]   Jesus did this, the first of his signs, in Cana of Galilee, and revealed his glory; and his disciples believed in

revealing something of Jesus' identity through associations with the Old Testament. Such a miracle might suggest, for example, the deeds of Elijah (1 K 17.7-16) or Elisha (2 K 4.1-7[1]). More specifically, the promised time of restoration is expressed in the imagery of marriage (Is. 54.4-8;[2] 62.4-5[3]) and of an abundance of wine (Is. 25.6;[4] Jer. 31.12;[5] Amos 9.13-14[6]). Indeed, in Hosea these images appear together (Hos.2.14-23[7]). Thus, through both the supernatural power of the miracle and the imagery associated with it the disciples' confessions of Jesus in the first chapter are confirmed. Here indeed

---

him.

[1] Now the wife of a member of the company of prophets cried to Elisha, 'Your servant my husband is dead; and you know that your servant feared the Lord, but a creditor has come to take my two children as slaves.' Elisha said to her, 'What shall I do for you? Tell me, what do you have in the house?' She answered, 'Your servant has nothing in the house, except a jar of oil.' He said, 'Go outside, borrow vessels from all your neighbours, empty vessels and not just a few. Then go in, and shut the door behind you and your children, and start pouring into all these vessels; when each is full, set it aside.' So she left him and shut the door behind her and her children; they kept bringing vessels to her, and she kept pouring. When the vessels were full, she said to her son, 'Bring me another vessel.' But he said to her, 'There are no more.' Then the oil stopped flowing. She came and told the man of God, and he said, 'Go, sell the oil and pay your debts, and you and your children can live on the rest.'

[2] Do not fear, for you will not be ashamed; do not be discouraged, for you will not suffer disgrace; for you will forget the shame of your youth, and the disgrace of your widowhood you will remember no more. For your Maker is your husband, the Lord of hosts is his name; the Holy One of Israel is your Redeemer, the God of the whole earth he is called. For the Lord has called you like a wife forsaken and grieved in spirit, like the wife of a man's youth when she is cast off, says your God. For a brief moment I abandoned you, but with great compassion I will gather you. In overflowing wrath for a moment I hid my face from you, but with everlasting love I will have compassion on you, says the Lord, your Redeemer.

[3] You shall no more be termed Forsaken, and your land shall no more be termed Desolate; but you shall be called My Delight Is in Her, and your land Married; for the Lord delights in you, and your land shall be married. For as a young man marries a young woman, so shall your builder marry you, and as the bridegroom rejoices over the bride, so shall your God rejoice over you.

[4] On this mountain the Lord of hosts will make for all peoples a feast of rich food, a feast of well-matured wines, of rich food filled with marrow, of well-matured wines strained clear.

[5] They shall come and sing aloud on the height of Zion, and they shall be radiant over the goodness of the Lord, over the grain, the wine, and the oil, and over the young of the flock and the herd; their life shall become like a watered garden, and they shall never languish again.

[6] The time is surely coming, says the Lord, when the one who ploughs shall overtake the one who reaps, and the treader of grapes the one who sows the seed; the mountains shall drip sweet wine, and all the hills shall flow with it. I will restore the fortunes of my people Israel, and they shall rebuild the ruined cities and inhabit them; they shall plant vineyards and drink their wine, and they shall make gardens and eat their fruit.

[7] Therefore, I will now persuade her, and bring her into the wilderness, and speak tenderly to her. From there I will give her her vineyards, and make the Valley of Achor a door of hope. There she shall respond as in the days of her youth, as at the time when she came out of the land of Egypt. On that day, says the

is the one they have been waiting for. He himself is the good wine that has been kept back until now.

The 'sign' at the Wedding Feast of Cana raises more questions than it answers. The dominating theme of the Evangelist's narrative is that of salvation-history, i.e., that the 'hour' of Jesus has come and in this hour he reveals his glory. The narrative emphasis is on this 'hour' as a result of Mary's premature pressurising of Jesus. Yet the conversation between Mary and Jesus is not finished: *they have no wine-what is that to me-my hour is not yet-do whatever he tells you.* The last phrase has no context other than Mary leaving the initiative to Jesus: he will act or he will not, it is up to him. What did she expect him to do? Catholics will often use this moment of Mary approaching Jesus to give support to their belief in Mary's intercessory powers, but this is not what is in the mind of the Evangelist as the reason for her statement. At Jn. 2.11 the Evangelist gives us his own point of the narrative: the sign is accomplished and through this sign Jesus let his glory be seen and the disciples believed in him,

> Jesus made this to be, the first of his signs in Cana in Galilee, he
> allowed his glory to be seen and his disciples believed him.

What began as an approach by Mary in a situation of crisis ends with the decisive breakthrough of the promised salvation. But all must wait their time for this because the time of Jesus is appointed by the Father. Mary stands for the impatient yet believing Israel which waits for the fulfilment of the promises. So we might break down the temporality of the sign thus:

Lord, you will call me, 'My husband', and no longer will you call me, 'My Baal'. For I will remove the names of the Baals from her mouth, and they shall be mentioned by name no more. I will make for you a covenant on that day with the wild animals, the birds of the air, and the creeping things of the ground; and I will abolish the bow, the sword, and war from the land; and I will make you lie down in safety. And I will take you for my wife for ever; I will take you for my wife in righteousness and in justice, in steadfast love, and in mercy. I will take you for my wife in faithfulness; and you shall know the Lord. On that day I will answer, says the Lord, I will answer the heavens and they shall answer the earth; and the earth shall answer the grain, the wine, and the oil, and they shall answer Jezreel; and I will sow him for myself in the land. And I will have pity on Lo-ruhamah, and I will say to Lo-ammi, 'You are my people'; and he shall say, 'You are my God.'

> They have *no wine what is that to me*
> my hour is *not yet* come
> *Do what he tells you*
> Fill the jars to the brim
> Draw some out *now*
> The best until *now*

It is the word of the ignorant, independent objective steward here that emphasises how the time of fulfilment has broken through in Jesus whose *not yet* has become the *now*. For in the moment Jesus tells the stewards to *draw some out now*, the hour that was not yet is come. Some have sought to interpret the wedding imagery in a different manner by associating the wine with the 'messianic wedding'. It is certainly true that wine in plenty is an image which is used for the coming glory of God as the references in the previous page indicates and Jesus himself uses wine as a parabolic image of the coming of the kingdom (Mk. 2.22[1]) so joy and plenty are usually associated with this parabolic imagery. Some may even interpret the wine in the Cana narrative eucharistically but this is not the main intention of the Evangelist. Jesus, while certainly the host at the Last Supper, is not the host here; nor is he the bridegroom. While the first sign takes place at a wedding, the wedding itself is in the background. The Evangelist is rather making something else clear: the *first* sign has the same purpose that all the *following* signs will have: *revelation about the person of Jesus*.

Scholarly interpretations to the contrary, John does not put primary emphasis on the replacing of the water for Jewish purification, or on the change from water to wine, or even on the resulting wine. John does not focus on Mary and her intercession, nor on why she made the request or whether she pursued it further after Jesus' initial response. John does not focus on the reaction of the master of the feast or the bridegroom. The primary focus, as for all the Johannine stories, is on *Jesus as the One sent by*

---

[1] And no one puts new wine into old wineskins; otherwise, the wine will burst the skins, and the wine is lost, and so are the skins; but one puts new wine into fresh wineskins.'

the Father to bring salvation to the world. What shines through is his 'doxa' (doxa/glory), and the only reaction emphasized is that of his disciples when they believed in him. The Evangelist reinforces in this dramatic narrative that all is to be found in Jesus; that what was said of Jesus in the Prologue is now present and real. This is the first mention of the word glory since Jn. 1.14.[1] Obviously John understands the miracle at Cana to reveal the glory of God. Jn. 1.14 had said that we saw that glory in the Word made flesh. At Cana a small portion of the world understood that God was present. In a humble village wedding, with rough stone water jars, unobtrusively, God was there. Shortly after the first wedding mentioned in Gen. 2 the glory of God was lost. At Cana, the glory of God was back at a wedding again, a sign of a new beginning. In the place of the Law given by Moses (the rites of purification/the water jars) the fullness of grace and truth and all they imply is now present in the time of fulfilment through Jesus. What unfolds in the gospel of John from this point onward is the ever deepening and truer showing of the glory that Jesus allows to be seen at Cana.

At this point there are two major questions that need to be asked about the sign given at Cana:

> 1. How does the sign at Cana reveal the glory of Jesus in the narrative context?
> 2. How did the sign reveal the glory of Jesus to the disciples?

In relation to (1) the Evangelist tells the reader that this is the *first* of the signs (Jn. 2.11) and so Cana is to be seen in relation to the other signs that will follow in the gospel (Jn. 2.1-12.50). On of the key elements of Jn. 2-4 is the replacing of the institutions and celebrations of Judaism and Jn. 5-10 emphasises Jesus actions and teaching on the Jewish feasts, (in many cases by the symbolism of replacement: Jesus is the true temple (Jn. 2.13-

---

[1]   And the Word became flesh and lived among us

22[1]); worship at Jerusalem will be replaced by worship in spirit and truth (Samaritan woman (Jn. 4.1-42); his body and blood will give life in a way the Exodus manna could not (Jn. 6 Tabernacles); Jesus is the living water; Jesus is the true light not the light of the Temple (Jn. 8.12-20[2]); Jesus is consecrated to God not the altar (Dedication). Viewed in the context of the 'replacement' motif, the *first* of the signs at Cana establishes the theme of replacement through the changing of the water of the Jewish purification rites into the new wine of fulfilment. The sign at Cana reveals the glory of Jesus as the one sent by the Father and in replacing the water of Judaism with the *best* wine kept until 'now', all previous religious institutions, feasts, customs are no longer relevant: Jesus is the only way to the Father.

(2) is the much more difficult question to answer: the disciples were not aware that Jesus was replacing the older Jewish institutions and feasts with his own self, how then were the disciples supposed to have seen the glory of Jesus manifested at Cana so that they *believed in him*? To try and answer this we need to return to the some of the symbolism used in the Hebrew Scriptures, symbolism which we would not be unreasonable in presuming the disciples had some knowledge of. The sign narrative takes

---

[1]   The Passover of the Jews was near, and Jesus went up to Jerusalem. In the temple he found people selling cattle, sheep, and doves, and the money-changers seated at their tables. Making a whip of cords, he drove all of them out of the temple, both the sheep and the cattle. He also poured out the coins of the money-changers and overturned their tables. He told those who were selling the doves, 'Take these things out of here! Stop making my Father's house a market-place!' His disciples remembered that it was written, 'Zeal for your house will consume me.' The Jews then said to him, 'What sign can you show us for doing this?' Jesus answered them, 'Destroy this temple, and in three days I will raise it up.' The Jews then said, 'This temple has been under construction for forty-six years, and will you raise it up in three days?' But he was speaking of the temple of his body. After he was raised from the dead, his disciples remembered that he had said this; and they believed the scripture and the word that Jesus had spoken.

[2]   Again Jesus spoke to them, saying, 'I am the light of the world. Whoever follows me will never walk in darkness but will have the light of life.' Then the Pharisees said to him, 'You are testifying on your own behalf; your testimony is not valid.' Jesus answered, 'Even if I testify on my own behalf, my testimony is valid because I know where I have come from and where I am going, but you do not know where I come from or where I am going. You judge by human standards; I judge no one. Yet even if I do judge, my judgement is valid; for it is not I alone who judge, but I and the Father who sent me. In your law it is written that the testimony of two witnesses is valid. I testify on my own behalf, and the Father who sent me testifies on my behalf.' Then they said to him, 'Where is your Father?' Jesus answered, 'You know neither me nor my Father. If you knew me, you would know my Father also.' He spoke these words while he was teaching in the treasury of the temple, but no one arrested him, because his hour had not yet come.

places during a *wedding* which in the Hebrew bible comes to symbolise the messianic age and Jesus used wedding symbolism himself (Mt. 8.11,[1] Lk. 22.16-18[2]). Jesus also replaces the water with *best wine* and in the Synoptic tradition (Mk. 2.19[3]), he uses the imagery of old and new wine skins to compare his teaching with the of the Pharisees. It is perfectly reasonable, therefore to see the chief steward's statement *You have kept the best wine until now* as an announcement of the coming of the messianic days. In this light Mary's statement *They have no wine* might indicate the emptiness of Jewish ritual and purification.

If one takes into account the amount of wine (perhaps as much as 162 gallons) then the imagery of *abundance* becomes clear: abundance of wine is one of the recurring images for joy in the Hebrew Scriptures and Enoch 10.19 predicts that the vine shall yield wine in abundance; and in 2 Bar. 29. 5 (a Jewish apocryphon almost contemporary with the Fourth Gospel) we find an exuberantly fantastic description of this abundance: the earth shall yield its fruit ten thousand fold; each vine shall have 1000 branches; each branch 1000 clusters; each cluster 1000 grapes; and each grape about 120 gallons of wine. It is through knowledge of such symbolism so important to their own religious tradition that the disciple could have seen the sign at Cana as the beginning of the messianic age and time of fulfilment (in the same way they would have understood Jesus' statement about new wine for new wine skins). One final point: others were present when this sign occurred but John does not mention them as coming to belief, only the disciples are mentioned as believing in him (this is not to say that Jesus was not calling those present to belief). The disciples were those who were with Jesus from the beginning, from the *first of the signs* and as witnesses to his

---

[1] I tell you, many will come from east and west and will eat with Abraham and Isaac and Jacob in the kingdom of heaven

[2] For I tell you, I will not eat it until it is fulfilled in the kingdom of God.' Then he took a cup, and after giving thanks he said, 'Take this and divide it among yourselves; for I tell you that from now on I will not drink of the fruit of the vine until the kingdom of God comes.'

[3] Jesus said to them, 'The wedding-guests cannot fast while the bridegroom is with them, can they? As long as they have the bridegroom with them, they cannot fast.

glory from the beginning (Jesus makes this clear in Jn. 15.27[1]) it was this witness to the glory of Jesus that brought others to faith in Jesus as the Christ the Son of God (which the Evangelist says is the purpose of *these things* he has written (Jn. 20.31[2]). John is writing his gospel to strengthen the faith of his own apostolic community as the Synoptics are written for others: the disciples, as the first witnesses of Jesus' glory, were not only the founders of those communities (the Church) but, with Mary (if she became a disciple at Cana which is by no means certain), also the first representatives of its faith.

e. The Women Gathered Near The Cross (Jn. 19.25)

> Meanwhile, standing near the cross of Jesus were his mother, and his mother's sister, Mary the wife of Clopas, and Mary Magdalene.

It is only in the gospel of John that the *mother of Jesus* is included in the list of women gathered the foot of the cross which might indicate that John got this story from an independent tradition (Salezer 2006:115) but this should be treated with caution since it is only John who has the 'Beloved Disciple' (son) - Mary (mother) scene. And it is more than likely that this scene is not historical (Barrett 1978:551) but symbolic where the *mother of* Jesus and the 'Beloved Disciple' are representative of the new community 'gathered around' Jesus (Salezer 2006:115). John has presented other 'groups' present at the death of Jesus: those who are demanding that Pilate remove the placard which reads *Jesus of Nazareth King of the Jews* (Jn. 19.19-22), and the soldiers who cast lots for his tunic (Jn. 19.23-24). It would not have been unusual for people to gather around the site of the execution of prisoners either to jeer and mock them, or family members to grieve and

---

[1] You also are to testify because you have been with me from the beginning.
[2] But these are written so that you may come to believe that Jesus is the Messiah, the Son of God, and that through believing you may have life in his name.

mourn (cf. *t. Gittin* 7.1, 330; b. *Baba Metzia* 83b).

Mark says there was quite a group of women present (Mk. 15:41), but John focuses on a handful near the cross. The list of women most likely refers to four individuals. Mark names three women in particular who were present, *Mary Magdalene, Mary the mother of James the younger and of Joses, and Salome* (Mk. 15.40). The mother of James and Joses has always been understood as the one referred to in John as *Mary, the wife of Clopas* (Jn. 19.25) and that Salome is the one John calls *his mother's sister* (Jn. 19.25). Salome, is further identified with the mother of the sons of Zebedee, by Matthew's (Mt. 27.56) which would mean that the sons of Zebedee were Jesus' cousins but this identification is dubious because the texts do not admit certainty, since, as Mark says, there were a *number of women* present (see discussion in Brown 1999:905. However, if the 'Beloved Disciple', taken to be John, the son of Zebedee, (by no means certain either), is Jesus' cousin, then Jesus' commending his mother to his care corresponds a little more with normal family patterns, though much more is involved as we will soon see (see Ridderbos 1991:611; Mullins 2002:383). Furthermore, it is striking that neither Jesus' mother nor his aunt are named, a trait they share with the 'Beloved Disciple'. Now he shows us a group of women and one man (making the presumption on the basis of tradition that the 'Beloved Disciple' was male) gathered around the foot of the cross.

f. The Mother of Jesus and 'Beloved Disciple' (Jn. 19.26-27)

> When Jesus saw his mother and the disciple whom he loved standing beside her, he said to his mother, 'Woman, here is your son.' Then he said to the disciple, 'Here is your mother.' And from that hour the disciple took her into his own home.

At the literal and historical level this episode portrays Jesus as a loving son providing social security for his mother. However, John's gospel has not given much attention to Jesus' compassion and kindness to anyone. If would be unusual for John to report this event at the cross and to see no theological importance to it. There have been many attempts to provide theological and allegorical interpretations of Jesus' provision for his mother. It is significant that it was the 'Beloved Disciple' to whom Jesus gave the care of his mother. Church tradition sees John the son of Zebedee as the 'Beloved Disciple' (cf. Barraett 1985:552). However, the 'Beloved Disciple' functions in a symbolic way in this gospel for the ideal Christian believer. With these supporters standing near him, Jesus focuses on his mother and the 'Beloved Disciple' (vv. 26-27) (see Brown's interesting observation in 1999:906). Jesus says to his mother, *Woman, behold your son*, and to the 'Beloved Disciple', *Behold your mother*. Similar language was used in connection with betrothal (Tob. 7.12[1]) and thus seems to signal some change of relationship. Jesus' mother is now brought under the care of the 'Beloved Disciple' (v.27). In this Gospel there is a symbolic role for both the *mother of Jesus* and the 'Beloved Disciple', for they are both examples of true discipleship (cf. Jn. 2.1-11;[2] 13.23). So in changing the relationship they have to one another, Jesus is completing the formation of the community gathered around him, gathered around him precisely as he is on the cross (Salezer 2006:117). The new community is now seen to be a new family (cf. Jn. 20.17).

A great deal has been made of this text. Many have understood Jesus' mother to be a symbol of Eve, the mother of the living, or a symbol of the

---

[1] Then Raguel summoned his daughter Sarah. When she came to him he took her by the hand and gave her to Tobias, saying, 'Take her to be your wife in accordance with the law and decree written in the book of Moses. Take her and bring her safely to your father. And may the God of heaven prosper your journey with his peace.'

[2] On the third day there was a wedding in Cana of Galilee, and the mother of Jesus was there. Jesus and his disciples had also been invited to the wedding. When the wine gave out, the mother of Jesus said to him, 'They have no wine.' And Jesus said to her, 'Woman, what concern is that to you and to me? My hour has not yet come.' His mother said to the servants, 'Do whatever he tells you.' Now standing there were six stone water-jars for the Jewish rites of purification, each holding twenty or thirty gallons. Jesus said to them, 'Fill the jars with water.' And they filled them up to the brim. He said to them, 'Now draw some out, and take it to the chief steward.' So they took it. When the steward tasted the water that had become wine, and did not know where it came from (though the servants who had drawn the water knew), the steward called the bridegroom and said to him, 'Everyone serves the good wine first, and then the inferior wine after the guests have become drunk. But you have kept the good wine until now.' Jesus did this, the first of his signs, in Cana of Galilee, and revealed his glory; and his disciples believed in him.

church. Quite often it has been assumed that the disciple is given into the care of the mother, which has contributed to the development of views regarding Mary's role in the lives of Christians, who are symbolised by the 'Beloved Disciple'. Such symbolism is a further development of John's own focus, which is on the new family formed among the disciples of Jesus, with the 'Beloved Disciple', who is the witness to Jesus par excellence, as the one exercising care. The mother and the 'Beloved Disciple' together symbolise the new community. If at the end of the Cana story, it was not clear whether the mother of Jesus became a disciple or not, at the foot of the cross, this is clearly established. The fact that there is one clear Marian passage in the last half of the gospel is significant because in this part of the gospel there is more instruction and care for those whom Jesus would consider his disciples. To introduce the mother of Jesus into this atmosphere is to bring her into the context of discipleship. Mary now becomes the mother of the disciple par excellence and so, becomes herself a model of belief and discipleship (cf. Salezer 2006:118; Treanor 1997:216).

g. The Death of Jesus (Jn. 19.1-22)

> After this, when Jesus knew that all was now finished, he said (in order to fulfil the scripture), 'I am thirsty.' A jar full of sour wine was standing there. So they put a sponge full of the wine on a branch of hyssop and held it to his mouth. When Jesus had received the wine, he said, 'It is finished.' Then he bowed his head and gave up his spirit

The death of Jesus happens while his mother and his 'Beloved Disciple' are still at the foot of the cross. This scene is often read as a parallel to Acts 1.14 and Pentecost when the scared disciples in the upper room received God's spirit manifested by the tongues of fire that settled on their heads. In John, the giving of the Spirit to the disciples happened at the foot of the cross when Jesus *gave up his spirit*. It is interesting to note that the mother of Jesus was there when this happened.

h. The Piercing of Jesus' Side (Jn. 19.31-37)

> Since it was the day of Preparation, the Jews did not want the bodies left on the cross during the Sabbath, especially because that Sabbath was a day of great solemnity. So they asked Pilate to have the legs of the crucified men broken and the bodies removed. Then the soldiers came and broke the legs of the first and of the other who had been crucified with him. But when they came to Jesus and saw that he was already dead, they did not break his legs. Instead, one of the soldiers pierced his side with a spear, and at once blood and water came out. (He who saw this has testified so that you also may believe. His testimony is true, and he knows that he tells the truth.) These things occurred so that the scripture might be fulfilled, 'None of his bones shall be broken.' And again another passage of scripture says, 'They will look on the one whom they have pierced.'

The Johannine Mary was a witness not only to the death of her son but even to the piercing of his side. This episode is found only in John's gospel. Jn. 19.31-37 describes the piercing of Jesus' side. For strong and stubborn men crucifixion was often a long process. Several days might pass before the criminal finally died. The Romans were happy to leave a victim moaning on the cross. It strengthened the deterrent aspect of crucifixion This is the climax of Jesus hour, the piercing of his side and the unusual flow of blood and water from his (pierced) side. This scene too is interpreted symbolically, especially in relation to the lines in the Old Testament that are being fulfilled. In this scene, a twofold prophecy is fulfilled: First, that which says *No bones of his will be broken* and the other, which says *They will look on him whom they have pierced*. The double fulfilment plainly shows that God's plan of salvation is fulfilled in this event, and that the crucified Jesus is the promised bringer of salvation. For the fourth evangelist, Jesus is the true Passover Lamb whose blood flowed out for humankind and whose dying has brought new life. It is possible to seethe piercing of Jesus' side and the flow of blood and water in maternally symbolic terms. The mingling of water and blood is particularly evocative of childbirth in which both elements flow. In this scene, Jesus' death can be read as the sorrowful labour that brings forth the joy of life. and his wounded side is also the 'womb' that produces life. The ones who gaze on him 'whom they have pierced' reveal themselves then to be children of God, born of divine love through the labour of Jesus and the Spirit.

It is clear from verses Jn. 19.36, 37 that these first events following Jesus' death fulfilled Scripture. Ex.12.10, 46[1] specifically state that no bones are to be broken in the Passover Lamb. Ps. 34.20[2] also declares that the righteous sufferer's bones will not be broken. Zech.12.10[3] speaks of looking at the one they have pierced. The emphasis on blood and water bursting from Jesus' side may have also been motivated by John's desire to combat rising Docetism (a heresy which denied the reality of Jesus' humanity). The literal, physical death of Christ is strongly affirmed by the statement about blood and water. Throughout Christian history there have been interpreters who believed John mentioned the blood and water for symbolic or theological reasons. The most common symbolism expressed is that the blood refers to the Eucharist or Lord's Supper and the water refers to baptism. This raises the question of sacramental symbolism in the Fourth Gospel. John is never explicit in referring to the sacraments preferring to always hint when dealing with them. However, in this passage the sacramental implication is secondary at best. The blood most normally would point to the sacrificial death of the Passover Lamb. The purpose of

---

[1] You shall let none of it remain until the morning; anything that remains until the morning you shall burn. It shall be eaten in one house; you shall not take any of the animal outside the house, and you shall not break any of its bones.

[2] He keeps all their bones; not one of them will be broken.

[3] And I will pour out a spirit of compassion and supplication on the house of David and the inhabitants of Jerusalem, so that, when they look on the one whom they have pierced, they shall mourn for him, as one mourns for an only child, and weep bitterly over him, as one weeps over a firstborn.

mentioning the blood was expressed in 1 Jn. 1.7, *The blood of Jesus his Son cleanses us from all sin*. John may well have thought of baptism when he mentioned the water; however, the usual symbolism of water in John's gospel is the Holy Spirit (Zech.12.10 also speaks of *the Spirit of* grace). Atonement from sin and the gift of the Holy Spirit are the two main results of Jesus' death. Here the desire is to suggest the theological meaning of the death of Jesus as the opening of a fountain of grace. No sooner is Jesus' sacrifice complete than the flow of life for the world begins.

i. John's Portrayal of Mary in His Gospel

Though there are only two scenes in which the *mother of Jesus* appears (Jn 2.1-12; 19.25-27) she is also referred to at Jn. 6.42, They were saying:

> Is not this Jesus, the son of Joseph, whose father and mother we
> know? How can he now say, "I have come down from heaven"?

Mary is never named and aside from the designation of her as *the mother of Jesus* the only other time she is addressed is as *Woman* by Jesus both at Cana and at the foot of the cross. Other than the one reference to the father of Jesus (Jn. 6.42[1]), there are not other references to him which may indicate that by the time of Jesus' death Mary was already a widow. Reference is made the *brothers* of Jesus (Jn. 2.12;[2] 7.1-10[3] which may mean that these

---

[1] They were saying, 'Is not this Jesus, the son of Joseph, whose father and mother we know? How can he now say, "I have come down from heaven"?'

[2] After this he went down to Capernaum with his mother, his brothers, and his disciples; and they remained there for a few days.

[3] After this Jesus went about in Galilee. He did not wish to go about in Judea because the Jews were looking for an opportunity to kill him. Now the Jewish festival of Booths was near. So his brothers said to him, 'Leave here and go to Judea so that your disciples also may see the works you are doing; for no one who wants to be widely known acts in secret. If you do these things, show yourself to the world.' (For not even his brothers believed in him.) Jesus said to them, 'My time has not yet come, but your time is always here. The world cannot hate you, but it hates me because I testify against it that its works are evil. Go to the festival yourselves. I am not going to this festival, for my time has not yet fully come.' After saying this, he remained in Galilee.

were his siblings or other relatives (as already noted the former of these would cause difficulties for those of the Roman Catholic and Orthodox traditions). John does not appear to be concerned to give information that is of a general nature and the only thing that is certain is that this woman is the *mother of Jesus*.

The *mother of Jesus* is present at two defining moments in the life of Jesus: at Cana, where he let his glory be shown (Jn. 2.11) and at his death (Jn. 19.17-37). That John has placed the *mother of Jesus* at these two significant and defining moments of Jesus' life would seem to indicate the *mother of Jesus* is herself a significant character and her significance lies in her being 'present'. From this, it is not unreasonable to suggest that the gospel writer saw the *mother of Jesus* not only being significant in herself but also significant in the community (Salezer 2006:119). This is further strengthened by the fact that when John names those at the foot of the cross the *mother of Jesus* is placed first (Jn. 19.25b) (see table and discussion in Brown 1999:905) and the same placing can be found at Cana, she is named before Jesus. Again the same placing can be found in the transition verse of Jn. 2.12:

> After this he went down to Capernaum with his mother, his brothers, and his disciples; and they remained there for a few days.

Mary is once again given prominence in the group of people gathered around Jesus which highlights her significance and primacy. John, therefore, firmly establishes the prominence and significance of Mary from the very beginning of Jesus' ministry to the very end and this is determinative of her character. It might be noted here that although John names her first at the beginning of the Cana narrative, he does not mention her at the end stating only (Jn. 2.11):

> Jesus did this, the first of his signs, in Cana of Galilee, and revealed his glory; and his disciples believed in him.

What might be implied in this? Had John forgotten that she was at Cana, or has he set her aside since she has fulfilled her function in the narrative and so need not appear again? John says that the *disciples believed in him*, does this imply that the *mother of Jesus* did not? This seems unlikely since she is placed first among the group that goes down to Capernaum with Jesus and in Jn. 19 she is to be found placed first among those named at the foot of the cross thus indicating that the response her response was that of the disciples, i.e., belief. In relation to the *mother of Jesus* there are other characters in the gospel who interact or react to her, primarily:

- Jesus at Cana
- The servants at Cana
- the 'Beloved Disciple' at the cross

The reaction of Jesus to his mother at Cana confirms what John has already told us about her in her words and actions. In his answer to her statement that the wine had run out, Jesus initially refuses to take any action over it by indicating that the problem was nothing to do with him and that his *hour* had not yet come. So, Jesus' *hour* takes precedence over the immediate situation of Mary's highlighting the embarrassing predicament the wedding couple face in relation to providing for their guests. And Mary's response to the servants that they do whatever Jesus tells them to do is again indicative of her role and character. In this respect this is a healthy and mature relationship between mother and son since the adult Jesus does not feel obliged to simply do whatever his mother tells him to do, he has his own authority of person now whereas as Luke tells us after the incident of being found in the Temple, he went down to Nazareth and lived under their obedience (Lk. 2.51[1]). That Jesus commands the servants to do what he tells them and so changes the water into wine does not mean that he has acceded to his mother's request since he has already refused to get involved and the

---

[1] Then he went down with them and came to Nazareth, and was obedient to them. His mother treasured all these things in her heart.

sign at Cana is to reveal his *glory* not to give his mother what she wants (in whatever was implied in her statement to him). In this respect then, Mary's statement (request?) is entirely consistent with the intentions of Jesus and an affirmation that she is present to the situation of the wedding couple, the guests and her own in a sensitive way. At the foot of the cross, Jesus gives his mother to the 'Beloved Disciple' as a mother, and gives the 'Beloved Disciple' to her as son. Here, Jesus confirms that she is his mother, and as he dies he provides a family for her (this may be consistent with the possibility inferred from the general information that Mary was already a widow at the time of Jesus' death). the 'Beloved Disciple' *took her into his own home,* thus *the mother of Jesus*, was not alone. but had a new family in the person of the 'Beloved Disciple'.

Mary, therefore, in the gospel of John is to be viewed in the same way the other women in the gospel of John are:

- the Samaritan Woman (Jn. 4.1-42) (see next chapter) who believed that Jesus was the Messiah;
- the woman caught in adultery (Jn. 8.1-11) who also believed in Jesus;
- Martha at the raising of Lazarus (Jn. 11.17-27) who believed Jesus was the Christ, the Son of God, and
- Mary Magdalene at the empty tomb (Jn. 20.1-18) who met the risen Jesus and believed and who became the 'Apostle to the Apostles'.

It is from the gospel of John especially that Christianity in its depiction of the *mother of Jesus* has received the image of her as mother and disciple. John, in a sense, takes Mary on a journey from motherhood to discipleship though, of course, she is always the *mother of Jesus*. Indeed, it is true to say that her role as 'mother' is widened since she becomes the mother of the 'Beloved Disciple' who is symbolic of the new community gathered around

Jesus. As John presents her, Mary is not simply the *mother of Jesus* who happened to become a disciple, or a disciple who happened to be the *mother of Jesus, she* is mother-disciple at one and the same time: the *woman* of Cana and *woman* the cross is also the *mother* and *disciple* in both incidents.

CHAPTER TEN

JESUS AND THE WOMEN IN JOHN

The Samaritan Woman (Jn. 4.1-42)

and the

The Woman Caught In Adultery (Jn. 7.53-8.11)

The Narrative Context

In this brilliantly written and structured narrative, John shows Jesus as the gift of God who can give humanity living water (Jn. 4.10) which will well up within them to eternal life (Jn. 4.14). This recalls the imagery of God as the *fountain of* life in Ps. 36.9 and the *spring of living waters* in Jer. 2.13. Jesus is thus portrayed as fulfilling what God would be for and to his people and his words echo Old Testament images of God being a source of water which satisfies thirst (Ps. 23.2;[1] 46.4;[2] Is. 44.3-4;[3] 48.21;[4] 55.1[5] and this includes the famous image of the Word of God as the rain and snow which produces life in Is. 55.10-11[6]). Other allusions may be Is. 32.1-2 (the coming king who will be like the river of water in dry places); Is. 35.2-7 (the mirage of the pool and the ground springs of water when the blind and lame are healed). These are prophesies of the Restoration, the days of the

---

[1] He makes me lie down in green pastures; he leads me beside still waters.

[2] There is a river whose streams make glad the city of God, the holy habitation of the Most High.

[3] For I will pour water on the thirsty land, and streams on the dry ground; I will pour my spirit upon your descendants, and my blessing on your offspring. They shall spring up like a green tamarisk, like willows by flowing streams.

[4] They did not thirst when he led them through the deserts; he made water flow for them from the rock; he split open the rock and the water gushed out.

[5] Ho, everyone who thirsts, come to the waters; and you that have no money, come, buy and eat! Come, buy wine and milk without money and without price.

[6] For as the rain and the snow come down from heaven, and do not return there until they have watered the earth, making it bring forth and sprout, giving seed to the sower and bread to the eater, so shall my word be that goes out from my mouth; it shall not return to me empty, but it shall accomplish that which I purpose, and succeed in the thing for which I sent it.

Messiah, so Jesus may be understood here to laying claim to be both Messiah and Son of God. This reinforces what Jesus spoke about in Jn. 3 and the Spirit which *blows where it wills* (Jn. 3.8) and the imagery of life-giving water which used again to refer to the spring which bubbles up within men and women to give eternal life. The 'rain of heaven' is falling and men and women can drink of its abundance, for Jesus now sees that the Spirit is at work in men and women. Once again John contrasts the old with the new, the lifeless with the life-giving: the old water of Jacob's well is replaced with the new water of life which through Jesus is the gift of God; the old worship in Jerusalem and Gerizim is replaced by the new worship in Spirit and truth. The narrative then mounts to the climax of Jesus' revelation to the Samaritan woman that he is the Messiah (Jn. 4.26) while the Samaritans themselves declare that he is the saviour *of the world* and though revealed by Jesus at the end of the narrative, the Messiahship of Jesus is present in this narrative from beginning to end.

The Samaritans were a people despised by the Jews, and yet not looked on as Gentiles. It is doubtful if they were descended from the inter mixture of the Israelites left in the land when Samaria was sacked in 722 BC, and the people brought in from other lands to replace those who had been deported, with whom they intermarried. They may, however, have been descended from YHWH worshippers who had remained in the land and had come together to form a community in order to preserve their own form of worship. Or they may have resulted from a group who arrived later seeking a home for themselves where they could follow their own religious beliefs. Certainly some of the people left in the land by the Assyrians had at least continued to look to the Temple at Jerusalem (Jer. 41.5[1]), but after Judah's exile, when the Temple was being restored, the Samaritans had offered their help, and had been refused any part in it. They were looked on as being religiously unacceptable. And there is no doubt that their religion was not orthodox Judaism. The Hellenisation of that part of the world by

---

[1] Eighty men arrived from Shechem and Shiloh and Samaria, with their beards shaved and their clothes torn, and their bodies gashed, bringing grain-offerings and incense to present at the temple of the Lord.

Alexander the Great had resulted in the disappearance of most people in the region into the mass of Hellenists. The Samaritans stood out among them, being centred around Shechem and following a distorted form of Yahwism. Certainly it seems that the later 'Samaritans' were connected with the area around Shechem (Eccl. 50.26;[1] 2 Macc. 5.22;[2] 6.2[3]), and one of Josephus' sources describes them as 'Shechemites'. After a long period of desolation Shechem had been rebuilt in the late 4th century BC, and at that stage they had built their own Temple, with a genuine Aaronic priesthood, on Mount Gerizim, which was later destroyed by John Hyrcanus (about 128 BC) (cf. Barrett 1985:230-231). They accepted the Law, but had their own version of it in the Samaritan Pentateuch, which named Mount Gerizim as the place of sacrifice (cf. Mullins 2002:151). They believed in the one God, and the coming of a deliverer, 'the Taheb (restorer)', identified by them with *the prophet* in Deut. 18.15. They were therefore not looked on as pagans, but as second rate worshippers of the one God, and for that reason tolerated, but only in order to be dismissed as heretics (Williamson 1992:726). Thus their connections with the earlier 'Samaritans' may have been tenuous. They may have been a group who had kept themselves relatively clean from the introduction of the various gods of the nations, and maintained their own relatively pure system of worship, or they may have been a group that arrived later and settled there. They were, however, despised by men like the Judaisers, and indeed by most Jews.

Nothing therefore would have seemed less likely to most Jews than the spiritual transformation of a despised Samaritan (see reflection by Sloyan 1983:10). Yet here at the beginning of Jesus' ministry he demonstrates that there are no barriers of race or past morals to prevent anyone from coming to God once the heart is set in the right direction and that God is ready to accept them.

---

[1] Those who live in Seir, and the Philistines, and the foolish people that live in Shechem.

[2] He left governors to oppress the people: at Jerusalem, Philip, by birth a Phrygian and in character more barbarous than the man who appointed him

[3] Also to pollute the temple in Jerusalem and to call it the temple of Olympian Zeus, and to call the one in Gerizim the temple of Zeus-the-Friend of Strangers, as did the people who lived in that place.

a. The Structure of the Narrative

The narrative of Jesus and the Samaritan Woman is the first of three major narratives in John who often uses stories to introduce dialogue around the identity of Jesus, as for example the conversation between Jesus and Nicodemus in Jn. 3. At the beginning of the chapter Nicodemus and Jesus are in conversation until Nicodemus is silent and John offers a sustained reflection on the identity of Jesus. However, the narrative of Jesus and the Samaritan Woman is sustained over forty two verses and in this sense it is similar to the narrative of the man born blind in Jn. 9 and the raising of Lazarus from the dead in Jn. 11 where these three stories interweave dialogue with characterisation.

The actual literary structure of the narrative is a very careful composition (see, Brown 1999:177-178). John uses various literary techniques to both focus and move the dialogue forward: misunderstanding (Jn. 4.11), irony (Jn. 4.12), an embarrassing subject quickly changed (Jn. 4.19), and front and back stage effects (Jn. 4.29). There are two main sections or 'acts':

1. Dialogue one: the Samaritan Woman (Jn. 4.2-29)
2. Dialogue two: the disciples (Jn. 4.27-38)

The two 'acts' are then drawn by John for an appropriate conclusion.

Act One, Scene One: The dialogue about the identity of Jesus and *living water*.

1. The Samaritan woman fails to understand Jesus (He is less than Jacob) (Jn. 4.11-12)
3. Jesus clarifies his reference to water (Jn. 4.13-14)
4. The woman asks for the water (Jn. 4.15)

The main section of this 'scene' in Act One, therefore, has been the *living water,* what has not been spoken about is the identity of Jesus and this is dealt with in Scene Two:

Act One, Scene Two: the dialogue on *true worship* of the Father (Jn. 4.16-26). This portion also has two brief dialogues with three lines in each:

1. Jesus reveals himself by discernment of her (Jn. 4.16)
2. The woman becomes evasive (Jn. 4.17)
3. Jesus uncovers her past (Jn. 4.18)

In Jn. 3.19-21 Jesus said,

> And this is the judgement, that the light has come into the world, and people loved darkness rather than light because their deeds were evil. For all who do evil hate the light and do not come to the light, so that their deeds may not be exposed. But those who do what is true come to the light, so that it may be clearly seen that their deeds have been done in God.'

This is a critical moment in the 'act' because the past 'evil' of the woman has now been brought to light by Jesus and judgement has come to her. How will she respond; will she continue to live in *darkness* or will she move towards the *light which enlightens all people* (Jn. 1.9) and which has *come into the world,* the *light the darkness could not overpower?* (Jn. 1.5)?

1. The woman is still evasive but open by her comment about worship (Jn. 4.19-20)
2. Jesus explains *true* worship (Jn. 4.21-24)
3. The woman recognises and confesses Jesus (Jn. 4.25-26)

Act Two (Jn. 4.27-38) concerns itself with the return of the disciples and the conversation with ensues between them and Jesus. While at first seemingly nothing to do with the Samaritan Woman as such, the actuality is more complex for it is the return of the Samaritan Woman to the city and her proclamation to the people which sets the context for what follows which is the coming of people (symbolised in the Samaritans coming out to meet him) to Jesus. So, this section of the narrative may outlined thus:

1. The conversation with the disciples after their return from the city (Jn. 4. 37-38)
2. The proclamation of the Samaritan Woman to the people of the city about Jesus as the context for what follows (Jn. 4.27-30)
3. The misunderstanding of the disciples about the *food* Jesus speaks of (Jn. 4.31-33) which echoes the misunderstanding about *water* (Jn. 4.7-11)
4. Jesus clarifies the misunderstanding (Jn. 4.34)
5. Jesus' symbolic reference to *food* paves the way for Jn. 4.35-38.

Jn. 4.35-38 contains two parables with a commentary

1. The parable of the harvest (Jn. 4.35)
2. The comment on the parable (Jn. 4. 36)
3. The parable on sowing (Jn. 4.37)
4. The comment on the parable (Jn. 4.38)

Finally, John draws the two scenes together and to an evangelistic conclusion in vv. 39-42. The harvest that Jesus had described in Act Two is brought to completion as the Samaritans believe for themselves. The preparatory work of Jesus and the woman is acknowledged as an important part of the process leading to the Samaritans' believing. Their faith is another instance of the purpose of John's gospel being illustrated.

b. Jesus and the Samaritan Woman (Jn. 4.4-26)

This narrative of the encounter between Jesus and the Samaritan woman in Jn. 4.4-26 is one of the most well known 'encounter' stories associated with Jesus in John (Nicodemus, Jn. 3.1-17 and Lazarus, Jn. 11.1-44, being the others). Detailed, graphic and brilliantly constructed as a literary edifice, its two central themes: water and worship, are contextualised within sub strata of other discussions on spirit, word, 'messianic' understandings, marriage, bridegroom implications, individual and corporate responses to Jesus and many others (cf. Brown 1978:180; see also Mullins 2002:153). However, this is a pleasant, irenic and, at least in one place, humorous interchange between Jesus and the woman. But even given this, the encounter between Jesus and the Samaritan Woman has at its core serious issues. The narrative shows a skilled literary hand at work and it is structured very carefully around the questions of the woman, Jesus' replies, her misunderstandings, Jesus' ever deepening explanations, her growing insight into his identity, and her response to him (see above). At the same time this is more than an individual encounter: the enthusiastic announcement of the woman to her own villagers and their initial response to her, then their response to Jesus indicate that one of the underlying themes of this narrative is the eschatological fulfilment in the coming of Jesus who, as he has done at Cana, transforms, changes and reshapes the very nature of salvation history.

The narrative is preceded by what is best described as a 'transitional' passage Jn. 4.1-3. This section deals with Jesus' departure from Judea and his return to Galilee. The only reason given for this is that Jesus had learned that the:

> Pharisees had heard that he was winning and baptising more
> disciples than John

So given what had happened to John the Baptist, it would seem that Jesus makes a tactical withdrawal for his own security and safety. An interesting insertion takes place at this point which may indicate more than one hand at work in the construction of John

> however, it was not Jesus himself who was baptising but his disciples

This is a direct contradiction of Jn. 3.22 where we are told that Jesus did baptise and the emendation here would seem to be made as a pre-emptive strike against any suggestion from the disciples of John the Baptist that Jesus was imitating John the Baptist.

The narrative proper begins at Jn. 4.4 with the phrase *he had to* (it was *necessary) pass through Samaria*. In fact, this was not a necessity from a geographical point of view, so how much weight is to be given to *had to/necessary* is difficult to determine (cf. Brown 1978:169; Barrett 1985:230). The main road from Judea to Galilee ran through Samaria. Jn. 3.22 tells us that Jesus was in the Jordan valley and so he could, quite easily, have gone north up through the valley, through the Bethshan gap and then into Galilee. But he did not do this, choosing instead to go through Samaria. In this context, therefore, while not *geographically* necessary, the deeper necessity (the necessity of God's will) may also be implied.

c. The Dialogue With The Woman (Jn. 4.4-26)

Jn. 4.5-7 presents us with a quite ordinary picture: Jesus, tired and thirsty from walking in the noonday heat, sits down at the well and asks a woman who has come to draw water from it for a drink. Since we are also told that the disciples have gone into the town to buy food, Jesus must rely on the near eastern custom of hospitality to the traveller from the woman. It is ordinary, natural and human but it is also packed with symbolism and significance. The well is situated near 'Sychar' but where this is is difficult to determine (cf. Brown 1978:169; Barraett 1985:231. Some try to locate it as Tell 'Askar but that is nearly a mile away from the well of Jacob. A scribal error may have changed 'Sychem' in to Sychar. No evidence of a town called 'Sychar' has been found in Samaria despite some ancient reports. Askar had its own well which would make the long journey the woman would have taken curious if not inexplicable. However, if the reading is Shechem then everything would fall into place. Gen. 3.18;35.4 explicitly mentions Shechem can the same name is connected with the land that Joseph's descendant inherited from Jacob (Gen. 48.22). While the well of Jacob itself is not mentioned in the Old Testament, there was a well about 10 feet deep mentioned in this area by early Christian pilgrims (see, Brown 1978:160. Today it identified as being at the foot of Mt. Gerezim which is broadly accepted. What is interesting is that the geographical knowledge used in Jn. 4 shows a familiarity with not just Palestine but with a specific location. It may well be that Jesus knew the site and naturally oriented himself towards it for some rest weary as he was from his walking. John gives the time of day as *noon*, the hottest part of the day. The description of Jesus as tired, thirsty, needing to sit down because it is hot, are all part of John's intention to allow some glimpse of the humanity of Jesus and therefore dispel any notion of Docetism (the idea that Jesus only 'seemed' or 'appeared' to be human) of which John is sometimes accused. Some have sought to find significance in the fact that John specifically mentions the time as *noon* and thereby seek to link to the crucifixion of Jesus where noon is also the *hour* (Jn. 19.14) where Jesus says that he is *thirsty* (Jn. 19.28) but this seems to see significance where there is none.

Once John has set the naturalness of the scene he introduces the woman at Jn. 4.7 with the description *a Samaritan woman came to draw water*, he offers no other description of her yet in this simple phrase has said everything that is important: she is *Samaritan,* a *woman* and she has come for *water*. Meetings at wells are a common feature of Old Testament encounters e.g. Gen. 24.11;[1] 29.2;[2] Ex. 2.15.[3] At one level there is nothing extraordinary about the encounter, Jesus, relying on oriental customs of hospitality, simply asks for a drink. But the location and the persons involved are what make it unusual and it is the woman who points this out in her reply to Jesus, she does not refuse to give him a drink, but she surprised by and perhaps suspicious of the request (Jn. 4.9):

> What? You a Jew ask me, a woman of Samaria for a drink?

The narrator inserts the explanatory phrase *Jews use nothing in common with Samaritans*. (see extensive comment by Barrett 1985:233 and Brown's brief comment 1978:170) This is an aside which highlights the deep seated dislike or even hatred that the Jews felt for the Samaritans and vice versa stemming from the fact that the Samaritans were the descendants of two groups: those who were left behind following the destruction of the Northern Kingdom in 722 BC and colonists imported by the Assyrians from Babylonia and Media. But there were also political and religious differences. The Samaritans had persistently thwarted attempts by the Jews to restore the Temple after the Babylonian exile and in second century BC they collaborated with the Syrians in their war against the Jews. They refused to worship at Jerusalem and worshipped at Mt. Gerezim (the temple there was burned in 128 BC by the Jewish High Priest), accepted only the Five Books of Moses and had a different understanding of the Messiah (see below). It is this historical background which explains *Jews use nothing in common with Samaritans*. It may be that the Evangelist has in mind here the Jewish suspicion about the ritual uncleanness of Samaritans. A regulation from 65-66 AD considered that Samaritan women were *menstruants from the cradle*

---

[1] He made the camels kneel down outside the city by the well of water; it was towards evening, the time when women go out to draw water.

[2] As he looked, he saw a well in the field and three flocks of sheep lying there beside it; for out of that well the flocks were watered. The stone on the well's mouth was large.

[3] When Pharaoh heard of it, he sought to kill Moses. But Moses fled from Pharaoh. He settled in the land of Midian, and sat down by a well.

and thus one could not be certain that they were ritually clean (Mullins 2002:152 n.89). Some have tried to suggest that this shows that Jesus is challenging the cultural and religious mores of his own time and being deliberately provocative, whatever the case may be in relation to this idea, Jesus is not openly challenging the ritual regulations' understanding of Samaritans, he is simply ignoring them as they have nothing to do with what is about to unfold. He is simply tired, hot and thirsty and has asked from water. That question sets in train a wonderful narrative that relies on question, answer, misunderstanding, explanation, literalness, irony; soliloquy and chorus.

Jesus does not bother to refer to the issues of divisiveness which the Samaritan Woman has highlighted (Jn. 4.10). As in his conversation with Nicodemus in the previous chapter, Jesus moves the discussion to another plane altogether where such divisions simply do not exist (Jn. 4.10):

> If you knew the gift of God and who it is that is saying to you
> 'Give me a drink' you would have asked him and he would have
> given you living water

Some have tried to suggest that *gift of God* refers to Jesus himself but it is more likely that it refers to the gift that God will give in and through Jesus (his teaching, revelation, the Spirit all of which have been mentioned in the conversation with Nicodemus). If the woman knew that and the one who was speaking, then she would not be preoccupying herself with ancient problems between the Jews and Samaritans, she would be asking for such water immediately. However, the woman has no idea what he is talking about, in fact, her reply demonstrates the extent of her lack of understanding. She concentrates on the very real practical issue of how the water Jesus wants to drink is to be obtained, after all, he has no bucket and it is a deep well. She may still be making a reference to the non sharing of drinking vessels between Jews and Samaritans since Jesus brought nothing to put into the well, whereas she has brought her own vessel. But she may be trying to work out what Jesus means: living *water* was water that flowed from a spring just like the water in the well they were both at, Jacob's Well and that was a gift of God insofar as God gave it to Jacob and Jacob gave it to the his people (Jn. 4.12). Where is she expected to get such water? And is Jesus suggesting that he is is greater than our father Jacob? This is an example of the irony that is to be found in John's gospel as a literary device. The woman is unconsciously stating a truth in the form of a sarcastic question. The word for *well* used in Jn. 4.11-12 is 'phrear' but in Jn. 4.6 it is 'pēgē' while there is not much to distinguish these two terms, the former has more of the meaning 'cistern' whereas the latter could be understood as 'fountain' (cf. Mullins 2002:255; Brown 1978:170). John could be suggesting that while Jacob's Well in the early reference is a fountain, when the conversation turns to Jesus' explanation of living water, it is Jesus who is now the fountain and Jacob's Well a mere cistern.

What is implicit in the narrative is that Jesus is greater than Jacob but he does not state this openly, instead using water both as reality and image, Jesus contrasts *this water* of Jacob with the water he offers (Jn. 4.3-14). Jesus is not saying there is something wrong with water or that it does not quench thirst, he had himself asks for water from the well but what he is saying that it quenches the physical thirst but that is all it can do. Whoever drinks the water from the well will be thirsty again but the gift Jesus offers *the water I will give* will quench thirst forever. This is water that a person will not have to travel miles for in the hot, dusty noon day sun but it will be inside them as a *spring leaping up inside them.* The word Greek word for springing/leaping is used of beings that move/dart very quickly and this is the only time it is applied to water (cf. Mullins 2002:155; see Barrett's comment 1985:234-235). In the Septuagint it is used of the spirit of God as it rests on Samson, Saul and David (which may suggest that in the Fourth Gospel the living water is the Spirit). This will spring up within a person and so one drink will not satisfy but as the gift of God it is eternal and a renewing source of life. Some have sought to see in this contrast some form of Hellenistic dualistic background but this may be reading too much into the text or failing to forcefully highlight the context in the overall replacement motifs that dominate the gospel. The contrast is being made between what Jacob, the Patriarch of the Samaritans gave to his own people (or children since the woman refers to as *our father*) and what Jesus will give. The limitations of Jacob's water have already been mentioned as will the limitations of the 'food' that Moses gave in the desert contrasted with the food that Jesus will give (Jn. 6). As the woman will ask for *this water,* so the crowd will ask for this bread and while there may be elements of contrast between illusion (the Samaritan woman asking for physical water) and reality (the symbolic living water of Jesus), the narrative sets itself within the history of salvation in the revelation of God to Israel and Jesus is indeed the revelation for all Jews and Gentiles but is this precisely as the Messiah that Israel (and the Samaritans in their understanding) longed for. Joseph had given the well to Jacob, thus the water that was a reminder to the Samaritans that God was involved with his people.

Jesus may have in mind the same tradition when he speaks of *living water* for images of water as the gift that the people desired from God abound throughout the Old Testament, e.g., Ps. 12.3;[1] 23.2ff;[2] 36.8;[3] in Ps. 42.1 the soul *thirsts for God,* in Ps. 39.9 God is the *fountain of life;* in Jer. 2.13 he is *the fountain of living waters;* in Is. 55.1f salvation is the living water *for those who are thirsty.* And the Wisdom tradition uses many such images, e.g., Prov.13.14;[4] 18.4;[5] Sir. 24.4.[6] And Jesus using the images and symbols of the understanding of salvation history among the Jews is seen elsewhere *bread from heaven, light of the world* (both for Torah). Thus, it does not seem to be that the Evangelist is using these as terms which point to an antithesis between an illusory world and a real world but rather from the point of salvation-history in the sense that it is Jesus who brings fulfilment to this tradition for it is he who brings the truth and the fullness

---

[1] He makes me lie down in green pastures; he leads me beside still waters

[2] They feast on the abundance of your house, and you give them drink from the river of your delights.

[3] May the Lord cut off all flattering lips, the tongue that makes great boasts

[4] The teaching of the wise is a fountain of life, so that one may avoid the snares of death.

[5] The words of the mouth are deep waters; the fountain of wisdom is a gushing stream.

[6] dwelt in the highest heavens, and my throne was in a pillar of cloud.

of God. Exactly how Jesus is the fulfilment of this he does not say but what is clear is that in Jesus this gift of God for which the people longed is already present.

Her respectful reply to Jesus at Jn. 4.15, therefore, (from the point of view of where she is) is not unreasonable:

> Sir, give me this water so that I may never be thirsty and not
> have to come here to draw water

The woman still does not grasp what Jesus is saying and while her attitude shifts slightly it is still preoccupied with the more practical realisations of this. Jesus makes no reply this is but rather suddenly introduces a topic into the conversation that seems out of place with what has gone before and it is necessary to quote the entire section of conversation (Jn. 4.16-19)

> Go, call your husband and return here. The woman answered
> him, I have no husband. Jesus said to her, You are right in
> saying I have no husband, for you have had five husbands and
> the one you have now is not your husband. What you have said
> is true. The woman said to him, Sir, I see you are a prophet.

Where has this come from? Why does Jesus shift the conversation? What is his purpose in doing this? Many explanations have been offered for this seemingly disjointed insertion into the conversation with the woman (cf. Mullins 2002:156; Brown 1978:171; Barrett 1985:235). One of the most popular views is that the question of Jesus is a lead in to the issue of worship which follows and that what is strong here is marriage allegory. The five husbands are deemed to be the gods of the five nations which settled in Samaria from Assyria (2 K 17.24[1]), while the husband Jesus invites her to call is the present form of Samaritan (and by Jewish standards illicit)

---

[1] The king of Assyria brought people from Babylon, Cuthah, Avva, Hamath, and Sepharvaim, and placed them in the cities of Samaria in place of the people of Israel; they took possession of Samaria, and settled in its cities.

worship. As interesting as this sounds there are serious flaws with it: there were not five but seven nations that worshipped their gods and this they did simultaneously not successively (2 K 17.29[2]) and there is no way that Yahweh could be called the *illicit* husband of Samaritans. But there is no evidence for this allegorical interpretation in the text and John uses symbolic interpretation in his gospel not allegorical further the five god allegory would have had to have been well known among Jews and Samaritans for it to have have any impact here and how far such an allegory was known cannot be determined.

The other popular way of looking at the question and the five husbands issue is to see it as Jesus acting in a pastoral manner insofar as he is attempting to bring the woman to a realisation of the sinfulness of her own life (see, Ridderbos 1991:160). This would mean that the woman's answer at Jn. 4.17, *I have no husband,* would be a way of trying to extricate herself from an uncomfortable kind of questioning which does not work since Jesus pursues the natter even deeper. She then introduces a seemingly unconnected issue (where *true worship* takes place) to try and knock Jesus off the subject. Elements of this interpretation are plausible, e.g., Jesus trying to lead the woman to an acknowledgement of her situation (though not by any supernatural knowledge on his part) and what Jesus brings out of her does not cast her in a good moral light. But in essence what Jesus has done is develop the conversation with the Samaritan Woman by moving it onto a deeper level (see, Mullins 2002:156; Brown 1978:171). The woman offers not further explanation or clarification and Jesus does not condemn or judge her for her answer *what you have said is true* (Jn. 4.18c) and we can take from this that the woman is well aware of her own situation and does not need Jesus to point it out. There seems no good reason, therefore, not to take the words of Jesus literally as a manifestation of his supernatural knowledge and the only response the woman makes to Jesus is more about him that it is about her *Sir, I see you are a prophet.* This style of

---

[2]   But every nation still made gods of its own and put them in the shrines of the high places that the people of Samaria had made, every nation in the cities in which they lived.

supernatural knowledge was present in Jn. 1.47 when Nathaniel comes to Jesus and Jesus is able to share his insight with Nathaniel and elicits the response *Rabbi, you are the Son of God, you are the King of Israel* in the same way the woman responds with *Sir, I see you are a prophet*. What Jesus has done, therefore, is not bring the woman to any awareness about who she is, or what her state in life is, but rather brought her to an awareness of who *he* Is. The woman has thus moved in the conversation from referring to Jesus as *a Jew* to *a prophet* but this is as far as she has got (Mullins 2002:156; Brown 1978:171). But even so, the woman does seem to be articulating the idea that a prophet was someone who was gifted with supernatural knowledge and through whom a person could her the word of God pronounced and while the Samaritans did not accept the prophetical books of the Old Testament, they did accept the Five Books of Moses so her understanding of prophet here is probably derived from Deut. 18.15-22 (see Barrett 1985:236).

Having initially been distrustful of Jesus, the woman has moved from addressing him as *a Jew* to *Sir* to *a prophet*. She has listened and though misunderstood, she has tried to grasp what Jesus was saying about *gift of God* and *living water*. At Jn. 4.20 she seems to have enough confidence to ask Jesus' opinion about a fundamental issue of division between the Jews and Samaritans (perhaps because she has identified him as a prophet who could speak authoritatively on such matters?) and that is the proper place wherein God is to be worshipped. The Samaritan Pentateuch in Deut. 27.4[1] tells of the instruction given to Joshua to build a shrine on Mt. Gerizim, the sacred mountain of the Samaritans, which was situated near Jacob's Well. In due course they built a temple there which was destroyed in 128 BC but religious worship continued there and it remained a major source of contention and division between the Jews and the Samaritans. The woman locates herself firmly within her own ancestral religious tradition while at the same time highlighting the difference between Samaritans and Jews:

---

[1] Therefore it shall be when you have gone over Jordan, [that] you shall set up these stones, which I command you this day, in mount Ebal, and you shall plaster them with plaster.

> our fathers worshipped on this mountain but you say the place
> where people must worship is Jerusalem

Notice the way in which the pronouns are used *our..you..people:* she stands as a representative of her people (*our*) and addresses Jesus as representative of the Jews (*you*) and speaks in indefinite collective terms of all *people.* There is a sense in which the *mountain* under which they meet and its meaning has been present throughout the conversation: given that there has been much talk of the well, water, Patriarchal ancestors, it was inevitable that the issue of the significance of the mountain would emerge (see Brown 1978:171). Jesus does not circumvent the question, he rather shifts the parameters by moving the contentious question of *place* of worship to the question of the nature and universality of worship itself.

Jesus begins with, *Believe me woman* which carries the same weight as the solemn declarations which later in appear in John which begin *amen, amen, I say to you* and which indicate that what follows is a solemn pronouncement by Jesus. Here the solemn pronouncement is the arrival of an *hour* when the Samaritans (her included (*you*) will worship not in places such as the hallowed Gerizim or Jerusalem but in another 'place' which is not geographical. This does not mean that Jesus is equating Gerizim and Jerusalem: he points out the misguidedness of the Samaritans (at best) and at worst their ignorance (Jn. 4.22):

> You worship what you do not know, we (the Jews) worship
> what we do know for salvation is of the Jews

Some would suggest that this is an addition or a gloss since it appears antithetical to the manner in which Jesus clashes harshly with 'the Jews' in later sections of the gospel (e.g. Jn. 8.41;[1] 10.34;[2] 13.33[3]) and the Jesus of

---

[1]   You are indeed doing what your father does.' They said to him, 'We are not illegitimate children; we have one father, God himself.'

[2]   Jesus answered, 'Is it not written in your law, "I said, you are gods"?

[3]   Little children, I am with you only a little longer. You will look for me; and as I said to the Jews so now I say to you, "Where I am going, you cannot come."

John would never have made a remark like this. The use of the term 'the Jews' in the main refers to the leaders of the Jewish people who are outwardly contentious and hostile to Jesus and does not refer to the whole people. The term *the Jews*, therefore, does not always carry the antithetical meaning in John. Jesus, as a Jew, is speaking to a Samaritan, a foreigner and is placing great significance on the fact that the revelation is given to Israel and so any form of worship which opposes this revelation is, in reality, no form of worship at all but simply a self choice (see, Ridderbos 1991:163). To interpret Jesus' use of 'the Jews' in every case as antithetical is to misunderstand John's intention in those sections where he is quite deliberately referring to the religious leaders and not the whole people. Further, is it to place upon the gospel an anti-Semitism that is simply not present either in intention or text. It is undoubtedly true that in the Fourth Gospel Jesus does distance himself from 'the Jews' (understood as the leaders of the people) and 'their' law and has some very harsh and brutal things to say to and about them; however, it is equally true that the mission of Jesus in John is firmly fixed in the revelation of God and his salvation to Israel. Thus *salvation is from the Jews* cannot be interpreted as a gloss or a comment inserted later but must be understood as a genuine part of the verse.

Jesus now moves his pronouncement to an even deeper level. Having asserted that the *hour is coming* when 'place' will not be the crucial factor in worship and that salvation is rooted in the revelation to Israel, Jesus re-emphasises that statement at Jn. 4.23 *But the hour is coming, and is now here* (see also Jn. 5.25) and the use of the future tense indicates that this hour lies in the future while the present indicates that it has already dawned. John has the same paradox about the eschatological moment that the Synoptics have when they speak about the kingdom being here but lying in the future. Jesus has already told the woman that worship will happen in a different 'place' when that hour comes and the new 'place' is in *spirit and truth* and this will be the characteristic of *true worshippers*. This form of worship replaces and supersedes geographical locations but it does not mean that true worship exists or consists in worshipping in some transcendental realm above and beyond the existential reality of the visible world. *Spirit and truth* the descriptors of the new relationship that exists between *true worshippers* and God who has realised the future *hour* in the present sending of his Son because *he so loved the world* (Jn. 3.16). This new relationship between God and humanity is not expressed, in the first instance, through place, cult, or its various liturgical forms but through the Spirit of God. And that relationship is *now here* because it is Jesus who is the 'way and the truth' to the 'life' that is new relationship to, worship of God who *is spirit*.

This statement of Jesus in itself brings no response from her, however, she does intuit, perhaps because Jesus says believe *me woman the hour is coming*, that it has something to do with expectations of the future and this she appears either not to have heard or ignoring Jesus other words *and is now here* when she makes reference to the 'Messiah' who will come. However, the woman is a Samaritan and the Samaritans did not share the same notion of the 'Messiah' as the Jews did, in fact, their name for this coming person was Taheb (which means *one who returns*) and *when he comes he will show us all things* (Jn. 4.25) (see, MacDonald 1964:362-65; Dexinger 1989:272-76). Exactly how the Samaritans understood the Taheb cannot be adequately determined because of lack of historical reference (Brown 1978:172). But the Samaritans did accept the Pentateuch and so she must have in mind here the *prophet-like-Moses* (Deut. 18.18[1]) who would settle issues about the Law and who would restore proper worship. The woman feels comfortable enough in her own understanding of this prophet of the future (and she has already referred to Jesus as *a prophet*) to make the leap of connectedness between what Jesus is saying and her own understanding. Jesus himself does not engage in fine tuning her understanding of 'Messiah' but meets the woman where she is in her own understanding by focusing the *hour* that is *now* in the person who is *here*

---

[1]   I will raise up for them a prophet like you from among their own people; I will put my words in the mouth of the prophet, who shall speak to them everything that I command.

when he responds to her *I who speak to you am he*. By making this statement, Jesus is telling the woman that all the prophets, all the expectation that she has voiced *I know that the Messiah will come..and he will tell us everything* find in him their realisation and fulfilment. It is the one who speaks to her is the one she and the Jews have been waiting for. All history, all revelation, all salvation is present in the person of Jesus and not just for the Samaritans and Jews but for everyone (cf. Mullins 2002:159).

d. The Dialogue With The Disciples (Jn. 4.27-42)

At this point the conversation is interrupted for the disciples return (Jn. 4.27-42) and the Samaritan woman returns to her own people. But John masterfully and with great conciseness presents us with a 'split screen' scene: in one frame the astonishment of the disciples that Jesus has been alone in conversation with a woman which was not considered the done thing by the social mores of his time, and this is further exacerbated by the fact it was a Samaritan woman. Yet none of the disciples ask him what he thinks he is playing at! They remain silent, though John articulates the questions that they undoubtedly desired to ask or is it perhaps that they know that Jesus' motivations for speaking with the woman are in accord with his reasons which have nothing to do with social conventions or religious differentiation or contention? Perhaps it was the return of the disciples that prompted the woman to leave but John makes it clear that she returns with haste and *left the water jar* (Jn. 4.28). Since it was with the water jar that she had come to the well to draw water, she has forgotten the original intention and left the 'reason' for it behind. But John is not highlighting her absent mindedness but rather her enthusiasm to share her discovery with her own townspeople. There is wonderful interweaving of idea and association in this scene of enthusiasm when the woman speaks to her own people (Jn. 4.28-29). The woman has been impressed and not a little amazed at the knowledge Jesus has shown of her life and history; this led her to move from calling Jesus a *Jew* to a *prophet* and now something much more profound is in her mind and heart: *could this person really be the Messiah*? The question must be seen a rhetorical device: it is hardly likely that the woman would have forgotten her water jar and rushed back to the city to bring the inhabitants out to see a mere prophet. The townspeople want to see for themselves, perhaps to make their own mind up, or perhaps they are nonplussed at the woman's enthusiasm. So, having heard the woman's statement and on her word alone, they leave the city and begin to make their way to Jesus. The Samaritan Woman, isolated and alienated within her own community because of her unseemly lifestyle becomes one of the major witnesses to Jesus in the gospel of John. Thus far in the gospel the encounter that Jesus has had have been individual: the disciples who follow him in Jn. 1, the conversation with Nicodemus in Jn. 3.1-17, the conversation with the woman in Jn. 4.1-42 but now for the first time we get the appearance of the 'crowd' how, John tells us *left the city and were on their way to him* (Jn. 4.30).

While the woman is giving her witness to Jesus as the Messiah, the disciples are urging Jesus to take care of more mundane matters by encouraging him to eat something. At the beginning of Jn. 4.8 we have been told that *his disciples had gone into the city to buy food*, so on their return it is not unnatural that they should try to get Jesus to eat given the fact that he is already tired, hungry and thirsty from the journey which is what prompts him to it at the well and ask for something to drink. Food becomes an important motif in this pericope and provides the primary imagery by which Jesus shifts the perspective from earthly food to something much more profound (as he will do in Jn. 6) (cf. Ridderbos 1985:167). Food, eating, water, drinking, harvests all these important images are woven together by John in this conversation and referring back to the 'split screen' while this conversation is taking place the Samaritans are coming to Jesus because it is they who are the first fruits of the 'harvest' (Jn. 4.35-37). The reply that Jesus gives to their insistence that he eat something call us back to the beginning of his conversation with the woman: there Jesus after asking for a drink and the woman highlighting some of the practical issues involved (he has no bucket, the well is deep) Jesus uses the image of water and drinking to lead the woman into deeper understanding and recognition. His understanding and use of these ordinary everyday things are not the same as hers. So too here, Jesus' enigmatic and confusing reply to their insistence that he (Jn. 4.32):

> eat something.. I have food to eat that you do not know about

is completely misunderstood by the disciples who can do no more than ask what is, in the end, a ridiculous question to each other and not to him: *surely no one has brought him something to eat?* The lack of understanding of the disciples, is not used by John (as it is say by Mark) (Ridderbos 1985:167) to demonstrate lack of faith more a lack of insight, as for example here: Jesus has just revealed himself as the Messiah not just for Jews but for everyone, yet when pressing him to eat the disciples refer to him as 'Rabbi'. Yet as the gospel unfolds Jesus continues to patiently teach and form the disciples so that with the resurrection their insights are deepened and their understanding clear. But that is some way off yet.

Jesus continues in the enigmatic vein by telling them that *my food* (Jn. 4.34), what gives him life, sustains, nourishes him is to *do the will of him who sent me*. Matthew tells us that Jesus considered his first priority to be the *lost sheep of the house of Israel* (Mt. 10.6; 15.24), this is undoubtedly his priority but now he sees the Samaritans included in that number since they too worshipped the God of Abraham and Moses perhaps this is what Jesus had in mind when he said, *Four months more, then comes the harvest,* may have been a well known proverb indicating that something was certain to come but the time for it to do so was not known or delayed or it may simply have indicated the time of year, but the Samaritans do not have to wait for the 'harvest time' for Jesus says, *look around you, and see how the fields are ripe for harvesting* for the time for the harvest has arrived (on this point see, Barrett 1985:241). Jesus has done the *will of the Father* and the fruit of that labour is the fact that Samaritans come out to meet him and they ask *him to stay with them; and he stayed there for two days.* In John 1 the first disciples had asked Jesus where he lived Jesus replied *come and see,* they followed him to his dwelling and *stayed with him the rest of that day* (Jn. 1.35-42). It was following this encounter with Jesus that Andrew found his brother Peter and brings him to Jesus, and after Philip has been called by Jesus he in turn brings Nathaniel to him. This is what the Samaritan woman does when she says to her own people (Jn. 4.29)

> Come and see a man who told me everything I have ever done!
> He cannot be the Messiah, can he?'

On hearing this, the Samaritans *left the city and were on their way to him.* These terms, therefore, *come and see,* and *stayed with/there* indicate the invitation to and experience of discipleship. The Samaritan woman, therefore, is a disciple who brings others to Jesus but it is their personal experience of being with Jesus that leads them to say to her (Jn. 4.42):

> It is no longer because of what you said that we believe, for we
> have heard for ourselves, and we know that this is truly the
> Saviour of the world.

The word John uses for *what you have said* is 'lalia/lal-ee-ah' and means, speech, talk but can also mean babbling or gossip. It should not be taken to mean 'babble' here but rather that she got excited when she was speaking to her own people about Jesus. The Samaritans believe 'because of her word' (Jn. 4.39). This expression is significant because it recurs in Jesus' 'priestly' prayer (Jn. 17.20) for his disciples where he says:

> It is not for these alone that I pray, but also for those who
> believe in me "through their word

John describes the Samaritan woman's work in that village in precisely the same language he uses to describe the disciples' ministry. The key, however, is that it is direct experience of Jesus that leads to faith for Jesus is not simple professed as the Jewish Messiah or the Samaritan Taheb but *Saviour of the world*. This same universal title is used in I Jn. 4.14 and in the first century this phrase was often used of Caesar. Roman persecution occurred because Christians used this title exclusively for Jesus and John may be emphasising this to his community: it is Jesus who is the true *Saviour of the world* and not any worldly emperor.

e. The Faith of the Samaritan Woman

Some of the approach to this narrative focuses on the moral state of the Samaritan Woman but her role in this narrative is much more complex and revealing than that. Before proceeding to explore this, it may be worthwhile just to rehearse once again the cultural context of the narrative. In this encounter Jesus crosses not just the geographical 'border' of Samaria but also crosses the 'borders' of the religious, cultural and social divide since he speaks openly with a Samaritan and a Samaritan who was a woman. Such open and public conversation was looked upon as inappropriate in Jewish society and if such conversations with Jewish women was seen to be inappropriate then even more so with Samaritan women who were considered to be perpetually 'unclean'. This explains why the woman is surprised at Jesus' request she give him a drink for in doing so Jesus would have been rendered unclean by the dictates of Jewish law. It is worth noting here that when the disciples return their surprise is not that he is talking to a Samaritan but that he is talking to a woman so openly.

Women were considered to be incapable of beign taught or of engaging in in depth theological discussion. Study of the Torah was forbidden them as this was considered the 'business' of men, indeed, one Rabbi said that if a man taught his daughter the Torah then he might as well teach her 'lechery' and another said that that rather than teach a woman the Torah, it should be burned. Because of their intellectual weakness and what

Josephus called their 'flightiness' and 'brashness', they could not give witness. However, in his encounter with the Samaritan woman Jesus does not so much challenge these religious, cultural and social mores, as ignore them completely. He takes the Samaritan woman on an unfolding journey of faith through a complex theological reflection and discourse on the *living water,* the *nature of true worship*, the nature of God who is *spirit* and at every stage the Samaritan woman, though she may not understand completely what Jesus is saying, asks her questions, makes her own responses, expresses her own faith until finally Jesus, in answer to her clear statement (Jn. 4.25):

> I know that Messiah is coming' (who is called Christ). 'When he
> comes, he will proclaim all things to us

he reveals to her that he is the one she speaks of. When the disciples arrive back, the Samaritan woman departs to her own village but in doing so she leaves behind her *water pots* (Jn. 4.28) and bears witness to Jesus by her proclamation (Jn. 4.29):

> Come and see a man who told me everything I have ever done!
> He cannot be the Messiah, can he?'

and the response of her own village is that they come out to meet Jesus at the well.

f. The Samaritan Woman As Disciple (Jn. 4.27-30)

Three observations are worth making at this point which allow the Samaritan woman to be understood in terms of discipleship:

- she leaves her water pots behind
- she proclaims her grasp of Jesus' identity to her
- the Samaritans respond to her and go to Jesus

In Mk. 1.16-20 Jesus calls Simon and Andrew to be his disciples and *immediately* they leave their *nets* and follow him; James and John *immediately* leave their *father in the boat* and the *hired hands* and the *nets*. In other words, the first group of disciples leave everything (symbolised by the *nets, father, boat, hired hands*) and follow Jesus as his disciples. In Mk. 2.13-14[1] Levi (Matthew) is *sitting at the tax booth*, Jesus calls him and Levi *got up and followed him* thus leaving behind everything (symbolised by the tax booth) for discipleship of Jesus. In Mk. 10.46-52,[2] the narrative of 'blind Bartimaeus', Bartimaeus, *throwing off his cloak* came to Jesus and after his healing *followed him on the way*. As the cloak was everything that Bartimaeus owned he leaves this behind and follows Jesus as a disciple. In Mk. 10.28-30, Jesus reassures those who have *left everything* to follow him that they will be rewarded a *hundred fold*. And in Jn. 1.35-42, the disciples of John the Baptist, one of whom is Andrew, leave John and *follow after* Jesus. Andrew in turn brings his brother Simon to Jesus (Jn. 1.41-42) and later in Jn. 1.44-47 Philip finds Nathaniel and brings him to Jesus. It is in this light of leaving *everything* behind to follow after Jesus and bringing other to Jesus that the Samaritan woman can be viewed as a disciple since she leaves behind her *water pots*, tells the Samaritans about Jesus (as does Andrew to Peter and Philip to Nathaniel) who then come *out* to him (see, Hall 1971/72:56-57; Daube 1950:37-47). The Samaritan woman, therefore, is clearly to be understood as a disciple (Mullins 2002:160). It is also worth noting that the words she uses to the Samaritans, *come and see* (Jn. 4.29) are the same words of invitation Jesus speaks to the first two disciples in Jn.

---

[1] Jesus went out again beside the lake; the whole crowd gathered around him, and he taught them. As he was walking along, he saw Levi son of Alphaeus sitting at the tax booth, and he said to him, 'Follow me.' And he got up and followed him.

[2] They came to Jericho. As he and his disciples and a large crowd were leaving Jericho, Bartimaeus son of Timaeus, a blind beggar, was sitting by the roadside. When he heard that it was Jesus of Nazareth, he began to shout out and say, 'Jesus, Son of David, have mercy on me!' Many sternly ordered him to be quiet, but he cried out even more loudly, 'Son of David, have mercy on me!' Jesus stood still and said, 'Call him here.' And they called the blind man, saying to him, 'Take heart; get up, he is calling you.' So throwing off his cloak, he sprang up and came to Jesus. Then Jesus said to him, 'What do you want me to do for you?' The blind man said to him, 'My teacher, let me see again.' Jesus said to him, 'Go; your faith has made you well.' Immediately he regained his sight and followed him on the way.

1.39 and they *went with him and remained the rest of that day with him* (again it is worth noting that to remain, abide with Jesus is to be his disciple cf. Jn. 15.1-11). They are also the words used by Philip to Nathaniel in Jn. 1.46. When the Samaritan woman makes the invitation to her own village, they go out to meet Jesus and as Jesus invited the first disciples to spend the day with him, the Samaritans invite Jesus to spend time with them (Jn. 4.40a) and he stays *two days* with them (Jn. 4.40c).

Two other observations strengthen the image of the Samaritan woman as a disciple. The first can be found in the statement that Jesus makes to the disciples when he says (Jn. 4.38):

> I sent you to reap that for which you did not labour. Others have
> laboured, and you have entered into their labour

and the other is to be found in the words of the Samaritans to the woman (Jn. 4.42):

> It is no longer because of what you said that we believe, for we
> have heard for ourselves, and we know that this is truly the
> Saviour of the world

Jn. 4.38 is from the 'parable' of the harvest that Jesus shares with the disciples. The Samaritan woman has gone off to her village and is proclaiming Jesus to the Samaritans, they in response come out to meet him, as Jesus speaks to the disciples he looks up and sees the Samaritans (the harvest) coming to him. But this is not the work of the disciples, it is the work of the Samaritan woman. The Greek verb John uses for *sent* is 'apesteila' (apes-teel-a) may also be applied to the Samaritan woman for she is the one 'sent' by Jesus after her encounter (though not explicit in the text it can be read as such) since she immediately returns to her village and proclaims him to them as the 'Taleb' (Messiah). Thus the Samaritan woman engages in apostolic evangelical missionary activity (as the disciples are commissioned to cf. Mk. 6.6b-13;[1] Mt. 10.5-15;[2]). Jn. 4.42 may also be seen in the same light. Andrew brought Simon to Jesus 'through his word' (Jn. 1.40-41) and Philip brought Nathaniel to Jesus 'through his word' (Jn. 1.43-47) and later at Jn. 17.20 Jesus will say:

> It is not for these alone that I pray, but also for those who believe in me *through their word*

What is of importance here, therefore, is that Jesus uses the same language of the Samaritan woman. Thus, Jesus ignores the restrictions that culture, race, or religious understanding would place on him and the woman in these 'border' crossings and treats the Samaritan woman not as someone who cannot be taught theology or be a witness, but as the direct opposite. Her response to her encounter with Jesus is discipleship and apostolic evangelical ministry. It is also worth taking note of where the encounter with the Samaritan woman appears, i.e., after the encounter with Nicodemus. Even a cursory glance at the two narratives highlights the differences between him and the Samaritan woman:

---

[1]   Then he went about among the villages teaching. He called the twelve and began to send them out two by two, and gave them authority over the unclean spirits. He ordered them to take nothing for their journey except a staff; no bread, no bag, no money in their belts; but to wear sandals and not to put on two tunics. He said to them, 'Wherever you enter a house, stay there until you leave the place. If any place will not welcome you and they refuse to hear you, as you leave, shake off the dust that is on your feet as a testimony against them.' So they went out and proclaimed that all should repent. They cast out many demons, and anointed with oil many who were sick and cured them.

[2]   These twelve Jesus sent out with the following instructions: 'Go nowhere among the Gentiles, and enter no town of the Samaritans, but go rather to the lost sheep of the house of Israel. As you go, proclaim the good news, "The kingdom of heaven has come near." Cure the sick, raise the dead, cleanse the lepers, cast out demons. You received without payment; give without payment. Take no gold, or silver, or copper in your belts, no bag for your journey, or two tunics, or sandals, or a staff; for labourers deserve their food. Whatever town or village you enter, find out who in it is worthy, and stay there until you leave. As you enter the house, greet it. If the house is worthy, let your peace come upon it; but if it is not worthy, let your peace return to you. If anyone will not welcome you or listen to your words, shake off the dust from your feet as you leave that house or town. Truly I tell you, it will be more tolerable for the land of Sodom and Gomorrah on the day of judgement than for that town.

Nicodemus	Samaritan Woman
Male	Female
Jewish	Samaritan
Pharisee	Unclean
Teacher	Uneducated
Comes by night	Comes at noon
Asks questions but does not understand	Asks questions and though does not understand persists
Not convinced by Jesus	Accepts Jesus immediately
No revelation to Nicodemus about identity given by Jesus	Revelation to woman that he is the Messiah
Disappears from discourse	Returns to own village, proclaims Jesus as Messiah
	Samaritans come to Jesus

Nicodemus, the influential, male teacher in Israel, member of the ruling council struggles to 'tune into' what Jesus is teaching him and in the end remains confused or unconvinced by Jesus' words. He does not appear again in the gospel until Jn. 7.50-51[1] where he insists that Jesus must be given a fair hearing, and at the end when he is involved in the burial of Jesus (Jn. 19.38-42[2]) which does seem to indicate that Nicodemus had come to discipleship. The Samaritan woman, outcast, marginalised, disrespected, of dubious moral life, regarded as 'perpetually unclean' by Jewish society and

---

[1] Nicodemus, who had gone to Jesus before, and who was one of them, asked, 'Our law does not judge people without first giving them a hearing to find out what they are doing, does it?'

[2] After these things, Joseph of Arimathea, who was a disciple of Jesus, though a secret one because of his fear of the Jews, asked Pilate to let him take away the body of Jesus. Pilate gave him permission; so he came and removed his body. Nicodemus, who had at first come to Jesus by night, also came, bringing a mixture of myrrh and aloes, weighing about a hundred pounds. They took the body of Jesus and wrapped it with the spices in linen cloths, according to the burial custom of the Jews. Now there was a garden in the place where he was crucified, and in the garden there was a new tomb in which no one had ever been laid. And so, because it was the Jewish day of Preparation, and the tomb was nearby, they laid Jesus there.

religion, embraces Jesus immediately as the Messiah and brings others to him, who in turn come to believe that he is the *saviour of the world*. Unlike Nicodemus she does not hide her acceptance of Jesus but boldly proclaims it. John, therefore, has chosen to place the revelation of Jesus as the Messiah not to the learned intelligentsia of the Jews but to an uneducated despised Samaritan woman. The Samaritan woman, therefore, can be seen as representative not just of individuals who are open and receptive to Jesus but of whole groups (cf. Mullins 2002:161). And in this sense, she is both a disciple and an apostle and so stands for those women, possibly in the Johannine community, who had roles as teachers, preachers and other forms of apostolic ministry.

The Woman Caught In Adultery (Jn. 7.53-8.11)

The Narrative Context

This narrative, which has become known as the 'Woman Caught in Adultery', while it is a wonderful story that illustrates the compassion of God expressed through the actions of Jesus, is not to be found in the oldest and best five manuscripts of the Greek New Testament (see, Salvoni 1960:11-15). Some of the MSS (manuscripts) place it in different places in John, e.g., after Jn. 7.26, at the end of Jn. 21 and the middle of Lk. 21 and in some MSS marks appear to indicate that the scribes/copyists were not convinced of its provenance (Metzger 1994:189). However, there is some indication that it may have been known very early in the second century, perhaps the early 100's (Hodges 1979:318-32). The story shares some features more common with Synoptic materials than John and that may indicate that the early Church felt that this narrative, given the nature of its content, was too important to completely leave out of the New Testament (see discussion in Brown 1978:335). Most of Christendom, however, has received this story as authoritative, and modern scholarship, although concluding firmly that it was not a part of John's Gospel originally, has generally recognised that this story describes an event from the life of

Christ. Furthermore, it is as well written and as theologically profound as anything else in the Gospels.

How then is this narrative to understood in the context in which it appears? The first thing to note is that it is highly unlikely that it was originally part of John's gospel, it is missing from the most important MSS and it seemingly interrupts the flow of the dialogue/discourse at the Feat of the Tabernacles that precedes it (but see below). But this does not mean that the narrative is false: the early church would not make up a story about the forgiveness of an adulteress. Its purpose was to provide an illustration of Jesus' words in Jn. 8.15: *You judge according to the flesh, but I judge no one.* What we have here, then, is a bit of Synoptic-like material stuck in the middle of John's Gospel. Its presence highlights some of the similarities and differences between John and the Synoptics. The setting is one of controversy in the temple, though the way this is introduced in Jn. 7.53-8.2 is much more like Luke's style (cf. Lk. 19.47;[1] 20.1;[2] 21.37[3]) than John's. Furthermore, the theme of judgement also corresponds to the theme of the larger section in the gospel (Jn. 7.24;[4] 8.15-16[5]). This setting and theme probably led to its inclusion in John at this point. It is usually said that this story interrupts John's flow of thought, as though a patch of a different pattern has been sewn onto a piece of cloth. On the contrary, while the style of Jesus' self-revelation is quite different in John, this added story contains an example of the Synoptic form of revelation, which shows that Jesus is more than a human prophet. So although there is a patch, the patch is of the same pattern as the whole, albeit less bright. While the style of the material is very different, the substance is quite similar. This specific story is a case

---

[1] Every day he was teaching in the temple. The chief priests, the scribes, and the leaders of the people kept looking for a way to kill him.
[2] One day, as he was teaching the people in the temple and telling the good news, the chief priests and the scribes came with the elders.
[3] Every day he was teaching in the temple, and at night he would go out and spend the night on the Mount of Olives, as it was called.
[4] Do not judge by appearances, but judge with right judgement.'
[5] You judge by human standards; I judge no one. Yet even if I do judge, my judgement is valid; for it is not I alone who judge, but I and the Father who sent me.

in point of what is generally true of the relation between the Synoptics and John. The Synoptics have as high a Christology as John does, though they express it differently.

a. The Woman Caught In Adultery (Jn. 7.53-8.11)

While Jesus went to the Mount of Olives. Early in the morning he came again to the temple. All the people came to him and he sat down and began to teach them. The scribes and the Pharisees brought a woman who had been caught in adultery; and making her stand before all of them, they said to him, 'Teacher, this woman was caught in the very act of committing adultery. Now in the law Moses commanded us to stone such women. Now what do you say?' They said this to test him, so that they might have some charge to bring against him. Jesus bent down and wrote with his finger on the ground. When they kept on questioning him, he straightened up and said to them, 'Let anyone among you who is without sin be the first to throw a stone at her.' And once again he bent down and wrote on the ground. When they heard it, they went away, one by one, beginning with the elders; and Jesus was left alone with the woman standing before him. Jesus straightened up and said to her, 'Woman, where are they? Has no one condemned you?' She said, 'No one, sir.' And Jesus said, 'Neither do I condemn you. Go your way, and from now on do not sin again

A close examination of the narrative shows that it develops in four scenes or episodes:

Scene One: Setting the scene (Jn. 7.53-8:2)
Scene Two: The challenge presented to Jesus by the Jewish
           leaders (Jn. 8.3-6)
Scene Three: Jesus' response to the opponents (Jn. 8.6-9)

Scene Four: Jesus' response to the woman (Jn. 8.10-11)

b. Scene One (Jn. 7.53-8.2)

The meeting of the chief priests and Pharisees with their servants, the temple guards (Jn. 7.45-52), presumably took place on the last (and seventh) day of the feast (cf. 7.37). As this passage stands in this context, Jesus is coming early to the temple to teach on the morning of the added eighth day of the feast, which was a day of rest (Lev. 23.39[1]).

c. Scene Two (Jn. 8.3-6)

At the outset the treatment of the woman here is both humiliating and publicly demeaning, which perhaps is the intention of *the scribes and the Pharisees* who bring her to Jesus (see Brown 1978:337 for a discussion of this topic). Since it is *early in the morning* it may be reasonable to assume that she had been *caught in the act of adultery* the previous evening and had therefore been held all night. If the woman had indeed been caught in the very act of adultery her trepidation would have been for as the Pharisees and scribes point out *the law Moses commanded us to stone such women* (cf. Ridderbos 1985:287. However, there is a certain chauvinism (or even misogyny) here for the *law of Moses* says that the *man* and woman must be put to death (Lev. 20.10;[2] Deut. 22.22-24[3]):

> If a man commits adultery with the wife of his neighbour, both
> the adulterer and the adulteress shall be put to death.

---

[1]   Now, the fifteenth day of the seventh month, when you have gathered in the produce of the land, you shall keep the festival of the Lord, lasting seven days; a complete rest on the first day, and a complete rest on the eighth day.

[2]   If a man commits adultery with the wife of his neighbour, both the adulterer and the adulteress shall be put to death.

[3]   If a man is caught lying with the wife of another man, both of them shall die, the man who lay with the woman as well as the woman. So you shall purge the evil from Israel. If there is a young woman, a virgin already engaged to be married, and a man meets her in the town and lies with her, you shall bring both of them to the gate of that town and stone them to death, the young woman because she did not cry for help in the town and the man because he violated his neighbour's wife. So you shall purge the evil from your midst.

> If a man is caught lying with the wife of another man, both of them shall die, the man who lay with the woman as well as the woman. So you shall purge the evil from Israel.

The Pharisees and scribes are certainly zealous for the Law but it is shallow and superficial since their motivation is not the truth of the Law or its justice their approach to Jesus is pernicious and shabby (Jn. 8.6):

> They said this to test him, so that they might have some charge to bring against him

But they are also being disingenuous because there is no evidence that this sentence was ever carried out. Indeed, John's gospel indicate elsewhere that the Sanhedrin did not have the power to exact a capital punishment (perhaps reflecting the tradition that the Romans withdrew this right from them in c.30 AD) (see point made by Ridderbos 1985:288). Another question which emerges is: has the woman already been sentenced or has she not yet been tried? If it is the former, then why is she being brought to Jesus? Are the Pharisees and scribes asking Jesus to decide whether or not she should be stoned, as the Law says? Or if she has not been tried then what are they asking Jesus' opinion for? (see, Mullins 2002:219). There is also more than a little deceit here because they are asking a question in supposed loyalty to Moses about an aspect of the Law of Moses which they themselves most likely have not kept. Furthermore, since the law says both the man and the woman who commit adultery are to be killed, we are left wondering why the man was not brought in as well. It may be that he had escaped, but the fact that only the woman is brought raises suspicions and does not speak well of their zeal for the law of Moses; for if they were really committed, they would have brought the man as well. Indeed, the law makes it clear that stoning could only take place after a careful trial, which included the chance for the condemned to confess his or her wrong (*m. Sanhedrin* 6:1-4). The hypocrisy of the opponents is evident. If the Sanhedrin did not have the right to exact a capital punishment, then the reason for bringing the woman to Jesus and the nature of the trap they have set becomes clear. If Jesus is laissez faire towards the Law then he stands condemned before the Pharisees, scribes and people. If he agrees with the woman's accusers then he would find himself in a great deal of trouble with the Romans since it is entirely possible that he would be held responsible for the stoning and subsequent death of the woman (see, Mullins 2002:220-221). The leaders of Israel are putting God to the test in the person of his Son, repeating the Israelites' historical pattern on more than one occasion in the wilderness at Meribah and Massah (Ex. 17.2; Num. 20.13; cf. Deut. 6.16; Pss. 95.8-9; 106.14).

d. Scene Three: (Jn. 8.6-9)

This is one of the most memorable scenes in the gospels. Jesus, having heard the accusation, bends over and writes in the dust with his finger. There has been a great deal of speculation as to what Jesus actually wrote. One suggestion is that since it was unlawful to write even two letters on the Sabbath but that writing with dust was permissible (*m. shabbat* 7.2; 12.5). If this were the eighth day of the feast, which was to be kept as a day of rest, then Jesus' writing on the ground would show that he knows well not only the law but also the oral interpretations. Two of the most popular are that Jesus is following the practice of Roman law where a judge wrote down the verdict before it was known and the second, commented on by Ambrose and Augustine (and finding great favour today) is that his writing echoes an Old Testament passage, thereby turning it into a symbolic action (Jer. 17.13):

> O Lord, the hope of Israel, all who forsake you will be put to shame. Those who turn away from you will be written in the dust because they have forsaken the Lord, the spring of living water.

Here *written in the dust* probably means the opposite of being written in the book of life (Ex. 32.32;[1] Dan. 12.1[2]); those who have turned away are consigned to death because they have rejected the one who is the source of the water of life (cf. Mullins 2002:221). Thus it appears that Jesus is associating his opponents with those whom God condemns for forsaking himself and whom he consigns to death. The judgement that they suggest Jesus execute on this adulterous woman is in fact the judgement that he visits upon them for their rejection of him, the one who has offered them God's living water (Jn. 7.38-39). In rejecting Jesus, they are forsaking God, and thereby committing a most shameful act. Adultery is shameful, certainly, but they themselves are acting in a shameful way worthy of death. Both of these interpretations are dubious. However, the first of these is overly argued. Would Jesus really have needed to write in the dust on the eighth day of the feast to demonstrate that he knew the oral interpretations of the Law when he demonstrated on more than one occasion that he knew and understood them very well? It seems highly unlikely that Jesus would use a custom from the occupying Romans to make a point in Jewish territory to those who would have been fiercely anti-Roman. In relation to the symbolic action based around Jer. 17.13[3], even for Jesus this would have been an overly subtle way to remind those in front of him about Jeremiah's words. But in the end it is not *what* he wrote that is important but *that* he wrote. If we apply a combination of Sherlock Home's maxim, *when you eliminate the impossible, whatever is left, no matter how improbable, must be the truth* and Occam's Razor, *no multiplication of things without necessity* (better paraphrased as *the simplest solution is the best*), then the simplest reason why Jesus wrote is that it was a delaying tactic, a 'cooling off' moment, a time for him to gather his own thoughts before speaking (see, Ridderbos 2002:289). So he distracts the accusers with an unusual,

---

[1] But now, if you will only forgive their sin but if not, blot me out of the book that you have written.'

[2] 'At that time Michael, the great prince, the protector of your people, shall arise. There shall be a time of anguish, such as has never occurred since nations first came into existence. But at that time your people shall be delivered, everyone who is found written in the book.

[3] O hope of Israel! O Lord! All who forsake you shall be put to shame; those who turn away from you shall be recorded in the underworld, for they have forsaken the fountain of living water, the Lord.

seemingly bizarre gesture. It also has the appearance of a 'dampener', in other words: the seeming urgency of the woman's situation as understood by the accusers is not perceived as such by Jesus.

When Jesus calls for the one without sin *to cast the first stone* he accomplishes several things: it relieves him from the charge of having instigated a stoning; it ensures there will not be a stoning, since none of the accusers will want to take responsibility for it; and it causes them to reflect on their own sinfulness before God. It is also a challenge for them to fulfil the requirements of the same Law which they have cited as demanding the woman's stoning because Deut. 13.9 says:

> your own hand shall be first against them to execute them, and afterwards the hand of all the people

and Deut. 17.7 says,

> The hands of the witnesses shall be the first raised against the person to execute the death penalty, and afterwards the hands of all the people. So you shall purge the evil from your midst

So the witnesses to a crime which requires capital punishment are those who must raise their hands first. But while Jesus may be using the language of the Law, he makes an addition that it be those *with* sin who raise their hand first. By saying this Jesus issues his own challenge: as they have brought the woman before him under an accusation of the Law, so now they have to face the seriousness of the Law itself: not so that the actual just judgement of the Law is made impossible, but to challenge those who would want to apply it without compassion or mercy. It has often been suggested that the eldest accusers were the first to leave (Jn. 8.9) because they recognised their own sinfulness more readily. However, leaving in this order may simply reflect the custom of deferring to the elders. In any case, their withdrawal was in fact a confession of sin. Those who came to condemn ended up condemning themselves by not casting a stone.

e. Scene Four: (Jn. 8.10-11)

It is only when the crowd have departed that Jesus looks up and finds himself alone with the woman, or as Augustine wrote in his beautiful sentence, *there are two left alone, misera* (a wretched woman) *and misericordia* (mercy) (Augustine, *On John,* 33.5) (see Mullins 2002:222). He stands up straight and asks, *Where are your accusers? Has no one condemned you?'* As if he has been completely oblivious of what has just transpired, or indeed, that anything had transpired. She had been brought to him and had been accused but the accusers have not condemned because they are gone and she is still there unstoned. The question that Jesus asks, therefore, is on the surface superfluous but it is said without a hint of irony or gloating and it serves to bring home to the woman the stark reality of the situation she now finds herself in: she need not fear those who sought her life because they have not judged or condemned. However, there is one remaining who can pass judgement, which is what the crowd of accusers wanted in the first place, not for the justice of the Law but as a cynical and shabby ploy to trap him and they were prepared to throw away a life to do so. We can only speculate as to whether the woman was familiar with Jesus and his embodiment of the mercy of God. In any case, she becomes a memorable example of the fact that God did not send his Son into the world to condemn the world, but to save the world through him (Jn. 3.17). Jesus says to her (Jn. 8.11), *Neither do I condemn you. Go, and from now on no longer sin.* By adding *then* to the beginning of this sentence some translations allow the most unfortunate suggestion that Jesus' response was caused by the response of the teachers of the law and the Pharisees. The translation of the end of the verse is some translation is also unfortunate, since *leave your life of sin* almost paints the woman as an habitual whore which cannot be borne out by the Greek.

f. Interpreting The Narrative

The consensus of ancient and modern authorities is that the story of the woman caught in adultery does not belong to John's gospel but in reality it does not matter that it does not (see interpretation of Brown 1978:29-30). And it does not matter because it is a perfect jewel: simply written, dramatic, tense and with an air of doom laden threat at the beginning, as it unfolds a great serenity descends over the scene that John (since it appears in his gospel) depicts. The intensity and ferocity of the crowd of legal zealots in their accusation of the woman, their public humiliation and demeaning of her is contrasted with the calm, serene gesture and pose of Jesus who, on hearing the accusation, offers no word but the silence of a gesture whose content, pointed or otherwise, will be unknown for all time. In his statement to them he, on the one hand, recognises the truth of their case, if indeed, as they make it clear, she has been caught 'red handed', then the Law is non-negotiable: her sin has found her out and she must pay the price but on the other hand, he challenges them (and by extension the Law) about who is sinful and who is not. And thus, the one who is without sin (which the Law is unambiguous about) must raise their hand first. Mercy and compassion meet the rigidity of legalism; justice and love meets crime and punishment. Jesus is not saying that the woman is without guilt or sin, or, indeed, that she should not be punished according to the dictates of the Law, but he is saying that there are some things greater than the legalism and rigidity of the unflinching Law, i.e., mercy and compassion. Love does not replace Law but it does supersede it. Jesus, it might be noted, grants pardon, not acquittal, since the call to leave off sinning shows he knew she was indeed guilty of the adultery. His non condemnation is quite different from theirs. They wanted to condemn but lacked the opportunity; he could have done so, but he did not. Here is mercy and righteousness. He condemned the sin and not the sinner (Augustine, *On John* 33.6). But more than that, he called her to a new life. The gospel is not only the forgiveness of sins, but a new quality of life that overcomes the power of sin (cf. Jn.

8.32-36;[1] 1 Jn. 3.4-6[2]). This passage also contains an extremely significant revelation of Jesus' identity. The fact that it comes in this Synoptic style and yet fits so well in this context in John makes it all the more remarkable. The opponents challenged Jesus regarding the law of Moses by saying, essentially, Moses tells us to stone such a person, but you what do you say? (Jn. 8.5, *you* is emphatic in the Greek). Jesus sets aside Moses' clear command, albeit one that few ever acted on in Jesus' day. He does not follow through on Moses' command even when challenged to do so, which leads us to believe that he is more than just a prophet cf. Jn. 9.34[3]). Jesus does not say explicitly that he forgives the woman, but such is the implication of his saying he does not condemn her and then telling her to not sin again. So here we seem to have another occasion when Jesus mediates the forgiveness of God (Lk.7.36-50[4]). In doing so, he is bypassing the temple and acting in a divine role. This revelation of Jesus' divinity is as

---

[1]   And you will know the truth, and the truth will make you free.' They answered him, 'We are descendants of Abraham and have never been slaves to anyone. What do you mean by saying, "You will be made free"?'

[2]   Everyone who commits sin is guilty of lawlessness; sin is lawlessness. You know that he was revealed to take away sins, and in him there is no sin. No one who abides in him sins; no one who sins has either seen him or known him.

[3]   They answered him, 'You were born entirely in sins, and are you trying to teach us?' And they drove him out.

[4]   One of the Pharisees asked Jesus to eat with him, and he went into the Pharisee's house and took his place at the table. And a woman in the city, who was a sinner, having learned that he was eating in the Pharisee's house, brought an alabaster jar of ointment. She stood behind him at his feet, weeping, and began to bathe his feet with her tears and to dry them with her hair. Then she continued kissing his feet and anointing them with the ointment. Now when the Pharisee who had invited him saw it, he said to himself, 'If this man were a prophet, he would have known who and what kind of woman this is who is touching him, that she is a sinner.' Jesus spoke up and said to him, 'Simon, I have something to say to you.' 'Teacher,' he replied, 'speak.' 'A certain creditor had two debtors; one owed five hundred denarii, and the other fifty. When they could not pay, he cancelled the debts for both of them. Now which of them will love him more?' Simon answered, 'I suppose the one for whom he cancelled the greater debt.' And Jesus said to him, 'You have judged rightly.' Then turning towards the woman, he said to Simon, 'Do you see this woman? I entered your house; you gave me no water for my feet, but she has bathed my feet with her tears and dried them with her hair. You gave me no kiss, but from the time I came in she has not stopped kissing my feet. You did not anoint my head with oil, but she has anointed my feet with ointment. Therefore, I tell you, her sins, which were many, have been forgiven; hence she has shown great love. But the one to whom little is forgiven, loves little.' Then he said to her, 'Your sins are forgiven.' But those who were at the table with him began to say among themselves, 'Who is this who even forgives sins?' And he said to the woman, 'Your faith has saved you; go in peace.'

profound as other such revelations in this Gospel, though it is expressed in the form it takes in the Synoptics. This patch of cloth sown onto John's Gospel has the same pattern as the whole, even if the colours are somewhat different.

CHAPTER ELEVEN

JESUS AND THE WOMEN IN JOHN

Martha and Mary of Bethany (Jn. 11.1-44; 12.1-8)

The Narrative Context

This chapter of John can be viewed as a transitional chapter which recapitulates motifs that have gone before it and as an introduction to the Passion Narrative. The motif of light found in Jn. 8 and 9 continues (Jn. 11.9-10[1]), the purpose given for the illness of the blind man is similar to that given for Lazarus' death (Jn. 9.3;[2] 11:4[3]), and the healing of the blind man is referred to (Jn. 11.37[4]), as is the conflict with the Jewish authorities in chapter 10 (Jn. 11.8[5]). Certainly one purpose of it from John's point of view was to illustrate the earlier statements made by Jesus to the effect that he is the one who gives spiritual life to men and on the last day will physically raise the dead (cf. Jn. 5.24-29[6]). There are also larger connections, for the raising of Lazarus is the last of a series of Jesus' signs that began in Jn. 2

---

[1] Jesus answered, 'Are there not twelve hours of daylight? Those who walk during the day do not stumble, because they see the light of this world. But those who walk at night stumble, because the light is not in them.'

[2] Jesus answered, 'Neither this man nor his parents sinned; he was born blind so that God's works might be revealed in him.

[3] But when Jesus heard it, he said, 'This illness does not lead to death; rather it is for God's glory, so that the Son of God may be glorified through it.'

[4]

[5] The disciples said to him, 'Rabbi, the Jews were just now trying to stone you, and are you going there again?'

[6] Very truly, I tell you, anyone who hears my word and believes him who sent me has eternal life, and does not come under judgement, but has passed from death to life. 'Very truly, I tell you, the hour is coming, and is now here, when the dead will hear the voice of the Son of God, and those who hear will live. For just as the Father has life in himself, so he has granted the Son also to have life in himself; and he has given him authority to execute judgement, because he is the Son of Man. Do not be astonished at this; for the hour is coming when all who are in their graves will hear his voice and will come out, those who have done good, to the resurrection of life, and those who have done evil, to the resurrection of condemnation.

(see below); both the first and last of the signs in this series (Jn. 2.11;[1] 11.4) are explicitly linked with the revelation of God's glory. All of the signs were revelations of who Jesus is and what he offers. The final sign, the raising of Lazarus, points most clearly to what has been at the heart of the revelation all the way through and what was emphasized in Jesus' keynote address (Jn. 5.19-30[2]) that Jesus is the one who gives life. The irony, of course, is that he gives life by giving up his own life on the cross. A further irony is that by giving life to Lazarus, Jesus sets in motion his own death. That far off event of the general resurrection is brought home emphatically by what happened here in the raising of Lazarus from the tomb (cf. Jn. 5.28-29). It is a fitting cap on the ministry of Jesus (see, Mullins 2002:259). The raising of Lazarus, then, is the final sign before the event that actually accomplishes what all the signs have pointed toward: the provision of life through the death of the Son of God. So we may see what is to happen to Lazarus as both the climax of Jesus' ministry before his final days, and as a contribution to the finality of those days. In a sense we may see the first part of the Gospel as reaching a conclusion in the resurrection of a believer which is a clear picture of the coming resurrection which will take place at Jesus Christ's behest, illustrating the success of his ministry. While in the second part, which will close with the resurrection of Jesus Christ himself as the first fruits of that coming resurrection, all is concentrated on the preparation for his death and its carrying through, culminating in death's defeat as Jesus is revealed as the Lord of Glory. Alternately we could concentrates on seeing the Passion narrative as sandwiched between two depictions of the resurrection to life. Both emphases are true.

---

[1] Jesus did this, the first of his signs, in Cana of Galilee, and revealed his glory; and his disciples believed in him.

[2] Jesus said to them, 'Very truly, I tell you, the Son can do nothing on his own, but only what he sees the Father doing; for whatever the Father does, the Son does likewise. The Father loves the Son and shows him all that he himself is doing; and he will show him greater works than these, so that you will be astonished. Indeed, just as the Father raises the dead and gives them life, so also the Son gives life to whomsoever he wishes. The Father judges no one but has given all judgement to the Son, so that all may honour the Son just as they honour the Father. Anyone who does not honour the Son does not honour the Father who sent him. Very truly, I tell you, anyone who hears my word and believes him who sent me has eternal life, and does not come under judgement, but has passed from death to life.

So we have in this chapter the seventh of the signs specifically brought out by John, closing off the seven signs and culminating the whole, and suggesting that now Jesus has been fully and perfectly revealed. (In contrast the seven 'I am' sayings cover almost the whole Gospel, so we must not make too great a distinction between the two parts). The previous signs have been:

Jn. 2.1-11.	The turning of water into wine	Illustrating the new truth which Jesus has brought into the world as something which is replacing the old well-loved ritual.
Jn. 4.46-54.	The healing at a distance of the court official's son	Which reveals the fact that Jesus can work at long range in response to faith and giving life to the dying
Jn. 5.2-9.	The healing of the disabled man	Which reveals that He can heal a crippled Israel and restore it to wholeness
Jn. 6.1-14.	The miraculous feeding of the crowds	Which reveals the fact that Jesus can feed the souls with the bread of life
Jn. 9.1-41.	The healing of the man blind from birth	Which reveals the fact that he has come in order to open eyes so that they may see.

Furthermore, each has pointed to Jesus either as Messiah or true Son of God, or indeed as both. And now in Jn. 11.1-42 we are to see a culminating sign which is directly related to his Messiahship and Sonship, and which emphasises the fact that he gives eternal life to all who believe in him, revealing at the same time that he will be the one who raises the dead in the last day. It is a fitting climax to the whole. In this passage we also have the next 'I am' saying. These 'I am' passages are self-revelatory, and are spread between Jn. 8.12 and Jn. 15.1, thus coming late in his ministry. Their spread should prevent us from too sharply differentiating two sections in the Gospel. John saw his Gospel as one whole. In them Jesus declares:

Jn. 6.35.	I am the Bread of Life	Who gives life to all and satisfies the hunger and thirst of their hearts
Jn. 8.12.	I am the Light of the world	So that those who follow me will not walk in darkness but will have the light of life
Jn. 10.9.	I am the Door	By me if anyone enters in they will be saved'
Jn. 10.12.	I am the Good Shepherd	Who leads his own sheep in and out and gives his life for the sheep
Jn. 11.25.	I am the Resurrection and the Life	Who gives life to those who believe in him, both in he present and in the future
Jn. 14.6.	I am the Way, the Truth and the Life	Through whom all come to the Father
Jn. 15.1.	I am the True Vine	The root and trunk of the true people of God, by union with Whom they become fruitful

In all this he reveals his uniqueness as the Lord of glory. Note the emphasis in the sayings on life and salvation: Jesus has come as the life-giver and the Saviour. Truly 'no man ever spoke like this man'. This narrative also continues to develop the theme of faith. Jesus has just made a very clear statement of his unity with the Father (Jn. 10.30, 38[1]), and many have believed in him (Jn. 10.42). Often in this gospel Jesus reacts to faith by doing or saying something scandalous or cryptic. Although these people

---

[1] The Father and I are one.' But if I do them, even though you do not believe me, believe the works, so that you may know and understand that the Father is in me and I am in the Father.'

who have faith are not present at the raising of Lazarus, the raising can perhaps be seen as a further revelation in response to their faith, as they represent a general turn upward in his popularity.

a. Setting The Scene: The Illness of Lazarus (Jn. 11.1-6)

Now a certain man was ill, Lazarus of Bethany, the village of Mary and her sister Martha. Mary was the one who anointed the Lord with perfume and wiped his feet with her hair; her brother Lazarus was ill. So the sisters sent a message to Jesus, 'Lord, he whom you love is ill.' But when Jesus heard it, he said, 'This illness does not lead to death; rather it is for God's glory, so that the Son of God may be glorified through it.' Accordingly, though Jesus loved Martha and her sister and Lazarus, after having heard that Lazarus was ill, he stayed two days longer in the place where he was. Then after this he said to the disciples, 'Let us go to Judea again.' The disciples said to him, 'Rabbi, the Jews were just now trying to stone you, and are you going there again?' Jesus answered, 'Are there not twelve hours of daylight? Those who walk during the day do not stumble, because they see the light of this world. But those who walk at night stumble, because the light is not in them.' After saying this, he told them, 'Our friend Lazarus has fallen asleep, but I am going there to awaken him.' The disciples said to him, 'Lord, if he has fallen asleep, he will be all right.' Jesus, however, had been speaking about his death, but they thought that he was referring merely to sleep. Then Jesus told them plainly, 'Lazarus is dead. For your sake I am glad I was not there, so that you may believe. But let us go to him.' Thomas, who was called the Twin, said to his fellow-disciples, 'Let us also go, that we may die with him.'

With this story John leads the way into the Passion narrative. We are given a foretaste of the resurrection. and in consequence of what happens the

Sanhedrin semi-officially determine on his death (Jn. 11.47-52[1]), a verdict linked with the raising of Lazarus (Jn. 11.46[2]), while it is followed immediately by a description of Mary's anointing of Jesus in preparation for his death, also linked with Lazarus (Jn. 12.1-8[3]). At the same time he is putting the cap on the seven signs of Jesus' Messiahship and Sonship, thus finalising the impact of Jesus during his life and ministry (Mullins 2002:259; Ridderbos 1985:384).

John does not say exactly when this event took place, only that it was sometime during the four months, roughly, between the Feast of Dedication and Passover. But he is careful to name the three siblings and where they lived, *Lazarus* who was *brother* to *Martha and Mary* and they lived at *Bethany*. This Bethany is a little less than two miles southeast of Jerusalem on the road to Jericho (Jn. 11.18). It is to be distinguished from the Bethany where John had been baptising (Jn. 1.28) and to which Jesus had just returned (Jn. 10.40), which is either in Perea at the Jordan a few miles north of the Dead Sea, about a day's journey from Jerusalem, or up north in Batanea, several days journey away. Jn. 11.1 introduces these siblings for the first time in the New Testament. Neither Lazarus nor his sisters have been mentioned previously in John's gospel. Mary and Martha appeared in

---

[1] So the chief priests and the Pharisees called a meeting of the council, and said, 'What are we to do? This man is performing many signs. If we let him go on like this, everyone will believe in him, and the Romans will come and destroy both our holy place and our nation.' But one of them, Caiaphas, who was high priest that year, said to them, 'You know nothing at all! You do not understand that it is better for you to have one man die for the people than to have the whole nation destroyed.' He did not say this on his own, but being high priest that year he prophesied that Jesus was about to die for the nation, and not for the nation only, but to gather into one the dispersed children of God.

[2] But some of them went to the Pharisees and told them what he had done.

[3] Six days before the Passover Jesus came to Bethany, the home of Lazarus, whom he had raised from the dead. There they gave a dinner for him. Martha served, and Lazarus was one of those at the table with him. Mary took a pound of costly perfume made of pure nard, anointed Jesus' feet, and wiped them with her hair. The house was filled with the fragrance of the perfume. But Judas Iscariot, one of his disciples (the one who was about to betray him), said, 'Why was this perfume not sold for three hundred denarii and the money given to the poor?' (He said this not because he cared about the poor, but because he was a thief; he kept the common purse and used to steal what was put into it.) Jesus said, 'Leave her alone. She bought it so that she might keep it for the day of my burial. You always have the poor with you, but you do not always have me.'

Lk. 10. 38-42,[1] but no mention of Lazarus is made in those verses. Lazarus is the name applied to the poor beggar in the parable of the Rich Man and Lazarus in Lk. 16.19-31[2]. However, there appears to be no connection between the literary figure in that parable and the brother of Mary and Martha. The name Lazarus is known from archaeology and Josephus as a common name in first century Palestine. It is the Greek form of Eleazar which means, 'God helps,' though John makes nothing of that original meaning (Moloney 1998:335). It may well have been at their house that Jesus tended to stay when he was in Jerusalem (Mt. 21.17; [3] Mk. 11.11;[4] Lk. 10.38-42, cf. Jn. 12.1-8[5]), and it could well have been their ass on which He

---

[1] Now as they went on their way, he entered a certain village, where a woman named Martha welcomed him into her home. She had a sister named Mary, who sat at the Lord's feet and listened to what he was saying. But Martha was distracted by her many tasks; so she came to him and asked, 'Lord, do you not care that my sister has left me to do all the work by myself? Tell her then to help me.' But the Lord answered her, 'Martha, Martha, you are worried and distracted by many things; there is need of only one thing. Mary has chosen the better part, which will not be taken away from her.'

[2] 'There was a rich man who was dressed in purple and fine linen and who feasted sumptuously every day. And at his gate lay a poor man named Lazarus, covered with sores, who longed to satisfy his hunger with what fell from the rich man's table; even the dogs would come and lick his sores. The poor man died and was carried away by the angels to be with Abraham. The rich man also died and was buried. In Hades, where he was being tormented, he looked up and saw Abraham far away with Lazarus by his side. He called out, "Father Abraham, have mercy on me, and send Lazarus to dip the tip of his finger in water and cool my tongue; for I am in agony in these flames." But Abraham said, "Child, remember that during your lifetime you received your good things, and Lazarus in like manner evil things; but now he is comforted here, and you are in agony. Besides all this, between you and us a great chasm has been fixed, so that those who might want to pass from here to you cannot do so, and no one can cross from there to us." He said, "Then, father, I beg you to send him to my father's house, for I have five brothers, that he may warn them, so that they will not also come into this place of torment." Abraham replied, "They have Moses and the prophets; they should listen to them." He said, "No, father Abraham; but if someone goes to them from the dead, they will repent." He said to him, "If they do not listen to Moses and the prophets, neither will they be convinced even if someone rises from the dead." '

[3] He left them, went out of the city to Bethany, and spent the night there.

[4] Then he entered Jerusalem and went into the temple; and when he had looked around at everything, as it was already late, he went out to Bethany with the twelve.

[5] Six days before the Passover Jesus came to Bethany, the home of Lazarus, whom he had raised from the dead. There they gave a dinner for him. Martha served, and Lazarus was one of those at the table with him. Mary took a pound of costly perfume made of pure nard, anointed Jesus' feet, and wiped them with her hair. The house was filled with the fragrance of the perfume. But Judas Iscariot, one of his disciples (the one who was about to betray him), said, 'Why was this perfume not sold for three hundred denarii and the money given to the poor?' (He said this not because he cared about the poor, but because he was a thief; he kept the common purse and used to steal what was put into it.) Jesus said, 'Leave her alone. She bought it so that she might keep it for the day of my burial. You always have the poor with you, but you do not

entered Jerusalem' (Mk. 11.1[1]). He is constantly shown as having a close relationship with the family. The fact that Lazarus was identified by his relationship to Mary and Martha demonstrates that the author expected the latter to be well known to his readers. This confirms that the Gospel was written against a background of known material. As they appeared in Lk. 10.38-42, this may suggest that he knew that his readers would be familiar with the tradition behind Luke's Gospel.

Jn. 11.2 is also interesting. The incident John mentions has not yet been recorded (Jn. 12.1-8) (Moloney 1998:329; Mullins 2002:262). This again suggests that John expected that the incident was also well known to his readers, even before he himself wrote about it (see, Ridderbos 1991:386). Thus it is clear that John, in writing, depended on the fact that his readers already had a solid background of knowledge about the life of Jesus gained from the tradition (something possibly known as, 'The Testimony of Jesus Christ' (Rev.1.2, 9;[2] 12.17;[3] 19.10;[4] cf. 2 Tim.1.8[5]). Some scholars have seen this strange order as evidence of an earlier edition of John with a different order.

It is apparent that Lazarus was very ill, and his sisters therefore turned to the only one whom they felt could help them. They sent him a message, *Lord, he whom you love is ill*. They describe their brother as the one whom Jesus loves. The Greek word for *love* here is 'phileo' not 'agape'. For this reason some translations describe Lazarus as Jesus' 'friend'. On the basis of this verse some scholars believe that Lazarus was the 'Beloved Disciple' (Jn.

---

always have me.'

[1] When they were approaching Jerusalem, at Bethphage and Bethany, near the Mount of Olives, he sent two of his disciples

[2] Who testified to the word of God and to the testimony of Jesus Christ, even to all that he saw. I, John, your brother who share with you in Jesus the persecution and the kingdom and the patient endurance, was on the island called Patmos because of the word of God and the testimony of Jesus.

[3] Then the dragon was angry with the woman, and went off to make war on the rest of her children, those who keep the commandments of God and hold the testimony of Jesus.

[4] Then I fell down at his feet to worship him, but he said to me, 'You must not do that! I am a fellow-servant with you and your comrades who hold the testimony of Jesus. Worship God! For the testimony of Jesus is the spirit of prophecy.'

[5] Do not be ashamed, then, of the testimony about our Lord or of me his prisoner, but join with me in suffering for the gospel, relying on the power of God.

13:23; 19:26, etc) (cf. e.g., Sanders 1954-55:33. These words emphasise the close friendship there was between Jesus and the family. Jesus is seen to be human and to have close personal friends. The use of *Lord* here goes beyond just a formal greeting. It is not to be seen as over-theological in its use by Martha and Mary, but rather as an acknowledgement of the respect in which they held Jesus (cf. Mullins 2002:262;. It was probably otherwise in the mind of the writer who wants us to see him as Lord over all.

This request is very similar to Jesus' mother's request at the wedding of Cana (Jn. 2.4). It presents a need but does not dictate to Jesus how he should respond. Such humility and submission are key characteristics of true disciples. Mary and Martha must have known how dangerous it had become for Jesus to be in the vicinity of Jerusalem. They might have known that Jesus could heal at a distance (cf. Jn. 4.49-53[1]), yet they seem to want him to come to heal Lazarus (Jn. 11.21, 32[2]). Perhaps their anxiety for their brother led them to summon Jesus. But love is the laying down of life (cf. 1 Jn 3.16[3]), and the sisters seem to think that Jesus would be willing to risk his life for the sake of their brother, whom he loves. Whatever they may have been thinking, we see that Jesus, the Good Shepherd, was indeed willing to risk his life for his friend (cf. Jn. 10.11,15[4]), though he was under no real danger since he was doing the Father's will and under his protection (Jn. 10.39[5]; cf. Jn. 10.29[6]).

Jn. 11.4 is an important verse because on the surface it appears that

---

[1] The official said to him, 'Sir, come down before my little boy dies.' Jesus said to him, 'Go; your son will live.' The man believed the word that Jesus spoke to him and started on his way. As he was going down, his slaves met him and told him that his child was alive. So he asked them the hour when he began to recover, and they said to him, 'Yesterday at one in the afternoon the fever left him.' The father realized that this was the hour when Jesus had said to him, 'Your son will live.' So he himself believed, along with his whole household.

[2] Martha said to Jesus, 'Lord, if you had been here, my brother would not have died. When Mary came where Jesus was and saw him, she knelt at his feet and said to him, 'Lord, if you had been here, my brother would not have died.'

[3] We know love by this, that he laid down his life for us, and we ought to lay down our lives for one another.

[4] 'I am the good shepherd. The good shepherd lays down his life for the sheep. just as the Father knows me and I know the Father. And I lay down my life for the sheep.

[5] Then they tried to arrest him again, but he escaped from their hands.

[6] What my Father has given me is greater than all else, and no one can snatch it out of the Father's hand.

Jesus got it wrong, *this sickness is not death* he declares when the story makes it clear that Jesus had divine knowledge of Lazarus' death. However, the Greek construction suggests a translation something like, 'this sickness is not to end in death'. John seems to be playing on words. Though Lazarus was soon to die his sickness did not end up in death because Jesus was going to bring him back to life. The restoration of Lazarus' physical life would function as a sign of the eternal life promised and about to be provided by Jesus. The whole incident was to be a means by which the God's glory would be manifested, and the glorious reality of the resurrection would be revealed in picture form (cf. Brown 1978:431; see, Ridderbos 1991:387).

But it would also be an incident which would arouse his enemies and finally result in his death, because they were so blinded that, instead of glorying in a wonderful miracle, they resented the influence that it gave him (Jn. 11.45-53[1]). Although in contrast to this was the fact that some did believe (v.45). Thus Jesus specifically declared that by it he, 'the Son of God' (the God-sent Messianic prince, the only true Son of God) would be glorified in two senses. Firstly in that his power to raise the dead, including the dead at the last day, would be amazingly revealed. But secondly because through it he would be glorified by being raised up on a cross, in order that through his death he might perform the work that would make the resurrection possible (Jn. 12.23[2]). He was both challenging the power of death and challenging his adversaries, knowing in both cases what the consequences would be. The term 'Son of God' would be understood by listeners as signifying the one chosen and appointed by God. To Jesus and to the readers, in the light of Jn. 1, it signifies that he is God's only Son. For

---

[1] Many of the Jews therefore, who had come with Mary and had seen what Jesus did, believed in him. But some of them went to the Pharisees and told them what he had done. So the chief priests and the Pharisees called a meeting of the council, and said, 'What are we to do? This man is performing many signs. If we let him go on like this, everyone will believe in him, and the Romans will come and destroy both our holy place and our nation.' But one of them, Caiaphas, who was high priest that year, said to them, 'You know nothing at all! You do not understand that it is better for you to have one man die for the people than to have the whole nation destroyed.' He did not say this on his own, but being high priest that year he prophesied that Jesus was about to die for the nation, and not for the nation only, but to gather into one the dispersed children of God. So from that day on they planned to put him to death.

[2] Jesus answered them, 'The hour has come for the Son of Man to be glorified.

John the ultimate glorification of Jesus comes through the death, resurrection, and ascension of Christ (Mullins 2002:265; cf. Brown 1978:431; Ridderbos 1991:388). There are several clues throughout this passage that suggest that John is already thinking very much about Jesus' death as he tells about Lazarus' death, because Jesus' whole life and ministry, death and resurrection arise from the will of the Father. Thus the glorification of Jesus leads to the glory of God (cf. Cadman 1959:423-34).

John's ordering of the material in Jn. 11.5,6 is very effective. By mentioning Jesus' love for the family before describing his delay, greater attention is drawn to the delay (see Mullins 2002:265). If he really loved Martha and her sister and Lazarus, why would he wait several more days before going to see them? Thus the reader is drawn more emotionally into the story. But Jesus is not moved by emotion; it is the will and timing of the Father that propels him through life. The hour has not yet come; he will not go to Bethany just because of Lazarus' need. Jesus goes when the Father sends him.

b. On The Way To Bethany (Jn. 11.7-16)

Jn. 11.7 begins the with the return of Jesus and his disciples to Bethany in Judea and the conversation they have either before they set out or as they are on the road. There are some very important features to this section of the narrative. When Jesus announces that they are to return to Judea (Jn. 11.7), his disciples remind him that the Jewish opponents had just been trying to stone him there (Jn. 11.8) (cf. Brown 1978:432). The disciples are taking their cues from their circumstances rather than from the Father. They are very aware of the danger their opponents present, but they are not in tune with the voice of the Father. Jesus responds with a cryptic saying, which, as usual, directly addresses the issue at hand but is not able to be understood (Jn. 9-10). He uses the imagery of light to put things into perspective for them. In the natural realm one is able to walk without stumbling while there is light, and there is light for a set period of time. One need not worry about stumbling while it is day. But Jesus is not making a reference to how the Jews kept time but something much more profound than that. The Jewish (and Roman) day was divided into twelve equal hours. This meant that a winter hour was shorter than a summer hour. Because lighting was difficult and expensive most activity ended at sundown. The daylight opportunity was limited; when night came opportunity ended. Jesus' observation that there are twelve hours in the day is more than a statement about Jewish time. It also means that Jesus' ministry was a (day) window of opportunity. What was to be done had to be done before the opportunity disappeared. The threat of death was real, but it could not paralyse Jesus from doing what God had sent him to do (cf. McNeil 1974: 269-75). In that sense as long as Jesus walked in the day (doing the will of God) he would not stumble (would not be killed). The point is that they need not worry about what will happen to them for they have the Light of the World with them (Jn. 8.12), for with him they are able to get on with the work of the Father (Jn. 9.4). With the psalmist they can say, *The Lord is my light and my salvation whom shall I fear?* (Ps. 27.1). They must remain with Jesus even when he seems to lead them into danger, for no matter what happens it will work out for the best, even as Lazarus' illness will work for the glory of God.

At that point in the saying Jesus shifts his illustration. Jn.11.10 assumes that Jesus is the light. Thus when Jesus is present, there is no darkness and one will not stumble. This means that the disciples can safely follow Jesus to Judea. Another important feature of the narrative is that Lazarus' death is revealed in this paragraph. Jesus uses the metaphor of sleep to describe Lazarus' death (The New Testament constantly refers to death as 'sleep' in the context of resurrection (e.g., Mk. 5.39;[1] Lk. 8.52;[2] Acts 7.60;[3] 1

---

[1] When he had entered, he said to them, 'Why do you make a commotion and weep? The child is not dead but sleeping.'

[2] They were all weeping and wailing for her; but he said, 'Do not weep; for she is not dead but sleeping.'

[3] Then he knelt down and cried out in a loud voice, 'Lord, do not hold this sin against them.' When he had said this, he died.

Cor.11.30;[1] 15.6, 18, 51;[2] 1 Thess.4.13-15;[3] 2 Pet.3.4[4]). He also uses the metaphor of awakening in Jn. 11.11 to describe the impending raising of Lazarus. Though it is perfectly understandable, the misunderstanding of the disciples fits in with John's pattern of writing. Ironically, in Jn. 11.12 the disciples state what is about to happen without knowing it. If he is sleeping he will recover. The Greek word usually translated *recover* literally means *to be saved* or *to be rescued, delivered*. It was often used in New Testament times (and in the New Testament) to mean *healed*. There is a play on words here. If Lazarus is sleeping that will mean healing or recovery for him. Yet the Christian reader knows that the rescue is not just from sickness but also from death. One of the early copies of the New Testament contains the word *raised* instead of *recovered*. That scribe knew the rest of the story. Since the disciples do not understand that Jesus is speaking of Lazarus' death, he has to explain it to them (Jn. 11.14) and thereby give them his perspective on this opportunity: *for your sake I am glad I was not there, so that you may believe* (Jn. 11.15). Jn. 11.15 must also be qualified by Jn. 11.33-36. The rejoicing of Jesus is not over Lazarus' death nor the sorrow of the family and friends. Jn. 11.33-36 reveal genuine sorrow and sympathy on Jesus' part. It is important that the disciples have their faith established as they approach the critical moment of Jesus' death. The death of Lazarus provides an opportunity for the faith of the disciples to be built up in preparation for the difficult days ahead. For that reason Jesus rejoices. The Bible does not indicate that God causes or rejoices over the tragedies and difficulties of our lives. However, it does indicate that he knows, rejoices over, and actively

---

[1] For this reason many of you are weak and ill, and some have died.

[2] Then he appeared to more than five hundred brothers and sisters at one time, most of whom are still alive, though some have died. Then those also who have died in Christ have perished. Listen, I will tell you a mystery! We will not all die, but we will all be changed,

[3] But we do not want you to be uninformed, brothers and sisters, about those who have died, so that you may not grieve as others do who have no hope. For since we believe that Jesus died and rose again, even so, through Jesus, God will bring with him those who have died. For this we declare to you by the word of the Lord, that we who are alive, who are left until the coming of the Lord, will by no means precede those who have died.

[4] 'Where is the promise of his coming? For ever since our ancestors died, all things continue as they were from the beginning of creation!'

works to bring about good in and for us in the midst of the difficulty. He has no doubt that he could have cured Lazarus if he had been there, but something even more helpful for their faith is now going to take place. To have faith in the Son of God is far more important than to have health and comfort in this life. Such faith leads to eternal life (Jn. 20.31), as this miracle will symbolise. This faith is a progressive thing, for here Jesus is talking to those who have believed in him already, and yet he says this miracle is *so that you may believe.*

Jesus may be rejoicing, but Thomas, and presumably the other disciples, is not. We usually think of Thomas as *doubting Thomas* from his reactions after the resurrection of the Lord (Jn. 20.24-28[1]). In the present story we see another facet of Thomas: his loyalty. This is the response of a true disciple. Just as Peter remains with Jesus even though he does not understand what Jesus is talking about regarding eating his flesh and drinking his blood (Jn. 6.68[2]), so Thomas is willing to go with Jesus to death (Jn. 11.16[3]) (Mullins 2002:265). He is still fixated with the evident danger (Jn. 11.8), and he does not understand the encouraging words Jesus has just spoken, but he is attached to Jesus and is going to stay with him, even though he does not see how Jesus' decision makes any sense. Here is an incredible picture of faith. He is not following because he sees how it all fits; he is following out of loyalty to Jesus himself. He is a model disciple at this point. As Thomas follows Jesus into what he thinks is death he is answering the call, expressed in the Synoptics, that (Mk. 8.34-35):

> if anyone would come after me, he must deny himself and take up
> his cross and follow me. For whoever saves his life will lose it and

---

[1] But Thomas (who was called the Twin), one of the twelve, was not with them when Jesus came. So the other disciples told him, 'We have seen the Lord.' But he said to them, 'Unless I see the mark of the nails in his hands, and put my finger in the mark of the nails and my hand in his side, I will not believe.' A week later his disciples were again in the house, and Thomas was with them. Although the doors were shut, Jesus came and stood among them and said, 'Peace be with you.' Then he said to Thomas, 'Put your finger here and see my hands. Reach out your hand and put it in my side. Do not doubt but believe.' Thomas answered him, 'My Lord and my God!'

[2] Simon Peter answered him, 'Lord, to whom can we go? You have the words of eternal life.

[3] Thomas, who was called the Twin, said to his fellow-disciples, 'Let us also go, that we may die with him.'

whoever loses his life will save it

c. The Arrival At Bethany (Jn. 11.17-19)

The previous pages serve to highlight not just the literary structural elements or simple narrative contextuality but also the importance of Jesus intentions, *our friend Lazarus has fallen asleep and I am going to wake him*, and his dialogue about light and life with the disciples as they make their way to Bethany. To this point the two sisters have not been referred as such. John spells out that Bethany is quite near Jerusalem (Jn. 11.18). This note heightens the drama. Jesus had said he was returning to Judea (Jn. 11.7), which the disciples recognised as the place of hostility. Now John makes sure we understand that Jesus has come back to the region of Jerusalem itself, the very heart of the opposition. Jerusalem is also the key place for revelation, and the greatest of all revelations is now starting to unfold. Now Jesus arrives at Bethany only to find that Lazarus has been dead for *four days*. The specific time reference is important in a Jewish context because it emphasises the finality of Lazarus' death, it probably signifies that Lazarus is clearly dead and beginning to decay (cf. *m. Yeb.* 16.3). A later Jewish text that cites an authority from the early third century A.D. says the mourners should continue to come to the tomb for three days because the dead person continues to be present. Mourning is at its height on the third day, presumably because it is the last time the dead person will be present there. Bar Kappara taught (*Gen. Rab.* 100.7):

> Until three days (after death) the soul keeps on returning to the grave, thinking that it will go back (into the body); but when it sees that the facial features have become disfigured, it departs and abandons it (the body)'

Thus, the reference to the fourth day may be quite significant for setting the scene for another dramatic miracle. Lazarus is dead; there is no hope of the kind of rescue from death that was experienced by widow of Nain's son or

Jairus daughter or the lad raised by Elijah according to 1 K 17.17-23.[1] (Mullins 2002:266) Mary and Martha are surrounded by their friends trying to comfort them. It is a rare positive picture of the Jews from Jerusalem that John presents in v.19. The healings in this Gospel have taken place in response to desperate needs from the son of the royal official who was close to death (Jn. 4.49), to the man who was paralysed for thirty-eight years (Jn. 5.5), to the man born blind (Jn. 9.1). Now we come to the climax of this sequence.

d. The Dialogue With Martha (Jn. 11.20-27)

The heart of this section appears in Jn. 11.21-27 in the dialogue between Jesus and Martha. In a real sense the meaning of their discussion is faith. Martha believes in Jesus. She is confident that if he had been present before Lazarus had died Jesus would have healed him. She was aware of other healing miracles and believed that Jesus could have done the same for her brother. Jesus pushes her toward a deeper faith that is not dependent on the word *if* and a faith that focuses on him alone. As Jesus approaches, Martha comes out to meet him. It is unclear why Jesus halted and met her in this way. Some have suggested the desire for relative privacy, but perhaps more likely this reflects the danger he is in by returning to the suburbs of Jerusalem. The crowd of mourners may well contain those who would inform the authorities of Jesus' presence, as indeed does happen after the raising of Lazarus (Jn. 11.46). Martha says (Jn. 11.21),

---

[1] After this the son of the woman, the mistress of the house, became ill; his illness was so severe that there was no breath left in him. She then said to Elijah, 'What have you against me, O man of God? You have come to me to bring my sin to remembrance, and to cause the death of my son!' But he said to her, 'Give me your son.' He took him from her bosom, carried him up into the upper chamber where he was lodging, and laid him on his own bed. He cried out to the Lord, 'O Lord my God, have you brought calamity even upon the widow with whom I am staying, by killing her son?' Then he stretched himself upon the child three times, and cried out to the Lord, 'O Lord my God, let this child's life come into him again.' The Lord listened to the voice of Elijah; the life of the child came into him again, and he revived. Elijah took the child, brought him down from the upper chamber into the house, and gave him to his mother; then Elijah said, 'See, your son is alive.'

> Lord, if you had been here, my brother would not have died.
> But I know that even now God will give you whatever you ask

It is difficult to know how to understand this statement (cf. Ridderbos1991:394). It is possible to find in her first sentence a rebuke of Jesus and in her second sentence a very defective view of Jesus: she regards Jesus as an intermediary who is heard by God (Jn. 11.22), but she does not understand that he is life itself (Jn. 11.25). The fact that she says, literally, *I know that whatever you ask of God, God will give you* suggests a distance between Jesus and God through the repetition of the word *God*. Also, the word she uses for *ask* (aiteo='I ask', 'request', 'beg', 'petition') is not the word used by Jesus for his own prayer to the Father but the word he uses of the disciples' prayer (see, Mullins 2002:266). She sees Jesus as a holy person who can get his prayers answered but she does not yet understand that Jesus is the agent through whom God is making resurrection possible for human beings. Thus, there is no doubt that her view of Jesus is defective. Indeed, in this very interchange Jesus is revealing himself more perfectly to her, as he revealed himself to the Samaritan woman, despite her defective views. But we should also see here a genuine, though defective, faith. Her initial statement (Jn. 11.21) need not imply a rebuke. It could simply be a lament, and although her knowledge of Jesus is defective, nevertheless, she does believe Jesus could have healed Lazarus. And her belief that Jesus' prayers are answered does pick up on the truth of Jesus' dependence upon the Father, as will be illustrated later in this story (Jn. 11.41-42). So there is more here than simple unbelief or defective belief (see Schnackenburg's view of this statement II:329).

Indeed, her statement at Jn. 11.22 is an extraordinary expression of faith but what is she asking of Jesus or saying about him? It may be that Martha thought that God, through Jesus, could raise Lazarus but her reaction when Lazarus is indeed raised does not seem to fit with that (Jn. 11.39). But the key to what Martha is saying lies in the two simple words *even now* because she continues to have faith in him even though the death of Lazarus has seemed to shatter as illusory Jesus' own words, *this sickness is not unto death* (Jn. 11.4). Jesus delayed in coming to help Lazarus yet *even now* Martha continues to trust that Jesus is the agent of God's graciousness and mercy even though that graciousness and mercy was not present for her brother (but see Brown's comment 1978:434). Her trust in Jesus as God's agent is not shaken by an apparent indifference (cf. Job 13.15;[1] Hab. 3.16-19[2]). Martha, therefore, is an example of extraordinary faith (even though it may be defective) (cf. Moloney 1994:471-493).

Jesus comment at Jn. 11.23 can be interpreted in several ways (Brown 1978:434; Ridderbos 1991:396-97; Mullins 2002:266; Moloney 1994:485). *Your brother will rise again* could mean a resuscitation in which Lazarus is returned to life. In the context that is the most natural meaning and it is, in fact, what happened. It is also possible to take Jesus' words as a reference to the general resurrection at the end of time. Not all Jews (the Sadducees for example) believed in the resurrection. However, the Pharisees had widely taught this doctrine and Jn. 11.24 shows that Martha understood Jesus in this second sense: *I know that he will rise again in the resurrection on the last day* which is another case of misunderstanding. Not that her belief in the future resurrection is wrong, indeed, it is confirmed by what takes place. But Jesus is speaking of something more profound, the very foundation upon which the future resurrection itself rests. As almost always in John's Gospel, the key to unlocking Jesus' cryptic sayings is Jesus' own identity. Another way to understand his statement is to suggest that he was describing a new kind of existence beyond death that was available before the general resurrection. The context suggests that Jesus has this third meaning in mind without denying the reality or possibility of the first two. It is not surprising that Martha did not understand this. It is the new teaching that Jesus was in

---

[1]   See, he will kill me; I have no hope; but I will defend my ways to his face.

[2]   I hear, and I tremble within; my lips quiver at the sound. Rottenness enters into my bones, and my steps tremble beneath me. I wait quietly for the day of calamity to come upon the people who attack us. Though the fig tree does not blossom, and no fruit is on the vines; though the produce of the olive fails and the fields yield no food; though the flock is cut off from the fold and there is no herd in the stalls, yet I will rejoice in the Lord; I will exult in the God of my salvation. God, the Lord, is my strength; he makes my feet like the feet of a deer, and makes me tread upon the heights.

the very process of revealing. But it is also what John wants his readers to understand.

Martha has expressed her faith in the future resurrection and her brother's place in it (Jn. 11.24). Jesus responds to this statement of faith by challenging her with a deeper revelation of himself (Jn. 11.25-26):

> I am the resurrection and the life. He who believes in me will
> live, even though he dies; and whoever lives and believes in me
> will never die

All the *I am* sayings have to do with Christ as the life-giver, as is clearly the case here where we see that he does not just give life, but is life itself. As is made evident in some of the other *I am* sayings, he gives life by becoming our life (for example, Jn. 6.51;[1] 15.1[2]). The tenses of the verbs are important: *I Am* (another *ego eimi* expression) *the resurrection and the life,* i.e., Jesus is presently and always resurrection and life. Jesus is the resurrection and the life; apart from him there is no resurrection and no life, and where he is, resurrection and life must be. The resurrection is not to be understood simply as a future event at the end of time. Where Jesus is, the resurrection is present and active. The person who is presently believing in Jesus is assured of life. In fact, the continual present believing in Christ reverses the very meaning of death. Obviously Jesus is not promising that no believer will ever go through the pain of death, millions have. But the essence of death, its capacity for ultimate separation, its terminal character, its role as punishment for sin has ended for the one who totally trusts in Christ. The main point is that Jesus' own identity spans the gap between the already and the not yet: *The resurrection because the life* (Augustine, *On John* 49.14). Life is the more basic term, and the life Jesus is talking about even encompasses the resurrection life of the world to come. This 'already'

---

[1] I am the living bread that came down from heaven. Whoever eats of this bread will live for ever; and the bread that I will give for the life of the world is my flesh.'

[2] I am the true vine, and my Father is the vine-grower.

and 'not yet' was met earlier (Jn. 6.54;[1] cf. Jn. 5.24-29[2]). So we have in the raising of Lazarus a revelation of Jesus' authority and his identity as life-giver because he is life itself. Jesus' role goes far beyond our earthly existence (see Brown's comments 178:434).

The two terms Jesus uses, *resurrection* and *life,* are unpacked in the statements that follow. *I am the resurrection*: *He who believes in me will live, even though he dies* (Jn. 11.25). This statement addresses Martha directly in the situation she is experiencing with the death of her brother. Jesus' claim is mind-boggling. He says it is faith in him that brings one back to life at the resurrection at the last day. He is the ground of eschatological hope. But then he goes even further (Jn. 11.26):

I am the life: and whoever lives and believes in me will never die

The life that comes through believing in Jesus is not interrupted by physical death (cf. Moule 1975:114-125). The topic is the nature of the life that the believer has, namely one that death cannot destroy since the believer is in union with him who is the *Life*. By taking humanity into himself he has revealed the permanence of humanity's individuality and being. But this permanence can be found only in union with him. Thus two main thoughts are laid down: *Life* (resurrection) is present, and this *Life* is in a *Person*.

Martha has confessed her faith in the resurrection (Jn. 11.24), and now Jesus has revealed himself to be the source of resurrection and life itself. He asks her, *Do you believe this?* (Jn. 11.26). She, like the former blind man (Jn. 11.9.35-38), is given the opportunity to make a confession of faith. She does so in a statement that echoes earlier confessions in the

---

[1] Those who eat my flesh and drink my blood have eternal life, and I will raise them up on the last day

[2] Very truly, I tell you, anyone who hears my word and believes him who sent me has eternal life, and does not come under judgement, but has passed from death to life. 'Very truly, I tell you, the hour is coming, and is now here, when the dead will hear the voice of the Son of God, and those who hear will live. For just as the Father has life in himself, so he has granted the Son also to have life in himself; and he has given him authority to execute judgement, because he is the Son of Man. Do not be astonished at this; for the hour is coming when all who are in their graves will hear his voice and will come out, those who have done good, to the resurrection of life, and those who have done evil, to the resurrection of condemnation.

Gospel (Jn. 1. 42,49[1]) and anticipates the statement of its purpose in Jn. 20.30-31. She responds (Jn. 11.27):

> Yes, Lord, I believe that you are the Christ, the Son of God,
> who was to come into the world

She does not repeat the terms Jesus has used, but she combines two of the most common titles used for Jesus in this Gospel. It would seem that she does not really grasp what Jesus is saying, as will be clear from her response when he does raise Lazarus (Jn. 11.39). So her use of more common titles may be a sign that she has not understood him. But her faith is still genuine and solid, for it is in Jesus himself. She is not grasping all that he is saying about himself, but she is staying with him and confessing as much as she knows, which is what faith is about. As the events of the raising of Lazarus unfold Jesus will instruct her in what he has just claimed, thus bringing her step by step in her knowledge of who he is and what he is offering so she may respond in faith. The relevance of faith lies not in the power of faith as such, but in the fact that faith creates communion with Jesus and that through Jesus believers receive the gift of life. While Martha's use of terms may suggest her lack of comprehension, the effect her statement has in the unfolding revelation in this Gospel is more positive. Jesus' language of resurrection and life is combined with a common Jewish term, *Christ*, and John's favourite title for Jesus, *Son* (of God). This combination brings together several strands of thought and makes them interpret one another. The most fundamental category in John is life. At this point, when Jesus most clearly speaks of himself as life, other major terms are brought in, thus suggesting that they should be interpreted in the light of this theme of life as well. Thus, Martha's confession and Jesus' claim provide a major point of revelation in this Gospel.

---

[1] He brought Simon to Jesus, who looked at him and said, 'You are Simon son of John. You are to be called Cephas' (which is translated Peter); Nathanael replied, 'Rabbi, you are the Son of God! You are the King of Israel!'

e. The Encounter With Mary (Jn. 11.28-33)

This paragraph consists mostly of a narrative description of how Mary came to Jesus' feet. Her words are identical to those of Martha in Jn. 11.21. However, this paragraph is the transition to the raising of Lazarus and no dialogue like that of Martha and Jesus is reported (Brown 1978:435). That does not mean that no dialogue took place or that Mary did not come to the same confession of faith that Martha did. Rather, John repeats the opening line of the dialogue in Jn. 11.32. After Martha made her confession of faith Jesus apparently sent her to call her sister Mary, since she tells Mary, *The Teacher is here and is asking for you* (Jn. 11.28; more literally, *he is calling you*). The designation of Jesus as *Teacher* is interesting after the more exalted terms of Martha's confession. But it is appropriate since he had just given her a teaching. Mary runs to Jesus (Jn. 11.29), as had Martha (Jn. 11.20), showing that they had a great attachment to Jesus, which reciprocated his love for them. In coming to Jesus in the midst of suffering the sisters provide a model for all believers. John tells us that Martha gives her message secretly (Jn. 11.28) and that Mary and Jesus meet apart from the crowd (Jn. 11.30) so it would seem Jesus desires privacy, perhaps, as noted above, because he is a marked man in this region. But his desire for privacy is subverted when those who were mourning with Mary follow her, thinking she was going to wail at the tomb (Jn. 11.31). So all the mourners in the house gather at the tomb, providing witnesses to what is about to happen and thus giving them the opportunity to believe and others as well through their testimony.

When Mary reaches Jesus, she falls at his feet and says, *Lord, if you had been here, my brother would not have died* (Jn. 11.32). This is exactly what her sister had said (Jn. 11.21). Indicating, perhaps, that the sisters had been sharing this thought with one another. Whether her statement is rebuke or lamentation is unclear, as it is in the case of Martha. It could have elements of both, though the fact that she is wailing (Jn. 11.33) suggests lamentation is her main response. Mary does not add an expression of faith as Martha does (Jn. 11.2), though falling at Jesus' feet may suggest a similar attitude. That should be sufficient to remind us of the issue of faith. Instead of repeating all the words, Jesus now moves toward acting out the meaning of being resurrection and life by the miracle of raising Lazarus. Jn. 11.33 is a transition verse that belongs to both this and the next paragraph. It expresses Jesus' awareness of and response to Mary's grief. In expressing awareness it belongs with Jn. 11.28-32, in responding it belongs with Jn. 11. 34-44 for Jesus' response culminating in the raising of Lazarus.

f. Martha And Mary: Women of Faith

John introduced the three characters involved in the narrative in Jn. 11.1. It is of note that he portrays Lazarus in terms of his relationship to Mary and Martha (cf. Brown 1975:688-699). It seems likely that in the eyes of the Evangelist, both Martha and Mary were more prominent than Lazarus. The author obviously expects the story of Mary's anointing of Jesus to be familiar to his readers since he refers to it in Jn. 11.2 but has not yet narrated the event itself (cf. Jn. 12.1-8). Jesus names Martha, Mary and Lazarus as objects of Jesus' love (Jn. 11.5). The only other individual in John of whom this is said is the 'Beloved Disciple', this may imply that Mary and Martha as well as Lazarus were disciples of Jesus. In Jn. 11.3 the narrator encourages us to see Mary and Martha as persons of faith. The message they send to Jesus telling him of Lazarus' illness hints that they believe only Jesus can deal with their drastic situation. This impression is strengthened when Martha tells Jesus that if he had been there her brother would not have died. Martha's response to Jesus' assurance that her brother will rise again (Jn. 11.23) gives evidence of her theological awareness, expressing the belief of Pharisaic Judaism in the resurrection of the dead at the last judgement. It is at this point that Jesus attempts to move Martha from her affirmation of traditional eschatological expectations to a realization that he is the one who fulfils Jewish expectations. Jesus addresses one of his *I am* sayings to a woman, and Martha responds with a climactic confession of Jesus as the *Christ, the Son of God, who was to come into the world* (Jn. 11.27). Her confession is similar to Simon Peter's great confession in Mt. 16.15-19[1], which has often been viewed as related to his position of leadership. In fact, this is the closest parallel to Peter's confession found anywhere in the Gospels.

The narrative of Jn. 11 is the longest narrative found in the Fourth Gospel apart from the Passion account. It is also the climactic sign of Jesus' ministry as it immediately precedes the account of his own death and resurrection. It is significant that John chooses to highlight a story which makes a woman the recipient of one of Jesus' most profound statements about himself and in which a woman makes an accurate and appropriate response to his declaration. The dialogue between Jesus and Martha is one of the most magnificent revelations of himself which the Son of God ever made. Hers is one of the most unreserved confessions.

John presents Martha as the ideal of discerning faith. Martha's confession is notably fuller and perhaps even more satisfactory than the Petrine confession in Jn. 6.68-69.[2] It is Martha, rather than Peter, who serves as the Johannine model of discerning and steadfast faith (see, Mullins 2002:270). Within a culture which placed little value on the word and witness of women, John portrays Martha as an exemplary model of what it means to confess the truth about Jesus. Jesus transcends the typecasting of his day and views Martha as a person capable of a perceptive and discerning faith. The account illustrates the Fourth Gospel's conviction that women have a right to be taught even the mysteries of the faith, and that they are capable of responding in faith with an accurate confession. In short, they are capable of being full-fledged disciples of Jesus (Brown 1975:698; cf. Also Sneiders 1982:35-45).

---

[1] He said to them, 'But who do you say that I am?' Simon Peter answered, 'You are the Messiah, the Son of the living God.' And Jesus answered him, 'Blessed are you, Simon son of Jonah! For flesh and blood has not revealed this to you, but my Father in heaven. And I tell you, you are Peter, and on this rock I will build my church, and the gates of Hades will not prevail against it. I will give you the keys of the kingdom of heaven, and whatever you bind on earth will be bound in heaven, and whatever you loose on earth will be loosed in heaven.'

[2] Simon Peter answered him, 'Lord, to whom can we go? You have the words of eternal life. We have come to believe and know that you are the Holy One of God.'

Mary Anoints Jesus At Bethany (Jn. 12.1-8)

The Narrative Context

The raising of Lazarus from the dead is the apex of John's gospel and immediately afterwards John moves from the raising of Lazarus to a meeting of the Sanhedrin (Jn. 11.45-54). The decision of kill Jesus is approved and then the final journey to Jerusalem begins (Jn. 12.12-19). From a literary point of view Jn. 12 is somehow disorganised in that it is more a series of episodic scenes than a coherently flowing narrative. But John is more interested in what these episodes mean than the literary construction of them. There five episodes or scenes:

> Episode One: The Plot to Kill Jesus (Jn. 11.45-54)
> Episode Two: Passover material, Mary's anointing of Jesus, the plot against Lazarus (John 11.55-12.11)
> Episode Three: The Triumphal Entry (Jn. 12.12-19)
> Episode Four: The Greeks (12.20-36)
> Episode Five: The close of Jesus' public ministry, another condemnation of the rejection of Jesus, a final statement of his teaching (12.37-50).

It is within this broad canvas that John sets the anointing of Jesus by Mary between the plot to kill him (Jn. 11.45-54[1]) and the plot to kill Lazarus (Jn. 12.9-11[2]). As a result of the raising of Lazarus from the dead there is again

---

[1] Many of the Jews therefore, who had come with Mary and had seen what Jesus did, believed in him. But some of them went to the Pharisees and told them what he had done. So the chief priests and the Pharisees called a meeting of the council, and said, 'What are we to do? This man is performing many signs. If we let him go on like this, everyone will believe in him, and the Romans will come and destroy both our holy place and our nation.' But one of them, Caiaphas, who was high priest that year, said to them, 'You know nothing at all! You do not understand that it is better for you to have one man die for the people than to have the whole nation destroyed.' He did not say this on his own, but being high priest that year he prophesied that Jesus was about to die for the nation, and not for the nation only, but to gather into one the dispersed children of God. So from that day on they planned to put him to death.

[2] When the great crowd of the Jews learned that he was there, they came not only because of Jesus but also to see Lazarus, whom he had raised from the dead. So the chief priests planned to put Lazarus to death as

a variety of responses (Mullins 2002:277). Many put faith in Jesus (Jn. 11.45), but others inform the authorities (Jn. 11.46). John does not make clear whether their trip to the authorities is innocent or a betrayal of Jesus. At an earlier stage the crowd was well aware of the authorities' concerns over Jesus (Jn. 11.7.13,25[1]), and their animosity deepened significantly at the Feast of Dedication (Jn. 10.31-39[2]), leading Jesus to withdraw from the area (Jn. 10.40-42). So it may well be that this is another betrayal of Jesus, similar to the lame man's betrayal earlier in Jesus' ministry (Jn. 5.15).

The report alarms the Pharisees, and so *the chief priests and the Pharisees called a meeting of the Sanhedrin* (Jn. 12.47). The Sanhedrin was the supreme Jewish court in Jerusalem, which, under Roman oversight, had both religious and political powers and comprised the elite (both priestly and lay) of society. Both Sadducees and Pharisees were part of the Sanhedrin. Which of the two was the dominate part is uncertain, though John implies it was the *chief priests* (Jn. 7.45,48;[3] cf. Jn. 12.10[4]). The *chief priests* were members of high-priestly families, along with others from prominent priestly families (cf. Acts 4.6[5]), including, perhaps, temple officers like the treasurer and captain of police. Of the fifty-four references to *chief priests* in the Gospels, all of them are associated with Jerusalem, and almost all of them

---

well, since it was on account of him that many of the Jews were deserting and were believing in Jesus.

[1] Then after this he said to the disciples, 'Let us go to Judea again.'; Jesus, however, had been speaking about his death, but they thought that he was referring merely to sleep; Jesus said to her, 'I am the resurrection and the life. Those who believe in me, even though they die, will live,

[2] The Jews took up stones again to stone him. Jesus replied, 'I have shown you many good works from the Father. For which of these are you going to stone me?' The Jews answered, 'It is not for a good work that we are going to stone you, but for blasphemy, because you, though only a human being, are making yourself God.' Jesus answered, 'Is it not written in your law, "I said, you are gods"? If those to whom the word of God came were called "gods" and the scripture cannot be annulled can you say that the one whom the Father has sanctified and sent into the world is blaspheming because I said, "I am God's Son"? If I am not doing the works of my Father, then do not believe me. But if I do them, even though you do not believe me, believe the works, so that you may know and understand that the Father is in me and I am in the Father.' Then they tried to arrest him again, but he escaped from their hands.

[3] Then the temple police went back to the chief priests and Pharisees, who asked them, 'Why did you not arrest him?': Has any one of the authorities or of the Pharisees believed in him?

[4] So the chief priests planned to put Lazarus to death as well.

[5] And calling together all the chief priests and scribes of the people, he inquired of them where the Messiah was to be born.

concern Jesus' final conflict (the exceptions are Mt. 2.4;[1] Jn. 7.32,45). In John's Gospel the Pharisees are also closely associated with Jerusalem.

Thus the two chief components of the Sanhedrin now call the Sanhedrin together. Both the Pharisees and the chief priests had attempted to apprehend Jesus earlier (Jn. 7.32, 45), but now the situation is reaching a crisis, as they see his popularity rising. The low point after the Feeding of the Five Thousand, at which almost everyone deserted Jesus (Jn. 6.66), is now past and many are believing in him. Like many religious leaders since, Jesus is accused of being a threat to national security. Jesus' popularity could look like a popular uprising that would require calling in the Roman legions (cf. Acts 19.23-41, especially 19.40[2]), who would *come and take away both our place and our nation* (Jn. 11.48). The position of the word *our* is emphatic. In fact, this could be translated, *will come and take away from us both our place and our nation*. While they seem concerned for the nation, John says they are actually concerned about their own self-interests, as are the hirelings Jesus condemned earlier (Jn. 10.12). The irony is that they do destroy the temple of Jesus' body (cf. Jn. 2.19, 21), but this does not prevent the Romans from destroying their Temple and their nation, nor does it prevent increasing numbers of people from believing in Jesus. Their plot prevented neither of the things they feared, even though they succeeded in getting Jesus killed.

a. Mt. 26.6-13; Mk. 14.3-9; Jn. 12.1-8

It is against this background of plotting and the rationale behind it and the sense of danger that ends Jn. 11 that John sets the anointing of Jesus by Mary at Bethany during the preparations for the Passover. Throughout his gospel John has placed Jesus in Jerusalem during all the major feasts. However, at Jn. 11.55-12.1 he places particular emphasis on the Passover

---

[1] The Pharisees heard the crowd muttering such things about him; and the chief priests and Pharisees sent temple police to arrest him. Then the temple police went back to the chief priests and Pharisees, who asked them, 'Why did you not arrest him?'

[2] For we are in danger of being charged with rioting today, since there is no cause that we can give to justify this commotion.'

and the repetition of *Passover* heightens the effect that Jesus is now in the process of undertaking his most important and definitive journey to Jerusalem. As the original Passover concerned itself with the freedom (or freeing) of the people of Israel, so too this Passover concerns itself with the freedom God has commissioned Jesus to effect. At Jn. 11.55, the Evangelist makes an important reference when he writes,

> many went up from the country to Jerusalem before the Passover to purify themselves.

While Ex. 19.10-11 gives the reasoning behind the purification:

> The Lord said to Moses: 'Go to the people and consecrate them today and tomorrow. Have them wash their clothes and prepare for the third day, because on the third day the Lord will come down upon Mount Sinai in the sight of all the people

Num. 9.10 makes it clear that anyone who had been on a long journey had to purify themselves for the Passover:

> Speak to the Israelites, saying: Anyone of you or your descendants who is unclean through touching a corpse, or is away on a journey, shall still keep the passover to the Lord

This process of Passover purification, however, is not a sufficient indicator for the sanctification/consecration of Jesus on the night before he died which is more fully expressed in Jn. 17.9. That consecration of Jesus for the work of redemption is part of the role that the anointing by Mary articulates. Where John places this narrative in his gospel is also of some interest. This narrative also appears in Lk. 7.36-38 and there are discernible similarities between Mt. 26.6-13; Mk. 14.3-9 and Jn. 12.1-8 they:

- are before the Passover,
- are in Bethany,
- describe the perfume as coming from pure nard,
- mention a value of the perfume at three hundred denarii,
- conclude with Jesus' defence of the woman
- mention the poor being always present, leaving the woman alone, and burial.

It is easy to see why, therefore, some would argue that Mt. 26.6-13; Mk. 14.3-9; Jn. 12.1-8 are, in fact, different versions of the same story. However, there are some fundamental differences between these versions (see, Brown 1978:450):

Matthew/Mark	John
• two days before the Passover, • after the Triumphal Entry	• six days before the Passover • before the Triumphal Entry
• no mention of Lazarus, Martha, Mary • at house of Simon the Leper	• Mary, Martha, and Lazarus • at their house
• Jesus' head is anointed	• Jesus' feet are anointed

It is also worth noting that in Lk. 7.36-38 the narrative takes place at the house of Simon *the Pharisee* and the anointing happens much earlier in the Galilean ministry. The fact that Jn. 11.2 has already mentioned the anointing which does not take place until Jn. 12.1-8 is somewhat confusing and it is not the way we would remember or even record what we considered to be a historical event today. These text issues surrounding the anointing of Jesus may never be resolved but it is clear for John (as it is for the other Evangelists) that this event was important and serves a number of functions:

- it is part of the consecration of Jesus for his death it contrasts with the purification that the Jews were undergoing in Jn. 11.55
- it is a preparation for burial
- John especially emphasises that the anointing points to Jesus' burial in Jn. 12.7
- the anointing represented the anointing of Jesus as king
- next event to be narrated in John is Jesus' Triumphal Entry as the King

These are important theological reasons for John to place this narrative before the 'Triumphal Entry' which clearly marks the beginning to the Johannine Passion Narrative.

b. Mary Anoints Jesus At Bethany (Jn. 12.1-8)

Six days before the Passover Jesus came to Bethany, the home of Lazarus, whom he had raised from the dead. There they gave a dinner for him. Martha served, and Lazarus was one of those at the table with him. Mary took a pound of costly perfume made of pure nard, anointed Jesus' feet, and wiped them with her hair. The house was filled with the fragrance of the perfume. But Judas Iscariot, one of his disciples (the one who was about to betray him), said, 'Why was this perfume not sold for three hundred denarii and the money given to the poor?' (He said this not because he cared about the poor, but because he was a thief; he kept the common purse and used to steal what was put into it.) Jesus said, 'Leave her alone. She bought it so that she might

> keep it for the day of my burial. You always have the poor with
> you, but you do not always have me.'

Jn. 11.55 has heightened both the tension and the sense of danger that Jesus is in for the

> the chief priests and the Pharisees had given orders that anyone
> who knew where Jesus was should let them know, so that they
> might arrest him.

And now he has returned to Bethany and the site of the raising of Lazarus from the dead (Jn. 12.1). It is while he is there that a meal is prepared for him (Jn. 12.2). Unlike Mt. 26.6-13; Mk. 14.3-9, who locate this event in the house of Simon the Leper, John does not give the venue though from Jn. 12.1-2 it is not unreasonable to assume that it was at the house of the siblings. Lazarus is also present (Jn. 12.2c). Martha, in keeping with the picture presented of her elsewhere (Lk. 10.38-42) is serving. John depiction of Mary is also true to that of Lk. 10.38-42 for he presents her as a devoted disciple who quite definitively sets aside or ignores the societal, cultural and religious taboos in how she approaches and behaves with Jesus. In Luke she *sat at the Lord's feet and listened to what he was saying* (Lk. 10.39b) but while *sitting* at the feet of a male (the attitude a disciple adopts to a teacher) was not the place for a woman but serving the meal (Martha's complaint), Jesus commends her for *she has chosen the better part* (Lk. 10.42b). John, however, now shows her behaviour and deportment in an even more shocking and scandalous way for she pours expensive ointment over Jesus' feet, anoints them and then wipes it with her hair (Jn. 12.3).

In the accounts in Matthew and Mark, she anoints Jesus' head, while in John it is his feet. Obviously, it could have been both, and with so much ointment to use with she could have anointed his whole body. Indeed, since he interprets this as an anointing for his burial (Jn. 12.7) it seems she did anoint more than his head and feet, as Matthew and Mark suggest (Mt. 26.12; Mk 14.8). The other part of her action that would have been quite disturbing was the wiping of his feet with her hair. Jewish women did not let down their hair in public. This is an expression of devotion that would have come across as extremely improper and even somewhat erotic, as indeed it would in most cultures. There is no indication of why Mary did this act. The most obvious possibility was her sheer gratitude for what Jesus had done for her brother and the revelation it brought to her of Jesus' identity, power, authority and grace. John's focus on her anointing Jesus' feet points to Mary's great humility. As she has come to realise a bit more of the one who has been a friend to her and her brother and sister, her faith deepens and she recognises her unworthiness. The humility of her act prepares us to be all the more scandalised when Jesus himself washes his disciples' feet in the next chapter.

It was bad enough for a woman to let her hair down in public with the associations attendant upon such an action (the suggestion of prostitution) but the scandalous nature of this act is compounded by the type of ointment she uses, very expense imported nard. The other part of her action that would have been quite disturbing was the wiping of his feet with her hair. Jewish women did not let down their hair in public. This is an expression of devotion that would have come across as extremely improper and even somewhat erotic, as indeed it would in most cultures. There is no indication of why Mary did this. The most obvious possibility was her sheer gratitude for what Jesus had done for her brother and the revelation it brought to her of Jesus' identity, power, authority and grace. John's focus on her anointing Jesus' feet points to Mary's great humility. As she has come to realise a bit more of the one who has been a friend to her and her brother and sister, her faith deepens and she recognises her unworthiness. The humility of her act prepares us to be all the more scandalised when Jesus himself washes his disciples' feet in the Jn. 13.1-11. This was an extravagance that was outrageous. John says that it was Judas who pointed out that this expensive ointment (worth a year's wages) could have been sold and the money given to the poor (Jn. 12.5) (though Mark says that the *disciples* complained about the waste cf. Mk. 12.). It is clear that Jesus' teaching on the wise use of possessions had sunk in, but as can often happen, a certain hardness had also crept into the thinking of some of the disciples articulated by Judas. Jesus would remind them that a balance needs to be struck. Their hardness contrasted with Mary's generosity of spirit. Jesus, therefore, sees this is in a different light and springs to Mary's defence (Jn. 12.7-8):

> 'Leave her alone. She bought it so that she might keep it for the day of my burial. You always have the poor with you, but you do not always have me

Interestingly Jesus' comment both approves of their general attitude while at the same time gently rebuking their lack of insight. Mark says *she has done what she could, she has anointed my body beforehand for burial*. What Jesus therefore intended them to understand was that this moment must not be spoiled by arguments. As with the High Priest earlier (Jn. 11.49-51) her act was unconsciously a prophetic action (although possibly subconsciously it held within it a hint of prophecy, it is such as Mary who sometimes have a presentiment of doom, and she would know of his earlier teaching about his future suffering at the hands of the Jewish leaders, and she would be well aware of the threats that were going around). She had by it anointed him for his burial in advance. So he means 'let her keep what she has done for the day of my burial' - when that day came and he was buried unanointed, she would say to herself 'I anointed him in readiness for this' and be comforted. What seemed like extravagance would be seen to have been a necessity. So whatever Mary's intentions and reason for her action, Jesus sees it in reference to his coming death (Jn. 12.7). Jesus sees cryptic significance in another person's actions instead of making his more usual cryptic explanation of his own activity. There is no reason to think Mary knew the full import of what she was doing, any more than Caiaphas knew what he was saying (Jn. 11.49-51). The people around Jesus are being caught up in the climax of all of salvation history. They are acting for their own reasons, yet they are players in a drama that they do not understand, doing and saying things with significance beyond their imaginings. Mary in her devotion unconsciously provides for the honour of the dead. Judas in his selfishness unconsciously brings about the death itself. Jesus' statement in Jn. 12.8, *You will always have the poor among you, but you will not always have me,* must be understood in its context both within Judaism and salvation history. On one level Jesus is simply reminding Judas and the others of priorities as understood within Judaism. He is alluding to the Scripture *there will always be poor people in the land* (Deut. 15.11) and perhaps also to the notion that acts of kindness, such as burial, are higher than works of charity, which would include giving alms to the poor (*b. Sukka* 49b). This view is based, in part, on the fact that kindness can be shown to the living and the dead (through funerals and burials), whereas charity can only be shown to the living. So the fact that Jesus is about to die (cf. Jn. 12.35-36) justifies Mary's action. But on another level, the identity of Jesus also justifies this action. In the Synoptics even the burying of one's father is put second to responding to Jesus and the call of the kingdom (Mt. 8.22; Lk. 9.60). So this anointing also makes sense given who Jesus is and the awesome events unfolding in salvation history.

Mary, then, is presented as a loving disciple literally at the feet of Jesus who is not afraid to shatter the taboos of her society, whether they be social or religious and faithfully prepares Jesus for burial in a profound act of loving service. In this respect she is to be seen as the disciple par excellence.

CHAPTER TWELVE

JESUS AND THE WOMEN AT THE CROSS

The Narrative Context

All four gospels are in agreement that there were women gathered at the foot of the cross:

Mk. 15.40-41:

> There were also women looking on from a distance; among
> them were Mary Magdalene, and Mary the mother of James the
> younger and of Joses, and Salome. These used to follow him
> and provided for him when he was in Galilee; and there were
> many other women who had come up with him to Jerusalem.

Mt. 27.55-56:

> Many women were also there, looking on from a distance; they
> had followed Jesus from Galilee and had provided for him.
> Among them were Mary Magdalene, and Mary the mother of
> James and Joseph, and the mother of the sons of Zebedee.

Lk. 23.49:

> But all his acquaintances, including the women who had
> followed him from Galilee, stood at a distance, watching these
> things

Jn. 19.25b:

> Meanwhile, standing near the cross of Jesus were his mother,
> and his mother's sister, Mary the wife of Clopas, and Mary

Magdalene

That women were an integral and essential part of Jesus' life and ministry need not be gainsaid. Of special mention, of course, is Mary Magdalene who will be treated of in a moment. As Lk. 23.49 mentions *the women who had followed him from Galilee*, if we return to Galilee through using Lk. 8.1-3 then we read:

> Soon afterwards he went on through cities and villages, proclaiming and bringing the good news of the kingdom of God. The twelve were with him, as well as some women who had been cured of evil spirits and infirmities: Mary, called Magdalene, from whom seven demons had gone out, and Joanna, the wife of Herod's steward Chuza, and Susanna, and many others, who provided for them out of their resources

The text says that Mary Magdalene was the one what had *seven demons* cast from her but the context also suggests that Joanna and Susanna had also been in some difficulty physical or spiritual and had been healed by Jesus. One of the key phrases in this text is *with Jesus* and while this is specified of *the Twelve* the women are connected by *as well as*. These women, therefore, are *with* Jesus and are an integral part of the community that had gathered around Jesus and which they supported from their *own means*. That Luke considered these women to be important can be seen when the structure of 'disciple' names narratives is compared:

Lk. 6.12-16	Lk. 8.2-3
Now during those days he went out to the mountain to pray; and he spent the night in prayer to God. And when day came, he called his disciples and chose twelve of them, whom he also named apostles: Simon, whom he named Peter, and his	as well as some women who had been cured of evil spirits and infirmities: Mary, called Magdalene, from whom seven demons had gone out, and Joanna, the wife of Herod's steward Chuza, and Susanna, and many others, who provided

brother Andrew, and James, and John, and Philip, and Bartholomew, and Matthew, and Thomas, and James son of Alphaeus, and Simon, who was called the Zealot, and Judas son of James, and Judas Iscariot, who became a traitor.	for them out of their own resources

This can be demonstrated further when the structural elements of Lk. 4.31-6.49 and Lk. 7.1-8.21 are compared. Again, it is worth noting that Lk. 8.1-3 can be structured thus:

A. Soon afterwards he went on through cities and villages, proclaiming and bringing the good news of the kingdom of God. The twelve were with him	A. Mary, called Magdalene, from whom seven demons had gone out, and Joanna, the wife of Herod's steward Chuza, and Susanna, and many others, who provided for them out of their resources.
B. as well as some women who had been cured of evil spirits and infirmities	

So that here one may argue that the ministry of Jesus in Galilee and the disciples *with him* can be set alongside *as well as* the *some women* so that the women also have role in the Galilean ministry of Jesus. Precisely what that role is is hard to determine save that Luke says they *provided for them out of their own resources*. Is the text saying that the women in fact are *not* disciples in the commonly understood sense of the term but rather wealthy women who have become his benefactoresses? Does the fact they provide *for them* that since they are not providing for Jesus himself they cannot be considered *disciples* in the strict sense of the term? Opinions differ on how precisely the women are to be understood within the context of the group with some scholars suggesting they are to be considered 'disciples' while others suggest they are not 'disciples' in the strict sense of the term but rather a 'support group' for Jesus and the male disciples. However, the women are in the group that *follow* Jesus and they are *with him*, plus they provide for the group out of their own resources and so they can be understood as not only supporting the mission but as actively participating in it.

Lk. 8.1-3 shows a group of women who are alongside Jesus and the male disciples, participating in the activity of the group, ministering to it from their own resources and supporting it. Further, the way Lk. 8.1-3 is structured indicates that these women have, in some way, encountered Jesus in a healing experience either from evil spirits (Mary Magdalene) or illness and infirmity. This 'possession' or these illnesses, as with others in the gospels, would have resulted in alienation, isolation and marginalisation either within or from the community. Aside from the healing restoring them to the Jewish community, they are now part of the community of Jesus and their relationship with Jesus is contextualised or identified by that healing and restoration. It might also be noted here that Luke, in naming the women and their role and function within the group, does not present their presence in the wandering community of Jesus as something unusual in the sense that while their own society may have found their very public presence in such a group as questionable and scandalous, their presence in the community around Jesus was normal.

Mary Magdalene appears in all four gospels as one of the women who was at the foot of the cross, saw where Jesus was buried and was at the tomb on the first day of the week (see below). Neither Joanna or Susanna is mentioned anywhere other than Luke and Joanna is mentioned in relation to her husband who himself is mentioned in relation Herod. This is interesting insofar as while being associated with Herod's house through her husband may have given her independent financial and social standing, her association with Herod may well have been viewed with suspicion. Her identity now, however, is to be found in the fact that she was healed by Jesus, is in relation to him and is part of his wandering community (the same is applicable to Susanna, also healed by Jesus). These women, therefore, are now seen in the relation to Jesus and his wandering community in which they have found a new place and new role. Their ministering to the community's needs from their own resources is to be seen, therefore, as their expression of their discipleship rather than simply 'tagged on' to the activity of the male disciples within the same community.

a. Mk. 15.40-41

> There were also women looking on from a distance; among them were Mary Magdalene, and Mary the mother of James the younger and of Joses, and Salome. These used to follow him and provided for him when he was in Galilee; and there were many other women who had come up with him to Jerusalem

Mk.15.40-41 is the first mention in the gospel tradition of the presence of women at the foot of the cross and sets the scene and tone for their mention in the other Synoptics and John. This section will not treat of the presence of the women at the cross in Matthew or Luke but concentrate on Mark and Mary Magdalene in Jn. 20.1-18. Mark names them as *Mary Magdalene, and Mary the mother of James the younger and of Joses, and Salome* (Mk. 15.40) and identifies them as those who *used to follow him and provided for him when he was in Galilee* (as Luke, see above, has also mentioned a group of women who followed and looked after him). Mark has other narratives where women appear (Simon's mother-in-law, the woman with the haemorrhage, Jairus' daughter, the Syro-Phoenician woman, the woman who anoints him at Bethany) (cf. Malbon 1983:36-37) but this is the first time he has mentioned this group as having followed Jesus from Galilee (cf. Miller 2002:212). The women of the previous narratives have been portrayed in a very positive light and one might wonder why Mark has not mentioned the group who followed Jesus in Galilee up to this point.

The first one in the list, Mary Magdalene, holds a special place in the imagination and story of the Christian community to the extent that the legend has obscured the reality. She appears in all four gospels in the narratives of death, burial and resurrection of Jesus (Mt. 28.1-10; Lk. 24.1-12; Jn. 20.1-18). Variously, Mary Magdalene is understood to be the woman caught in adultery (Jn. 7.35-8.11), that she was a sinner, that she anointed Jesus at Bethany Mk.14.3-9; Mt. 26.6-13) that she was a prostitute (for which there is no substance at all). None of these, however, are to be found in the gospels texts, only Luke says that she had *seven devils* exorcised from her by Jesus (Lk. 8.1). Throughout the gospels the women have been set in relation to the men, i.e., Mary and Martha in relation to their sibling, Lazarus, Jairus' daughter, Joanna, the wife of Chuza, Mary, the mother of Jesus, Mary the mother of James and Joses etc. Mary Magdalene, however, is set in relation to her home town, Magdala in the north west of Galilee. Mary. Therefore, like Jesus and the Twelve is from Galilee. If Mary left her home town in Galilee to follow Jesus and was with him right up to the cross (and beyond), then she can be understood as a disciple in the same way the first Galilean disciples of Jesus are understood. They left their homes and everything else to follow Jesus, so too did Mary Magdalene. Mark gives no other information about Mary Magdalene other than her home town and that she followed Jesus on his ministry in Galilee and then, finally, into Jerusalem and to the cross (cf. Martin 2005:442). The fact that Mark gives no other information about her (though the so-called 'Longer Ending of Mark', Mk. 16.9 refers to her the one who had *seven demons cast from her* but this may a conflation of Lk. 8.1 in this later addition to Mark's ending) would seem to indicate that she was well known in the Markan community and therefore he did not need to supply extra material about her.

Mary, *the mother of James and Joses* cannot be identified with any certainty (cf. Gundry 1993:977). Possibly the same woman as *Mary of Joses* (Mk. 15.47) and *Mary of James* (Mk. 16.1). The differing descriptions may indicate different sources for his material or just deliberate variation. She may also be 'the other Mary' (Mt. 27.61; 28.1 compare

27.56). But Mary the mother of Jesus could also have been called the mother of James and Joses (Mk. 6.3), and it is interesting that John alone otherwise mentions her presence at the cross (and does not mention Mary the mother of James and Joses). But this is unconvincing because, aside from the difficulties this would pose for Roman Catholic and Orthodox Christians, Mark always mentions the mother of Jesus specifically as such (cf. Mk. 3.31, 32; 6.3) and does not say that *Mary, the mother of James and Joses* is the mother of Jesus and only gives two names here rather than the four at Mk. 6.3. Further, Matthew and Luke do not make this association. Identification of a woman by a son's name was commonplace among the Arabs and was probably Semitic custom if the husband was dead. James may have been called 'James the less' because he was small or simply because he was the younger brother. We do not know whether he can be connected with James the son of Alphaeus (Mk. 3.18). The identification of *Mary the mother of James and Joses*, therefore, with Mary the mother of Jesus is to be treated with great caution.

The woman named as *Salome,* possibly the wife of Zebedee, and mother of James and John (Mt. 27.56), but Mark makes no mention of her as the mother if these disciples. Lk. 23.49 refers to *the women who had followed him from Galilee* but does not list their names but at Lk. 24.10 he lists the women who go the tomb as *Mary Magdalene, Joanna, and Mary the mother of Joses,* (as well as other unnamed women). No mention is made of any husbands for Mary Magdalene and Salome and Mary the mother of James and Joses is not presented in relation to her husband but her sons, possibly indicating she was a widow. However, all this may simply mean that in the community gathered around Jesus women acted independently of their husbands (cf. Miller's comment 2002:210). The actual naming of the woman is significant since earlier in Mark the women are anonymous (except for Herodias, Mk. 6.14-29) and their significance lies in not just the fact that they were at the foot of the cross but that they saw where Jesus were buried (Mk. 15.47), went to anoint him and found the tomb empty (Mk. 16:1). These women, therefore, have an extraordinary importance in the early Christian community as witnesses to the Resurrection and this would explain their naming and prominence (see, Munro 1982:236) Mark describes *many other women who had come up with him to Jerusalem* (Mk. 15.41). All the evangelists speak of the crowds that *follow* Jesus and women were present in these crowds (it is worth noting that the woman with the haemorrhage emerges out of the crowd(Mk. 5.27):

> She had heard about Jesus, and came up behind him in the crowd and touched his cloak

and Mk. 10.32 says,

> They were on the road, going up to Jerusalem, and Jesus was walking ahead of them; they were amazed, and those who followed were afraid

where being 'on the road' to Jerusalem with Jesus is to be understood to be in discipleship and it is entirely possible that the group of women *who had come up with him to Jerusalem* were part of this group (cf. Selvidge 1983:. The women at the foot of the cross, therefore, are to be clearly understood as disciples, i.e., those who had left homes, husbands (perhaps) and previous ways of life to 'follow Jesus' on the *road to Jerusalem*.

The women at the foot of the cross have been constant members of the group that have followed Jesus from Galilee to Jerusalem for the Passover (Corley 2002:198) and they are portrayed by Mark in a more positive light than the male disciples who betrayed him (Mk. 14.44) (see, Sweetland 2007:200) deserted him (Mk. 14.50), denied him (Mk. 14.66-72). The male disciples were the ones Jesus called originally to follow him and be with him (Mk. 3.14) and they have been with him until the time of his arrest (Mk. 14.50). Matthew makes no reference to the disciples at the cross and Luke tries to rehabilitate them by not mentioning their desertion of Jesus in Gethsemane and by suggesting that at least a few were present at the cross (Lk. 23.49). John places the 'Beloved Disciple' at the cross with the mother of Jesus, Mary Magdalene and Mary the wife of Clopas (Jn. 19.25-27). However, it might be noted that while Mark presents the women in a more positive light than the male disciples, they may not be being presented entirely as such for they watch *at a distance* (Mk. 15.40), the same phrase is used on Peter in Mk. 14.54 and *at a distance* is the opposite of *with him* which the disciples were called to be (cf. Mullins 2002:437). Peter still follows Jesus but *at a distance* meaning that he does not want to be identified with him, in other words, Peter's distance from Jesus is a failure.

Whether the women *standing at a distance* is to be understood in this way is a matter of some debate (see, Selvidge's interesting idea on this 1983:399). In Peter's case Mark intends to show Peter's failure, in the case of the women standing at the foot of the cross their *distance* may not be implying failure because it does not follow that they stood *at a distance* because they did not want to be associated with Jesus too closely (Tolbert 1989:192). While it is true that families of those being crucified were often present at such executions, it is well attested in extra biblical sources that the families of the 'criminal' could also face retribution and suffering (Tacitus *Annals* 6: 10,19; Josephus, *Jewish War.* 2.253), so the women may have stood at a distance because of the presence of the Roman soldiers and the Chief Priests (Mk. 15.31) (Schotroff 1993:170-172) Given the nature of the charges levelled against Jesus, that he is treated as a seditionist (Mk. 14.48), that is is crucified with two other seditionists (M.15.27), that before Pilate he is accused of claiming to be a king (Mk. 15.2) and the statement of the placard on the cross (Mk. 15.26), all of which add up to 'political' crimes, it is entirely possible that the women feared for their own safety and so kept their distance. The presence of the women at the cross continues after the death of Jesus since *Mary Magdalene and Mary the mother Joses saw where the body was laid* (Mk. 15.47; Lk. 23.55). The women are watching and are involved in the hasty burial of Jesus undertaken by Joseph of Arimathea

(Mk. 15.42-46). As a respected member of the Sanhedrin, Joseph of Arimathea was in a better position to petition Pilate for Jesus' body than the women who would have been regarded as having little or no social status or authority. It has been suggested that Joseph may have been present at the 'Jewish Trial' of Jesus and therefore have condemned him to death, in which case his petitioning for the body has more to do with the holiness of the Passover than care of Jesus (see, Brown 1988:23-45). This is unconvincing: Joseph does not ask for the bodies of the other two crucified with Jesus, he wraps Jesus in a shroud and places him in an unused tomb then seals it with the stone (Mk. 15.46). This is an extraordinary length to go to care for the dead body of someone he has condemned to death wherein if this were the case he would have regarded Jesus as a blasphemer just as the High Priest proclaimed (Mk. 14.63). These actions on the part of Joseph for the body of Jesus do not suggest one who is antagonistic towards Jesus but rather seem to be the actions of one who respected, admired and loved Jesus.

Similarly, the suggestion that the women are to be viewed negatively because they do not assist Joseph in this important Jewish custom of care for the dead must also be rejected (cf. Brown 1994:2.1158). The women stood at a distance because the possibility existed that they too would have been persecuted (and perhaps even killed) for their association with Jesus (Miller 2002:229). They will, however, return at the first opportunity they can to perform those rituals which Jesus was denied in such haste (Mk. 16.1-8). It is further interesting to note that they return without, it seems, having conferred with anyone (including Joseph of Arimathea and the disciples) about doing so since they have a very practical discussion about who will roll always the stone for them (Mk. 16.3). The women at the foot of the cross, therefore, stand as witnesses to the death of Jesus and are aligned with the passion and death of Jesus (Byrne 2002:249; see Gnilka's observation on this 1978:2.334; see, Brown 1994:2.1157-1158)). The women have followed Jesus from Galilee to Jerusalem and remained with him while the male disciples have abandoned him and fled into hiding. The women stay with Jesus from the moment of his crucifixion up to the moment he is placed into the tomb and intend to return after the Sabbath to perform for him those duties to the dead that were so sacred among the Jews. The women at the foot of the cross, therefore, are true, faithful and loving disciples who care for and serve Jesus even after his death.

CHAPTER THIRTEEN
JESUS AND THE WOMEN AT THE EMPTY TOMB
Mk. 16.1-8 & Jn. 20.1-20

The Narrative Context

In Mk. 16.1-8 the women who were at the cross and who saw where Jesus was laid make their way to the tomb at first light on the *first day of the week* with the intention of performing for Jesus those rites of the dead which he was denied in his hasty burial. They wonder who will move the stone away for them but on arriving at the tomb they find it already moved back, the body of Jesus not in the tomb and a young man who tells them that Jesus is risen and that he has gone to Galilee to meet the disciples there as he said. The women flee the tomb in terror and tell no one. In Mt. 28.1-10, Mary Magdalene and *the other Mary* make their way to the tomb, there is a great earthquake, an angel appears rolled back the stone and sat upon it. The angel tells the women not to be afraid, that Jesus is risen and that he has gone to Galilee and will meet the disciples there. The women run from the tomb in fear and joy to tell the disciples but they are met by Jesus who greets them and they fall at his feet and worship him. Jesus himself then tells them not to be afraid and to go and tell the disciples he will see them in Galilee. Lk. 24.1-12 has the women coming to the tomb who found the stone rolled away, going in thy did not find the body. Then two men in dazzling clothes stand in front of them tell and them that Jesus is risen. They return to tell the male disciples who do not believe them and who come to the tomb, Peter goes inside, sees the burial cloth lying there and believes. Jn. 20.1-10;11-18 has Mary Magdalene come to the tomb, find the stone rolled back, the body of Jesus not here. She runs back to tell the disciples, run to the to, themselves, Peter goes inside, while the 'Beloved Disciple' stays outside, sees the burial cloths rolled up and believes and then returns home. Later, Mary Magdalene returns to the tomb and encounters someone she believes to be the gardener until it is revealed to her that it is Jesus himself. The preceding paragraph is obviously a weak paraphrase of the content of the resurrection narratives but while there are disagreements between the narratives the fundamentals of the narratives do not change:

- Mary Magdalene and others come to the tomb
- It is the first day of the week
- It is not yet light
- The stone is rolled back
- Heavenly beings are present
- They announce that Jesus is risen

These are the core features of the experience of the women at the tomb. It will not be the intention here to deal with all the accounts of the women at the empty tomb so the concentration will be given to Mark (as the first written account) and John (as the last written account). But also because Mary Magdalene features in all the accounts of the women at the tomb and her role is prominent in Mark and John.

a. The Markan Account (Mk. 16.1-8)

When the Sabbath was over, Mary Magdalene, and Mary the mother of James, and Salome bought spices, so that they might go and anoint him. And very early on the first day of the week, when the sun had risen, they went to the tomb. They had been saying to one another, 'Who will roll away the stone for us from the entrance to the tomb?' When they looked up, they saw that the stone, which was very large, had already been rolled back. As they entered the tomb, they saw a young man, dressed in a white robe, sitting on the right side; and they were alarmed. But he said to them, 'Do not be alarmed; you are looking for Jesus of Nazareth, who was crucified. He has been raised; he is not here. Look, there is the place they laid him. But go, tell his disciples and Peter that he is going ahead of you to Galilee; there you will see him, just as he told you.' So they went out and fled from the tomb, for terror and amazement had seized them; and they said nothing to anyone, for they were afraid.

Mark's account of the experience of the women at the tomb of Jesus is telescoped and it is stark. He does not fill in any of the details but gives the barest minimum of information. He tells us first that these three had to buy more spices once the Sabbath was over. They had discovered that they did not have sufficient, but the arrival of the Sabbath had cut short their plans and nothing could be done on the Sabbath. The purchase of spices and their application to the body were forbidden on the Sabbath. So they waited until after sunset on that day and then went out and purchased what they needed. We should perhaps note the love revealed by their actions (see, Hooker 1991:383). Jesus had now been dead for over a day, and by the time they reached it a day and a half, yet they were determined that he should be anointed, come what may. Mark says nothing about Mary Magdalene, the youngest and most agile, leaving the others in their preparation, going on ahead to discover what was happening at the tomb, her subsequent experiences and her meeting up with Jesus Himself (Jn. 20.1-18). For what Mark concerns himself with is the experience of the whole band of women who had shared the vigil at the cross.

Mark names the women again as he had done as they stood at the foot of the cross and in doing so he highlights their importance as witnesses. Since these were the women who were present at the cross, they can therefore witness to his death, and further, since these are the women who see where Jesus was buried they witness to his burial. In this context, therefore, the suggestion that the woman went to the wrong tomb on the Sunday morning has to be rejected. Since they come to the right tomb, they also serve as witnesses to the resurrection. It might be noted at this point that women are the key witnesses in all the resurrection accounts since they are the first ones at the tomb (Mt. 28.1-10; Lk. 24.1-11; Jn. 20.11-18).

Mary Magdalene and the other Mary are present at the foot of the cross as is Salome who is also at the tomb. Mary Magdalene figures in all four accounts and since she is mentioned first this highlights her prominence and importance in the community as a witness. Thus, the role and function of the women as witnesses to the empty tomb, the angel's message, and the resurrection, is of vital importance and significance.

b. The Women As Witnesses

However, this raises the crucial point of the validity of their witness. Women could not be witnesses (Josephus notes this, cf. *Antiquities* 4.219) which may explain why the males disciples did not originally believe their testimony (Lk. 24.11; Jn. 20.2-8). There are, however, passages in the Mishnah which do accept the testimony of women (*m. Yebam.* 16: 5; b. *Bek.* 46b). The Mishnah does not explicitly exclude the testimony of women it rather assumes that women do not act as witnesses (*m. Sanh.* 3:3-4) (Ilan 1995:163-66). In Lev.5.1 the Law relating to testimony applied to men but not to women but there were exceptions to this rule (*m. Ketub.* 1.6-7; 2:5-6; *m. Yebam.* 15.1-2; 16.7; *in. Sebu.* 5.1; 6.1; 7.8). But how far the Mishnah was in use during New Testament period is a matter of some debate (Wenger 1988:120ff.). The strange ending of Mark which depicts the women fleeing from the empty tomb in terror (Mk. 16.8), telling *no one* because they *were afraid* is interpreted to mean that Mark depicts the women as failures and Luke is clear that the males disciples regarded what they heard from the women as an *idle tale and did not believe them* (Lk. 24.11). It is clear, however, that the women do witness to the resurrection, whether in the first instance they are believed or not.

c. The Intention To Anoint (Mk. 16.1)

Mark shows the women to be true observers of the Law since they wait until Sabbath is over to go to anoint the body of Jesus. Further, he touches on something of their compassion and love for Jesus because although Joseph of Arimathea has done what he could for Jesus (Mk. 15.42-43), the women do not feel that Jesus has had the proper treatment that Jewish piety demands. This action of the women can be contrasted with the inaction of the disciples who are nowhere to be seen and unlike the disciples of John the Baptist, they offer no final farewell to their Master (Mk. 6.14-29). Further, the intention to anoint the body of Jesus recalls the anointing at Bethany (Mk. 14.3-9) (Mullins 2002:441). On that occasion, the anointing had messianic significance insofar as Jesus is anointed as King and he interprets it as a preparation for his own burial as the crucified King of the Jews. So, an anointing of the body of Jesus by a woman frames the beginning of the Passion Narrative and the desire to anoint the body of Jesus frames the end of the Passion Narrative: the anointing at Bethany points to the death of Jesus, the intention of the women to anoint the dead body of Jesus points to the resurrection (cf. Mullins 2002:442). The women who come to the tomb, therefore, show themselves to be true disciples of Jesus in that they 'stand beside' him in solidarity and faithfulness. This is contrasted with the male disciples who have abandoned him and are nowhere to be seen after his death.

The women who go to the tomb have followed Jesus from Galilee and have, therefore, been involved in his ministry there and have faithfully been with him *on the road* as he journeyed to Jerusalem. They are *with him* right to the end and they demonstrate their fidelity and courage by standing at the foot of the cross and then visiting the tomb in the early hours of the Sunday morning to anoint his body. Aside from Joseph of Arimathea, all the males who interact with Jesus in the Passion narrative do so negatively and destructively and in some cases (the Chief Priests, Pilate, the soldiers) they are men of great power. The women who followed Jesus to the cross interact with Jesus positively and lovingly but they are powerless (even down to their question about who will move the stone for them, love has not reasoned out their situation!). But even given this, it is the women who decide to go to the tomb and they fully expect to find the body of Jesus, they do not expect to find it empty. It may be argued that there is some foolishness in their going to the tomb because Jesus had already predicted his rising on the third day in the Passion Prophecies while on the road to Jerusalem from Galilee (Mk. 8.31;[1] 9.31;[2] 10.33-34[3]). But this is to presume that the women heard the prophecies which is by no means made clear by Mark. It is possible they heard the first two but the third prophecy is given to the Twelve alone (Mk. 10.33-34). It cannot be argued, therefore, that the women had any inkling or expectation of the resurrection. What is clear, however, is their loyalty and faithfulness to Jesus in intending to go to the tomb to anoint him.

d. The Women At The Tomb (Mk. 16.5-8)

> As they entered the tomb, they saw a young man, dressed in a white robe, sitting on the right side; and they were alarmed. But he said to them, 'Do not be alarmed; you are looking for Jesus of Nazareth, who was crucified. He has been raised; he is not here. Look, there is the place they laid him. But go, tell his disciples and Peter that he is going ahead of you to Galilee; there you will see him, just as he told you.'

The difficulty the women who go to the tomb face is enhanced by the discussion the women have about a very practical issue, viz., *Who will roll away the stone for us from the entrance to the tomb?* They had brought no help with them and they seem to be indicating that they could not roll back the large stone by themselves even if there were a group of them. What they were not expecting was that the stone *which was very large, had already been rolled back.* Mark highlights the enormity of their task of rolling away

---

[1] Then he began to teach them that the Son of Man must undergo great suffering, and be rejected by the elders, the chief priests, and the scribes, and be killed, and after three days rise again.

[2] For he was teaching his disciples, saying to them, 'The Son of Man is to be betrayed into human hands, and they will kill him, and three days after being killed, he will rise again.'

[3] 'See, we are going up to Jerusalem, and the Son of Man will be handed over to the chief priests and the scribes, and they will condemn him to death; then they will hand him over to the Gentiles; they will mock him, and spit upon him, and flog him, and kill him; and after three days he will rise again.'

the stone by stating that it was *very large* but it had already been rolled back (cf. Mullins 2002:442; Byrne 2008:254). For all their practical questioning about who would roll the stone back for them, they had not factored in what God could do: the reference to the *very large* stone emphasises the power of God not just in rolling back the stone but in 'rolling back' death itself (from Mt. 28.2 it seems that the stone was knocked out of its groove by an earthquake caused by an angel, and it was lying on its side).

> As they entered the tomb, they saw a young man, dressed in a
> white robe, sitting on the right side; and they were alarmed.

Mark does not say who this *young man* was but he undoubtedly means an angel (Matthew says it was *an angel of the Lord*) (cf. Mullins 2002:442; Byrne 2008:255-256). The response of the women to this young man is terror: the Greek verb Mark uses to describe this 'ekthambeó', means, 'astonished', 'awe-struck', 'to be out of one's senses' and is used only by Mark (see, Lane 1974:591; Mullins 2002:442 esp. n.123). In other words, the women are frightened out of their skin and this is a natural reaction: they had expected to find the body of Jesus but instead they find the stone rolled away, no body, and a *young man* sitting there. Terror, therefore, is a natural reaction from the women (cf. Donahue and Harrington 2002:458). But they are encouraged by the *young man* (in the manner of all biblical encounters with heavenly beings) with the words *Do not be alarmed* and he then tells them that he knows why they have come,

> you are looking for Jesus of Nazareth, who was crucified. He
> has been raised; he is not here. Look, there is the place they laid
> him.

The young man uses the formal mode of reference to Jesus, *Jesus of Nazareth who was crucified*. This was the name that had been written in the inscription on the cross, *Jesus of Nazareth, (King of the Jews)* so there is no mistaking the tomb (as some have tried to suggest as an argument against the resurrection). The young man's message to the women is straightforward and direct, *he has been raised, he is not here*. This announcement is simple: Jesus the Nazarene is no longer there for he is no longer dead. He is risen. The place where his body had been laid was empty because he was gone. He was indeed risen, bodily (cf. Byrne 2008:256). Death had been conquered: he who had cried out, *My God, My God, why have you forsaken me?* has not been forsaken. He has, like the Danielic Son of Man, been vindicated. God has not abandoned him; he who had been crucified has triumphed (see, Hooker 1991:385; Taylor 1957:607). Everything must now be rethought. Everything must begin anew. The young man's message to the women,

> go, tell his disciples and Peter that he is going ahead of you to Galilee; there you will see him, just as he told you.

recalls Jesus own words to the disciples at Mk. 14.28,

> I will strike the shepherd and the sheep will be scattered. But after I am raised up I will go ahead of you to Galilee.

At the end of the Galilean ministry when Jesus was going to Jerusalem and towards death, Mark had said he *went ahead* of them. In Jerusalem the disciples had faltered and failed through their betrayal, abandonment and denial of him and their absence at his death and burial. But now that the Shepherd is risen, he will make good his promise and go *ahead* to meet them in Galilee and it is there that they *will see him*. Galilee was the 'golden moment', it was the place where Jesus had first called Peter and Andrew and James and John; it was where the proclamation of the imminence of the kingdom was first preached; where Jesus taught in the synagogues, spoke in parables, healed, exorcised, controlled the power of nature, and raised the dead and first encountered the opposition over which he had now triumphed. The disciples had been present during all these events, now, through the message given to the women, they are being called back to Galilee so that they can once again be disciples. The risen Jesus restores those who failed him and abandoned him to the full stature of disciples: once again he will *go ahead* and they *will follow after* him.

e. The Women Leave The Tomb:(Mk. 16.8)

> So they went out and fled from the tomb, for terror and amazement had seized them; and they said nothing to anyone, for they were afraid

The effect on the women was predictable. They had been living with nerves stretched for some time. They were in a state of fear and uncertainty. And now this remarkable news from a stranger whom they did not know had taken them totally aback. It would only be afterwards that they would realise who and what he was. So they panicked and fled, overwhelmed by what they had witnessed and they were so *awestruck* that they did not even talk to each other, or anyone they met, as they hurried on their way. And as they hurried on, their minds would be in a whirl. He was not there. He was risen. Whatever could it mean? They must reach the disciples and tell them. This idea of 'fear' or 'awe' at seeing what has happened has been a feature of the Gospel, e.g., Mk. 4.40-41[1] with regard to the stilling of the storm; Mk. 6.50[2] with regard to his walking on the water; Mk. 10.32[3] with regard to his determination to get to Jerusalem; and compare Mk. 5.15, 33[4] where others

---

[1] He said to them, 'Why are you afraid? Have you still no faith?' And they were filled with great awe and said to one another, 'Who then is this, that even the wind and the sea obey him?'

[2] For they all saw him and were terrified. But immediately he spoke to them and said, 'Take heart, it is I; do not be afraid.'

[3] They were on the road, going up to Jerusalem, and Jesus was walking ahead of them; they were amazed, and those who followed were afraid. He took the twelve aside again and began to tell them what was to happen to him

[4] They came to Jesus and saw the demoniac sitting there, clothed and in his right mind, the very man who had had the legion; and they were afraid. But the woman, knowing what had happened to her, came in fear and trembling, fell down before him, and told him the whole truth.

were afraid at what they saw. It is a sign of the unexpected and of the truly awesome which they cannot understand. It is Matthew who tells us the sequel, (his account follows a similar pattern to that of Mark) that as they hurried to tell the disciples Jesus himself met with them and they worshipped him. He told them to do what the angel had said and inform his disciples that they were to go to Galilee where they would see him (Mt. 28.8-10[1]). And it is Luke who tells us that their words were to the disciples *as idle tales* so that they would not move from Jerusalem with the result that the resurrection appearances had to begin in Jerusalem (Lk. 24.11[2]). This was Jesus' gracious response to his disciples who did not believe right to the end until they were left with no choice. And with v. 8 the Gospel suddenly ends.

This ending has caused scholars a great deal of vexation and wonder (cf. Byrne: 2008:257; Mullins 2002:445). It is an ending which is as bizarre as it is strange and leads to all kinds of questions: did Mark really intend to end his gospel like this (hence the need for the so called *Longer Ending* of Mk. 16.9-19)?(cf. Lane 1974:110) Was there part of the gospel lost? The strangeness of the ending is further enhanced by the use of 'gar' for who ends a sentence let alone a whole 'book' on a preposition? (see, Van Horst 1972:121-124). It is almost as if Mark simply stopped dead. This leads to other questions: undoubtedly Jesus did fulfil his promise and meet the disciples in Galilee, but why does Mark make no mention of it other than the young man's words? At the death of Jesus everything seemed to have fallen apart, the great Jesus 'dream' of the kingdom of God on earth seems to have been wrecked at Golgotha. The great protestations of fidelity by the disciples have proved to be empty words and here Mark seems to give us no resolution to all this other than the statement that Jesus will go before the disciples to Galilee. Or is Mark doing something else? The commission of the angel was *Do not be alarmed/afraid..Go, tell* but Mark ends his gospel

---

[1] So they left the tomb quickly with fear and great joy, and ran to tell his disciples. Suddenly Jesus met them and said, 'Greetings!' And they came to him, took hold of his feet, and worshipped him. Then Jesus said to them, 'Do not be afraid; go and tell my brothers to go to Galilee; there they will see me.'

[2] But these words seemed to them an idle tale, and they did not believe them.

with *they said nothing to anyone for they were afraid*. In others words, they did not do what Jesus asked them to do through the agency of the young man. Is Mark saying, (despite what has been written above about returning to Galilee to be disciples once again) that even at the very end the disciples (the women who followed *him...provided for him*, who stood *far off*, who saw where he was laid, who came to anoint his body) failed? If that is so, then what does resurrection mean for Mark or indeed for his community? Or is Mark pointing to something much more profound, so profound that we cannot fully grasp it?

The Johannine Account (Jn. 20.1-18)

The Narrative Context

Early on the first day of the week, while it was still dark, Mary Magdalene came to the tomb and saw that the stone had been removed from the tomb. So she ran and went to Simon Peter and the other disciple, the one whom Jesus loved, and said to them, 'They have taken the Lord out of the tomb, and we do not know where they have laid him.' Then Peter and the other disciple set out and went towards the tomb. The two were running together, but the other disciple outran Peter and reached the tomb first. He bent down to look in and saw the linen wrappings lying there, but he did not go in. Then Simon Peter came, following him, and went into the tomb. He saw the linen wrappings lying there, and the cloth that had been on Jesus' head, not lying with the linen wrappings but rolled up in a place by itself. Then the other disciple, who reached the tomb first, also went in, and he saw and believed; for as yet they did not understand the scripture, that he must rise from the dead. Then the disciples returned to their homes.

The Resurrection Narrative of John (like his Passion Narrative) consists of a series of scenes or episodes where the tension is steadily built up. John unfolds the Resurrection calmly and without haste. There are no angels sitting on or in the tomb, there are no earthquakes (Mt. 28.2). There is simply the discovery of the empty tomb by Mary Magdalene and what follows afterwards (see Mullins 2005:401). The 'scenes' or 'episodes' can outlined thus:

Scene One	Jn. 20.1	Mary comes to the tomb and finds it empty.
Scene Two	Jn. 20.2	She returns to tell Peter and the 'Beloved Disciple' what she has discovered.
Scene Three	Jn. 20.4-7	Peter and the 'Beloved Disciple' reach the tomb. the 'Beloved Disciple' looks in sees the death linen and stays outside. Peter goes in.
Scene Four	Jn. 20.8	the 'Beloved Disciple' enters the tomb, sees the death linen and *believes*.
Scene Five	Jn. 20.9-10	They do not understand the significance of what they have seen and return home.

Like the Synoptic gospels, there is no description of the Resurrection itself in John, there is simply the discovery of the empty tomb by Mary Magdalene (see, Ridderbos 1991:631). With this narrative technique John is able to build the tension and the reader is brought into the very heart of the agony or wondering why the tomb is empty, what it means, and hopefully, like Mary Magdalene, experience the unbridled joy at the appearance of the Risen Lord. John unfolds the narrative slowly, step-by-step and in this way he can reveal the truth of the Resurrection gradually (which may indicate it was an independent and original unit) (see, Ridderbos 1991:631; Maloney 1974:171; Lindars 1960-61:142-147; Brown 1999:2.995) Like the Synoptic accounts, John says that (Jn. 20.1):

> Early on the first day of the week, while it was still dark, Mary Magdalene came to the tomb and saw that the stone had been removed from the tomb

The *first day of the week* could be any time after sunset on the Saturday evening but here it is the Sunday just before the sun rises and the use of *first day of the week* with *while it was still dark* seems to indicate an anticipatory sense of a new beginning (see, Brown 199:2.998; Mullins 2005:402). The Synoptics say that other women came with Mary (Mt. 28.1;[1] Mk. 16.1;[2] Lk. 23.55-24.1[3]), but John has Mary alone (see, Brown 1999:2.998). As with the Synoptics, Mary finds the stone removed (Mt. 28.1 says it had been removed by an *earthquake*). It might be noted here that it was not necessary that the stone be moved away but it was necessary that the emptiness of the tomb be seen. John might have used this moment to explain that Jesus had been raised from the dead but he says nothing about this, rather, he has Mary Magdalene in a great panic run back (Jn. 20.2)

> to Simon Peter and the other disciple, the one whom Jesus loved
> and say to them 'They have taken the Lord out of the tomb, and
> we do not know where they have laid him.'

The use of the title *the Lord* is significant here. It indicates great respect. Even though Jesus was dead Mary still saw him as her *Lord*, despite the fact that she had no hope of ever seeing him again. In their grief the last desire of Mary and the other women was to see him rightly treated in his burial.

At this point Mary drops out of the narrative (she will return in a moment) but John now concentrates on the two disciples and who runs the fastest, who gets to the tomb first and how they react to it. In the event it is the 'Beloved Disciple' who gets there first. Attention has been focused on the fact that the 'Beloved Disciple' gets to the tomb before Peter, *bent down, looked in and saw the linen wrappings lying there, but he did not go in* (Jn.

---

[1] After the Sabbath, as the first day of the week was dawning, Mary Magdalene and the other Mary went to see the tomb.

[2] When the Sabbath was over, Mary Magdalene, and Mary the mother of James, and Salome bought spices, so that they might go and anoint him.

[3] The women who had come with him from Galilee followed, and they saw the tomb and how his body was laid. Then they returned, and prepared spices and ointments. On the sabbath they rested according to the commandment. But on the first day of the week, at early dawn, they came to the tomb, taking the spices that they had prepared

20.5) (see observations of Ridderbos 1991:633). This has led some to suggest that John is highlighting the importance of the 'Beloved Disciple' and an implied criticism of Peter. But this cannot be read from the text for nowhere is Peter criticised. The suggestion that perhaps the 'Beloved Disciple' was driven by a greater love is eisogetically reasonable given that Peter's love had to be affirmed later (Jn. 21.15-17). One could also reasonable ask if the 'Beloved Disciple' had so much love for Jesus then why did he not go into the tomb as Peter does immediately he arrives? (see comment of Barrett 1978:563) These are interesting speculations but in the end that is all they are since no information on the internal motivations can be exegetically discerned in the text.

Much attention is given to the death wrappings (see, Brown 199:2.987). The 'Beloved Disciple' bends down sees them lying on the ground but does not go in, Peter goes in sees the death wrappings, including the cloth that covered Jesus' head, which is set aside in its own place (Jn. 20.6-7). It seems Jesus 'tidied' up before he left the tomb! Ideas that Jesus simply 'passed through' the death wrappings are interesting and suggest that Jesus did not 'rush' to get out of the tomb but took his time, however, John does not deal with the actual physicality of the Resurrection itself but with what it means. The folded death wrappings emphasise that Jesus was not there and that the body had not been 'taken' for grave robbers do not strip the corpse, fold up the shroud neatly, and then leave with a naked dead body! The point that John wishes to make is in the response of the 'Beloved Disciple' (Jn. 20.8):

> Then the other disciple, who reached the tomb first, also went in,
> and he saw and believed

The question that needs to be asked here is, what is this faith? John says in 20.9, *for as yet they did not understand the scripture, that he must rise from the dead.* Up to this point they had not accepted in their hearts the Scripture testimony to the resurrection of the Coming One. They had not 'known', the

Scripture that Jesus would rise from the dead (see below) but now he 'knew' and believed. It is quite probable that the writer saw the tradition of Jesus as Scripture, as well as the Old Testament. This kind of limited understanding that characterises the faith of the disciples has been present since the first sign in Jn. 2.11 (cf. Ridderbos 1991:635)) But it is a true faith, nonetheless, for it sees the presence of God in something which it does not fully comprehend or understand. the 'Beloved Disciple' saw the death wrappings, no body of Jesus, and believed without fully understanding what this experience meant. John does not say whether Peter also believed at this point. But he does say that neither of them understood the Scripture regarding resurrection, thereby admitting his own ignorance at this point (seee Brown's comment on this lack of understanding 1999:2.987). Several texts of Scripture have been suggested as the ones to which John is referring (Ps. 16.10;[1] Hos. 6.2;[2] Jn. 1.17[3]), but he may simply mean the Scripture's witness as a whole, as when Paul says *Christ was raised on the third day according to the Scriptures* (1 Cor. 15.4;[4] cf. Lk. 24.44-47[5]). This confession of ignorance puts the 'Beloved Disciple' in the same boat as Peter, contrary to views that play the two disciples off against one another. They are able to bear witness to the empty tomb and the grave clothes, though not yet to the resurrection. But they do not bear witness at all. Rather, they simply return to the places where they are staying (Jn. 20.10). If they do speak to the other disciples, John does not mention it. This lack of witness is another sign that although the 'Beloved Disciple''s faith may be significant, it is still lacking. It is this experience of the two disciples at the empty tomb which sets the context for the experience of Mary Magdalene in Jn. 20.11-18.

---

[1]   For you do not give me up to Sheol, or let your faithful one see the Pit.

[2]   After two days he will revive us; on the third day he will raise us up, that we may live before him.

[3]   The law indeed was given through Moses; grace and truth came through Jesus Christ.

[4]   And that he was buried, and that he was raised on the third day in accordance with the scriptures,

[5]   Then he said to them, 'These are my words that I spoke to you while I was still with you, that everything written about me in the law of Moses, the prophets, and the psalms must be fulfilled.' Then he opened their minds to understand the scriptures, and he said to them, 'Thus it is written, that the Messiah is to suffer and to rise from the dead on the third day, and that repentance and forgiveness of sins is to be proclaimed in his name to all nations, beginning from Jerusalem.

Mary Magdalene Meets The Risen Jesus (Jn. 20.11-18)

a. Mary Encounters The Two Angels (Jn. 20.11-13)

> But Mary stood weeping outside the tomb. As she wept, she bent over to look into the tomb; and she saw two angels in white, sitting where the body of Jesus had been lying, one at the head and the other at the feet. They said to her, 'Woman, why are you weeping?' She said to them, 'They have taken away my Lord, and I do not know where they have laid him.'

Having focused on the two disciples, John returns to Mary Magdalene who must have followed them as they ran to the tomb. Mary is distraught and stands *weeping outside the tomb* (Jn. 20.11). Since it was the custom at this time to let grief have its full sway, Mary may well have been weeping loudly and vigorously and John places some emphasis on her *weeping* since he refers to again at Jn. 20.1, 11, 13, 15 and it is through this emphasis that John shows the great love Mary has for Jesus in the extent and depth of her grief (cf. Mullins 2005:405; Ridderbos 1991:635). And therefore she does not weep because Jesus is dead but because she thinks the body has been stolen (see Brown 1999:2.988) Like other disciples Mary thinks she is alone but on bending down to look into the tomb she sees (Jn. 20.12):

> two angels in white, sitting where the body of Jesus had been lying, one at the head and the other at the feet

Such heavenly messengers appear at many of the significant points in salvation history. Like the grave clothes, their presence witnesses that the powers of heaven have been at work here. The angels may have been seated as being temporary protectors of the place where Jesus had lain, just as the Cherubim had been protectors of the Ark. Or more likely (they had not been there when John and Peter arrived) they may have wished to draw attention to the exact spot where Jesus' body had been (none of his followers would otherwise have known at which spot his body had been placed). They may also have been present as an indication to all who saw that Jesus had been escorted by angels into God's presence. This would be in accordance with Lk. 16.22[1] which seemingly reflects Jewish tradition. Often in Scripture the person who encounters an angel is struck with terror. But if Mary felt such a reaction, John does not mention it. The angels ask her (Jn. 20.13):

> 'Woman, why are you weeping?' She said to them, 'They have taken away my Lord, and I do not know where they have laid him.'

Mary did not realise that the men in white were angels. So while the angels were seeking to deal with the source of her distress, she was too overwrought to listen to them. Her mind was filled with the question of what had happened to Jesus' body, and she turned away having automatically answered their question. The two men were irrelevant to her. She did not even ask herself what they were doing there. She was too distraught. In the face of this grief the angels do not bombard her with good news but rather ask the question that can lead to the healing word. This is in striking contrast with the angels' triumphant announcement of the resurrection recorded in the Synoptics (Mt 28.5-7; Mk 16.6-7; Lk 24.5-7). Mary's answer (Jn. 20.13b) shows that she is totally focused on the fact that Jesus' body is missing. He is still her *Lord* even though he is dead; her loyalty is still fixed on him. In saying she does not know where *they have put him* she seems to assume that Joseph of Arimathea had his workmen move Jesus to a more permanent site. Her answer gives the angels a perfect opportunity to proclaim the good news, but they are interrupted by the appearance of the Lord himself.

---

[1] The poor man died and was carried away by the angels to be with Abraham. The rich man also died and was buried.

b. Mary Encounters The Risen Jesus (Jn. 20.14-16)

> When she had said this, she turned round and saw Jesus
> standing there, but she did not know that it was Jesus. Jesus said
> to her, 'Woman, why are you weeping? For whom are you
> looking?' Supposing him to be the gardener, she said to him,
> 'Sir, if you have carried him away, tell me where you have laid
> him, and I will take him away.' Jesus said to her, 'Mary!' She
> turned and said to him in Hebrew, 'Rabbouni!' (which means
> Teacher)

It is important to note that this was the opposite of hallucination. In
hallucination you believe what you see, however amazing. But Mary was
too practically minded to hallucinate. She was actually seeing amazing
things and did not realise they were amazing, but interpreted them in
earthly, down-to-earth terms. She saw these figures as just men (Mk. 16.5)
who were there because they presumably had a job to do. She also only
dimly saw the man outside. The day was still just beginning and the light
was not good, and Mary's eyes were flooded with tears. She saw but a
vague figure standing before her. After all the last thing that she was
expecting to see was Jesus fully clothed presumably looking hale and
hearty. He would have looked very different from when she last saw him, a
broken bleeding figure on the cross. Such can be the blinding effect of
profound emotions. Indeed his appearance seems to have made him
partially unrecognisable. In this case her inability to recognise him also
seems to be due to the fact that Resurrection had clearly changed his
appearance somewhat as we would expect since such failure is typical of
encounters with him. Jesus recognises her grief when he asks her the same
question that the angels asked her, *'Woman, why are you weeping?* And then
makes the question more specific, *Who are you looking for?* (Jn. 20.15).

The good news is not just that Jesus arose but that the character of
God is revealed in Jesus. He is life, and he is also love. This question, the

first thing the risen Jesus says, echoes the very first thing he said at the beginning of this Gospel (Jn. 1.38). It is a question that reveals the heart. When the dimly discerned man asked her what was wrong, and why she was crying, she could only ask in tears what they had done with Jesus' body. She does not answer the question but assumes that Jesus is Joseph's gardener and that he knows whom she is looking for (Jn. 20.15) (see, Brown 1999:2.990; Ridderbos 1991:636). Her only concern was that the body of Jesus be treated with reverence. These words lay bare the heart of Mary. She did not stop to consider the difficulties. She longed only to ensure that the body of her crucified Master was given proper burial. Let this attendant but tell her what they had done with the body and she would take it off their hands. His appearance has given her hope, hope that she can now find Jesus' dead body. She wants to care for Jesus' corpse. So she plans a second burial for Jesus, while the living Jesus is there, and just about to lift her in the embrace of his manifested power and love.

Even when Jesus himself appeared to Mary, Jn. 20.15 tells us that she responded to him with the same despair with which she had addressed the angels. Jesus calls her by the name he used for her before, and she responds with the title she used before. Only when Jesus called her by name did recognition come (Jn. 20.16):

> Jesus said to her, 'Mary!' She turned and said to him in Hebrew, 'Rabbouni!' (which means Teacher)

Mary's response has occasioned much discussion. Jn. 20.16 states that she *turned* when she heard her name. The implication is that she was not facing Jesus. However, Jn. 20.14 seems to say that she had *turned* to Jesus then for the conversation of Jn. 20.14 and 15. The word *turned* was also used by the early church for the turning away from the former life into the life of faith. Some even translate it *be converted* in some contexts. Perhaps John meant to explain that at the sound of her voice Mary *was converted* or *turned* from the old life to her new life in Christ. She called Jesus, *Rabboni*. This word appears only here and in Mk.10.51 in the New Testament. It is a lengthened form of *rabbi* (see Brown's discussion of the term 1999:2.991). *Rabbi* meant *my great one* and was used as a title of respect for a teacher. *Rabboni* would have expressed greater respect and honour. There is no evidence that it showed any recognition of deity even though Jews sometimes called God by that very title. John's translation of *teacher* shows what he understood Mary to mean.

c. Mary Is Commissioned By Jesus (Jn. 20.17-18)

> Jesus said to her, 'Do not hold on to me, because I have not yet ascended to the Father. But go to my brothers and say to them, "I am ascending to my Father and your Father, to my God and your God." ' Mary Magdalene went and announced to the disciples, 'I have seen the Lord; and she told them that he had said these things to her

These verses raise one of the most puzzling parts of the story of Jesus' appearance to Mary Magdalene: Jesus' command, *do not cling to me* or *do not hold onto me* (Jn. 20.17) (for a discussion of possible explanations see, Brown 1999:2.992; cf. Barrett 1978:565)). Part of the problem is why Jesus should forbid Mary to touch him here when he will command Thomas to touch him in Jn. 20.27. It would appear that Mary must have been clinging to him as though she would never let him go, and so he gently removed her hands to let her know that there was a new beginning. The use of the present tense ('haptou') suggests in this context that he is not forbidding her to touch him but telling her to stop that which she is already doing. These words were intended to make clear to her that the old relationship no longer held. He was not to be seen as a man restored to life to live again on this earth. Rather he was about to ascend to his Father. Thus she must not cling to him and retain Him. She must let him go to become both Lord and Christ

(Acts 2.36[1]). From now on she must worship him in Spirit and in truth (Jn. 4.23-24[2]). Mary must not try to hold on to Jesus, cling fast to him, or restrict him in any way because he has *not yet ascended to the Father* (see, Brown 1999:2.992; Ridderbos 1991:638; Mullins 2005:406). Jesus is till here, still present on earth in his resurrected state but there is no singularity of relationship now; his relationship is not with individuals but with the whole of humanity. This statement of Jesus allows John to set up the next scene up the next scene of this post-resurrection appearance which is the commissioning of Mary Magdalene to announce the resurrection to *my brothers* (Jn. 20.17c). The commissioning of Mary Magdalene by Jesus that she:

> go to my brothers and say to them, "I am ascending to my
> Father and your Father, to my God and your God." '

emphasises the change in relationship that Jesus now has not just with Mary Magdalene but with the disciples. In essence it means the disciples but John also has in mind all those who *believe that Jesus is the Christ, the Son of the Living God* (Jn. 11) and who do the will of God (Mk. 3.35). The term *brother* (and *sister*) is a new one in their relationship with him; they have moved relationally from servant to *friend* (Jn. 15.15) to *brother/sister* (Rom. 8.29;[3] Heb. 2.11[4]). This is the first time in John that Jesus uses the term *brothers* of the disciples. This shows that Jesus has not abandoned his humanity in his resurrected state but that he has initiated a new, mysterious level of intimacy between him and his followers. The 'community' has now become the new 'family' Jesus established at the cross (Jn. 19.26-27). This new relationship is expressed in the message Mary is to announce (Jn.

---

[1] Therefore let the entire house of Israel know with certainty that God has made him both Lord and Messiah, this Jesus whom you crucified.'

[2] But the hour is coming, and is now here, when the true worshippers will worship the Father in spirit and truth, for the Father seeks such as these to worship him. God is spirit, and those who worship him must worship in spirit and truth.'

[3] For those whom he foreknew he also predestined to be conformed to the image of his Son, in order that he might be the firstborn within a large family.

[4] For the one who sanctifies and those who are sanctified all have one Father. For this reason Jesus is not ashamed to call them brothers and sisters.

20.17):

> tell them, 'I am returning to my Father and your Father, to my
> God and your God'.

It is perhaps surprising that his first message is not 'I have risen from the dead.' He does not focus on himself in this way; he focuses on himself in relation to his Father. Jesus had spoken of his going to the Father, both in his general teaching (Jn. 7.33-36[1]) and in the farewell discourse to his disciples (Jn. 13.3;[2] 14.2-4, 12;[3] 16.5, 10, 17, 28[4]). The Father is his centre of reference, and to return to him is his greatest joy and therefore the joy of his disciples (Jn. 14.28[5]). So the message *I am returning to my Father* expresses Jesus' great delight. He has finished the work (Jn. 19.30) and can now return to the Father. It might be noted here how Jesus does not speak of 'our Father' or 'our God'. His relationship to the Father is to be seen as distinctive from ours and unique, thus it is *my Father* and *your Father* and *my God* and *your God*. As the Son he spoke of *My Father*, whereas we would speak of *our Father*; as glorified representative Human he spoke of *My God*, we would speak of *our God*. But in both cases his relationship with

---

[1] Jesus then said, 'I will be with you a little while longer, and then I am going to him who sent me. You will search for me, but you will not find me; and where I am, you cannot come.' The Jews said to one another, 'Where does this man intend to go that we will not find him? Does he intend to go to the Dispersion among the Greeks and teach the Greeks? What does he mean by saying, "You will search for me and you will not find me" and, "Where I am, you cannot come"?'

[2] Jesus, knowing that the Father had given all things into his hands, and that he had come from God and was going to God.

[3] In my Father's house there are many dwelling-places. If it were not so, would I have told you that I go to prepare a place for you? And if I go and prepare a place for you, I will come again and will take you to myself, so that where I am, there you may be also. And you know the way to the place where I am going.' Very truly, I tell you, the one who believes in me will also do the works that I do and, in fact, will do greater works than these, because I am going to the Father.

[4] But now I am going to him who sent me; yet none of you asks me, "Where are you going?" about righteousness, because I am going to the Father and you will see me no longer; Then some of his disciples said to one another, 'What does he mean by saying to us, "A little while, and you will no longer see me, and again a little while, and you will see me"; and "Because I am going to the Father"?' I came from the Father and have come into the world; again, I am leaving the world and am going to the Father.'

[5] You heard me say to you, "I am going away, and I am coming to you." If you loved me, you would rejoice that I am going to the Father, because the Father is greater than I.

the Father was distinctive from ours. There is nothing surprising about his referring to *my God*. In his manhood he had regularly worshipped God, otherwise he would not have been truly human. This was simply an extension of the practise. It said nothing to diminish his divine status.

His returning to the Father is also good news for the disciples, not just because they share in his joy, but also for their own condition. For when Jesus returns to the Father he will send the Paraclete, who will teach them all things and complete their union with the Father and the Son (Jn. 16.7;[1] cf. 14.16-17, 28;[2] 15.26[3]). This new relationship has already been established through Jesus' death and resurrection, but the disciples will enter into it fully when the Spirit comes. The message Jesus gives Mary shows the Christological basis of the new relationship. Because God is Jesus' Father, he is also their Father; because he is Jesus' God, he is also their God. They are taken up into the fellowship that unites Jesus and the Father. Jesus is the point of contact between the disciples and the Father (cf. Jn. 17.21-22[4]). The Father is the Father of the disciples in this new intimacy precisely because he is Jesus' Father, for the disciples are now Jesus' brothers. Jesus characterizes the time of his resurrection appearances as the time when he is ascending to the Father. He has received his orders, and he is about to ship out. This focus implies a contrast between the passing nature of Jesus' presence in his post-resurrection appearances and the permanent nature of his presence in the Spirit. But it does not mean the resurrection and the ascension have somehow been blended into one another or that the one has

---

[1]   Nevertheless, I tell you the truth: it is to your advantage that I go away, for if I do not go away, the Advocate will not come to you; but if I go, I will send him to you.

[2]   And I will ask the Father, and he will give you another Advocate, to be with you for ever. This is the Spirit of truth, whom the world cannot receive, because it neither sees him nor knows him. You know him, because he abides with you, and he will be in you. You heard me say to you, "I am going away, and I am coming to you." If you loved me, you would rejoice that I am going to the Father, because the Father is greater than I.

[3]   'When the Advocate comes, whom I will send to you from the Father, the Spirit of truth who comes from the Father, he will testify on my behalf.

[4]   That they may all be one. As you, Father, are in me and I am in you, may they also be in us, so that the world may believe that you have sent me. The glory that you have given me I have given them, so that they may be one, as we are one,

been replaced by the other. Jesus must return to the Father before the Paraclete can come (Jn. 16.7). The fact that Jesus imparts the Spirit later this same day (Jn. 20.22) suggests to many that John does not view the ascension as a definite act as described by Luke (Lk. 24.51;[1] Acts 1.9-11[2]). But we will see that the account of Jesus' breathing impartation of the Spirit suggests his giving of the Spirit, like his ascension, was not a simple event. John may not describe the ascension, but his account assumes it, as becomes evident in his description of the impartation of the Spirit and what follows.

d. Mary Magdalene: Apostle And Teacher

Mary obeys this command of Jesus and returns to the disciples and tells them, *I have seen the Lord* and again in fidelity to Jesus' command *she told them that he had said these things to her* (Jn. 20.18c). We do not know exactly how this ties in with the appearance of the other women at the tomb. No one was trying to piece the incidents together. On the whole they were summarised and telescoped together (Mt. 28.5-6;[3] Mk. 16.1-8;[4] Lk. 24.1-9[5]). All had been in the original party of women who had planned to visit

---

[1] While he was blessing them, he withdrew from them and was carried up into heaven.

[2] When he had said this, as they were watching, he was lifted up, and a cloud took him out of their sight. While he was going and they were gazing up towards heaven, suddenly two men in white robes stood by them. They said, 'Men of Galilee, why do you stand looking up towards heaven? This Jesus, who has been taken up from you into heaven, will come in the same way as you saw him go into heaven.'

[3] But the angel said to the women, 'Do not be afraid; I know that you are looking for Jesus who was crucified. He is not here; for he has been raised, as he said. Come, see the place where he lay.

[4] When the Sabbath was over, Mary Magdalene, and Mary the mother of James, and Salome bought spices, so that they might go and anoint him. And very early on the first day of the week, when the sun had risen, they went to the tomb. They had been saying to one another, 'Who will roll away the stone for us from the entrance to the tomb?' When they looked up, they saw that the stone, which was very large, had already been rolled back. As they entered the tomb, they saw a young man, dressed in a white robe, sitting on the right side; and they were alarmed. But he said to them, 'Do not be alarmed; you are looking for Jesus of Nazareth, who was crucified. He has been raised; he is not here. Look, there is the place they laid him. But go, tell his disciples and Peter that he is going ahead of you to Galilee; there you will see him, just as he told you.' So they went out and fled from the tomb, for terror and amazement had seized them; and they said nothing to anyone, for they were afraid.

[5] But on the first day of the week, at early dawn, they came to the tomb, taking the spices that they had prepared. They found the stone rolled away from the tomb, but when they went in, they did not find the body. While they were perplexed about this, suddenly two men in dazzling clothes stood beside them. The women were terrified and bowed their faces to the ground, but the men said to them, 'Why do you look for

the tomb and had sent the two Marys on ahead. All came to the tomb at one time or another and heard what the angels had to say, and returned to tell the disciples. It was the message that was important not the detail. And in all cases the message was disbelieved. The disciples were in no state to accept the testimony of a bunch of women. Everyone knew what women were with their vivid imaginations and unreliable ideas. They even probably thought that Peter and John had got it wrong, although they at least did not claim to have seen Jesus at the tomb. But it was different when Peter himself claimed to have seen Jesus (Lk. 24.34; 1 Cor.15.5). Light was gradually dawning.

This highlights the way in which traditional scholarship has focused on the male dominated tradition of the post-resurrection appearances (cf. 1 Cor.15.1-7). Paul, for example, makes no mention of the women at the tomb and their role in witness to the resurrection. Yet the gospels make their witness central, even Peter and the 'Beloved Disciple' run to the tomb to either see for themselves or to determine the truth of Mary's announcement to them that the body of Jesus is missing. The fact remains that in the gospel tradition it is the women who find the tomb of Jesus empty and who are commissioned by the angel/s (Mt. 28.1-7; Mk. 16.1-8; Lk. 24.1-9) and in Jn. 20.17-18 it is Jesus himself who gives the commission, as it is in Mt. 28.10). The New Testament makes it clear that the Resurrection is the sine qua non of faith and belief (1 Thess. 4.14;[1] Rom. 10.9[2]) and therefore it cannot be without significance that the resurrected Jesus commissions a woman, Mary Magdalene, to announce this message to the disciples. Peter and the 'Beloved Disciple' experience the empty tomb in their own way but Jesus does not appear to them, he appears to Mary and *sends* her to announce the message that he is risen from the dead and this despite the fact

---

the living among the dead? He is not here, but has risen. Remember how he told you, while he was still in Galilee, that the Son of Man must be handed over to sinners, and be crucified, and on the third day rise again.' Then they remembered his words, and returning from the tomb, they told all this to the eleven and to all the rest.

[1] For since we believe that Jesus died and rose again, even so, through Jesus, God will bring with him those who have died.

[2] Because if you confess with your lips that Jesus is Lord and believe in your heart that God raised him from the dead, you will be saved.

that the witness of a woman was not acceptable in Jewish culture. This *sending* or commissioning of Mary Magdalene to announce *the* central message of New Testament, and thus, Christian faith and belief (the Resurrection) implies that Mary Magdalene, having been sent by the resurrected Jesus himself, is undertaking the role of an Apostle (and that in the traditionally understood sense of the term), indeed she is considered to the *Apostle to the Apostles*. In 1 Cor.15.3-11 Paul makes it clear that central to being understood or validated as an 'apostle' was seeing the Resurrected Jesus and being sent by him to proclaim that Resurrection (cf. 1 Cor. 9.1-2;[1] Gal.1.11-16[2]). Paul writes:

> For I handed on to you as of first importance what I in turn had received: that Christ died for our sins in accordance with the scriptures, and that he was buried, and that he was raised on the third day in accordance with the scriptures, and that he appeared to Cephas, then to the twelve. Then he appeared to more than five hundred brothers and sisters at one time, most of whom are still alive, though some have died. Then he appeared to James, then to all the apostles. Last of all, as to someone untimely born, he appeared also to me. For I am the least of the apostles, unfit to be called an apostle, because I persecuted the church of God. But by the grace of God I am what I am, and his grace towards me has not been in vain. On the contrary, I worked harder than any of them, though it was not I, but the grace of God that is with me. Whether then it was I or they, so we proclaim and so you have come to believe.

---

[1] Am I not free? Am I not an apostle? Have I not seen Jesus our Lord? Are you not my work in the Lord? If I am not an apostle to others, at least I am to you; for you are the seal of my apostleship in the Lord.

[2] For I want you to know, brothers and sisters, that the gospel that was proclaimed by me is not of human origin; for I did not receive it from a human source, nor was I taught it, but I received it through a revelation of Jesus Christ. You have heard, no doubt, of my earlier life in Judaism. I was violently persecuting the church of God and was trying to destroy it. I advanced in Judaism beyond many among my people of the same age, for I was far more zealous for the traditions of my ancestors. But when God, who had set me apart before I was born and called me through his grace, was pleased to reveal his Son to me, so that I might proclaim him among the Gentiles, I did not confer with any human being,

Paul, of course, makes no mention of Mary Magdalene, and other than his reference to *sisters* (v.6) he does not mention the women of the Resurrection narratives at all whose presence in the early formulation of the story was already present. However, Jn. 20 clearly indicates that Mary Magdalene meets all the criteria described by Paul: the Lord has appeared to her, she has *seen* him, she is sent by Jesus to proclaim the Resurrection and this is exactly what she does (Jn. 20.18):

> Mary Magdalene went and announced to the disciples, 'I have seen the Lord; and she told them that he had said these things to her

Mary is quite clearly commissioned by Jesus to both preach to and teach the disciples about the Resurrection even though in Jewish culture women could not be teachers. Mary Magdalene, therefore, does not have an apostolic role 'like' that of the male Apostles, rather she is an Apostle since she received from Jesus precisely that commission. This may also indicate that in the Johannine community women had equal status with men as teachers and preachers. Mary Magdalene, therefore, fittingly deserves the soubriquet: Apostle to the Apostles.

BIBLIOGRAPHY

Aune D. E., *The New Testament in its Literary Environment,* (Library of Early Christianity), Westminster Press, 1987.

Beavis, M. A., 'Women as Models of Faith in Mark, ' BTB 18 (1988), 3-9.

Benoit P.' L'enfance de Jean-Baptiste selon Luc. 1' NTS 3 (1956-57) 169-194.

Best, E., *The Temptation and the Passion: The Markan Soteriology* (2nd ed.; SNTSMS 2.Cambridge: Cambridge University Press, 1980; orig. 1965).

Bock, D. L., *Proclamation from Prophecy and Pattern: Lucan OldTestament Christology* (Journal for the Study of the New Testament Supplement Studies Series 12), Sheffield, 1986.

Brown R. E., 'The Meaning of the Manger: The Significance of the Shepherds', Worship 50 (1976), 528-538.

Brown R. E., *The Death of the Messiah: From Gethsemane to the Grave. A Commentary on the Passion Narratives in the Four Gospels.* ABRL. New York: Doubleday. 1994.

_____*The Birth of the Messiah: A Commentary on the Infancy Narratives in the Gospels of Matthew and Luke* (2nd ed.; ABRL; New York: Doubleday, 1993 (1977)

_____'The Burial of Jesus (Mark 15:4 2-47),' CBQ 50 (1988): 233-45.

_____. 'Gospel Infancy Narrative Research from 1976 to 1986: Part II

(Luke).' The Catholic Biblical Quarterly 48:4 (October 1986): 660-680.

_____ 'The Annunciation to Zechariah, the Birth of the Baptist, and the Benedictus (Luke 1:5-25, 57-80).' Worship 62 (November 1988): 482-496.

_____ 'The Annunciation to Mary, the Visitation, and The Magnificat (Luke 1:26-56).' Worship 62 (May 1988): 249-259.

_____ 'Roles of Women in Fourth Gospel' TS 36 (1975) 688-699.

Brown-Driver-Briggs, *Hebrew and English Lexicon,* Hendrickson Publishers 1996.

Brown, R E., Achtemeier, P. J., *Mary in the New Testament: A Collaborative Assessment by Protestant and Roman Catholic Scholars*. Paulist Press, 1978.

Burkill, T. A., "Historical Development of the Syrophoenician Woman," Novum Testamentum 9:173 (1967).

Cadman, W. H., 'The Raising of Lazarus,' *Studia Evangelica* 1 [= *Texte und Untersuchungen zur Geschichte der altchristlichen Literatur* 73] (Berlin: Akademie-Verlag, 1959): 423-34. Cambridge University Press, 1984.

Childs, B. S., *Isaiah*. Westminster John Knox Press. 2001

Clark, G., *Women in the Ancient World*, Oxford: Oxford University Press, 1989.

Cohen, S. J. D., 'Menstruants and the Sacred in Judaism and Christianity, ' in *Women's History and Ancient History* ed. S. B. Pomeroy, Chapel Hill, University of North Carolina Press, 1991.

Coleridge, M., *The Birth of the Lukan Narrative: Narrative as Christology in Luke 1-2,* Journal for the Study of the New Testament Supplement Series 88, Sheffield, JSOT Press, 1993.

Collins, A. Y., *Mark: A Commentary, Hermeneia: A Critical and Historical Commentary on the Bible,* ed. Harold W. Attridge , Minneapolis, Fortress Press, 2007.

Corley, K. E., 'Slaves, Servants and Prostitutes: Gender and Social Class in Mark, ' in A Feminist Companion to Mark (ed. AA. Levine; Sheffield: Sheffield 2001.

Cotter, W. J., 'For it was not the Season for Figs' Catholic Biblical Quarterly, 48 (1986) 62-66.

Davies W. D., and Allison, D. C., *A Critical and Exegetical Commentwy on the Gospel According to Saint Matthew,* Vol. 2. Edinburgh: T&T Clark, 1991.

De La Torre, M., 'Was Jesus a Racist?' Associated Baptist Press, February 23, 2009.

Derrett, J. D. A., 'Law in the New Testament: The Syrophoenician Woman and Jairus', ' NovT 15 (1973), 16.

Dewey, J., 'The Gospel of Mark, ' in *Searching the Scriptures,* Vol. 2 (ed. E. Schüssler Fiorenza; New York: Crossroad, 1994.

Dillon, R. J., 'The Benedictus in Micro and Macrocontext,' CBQ 68 (2006) 457-80.

Donahue, J. R. and Harrington, D. J., *The Gospel of Mark* , Sacra Pagina, vol. 2, Collegeville, MN.: The Liturgical Press, 2002.

Dornisch L., *A Woman Reads the Gospel of Luke*, Minnesota, The Liturgical Press, 1996.

Drury, J., 'Mark 1: 1- 15. An Interpretation, ' in Alternative Approaches to New Testament Study (ed. A.E. Harvey; London: SPCK, 1985), 25-36.

Evans C. F., *Saint Luke: New Testament Commentaries*, London, SCM, 1990.

Evans, C.F., *The Gospel of Luke*, SCM Press, 1990, Ed.2, 2009.

Finklestein, L., *The Pharisees: The Sociological Background of Their Faith*, Jewish Publication Society of America (Philadelphia), 1962

Fitzmyer, J., *The Gospel According to Luke,* Anchor Bible 28, 28A, New York, Doubleday, 1981.

Francis J. Moloney, Daniel J. Harrington, *The Gospel of John* Liturgical Press, 1998.

Gibson, B.,'Jesus' Wilderness Temptation according to Mark, ' ANT 53 (1994), 21-32.

Gnilka, J., *Das Evangelium nach Markus* (2 vols), EKKNT. Zurich: Benziger, 1978-79).

Gowan, D. E.*, The Westminster theological wordbook of the Bible* 2003

Green, J. B., *The New International Commentary on the New Testament: The Gospel of Luke,* Michigan: Eerdmans, 1997.

_____'The Social Status of Mary in Luke 1:5-2:52: A plea for Methodological Integration' Biblica 73 (1992) 457-472.

Green, M., *Matthew For Today: Expository Study of Matthew,* Word Publishing, Dallas, Texas, 1989.

Guelich, R. A., *Mark 1-8*: 26, WBC 34. Dallas, Word, 1989.

Gundry, R. H., Mark. A Commentary on His Apology for the Cross (Grand Rapids: Eerdmans, 1993.

Hodges, Z. C., 'The Woman Taken in Adultery (John 7:53-8:11): The Text,' *Bibliotheca Sacra* 136 (1979): 318-32.

Hooker, M. D., *A Commentary on the Gospel according to St Mark. Black's New Testament Commentaries* London, A&C Black, 1991.

Ilan, T., *Jewish Women in Greco-Roman Palestine: An Inquiry into Image and Status,* Tubingen: JCB Mohr (Paul Siebeck), 1995.

Jeremias J., *Jerusalem in the Time of Jesus*, Fortress Press, 1969.

_____*Jesus' Promise to the Nations,* trans. S. H. Hooke, SCM Press, 1958

Jones, D.R., 'The Background and Character of the *Lukan Psalms*,' JTS n.s. 19 (1968), pp. 19-50.

Kee, H. C., 'The Terminology of Mark's Exorcism Stories, ' NTS 14 (1967) 232-46.

Kelber, W. H., *Mark's Story of Jesus*, Fortress Press, 1979.

Kingsbury, J. D., *Conflict in Mark Jesus, Authorities, Disciples,* Augsburg Fortress, Publishers, 1989.

_____*Matthew: Structure, Christology, Kingdom,* 1975, reprint edition, Augsburg Fortress, Publishers, 1989.

Kopas, J., 'Jesus and Women in Mark's Gospel, ' Review for Religious 44 (1985) 912-20.

Krause, D., 'Simon Peter's Mother-in-Law – Disciple or Domestic Servant? Feminist Biblical Hermeneutics and the Interpretation of Mark 1: 29-31' in *A Feminist Companion to Mark* (ed. A. -J. Levine; Sheffield, Sheffield Academic Press,2001), 37-53.

Lane, W. L., *The Gospel of Mark.* NICNT. Grand Rapids, Eerdmans, 1974.

Laurentin R., *The Truth Of Christmas Beyond the Myths: The Gospels of the Infancy of Christ*, Fordham University Press, 1989.

Leonard M., *The Prophecy of Zechariah: A Study of the Benedictus in the Context of Luke-Acts,* Roma: Pontificia Università Gregoriana, 2000.

Loader, W., 'Challenged at the Boundaries: A Conservative Jesus in Mark's Tradition, ' JSNT 63 (1996): 45-61.

Loewe, R., *The Position of Women in Judaism.* S.P.C.K., London, 1966.

Longenecker, R. N, *Biblical Exegesis in the Apostolic Period*, 1975, edition 2, Wm. B. Eerdmans Publishing, 1999.

Malbon, E. S., 'Fallible Followers: Women and Men in the Gospel of Mark.' Semeia, 28 (1983): 29-48.

Malbon, E.S., 'Jewish Leaders in the Gospel of Mark', Journal of Biblical Literature, 108.2 Summer (1989) 283-300

Marcus, J. 'The Jewish War and the Sitz im Leben of Mark, ' JBL 111 (1992): 446-48.

Marshall, C. D., *Faith as a Theme in Mark's Narrative,* (SNTSMS 64. Cambridge, Cambridge University Press, 1989.

Marshall, I. H., *The Gospel According to Luke: A Commentary on the Greek Text* (Exeter: Paternoster, 1978).

Matera, F. J., 'The Prologue as the Interpretative Key to Mark's Gospel, ' ANT 34 (1988), 3-20.

Matera, F. J., *The Kingship of Jesus: Composition and Theology in Mark 15* SBLDS 66. Chico, California, Scholars Press, 1982.

McNeil, B., 'The Raising of Lazarus,' *Downside Review* 92 (1974): 269-75.

Meier, J. P., *A Marginal Jew: Roots of the Problem and the Person Rethinking the Historical Jesus,* Vols. 1-4 (Anchor Bible Reference), Yale University Press, Ed. 2, 2007-2009.

H. R. Moehring, 'The Census in Luke as an Apologetic Device,' in *Studies in the New Testament and Early Christian Literature: Essays in Honor of Allen P. Wikgren*, ed. D. E. Aune, Nov. T. Supp. 33 (Leiden: Brill, 1972): 144–60.

Miller, S., *Women in Mark's Gospel*, PhD Thesis, Glasgow, on line at *theses.gla.ac.uk/1427/1/2002**millerphd**.pdf*

_____*Women in Mark's Gospel*, Blommsbury, T&T Clark, 2004

Moloney, F. J., *The Gospel of Mark: A Commentary*, Peabody, Massachusetts, 2002.

_____'The Faith of Martha and Mary: A Narrative Approach to John 11.17-40', *Bib* (75), 1994, 471-493.

Mulholland, S., *Meeting Jesus in the Gospel of Mark*, 2 Vols, FISC Press, Canterbury, 2011-2012.

Mullins, M., *Mark*, Columba Press, Dublin, 2005

_____*John,* Columba Press, Dublin, 2005

Munro, W. 'The Anointing of Mark 14: 3-9 and John 12: 1-8. ' Pages 127-30 in SBLSP 1. Edited by P. J. Achtemeier. Missoula: Scholars Press, 1979.

_____'Women Disciples in Mark? ' CBQ 44 (1982) 225-41.

Neyrey, J. H., 'Ceremonies in Luke-Acts' in *The Social World of Luke-Acts: Models for Interpretation,* Ed. Jerome H. Neyrey (Massachusetts: Hendrickson, 1991 361- 387.

Nolland, J. L., *Word Biblical Commentary,* 35A, 35B, 35C; Waco, Texas: Word, 1989, 1993.

_____*The Gospel of Matthew: A Commentary on the Greek Text*, Grand Rapids, W. B. Eerdmans, 2005.

O Hanlon, J., *Mark My Words,* St Pauls Publishing, Reissue edition, 1994

Oliver, H. H., 'The Lucan Birth Stories and the Purpose of Luke-Acts,' NTS 10 (1963/64) 205-15.

Pokorny, P., 'From a Puppy to a Child: Some Problems of Contemporary Biblical Exegesis Demonstrated from Mark 7: 24-30/Matt 15: 21-28, ' NTS 41 (1995), 321-337.

Reicke, B., 'Jesus, Simeon, and Anna [Luke 2:21-40],' in *Saved By Hope*, ed. J. I. Cook [Grand Rapids: Eerdmans, 1978], 96-108.

Reid, B.E., *Choosing the Better Part? Women in the Gospel of Luke*, Minnesota: Liturgical, 1996.

Rhoads, D., 'Jesus and the Syrophoencian Woman in Mark: A Narrative-Critical Study, ' JAAR 62 (1994), 348-52.

Salvoni, F., 'Textual Authority for Jn. 7:53-8:11,' *Restoration Quarterly* 4 (1960): 11-15.

Schiissler Fiorenza, E., *In Memory of Her: A Feminist Theological Reconstruction of Christian Origins* (New York: Crossroad,1985), 320-22.

Schilling, F. A., 'The Story of Jesus and the Adulteress,' *Anglican Theological Review* 37 (1955): 91-106.

Schmitt, J., 'Women in Mark's Gospel: An Early Christian View of Woman's Role, ' BT 19 (1981).

Schottroff, L., *Let the Oppressed Go Free: Feminist Perspectives on the New Testament* Westminster, John Knox, 1992.

Seim, T. K., *The Double Message: Patterns of Gender in Luke & Acts*

Nashville: Abingdon, 1994.

Selvidge, M. J., 'And Those Who Followed Feared' (Mark 10: 32). ' CBQ 45 (1983): 396-400.

_____'Mark 5: 25-34 and Leviticus 15: 19-20: A Reaction to Restrictive Purity Regulations, ' JVL 103 (1984): 619-23.

Sweeney, M. A., *Isaiah 1–39: With an introduction to Prophetic Literature.* 1996.

Tannehill, R. C., *Luke* Abingdon New Testament Commentaries, Nashville: Abingdon, 1996.

Taylor, V., *The Gospel According to Saint Mark: The Greek Text With Introduction, Notes and Indexes,* London, Macmillan, 1957

Theissen, G., *The Gospels in Context: Social History and Political History in the Synoptic Tradition*, Minneapolis, Fortress, 1991.

Theissen, G., *The Miracle Stories of the Early Christian Tradition,* SNTW. Edinburgh, T&T Clark, 1983.

Thibeaux, E. R., 'Known to Be a Sinner: The Narrative Rhetoric of Luke 7:36-50' BTB23 (1993) 151-160.

Thrall, M. E., 'Elijah and Moses in Mark's Account of the Transfiguration. ' NTS 16 (1970): 305-17.

Thurston B., *The Widows: A Women's Ministry in the Early Church,* Minneapolis, Fortress, 1989.

Tolbert, M, A., 'Mark, ' in *Women's Bible Commentary*, ed. C. A. Newsom and S. H. Ringe; London, SPCK, 1992.

Tolbert, M.A., *Sowing the Gospel: Mark's Word in Literary-Historical Perspective*. Minneapolis, Fortress, 1989.

van Horst, P. W., 'Can a book end with γάρ? A note on Mark 16:8', in *JTS*, new series 23 (1972) pp. 121–124.

Wegner, J. R., *Chattel or Person? The Status of Women in the Mishnah*. Oxford, Oxford University Press, 1988.

Witherington, B., *Women in the Ministry of Jesus: a Study of Jesus' Attitudes to Women and their Roles as Reflected in his Earthly Life*. Cambridge, 1987.

_____'Birth of Jesus,' *DJG*, 69-70 in C. S. Keener, *The IVP Bible Background Commentary: New Testament*, 1994